**Northern Russia**
Pages 204–211

SIBERIA AND THE FAR EAST

Magadan

Kamchatka

Krasnoyarsk

Irkutsk

Sakhalin Island

Vladivostok

**Central and
Southern Russia**
Pages 220–235

**Siberia and
the Far East**
Pages 246–259

# RUSSIA

EYEWITNESS TRAVEL

# RUSSIA

DK

**DK** | Penguin Random House

**Managing Editor** MadhuMadhavi Singh
**Senior Editorial Manager** Savitha Kumar
**Senior Manager Design and Cartography** Priyanka Thakur
**Editors** Shreya Sarkar, Vatsala Srivastava
**Project Designer** Stuti Tiwari Bhatia
**Designer** Aradhana Gupta
**Senior Cartographic Manager** Uma Bhattacharya
**Cartography Manager** Suresh Kumar
**Senior Cartographer** Hassan Mohammmad
**Senior DTP Designer** Azeem Siddiqui
**DTP Designer** Rakesh Pal
**Picture Research Manager** Taiyaba Khatoon
**Senior Picture Researcher** Sumita Khatwani

**Contributors**
Catherine Phillips, Christopher Rice, Melanie Rice, Daniel Richardson, Matt Willis

**Photographers** Matt Willis, Katerina Zaharieva

**Illustrators**
Stephen Conlin, Richard Draper, Stephen Gyapay, Claire Littlejohn, Chris Orr & Associates,
Maltings Partnership, Arun Pottirayil, Paul Weston

Printed and bound in China

First American Edition, 2013
15 16 17 18 10 9 8 7 6 5 4 3 2 1

Published in the United States by DK Publishing, 345 Hudson Street,
New York, New York 10014

**Reprinted with revisions 2016**

Copyright © 2013, 2016 Dorling Kindersley Limited, London
A Penguin Random House Company

Published in the UK by Dorling Kindersley Limited.

A catalog record for this book is available from the Library of Congress.
ISSN 1542-1554
ISBN 978-1-4654-4133-1

Floors are referred to throughout in accordance with
European usage; ie the "first floor" is the floor above ground level.

MIX
Paper from
responsible sources
FSC™ C018179

**The information in this
DK Eyewitness Travel Guide is checked regularly.**
Every effort has been made to ensure that this book is as up-to-date as possible
at the time of going to press. Some details, however, such as telephone numbers,
opening hours, prices, gallery hanging arrangements, and travel information are
liable to change. The publishers cannot accept responsibility for any consequences
arising from the use of this book, nor for any material on third party websites, and
cannot guarantee that any website address in this book will be a suitable source of
travel information. We value the views and suggestions of our readers very highly.
Please write to: Publisher, DK Eyewitness Travel Guides, Dorling Kindersley,
80 Strand, London WC2R 0RL, UK, or email: travelguides@dk.com.

Front cover main image: Domed towers of the Monastery of the Saviour and
St Euphemius, Suzdal

◀ St Basil's Cathedral at twilight, Red Square

# Contents

How to Use this Guide **6**

The colourful domes of St Basil's Cathedral,
Red Square, Moscow

# Introducing
# Russia

Discovering Russia **10**

Putting Russia on
the Map **16**

A Portrait of Russia **18**

Russia Through
the Year **34**

The History of Russia **38**

Ballet troupe performing *Swan Lake* at the
Mikhailovskiy Theatre, St Petersburg

## Moscow
## Area by Area

Moscow at a Glance **50**

The Kremlin **52**

Red Square and
Kitay Gorod **64**

Garden Ring **76**

Zamoskvoreche **94**

Further Afield **102**

Beyond Moscow **112**

Shopping in Moscow **118**

Entertainment in
Moscow **120**

Moscow Street Finder **122**

A herd of reindeer migrating, northern Kamchatka

Further Afield **178**

Beyond St Petersburg **184**

St Petersburg Street
Finder **192**

## Russia Region
## by Region

Russia at a Glance **202**

Northern Russia **204**

Kaliningrad **212**

Central and Southern
Russia **220**

The Caucasus **236**

Siberia and the
Far East **246**

## Travellers' Needs

Where to Stay **262**

Where to Eat and
Drink **274**

Shopping in Russia **292**

Entertainment in
Russia **296**

Outdoor Activities **298**

## Survival Guide

Practical Information **302**

Travel Information **312**

General Index **318**

Phrase Book **332**

Detailed mosaic work in the Small Throne
Room at the Hermitage, St Petersburg

## St Petersburg
## Area by Area

St Petersburg at
a Glance **132**

The Islands **134**

Palace Embankment **144**

Gostinyy Dvor **158**

Sennaya Ploshchad **170**

The Kremlin, Presidential area, Moscow

# HOW TO USE THIS GUIDE

This Dorling Kindersley Travel Guide helps you to get the most from your visit to Russia. It provides detailed practical information and expert recommendations. *Introducing Russia* maps the country and its regions, sets them in their historical and cultural context and describes events through the year. *Russia Region by*

*Region* is the main sightseeing section, which covers all the important sights, with photographs, maps and illustrations. Information on hotels, restaurants, shops, entertainment and sports is found in *Travellers' Needs*. The *Survival Guide* has advice on everything from travel to medical services, banks and communications.

## Moscow and St Petersburg Area By Area

Russia's main cities have been dealt with in their respective sections. Both of these have been divided into six sightseeing areas. Each area has its own chapter, which opens with an introduction and a list of the sights described. All sights are plotted on an *Area Map*. The key to the map symbols is on the back flap.

**Sights at a Glance** lists the chapter's sights by category: Churches, Museums and Galleries, Historic Buildings, Parks and Gardens, and so on.

**All pages** relating to Moscow have red thumb tabs.

**2 Street-by-Street Map**
*This gives a bird's-eye view of a key area in each chapter.*

**A suggested route** for a walk is shown with a dotted red line.

**All pages** relating to St Petersburg have green thumb tabs.

**A locator map** shows where the area is in relation to other parts of the city.

**1 Area Map** *For easy reference, the sights are numbered and located on a map. Sights in each area are also shown on the Moscow and St Petersburg Street Finder maps on pages 126–9 and 196–9 respectively.*

**Stars** indicate the sights that no visitor should miss.

**3 Practical information**
*The main sights in both cities are described individually with addresses, information on opening hours, admission charges and websites.*

**Story boxes** explore specific subjects further.

**1 Introduction** *The landscape, history and character of each region is outlined here, revealing how the area has developed over the centuries and what it offers to the visitor today.*

## Russia Region By Region

Apart from Moscow and St Petersburg, the rest of Russia has been divided into five regions, each with a separate chapter. The most interesting places to visit have been numbered on a Regional Map at the beginning of each chapter.

**Each region** can be quickly identified by its colour coding, shown on the inside front cover.

**2 Regional Map** *This shows the road network and gives an illustrated overview of the whole region. All the sights are numbered here, and there are also useful tips on getting around the region by car and train.*

**Getting Around** gives tips on travel within the region.

**3 Detailed information**
*All the important places to visit are listed in order, following the numbering on the Regional Map. Each sight is described individually. Within each town or city, there is detailed information on major buildings and other sights.*

**The Visitors' Checklist** provides all the practical information needed to plan your visit.

**4 Town Map** *Major towns have a map showing the key sights, each of which is described in more detail.*

# INTRODUCING RUSSIA

Discovering Russia     **10–15**

Putting Russia on
the Map     **16–17**

A Portrait of Russia     **18–33**

Russia Through the Year     **34–37**

The History of Russia     **38–47**

# DISCOVERING RUSSIA

The following tours have been designed to take in as many of the country's highlights as possible, while keeping long-distance travel manageable. The first tours outlined here are both two-day tours of Russia's historic capitals: Moscow and St Petersburg. These itineraries can be followed individually or combined to form a longer tour, which can commence in either city. There is also a two-week tour that follows the mighty Volga river by boat all the way from the beautiful city of Nizhny Novgorod to the Caspian Sea. Finally, there is a seven-day tour of the Lake Baikal region, with the option of adding three days to include the 5,000-km (3,110-mile) Trans-Siberian rail journey from Irkutsk to Moscow. Choose and combine tours or dip in and out and be inspired.

**The Volga and Oka rivers, Nizhny Novgorod**
In the Tsarist era, the Volga and Oka rivers formed a natural moat around Nizhny Novgorod and protected it from invasions. Today, the dynamic city and its ancient Kremlin rise over the rivers' banks.

## Two weeks on the Volga river

- Marvel at the sheer size of the Volga from the Kremlin in **Nizhny Novgorod**. The city rises above the strategic confluence of the Oka and Volga rivers.

- Be awed by **Kazan's** illuminated Kremlin complex, which looks particularly striking at night.

- Join a boat trip to visit the pretty medieval churches in **Sviyazhsk**.

- Descend 30 m (100 ft) into Stalin's intriguing secret bunker in **Samara**.

- Stand in deferential silence beneath one of the world's largest freestanding statues at the Mamayev Kurgan war memorial complex in **Volgograd**.

- Allow time to visit **Volgograd's** superb Battle of Stalingrad Panorama Museum.

- Explore at leisure the glorious medieval churches and cathedrals within the formidable white-walled Kremlin in **Astrakhan**.

**Key**

— Two weeks on the Volga river

◀ The Kremlin, Moscow, from Kamennyy Most showing Vodovzodnaya Tower and Moskva river, 1819 by Maxim Nikiforovich Vorobiev

## A week in the Baikal region

- If the weather allows, sunbathe on Listvyanka's lakeside beach.

- Take a trip on the **Circum-Baikal Railway** and behold breathtaking views of the splendid lake.

- Sample smoked omul freshly caught from **Lake Baikal**.

- Admire the truly huge statue of Lenin's head installed at **Ulan-Ude**.

- Learn all about the region's fascinating Buryat culture at Ulan-Ude's Buryat History Museum and the outdoor **Taltsy Architectural and Ethnographic Museum** near Irkutsk.

- Seek solace in the brightly coloured temples of **Ivolginsky Datsan** – Russia's centre of Buddhism.

**Key**

— A week in the Baikal region

**Taltsy Architectural and Ethnographic Museum**
This delightful open-air museum displays preserved Siberian folk architecture and is the perfect place to experience the colourful culture of the people of Siberia.

## Two days in Moscow

*Russia's capital is a riveting blend of old and new, where onion-domed churches jostle for space with glass-fronted blocks and Communism's red stars still adorn many buildings.*

- **Arriving** Moscow's largest airports are Domodedovo and Sheremetyevo. Domodedovo is located 42 km (26 miles) southeast of the city centre, while Sheremetyevo is 28 km (17 miles) northwest of the city centre. Aeroexpress trains run from 5am till 12:30am and take around 20–40 minutes to reach Moscow's metro system.

- **Moving on** Moscow to St Petersburg by Sapsan train takes about 4 hours.

The remarkable skyline of Moscow, with St Basil's Cathedral dominating Red Square

### Day 1

**Morning** Whatever the weather, head straight for **Red Square** *(p68)* to marvel at the iconic gilded onion domes of **St Basil's Cathedral** *(pp70–71)*. Queue outside the **Lenin Mausoleum** *(p69)* for a brief glimpse of the great leader's embalmed remains. From here, head for the **GUM** shopping mall *(p69)*, commissioned by Catherine the Great in the late 19th century. Next, visit the **Historical Museum** *(p68)* that faces Red Square. A proud statue of World War II hero Marshal Georgi Zhukov stands in front of the museum beside Kilometre Zero, the point from where all distances in Russia are measured – line up with visiting Russian tourists to have your picture taken here as a keepsake.

**Afternoon** Dedicate the afternoon to a thorough exploration of the Kremlin. Among the highlights are the glorious **Cathedral of the Assumption** *(pp58–9)* where Ivan the Terrible was crowned in 1547, and the exquisitely decorated **Patriarch's Palace** *(p56)*. Be sure to check out the giant 16th-century **Tsar Cannon** *(p56)* and the 200-tonne (221-ton) Tsar Bell, the heaviest bell in the world. Save plenty of time for the **Armoury Chamber** *(pp62–3)*; star exhibits include Tsar Alexis's 17th-century diamond throne and a glittering selection of Fabergé eggs.

### Day 2

**Morning** Start off with a spell of art appreciation at the world's largest collection of Russian art, the **State Tretyakov Gallery** *(pp98–9)*. Then, tour the **Pushkin State Museum of Fine Arts** *(pp90–91)* where the superb collection includes the **Gallery of 19th- and 20th-Century European and American Art** *(p88)*. Be prepared for a long visit, as there is plenty to see.

**Evening** Explore the cavernous interior of the nearby **Cathedral of Christ the Saviour** *(p89)*, rebuilt in 2000 to replace the original that was demolished on Stalin's orders in 1931 to make way for the unrealized Palace of Soviets. From here take the metro to Arbatskaya to the busy **Arbat Square** *(p89)*. Stroll along the popular ulitsa Arbat, where buskers perform outside the many shops, cafés and bars. Do not miss the imposing Gothic **Ministry of Foreign Affairs** building *(p93)*, which towers over the end of the street.

> **To extend your trip...**
> Spend a day at the **Trinity Monastery of St Sergius** *(p114)*, 75 km (47 miles) north of Moscow and another at the UNESCO-listed settlement of **Suzdal** *(pp116–17)*.

Portraits of notable Russians on display at Moscow's Historical Museum

## Two days in St Petersburg

*Founded by Peter the Great in the early 18th century, St Petersburg was Russia's capital from 1732 to 1918. Much of its stunning architectural heritage has been remarkably well preserved.*

- **Arriving** Pulkovo is St Petersburg's main international airport, located 23 km (14 miles) south of the city. Buses link the airport to Moskovskaya metro station between 5:25am and 1:30am.

- **Moving on** Moscow is an hour and 20 minutes away by air, or approximately 4 hours by Sapsan train.

### Day 1

**Morning** Get a feel of both contemporary and historic St Petersburg with a stroll along **Nevskiy prospekt** (p166), the main street since the city was founded in the 18th century. Covering a length of 5 km (3 miles), it is jammed with monuments, churches and exquisite buildings. Look out for the **Cathedral of Our Lady of Kazan** (p168), a statue of Catherine the Great and the **Church on Spilled Blood** (p162), which was built as a memorial to Alexander II on the spot where he was assassinated. Its quintessentially Russian onion domes are reminiscent of Moscow's St Basil's Cathedral.

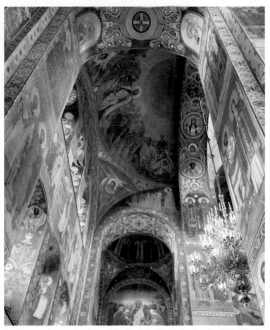

Stunning murals portraying the symbols of Orthodox Christianity, Church on Spilled Blood

Gilded domes adorning the grand palace at Peterhof

**Afternoon** Arrive at the vast **Palace Square** (p152), dominated by the monumental **Hermitage** (pp154–5). Spend time exploring the luxurious former residence of the tsars that now houses one of the world's largest and most illustrious art collections. Start with a tour of the magnificent interiors of the **Winter Palace** (pp156–7) to get a feel of the museum before progressing further. It is impossible to see everything in an afternoon, so choose one or two collections to focus on. Later, head to the well-manicured gardens in front of the nearby **Admiralty** building (p148) for a relaxing evening stroll.

### Day 2

**Morning** Begin the day with a hydrofoil trip to **Peterhof** (pp186–7), Peter the Great's magnificent complex of palaces and gardens that was built to rival the Gardens of Versailles in Paris. Spend the morning soaking up the imperial atmosphere – highlights include the opulent Throne Room, the Grand Cascade of bronze sculptures, fountains and water jets, and the Imperial Suite, featuring original 18th-century oak panelling.

**Afternoon** Wander through the historic **Peter and Paul Fortress** (pp136–7) that faces the Hermitage across the Neva river. The main attraction here is the **Cathedral of SS Peter and Paul** (pp138–9) where the Romanov family are buried. If the weather is suitable, consider joining the locals to sunbathe on the riverside beach. Afterwards, pay a late afternoon visit to the colossal **St Isaac's Cathedral** (pp150–51), Russia's largest church that took 40 years to construct and was finally opened in 1858. Round of the day with an evening ballet or opera performance at the renowned **Mariinskiy Theatre** (p174).

> **To extend your trip...**
> Take a day trip to the peaceful 18th-century palace at **Pavlovsk** (pp190–91). Located 26 km (16 miles) south of St Petersburg, it is refreshingly free of crowds.

## Two weeks on the Volga river

- **Airports** Fly from Moscow's Sheremetyevo Airport to Nizhny Novgorod International Airport and depart from Astrakhan's Narimanovo Airport.

- **Transport** Organized cruises run the length of the Volga from May till September. While it is possible to join shorter cruises between cities during the same period, services are unpredictable, so it is best to seek out the latest information at local river terminals or travel agencies. It may be necessary to travel by train when riverboats are unavailable for any part of the journey.

The exquisite Kul Sharif Mosque located within the Kremlin, Kazan

### Day 1: Nizhny Novgorod
The perfect preamble to this itinerary, **Nizhny Novgorod** offers many attractions. Devote a morning to exploring its Kremlin (p224), which occupies a superb vantage point overlooking the confluence of the Oka and Volga rivers. Visit the Church of the Blessed Virgin (p224), one of the many churches scattered around the city, and marvel at its multicoloured domes.

### Days 2 and 3: Kazan
From Nizhny Novgorod, take the riverboat (24 hours) to **Kazan**. Spend time in its historic centre, where the riverside Kremlin (p225) is the main attraction.

The nearby National Museum of the Republic of Tatarstan (p225) provides a fascinating insight into the region's complex history.

### Days 4 and 5: Sviyazhsk
Travel to **Sviyazhsk** on a riverboat (3 hours) to visit the meticulously restored Assumption Monastery (p226) that once served as a stronghold for Ivan the Terrible. Head back to Kazan and, in the evening, take the riverboat (24 hours) to Ulyanovsk.

### Day 6: Ulyanovsk
Most famous for being Lenin's birthplace, **Ulyanovsk** has several museums dedicated to the renowned Soviet leader, notable among which is the Lenin Memorial Centre (p227). Take time out to appreciate the town's well-preserved old quarter of 19th-century wooden houses.

### Days 7 and 8: Samara
Travel by boat (24 hours) to **Samara**. Wander through the atmospheric centre and along the pretty embankment of this city. Soak up some history at Stalin's Bunker (p228) and browse the exhibits at the splendid Samara Space Museum (p229). Consider joining a rafting trip to the Samara Bend.

### Days 9, 10 and 11: Volgograd
Take the riverboat (2½ days) to **Volgograd**. Visit the many memorials and museums dedicated to the Battle of Stalingrad,

Giant Soyuz rocket on display at the entrance to the Samara Space Museum

which destroyed the city during World War II. Behold the awe-inspiring statue of Mother Russia at the Mamayev Kurgan memorial complex (p232).

### Days 12 and 13: Astrakhan
Travel by riverboat (around 24 hours) to **Astrakhan**, where the Volga river meets the Caspian Sea. Spend time touring the city's splendid Kremlin (p233) and surveying its quarter of faded wooden Tatar houses.

### Day 14: Volga Delta
Join a boat tour of the labyrinthine **Volga Delta**, home to countless endemic and endangered species of wildlife. Spend a memorable night at one of the delta's floating wooden hotels.

The Church of the Blessed Virgin, Nizhny Novgorod

For practical information on travelling around Russia, see pp314–15

## A week in the Baikal region

- **Airports** Fly from Moscow's Sheremetyevo Airport to Irkutsk International Airport and depart from Ulan-Ude International Airport.

- **Transport** Take the 6-hour flight from Moscow to Irkutsk. The city makes the perfect base for day trips around the region. Local buses and the Circum-Baikal Railway serve destinations around Lake Baikal. The journey from Irkutsk to Ulan-Ude is 7 hours by train.

Rock projection from the amazing blue expanse of Lake Baikal

### Day 1: Irkutsk
Roughly halfway between Moscow and Vladivostok on the Trans-Siberian Railway is **Irkutsk**, a thoroughly enjoyable city to explore. Start at the Museum of City Life (p252) and the complex of preserved wooden mansions of Irkutsk's 19th-century Decembrist aristocrats. From here, follow the curve of the Angara river to ploshchad Kirova where the city's oldest churches stand side by side. Don't miss the brightly painted façade of the Epiphany Cathedral (p252).

### Day 2: Taltsy and Listvyanka
Take the minibus from Irkutsk to Listvyanka, which stops halfway at the **Taltsy Architectural and Ethnographic Museum** (p253). This museum offers an insight into Siberian culture and architecture. The wooded grounds of the museum are filled with traditional Buryat dwellings. Of special note are a complex of wooden Cossack homes and stalls selling traditional crafts. Continue to the lakeside village of Listvyanka in the afternoon and to the banks of Lake Baikal (p253). Sunbathe on the beach if the weather permits and sample freshly smoked omul – Lake Baikal's most famous fish. Head back to Irkutsk via minibus in the evening.

### Day 3: Circum-Baikal Railway
Catch the early morning minibus to Sludyanka. From here a local train operates daily on the Circum-Baikal Railway (p253) along the rocky shore of Lake Baikal. Enjoy the scenic views and quaint stations en route, but fight back the hunger pangs as refreshments won't be available until the train arrives at Port Baikal several hours later. Return to Irkutsk to catch the minibus to Olkhon Island the next morning.

### Day 4: Olkhon Island
Spend the day investigating this peaceful island (p253) dotted with ancient shamanic monuments and wooden houses. A day trip can easily be extended to an overnight stay at one of the island's many guesthouses.

### Day 5: Irkutsk to Ulan-Ude
Travel by train to Ulan-Ude and enjoy the stunning vistas the journey offers. The railway skirts the edge of Lake Baikal for more than a 100 km (62 miles), passing picturesque wooden cottages and offering stunning views of the lake to the north. Look out for the peaks of the Ardaban Mountains to the southeast as the train nears Ulan-Ude.

### Day 6: Ulan-Ude
Visit the world's largest statue of Lenin's head in the modern city centre of **Ulan-Ude** before inspecting the region's fascinating past at the Buryat History Museum (p256). Next, stop by the Ethnographic Museum (p256) to explore the nomadic roots and shamanic beliefs of the indigenous Buryats.

### Day 7: Ivolginsky Datsan
Minibuses regularly take tourists and locals out of Ulan-Ude and into the featureless plains beyond in the direction of **Ivolginsky Datsan** (p256). Visit the Buddhist monastery complex here that forms the spiritual heart of Russian Buddhism. The monastery's colourful temples make for a meditative day trip. Return to Ulan-Ude in the evening.

> **To extend your trip...**
> Catch the overnight train from Ulan-Ude to Irkutsk and then spend three days travelling to Moscow on the **Trans-Siberian Railway**, converting this into a 10-day itinerary.

Devotee practising temple rites at the Ivolginsky Datsan monastery complex

# Putting Russia on the Map

With an area of 17 million sq km (6.6 million sq miles), the Russian Federation was the greatest of the USSR's 15 republics and is now the world's largest country, almost twice the size of the US. Moscow, the capital with 12 million inhabitants, is the biggest city, followed by St Petersburg. At its widest point along a geodesic line, Russia measures 8,000 km (4,971 miles) from east to west, including the Kaliningrad region, an extraterritorial enclave on the Baltic.

*Arctic Ocean*

*Barents Sea*

*Kara Sea*

Oulu · Murmansk

FINLAND

*Baltic Sea*

Tallinn · Helsinki

RUS. FED.

Riga · ESTONIA · M10 · ST PETERSBURG · M18 · *White Sea* · Arkhangelsk

Kaliningrad · LATVIA · Pskov · Petrozavodsk

Vilnius · LITHUANIA · Novgorod

BELARUS · A14 · M8 · Vologda · Ukhta · Pechora · Vorkuta · Noril

M9 · M8 · Syktyvkar · **RUSSIA** · Novyy Urengoy

Kiev · MOSCOW · M7 · Nizhny Novgorod · *Urals*

UKRAINE · M4 · Lipetsk · P175 · Kazan · Ob

Voronezh · M5 · Nefteyugansk · Noyabrsk · Surgut · Nizhnevartovsk

Rostov-na-Donu · M4 · Saratov · Samara · Yekaterinburg · P404

Krasnodar · M6 · Ufa · M5 · P351 · Chelyabinsk · Severo-Yeniseyskiy

Sochi · Elista · Volgograd · Orenburg · M51 · P402 · Lesosibirsk

*Black Sea* · GEORGIA · A1 · M6 · Astrakhan · Omsk · M51 · Tomsk · Krasnoyarsk · M53

TURKEY · *Caspian Sea* · *Caucasus* · M38 · Novosibirsk · Abakan

ARMENIA · Yerevan · Astana · Barnaul · M54 · Kyz

AZERBAIJAN · Baku · K A Z A K H S T A N · *Altai Mountains*

Zhezkazgan · Karagandy

C H I N A

## St Petersburg and Environs

0 km    50
0 miles    50

Sosnovo · A129 · *Lake Ladoga*

Primorsk · A125 · M10 · Vaskelovo

A123

*Gulf of Finland*

Sosnovyy Bor · ST PETERSBURG · Novaya Ladoga · M18

A121 · Pulkovo

M11 · Gatchina · Tosno

Volosovo · M20 · Vyritsa · M10 · Kirishi · A115

### Key

✈ International airport
— Motorway
— Dual carriageway
— Main road
— International border

# A PORTRAIT OF RUSSIA

Straddling the vast Eurasian landmass, from the Baltic to the Pacific and the Arctic to the Caucasus, Russia is the world's largest nation, with an unparalleled ethnic and geographical diversity. The country's epic history is reflected in its rich culture of arts, literature, music, ballet and drama. The bustling cities of Moscow and St Petersburg are vanguards of Russian culture as well as being home to iconic onion-domed cathedrals, stunning imperial palaces and superb museums.

The low-lying Urals separate European Russia from the enormity of Siberia and the Far East. Split between Europe and Asia, Russia has an extraordinary diversity of indigenous people. In fact, the Russian language is the only element that unites the multi-ethnic society.

At the heart of most old Russian cities is a kremlin (fortress), a reminder of the land's many invasions and conquests. With a glittering skyline of gilded cupolas and red stars symbolizing the fusion of Holy Russia and Soviet power, Moscow's Kremlin serves as the seat of the Russian government. For over 200 years, however, the Tsarist Empire was ruled from St Petersburg, a splendid city aptly described as the Venice of the North. The decline of the Tsarist Empire marked the beginning of the Soviet era, with Russia as the leading constituent of the Soviet Union born of the October Revolution of 1917. As the world's first socialist state, it boasted of overthrowing capitalism and establishing a classless Communist utopia. However, the Soviet system failed to satisfy its citizens' material aspirations and fell behind its Western and Asian competitors. Its dissolution in 1991 led to Russia's transition from Communism to capitalism. Today's Russia comprises three-quarters of the territory of the former Soviet Union, whose legacy is manifest in everything from architecture to local slang.

Outside the booming urban hubs of Moscow and St Petersburg are charming historic cities, spa towns and a diverse landscape of great lakes, beaches, rolling plains and icy wastes. This vibrant mix of mesmerizing attractions, amazing landscapes and fascinating culture makes a visit to Russia a truly enriching experience.

The golden-domed St Isaac's Cathedral – one of St Petersburg's most iconic landmarks – seen from the Mojka Canal

◀ Traditional dancers in lavish costumes performing at ulitsa Arbat, Moscow

Rolling grasslands against a backdrop of the snow-capped peaks of the western Caucasus

## Land and Ecology

With an area of 17 million sq km (6.6 million sq miles), stretching from Europe to the Pacific Ocean, Russia is the world's largest country. Constituting 33 per cent of this total area, European Russia stretches south to the Caucasus and the Caspian Sea, and is flanked by Georgia, Armenia and Azerbaijan. Extending beyond the Urals, Asian Russia forms the larger half of the territory and shares borders with Kazakhstan, China, Mongolia and North Korea. Sandwiched between Poland and Lithuania, the Kaliningrad region is an extraterritorial enclave of Russia.

Due to its vast extent, Russia features a wide variety of terrain, distinguished by their different climates and vegetation. The far north is dominated by the tundra, which is characterized by moss, lichen and permafrost. Stunted trees mark the transition of these barren flatlands to the taiga forests. Covering most of Northern Russia, these dense coniferous forests account for a fifth of the world's forest reserves. Watered by the mighty Don and Volga rivers that flow into the Black and Caspian seas, southern Russia is the nation's granary. Dominated by steppes, or undulating grasslands, this region consists of fertile *chernozem* (black earth) or semi-arid salt-marshes. The rugged far east lays claim to being the wildest and most remote region, with taiga forests inhabited by a variety of fauna, notably tigers.

Russia's seemingly infinite resources have long encouraged rampant environmental exploitation. The country saw some of the worst ecological disasters during the Soviet era, when preservation of the environment was thought to be a hindrance to economic advancement. As a result, extensive oil and gas drilling activities in the Arctic and Siberian regions eventually led to the destabilization of the tundra ecosystem. In addition, water pollution caused by industrial and chemical waste contributed to the decimation of fish species in the Black and Caspian seas. Fortunately, the government of Russia today has recognized these problems and has made significant efforts to establish 101 *zapovedniki* (nature reserves) and 38 national parks to protect the country's ecosystem.

## Economy

Since the dissolution of the Soviet Union, Russia has moved from a largely isolated, centrally planned economy to a more market-based, globally integrated one.

Typical snow-covered Siberian landscape

Façade of the skyscraper housing Gazprom's headquarters, Moscow

Although the country is rich in natural resources such as oil, gas, coal and precious metals, most of these reserves are in inhospitable regions, requiring huge investments in infrastructure. Multinational corporations have been instrumental in developing new oil- and gasfields in joint ventures. However, their operations have often run into problems resulting from takeover bids by the Russian energy giants Gazprom and Sibneft.

Russia is the world's second-largest producer of natural gas after the United States and the world's largest producer of crude oil. State levies on oil and gas exports account for nearly half of Russia's revenue, making the economy critically dependent on commodity prices. Other sectors of the economy have seen rapid or fitful growth since the 1990s, notably services, industry and agriculture, which accounted for 58, 32 and 10 per cent of the national economy, respectively, in 2011. One-fifth of manufacturing jobs are in the defence sector, making Russia the world's second-largest exporter of weapons.

For a majority of Russians, life since the early 2000s has been better than before. The average monthly salary has increased eight-fold and the percentage of people living below the poverty line has fallen from 30 to 14 per cent.

## Politics and Government

Since the overthrow of Communism in 1991, Russia has experienced rapid change and bewildering dislocations. The break-up of the Soviet Union left Russia beset by hyper-inflation, mass unemployment and rampant criminality, with millions of ethnic Russians facing an uncertain future in newly independent states. Under President Boris Yeltsin, state assets, including oilfields, were privatized at knockdown rates, creating a new class of wealthy oligarchs, in league with organized crime, corrupt bureaucrats and politicians.

After the wild capitalism of the 1990s, Yeltsin's successor, Vladimir Putin, experienced a sweeping victory in the 2000 presidential elections. In contrast to Yeltsin, Putin consolidated the mafia-state and by curbing the oligarchs he convinced a majority of Russians that he was a man of the people. His second term in office saw Russia enriched by petrodollars with improved living standards in cities besides Moscow and St Petersburg.

In small towns across Russia, people are grateful for stability, and influenced by pro-regime TV. However, in major cities, the fact that wages and pensions are paid on time is no longer enough. Growing disparities between the super rich and the majority of the population continue to breed resentment in Russian society.

President Vladimir Putin speaking on the Day of Russia, Moscow

Graceful ballet dancers performing *The Sleeping Beauty* at the Bolshoi Theatre, Moscow

## Culture and Arts

Russians are intensely proud of their culture, language and arts. This pride stems from the Slavophile movement of the 19th century, which emphasized belief in the uniqueness of Russian traditions and culture. The movement included the composers Modest Mussorgsky and Alexander Borodin as well as the writers Nikolai Gogol and Fyodor Dostoevsky. For Slavophiles, Russia's Orthodox Church, mysticism and the concept of *sobornost*, which advocated cooperation between opposing ideas in favour of the ultimate, holy good, were infinitely superior to the Western values of rationalism, materialism and individualism. It is a view that still resonates today, much to the chagrin of the liberal-minded minority who cherish democracy and secularism.

Russian despotism, xenophobia and corruption have long been ascribed to the three centuries that the country spent under the Mongol yoke while Europe underwent the Renaissance. These political and social themes depicted in the Russian arts are a distinct mix of Western and indigenous styles. Although most Russians regard themselves as Europeans, they also

A symphony orchestra performing at the Mariinskiy Theatre, St Petersburg

acknowledge an Asian dimension to their national identity that sets them apart from their Western neighbours.

The psychological realism of Dostoevsky's novels, the naturalistic dialogue in Anton Chekhov's plays, the poet masterpieces of Alexander Pushkin, and Konstantin Stanislavskiy's method acting are all highly regarded around the world. The legacy of Russian creativity is further manifested in film maker Sergei Eisenstein's jump-cuts, Pyotr Tchaikovsky's symphonies and Vasily Kandinsky's abstract art.

Visitors to Russia can enjoy world-class ballet, opera and classical music in Moscow's Bolshoi Theatre (see pp82–3) and St Petersburg's Mariinskiy Theatre (see p174). Both cities have a thriving theatre scene too, with the Moscow Arts Theatre (see p84) and the Mikhaylovskiy Theatre (see p163) in St Petersburg staging the works of contemporary Russian playwrights. The cities are also at the cutting edge of Russian nightlife and fashion. Other urban locations such as Sochi, Yekaterinburg and Vladivostok host festivals that showcase contemporary culture not only from all over the country but also from around the world.

## People and Society

Russia's population has been declining. The 2010 census recorded a population of nearly 143 million, around 2 million fewer than 10 years earlier. Some trace the country's stunted demography back to the scores of people who died in wars, famines and purges during the 20th century; others blame a plummeting birth rate, endemic alcoholism and poor healthcare.

Despite the break-up of the Soviet Union, Russia is home to a great diversity of ethnic minorities, from camel-riding Kalmyks in southern Russia and reindeer-herding Nenets in Siberia to Tatars fishing on the Volga and Sakha in the Far East. Of the country's 160 recognized ethnic groups, nearly 81 per cent of citizens identify themselves as Russians. Tartars (4 per cent), Ukrainians (1 per cent), Bashkir (1 per cent), Chechens (1 per cent) and Armenians (1 per cent) form the largest minorities, amounting to two-thirds of the total ethnic-minority population.

While over 100 languages are spoken across the country, many are on the verge of extinction, particularly among the indigenous peoples of the far north. If anything unites this multicultural society, it is the Russian language, which is universally understood. Religion comes a poor second, with some 100 million citizens considering themselves Orthodox Christians. Muslims number between 9 and 20 million, but are undoubtedly the nation's fastest-growing demographic. As Orthodoxy has grown more assertive in Russia, and Islam has spread in the Caucasus, secularists, liberals, feminists and gays have been stigmatized and assaulted.

A Nenet man with his herd of reindeer in northwestern Siberia

Russia has seen rapid urbanization over the last century, with around three-quarters of its population now living in cities and towns. The life of most Russians has also vastly improved in contrast to Soviet times, or even the 1990s, when millions of families still struggled to make a living. Today, even provincial school teachers can afford a holiday abroad besides owning a car and a computer. Despite these advancements, Russian society is not devoid of disparities. At the start of this century, Moscow boasted more billionaires than any city in the world, while thousands of towns and villages languished in poverty. Such polarities exist in the societies of many countries, but are magnified in Russia due in part to the vast distances and climactic extremes.

Tourism is now a major industry in Russia. Although renowned for its cultural and historical attractions, the country is fast emerging as a prime destination for adventure sports enthusiasts, with activities ranging from pony trekking and caving to volcano-watching. Russia is also famous for its ornate folk arts and artisan crafts, such as amber jewellery, lacquered boxes, glazed earthenware and wood carvings. However, caviar, vodka and Soviet memorabilia remain the most sought-after souvenirs.

Beautifully carved wooden handicrafts on sale

# Landscape and Wildlife

Russia comprises nearly every kind of natural environment found in the northern hemisphere. From the windswept southern grasslands and the densely forested north to the cold seas and barren tundra bordering the Arctic coastline, the world's largest country is a land of incredible contrasts. This vast landmass is divided into European Russia and Siberia by the Ural Mountains, beyond which the great rivers of Siberia flow northwards into the Arctic Ocean. With one of the largest forest reserves in the world, Russia is home to diverse ecosystems. Notable among the many animal species found here are the Siberian tiger, Amur leopard, sturgeon and brown bear.

Snow-covered fir trees in the southern Ural region

## Steppe and Desert

The Eurasian steppes, or grasslands, extend from Hungary to Mongolia and are largely treeless lands. Some areas are semi-arid, merging into desert. Desertification of the Kalmyk Steppe and soil erosion in the *chernozem* belt of southern Russia are problems for these areas.

**Steppe marmots** are a common sight in the grasslands. They graze on the steppe's vegetation cover and have served as a natural food "reservoir", saving many Russians from starving to death during famines in the 20th century.

**The steppe eagle** breeds in southern Russia and winters in Africa. Its diet includes carrion of all kinds, but it also hunts rodents and other small mammals.

**Purple pasqueflowers** bloom on the steppes of the black-earth zone in mid-April when the snow melts.

## Rivers and Lakes

Of Russia's 10,000 rivers, the Volga is the longest in Europe, and the Siberian Ob, Yenisei, Lena and Amur are among the longest rivers in the world. Besides this, Russia also has Lake Baikal, the world's largest, deepest and purest freshwater lake – home to several unique species.

**Sturgeon** is the common name for some 26 species of fish prized for their roe, or caviar. Most are critically endangered due to over-fishing or pollution of the Caspian Sea, the Volga river and other breeding grounds.

**Nerpas** are the only freshwater seals in the world, unique to Lake Baikal. Their main breeding colony lies on the lake's western shores.

**The Sacred Lotus** blossoms on a bed of white water lily pads. It is chiefly found in the Astrakhan Biosphere Reserve *(see p233)* of the Volga Delta.

## Saving the Siberian Tiger

Also known as the Amur tiger, this is the world's largest sub-species of tiger, weighing up to 300 kg (660 lb). It is a critically endangered feline species: the Sikhote-Alin Mountains, to the northeast of Vladivostok, account for 90 per cent of the population in the wild, with an estimated 350–500 surviving adults. Under the Species Survival Plan of 1981, thousands of tigers have been bred in zoos in order to achieve maximum genetic diversity and stabilize their dwindling numbers. Their survival is also dependent on conserving prey such as roe, sika deer, wild boar and brown bear. Adult tigers are seasonal hunters and have been known to imitate bear calls to lure them into an ambush, springing from a rock or fallen tree to seize the bear's throat and sever its spinal column with a single bite.

The majestic Siberian tiger – the largest living felid in the world

## Forests and Tundra

Forests cover over half the territory of Russia, forming a great belt across Eurasia. The northern coniferous forest, or taiga, merges into mixed woodlands towards the south. To the north it is bounded by the treeless tundra, which is populated by reindeer, arctic foxes and wolves.

## Mountains and Coasts

The Caucasus boasts both alpine and sub-tropical flora and fauna around Sochi and Mount Elbrus, while Kamchatka is famed for its volcanoes and mud-geysers. Russia's 37,000-km-(22,991-mile-) long coastline borders the Arctic and Pacific oceans, and no fewer than nine seas.

**The brown bear** is the national animal of Russia. The country boasts a robust population of approximately 120,000 bears.

**The pincushion flower** turns alpine meadows violet-blue by the end of summer. Over 13,000 plant species have been identified within the Teberdinsky Nature Reserve near Dombay, 190 of them endemic to the Caucasus.

**Wolves** were once found throughout Russia. Today there are perhaps 30,000 left nationwide, with relatively few in central Russia but growing numbers in Chechnya and Kalmykia.

**The Pacific walrus** weighs over a ton and measures up to 4-m (13-ft) long. During the mating season, 80,000 walruses pack the coast of Wrangel Island, using their tusks to anchor themselves to ice floes.

**Amur leopards** are critically endangered by poaching and logging. Having lost 80 per cent of their habitat since the 1970s, leopards are now confined to the temperate forests between Vladivostok and the Chinese border.

**The polar bear** is the world's largest land carnivore and the walrus's only natural predator. Subsistence hunting was made legal for Chukotka natives in 2007 and has threatened the bear population in Russia.

# Russian Orthodox Church

In 988, Prince Vladimir made Byzantine Rite Christianity the official religion of the Kievan Rus. The newly created Russian Orthodox Church was subordinate to the Patriarch of Constantinople, who appointed its archbishop. Having gained autonomy a few years before the fall of Constantinople in 1453, the church saw itself as the rightful head of Eastern Orthodoxy. Moscow was heralded as the Third Rome, in accordance with a prophecy by the monk Philotey of Pskov, "two Romes have already fallen but the third remains standing and a fourth there will not be".

Prince Vladimir the Great, canonized as an Orthodox saint

## Early History

*Christianity is said to have been brought to Russia by the Apostle Andrew, who foretold the founding of a great Christian city where Kiev stands today. Princess Olga of Kiev was the first Russian ruler to convert to Christianity. Her grandson Vladimir made the Kievan Rus a Christian state.*

**Cyril and Methodius** were 9th-century Greek monks who tried to convert the Slavs. The Cyrillic script is named after St Cyril, who laid the foundation for the Cyrillic alphabet.

**Candles** are symbolic of the faith of the worshippers and the light of knowledge.

**Monasteries**, like the one at Suzdal *(see pp116–17)*, doubled as strategic fortifications. They were built overlooking a river or as part of a chain blocking an invasion route across the plain. Under the Mongol yoke *(see p40)*, they became important repositories of Russian culture and faith.

## Iconostasis

The iconostasis is a screen on which icons of saints are displayed. It separates the nave from the sanctuary and symbolizes the division between Earth and Heaven. It is usually made of wood, delicately carved with natural motifs and gilded.

**Warrior saints** such as Dmitri Donskoy (1350–89) embody the Church's historic association with the Russian nation state. In the post-Communist era, the church has exploited its constitutional status as one of the four "recognized" faiths (the other three being Islam, Judaism and Buddhism) to discourage other Christian denominations from evangelizing.

**Icons of Christ** and the saints play a major role in the Orthodox Church. The icon is a sanctified object that helps the faithful sense God's presence. This is why icons have always been highly stylized.

## Parts of a Church

*Orthodox churches are usually oriented on an east–west axis. Worshippers enter the church from the west (associated with sin) and head up the aisle towards the light of Truth (in the east). The plan of a church is often rectangular like a ship (or Ark) or cruciform (like the Cross). Inside, the main space is the nave, with walls usually decorated with frescoes and icons. The altar, in the sanctuary, is hidden from the worshippers behind the iconostasis, but is visible during services, when the Royal Doors are opened.*

**Beautiful frescoes** cover the walls of Russian churches. This one, adorning the Cathedral of the Annunciation *(see p57)* in Moscow, dates from the 16th century. A popular subject on the west walls of churches is the Apocalypse.

**The cross** is an important symbol of the Church and has been described as the joining of the heavenly and the earthly. The three-armed cross, found in Slavic countries, has an upper bar that represents the inscription over Christ's head, while the lower slanting bar represents the foot rest.

## Orthodox Worship

*Orthodox services can be very moving as the church is lit mainly by candles and the air is heavy with incense. The whole service is sung, since the human voice is believed to be the finest medium for praising the Lord. The service forms a sung dialogue between the clergy and the congregation. Traditionally, there are no chairs and everyone is expected to stand as a mark of respect.*

**Key**

- ☐ Prophets and Patriarchs
- ☐ Twelve Apostles
- ☐ The Holy Trinity
- ☐ The Deesis Row
- ☐ Christ Enthroned
- ☐ Twelve Liturgical Feasts
- ☐ The Sovereign Row
- ☐ The Holy Virgin
- ☐ Christ Pantokrator
- ☐ The Royal Doors
- ☐ The Deacons' Doors

**The order of icons** on an iconostasis is not rigid although it keeps roughly to the plan above. Rows may not follow the same sequence, and all five are not always featured. An icon of one of the church's patron saints sometimes takes the place of the icon of Christ Pantokrator.

**Mary** has always been venerated by the Orthodox Church. Russians refer to her as the *Bogomateri* or *Bogroditsa* (Mother of God).

# The Arts

Russia has made a vast contribution to the arts including music, drama, ballet, painting and cinema, not to mention literature, where the contribution of its poets and novelists is particularly remarkable. These cultural triumphs are all the more impressive for having frequently been made in the face of official repression under Tsarist or Soviet regimes. Artistes who were accused of subversion often suffered terrible persecution and exile.

A scene from *Swan Lake,* Mikhailovskiy Theatre, St Petersburg

Anton Chekhov with members of the Moscow Arts Theatre, 1899

## Drama

Medieval Russia was noted for its *skomorokhi* (minstrels), who recited fables, sang and danced at harvest festivals. Unfortunately, the Orthodox Church abhorred such pagan traditions and encouraged performances of biblical stories instead. These were staged at Russia's first ever theatre, established at the court of Tsar Alexis in 1672. His son, Peter the Great, had the first public theatre built on Moscow's Red Square in 1702, but it was in his new capital St Petersburg that European drama took root. During the late 18th and early 19th centuries, theatrical troupes comprising serfs were established in aristocratic estates in St Petersburg, Moscow and the provinces.

The mid-19th century saw Alexander Griboedov, Nikolai Gogol and Alexander Ostrovsky create a distinctively Russian canon, but the most significant development was the foundation of the Moscow Arts Theatre (1898) by Konstantin Stanislavskiy and Vladimir Nemirovich-Danchenko. It was this theatre that successfully staged Anton Chekhov's naturalistic drama *The Seagull* (*see p84*) after it had flopped in St Petersburg. Subsequently, director Stanislavskiy's theories of method acting became hugely influential abroad and inspired Hollywood actors such as Marlon Brando and Dustin Hoffman.

## Music and Ballet

Russian classical music began with Mikhail Glinka, whose *Life for the Tsar* (1836) and *Ruslan and Ludmila* (1842) initiated the genres of musical drama and folk opera, drawing on Orthodox chant and folk melodies. Glinka inspired the next generation of composers, known as The Mighty Five, which included Modest Mussorgsky, famous for *Pictures at an Exhibition* (1874), and Alexander Borodin, known for the opera *Prince Igor* (1887).

Pyotr Tchaikovsky (*see p115*) established Russian music on the world stage with his ballets *Swan Lake* (1876) and *The Nutcracker* (1892), performed at the Bolshoi and Mariinskiy. His successors included the experimentalist composers Alexander Scriabin and Igor Stravinsky, and Sergei Rachmaninov. The last two left Russia after the Revolution. Composers who remained in, or returned to, the USSR risked ideological criticism. After Shostakovich's opera *Lady Macbeth of Mtsensk* (1934) was condemned by the newspaper *Pravda*, he could only redeem himself with the *Leningrad Symphony* (1941), which had patriotic overtones. Sergei Prokofiev was more adept in pleasing the authorities with his composition *Peter and the Wolf* (1936).

Ballet moved from imitating foreign forms to becoming a national art of surpassing

Premiere of Glinka's opera *Ruslan and Ludmila* at the Bolshoi Theatre, Moscow

Fifteenth-century icons painted by Andrei Rublev on display in the State Tretyakov Gallery, Moscow

brilliance. Its heritage and hopes are embodied in two great rival institutions, the Bolshoi Theatre *(see pp82–3)* and the Mariinskiy Theatre *(see p174)*.

## Painting

Russia's steppe cultures had no tradition of painting, until Prince Vladimir's adoption of Orthodox Christianity introduced the Byzantine art of icon painting. As individual principalities became more independent, different schools developed in Vladimir, Suzdal, Novgorod and Pskov. Theophanes the Greek (around 1340–1405) was the first artist to imbue the subjects of his icons with human emotions, but it was only with Andrei Rublev (around 1360–1430) that a truly Russian school was created.

By the end of the 17th century, icon painting began to lose its significance, superseded by European portraiture. Peter the Great and his successors promoted the training of Russian artists abroad and established an Academy of Arts in St Petersburg. The academic style that developed here set the tone for Russian art until the middle of the 19th century.

After 14 of the academy's most talented students rebelled and launched themselves as a travelling art exhibition known as *Peredvizhniki* (The Wanderers) in 1870, Russian art changed irrevocably. Realist works such as *Barge-Haulers on the Volga* (1873) by Ilya Repin excoriated the ills of Tsarist society, while Symbolist and Primitivist

paintings by the likes of Mikhail Vrubel and Natalya Goncharova challenged every tenet of the academic style.

The five years before and after the Revolution saw the rise and fall of Futurism – a radical experiment in new forms of the visual arts, architecture and design, by Kazimir Malevich, Vasily Kandinsky and Vladimir Tatlin. While Kandinsky left Russia in 1921 to teach at the Bauhaus school, Malevich and Tatlin remained in Russia long after the regime had rejected Futurism for socialist realism, which was Stalin's version of the academic style.

## Cinema

Russian cinema came of age after the Revolution, when the Soviet state recognized the genius of Sergei Eisenstein (1898–1948). His silent master-

A poster of Eisenstein's masterpiece *Battleship Potemkin*

pieces *Battleship Potemkin* (1927) and *October* (1928) pioneered the jump-cut, which has been used in movies ever since. Eisenstein's historical epics *Alexander Nevsky* (1938) and *Ivan the Terrible* (1944, 1958) were overseen by Stalin, who rewrote the script to make Ivan's speeches more laconic, like his own

The Brezhnev era was the heyday of slapstick comedies such as *Operation Y*, the romantic *Irony of Fate* (still shown every New Year's day on TV) and *White Sun of the Desert* (a Soviet "Eastern" set in Central Asia). Andrey Tarkovsky's *Andrei Rublev* and Sergei Bondarchuk's *War and Peace* have won prizes.

Films long hidden in the archives, such as Aleksandr Askoldov's *The Commissar* (1967), were released during Gorbachev's presidency, before the collapse of state funding and a flood of Hollywood imports left Russia's film industry in dire straits. Directors had to master new genres and find investors in order to survive; only Nikita Mikhalkov, whose *Burnt by the Sun* (1994) won an Oscar, got state funding. Alexei Balabanov's gangster movie *Brother* (1997) was the first domestic blockbuster, followed by the supernatural thrillers *Night Watch* (2004) and *Day Watch* (2006), directed by Timur Bekmambetov. Alexander Sokurov's *Russian Ark* (2002) has the distinction of being filmed in a single 96-minute shot, the longest in the history of cinematography.

# Russian Literature

For a country where most of the population was illiterate before the October Revolution and where French was the *lingua franca* of the aristocracy, Russia has made a remarkable contribution to world literature. With its supple inflections, Russian is suited to poetic and psychological expression – a trait brilliantly exploited by great writers such as Dostoevsky Pushkin and Tolstoy. Often criticizing the draconian policies of the regime, poets and novelists have been regarded as the conscience of the nation in both Tsarist and Soviet times.

Leo Tolstoy (1828 –1910) with his wife Sonya in the garden of their Russian home

## Early Russian Literature

Russian literature is suffused with an oral heritage of folk mythology, ballads and slang. The tradition of *byliny*, or folk tales, told by minstrels in the courts of the Kievan Rus *(see p39)* over a millennium ago is preserved in the 12th-century epic poem *The Lay of Igor's Host*. The only manuscript of the poem was discovered in 1795. Excavations in Veliky Novgorod have unearthed love letters and poems written on birchbark dating from around 1400, imply-ing that literacy was widespread here. After the Mongol invasion *(see p40)*, hagiographies of Orthodox saints became virtu-ally the only form of literature besides the Gospels. Printing presses were initially regarded by the majority of Muscovites as satanic, and printing output remained constrained.

## Pushkin, Lermontov and Gogol

Russian literature came of age with Alexander Pushkin *(see p93)*, whose work ranged from short stories to poetry and even a novel in verse, *Eugene Onegin* (1832). Pushkin created a Russian literary idiom, expanding the language to explore nuances of feeling and sensation. His writing invited harsh censorship by Tsar Nicholas I, thus setting the precedent for dissent by future writers in opposition to autocracy.

Mikhail Lermontov expressed the existential angst of a gener-ation that felt both impotent and ignored in *A Hero for Our Time* (1840). Like Pushkin, Lermontov was exiled to the Caucasus and killed in a duel.

Nikolai Gogol was a master of the grotesque, satirizing the snobbery and corruption of St Petersburg society in short stories. His novel *Dead Souls* (1842) was written as he lapsed into religious melancholia. He burned the second part in the fireplace. Afflicted by cataleptic fits, Gogol was allegedly buried alive in a Moscow cemetery.

## Turgenev, Tolstoy and Dostoevsky

The next generation of writers was also dominated by a trio of titans. Ivan Turgenev made his name with short stories about the lives of serfs and went on to write *Fathers and Sons* (1862). The novel explores the conflict between generations and the dilemmas of liberals in an autocratic state. Leo Tolstoy *(see p106)* presented the stoical humility of the peasantry in sharp contrast to the decadence and hypocrisy of the nobility and bourgeoisie in his epic works *War and Peace* (1869) and *Anna Karenina* (1877). He was expelled from the Orthodox Church for espousing Christian anarchism.

On the other hand, Fyodor Dostoevsky *(see p177)* renounced his socialist ideals after exile in Siberia. He became a fervent upholder of autocracy and a savage critic of Russia's revolutionaries in such master-pieces as *Crime and Punishment* (1866), *Demons* (1872) and *The Brothers Karamazov* (1880). The psychological insights that these works offer had a lasting influence on Western literature.

Street scene from a 1997 film version of Tolstoy's eponymous novel *Anna Karenina*

## Chekhov

Dostoevsky's psychological realism was echoed in the works of playwright and novelist Anton Chekhov *(see p86)*. His collaboration with the director of the Moscow Arts Theatre, Konstantin Stanislavskiy, gave rise to the first "modern" plays, namely *The Seagull* (1896) and *Uncle Vanya* (1899). The characters' silences and non sequiturs conveyed their inner natures and feelings more effectively than conventional dialogue, while simultaneously presenting a subtle critique of social values.

Poster of Anton Chekhov, a dramatist associated with the Moscow Arts Theatre

## The Silver Age

The beginning of the 20th century was the Silver Age of Russian poetry. Unfortunately, the abundance of artistic talent was significantly reduced by the Revolution. Emotional honesty was the ethos of the Acmeist movement, advocated by Anna Akhmatova *(see p182)* and Osip Mandelstam. Both produced their greatest work in Soviet times. Subsequently Akhmatova endured the purges, which have been recounted in her famous poem *Requiem* (1935–40), while Mandelstam died in the Gulag for lampooning Stalin. Marina Tsvetaeva was another "spiritual exile" in Soviet Russia. Her works were banned by the regime but circulated clandestinely, along with those of Alexander Blok, who had heralded the Revolution with his poem *The Twelve* (1918).

Actors rehearsing a scene from *The Master and Margarita* by Mikhail Bulgakov

## Soviet and Émigré Writers

The Futurist Vladimir Mayakovsky *(see p75)* and the peasant poet Sergei Yesenin were supporters of the Bolshevik movement and their agitational propaganda was promulgated via their art. Both of them committed suicide in the 1920s. Isaac Babel's *Red Cavalry* (1924) enraged Marshal Budyonny to such an extent that Babel was later tortured to death. Stalin saw writers as "engineers of the human soul" and decreed socialist realism obligatory. The genre was epitomized by Nikolai Ostrovsky's *How the Steel was Tempered* (1936), but Mikhail Sholokhov's Cossack epic *And Quiet Flows the Don* (1928–40) is better known abroad.

Among the host of writers who fled Russia in the 1920s, Ivan Bunin became the first Russian ever to be awarded a Nobel Prize for Literature in 1933. Vladimir Nabokov wrote with equal brilliance in English, becoming famous the world over for *Lolita* (1955). Another novel that had a lasting impact abroad was Yevgeny Zamyatin's *We* (1927), which inspired George Orwell's *Nineteen Eighty-Four* and Aldous Huxley's *Brave New World*.

In Stalinist Russia, expulsion from the Writers' Union meant loss of privileges, arrest or even death. So harsh were the conditions that Mikhail Bulgakov worked in a theatre while secretly writing *The Master and Margarita* in the 1930s and Boris Pasternak eschewed poetry for translation work. His novel *Dr Zhivago* (1957) was written "for the desk drawer" and was only published during Khrushchev's reign. A few years later in 1962, the literary magazine *Noviy Mir* serialized Alexander Solzhenitsyn's *One Day in the Life of Ivan Denisovich*, which is about life in the Gulag.

After ideological conformity was re-imposed in the 1960s, the work of dissident writers could only be circulated as *samizdat* (clandestine copies) or smuggled abroad for publication. Solzhenitsyn was expelled from Russia in 1974 for his work *The Gulag Archipelago*. The poet Joseph Brodsky suffered a similar fate after a grotesque trial where the judge asked him, "Who has recognized you to be a poet?"

Vladimir Mayakovsky in Yalta in 1926, four years before he committed suicide

# Russian Architecture

The architectural landscape of Russia borrows elements from several different styles. While the architecture of the Kievan Rus was influenced by the Byzantine style, the medieval Novgorod and Pskov schools developed their own distinct features such as the onion dome. As the might of the Russian state grew, Ivan the Great invited Italian masters to build structures with Renaissance motifs. In the 18th century, Elizabeth favoured Bartolomeo Rastrelli and his Baroque style. A Russian version of Art Nouveau flourished before the Revolution, while postwar Constructivism influenced Modernist architecture worldwide.

Intricate wrought-iron Baroque gate of the Winter Palace, St Petersburg

## Early Russian Architecture

Russia's earliest buildings were constructed entirely from wood. The Kizhi *pogost (see p208)*, a complex with a pair of domed wooden churches, is a prime example of sophisticated wooden architecture. Although stone and brick began to be used to construct important buildings around the 14th century, wood continued to be the main building material. This practice continued until the 1812 Great Fire of Moscow *(see p42)* burnt the city to the ground.

Churches constitute a majority of Russia's oldest surviving buildings. One of the earliest among these is Vladimir's 12th-century Cathedral of the Assumption *(see p116)* in Moscow. Its namesake in the

Kremlin *(see pp58–9)* dates from the 14th century and is a fusion of the early-Russian style and Italian Renaissance features. This architectural confluence during the 15th and 16th centuries was a result of the imperial practice of inviting talented Italian architects to Russia. The Italian masters were assigned the task of constructing prestigious buildings befitting the reputation and stature of the ever-expanding Russian Empire.

Another architectural innovation in the 16th century was the spire-like tent roof, apparent in St Basil's Cathedral *(see pp70–71)* in Moscow. In the mid-17th century, Patriarch Nikon (1665–81) banned its use, insisting that plans for new churches must be based on ancient Byzantine designs.

Although most secular buildings from this period have not survived, Moscow's Palace of the Romanov Boyars *(see p72)* remains a notable exception.

## Baroque

The magnificent gate churches at the Novodevichiy Convent *(see pp104–105)* and the Upper Monastery of St Peter *(see pp84–5)* are representative of the Moscow Baroque, or Naryshkin, style of architecture. The filigree limestone trimmings and pilasters set against a redbrick background embody a fusion of early-Russian and European Baroque motifs.

European Baroque reached its apogee in St Petersburg under Empress Elizabeth. The Winter Palace *(see pp156–7)*, the Great Palace at Peterhof *(see pp186–7)* and the Catherine Palace at Tsarskoe Selo *(see pp188–9)* are the creations of her favourite architect, the Italian maestro Bartolomeo Rastrelli *(see p157)*. His flamboyant style was later superseded by Neo-Classical designs in St Petersburg and Moscow. However, archetypal Baroque features such as stucco mouldings and vibrantly coloured façades remained the leitmotif of architecture in provincial towns, as evinced by 19th-century merchants' villas in the old quarter of Ulyanovsk *(see p227)* in the Volga region.

Multi-domed wooden churches in Kizhi, an example of early Russian architecture

## Neo-Classicism

The accession of Catherine the Great to the throne in 1762 gave a new direction to Russian architecture. She favoured the Neo-Classical style, which derives from the architecture of Classical Greece and Rome. This style has been used to great effect in Moscow's Pashkov House *(see p88)*, thought to have been designed by Vasily Bazhenov.

Bazhenov's assistant, the prolific Matvei Kazakov, demonstrated the flexibility of Neo-Classicism in his designs for a range of buildings, including churches, hospitals and the Moscow Old University *(see p81)*. The huge fire that followed Napoleon's brief occupation of Moscow led to a wholesale reconstruction of the city In the fashionable Empire style, a grandiose form of Neo-Classicism typified by the work of Osip Bove and Carlo Rossi. Both architects created monumental public spaces, namely Bove's Theatre Square *(see p80)* in Moscow, and Rossi's General Staff Building *(see p152)* and Ostrovskiy Square *(see p167)* in St Petersburg.

## Historicism and Style-Moderne

Historicism replaced Neo-Classicism in the mid-19th century. It arose from a desire to create a national style by reviving architectural movements from the past. Moscow's Grand Kremlin Palace *(see p60)* and Armoury Chamber *(see pp62–3)*, designed by Konstantin Ton in the 1840s, combine features from various erstwhile styles including Renaissance, Classical and Baroque. Ton also designed the Byzantine-style Cathedral of Christ the Saviour *(see p89)*, which was finished in 1883 and rebuilt between 1994–7.

Traditional Russian wooden architecture and folk art were rich sources of inspiration for

Church on Spilled Blood exemplifying the Russian-Revival style, St Petersburg

the architects that formulated the Russian-Revival style. Moscow's Historical Museum *(see p68)* and the magnificent Church on Spilled Blood *(see p162)* in St Petersburg are outstanding examples of this genre.

Another radical architectural style that developed during this time was Style-Moderne, akin to Art Nouveau. Its greatest exponents were Fyodor Shekhtel in Moscow, who designed the extraordinary mansion that is now the Gorky House-Museum *(see p86)*, and the St Petersburg architect Fyodor Livdal, whose Kshesinskaya Mansion *(see p141)* uses mosaic friezes, glazed brick and stained glass to stunning effect.

## Architecture after the Revolution

Constructivism was a novel attempt to combine form and function in the decade after the October Revolution. Although many visionary projects were never realized, Moscow has two outstanding buildings by the architect Konstantin Melnikov: the Bakhmetevsky Bus Garage that is now the Jewish Museum and Tolerance

Centre, and the Melnikov House *(see p92)* that he built for himself shortly before his career stalled.

In the 1930s, Stalin decreed a plan to rebuild large areas of Moscow. Constructivism was abandoned in favour of a grand Soviet version of Neo-Classicism. Many of Moscow's metro stations are superb examples of design from this era. More obtrusive are the Stalin-Gothic skyscrapers known as the Seven Sisters, including the Ministry of Foreign Affairs *(see p93)* and the Moscow State University *(see p108)*.

The Stalin-Gothic Ministry of Foreign Affairs building, Moscow

# RUSSIA THROUGH THE YEAR

Russians love to celebrate and take their public holidays seriously. Almost all official holidays as well as local ones are marked with concerts and fireworks. Music, whether classical, folk or contemporary, is the central theme of many festivals, bringing in talent from all over the world. Flowers play a particularly important role in Russian society. Mimosas symbolize International Women's Day when men present women with flowers, whereas lilacs herald the advent of summer. Even without an official holiday, Russians love to get outdoors, whether to ski or ice-skate in winter, or gather mushrooms in late summer and autumn.

## Spring

When rooks appear, usually in late March, and snowdrops bloom, spring is reckoned to have arrived. To warm themselves up after the months of cold, locals celebrate *maslenitsa*, the feast of pancake-making before Lent. Once the snow has melted, city-dwellers make a visit to their *dacha* (country cottage) to put the garden in order.

### March
**Maslenitsa** *(end Feb–early Mar)*, nationwide. Pancake week heralds spring with events such as concerts and carnivals.
**International Women's Day**, *Mezhdunarodnyy den zhenshchin (8 Mar)*, nationwide. Men buy gifts for their womenfolk and congratulate them on the holiday with the words *"S prazdnikom"*, meaning "best wishes".
**Easter Sunday**, *Paskha (Mar–early May, following the Orthodox calendar)*, nationwide. Churches throng with chanting devotees. After the greeting *Khristos voskres* (Christ is risen) and the reply *Voistine voskres* (He is truly risen) are exchanged, people kiss one another three times.

### April
**Musical Spring in St Petersburg**, *Muzikalnaya Vesna v Sankt-Peterburge (mid-Apr)*. Concert halls host musical programmes.

### May
**Labour Day**, *Den truda (1 May)*, nationwide. In the Soviet era, parades lined Moscow's Red Square *(see p68)*. Today, the festivities are rather low-key, with concerts and fireworks.
**Victory Day**, *Den pobedy (9 May)*, nationwide. Wreaths are laid at war memorials in memory of the 1945 Nazi surrender. A parade, with soldiers in historic uniforms, takes place in Red Square. Residents of many cities participate in the Bessmertny Polk (Immortal Regiment) march where they walk with the portrait of a relative or an unknown war veteran.
**Peterhof Fountains**, *Fontany v Petergofe (weekend in mid-May)*, St Petersburg. Bands and orchestras accompany the switching on of the fountains at Peterhof *(see pp186–7)* under a colourful fireworks display.
**Day of Slav Culture**, *Den Slavyanskoe Kultury (24 May)*, nationwide. Religious

Soldiers in uniform at the Victory Day parade on Red Square, Moscow

processions are held in honour of the saints Cyril and Methodius, the "apostles of the Slavs".
**City Day**, *Den goroda (last week of May)*, St Petersburg. Events, mainly taking place around the Peter and Paul Fortress *(see pp136–7)*, mark the founding of the city on 27 May 1703.
**Moscow Stars**, *Moskovskyy Zvezdy (throughout May)*. Conductors, soloists and ensembles from around the world perform at Moscow's Conservatory *(see p87)* and Tchaikovsky Concert Hall.
**SKIF Festival** *(May)*, St Petersburg. Indie and avant-garde musicians, DJs and performance artists from Russia and abroad delight audiences at clubs and other venues.
**Stars of the White Nights**, *Zvezdy Belykh nochi (late May–early Jul)*, St Petersburg. First-class opera, classical music and ballet performances are held across the city during the famous White Nights, when the sun hardly sets.
**Cossack Fairs**, *Kazachi yarmarki (May–Sep, last Sun of the month)*, Starocherkassk. Horse-riding, singing, dancing and merry-making takes place in this Cossack village.

Easter celebrations outside the Cathedral of Our Lady of Kazan, Moscow

Crowds at the delightful hot-air balloon festival, Kungur

## Summer

Throughout summer, cities are almost empty during weekends, when people visit their *dachas*. Despite this, there are several major music festivals and other events, including an air show outside Moscow and a hot-air balloon festival in the Urals.

### June

**Trinity Sunday**, *Troitsa (50 days after Easter Sunday, according to the Orthodox calendar)*, nationwide. Believers and atheists alike go to the graves of their loved ones and raise a toast for their souls.

**Moscow International Film Festival** *(Jun)*. A glamorous event attended by both celebrities and the general public, and featuring the latest releases from all over the world.

**Sadko Folklore Festival**, *Mezhdunarodnyy folklore festival Sadko (7–10 Jun)*, Veliky Novgorod. An international festival of folklore and crafts that starts with a parade from the Kremlin to Yaroslav's Court *(see p210)*.

Young boys at the Night of Ivan Kupala near Veliky Novgorod

**St Petersburg Palaces**, *Dvortsy Sankt-Peterburga (early Jun–early Jul)*. An international festival of chamber music and fireworks at the imperial summer palaces of Peterhof, Tsarskoe Selo *(see pp188–9)* and Pavlovsk *(see pp190–91)*.

**Day of Russia**, *Den Rossii (12 Jun)*, nationwide. This official holiday marks the day when Russia became "independent" of the Soviet Union in 1991. It is celebrated with a fireworks display in cities across the country.

**Tsarskoe Selo Carnival**, *Tsarskoselskiy karnaval (last weekend of Jun)*. Funny costumes, music and mayhem fill the centre of Pushkin, the town surrounding the imperial palace of Tsarskoe Selo.

**Tales of the Boy Onfim**, *Skazi malchika Onfima (Jun, Jul and Sep)*, Veliky Novgorod. Russian fairy-tale heroes, show puppets and age-old myths come to life in the medieval Kremlin.

### July

**Sky Fair of the Urals**, *Nebesnaya yarmarka Urala (early Jul)*, Kungur. A week-long international hot-air balloon festival held near the Kungur Ice Cave *(see p235)*.

**US Independence Day** *(4 Jul)*, Moscow. Celebrated with rock bands, fashion shows and fireworks in the grounds of Kuskovo Palace *(see p109)*.

**Night of Ivan Kupala**, *Noch Ivana Kupala (around 6 Jul)*, near Veliky Novgorod.

Ostensibly dedicated to St John the Baptist, this nocturnal pagan fertility rite, marked by youths leaping over bonfires, is held beside Lake Ilmen.

**Grushinsky Festival**, *Vserossiyskiy festival avtorskoy pesni (first weekend of Jul)*, Samara. Two rival festivals devoted to Bard music, a Soviet genre of acoustic ballads. One is held by the Mastryukovskie lakes near Samara *(see pp228–9)*; and the other outside Tolyatti, in the Samara region.

**Amber Beach** *(mid-Jul)*, Kaliningrad. A Baltic pop festival held in the Kaliningrad region.

**Navy Day**, *Den voenno-morskovo flota (last Sun in Jul)*, port cities. Naval regattas of warships and submarines are held in St Petersburg's Neva basin and Vladivostok's harbour, plus there are celebrations in many other cities that have a waterfront.

**Kamwa Festival**, *Etnofuturisticherskiy festival KAMWA (late Jul–early Aug)*, Perm. Russia's answer to WOMAD, this ethno-futuristic festival brings together ancient Ugric traditions and modern art, music and fashion.

Aircraft trailing the colours of the Russian national flag, MAKS Air Show 2009

### August

**MAKS Air Show** *(mid-Aug)*, Zhukovskiy Airbase, 20 km (12 miles) southeast of Moscow. Aerial displays by Russia's latest and vintage warplanes.

**Kizhi Volost Festival** *(mid-Aug)*, Kizhi. Folk music, dancing and a handicrafts display on the remote island in Lake Onega *(see p208)*.

**Novorossiysk Bikers' Festival** *(last weekend of Aug)*. This Black Sea port hosts Russia's biggest bikers' festival, which President Putin attended in 2011, riding a Harley Davidson.

## Autumn

City life begins to gain pace as people return from their *dachas* and families begin to prepare for the start of school. In September, when theatres re-open after the summer break, cultural life resumes. October marks the beginning of the festival season in Moscow and St Petersburg, with musicians and theatre groups from all over the world taking part. Autumn is ideal for gathering mushrooms in the forests. Locals are skilled at identifying edible mushrooms, but amateur pickers should beware the dangers of poisonous ones.

President Putin laying a wreath in memory of victims of the Siege of Leningrad

### September

**Knowledge Day**, *Den znaniy (1 Sep)*, nationwide. Children and parents celebrate the start of the new academic year by bringing flowers to teachers.

Knowledge Day, celebrated with balloons and flowers at a school in Vladimir

**Battle of Borodino**, *Borodinskaya bitva (first Sun of Sep)*, Borodino. A re-enactment of the famous 1812 battle.

**City Day**, *Den goroda (first weekend of Sep)*, Moscow. A carnival on ulitsa Tverskaya and a pageant at the royal estate of Kolomenskoe are organized.

**Peterhof Fountains** *Fontany v Petergofe (second weekend of Sep)*, St Petersburg. Celebrations with fireworks mark the switching off of the famous fountains.

**Siege of Leningrad Day**, *Den Blokady Leningrada, (8 Sep)*, St Petersburg. Commemorated by wreath-laying ceremonies at the Piskarevskoe Memorial Cemetery and events and concerts for war veterans and siege survivors.

**International Early Music Festival**, *Mezhdunarodnyy Festival Early Music (late Sep–mid-Oct)*, St Petersburg, Moscow,

Nizhny Novgorod, Yekaterinburg, Perm and Novosibirsk. Soloists and ensembles perform music from the Middle Ages, Baroque, Renaissance and Classical times.

### October

**Baltic House**, *Baltiyskiy dom (Oct)*, St Petersburg. Actors, clowns and pantomime artists from the Baltic countries perform in theatres and on the streets for over two weeks.

**Autumn Rhythms**, *Osenie Ritmy (mid-Oct–mid-Nov)*, St Petersburg. A month-long international festival that segues from Ballroom and Latin dancing into jazz, held at clubs and concert halls.

**Halloween Night** *(31 Oct)* nationwide. Despite Halloween being anathematized by the Russian Orthodox Church as a pagan celebration, the country's

## Climate Of Russia

Russia experiences climatic extremes. Most of European Russia, southwestern Siberia and the southern Pacific coast have a continental climate, with cold winters and hot summers. Extremely severe winters characterize Russia's sub-arctic and polar regions, while the Black Sea coast has a humid subtropical climate with wet winters.

**Moscow** has a continental climate, characterized by cold winters, and warm, often hot summers. During heat waves, daytime temperature exceeds 30°C (86°F). In the winter months precipitation falls mainly as snow.

### MOSCOW

| °C | Apr | Jul | Oct | Jan |
|---|---|---|---|---|
| | 11 | 24 | 9 | |
| | 2 | 14 | 3 | |
| | | | | -4 |
| | | | | -9 |
| ☀ | 6 hrs | 9 hrs | 3 hrs | 1 hr |
| ☂ | 37 mm | 85 mm | 71 mm | 52 mm |
| month | Apr | Jul | Oct | Jan |

youth enjoy dressing up as vampires and werewolves for a night's clubbing.

### November
**Day of National Unity**, *Den' narodnogo yedinstva (4 Nov)*, nationwide. Originally meant to commemorate the liberation of the country, when all members of Russian society united to expel the Polish-Lithuanian forces in 1612, this official holiday has now been hijacked by far-right groups that proclaim "Russia is for Russians".

## Winter

As the ice thickens on the waters and the snow deepens, Russians head for the outdoors. Sledging,

A Russian Orthodox archbishop performing the evening service on Christmas Eve

ice-skating and cross-country skiing are popular wherever the topography allows. Hardy "Walruses" breaking the ice to take an early morning dip and fishermen sitting over holes drilled in the ice are a common sight.

### December
**Four Nations Tournament**, *Turnii chetlryy natsyy (mid-Dec)*, Moscow, Podolsk and other cities. Ice-hockey teams from Russia, Sweden, Finland and the Czech Republic compete.
**Moscow Forum**, *Moskovskyy Forum (Dec or Jan)*. Annual festival of contemporary music held at various venues.
**New Year's Eve** *Novyy god (31 Dec)*, nationwide. New Year's Eve is a family celebration, with visitors dressed as *Ded Moroz* (Grandfather Frost, the Russian equivalent of Santa Claus) or his sidekick *Snegurochka* (Snow Maiden), the bearer of gifts.
**Russian Winter Festival** *(mid-Dec–early Jan)*, Moscow. Folk music performances and *troika* (sleigh) rides can be enjoyed at Izmaylovo Park, with plenty of vodka to keep warm amid the freezing temperatures.

### January
**Russian Orthodox Christmas**, *Rozhdestvo (7 Jan)*, nationwide. Christmas is celebrated in a quieter fashion than Easter, with

attendance at the evening service on Christmas Eve (6 Jan) a tradition.
**Old New Year**, *Staryy Novyy god, (night of 13 Jan)*, nationwide. Orthodox Christians and die-hard party-goers welcome the New Year according to the defunct Julian calendar.
**Svyatki Masquerades**, *Svyatki (Sun nearest 19 Jan)*, Moscow. Bell-ringing and the blessing of the water at Kolomenskoe.

### February
**Defender of the Fatherland Day**, *Den zashchitnika Otechestva (23 Feb)*, nationwide. Men are given flowers and presents, and Russia's armed forces are honoured.
**Buddhist New Year** *Tsagaalgan (late Feb–early Mar)*, Siberia. A 16-day festival marking the lunar New Year, with offerings at Buddhist temples and family feasting. The festival is known as *Shagaa* here.

> ### Public Holidays
> **New Year** (1–8 Jan)
> **Russian Orthodox Christmas** (7 Jan)
> **Defender of the Fatherland Day** (23 Feb)
> **International Women's Day** (8 Mar)
> **Labour Day** (1 May)
> **Victory Day** (9 May)
> **Day of Russia** (12 Jun)
> **Day of National Unity** (4 Nov)

---

**St Petersburg** enjoys a mild maritime climate. Summers are warm and humid, particularly during the White Nights (mid-Jun–mid-Jul). In winter the Neva river freezes over, not thawing until late March or April.

**Sochi**, on the Black Sea coast, is on the same latitude as Nice in France, with a humid subtropical climate. However, winters are colder due to chill winds from Asia, and the temperature can even drop below freezing point.

**Khabarovsk** boasts of being the world's coldest city, with a population of over half a million people. Winter temperatures can approach -30°C (-22°F), with the lowest temperature recorded at -41°C (-42°F).

### ST PETERSBURG

| °C | Apr | Jul | Oct | Jan |
|---|---|---|---|---|
| high | 9 | 23 / 15 | 9 | 2 |
| low | 1 | | 4 | -3 / -8 |
| hrs | 6 | 9 | 2 | 2 |
| mm | 33 | 78 | 67 | 40 |
| month | Apr | Jul | Oct | Jan |

### SOCHI

| °C | Apr | Jul | Oct | Jan |
|---|---|---|---|---|
| high | 16 | 27 / 19 | 20 / 12 | 10 |
| low | 9 | | | 3 |
| hrs | 5 | 9 | 6 | 3 |
| mm | 116 | 124 | 167 | 181 |
| month | Apr | Jul | Oct | Jan |

### KHABAROVSK

| °C | Apr | Jul | Oct | Jan |
|---|---|---|---|---|
| high | 10 | 27 / 17 | 10 | 5 |
| low | 0 | | 1 | -16 / -23 |
| hrs | 7 | 8 | 6 | 5 |
| mm | 43 | 133 | 50 | 14 |
| month | Apr | Jul | Oct | Jan |

# THE HISTORY OF RUSSIA

From a few medieval principalities based around European Russia's inland waterways, Russia has grown to encompass one-sixth of the world. The story of its rise is marked by triumphs and tragedies on an epic scale, including such historic watersheds as the Mongol invasion that laid waste to its medieval civilization, and the creation and collapse of the Soviet Union. Modern-day Russia continues to surge ahead with a flourishing economy and achievements in science and industry.

According to Herodotus's *The Histories*, nomadic tribes known as the Scythians made the steppes of southern Russia their home between the 9th and 3rd centuries BC. Frozen tombs in the permafrost of the Altai Mountains and *kurgans* (burial mounds) on the steppes have yielded mummified humans and horses as well as magnificent gold jewellery. The Scythian empire stretched from southern Russia to the borders of Persia. Despite being scorned as barbarians by outsiders, the Scythians cross-fertilized numerous civilizations. They settled on the northern shores of the Black Sea, but were eventually displaced or absorbed by later nomadic invaders such as the Sarmatians, Huns, Goths and Khazars. The Khazar state, which ruled the lower Volga basin from the 5th to the 11th centuries AD, was a vital link in the Silk Road from Asia to Europe.

The Slavs were relative latecomers from the Pripet Marshes of what is now Belarus. They spread eastwards after the 7th century. Early Slav pottery in Moscow's Historical Museum suggests a primitive peasant culture, but the Slavs proved to be enduring and adaptable on the Eurasian landmass.

## Kievan Rus

In the mid-9th century, a Scandinavian people known as the Varangians (Vikings) ventured along inland waterways from the Baltic to the Black and Caspian seas, where they came in contact with the Slavs of Novgorod. Constant in-fighting between the Slavic tribes was quelled when the Varangian prince Rurik took control of the region in 860. His successor Oleg took Kiev, a Slavic city, and made it his capital, creating an alliance of principalities controlling the river trade routes for furs and slaves between Scandinavia and Byzantium. Kievan Rus absorbed the Viking minority into a Slavic alliance, ruled by feuding *boyars* (nobles).

In 988, Prince Vladimir of Kiev (r.980–1015) took the historic step of adopting Byzantine Orthodox Christianity and imposing it on his pagan subjects by mass baptism. This move deeply affected the future of Russia, whose main religion continues to be Orthodox Christianity. The Kievan state flourished under Vladimir's son Yaroslav the Wise (r.1019–54). But feuding among his successors weakened the state just as a deadly threat emerged from the east in 1223.

**400 BC** Sarmatian female warriors buried at Pokrovka, near modern-day Kazakhstan

**860** Varangian prince Rurik crowned by Slavs of Novgorod; Rurik dynasty created, which endured until 1598

**1223** First Mongol raid

| 600 BC | AD 1 | 425 | 725 | 1025 |

**500 BC** Tattooed mummies dating to this era found in the Altai Mountains of western and southern Siberia in the 1930s

**1050** Completion of St Sophia Cathedral in Novgorod

*Portrait of Rurik*

◀ A 1901 painting depicting Russians fighting off Tartars during one of their numerous clashes

### The Mongol Yoke

Between 1237 and 1240, Russia was invaded from the east by the fearsome Mongol horde led by Genghis Khan's grandson Batu Khan. They swept across the steppe, destroying everything in their path.

While Batu later withdrew to Central Asia, he left behind a detachment known as the Golden Horde that dominated Russia for the next 250 years, exacting tribute in the form of gold, furs and slaves. In the 14th century, the Mongols chose Grand Prince Ivan I of Muscovy (as the principality of Moscow was known) to collect tributes from all their conquered principalities, giving the city supremacy over its neighbours.

Muscovy owed its rise not just to bribery, but to its position at the centre of Russia's river trade routes. In 1380, an army led by Prince Dmitri Donskoy won a victory, the first of its kind, over the Mongols at Kulikovo on the Don river, and the idea of a Russian nation was born. The Orthodox monk Sergius of Radonezh (c.1319–92) was instrumental in uniting the *boyars* behind this patriotic crusade, cementing the Church's place at the heart of the Russian nation state.

The people of Kazan submitting to Ivan the Terrible, the first tsar of Russia

### Ivan the Great and Ivan the Terrible

During the long reign of Ivan III, known as "the Great" (r.1462–1505), the Mongols were forced back to the lower Volga region. Even independent Novgorod was forced to submit to Muscovy's authority. Furthermore, Ivan the Great's marriage to the niece of the last emperor of Byzantium increased Moscow's prestige, particularly her claim to being the last defender of true Orthodoxy.

Ivan the Great's grandson, Ivan IV "the Terrible" (r.1533–84) was the first to be called "Tsar of All the Russias". It was during his reign that the Mongol strongholds of Kazan and Astrakhan were captured. Russia expanded beyond the Urals into Siberia and strong trade links were established with England. The power of the *boyars* was broken by exiling them to remote provinces. But after killing his son and intended heir in a fit of rage, Ivan the Terrible's dynastic hopes rested on a retarded elder son, Fyodor, and an infant, Dmitri.

### The Time of Troubles

For 14 years, Fyodor (r.1584–98) ruled under the guidance of Boris Godunov, a former much-hated member of the *oprichniki* (state police). After Fyodor died childless, bringing the Rurik dynasty to an end, Godunov staged his own accession, but his wiles were no match for a run of disasters after 1601.

Two imposters claiming to be Tsarevich Dmitri invaded Russia one after the other. The first "False Dmitri" invaded

**1325–40** Ivan I rules Moscow and strengthens its position

**1453** Constantinople, previously Moscow's Orthodox ally, falls to the Ottomans; the emperor of Byzantium flees the city

**1533–84** Reign of Ivan the Terrible

**1462–1505** Reign of Ivan the Great

**1350**    **1400**    **1450**    **1500**

**1380** Dmitri Donskoy defeats the Mongols at the Battle of Kulikovo

*Statue of Dmitri Donskoy*

**1476** Ivan the Great stops paying tribute to the Mongols

**1478** Ivan the Great revokes Novgorod's charter of independence

Coronation of Ivan V and Peter I as co-tsars in 1682

Russia with Polish help and was crowned in 1605, but he soon alienated Muscovites and was torn to pieces by a mob. In 1607, the second "False Dmitri", backed by a Polish-Lithuanian army, began five years of invasions, civil war and banditry. This period came to be known as the Time of Troubles.

Only after the abbot of the Trinity Monastery of St Sergius declared a holy war to liberate Moscow did the *boyars* rally behind Prince Pozharskiy of Suzdal, and Kuzma Minin, a butcher from Nizhny Novgorod. They led an army that expelled the Poles in 1612. A monument in Moscow's Red Square commemorates the event.

### The First Romanovs

To avert further strife among the *boyars*, the abbot of the Trinity Monastery proposed Mikhail Romanov (r.1613–45), brother of Ivan the Terrible's first wife, as tsar, thus initiating the 300-year rule of the Romanovs. Under

Mikhail, Moscow made a dramatic recovery with a spate of new stone churches in the tent-roofed style, symbolizing the unity of Church and State. His successor, Alexis (r.1645–76), took the first steps to modernizing Russia by bringing in foreign soldiers, doctors and other professionals.

Alexis was succeeded by his sickly son Fyodor (r.1676–82), whose demise left his 10-year-old half-brother, Peter, heir to the throne. The powerful Miloslavskiy family along with Peter's half-sister Sophia instigated the 1682 Streltsy Revolt of Kremlin musketeers to force Peter's retarded other half-brother Ivan V to be recognized as co-tsar, under the regency of Sophia.

### Peter the Great

By the time Ivan V died in 1696, Peter had grown into a 24-year-old giant with willpower and energy to match. In 1697, he went on a European tour to study shipbuilding and other technological advances. On returning to Russia, he lost no time in enforcing Westernized reforms, using his fledgling Guards regiments to crush the Streltsy, when they revolted again in 1698.

Tsar Peter I, known as "the Great" (r.1682–1725)

It was Peter's determination to establish a northern port with an unrestricted passage to the Baltic that led to war with Sweden. In 1703, he began to fortify the Neva delta and founded the city of St Petersburg. After victory at Poltava in 1709 diminished the Swedish threat, St Petersburg was proclaimed the capital of Russia in 1712. By the time of Peter's death it had 40,000 inhabitants.

**1552** Mongol capital of Kazan captured; Ivan the Terrible builds St Basil's Cathedral to celebrate

**1598–1605** Reign of Boris Godunov

**1613** Coronation of Mikhail Romanov marks the end of the Time of Troubles and the birth of the Romanov dynasty

*Mikhail Romanov*

**1700–21** Great Northern War against Sweden

**1712** St Petersburg becomes the Russian capital

**1550**

**1600**

**1650**

**1700**

**1584** Ivan the Terrible dies and is succeeded by his son Fyodor

**1610** Moscow falls to the Poles but they are driven out two years later

**1654–67** Second war with Poland

**1682** The Streltsy Revolt; Peter I and his half-brother Ivan V become co-tsars with Sophia as regent

**1725** Peter the Great is succeeded by his widow Catherine I

## The Petticoat Period

For most of the rest of the 18th century Russia was ruled by women, whose taste did much to set the celebrated architectural tone of St Petersburg.

During the brief reigns of Peter's widow Catherine I (r.1725–7) and his grandson Peter II (r.1727–30), the court abandoned this frontier city for Moscow. But when the throne passed to Anna Ioannovna (r.1730–40), the daughter of Ivan V, she set about creating a European court in St Petersburg. Fashion was imported from France and opera from Italy. Many of her ministers were German, including her lover, Count Biron.

In 1741 Peter the Great's daughter, Elizabeth I was crowned tsarina after she staged a coup backed by the Imperial Guards. Her chief legacy is the splendid architecture she commissioned, mainly by her favourite architect, Bartolomeo Rastrelli.

Elizabeth was also responsible for choosing a German princess, Catherine, as wife for her heir, Peter III. By the time Peter III became tsar in 1761, Catherine had lived in Russia for 18 years, spoke fluent Russian and was steeped in Russian culture – unlike her husband, who alienated the nobility with

Portrait of Catherine II by
Alexander Roslin

his Germanic ways. Six months into Peter's reign, Catherine and her allies in the guards deposed the tsar, who was murdered within days of her coronation as Catherine II.

Catherine II, known as "the Great", was an enlightened ruler who reformed the legal system and built hospitals and schools. By the end of her reign, she had left Russia vastly enlarged after successful campaigns against Turkey and Poland, and donated a superb art collection that formed the basis of the Hermitage (see pp154–5).

## War and Peace

Under Catherine II's grandson Alexander I, Russia finally took her place alongside the great European powers during the Napoleonic wars. Alexander I's first campaign against Napoleon was a disaster, leading to the Treaty of Tilsit in 1807, which divided Europe into French and Russian spheres. In 1812, Napoleon advanced on Moscow with a Grande Armée of 600,000 men. However, the Russian Army evacuated, set fire to the city and fled. In just four days, two-thirds of the city burnt down, leaving the French Army without shelter or provisions. Facing winter without supplies, the army began its retreat in October. In celebration, Alexander I commissioned imposing public edifices in the Empire style, which became the dominant movement during the reconstruction of Moscow.

Russian officers who had witnessed the freedom of democratic Europe were frustrated by Alexander I's refusal to consider constitutional reform. When his autocratic

Napoleon and Alexander I drawing up the Treaty of Tilsit in 1807

**1741** Elizabeth I takes power, supported by the Imperial Guards

**1762** Catherine II deposes her husband and is coronated in Moscow

**1750**

Elizabeth I of Russia

**1768–74** First Russo-Turkish War

**1773** Pugachev Rebellion begins

**1787–92** Second Russo-Turkish War

**1775**

**1796** Paul, son of Catherine II, becomes tsar

**1801** Paul is murdered; Alexander I becomes tsar

**1800**

**1805–7** War with France: Russia is defeated at battles of Austerlitz and Friedland

**1825** Nicholas I becomes tsar; the Decembrist Rebellion is crushed

182

THE HISTORY OF RUSSIA | 43

brother Nicholas I was declared tsar in December 1825, they rallied their troops in revolt in what is now Senate Square in St Petersburg. This Decembrist Rebellion was rapidly crushed and Nicholas personally sentenced five ringleaders to death by hanging and over a hundred rebels to exile in Siberia.

## Progress and Reaction

After the unrelenting autocracy of Nicholas I, liberals welcomed the reign of his enlightened son Alexander II (r.1855–81). In 1861, the tsar passed the Edict of Emancipation, abolishing serfdom, but requiring peasants to buy their land at rates that proved ruinous. Industrialization took off as peasants flocked to the big cities to work in factories.

As reforms faltered, revolutionary groups known as Nihilists waged a campaign of terror, killing state officials and, in 1881, Alexander II himself. He was succeeded by Alexander III, an iron-fisted reactionary who forced the revolutionaries underground. As Russia industrialized at breakneck speed, his ministers diverted popular discontent by staging anti-Semitic pogroms. Nobody anticipated that the tsar would die at the age of 47, leaving Alexander II's son Nicholas II (r.1894–1917) to inherit the throne.

## The Death of Tsarist Russia

Nicholas II was chronically indecisive and unfit to rule. An unsuccessful war with Japan (1904–5) was followed by the massacre of Bloody Sunday. On 9 January 1905, peaceful demonstrators were killed in St Petersburg, sparking strikes and uprisings across Russia. To avert further disaster, Nicholas promised an

Bloody Sunday depicted in a painting by Vladimir Makovsky

elected Duma (Parliament), which convened in 1906. However, the tsar simply dissolved the Duma whenever it displeased him and fired ministers at whim. Furthermore, society was scandalized by lurid rumours about the friendship between the royal family and Rasputin (see p176). However, the regime might have survived had Nicholas not committed Russia to war against Germany in 1914.

By late 1916, Russia had lost 3.5 million men, morale at the front was low and food supplies at home were scarce. In February 1917, strikes broke out in St Petersburg, then called Petrograd. The tsar was forced to abdicate, bringing 300 years of Romanov rule to an inglorious end.

A provisional government was formed, which decreed human rights for all, but it fatally undermined its popularity by continuing the war. Its authority was challenged by the Petrograd Soviet of Soldiers, Workers and Peasants, whose "Order No.1", authorizing the formation of *soviets* (local revolutionary councils) throughout the army, threatened what discipline remained. By the autumn of 1917, the provisional government was ripe to be overthrown by more radical revolutionaries.

*Alexander Pushkin*

**1853** Crimean War begins

**1881** Alexander II is assassinated by terrorists; Alexander III becomes tsar

*Tsar Nicholas II*

**1914** Outbreak of World War I, St Petersburg changes name to Petrograd

**1850**          **1875**          **1900**

**1833** Pushkin writes *The Bronze Horseman*

**1861** Emancipation of serfs

**1855** Death of Nicholas I; Alexander II succeeds him

**1894** Alexander III dies; throne passes to Nicholas II

**1917** Tsarist regime falls in February

*February 27, 1917*, a painting by Boris Kustodiev

## Revolution and Civil War

The Bolsheviks were an extreme faction of Russian Marxists, who had split from the more moderate Mensheviks at the party's 1902 congress in Brussels. Under their leader-in-exile, Vladimir Lenin, the Bolsheviks built up an underground network of activists in Russia that awaited Lenin's return following the overthrow of tsarism in February 1917. Lenin lost no time in denouncing the provisional government for its continuation of the war against Germany and in October 1917 the Bolsheviks were able to stage a coup in Petrograd under the slogan "All power to the Soviets".

The October Revolution was the harbinger of a savage Civil War (1918–21) that engulfed all Russia from the Polish border to the Pacific coast of Siberia. The Reds (Bolsheviks) were opposed by a diverse coalition of anti-revolutionary groups that came to be known as the Whites, initially supported by foreign intervention.

By the time the Whites were beaten by the Red Army, Soviet Russia was devastated by years of conflict and Lenin's policy of War Communism, whereby crops were seized from the peasantry to feed the urban proletariat who laboured under military discipline. To revive the shattered economy, Lenin introduced the New Economic Policy, allowing limited private enterprise while retaining state control over the "commanding heights" of the economy. Enfeebled by strokes, Lenin died in 1924, when the Soviet state was still in its infancy.

## The Stalin Years

In the first five years after Lenin's death, Joseph Stalin used his position as General Secretary of the Communist Party to eliminate all rivals and establish a brutal dictatorship that utterly transformed Soviet society, dragging a nation still using horse-drawn ploughs into the nuclear age.

The collectivization of agriculture under the first Five-Year Plan (1928–33) forced peasants to surrender all livestock, machinery and land to collective farms. Up to 10 million peasants are thought to have died during the famine of 1931–2, or in the slave-labour camps of the Gulag, building such "hero projects" as the White Sea Canal. In December 1934, the assassination of the Bolshevik leader Sergei Kirov gave Stalin the pretext for a nationwide purge lasting five years. During this

*Portrait of Joseph Stalin (1879–1953)*

*Lenin (1870–1924)*

**1917** The October Revolution

**1924** Lenin dies; Petrograd is named Leningrad

**1934** Assassination of Party Secretary Kirov triggers the Great Terror

**1942** Shostakovich's *Leningrad Symphony* is broadcast while the city is besieged

**1920**

**1930**

**1940**

**195**

**1918** Civil War begins; the capital moves to Moscow

**1929** Collectivization of private land begins

**1941** Nazi Germany invades Russia; Siege of Leningrad begins

**1945** The Red Army captures Berlin

**1947** The term "Cold War" is coined

Soldiers commemorating their victory over Nazi Germany

period (known as the Great Terror), some 15 million people were arrested, over a million executed and the rest sent to the Gulag.

In 1937–8, the Red Army was included in this purge, which left it ill-prepared for the Nazi invasion of Russia in June 1941. Within months, the Germans had encircled Leningrad, subjecting the city to a 900-day siege that killed 670,000 citizens. The tide turned only at Stalingrad, where the Russians trapped the German Sixth Army in 1943. When the Soviet people celebrated victory over Nazi Germany in 1945, they also mourned 27 million dead and the devastation of much of western Russia, whose cities lay in ruins.

Stalin's iron grip now held Eastern Europe as well as the Soviet Union, as the Cold War with the West began. A new wave of purges was only halted by Stalin's death in 1953.

## Thaw and Stagnation

Stalin's successor, Nikita Khrushchev, denounced Stalin's crimes at the 20th Party Congress – initiating what Russians call "the Thaw". Political prisoners were released and Aleksandr Solzhenitsyn's book, *One Day in the Life of Ivan Denisovich*, about life in the Gulag, was published. The launch of Sputnik in 1957 and Yuri Gagarin's pioneering journey into space four years later made Khrushchev's

boast that Russia would overtake the West sound credible, and new housing and consumer goods seemed a foretaste of future prosperity for Soviet citizens.

However, Khrushchev's decision in 1962 to station nuclear missiles in Cuba brought the world to the brink of nuclear war. In 1964, Khrushchev was deposed by Politburo rivals, but was allowed to live on in obscurity rather than being shot, as disgraced leaders had been previously – a sign of how much had changed since Stalin's time.

When Leonid Brezhnev took over, the intellectual climate froze once more and the persecution of dissidents was stepped up. The first decade of Brezhnev's rule was a time of relative plenty, but beneath the surface a vast black market and network of corruption was growing. Party *apparatchiks* (functionaries), who benefited most from the corruption, had no interest in rocking the boat. When Brezhnev died in 1982, the politburo's choice of two geriatric leaders in succession, Yuri Andropov and Konstantin Chernenko, confirmed that Russia was living in an Era of Stagnation.

Sputnik I in the Soviet pavilion at Brussels World's Fair in 1958

**1953** Stalin dies

**1961** Cosmonaut Yuri Gagarin becomes the first human in space

**1968** Soviet troops enter Czechoslovakia to suppress the "Prague Spring"

*Aleksandr Solzhenitsyn*

**1982** Brezhnev dies and is replaced by Yuri Andropov

**1960**

**1970**

**1980**

**1964** Khrushchev is ousted; Brezhnev becomes General Secretary

**1970** Solzhenitsyn wins the Nobel Prize for Literature for *One Day in the Life of Ivan Denisovich*

**1979** Soviet forces invade Afghanistan

*Yuri Gagarin*

## Glasnost and Perestroika

When 53-year-old Mikhail Gorbachev announced his policies of *glasnost* (openness) and *perestroika* (restructuring) after taking over in 1985, he had no idea of what would follow. The elections for the Congress Peoples' Deputies in 1989 were the first free elections in the Soviet Union since 1917 and contained an element of genuine choice, with rebels such as Boris Yeltsin winning seats.

Mikhail Gorbachev

It was 1989 onwards that local elections brought nationalist candidates to power in the Soviet republics, and democrats to the major Russian city councils. By 1991, the Baltic Republics and a number of other republics had seceded from the Soviet Union. Economic crisis and rising criminality due to slack Soviet law and order led to Communist hardliners pressing for radical reforms to save the country.

In August 1991, die-hard Communists staged a coup against Gorbachev while he was on holiday in Crimea. Military tanks reached the Russian Parliament building

in Moscow, declaring a state of emergency. But Yeltsin, then the President of the Russian Republic, led the popular protest against the coup along with the presidents of other Soviet republics. After three days of confrontation, the coup collapsed with the retreat of the Communist hardliners. Upon Gorbachev's return from house arrest in the Crimea, Yeltsin forced him to outlaw the Communist Party, and in December, the secession of Ukraine and Belarus marked the break-up of the Soviet Union. On 25 December, Gorbachev resigned as president of a state that no longer existed; that evening, the Soviet flag was lowered over the Kremlin and replaced by the Russian tricolour.

## Wild Capitalism

In January 1992, President Yeltsin lifted price controls on subsidized products, sending inflation soaring. Sixteen thousand state enterprises were privatized and citizens given vouchers to "invest" in them, even as wages went unpaid for months. This enabled speculators to buy vouchers for a pittance, thereby gaining ownership of invaluable assets. In Moscow, shoot-outs and car-bombings became common as rival mafia gangs battled over territory.

The social and economic meltdown of "wild capitalism" was exacerbated by a political deadlock between Yeltsin's arch-reformers in the Kremlin and the "red-brown" coalition of Communists and radical nationalists in parliament. The conflict

Boris Yeltsin (1931–2007) defying the August Coup

**1986** Chernobyl reactor fire contaminates 1 million hectares of Belarus and Ukraine

*Chernobyl Nuclear Power plant*

**1988–1990** Estonia declares independence from the USSR, followed by Latvia and Lithuania

**2000** Vladimir Putin becomes President of Russia

**1991** Boris Yeltsin elected President of Russia; dissolution of the Soviet Union

**1996** Yeltsin re-elected president

**1985**

**1985** Gorbachev becomes Soviet leader, espousing *glasnost* and *perestroika*

**1989** First multi-candidate elections for Congress of People's Deputies

**1990**

**1990** Boris Yeltsin declares Russian independence from the USSR

**1993** Conflict between Yeltsin and parliament climaxes in the bombardment of the Russian White House

**1995**

*Vladimir Putin*

200

climaxed in October 1993 when demonstrators descended on the Russian White House and took over the Mayor's offices. The army, on Yeltsin's orders, stormed the building and arrested the ringleaders bringing an end to the conflict.

In December 1994, the Kremlin embarked on a war in Chechnya to subdue the breakaway republic. This left the Chechen capital, Grozny, in ruins with 120,000 dead – including thousands of Russian conscripts. Yeltsin looked set to be defeated in the 1996 presidential election until Russia's financiers and journalists united behind him.

Once the Communist threat was dispelled, the financial oligarchs behind Yeltsin's re-election fell out over the spoils. Vladimir Potanin acquired 30 per cent of the world's nickel reserves for a mere US$70 million, while Boris Berezovsky, Vladimir Gusinsky, Roman Abramovich and Mikhail Khodorkovsky made similar fortunes from oil, gas, telecoms and the media.

## Managed Democracy

By the late 1990s, the ailing Yeltsin needed a successor who could guarantee his family's security and wealth. His chosen heir was Vladimir Putin, an ex-KGB officer made acting prime minister shortly before a wave of apartment-block bombings that killed over 300 people in September 1999. Most Russians readily believed that Chechen terrorists were responsible and applauded Putin's vow to "wipe out terrorists wherever we find them – even on the toilet".

Within weeks, Russia launched a second war on Chechnya as Berezovsky's media empire went into overdrive, casting Putin

Vladimir Putin and Dmitri Medvedev at the Kremlin on 7 May 2008

as the resolute leader that Russia needed. Yeltsin's surprise resignation during his New Year message to the nation on the last night of the old millennium set the stage for Putin's inauguration as president in May 2000. Putin advocated a "strong vertical", appointing governors and mayors from the senior ranks of the armed forces and security services. He slaked the public thirst for vengeance against the oligarchs by forcing two into exile and sending another to a labour camp – but allowed the others to continue enriching themselves provided they courted his favour. The nexus of power and corruption forged in the 1990s reached its zenith in a "mafia state".

Barred by the constitution from a third consecutive term, Putin became prime minister under a new president, Dmitri Medvedev, who pledged to make Russia "a law-based state", but nothing really changed. While Putin's decision to run again as president was expected, the blatantly rigged parliamentary elections of 2011 provoked a wave of protests that caught the Kremlin by surprise.

Although Putin claimed victory in the 2012 election, his "managed democracy" looked threadbare and few believe that another, fourth term as president is feasible.

**2004** Chechen separatists seize a school in Beslan; more than 300 left dead after special forces storm the building

*Protests against election rigging*

**2012** Putin claims victory in presidential election; ascribes protests to "foreign meddling"

**2018** Russia to host the FIFA World Cup"

**2005**

**2010**

**2015**

**2008** Putin becomes prime minister and Dmitri Medvedev is made president

**2011** Rigged elections provoke protests in major cities

**2014** Winter Olympics in Sochi and Krasnaya Polyana

**2015** Opposition activist and former first deputy prime minister Boris Nemtsov is shot dead in Moscow in February

# MOSCOW
# AREA BY AREA

| | |
|---|---|
| The Kremlin | 52–63 |
| Red Square and Kitay Gorod | 64–75 |
| Garden Ring | 76–93 |
| Zamoskvoreche | 94–101 |
| Further Afield | 102–111 |
| Beyond Moscow | 112–117 |

# Moscow at a Glance

The capital city of Russia, Moscow, lies at the heart of European Russia. Spread over an area of 2,510 sq km (970 sq miles), the city grew up around a hilltop citadel, or Kremlin. In medieval times, the adjacent quarter of Kitay Gorod was Moscow's commercial hub. In 1812, almost the entire city was burnt to the ground in a great fire, lit deliberately by Muscovites to deny Napoleon possession of the city. Home to around 10 million today, Moscow is a melange of beautiful pre-Revolutionary architecture and Communist landmarks from the Soviet era. Most of the sights are situated in the city centre, within the area bounded by the Garden Ring and the Boulevard Ring.

**Locator Map**

**Garden Ring**
*(see pp76–93)*

**Bolshoi Theatre** *(see pp82–3)* is Moscow's most iconic cultural landmark. Founded in 1776, the grand six-tiered auditorium stages excellent ballet and opera performances.

**Pushkin State Museum of Fine Arts** *(see pp90–91)* is renowned for its impressive collection of art. In addition to altarpieces by Botticelli and biblical scenes by Rembrandt, the museum houses German archaeologist Heinrich Schliemann's *Treasures of Troy* artifacts.

◀ Bronze monument to Minin and Pozharskiy at the entrance to St Basil's Cathedral, Moscow

**St Basil's Cathedral** (see pp70–71), located in Red Square, is considered to be Russia's most enduring image. The cathedral was built by Ivan the Terrible in 1552 to mark the capture of the city of Kazan.

| 0 metres | 600 |
| 0 yards | 600 |

Bolshoi Theatre

Kremlin
(pp52–63)

Red Square and Kitay Gorod
(see pp64–75)

Zamoskvoreche
(see pp94–101)

**Cathedral of the Assumption** (see pp58–9) served as the venue for coronations and solemn ceremonies of the state until the end of the Romanov dynasty. A magnificent cathedral, it was built between 1475–9.

**The State Tretyakov Gallery** (see pp98–9) showcases the world's largest collection of pre-Revolutionary Russian art, with more than 170,000 works filling its rooms.

# THE KREMLIN

Citadel of the tsars, headquarters of the Soviet Union and now residence of the Russian president, the Kremlin has been a symbol of the power of the State for centuries. In 1156, Prince Yuri Dolgorukiy chose the confluence of the Moskva and Neglinnaya rivers as the site for the first wooden kremlin (*kreml* means fortress). Later, in the 15th century, Tsar Ivan the Great organized a large-scale reconstruction project, inviting several Italian masters to build a sumptuous new complex. They designed the present magnificent ensemble of cathedrals and the Faceted Chamber, among other buildings, in a fascinating fusion of early-Russian and Renaissance styles. Unfortunately, the Kremlin could not escape the architectural vandalism of the 1930s, when it was closed and several of its churches and palaces were destroyed on Stalin's orders. Only in 1955, two years after his death, was the Kremlin partially reopened to the public.

## Sights at a Glance

### Historic Buildings and Monuments
1. Trinity Tower
2. State Kremlin Palace
4. Tsar Cannon
5. Ivan the Great Bell Tower
9. Grand Kremlin Palace
11. Terem Palace
12. Faceted Chamber

### Museums
3. Patriarch's Palace
13. *Armoury Chamber pp62–3*

### Churches and Cathedrals
6. *Cathedral of the Assumption pp58–9*
7. *Cathedral of the Archangel*
8. *Cathedral of the Annunciation*
10. Church of Laying Our Lady's Holy Robe

### Gardens
14. Alexander Gardens

**Locator Map**
*See Street Finder, maps 3 & 4*

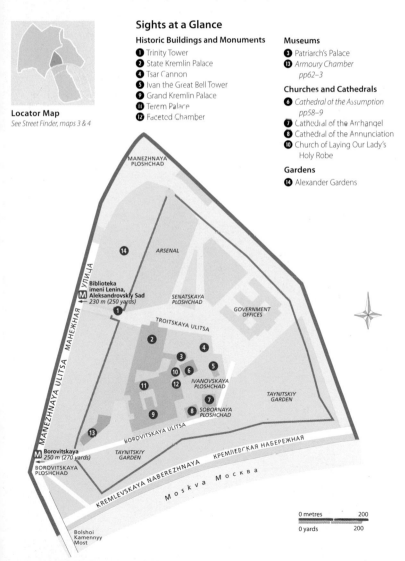

Golden-domed Cathedral of the Annunciation, Kremlin's main square

**For keys to symbols** *see back flap*

# Street by Street: The Kremlin

The Kremlin is home to the Russian president and is the seat of his administration. As a result, less than half of it is accessible to the public, but highlights including the Armoury Chamber, the Patriarch's Palace and the churches in Cathedral Square are open to visitors. Christians have worshipped at this site for more than eight centuries, but their early stone churches were demolished in the 1470s to make way for the present magnificent ensemble of cathedrals. In imperial times, these were the settings for great state occasions such as coronations, baptisms and burials.

Ticket office

**❶ The Trinity Tower** is the gate through which Napoleon marched in triumph when he entered the Kremlin in 1812 (see p42). He left after his defeat a month later.

**❷ The State Kremlin Palace** was originally built in 1961 for Communist Party congresses and is now used for a range of cultural events.

**⓫ The Terem Palace** has a chequered roof and 11 golden cupolas topped by crosses – the only visible part of this hidden building.

**❾ Grand Kremlin Palace**
The palace contains several vast ceremonial halls. The sumptuous stucco work of St George's Hall provides a magnificent backdrop for state receptions. Its marble walls are inscribed with the names of military heroes.

**⓭ ★ Armoury Chamber**
The Armoury Chamber was designed by Konstantin Ton to complement the Grand Kremlin Palace. Constructed in 1844–51, the building is now a museum. It houses the stunning imperial collections of decorative and applied art and the priceless State Diamond Fund.

**Borovitskaya Tower** and entrance if visiting the Armoury Chamber only.

**Key**

— Suggested route

0 metres 50
0 yards 50

**10 Church of Laying Our Lady's Holy Robe**
This served as the domestic church of the metropolitans and patriarchs.

Area illustrated

**3 The Patriarch's Palace** was rebuilt for Patriarch Nikon in 1652–6, and now houses the Museum of 17th-Century Life and Applied Art.

Church of the Twelve Apostles *(see p56)*

**4 The Tsar Cannon**, cast in 1586, weighs a massive 40 tonnes (44 US tons).

**5 The Ivan the Great Bell Tower** became the tallest building in Russia after a third storey was added to this beautiful octagonal tower in 1600.

**6 ★ Cathedral of the Assumption**
This 12th-century painting of St George the Warrior is one of the oldest surviving Russian icons. It forms part of the iconostasis in the cathedral's richly decorated interior.

**7 The Cathedral of the Archangel** has many elaborate tombs including that of Tsarevich Dmitri, the younger son of Ivan the Terrible.

Cathedral Square

**12 The Faceted Chamber** was constructed by two Italian architects, Marco Ruffo and Pietro Solario, between 1485 and 1491.

**8 Cathedral of the Annunciation**
Frescoes cover the walls and ceiling of this cathedral. In the dome above the iconostasis is a painting of Christ Pantokrator, above tiers of pictures of angels, prophets and patriarchs.

## ❶ Trinity Tower

Троицкая башня
*Troitskaya bashnya*

The Kremlin. **Map** 3 C1.

This tower is named after the Trinity Monastery of St Sergius *(see p114)*. The tower's Trinity Gate was once the entrance for patriarchs and the tsars' wives and daughters. At 76 m (249 ft), the Trinity Tower is the Kremlin's tallest. Built in 1495–9, it was linked by a bridge over the Neglinnaya river to the Kutafya Tower – the sole survivor of the circle of towers that was originally built to defend the Kremlin walls. In September 1812, Napoleon marched his army into the Kremlin through the Trinity Gate – they left only a month later, when the Russians set fire to the city.

The seven-storey Trinity Tower, the tallest tower in the Kremlin

## ❷ State Kremlin Palace

Государственный
Кремлёвский дворец
*Gosudarstvennyy Kremlevskiy dvorets*

The Kremlin. **Map** 3 C1. **Open** for performances only.

Sunk 15 m (49 ft) into the ground so as not to dwarf the surrounding buildings, the State Kremlin Palace is the Kremlin's only modern building. It was built in 1961 to host Communist Party conferences. Today, its 6,000-seat auditorium is a venue for ballet, opera and rock concerts.

## ❸ Patriarch's Palace

Патриарший дворец
*Patriarshiy dvorets*

The Kremlin. **Map** 4 D1. **Open** 10am–5pm Fri–Wed. 🖼

The metropolitans of the Russian Orthodox Church lived on the site of the current Patriarch's Palace for many years. When Nikon became the patriarch in 1652, he had the residence extended and renovated to create the Patriarch's Palace, with its integral Church of the Twelve Apostles. The palace now houses the Museum of 17th-Century Life and Applied Art, displaying more than 1,000 exhibits drawn from the Armoury Chamber collection *(see pp62–3)* and from churches and monasteries that were destroyed by Stalin in the 1930s.

Entry to the museum is up a flight of stairs. To the left is the Cross Chamber; when built, it was the largest room in Russia without columns supporting its roof. Consecrated oil called *miro* was produced here and the silver vats and ornate stove used in its production can still be seen.

Located to the right of the stairs, the Church of the Twelve Apostles houses some brilliant icons, including works by Simon Ushakov (1626–86). The iconostasis dates from around 1700 and was brought to the church from the Kremlin Convent of the Ascension before it was demolished in 1929.

The Gala Antechamber has a dazzling array of 17th-century patriarchs' robes, including some of Nikon's own vestments as well as regalia.

The grandiose Patriarch's Palace, former residence of Patriarch Nikon (1605–81)

## ❹ Tsar Cannon

Царь-пушка
*Tsar-pushka*

The Kremlin. **Map** 4 D1.

Cast in 1586, the Tsar Cannon is one of the largest cannons ever made; its bronze barrel weighs 40 tonnes (44 US tons) and has a calibre of 89 cm (35 inches). It was originally intended to guard the Saviour's Tower, but has only ever been used to blast the ashes of the False Dmitri *(see p40)* back towards Poland.

## ❺ Ivan the Great Bell Tower

Колокольня Ивана Великого
*Kolokolnya Ivana Velikovo*

The Kremlin. **Map** 4 D1.

Built to a design by Marco Bon Friazin, this 16th-century bell tower takes its name from the Church of St Ivan Climacus, which stood here in the 14th century. It became the tallest building in Moscow in 1600 when Tsar Boris Godunov added a third storey, extending it to a height of 81m (266 ft).

The massive Tsar Cannon, decorated with reliefs

Beside the tower rises the Assumption Belfry, with its single gilded dome, built in 1532–43. It holds 21 bells, the largest of which, the 64-tonne (71-ton) Assumption Bell, was traditionally tolled three times when the tsar died.

The colossal Tsar Bell, weighing over 200 tonnes (221 US tons), stands at the foot of the bell tower. When the original bell fell from the tower and shattered in a fire in 1701, the fragments were used in a second bell, which was still in its casting pit when the Kremlin caught fire again in 1737. When cold water was poured over the hot bell, a large piece, displayed beside the bell, broke off.

*Tsar Bell, the largest bell in the world*

## 6 Cathedral of the Assumption

*See pp58–9.*

## 7 Cathedral of the Archangel

Архангельский собор
*Arkhangelskiy sobor*

The Kremlin. **Map** 4 D1.

Commissioned by Ivan the Great shortly before his death in 1505, this was the last of the great cathedrals to be built in the Kremlin. Its Venetian architect, Aleviz Novyy, incorporated elements from early-Russian and Italian Renaissance architecture in its design. The cathedral served as the burial place for Moscow's tsars, whose white stone sarcophagi with bronze covers fill the nave. The tsars were no longer buried here after the capital city was moved to St Petersburg in 1712, with the exception of Peter II, who died of smallpox in Moscow in 1730.

The walls, pillars and domes of the cathedral are covered with frescoes painted in 1652–66 by a team of artists led by Simon Ushakov. There are over 60 full-length portraits of Russian rulers, and some images of the Archangel Michael, traditionally the protector of the

early Muscovite rulers. The fresco in the central cupola depicts the triune God. The Father holds the Son on his lap and the Holy Spirit, in the form of a white dove, hovers nearby. The cathedral's four-tiered iconostasis was built in 1680–81.

## 8 Cathedral of the Annunciation

Благовещенский собор
*Blagoveshchenskiy sobor*

The Kremlin. **Map** 4 D1.

Unlike the other Kremlin cathedrals, which were created by Italians, this cathedral is a wholly Russian affair. Ivan the Great commissioned it in 1484 as a royal chapel. It originally had open galleries on all sides but, after a fire in 1547, the corner chapels were added and the galleries were enclosed. On the south façade is the Groznenskiy Porch, from which Ivan the Terrible watched religious services through a grille. He was barred from attending them, having contravened church law by marrying for the fourth time.

The interior of the cathedral is painted with frescoes in warm colours, creating an atmosphere of intimacy. The vertical thrust of the pillars draws the eye upwards to the cupola and its awe-inspiring painting of Christ Pantokrator (Christ as Ruler of All). Three of Russia's greatest icon painters contributed to the iconostasis. Theophanes the Greek painted the images of Christ, the Virgin and the Archangel Gabriel; Andrey Rublev, *The Icon of the Archangel Michael*, *The Annunciation* and *The Nativity*; and Prokhor Gorodetskiy, *The Last Supper* and *The Crucifixion*.

The golden onion-shaped domes of the Cathedral of the Annunciation

# ⑥ Cathedral of the Assumption

Успенский собор

*Uspenskiy sobor*

From the early 14th century, the Cathedral of the Assumption was the most important church in Moscow. It was here that princes were crowned and the metropolitans and patriarchs of the Orthodox Church were buried. In the 1470s, Ivan the Great decided to build a cathedral to reflect the growing might of the nation during his reign. When the first version collapsed, possibly in an earthquake, Ivan summoned to Moscow the architect Aristotele Fioravanti, who designed a spacious masterpiece in the spirit of the Renaissance.

**★ Frescoes**
In 1642–4, a team of artists headed by Sidor Pospeev and Ivan and Boris Paisein painted these frescoes. The walls of the cathedral were first gilded to give the look of an illuminated manuscript.

## KEY

① **The tabernacle** contains holy relics including the remains of Patriarch Hermogen, who starved to death in 1612 during the Polish invasion.

② **Metropolitans' and patriarchs' tombs** line the walls of the nave and the crypt. Almost all the leaders of the Russian Orthodox Church are buried in the cathedral.

③ **The Tsarina's Throne** (17th–19th centuries) is gilded and has a double-headed eagle crest.

④ **The iconostasis** dates from 1652. The haunting 14th-century *Icon of the Saviour Not Made With Hands* is one of several icons forming part of the glorious iconostasis.

⑤ **Orthodox cross**

⑥ **The golden domes** stand on towers inset with windows, which allow light to flood into the interior of the cathedral.

⑦ **Frescoes in the central dome**

⑧ **The pillars** that stand in the centre of the cathedral are painted with over 100 figures of canonized martyrs and warriors.

⑨ **Royal gate**

⑩ **The Harvest Chandelier** contains silver recovered from the French after their occupation of the city in 1812 (see p42).

⑪ **The Patriarch's Seat** was carved from white stone in 1653 for use by the head of the Russian Orthodox Church.

⑫ **Monomakh Throne**

Western door and main entrance

★ **Scenes from the Life of Metropolitan Peter**
This 15th-century icon was made in the workshop of the artist Dionysius, albeit not by the master himself. Located on the cathedral's southern wall, it depicts events in the life of the religious and political leader.

## The Monomakh Throne

The royal seat of Ivan the Terrible is decorated with carvings relating the exploits of Prince Vladimir Monomakh (1053–1125). The panels depict his military campaigns and one shows him receiving the crown from the Byzantine Emperor Constantine Monomachus. This legend was used to confer legitimacy to the idea that the Russian monarchs were the heirs to Byzantium.

Inscribed legend of Prince Vladimir

Panels depicting scenes from Vladimir's life

**South Portal**
This splendid arched portal, decorated with 17th-century frescoes, was the entrance used for royal processions. Brought to Moscow from Suzdal (see p116) in 1401, the door's reverse side is engraved with scenes from the Bible.

## ❾ Grand Kremlin Palace

Большой Кремлёвский дворец
*Bolshoy Kremlyovskiy Dvorets*

The Kremlin. **Map** 3 C1. **Closed** to public.

The grand 125-m (410-ft) façade of this yellow-and-white palace is best admired from the Kremlin embankment. Built to replace an 18th-century palace that previously stood on the site, the Grand Kremlin Palace became the Moscow residence of the royal family. Built between 1837 and 1849, it was designed by a team of architects led by Konstantin Ton *(see p33)*. Ton's design integrated the Terem Palace and Faceted Chamber with the new palace, creating a single complex.

On the ground floor are the private rooms of the royal family, which are offered to visiting heads-of-state. The first-floor state chambers include many ceremonial halls. The St George's Hall has white walls engraved in gold with the names of those awarded the Order of St George, one of Russia's highest military decorations. Grander still is the green and gold St Andrew's Hall, named after the supreme award in the Tsarist Empire, bestowed in post-Soviet times on the Nobel Laureate Alexander Solzhenitsyn, and the inventor of the AK-47 rifle, Mikhail Kalashnikov. Today, the palace serves as the Russian President's residence.

Four of the eleven ornate domes of the Terem Palace churches

## ❿ Church of Laying Our Lady's Holy Robe

Церковь Ризоположения
*Tserkov' Rizopolozheniya*

The Kremlin. **Map** 4 D1.

Crowned by a single golden dome, this church was built in 1484–5 by architects from Pskov *(see pp210–11)*. It is named after a Byzantine feast day that celebrates the arrival, in Constantinople, of a robe supposed to have belonged to the Virgin Mary. The robe is believed to have saved the city from invasion several times.

The church's exterior has distinctive ogee arches shaped like the cross-section of an onion, a feature of many Russian churches from this period and a favourite device of the Pskov school of architecture. Inside the church, the walls and columns are covered with 17th-century frescoes depicting scenes from the lives of the Virgin, Christ, the prophets, royalty and the Moscow metropolitans. The impressive iconostasis created by Nazariy Istomin dates from 1627. To the left of the royal gate is a splendid image of the Trinity, and the *Icon of the Laying of the Virgin's Holy Robe* is to the right.

## ⓫ Terem Palace

Теремной дворец
*Teremnoy dvorets*

The Kremlin. **Map** 3 C1. **Closed** to public.

Built beside the Faceted Chamber in 1635–6, at the behest of Tsar Mikhail Romanov, the palace takes its name from the *terem*, a pavilion-like structure with a red-and-white chequered roof atop the main building. Here, royal wives and concubines were secluded in small, low-vaulted, simply furnished rooms. The tsar had five sumptuous rooms situated on the third floor of the palace, where he selected his bride from a group of virgins ostensibly asleep on eiderdowns, in a ritual known as the *smotriniy* (viewing).

Impressive façade of the Grand Kremlin Palace, as seen from the Kremlin walls

Magnificent vaulted ceiling of the main hall of the Faceted Chamber

The anteroom, where *boyars* and foreign dignitaries waited to be received, leads into the council chamber, where the tsar held these meetings. Beyond this are the throne room, the tsar's bedchamber and a small prayer room.

As a constituent building of the Grand Kremlin Palace, the Terem Palace is part of the residence of the Russian President. Most of the spectacular palace is not visible from the areas of the Kremlin to which the public have access. The eleven ornately decorated, gilded onion domes of the four palace churches, at one end of the palace, are all that can be seen.

## ⑫ Faceted Chamber
Грановитая палата
*Granovitaya palata*

The Kremlin. **Map** 4 D1. **Closed** to public.

Named after its distinctive stonework façade, the Faceted Chamber is all that is left of a larger 15th-century royal palace. It was commissioned by Ivan the Great in 1485, designed by two Italian architects, Marco Ruffo and Pietro Solario, and built over a period of six years. The chamber's first floor comprises the vaulted main hall and adjoining Sacred Vestibule, both decorated with rich frescoes and gilded carvings.

With an area of about 500 sq m (5,380 sq ft), the main hall was the tsars' throne room and banquet hall. Today, it serves as a venue for diplomatic receptions.

On the chamber's southern façade is the Red Staircase. Monarchs passed down this ceremonial staircase en route to the Cathedral of the Assumption *(see pp58–9)* for their coronations. The last such procession was at the coronation of Nicholas II in 1896. During the Streltsy Revolt of 1682 *(see p41)*, many of Peter the Great's relatives were hurled down the Red Staircase on to the pikes of the Streltsy guard. Demolished by Stalin in the 1930s, the staircase was rebuilt in 1994 at great expense.

## ⑬ Armoury Chamber
*See pp62–3.*

## ⑭ Alexander Gardens
Александровский сад
*Aleksandrovskiy sad*

The Kremlin. **Map** 3 C1.

These gardens are named after Tsar Alexander I, who presided over the restoration of the city after the Napoleonic Wars. Before they were laid out in 1821, the Neglinnaya river, part of the Kremlin moat, was channelled underground. The only reminder of its presence is a stone bridge linking the Kremlin's Kutafya and Trinity towers.

An obelisk erected in 1913 in the Upper Garden marks 300 years of the Romanov dynasty. After the 1917 October Revolution, its imperial eagle was removed and the inscription was replaced by the names of thinkers such as Karl Marx and Friedrich Engels.

A short distance away is the marble Tomb of the Unknown Soldier, unveiled in 1967. Its eternal flame, lit with a torch kindled at the Field of Mars in St Petersburg, burns for all the Russians who died in World War II. The body of a nameless soldier is buried beneath the monument, which is inscribed with the words, "Your name is unknown, your deeds immortal."

To the north of the gardens, whimsical statues based on Russian fairy tales such as the *The Frog Princess* welcome visitors to an underground shopping mall. It was opened in 1996 as part of Mayor Yuri Luzhkov's campaign to re-brand Moscow as an affluent, fun-loving metropolis.

Relaxing in Alexander Gardens, one of the first public parks in Moscow

# ⓭ Armoury Chamber

Оружейная палата

*Oruzheynaya palata*

The collection of the Armoury Chamber represents the wealth accumulated by Russian princes and tsars over many centuries. The first mention of a state armoury occurs in 1508, but there were forges in the Kremlin producing weapons and armour as early as the 13th century. Later, gold- and silversmiths, workshops producing icons and embroidery and the Office of the Royal Stables all moved into the Kremlin. The original armoury was demolished in 1960 to make way for the State Kremlin Palace. The current state armoury was built as a museum on the orders of Nicholas I. It was designed by Konstantin Ton in 1844 and completed in 1851.

★ **Fabergé Eggs**
This egg, also a musical box, was made in 1904 in the St Petersburg workshops of the famous House of Fabergé. The egg forms part of a stylized model of the Kremlin.

**Arms and armour** made in the Kremlin workshops are on show here, along with items from Western Europe and Persia.

**Carriages and Sledges**
This magnificent collection includes the beautiful gilded summer carriage presented to Catherine the Great by Count Orlov. The oldest carriage displayed in this collection was a gift from King James I of England to Boris Godunov.

First floor

**The State Diamond Fund**

This dazzling exhibition of diamonds, crowns, jewellery and state regalia includes the famous Orlov Diamond. Taken from an Indian temple, it was one of many presents given to Catherine the Great by her lover Count Grigori Orlov. The tsarina had it mounted at the top of her sceptre. Also on show are Catherine's imperial crown, inset with almost 5,000 gems, and the Shah Diamond, which was given to Tsar Nicholas I by Shah Mirza.

Great Imperial Crown, made for Catherine the Great's coronation

Ground floor

**Ambassadors' gifts**
presented by visiting emissaries from the Netherlands, Poland, England and Scandinavia are displayed here.

Main entrance from the Kremlin grounds

### ★ Crown of Monomakh

Emperor Constantine Monomachus was said to have given this 13th- or 14th-century gold crown to Vladimir Monomakh. Decorated with sable and gems, it was used at royal coronations until 1682.

**Catherine the Great's Coronation Dress** is among the many richly decorated clothes from the royal court on display. An ornate brocade gown embroidered with double-headed eagles in gold thread, it was made in 1762 for the queen's coronation.

Stairs to first floor

Stairs to ground floor

## VISITORS' CHECKLIST

**Practical information**
The Kremlin. **Map** 3 C1. **Tel** (495) 695 41 46. **Open** admittance at 10am, noon, 2:30pm and 4:30pm Fri–Wed. 🕙 Visitors can buy entrance tickets online at www. kreml.ru 🔲 English, call (495) 695 41 46 to book excursions. 🔲 📷
State Diamond Fund: **Tel** (495) 629 20 36. **Open** 10am–1pm and 2–5pm Fri–Wed. 🕙
🎫 English. 📷

**Transport**
Ⓜ Alexandrovskiy sad, Biblioteka imeni Lenina, Borovitskaya.

**Precious fabrics** encrusted with jewels and garments worn by the tsars are on display here.

### ★ Anna of Russia's Coronation Dress

It was in this dress that Anna Ioannovna, niece of Peter the Great, was crowned the Empress of Russia in 1730. Although the original pink colour of the dress has faded due to exposure to light over time, it remains preserved in the folds.

State Diamond Fund entrance

## Gallery Guide

*Tickets for the Armoury Chamber are sold at the Kremlin's main ticket office near Trinity Tower. If visiting in conjunction with other sights in the Kremlin, continue through the Trinity Tower. If only visiting the Armoury Chamber halls, entry is via the Borovitskaya Tower. The State Diamond Fund, a separate museum, is housed within this building.*

**Harnesses** and other equipment, originally produced for the Office of the Royal Stables, can be seen here.

### Key to Floorplan

- 🟨 Russian gold and silver
- 🟫 Arms and armour
- ⬜ Works by European craftsmen
- 🟦 Russian dress and fabrics
- 🟦 Carriages and harnesses
- ⬜ State regalia
- ⬜ Non-exhibition space

**Diamond Throne**
Made in Persia in 1659, this throne was presented to Tsar Alexis by an Armenian trading company. It is encrusted with 900 diamonds and turquoises and is the most valuable throne in the collection.

# RED SQUARE AND KITAY GOROD

Moscow's first suburb, Kitay Gorod was settled in the 12th century by tradesmen and artisans employed by the tsar. In fact, the word *kitay* is thought to refer to the wattle used to build the ramparts around the suburb. Red Square was created as a market square beside the Kremlin in the late 15th century. Behind it, trading rows were set up, with each line of wooden cabins specializing in a particular item, such as icons, pans or hats. In the 16th century, a number of *boyars*, including the Romanovs, built their estates nearby, while the presence of merchants from Novgorod and as far away as England was actively encouraged. In the 19th century, Kitay Gorod became Moscow's financial district, home to the city's first stock exchange and major banks. Today it is a major cultural and historic area.

## Sights at a Glance

### Streets and Squares

**1** Red Square
**7** Ulitsa Varvarka
**11** Ulitsa Ilinka
**12** Nikolskaya Ulitsa
**13** Lubyanka Square

### Historic Buildings and Monuments

**2** Resurrection Gate
**5** GUM

**8** Old English Court
**16** Sandunovskiy Baths

### Churches and Cathedrals

**3** Kazan Cathedral
**6** St Basil's Cathedral *pp70–71*
**10** Church of the Trinity in Nikitniki

### Museums

**4** Lenin Mausoleum
**9** Palace of the Romanov Boyars
**14** Polytechnical Museum
**15** Mayakovsky Museum

**Locator Map**
*See Street Finder, maps 2 & 4*

| 0 metres | 400 |
|---|---|
| 0 yards | 400 |

◀ *Kokoshniki* (tiered gables) adorning Kazan Cathedral, Red Square

**For keys to symbols** *see back flap*

# Street-by-Street: Kitay Gorod

Commerce and religion go hand-in-hand in this ancient part of the city. The heart of Moscow's financial district is Birzhevaya ploshchad, and the surrounding area has been home to traders for centuries. Among the banks and offices are numerous upmarket stores, especially lining Nikolskaya ulitsa, and the area now rivals Russia's best-known shopping arcade, GUM. At one time there were more than 40 churches and monasteries dotted about these narrow streets. Only around a dozen have survived, and most of these are now undergoing painstaking restoration.

**Ploshchad Revolyutsii metro station** has a splendid red marble central hall, flanked by 36 life-size bronze figures, personifying the defence of Soviet power and its achievements.

Russian Supreme Court

Red Square

**Key**

— Suggested route

0 metres          100
0 yards           100

NIKOLSKAYA ULITSA

BOGOYAVLENSKIY PEREULOK

VETOSHNYY PEREULOK

BIRZHEVAYA PLOSHCHAD

ULITSA ILINKA

KHRUSTALNYY PEREULOK

**⑫ Nikolskaya Ulitsa**
Well-heeled shoppers now head to this street's boutiques and jewellery shops. Among its more colourful sights is the Gothic-style Synodal Printing House, which dates from the 19th century.

**The Old Merchants' Chambers**
(Staryy Gostinyy Dvor), from the 18th–19th centuries, houses a shopping arcade.

**⑪ Ulitsa Ilinka**
Halfway along ulitsa Ilinka is Birzhevaya ploshchad, where the former Stock Exchange is located. Constructed in 1873–5 by Aleksandr Kaminskiy, this attractive, pink Neo-Classical building is now the home of the Russian Chamber of Industry and Commerce.

Church of St Barbara

**❼ Ulitsa Varvarka**
Several historic churches line this ancient route out of Moscow. Among them is the Church of St Maxim the Blessed, which was paid for by Novgorod merchants trading in Kitay Gorod and consecrated in 1698.

Area illustrated

**❿ ★ Church of the Trinity in Nikitniki**
Commissioned by the wealthy merchant Grigori Nikitnikov and completed in 1635, the Church of the Trinity in Nikitniki is famous both for its exuberant architecture and for the vivid frescoes that decorate its interior.

**This house** belonged to Simon Ushakov, a leading 17th-century icon and fresco painter. He worked on the nearby Church of the Trinity in Nikitniki.

**❾ ★ Palace of the Romanov Boyars**
This palace was originally occupied by powerful Muscovite *boyar* Nikita Romanov (c.1607–1654). It is now a museum evoking the life of noble families in the 16th and 17th centuries.

Church of St George

Monastery of the Sign

**❽ Old English Court**
Restored to its 17th-century appearance, this merchants' residence was given to visiting English traders by Ivan the Terrible in the hope of securing arms and other goods from them.

urch of St Maxim
e Blessed

Krasnaya ploshchad, or Red Square, with the Historical Museum at its far end

# ❶ Red Square

Красная площадь

*Krasnaya ploshchad*

**Map** 4 D1. Ⓜ Ploshchad Revolyutsii,
Okhotnyy Ryad. Historical Museum:
**Tel** (495) 692 40 19. **Open** 10am–
6pm Mon, Wed, Thu & Sun, 10am–
9pm Fri & Sat (last tickets 8pm).

🖼 📷 ♿

Originally a marketplace, this
area was popularly known as
Fire Square due to frequent fires
in its wooden stalls. The current
name, Krasnaya ploshchad,
dates from the 17th century and
derives from the Russian word
*krasnyy*, which originally meant
"beautiful" but later came to
denote "red". The coincidental
association between the colour
and Communism was fortuitous
for Russia's Soviet rulers.

The square is approximately
500 m (1,600 ft) in length, with a
slight curvature from one end to
another, as it slopes towards the
river. From the 14th century, this
was the setting for public
announcements and executions,
which were staged on a stone
dais called the Lobnoe Mesto.

## Red Square

Resurrection Gate
Kazan Cathedral
Red Square
GUM
Lenin Mausoleum
Lobnoe Mesto
St Basil's Cathedral

It was from this dais that tsars
addressed the people, and
patriarchs blessed the faithful
on Palm Sunday. In the
Soviet era, however, religious
processions were abolished and
military parades were staged
instead. On May Day and the
anniversary of the Revolution,
the line-up of Soviet leaders
atop the Lenin Mausoleum
was studied by foreign
"kremlinologists", trying to work
out the pecking order within
the regime. During the revolutionary utopianism of the 1920s,
Futurists dreamt of erecting a
396-m (1,300-ft) high Monument
to the Third International on the
square, while Stalin later
envisaged destroying its
most famous
landmark,
St Basil's Cathedral
*(see pp70–71)*.

Today, the square
is used for a variety
of cultural events,
concerts, firework
displays and other
public occasions. At
its northern end is the
red-brick **Historical
Museum**, built by
Vladimir Sherwood in the
Russian-Revival style. Among
its exhibits are a 5,000-year-old
oak longboat, Scythian gold-
work and Siberian funerary
masks. Behind the museum on
Manezhnaya ploshchad is an
equestrian statue of Marshal
Georgi Zhukov, the great Soviet
commander. It was erected on
the 50th anniversary of Russia's
victory in World War II.

# ❷ Resurrection Gate

Воскресенские ворота

*Voskresenskie vorota*

Krasnaya ploshchad. **Map** 2 D5.
Ⓜ Okhotnyy Ryad,
Ploshchad Revolyutsii.

This gateway, with its twin red
towers topped by green tent
spires, is a copy of the 17th-
century original, which Stalin
demolished to make Red Square
more accessible for tanks and
marchers. Rebuilt in the 1990s,
the gateway is notable for both
its mosaic icons – one of which
depicts Moscow's patron saint,
St George, slaying the dragon –
and the colourful Chapel
of the Iverian Virgin inside.
Whenever the tsar came to
Moscow, he would visit this
shrine before entering the
Kremlin. Visitors should try
to see the gate at night, when
it is impressively lit up.

# ❸ Kazan Cathedral

Казанский собор

*Kazanskiy sobor*

Nikolskaya ulitsa 3. **Map** 2 D5.
Ⓜ Okhotnyy Ryad. ✉

Besides the Resurrection Gate,
Stalin also demolished the
17th-century Kazan
Cathedral. A heroic
architect, Pyotr
Baranovskiy secretly
made plans to rebuild
it even as it was being
pulled down. He is
also known for saving
St Basil's from a similar
fate. Decades later,
his detailed plans
were used to faith-
fully reconstruct the
cathedral, which was
reconsecrated by
Patriarch Aleksey II in 1993.
The original cathedral housed
the *Icon of the Kazan Virgin*,
revered because it had
accompanied Prince Dmitri
Pozharskiy during his victorious
campaign against the invading
Poles in 1612. When the sacred
icon was stolen in 1904, the
Russians saw it as a bad omen.
The icon that is now on display
in the cathedral is a copy.

Icon of the Kazan Virgin,
Kazan Cathedral

## ❹ Lenin Mausoleum
Мавзолей ВИ Ленина
*Mavzoley VI Lenina*

Krasnaya ploshchad. **Map** 4 D1.
Ⓜ Ploshchad Revolyutsii, Okhotnyy
Ryad. **Open** 10am–1pm Tue–Thu,
Sat & Sun. ✉

Following Lenin's death in 1924,
and against his wishes, it was
decided to preserve the former
Soviet leader's body for posterity.
The body was embalmed and
placed in a temporary wooden
mausoleum in Red Square.
Once it became clear that the
embalming process had worked,
Aleksey Shchusev designed the
current mausoleum of a pyramid
of cubes cut from red granite
and black labradorite.

Paying one's respects to
Lenin's remains was once akin
to a religious experience and
queues used to trail all over
Red Square. Since 1993,
however, a lone militiaman
guards the mausoleum and it
now attracts mostly tourists.
Rumours that Lenin might be
moved from the mausoleum
have proved to be unfounded.

Behind the mausoleum at
the foot of the Kremlin Wall
are the graves of other famous
Communists. They include
Joseph Stalin, Leonid Brezhnev
and Yuri Andropov. Lenin's wife
and sister are also buried here,
as are the first man in space, Yuri
Gagarin, the novelist Maxim
Gorky and the American
journalist John Reed, honoured
for his sympathetic account of
the October Revolution in *Ten
Days that Shook the World*.

Lenin Mausoleum, final resting place of
the Russian leader

The impressive wrought-iron railings and walkways at GUM

## ❺ GUM
ГУМ
*GUM*

Krasnaya ploshchad 3. **Map** 4 D1.
**Tel** (495) 788 43 43. Ⓜ Ploshchad
Revolyutsii, Okhotnyy Ryad.
**Open** 10am–10pm daily. ♿
Ⓦ gum.ru

Before the Revolution, this building
was known as the Upper Trading
Rows after the covered market that
used to stand on the site. In fact,
lines of stalls used to run all the
way from here to the Moskva river.
The store's name, Gosudarstvennyy
Universalnyy Magazin, dates from
its nationalization in 1921.
The building was designed
by Aleksandr Pomerantsev in
1889–93 in the Russian-Revival
style, and the archways, wrought-
iron railings and stuccoed
galleries inside are especially
impressive when sunlight streams
through the glass roof.

There were once more than
1,000 shops here, selling goods
ranging from furs and silks to
humble candles. Nowadays,
Western firms such as Armani,
Max Mara and Dior dominate the
ground floor along with a variety
of cafés and restaurants.

### Embalming Lenin

Preserved body of Lenin

"Do not raise monuments to him, or palaces
to his name, do not organize pompous
ceremonies in his memory." Such were the
words of Lenin's widow, Krupskaya. Despite
this, Lenin's body was embalmed by two
professors and, after a delay to see if the
process had worked, put on display. A
laboratory is dedicated to preserving the
body, which needs regular applications of special fluids. Rumours that
parts of the body have been replaced with wax substitutes are denied.
Besides Lenin, the laboratory has also embalmed such Communist
leaders as Ho Chi Minh (1890–1969) and Kim Il Sung (1912–94).

# ❻ St Basil's Cathedral

Собор Василия Блаженного

*Sobor Vasiliya Blazhennovo*

Commissioned in 1552 by Ivan the Terrible to celebrate the capture of the Mongol stronghold of Kazan, and completed in 1561, this cathedral is reputed to have been designed by the architect Postnik Yakovlev. According to legend, Ivan was so amazed at the beauty of Postnik's work that he had him blinded so that he would never be able to design anything as exquisite again. The church was officially called the Cathedral of the Intercession because the final siege of Kazan began on the Feast of the Intercession of the Virgin. However, it is usually known as St Basil's after the "holy fool" Basil the Blessed whose remains are interred within. The cathedral's design, which was inspired by traditional Russian timber architecture, is a riot of gables, tent roofs and twisting onion domes.

**★ Domes**

Following a fire in 1583 the original helmet-shaped cupolas were replaced by ribbed or faceted onion domes. It is only since 1670 that the domes have been painted in bright colours; at one time St Basil's was white with golden domes.

**Entrance to the cathedral**

## KEY

① **The Chapel of St Basil**, the ninth chapel to be added to the cathedral, was built in 1588 to house the remains of the "holy fool", Basil the Blessed.

② **Chapel of the Three Patriarchs**

③ **Chapel of the Trinity**

④ **Bell tower**

⑤ **Tent roof on the Central Chapel**

⑥ **Chapel of St Nicholas**

⑦ **Chapel of St Varlaam of Khutynskiy**

⑧ **Tiered gables**

⑨ **The Chapel of the Entry of Christ into Jerusalem** was used as a ceremonial entrance during the annual Palm Sunday procession. On this day the patriarch rode from the Kremlin to St Basil's Cathedral on a horse dressed up to look like a donkey.

⑩ **Chapel of Bishop Gregory**

**Chapel of St Cyprian**

This is one of eight main chapels commemorating the campaigns of Ivan the Terrible against the city of Kazan, to the southeast of Moscow. It is dedicated to St Cyprian, whose feast is on 2 October, the day after the last attack.

**Central Chapel of the Intercession**
Light floods in through the windows of the tent-roofed central church, which soars to a height of 61 m (200 ft).

**★ Main iconostasis**
The Baroque-style iconostasis in the Central Chapel of the Intercession dates from the 19th century. However, some of the icons housed inside were painted much earlier.

**Minin and Pozharskiy**

A bronze statue by Ivan Martos depicts two heroes from the Time of Troubles (see pp40–41), the butcher Kuzma Minin and Prince Dmitri Pozharskiy. They raised a volunteer force to fight the invading Poles and, in 1612, led their army to victory when they drove the Poles out of the Kremlin. The statue was erected in 1818, in the triumphal afterglow of the Napoleonic Wars. Originally placed in the centre of Red Square facing the Kremlin, it was moved to its present site in front of St Basil's during the Soviet era.

**★ Gallery**
The gallery runs around the outside of the Central Chapel and connects it to the other eight chapels. It was roofed over at the end of the 17th century and the walls and ceilings were decorated with floral tiles in the late 18th century.

Monument to Minin and Prince Pozharskiy

## 7 Ulitsa Varvarka

Улица Варварка
*Ulitsa Varvarka*

**Map** 4 D1. Ⓜ Kitay Gorod.

Leading eastwards from St Basil's, ulitsa Varvarka is one of Moscow's oldest streets and the heart of the former merchants' quarter of Zaryade. It is named after the medieval Church of St Barbara (Varvara) the Martyr, which was demolished in 1796 to make way for a Neo-Classical church of the same name.

Further along is the Church of St Maxim the Blessed, built in 1698 by traders from Novgorod to house St Maxim's bones. Sandwiched between the two churches is the Old English Court, while across the road stand the Old Merchants' Chambers (Staryy Gostinyy Dvor), a market designed by Giacomo Quarenghi, an Italian architect, in 1790. Today, exhibitions and performances are held in its covered yard.

A little ahead, beside the Palace of the Romanov Boyars is the 17th-century Monastery of the Sign, whose red-brick cathedral is adorned with *kokoshniki* (tiered gables) and four onion domes covered in green-and-red shingles. The last in the row of historic churches is the Church of St George, built in 1657–8 by merchants from Pskov *(see pp210–11)*. A surviving section of Kitay Gorod's medieval walls can be seen in the subway entrance to the Kitay Gorod metro.

Domes of the historic Church of St George, ulitsa Varvarka

## 8 Old English Court

Старый английский двор
*Staryy angliyskiy dvor*

Ulitsa Varvarka 4a. **Map** 4 D1. **Tel** (495) 698 39 52. Ⓜ Ploshchad Revolyutsii, Kitay Gorod. **Open** 10am–6pm Tue, Wed, Fri–Sun & 11am–9pm Thu. **Closed** last Fri of the month. 🎧 📷 English, call (495) 606 06 05 to book.

This building is Moscow's earliest known diplomatic mission. In 1553, while searching for the northern coast of Russia for a passage to the east, the English merchant-adventurer Richard Chancellor was shipwrecked. He was taken to Moscow and received by Ivan the Terrible, whose desire to trade with England later led him to propose marriage to Queen Elizabeth I. On returning to Russia in 1556, Chancellor and his trading mission were given this property in Zaryade to serve as a depot, trading house and lodgings for English merchants.

The company exported furs, caviar and honey until it was expelled from Russia in 1649 by Tsar Alexis, who was enraged by the execution of Charles I. Pyotr Baranovskiy, who recognized the building's medieval origins, saved it from demolition in the 1960s and it reopened as a museum during the state visit of Queen Elizabeth II to Russia in 1994.

Exhibits include 16th–17th-century weapons and men's and women's English garments. Stone staircases lead down to the official chamber once used for negotiations and functions. English merchants fitted the Russian stove with an open hearth as a reminder of home.

Ornate dining room in the Palace of the Romanov Boyars

## 9 Palace of the Romanov Boyars

Палаты бояр Романовых
*Palaty Boyar Romanovikh*

Ulitsa Varvarka 10. **Map** 4 E1. **Tel** (495) 698 12 56. Ⓜ Kitay Gorod. **Open** 10am–6pm Thu–Mon, 11am–7pm Wed. **Closed** first Mon of the month. 🎧

Only the upper storeys of this palace can be seen from ulitsa Varvarka, since it is built on a steep slope that descends from the street towards the Moskva river. Originally built by the *boyar* Nikita Romanov in the 16th century, it was home to the Romanovs until 1613 when Mikhail Romanov *(see p41)* became tsar and the family moved to the Kremlin. The palace was restored on the orders of Nicholas I and has been protected as a museum since 1859.

A frozen ulitsa Varvarka, with the Old English Court in the background

Magnificent gilded iconostasis in the Church of the Trinity in Nikitniki

A double-headed eagle, the Romanov family crest, adorns the archway leading to the courtyard via which visitors enter the palace. The ground and first floors probably date from the 17th century. In the painted hall, personal effects of the early Romanovs are displayed, including gold dishes, ancient title deeds, ledgers inlaid with precious gems and the robes of Nikita's eldest son, Patriarch Fyodor Filaret. The rooms have been refurbished in the lavish style of the period, with walls covered in gilt-embossed leather or painted in accents of red, green and gold.

In the 16th and 17th centuries even the richest families had to tolerate rather cramped and dim conditions. The portals in the palace are so low that a man of average height has to stoop; the windows let in little light because they are made of mica, a translucent mineral, rather than glass. After a fire in 1674, a light and airy wooden upper storey was added to the palace, where the Romanov women-folk occupied their lives with weaving. The main hall on this level has a beautifully carved wooden ceiling.

## ❿ Church of the Trinity in Nikitniki

Храм Святой Троицы в Никитниках

*Khram Svyatoy Troitsy v Nikitnikakh*

Nikitnikov pereulok 3. **Map** 4 E1. **Tel** (495) 698 34 51. Ⓜ Kitay Gorod. **Closed** to public. Ⓦ **nikitniki.ru**

This splendid church is dwarfed by ugly 1970s buildings that were once Communist Party offices. When it was founded in 1635 by Grigori Nikitnikov, a wealthy merchant, the church would have dominated the local skyline with its five green domes, its profusion of decoration and painted tiles, and its tiers of *kokoshniki* (tiered gables). The equally elaborate tent-roofed bell tower, linked to the main building by an enclosed gallery, was

The pediment of the Russian Chamber of Industry and Commerce on ulitsa Ilinka

added shortly after construction was finished in 1653.

The church's frescoes were completed three years later, shortly before Nikitinikov died from the plague, which remained a scourge in Moscow until well into the 18th century. Many of the frescoes, such as *The Parable of the Rich Man*, portray scenes from the Gospels in direct, emotional terms, and are credited to the great fresco and icon painter Simon Ushakov (1626–86). He also painted several panels in the splendid gilded iconostasis, including *The Annunciation of the Virgin*, to the left of the Royal Doors (*see pp26–7*).

## ⓫ Ulitsa Ilinka

Улица Ильинка

*Ulitsa Ilinka*

**Map** 4 D1. Ⓜ Kitay Gorod.

Before the Revolution, this narrow street running alongside GUM was home to many banks and trading offices. Their colourful façades remain the highlight of a stroll along the street even today. Several important institutions are still located here, despite a wholly new financial district having sprung up a mile upriver from the Kremlin since the mid-1990s.

Russia's previous surge of capitalism – at the turn of the 19th and 20th centuries – was notable for its God-fearing entre-preneurs known as *Kuptsy*. When Moscow's first stock exchange opened in 1836, many merchants still wore long patriarchal beards and the traditional kaftan, and were used to dealing with one another in the street. They had to be coerced by the police to do business in the new premises on the corner of Birzhevaya ploshchad. The building now houses the Russian Chamber of Industry and Commerce. Across the street, a Russian-Revival-style pile built in 1876 is home to the Supreme Court, which has ruled on many disputes between oligarchs in the capitalist free-for-all of post-Communist Russia.

Gothic-style façade of the Synodal Printing House, Nikolskaya ulitsa

## ⑫ Nikolskaya Ulitsa
Никольская улица
*Nikolskaya ulitsa*

**Map** 2 D5. Ⓜ Lubyanka, Ploshchad Revolyutsii.

Named after the Kremlin's Nicholas's Tower, this street was settled by merchants and traders from the 12th century onwards. Long characterized by its shops, stalls and monasteries, Nikolskaya ulitsa underwent decades of dowdiness under Communism before reasserting its commercial vigour in the 1990s, when many designer clothes stores and jewellers opened up here.

Through the courtyard at No. 7 is a gateway leading into the Zaikonospasskiy Monastery, which was founded in the 15th century or earlier. The name means Saviour Beyond the Icons and recalls the time when there was a brisk trade in icons here. From 1687–1814 the monastery also housed Moscow's first institute of higher education, the Slavic Greek Latin Academy, whose pupils included the future founder of Moscow University, Mikhail Lomonosov.

At No. 15 are the Gothic-style spires of the Synodal Printing House. The pale blue building, with a lion and unicorn sculpted over its central window, dates from 1810–14. Its courtyard is enhanced by a colourful chequered roof and walls of blue and white tiles. In the chambers previously on this site Ivan Fyodorov produced Russia's first printed book, *The Acts of the Apostles* (1564), before being forced to flee by superstitious Muscovites incensed by what they saw as "Satan's work".

Next door, in the courtyard of No. 17, is the Slavyanskiy Bazaar restaurant, founded in 1870. Its former patrons include the theatre directors Konstantin Stanislavskiy and Vladimir Nemirovich-Danchenko, whose legendary 18-hour-long discussion led to the founding of the Moscow Arts Theatre *(see p84)*. The restaurant obligingly stayed open until two o'clock in the morning, when they finished talking.

## ⑬ Lubyanka Square
Лубянская площадь
*Lubyanskaya ploshchad*

**Map** 2 D5. Ⓜ Lubyanka.

For generations of Soviet citizens, the name Lubyanka was synonymous with the Communist secret police, which began life as the Cheka and evolved into the KGB of Cold War notoriety, before being renamed the Federal Security Service (FSB) in post-Communist Russia. The institution is inseparable from its headquarters in the former Rossiya Insurance building, taken over in 1918 by the Cheka's founder, "Iron" Feliks Dzerzhinskiy. His statue loomed over Lubyanka Square until it was toppled by a crowd following the unsuccessful coup against President Gorbachev in 1991 *(see p46)*.

While Dzerzhinskiy's statue has been relegated to the Muzeon *(see p107)*, the secret police are still ensconced in the Lubyanka, which was enlarged in the 1930s and 1940s to include an underground prison where thousands of people were interrogated, tortured and killed. The only monument to their fate is a boulder from the Solovetskiy concentration camp, embedded on the edge of Lubyanka Square near the Polytechnic Museum.

Far more prominent is Russia's largest toyshop, Tsentralnyi Detskiy Magazin (Central Children's Store), formerly known as Detskiy Mir (Children's World), which the Soviet authorities built just across from the Lubyanka in 1957 – supposedly as a tribute to Dzerzhinskiy, who chaired a committee on children's welfare after the Revolution.

The formidable FSB headquarters on Lubyanka Square

Sophisticated waiting area inside the plush Sandunovskiy Baths

The Polytechnical Museum, at the southern end of Lubyanka Square

# ⓴ Polytechnical Museum

Политехнический музей
*Politekhnicheskiy muzey*

Novaya ploshchad 3/4.
**Map** 2 E5. **Tel** (495) 625 06 14.
Ⓜ Kitay Gorod, Lubyanka.
**Closed** for renovation until 2018.
Ⓟ Ⓦ **polymus.ru**

The southern end of Lubyanka Square is dominated by the Polytechnical Museum, built in the 1870s. Many of its exhibits were originally assembled for an exhibition staged to mark the 200th anniversary of the birth of Peter the Great, but its collection has been expanded to trace the development of Russian science and technology from the 19th century onwards. Every two hours there are demonstrations of devices such as robots, sound equipment and working models.

# ⓯ Mayakovsky Museum

Музей-квартира ВВ Маяковского
*Muzey-kvartira VV Mayakovskovo*

Lubyanskiy proezd 3/6. **Map** 2 E5.
**Tel** (495) 621 93 87. Ⓜ Lubyanka.
**Open** 11am–7pm Fri–Tue, 1–9pm Thu.
**Closed** last Fri of the month. Ⓟ Ⓕ
Ⓦ **mayakovsky.museum**

Poet, iconoclast and self-publicist Vladimir Mayakovsky gave voice to the Revolution in his verses, plays, film scripts and poster art. Mayakovsky's provocative persona is reflected in this museum where artworks mingle with his belongings. Huge frameworks of metal bars lean at fantastic angles, providing a backdrop to chairs, old boots, typewriters, posters, sewing machines, photomontages and manuscripts.

Room designed to symbolize Mayakovsky's poetic origins

Mayakovsky actually lived in this block from 1919 until his death in 1930 – a single room on the fourth floor has been furnished to look as it would have done when he moved in. While living here, Mayakovsky continued his long-running love affair with Lilya Brik, the wife of his friend Osip Brik. The last part of the exhibition deals with Mayakovsky's suicide at the age of 37, following which Stalin praised him as the greatest of Soviet poets and continued to use his work for propaganda purposes.

# ⓰ Sandunovskiy Baths

Сандуновские бани
*Sandunovskie bani*

Neglinnaya ulitsa 14, building 3–7.
**Map** 2 D4. **Tel** (495) 625 46 31.
Ⓜ Kuznetskiy Most, Trubnaya.
**Open** 8am–10pm daily (last adm: 8pm). Ⓟ Ⓩ Ⓦ **sanduny.ru**

The back streets beyond Lubyanka harbour Moscow's famous Sandunovskiy Baths, founded in 1808 by the actor Sila Sandunov. A Beaux-Arts façade hides a sumptuous interior decorated in a mix of styles, inspired by the Alhambra Palace in Spain. The best, most expensive facilities are located on the first floor. Thrashing yourself with birch branches is an integral part of the Russian *banya* (steam bath) experience *(see p298)*.

# GARDEN RING

The Garden Ring *(Sadovoye Koltso)* marks the limit of what used to be the fortifications encircling the Kremlin and Kitay Gorod in the 17th century. After the 1812 Great Fire of Moscow destroyed the city centre, it was rebuilt in a mainly Neo-Classical style, in a patchwork of mansions and orchards, with a network of boulevards and side streets running along its perimeter. In Soviet times this leafy periphery was turned into a ring road dominated by Stalin-Gothic skyscrapers. The juxtaposition of Soviet gigantism and pre-Revolution elegance lends a unique character to this area. Alongside cultural landmarks such as the Bolshoi Theatre and Pushkin State Museum of Fine Arts is the grand Cathedral of Christ the Saviour. The atmospheric back-streets between the cathedral and the Old Arbat area, with its historic churches and early 19th-century mansions, make for a rewarding walk.

## Sights at a Glance

### Historic Buildings and Monuments
1 Hotel Metropol
4 House of Unions
5 Hotel National
10 Morozov Mansion
11 Upper Monastery of St Peter
15 Patriarch's Pond
21 Pashkov House
30 Melnikov House
32 Ministry of Foreign Affairs

### Streets and Squares
2 Theatre Square
6 Manège Square
7 Tverskaya Ulitsa
9 Bryusov Pereulok
12 Pushkin Square
20 Bolshaya Nikitskaya Ulitsa
26 Arbat Square
29 Spasopeskovskiy Pereulok

### Theatres and Concert Halls
3 *Bolshoi Theatre pp82–3*
8 Moscow Arts Theatre
19 Moscow Conservatory

### Museums
13 Museum of Contemporary History
14 Bulgakov House and Museum
16 Chekhov House-Museum
17 Gorky House-Museum
18 Stanislavskiy House-Museum
22 *Pushkin State Museum of Fine Arts pp90–91*
23 *Gallery of 19th- and 20th-Century European and American Art*
24 Glazunov Picture Gallery
27 Lermontov House-Museum
28 Skryabin House-Museum
31 Pushkin House-Museum
33 Shalyapin House-Museum

### Churches and Cathedrals
25 Cathedral of Christ the Saviour

**Locator Map**
*See Street Finder, maps 1, 2 & 3*

| 0 metres | 600 |
|---|---|
| 0 yards | 600 |

◀ The Patriarchal Bridge over the Moskva river leading to the Cathedral of Christ the Saviour

For keys to symbols *see back flap*

# Street-by-Street: Around Theatre Square

Moscow's theatreland is centred, quite appropriately, around Theatre Square (Teatrelnaya ploshchad). Dominating the square is one of the most famous opera and ballet stages in the world, the Bolshoi Theatre. The Malyy (Small) Theatre is on the east side of the square, while the Russian Academic Youth Theatre is on the west. Further to the west is the city's main shopping street, Tverskaya ulitsa, and two more theatres, the Yermolova Theatre and the Moscow Arts Theatre. There are also several excellent restaurants and bars in this neighbourhood.

**Yuri Dolgorukiy,** Moscow's founder, is depicted in this statue. It was unveiled in 1954, seven years after the city's 800th anniversary.

Pushkin Square

**❾ Bryusov Pereulok**
A granite archway leads from Tverskaya ulitsa to this quiet lane, once home to director Vsevolod Meyerhold. The 17th-century Church of the Resurrection is visible further down the lane.

Bolshaya Nikitskaya ulitsa

**❼ Tverskaya ulitsa**
is Moscow's main shopping street. Most of the imposing Stalinist blocks here date from the 1930s, but a few older buildings survive.

Central Telegraph Office

Yermolova Theatre

Lower Chamber of the Russian Parliament

**❽ Moscow Arts Theatre**
This famous theatre will always be associated with the dramatist Anton Chekhov (see p31). Several of his plays, including The Cherry Orchard, were premiered here.

Okhotnyy Ryad

**❺ Hotel National**
The National is a mix of Style-Moderne and Neo-Classical architecture. Now restored, its decor is as impressive as it was before the Revolution, when it was Moscow's finest hotel.

**❸ ★ Bolshoi Theatre**
Two earlier theatres on this site, including the first Bolshoi, were destroyed in fires. The current building was completed by Albert Kavos in 1856.

GARDEN RING

THE KREMLIN

☐ Area illustrated

**Petrovskiy Passage** is a fashionable shopping arcade (see p119).

Bolshoi Small Stage

**Key**

━ Suggested route

| 0 metres | 150 |
| 0 yards | 150 |

**The Malyy Theatre** is one of the oldest in Moscow. A statue of the great 19th-century playwright Aleksandr Ostrovskiy stands in front.

ULITSA PETROVKA

KUZNETSKIY MOST

DMITROVKA

M

OKHOTNYY RYAD

TSA

**❶ Hotel Metropol**
Built in 1899–1905 by Englishman William Walcot, the Metropol is one of Moscow's grandest hotels. This painted, glazed ceiling is the outstanding feature of the main dining room.

Russian Academic Youth Theatre

PLOSHCHAD REVOLYUTSII

Teatralnaya

Red Square

**❹ ★ House of Unions**
In the 1780s, architect Matvei Kazakov converted this Neo-Classical mansion into a noblemen's club. The trade unions took it over in the Soviet era, when it hosted Stalin's infamous show trials.

**❷ Theatre Square**
Laid out in its present form in the 1820s, Theatre Square served as a military parade ground between 1839–1911. Playbills around the city advertise performances in the theatres on the square.

## ❶ Hotel Metropol

Гостиница Метрополь
*Gostinitsa Metropol*

Teatralnyy proezd 2. **Map** 2 D5.
**Tel** (499) 501 78 00. Ⓜ Teatralnaya.

Built in 1899–1905, the Hotel Metropol is a fine example of Style-Moderne architecture *(see p33)* by William Walcot. *The Daydreaming Princess*, a large ceramic panel by Mikhail Vrubel, crowns its façade, and the hotel has a superb painted glass roof in its Metropol Zal restaurant. Its celebrity guests have included Irish dramatist George Bernard Shaw and Michael Jackson.

## ❷ Theatre Square

Театральная площадь
*Teatralnaya ploshchad*

**Map** 2 D5. Ⓜ Teatralnaya, Ploshchad Revolyutsii, Okhotnyy Ryad.

This elegant square is named after the theatres on three of its sides. Originally this area was marshy ground; in the 1820s the square was laid out to a design by Osip Bove. Today, Theatre Square is dominated by the Bolshoi Theatre. On the square's eastern side is the Malyy (Small) Theatre, where Aleksandr Ostrovskiy's satirical plays were staged. The Russian Academic Youth Theatre, with its elaborate Neo-Classical porch, stands on the square's western side, beside the Bolshoi Theatre's small stage.

To the northwest of Theatre Square is the Operetta Theatre. In the 1890s, the private opera company of the wealthy industrialist and arts patron Savva Mamontov (1842–1914) performed here. The opera singer Fyodor Shalyapin *(see p93)* and the famous pianist and composer Sergei Rachmaninov began their careers with Mamontov's company.

In the centre of the square is a granite statue of Karl Marx, erected in 1961, bearing the words "Workers of the world unite!"

## ❸ Bolshoi Theatre

*See pp82–3.*

## ❹ House of Unions

Дом Союзов
*Dom Soyuzov*

Bolshaya Dmitrovka ulitsa 1. **Map** 2 D5. **Tel** (495) 692 07 36. Ⓜ Teatralnaya, Okhotnyy Ryad. **Open** for performances only. Ⓦ **domsojuzov.ru**

This green and white Neo-Classical mansion built in the first half of the 18th century was converted into a noblemen's club in the early 1780s by architect Matvei Kazakov *(see p33),*

The elegant façade of the 18th-century House of Unions

who added a number of rooms including a magnificent ballroom known as the Hall of Columns. It was here, in 1856, that Tsar Alexander II addressed the Russian nobility on the need to emancipate the serfs.

After the Revolution, trade unions took over the building; in 1924 the hall was used for the lying in state of Lenin's body, when over a million citizens filed past his open coffin. Many of his closest colleagues, who formed the guard of honour, were later tried here during the infamous show trials of 1936–8 staged by Stalin, who lay in state here himself in 1953. Nowadays, the House of Unions is used for concerts and public meetings.

The luxurious Metropol Zal restaurant with its painted glass roof, inside the Hotel Metropol

## ❺ Hotel National

Гостиница Националь

*Gostinitsa Natsional*

Mokhovaya ulitsa 15/1. **Map** 1 C5.
**Tel** (495) 258 70 00. Ⓜ Okhotnyy
Ryad. 🛍 🍴 ♿

The Hotel National is an eclectic
mixture of Style-Moderne and
Classical-style architecture.
Its façade is topped by a mosaic
from the Soviet era featuring
factories belching smoke,
oil derricks, railway engines
and tractors.

Lenin stayed in Room 107
at the National for a week, in
March 1918, before moving
into the Kremlin. In the early
1990s, the hotel was totally
refurbished and its Style-
Moderne interiors were restored
to their original splendour.

The ornately painted façade and mosaic
of the Hotel National

## ❻ Manège Square

Манежная площадь

*Manezhnaya ploshchad*

**Map** 1 C5. Ⓜ Biblioteka Imeni Lenina,
Okhotnyy Ryad. Manège: **Tel** (495) 645
92 77. **Open** exhibitions only. 🎦 🖼
🌐 **moscowmanege.ru**

The square is named after the
Tsarist military riding school,
Manège, situated at its southern
end. Built in 1817 to a design by
General Augustin de Béthencourt,
the Manège's 45-m (148-ft) wide
roof had no supporting columns,
leaving an uninterrupted floor
space large enough for a squad-
ron of cavalry to manoeuvre.
In 1957, it became the Central
Exhibition Hall, where Nikita
Khrushchev *(see p45)* condemned abstract art at an
exhibition in 1962. Khrushchev
posthumously made amends to
the sculptor Ernst Neizvestniy –
whose work he had lambasted –
by specifying in his will that

The Manège, designed by Augustin de Bethencourt in 1817, lit up at night

Neizvestniy should design his
tombstone. Fire partly destroyed
the building in 2004, but it was
swiftly rebuilt and is still used
to house exhibitions.

The square itself underwent
substantial renovation in the
1990s. Mayor Yuri Luzhkov had
a shopping mall constructed
beneath the square in an effort
to humanize the bleak space.

The Moscow Old University is
another principal landmark here.
Founded by the polymath Mikhail
Lomonosov in 1755, the university
moved into this building in 1793.
Designed by Matvei Kazakov in
1782, it was rebuilt by Domenico
Gilardi after the 1812 Great Fire
and is an excellent example of
Neo-Classical architecture.

## ❼ Tverskaya Ulitsa

Тверская улица

*Tverskaya ulitsa*

**Map** 1 B3. Ⓜ Okhotnyy Ryad,
Tverskaya, Pushkinskaya.

During the 19th century,
Tverskaya ulitsa was the
grandest thoroughfare in

Elegant boutique lining Tverskaya ulitsa,
one of Moscow's main shopping streets

Moscow, renowned for its
restaurants, theatres, hotels and
purveyors of French fashions.
Stalin's reconstruction of Moscow
in the 1930s resulted in the road
being widened by 42 m (138 ft)
and renamed after the writer
Maxim Gorky. Many buildings
were torn down to make way
for apartment blocks to house
party bureaucrats, and others
were rebuilt further back on
the wider road. Now called
Tverskaya ulitsa again, the
street and surrounding area are
among Moscow's most popular
places to eat out and shop.

At No. 7 is the Central Telegraph
Office, a severe grey edifice,
outside which is an illuminated
globe, designed by Ilya Rerberg
in 1927. Through the arch on the
far side of the road is a green-
tiled building with floral friezes
and tent-roofed turrets, built in
1905 as the Moscow mission of
the Savvinskiy Monastery; it now
contains luxury flats and offices

Further up the street, Tverskaya
Square is dominated by the
red-and-white Mayor's office,
designed in 1782 by Matvei
Kazakov as the residence of
Moscow's Tsarist governor-
general. After the Revolution,
it became the Moscow City
Soviet or town hall.

Beyond Tverskaya Square, at
No. 14, is Moscow's pre-eminent
delicatessen, Yeliseyevsky Food
Hall. In the 1820s, this building
was the home of Princess Zinaida
Volkonskaya, whose soirées
were attended by great figures
of the day, including Alexander
Pushkin *(see p93)*. In 1898, Grigori
Yeliseev bought the building
and had it lavishly redecorated
with stained-glass windows,
crystal chandeliers, polished
wood counters and huge mirrors.

# ❸ Bolshoi Theatre

Большой театр

*Bolshoy teatr*

Established in 1776, the Bolshoi ballet and theatre companies
are among the oldest in the world. The first theatre building
opened in 1780, but was razed by fire in 1805, forcing the
company to perform at the Petrovsky Theatre. Soon this
building too was consumed by fire during Napoleon's
invasion. Its successor was completed in 1825 to a design
by Osip Bove and Andrei Mikhaylov. However, the building
was once again claimed by fire, in 1853, and was reconstructed by Albert Kavos in 1856. The building was closed for six
years of renovations in 2005. It finally reopened in 2011.

Elegant ballet dancers performing Victor Hugo's
*Esmeralda*, Bolshoi Theatre

**★ Apollo in the Chariot
of the Sun**
This eye-catching sculpture by
Pyotr Klodt, part of the original
1825 building, was retained by
Albert Kavos. It depicts Apollo
driving the chariot on which
he carried the sun
across the sky.

## KEY

① **Eight-columned portico**

② **The Neo-Classical pediment**
boasts a relief depicting a pair
of angels bearing aloft the lyre of
Apollo, the Greek god of music
and light. The relief was an
addition by Albert Kavos during
his reconstruction of the theatre.

③ **The auditorium** has six tiers and
a seating capacity of 1,740. When
Kavos rebuilt it he modified its
shape to improve the acoustics.

④ **Main stage**

⑤ **The upper stage** is where the
ballet dancers rehearse and perfect
their technique.

⑥ **Artists' dressing rooms**

⑦ **The exhibition foyer** extends
around the whole of the front of the
building on the first floor and hosts
temporary exhibitions that are open
to the public during performances.

**New Beethoven Concert Hall** is
an impressive 300-seat hall that
lies beneath Theatre Square
(Teatralnaya ploshchad) *(see p90)*. It
was added during the recent
renovation work and is accessed
from inside the Bolshoi Theatre. The
hall features moveable sections of
floor that can be lowered or raised to
transform it into an amphitheatre.

Entrance

**Vestibule**
Patrons entering the theatre find themselves in this
grand grey and white tiled vestibule. Magnificent
staircases, lined with white marble, lead up from either
side of the vestibule to the spacious exhibition foyer.

**Small Imperial Foyer**
This ornately decorated room was known as the Beethoven Hall in the Soviet era. It is now used for occasional exhibitions. The stuccoed decoration on the ceiling includes about 3,000 rosettes and the walls are adorned with delicately embroidered panels of crimson silk.

## VISITORS' CHECKLIST

**Practical information**
Teatralnaya ploshchad 1.
**Map** 2 D5.
**Tel** (495) 455 55 55.
**W** bolshoi.ru
**Open** Tue–Sun for performances.
**Closed** every year in August and reopens in the second week of September.
**in auditorium.**

**Transport**
12. **M** Teatralnaya. 2, 12.

**Apollo and the Muses**
The ten painted panels decorating the auditorium's ceiling are by Pyotr Titov. They depict Apollo dancing with the nine muses of Greek myth, each of which is connected with a different branch of the arts or sciences.

## The Bolshoi Ballet in the Soviet Era

In the 1920s and 1930s, new ballets conforming to revolutionary ideals were created for the Bolshoi, but the company's heyday was in the 1950s and 1960s. Ballets were produced and the dancers toured abroad for the first time to widespread acclaim. The distinguished

Soviet choreographer Yuri Grigorovich staged a number of productions for the Bolshoi, including *Spartacus*, *Ivan the Terrible* and *Golden Age*.

The Bolshoi Ballet Company's production of *Spartacus* (1954)

**★ Royal Box**
Situated at the centre of the gallery, the royal box, hung with crimson velvet, is one of over 120 boxes. The imperial crown on its pediment was removed in the Soviet era but has now been restored.

## ❽ Moscow Arts Theatre
### МХАТ имени АП Чехова
*MKhAT imeni AP Chekhova*

Kamergerskiy pereulok 3. **Map** 1 C5.
**Tel** (495) 629 87 60, (495) 646 36 46.
Ⓜ Teatralnaya, Okhotnny Ryad.
**Open** performances only. Ⓦ **mxat.ru**

The Moscow Arts Theatre (MKhAT) was founded by a group of young enthusiasts, led by the directors Konstantin Stanislavskiy and Vladimir Nemirovich-Danchenko and the first ever performance took place in 1898. The theatre made a name for itself with a production of Anton Chekhov's play *The Seagull* in its first year. When staged three years earlier in St Petersburg it was a disastrous flop, but performed using Stanislavskiy's new method acting *(see p28)*, it was rapturously received.

In 1902, architect Fyodor Shekhtel *(see p33)* reconstructed the theatre's interior, adding innovations such as a central lighting box and a revolving stage. The auditorium was sparsely decorated so that audiences were forced to concentrate on the performance.

The theatre's repertoire was restricted after the Revolution by state censorship. Most of the plays produced were written by Maxim Gorky, whose work was in favour with the regime. The frustrations and compromises of the period were satirized in the 1930s by Mikhail Bulgakov in his novel *Teatralnyy Roman*.

The Moscow Arts Theatre entrance with *The Wave* bas-relief above

There were still problems and in the 1980s part of the company moved to the Gorky Arts Theatre on Tverskoy bulvar.

Today, a variety of productions are staged at the Moscow Arts Theatre, including many of Chekhov's plays.

## ❾ Bryusov Pereulok
### Брюсов переулок
*Bryusov pereulok*

**Map** 1 C5. Ⓜ Okhotnyy Ryad, Arbatskaya.

A granite arch on Tverskaya ulitsa marks the entrance to this side street, named after the Bruces, a Scottish family who were involved with the Russian court.

In the 1920s, new apartments here were assigned to the staff of the Moscow state theatres. No. 12 was home to the avant-garde director Vsevolod Meyerhold, who lived here from 1928 until his arrest in 1939 at the height of Stalin's Great Terror. Next door, Nos. 8–10 were the headquarters of the Composers' Union, where composers Sergei Prokofiev and Dmitri Shostakovich were forced to read an apology for works that deviated from socialist realism *(see p107)*.

About halfway along Bryusov pereulok is the 17th-century single-domed Church of the Resurrection, one of the few churches to remain open during the Soviet era.

## ❿ Morozov Mansion
### Дом ЗГ Морозовой
*Dom ZG Morozovoy*

Spiridonovka ulitsa 17. **Map** 1 A5.
Ⓜ Mayakovskaya. **Closed** to public.

Fyodor Shekhtel built this striking house for Arseny Morozov, the nephew of his patron Savva Morozov, a wealthy textiles manufacturer, in 1893–1898. The Morozovs were one of the city's richest merchant families.

The mansion was built in Gothic and Neo-Romantic style to resemble a Moorish baronial castle, with carved turrets and arched windows. Some of the stained-glass windows were designed by the Symbolist artist Mikhail Vrubel.

## ⓫ Upper Monastery of St Peter
### Высоко-Петровский монастырь
*Vysoko-Petrovskiy monastyr*

Ulitsa Petrovka 28/2.
**Map** 2 D4. **Tel** (495) 623 75 80.
Ⓜ Pushkinskaya, Chekhovskaya.
**Open** 8am–7pm daily. 📞 call (903) 670 64 74 to book excursions in advance.

Founded in the reign of Ivan I, this monastery was rebuilt in the late 17th century with funding from the Naryshkin family, relatives of Peter the Great. Its six churches include the Church of the Metropolitan

Single-domed Church of the Resurrection on Bryusov Pereulok

*For hotels and restaurants in this area see p266 and pp280–82*

Iconostasis in the bell tower, Upper Monastery of St Peter

Peter, after which the monastery is named. It was built in 1514–17 to a design by Aleviz Novyy. The Church of the Icon of the Virgin of Bogolyubovo commemorates three of Peter the Great's uncles killed in the 1682 Streltsy Revolt. The Refectory Church of St Sergius has five cupolas and scallop-shell decoration. The complex includes a green-domed bell tower and monks' cells.

## ⓬ Pushkin Square

Пушкинская площадь
*Pushkinskaya ploshchad*

**Map** 1 B4. Ⓜ Pushkinskaya, Tverskaya, Chekhovskaya.

The square is named for a bronze statue of poet Alexander Pushkin, sculpted by Alexander Opekushin. It was unveiled in the presence of two other Russian literary giants, Fyodor Dostoevsky and Ivan Turgenev, in 1880. Pushkin has long epitomized the spirit of freedom in Russia, and, since the 1960s, his statue has been a rallying point for demonstrations, many of which have been broken up by the police.

The Rossiya Musical Theatre behind the statue is the venue for Moscow's International Film Festival and Russia's equivalent of the Oscars. It stands on the site of the 17th-century Convent of the Passion, which was demolished in 1935.

Beyond the theatre, at the beginning of Malaya Dmitrovka ulitsa, is the Church of the Nativity of the Virgin in Putinki. Built between 1649 and 1652, this attractive church has clustered tent roofs, tiered *kokoshniki* (tiered gables) and blue onion domes.

On the northeast corner of the square stand the offices of the newspaper *Izvestiya*, once an official mouthpiece of the Soviet government and now one of Russia's independent daily newspapers.

## ⓭ Museum of Contemporary History

Музей современной истории
*Muzey sovremennoy istorii*

Tverskaya ulitsa 21. **Map** 1 B4. **Tel** (495) 699 67 24. Ⓜ Pushkinskaya, Tverskaya. **Open** 11am–7pm Tue, Wed & Fri–Sun, noon–9pm Thu. English, book in advance. Ⓦ **sovr.ru**

A pair of stone lions guards this red mansion, built in the late 18th century. In 1831, it became the English Club, where the Muscovite aristocracy drank and gambled until 1917, after which it ironically – or fittingly – became the Museum of the Revolution. Since the break-up of the Soviet Union in 1991, its exhibits have reflected a more objective view of 20th-century Russian history, and the museum's name was changed to reflect this shift.

Laid out chronologically, the exhibits cover 1900–91. They include home-made grenades, a Maxim gun on a converted carriage (used in the Civil War), sweet wrappers depicting Marx and Lenin and former premier Nikita Khrushchev's camera from his 1959 trip to the United States. The so-called propaganda porcelain and gifts presented to Soviet rulers are also interesting.

Model of the five-pointed red star at the centre of the exhibition hall in the Museum of Contemporary History

### ⓮ Bulgakov House and Museum

Дом и музей Булгаков
*Dom i Muzey Bulgakova*

Bolshaya Sadovaya ulitsa 10.
**Map** 1 A4. Ⓜ Mayakovskaya.
Bulgakov Museum: **Tel** (495) 699 53
66. **Open** noon–7pm Tue, Wed & Fri–
Sun, 2–9pm Thu. Ⓦ **bulgakov
museum.ru/en** Bulgakov House:
**Tel** (495) 970 06 19. **Open** 1–11pm
Mon–Thu, 1pm–1am Fri, noon–1am
Sat, noon–11pm Sun. 🍴 Thu–Sun.
Ⓦ **dombulgakova.ru**

Mikhail Bulgakov (1891–1940)
wrote his classic satire of Stalinist
Russia, *The Master and Margarita*,
knowing that it would never
be published in his lifetime.
Although typed copies circulated
on the black market, it was only
published in Russia in the 1980s.
Today, there are two museums
in Bulgakov's honour, in the
building where many surreal
scenes from his novel are set.

An official **Bulgakov Museum**
occupies Flat 50, where the
author set portions of his
novel, while nearby is the rival
**Bulgakov House**. Both museums
organize performances, lectures
and excursions. A memorable
experience is the Bulgakov
House's night-ride around
central Moscow in a converted
trolleybus with its own buffet.

### ⓯ Patriarch's Pond

Патриаршие пруды
*Patriarshie prudy*

**Map** 1 A4. Ⓜ Pushkinskaya.

Just a few minutes' walk south
from the Bulgakov Museum is a
leafy, secluded square with the
Patriarch's Pond at its heart. The
pond was dug by a 16th-century
patriarch to drain a reputedly
haunted swamp. This association
with evil spirits and Christianity
inspired Bulgakov to make it the
setting for the opening scene in
*The Master and Margarita*, in which
the Devil appears in Moscow and
causes havoc. Locals have prevented the installation of giant sculptures illustrating Bulgakov's novel,
preferring instead to keep a bronze
statue of the 19th-century writer
of fables, Ivan Krylov, surrounded
by creatures from his stories.

Picture of Chekhov (left) with Leo Tolstoy,
in the Chekhov House-Museum

### ⓰ Chekhov House-Museum

Дом-музей АП Чехова
*Dom-muzey AP Chekhova*

Sadovaya-Kudrinskaya ulitsa 6.
**Map** 1 A5. **Tel** (495) 691 38 37.
Ⓜ Barrikadnaya, Krasnopresnenskaya.
**Open** 11am–6pm Tue & Wed, Sat &
Sun, 2–8pm Thu & Fri. **Closed** last day
of the month. 📷 🎫 book in
advance. ♿

Author Anton Chekhov (1860–
1904) lived in this two-storey
house in 1886–90. It was later
refurbished in consultation with
his widow, actress Olga Knipper-
Chekhova, and opened as a
museum in 1954. A brass plate
by the door testifies to Chekhov's
medical profession. Writing in his
spare time, it was here that he
created his first major play, *Ivanov*,
and wrote many short stories.

In the study, exhibits include
his doctor's bag, manuscripts
and pictures. Upstairs, Chekhov's
sister Mariya's room is the most
attractive in the house.

### ⓱ Gorky House-Museum

Дом-музей АМ Горького
*Dom-muzey AM Gorkovo*

Malaya Nikitskaya ulitsa 6/2. **Map** 1 B5.
**Tel** (495) 690 05 35. Ⓜ Pushkinskaya.
**Open** 11am–5:30pm Wed–Sun.
**Closed** last Thu of the month.
🎧 English, call (495) 690 51 30 to
book in advance.

A frieze of irises against a background of blue and purple
clouds runs around the top of
the yellow glazed-brick walls
of this mansion, a masterpiece
of Style-Moderne architecture
designed in 1900. In 1931, Stalin
presented the mansion as a gift
to the esteemed socialist writer

The spectacular Style-Moderne staircase in the Gorky House-Museum

*For hotels and restaurants in this area see p266 and pp280–82*

Maxim Gorky, who never got used to its luxury, nor produced much work while living here. However, Gorky's pre-revolutionary fame and support for the Bolshevik Party made him a useful propaganda tool for the Soviet government.

The interior of the house features ceilings with elaborate mouldings, stained-glass windows and carved door frames. The *pièce de résistance* is the staircase of polished Estonian limestone, which ends in a lamp resembling a jellyfish. On display are Gorky's hat, overcoat and walking stick, his collection of Japanese netsuke carvings and many of his letters and books.

Stunning stained-glass window in the Gorky House-Museum

## ⓲ Stanislavskiy House-Museum

Дом-музей КС Станиславского

*Dom-muzey KS Stanislavskovo*

Leontevskiy pereulok 6. **Map** 1 B5. **Tel** (495) 629 24 42. **Ⓜ** Arbatskaya, Tverskaya. **Open** noon–7pm Wed & Fri, 11am–8pm Thu, 11am–6pm Sat & Sun. **Closed** last Thu of the month.

This 18th-century mansion was the home of the director and actor Konstantin Stanislavskiy. Disillusionment with the conservative ethos of the old Moscow Theatre School led Stanislavskiy to found the Moscow Arts Theatre (MKhAT) in 1898 *(see p84)*. After moving into this flat, he converted its ballroom into a makeshift theatre where he rehearsed his experimental Opera Dramatic Group. The actors would step on stage from the adjacent Red Room, which served as a make-up studio.

Stanislavskiy was indifferent to his surroundings and, for most of his life, slept in his study. He died here in 1938.

The opulent Bolshoi Zal in the Moscow Conservatory

## ⓳ Moscow Conservatory

Московская консерватория

*Moskovskaya Konservatoriya*

Bolshaya Nikitskaya ulitsa 13/6. **Map** 1 B5. **Tel** (495) 629 94 01. **Ⓜ** Arbatskaya, Pushkinskaya. **Open** performances only. **ⓦ** mosconsv.ru

Russia's premier music school was founded in 1866 by Nikolai Rubinstein, the brother of pianist and composer Anton Rubinstein. One of the Conservatory's teachers was the young Pyotr Tchaikovsky. In the forecourt is his statue wielding a baton, and the railings are patterned with the opening notes of his symphonies.

Portraits of famous composers adorn the walls of the light, airy Bolshoi Zal (Great Hall), which hosts the prestigious Tchaikovsky International Competition. A museum that is open during performances celebrates alumni such as the pianist-composers Sergei Rachmaninov and Dmitri Shostakovich.

Globe-shaped sign outside the ITAR-TASS news agency, Bolshaya Nikitskaya ulitsa

## ⓴ Bolshaya Nikitskaya Ulitsa

Большая Никитская улица

*Bolshaya Nikitskaya ulitsa*

**Map** 1 B5. **Ⓜ** Arbatskaya, Okhotnyy Ryad, Biblioteka imeni Lenina.

This street, once the main road to Novgorod, is named after the 16th-century Nikitskiy Convent, demolished in the 1930s. Prominent aristocratic families built their palaces here in the 18th century. The finest among them is the former residence of Prince Sergei Menshikov, with its pale blue façade, reconstructed after the 1812 Great Fire of Moscow.

Opposite the Moscow Conservatory is the Church of the Little Ascension. Behind it is the Gothic tower of St Andrew's Anglican Church, built for the city's English community in 1882.

The heavily ornamented red-brick building at Nos. 19–20 is the Mayakovsky Theatre, which premiered Mayakovsky's plays *The Bath House* and *The Bed Bug* in 1928–9. Both were staged by the great avant-garde director Vsevolod Meyerhold, who was tortured and executed by the Soviet regime in 1940.

About halfway along the road is Nikitskie Vorota ploshchad, named after the medieval gate that used to stand here. The building with a sign in the shape of a large globe is Russia's main news agency, the ITAR-TASS.

Opposite is the Church of the Great Ascension. Alexander Pushkin married Natalya Goncharova here in 1831.

The imposing Pashkov House elevated on an enormous stone base

# ㉑ Pashkov House

Дом Пашкова

*Dom Pashkova*

Ulitsa Znamenka 6. **Map** 3 C2.
Ⓜ Borovitska, Biblioteka imeni Lenina. **Closed** to public.

This mansion built in the Neo-Classical style between 1784 and 1788 was once the finest private house in Moscow and enjoys a hilltop location overlooking the Kremlin. The mansion's height was achieved by placing it on an enormous stone base. The building is surmounted by a perfectly proportioned rotunda. The most impressive façade is at the rear of the building, which originally led to a garden. The Moscow Institute for Nobles occupied the house from 1839 to 1861, when it was taken over by the Rumyantsev Museum. Once part of the National State Library, the restored building can be hired for special events.

# ㉒ Pushkin State Museum of Fine Arts

*See pp90–91.*

# ㉓ Gallery of 19th- and 20th-Century European and American Art

Музей Галерея искусства стран Европы и Америки XIX–XX веков

*Galeryeya Iskusstva Stran Evropi I Ameriki X1X–XX Vekov*

Ulitsa Volkhonka 14.
**Map** 3 C2. **Tel** (495) 697 15 46.
Ⓜ Kropotkinskaya. **Open** 11am–8pm Tue & Wed, Sat & Sun, 11am–9pm Thu & Fri. 🖼 🔊 🅰 ♿ 💻 📷
Ⓦ **newpaintart.ru**

Before the Revolution, this building housed the Kanyazhiy Dvor Hotel, whose guests included Maxim Gorky and Ilya Repin. Now it is a museum displaying Impressionist and Post-Impressionist paintings that were previously shown in the Pushkin State Museum of Fine Arts next door, plus works from the Hermitage in St Petersburg.

The first of the three floors displays mainly European oil paintings from the first half of the 19th century, but the real masterpieces are upstairs. On the second floor are paintings by Vincent van Gogh, including *The Red Vineyard at Arles* (1888) and *Prisoners Exercising* (1890) as well as Pierre Auguste Renoir's *Nude* (1876) and *Bathing on the*

*Seine* (1879). The same floor also holds Paul Cézanne's *Mont Ste Victoire* (1905) and a series of paintings by Paul Gauguin.

The third floor features works by Henri Matisse, including *Goldfish* (1911–12), and Pablo Picasso's *Girl Standing on a Ball* (1905). Russia is also represented, with paintings by Vasily Kandinsky, including *Improvisation No. 20a* (1911).

# ㉔ Glazunov Picture Gallery

Картинная галерейя Илйи Глазунова

*Kartinnaya galereya Ilyi Glazunova*

Ulitsa Volkhonka 13.
**Map** 3 C2. **Tel** (495) 691 69 49.
Ⓜ Kropotkinskaya. **Open** 11am–7pm Tue, Wed & Fri–Sun, 11am–9pm Thu.
Ⓦ **glazunov.ru**

This gallery showcases the work of Russia's most famous living artist, Ilya Glazunov. His fascination for Orthodox and Tsarist culture led to him being exiled to the provinces in the 1970s. His dissident mystique was enhanced by tales of a giant painting called *The Mystery of the Twentieth Century*, and senior Communists were said to secretly collect his work. Glazunov's retro-patriotism is typified by a picture called *Eternal Russia*, and his scathing view of Russian capitalism by another canvas, *The Market of Our Democracy*. His polemical art resonates with many Russians even if Moscow's intelligentsia despise it.

The well-lit façade of the Glazunov Picture Gallery

Frescoes adorning the central dome of the Cathedral of Christ the Saviour

## ㉕ Cathedral of Christ the Saviour

Храм Христа Спасителя
*Khram Khrista Spasitelya*

Ulitsa Volkhonka 15. **Map** 3 C2.
Ⓜ Kropotkinskaya.

The rebuilding of this vast cathedral in the late 1990s was the most ambitious of the construction projects undertaken by Moscow's then mayor, Yuri Luzhkov. The project courted controversy from the start, both on grounds of taste and cost. A presidential decree declared that no taxpayers' money should be spent on it – funds were to be raised through donations from the public, the Orthodox Church, foreign corporations and local oligarchs. In reality, the better part of the total bill of over US$200 million came from the state budget at a time when many Russians were suffering extreme poverty.

The original cathedral was built to commemorate Russia's victory over Napoleon's Grande Armée *(see p42),* by architect Konstantin Ton. When completed in 1883 it was the tallest building in Moscow, its 103-m (338-ft) high gilded dome dominating the skyline. The cathedral was blown up on Stalin's orders in 1933 to make way for the never-built Palace of Soviets that was eventually superseded by an outdoor swimming pool in 1959.

In 2007, the rebuilt cathedral hosted the lying in state of former president Boris Yeltsin. The dome proffers spectacular views of Moscow.

## ㉖ Arbat Square

Арбатская площадь
*Arbatskuyu ploshchad*

**Map** 3 B1. Ⓜ Arbatskaya.

A chaotic mass of traffic and underpasses, Arbat Square is the link between the vividly contrasting areas of Old (ulitsa Arbat) and New Arbat (ulitsa Novy Arbat). Beneath the square, the underpasses contain a society of their own. Expect to come across an impromptu rock concert, kittens and puppies for sale and, in late summer, pensioners selling wild mushrooms, though these are not always safe to buy.

The Old Arbat, a narrow thoroughfare that was once the heart of bohemian Moscow is celebrated in a famous ballad by Bulat Okudhava. Today, it lures tourists with its street-performers, portrait artists and souvenir stalls. The New Arbat was built in the 1960s on an inhuman scale. One side is lined with 24-storey apartment complexes, once awarded to People's Artists. The other side features office blocks overlaid by a synchronized neon light display that visitors can view from aboard trolleybus 2.

### Stalin's Plan for a Palace of Soviets

The original Cathedral of Christ the Saviour was to have been replaced by a Palace of Soviets – a tower, 315 m (1,033 ft) high, topped by a 100-m (328-ft) statue of Lenin. It was designed as the highlight of Stalin's reconstruction of Moscow, much of the rest of which was realized: skyscrapers, boulevards and the metro system are now familiar features of the city. In the process, many supposedly unnecessary buildings were destroyed, but the intended centrepiece of Stalin's plan was never built due to the swampy subsoil in this locality. Devout Russians whispered that it was God's vengeance that thwarted Stalin's "Tower of Babel".

Palace of Soviets as envisioned by an artist

# ㉒ Pushkin State Museum of Fine Arts

## Музей изобразительных искусств имени АС Пушкина
*Muzey izobrazitelnykb iskusstv imeni AS Pushkina*

Founded in 1898, the Pushkin State Museum houses a fine collection of works from antiquity to the early 19th century in its main building. Following the collapse of the Soviet Union, the curators admitted that they had countless works of art hidden away. Some of these are now on show, including Heinrich Schliemann's *Treasures of Troy* excavations, which were taken from the Museum of Ancient History in Berlin by Soviet military authorities in 1945. The building was designed by Roman Klein. It was first built to house plaster casts of Classical sculptures for art students to use for research. The museum remains open while undergoing a major renovation programme. There are plans to open new galleries and an exhibition hall.

**Museum Building**
The design of the building borrows from Ancient Greece, Italy, France and Germany to create a suitably impressive façade and interior.

**Room 23**
houses mostly 18th–19th-century French paintings.

Stairs to ground floor

First floor

**★ Annunciation**
Painted around 1490 by Italian artist Sandro Botticelli, this work was originally part of a large altarpiece. It shows the angel Gabriel telling the Virgin Mary that she is to bear the Son of God.

**Room 3** houses Schliemann's *Treasures of Troy.*

### Key to Floorplan

- Collection of plaster casts
- Art of ancient civilizations
- 13th–16th century Byzantine and Italian art
- 15th–17th-century German, Dutch, and Flemish art
- 17th–18th-century Spanish and Italian art
- 17th–early 19th-century French art
- Temporary exhibition space

## Gallery Guide

*The ticket office is in the entrance hall. The displays are spread over two floors. Although the museum halls are numbered, the layout is not strictly chronological. The ground floor houses all of the works from ancient civilizations as well as Byzantine art and Italian, Dutch and Flemish art from the 13th to the 17th centuries. Spanish, Italian and French art from the 17th to the early 19th centuries is upstairs. The cloakroom and toilets are in the basement.*

**Bucentaur's Return to the Pier by the Palazzo Ducale**
(1729–30)
Venetian landscape painter, Canaletto, was known for his bold use of colour, exemplfied in this scene of the Grand Canal.

**Ahasuerus, Haman and Esther** (1660)
In this biblical scene by Rembrandt, the Persian king, Ahasuerus, is flanked by his Jewish wife Esther and his minister, Haman. Esther, lit by a single ray of light, accuses Haman of plotting to destroy the Jews.

**Room 10**
is dedicated to Rembrandt and his school and includes drawings, etchings and six paintings by the great master.

Stairs to first floor

★ **Bacchanalia** (around 1615)
Based on the myth of the god of nature, vegetation and viniculture, Dionysus-Bacchus, this splendidly exuberant, sensual painting was in the possession of its artist, Peter Paul Rubens, his entire life.

Tickets and information

★ **Fayoum Portrait**
Painted in the 1st century AD, this is one of a collection of portraits discovered at a burial ground at the Fayoum oasis in Egypt in the 1870s. They were painted while the subjects were alive, to be used as death masks on their mummies when they died.

Entrance

Ground floor

## ㉗ Lermontov House-Museum

Дом-музей МЮ Лермонтова

*Dom-muzey MYu Lermontova*

Ulitsa Malaya Molchanovka 2. **Map** 3 B1. **Tel** (495) 691 52 98. Ⓜ Arbatskaya. **Open** 11am–6pm Tue & Fri–Sun, 2–8pm Wed & Thu. **Closed** last day of the month.

Tucked away behind the tower blocks of the New Arbat is the house where the Romantic poet and novelist Mikhail Lermontov lived with his grandmother from 1829–32, when he was a student at Moscow University.

More interested in writing poetry than in his studies, Lermontov left university without graduating, becoming a guardsman. In 1937, he was exiled to the Caucasus for criticizing the authorities in a poem about the death of Pushkin. This marked a turning point in Lermontov's writing, presaging his most famous work, the novel *A Hero of our Time*, written in 1840. He was killed in a duel the next year, when he was only 26.

There are five rooms in the museum, and each bears testament to Lermontov's intellectual gifts and zest for life. In the study he would play the guitar, piano and violin, and compose music. The drawing room was often the site of dancing, singing and masquerades. Many of his manuscripts are displayed downstairs, together with watercolours of the Caucasus, some by Lermontov himself.

The elegant drawing room in the Lermontov House-Museum

Sitting room with one of Skryabin's pianos, Skryabin House-Museum

## ㉘ Skryabin House-Museum

Дом-музей АН Скрябина

*Dom-muzey AN Skryabina*

Bolshoi Nikolopeskovskiy pereulok 11. **Map** 3 A1. **Tel** (499) 241 19 01. Ⓜ Smolenskaya, Arbatskaya. **Open** 11am–7pm, Wed & Fri–Sun, 1–9pm Thu. **Closed** last Fri of the month. 🎨

Pianist and composer Aleksandr Skryabin (1872–1915) lived in this apartment from 1912 until his death at the age of 43. A graduate of the Moscow Conservatory with an international reputation as a concert pianist, he was also a composer and theorist, best known for orchestral works such as *Prometheus*. He was a a key proponent of associating music with colours.

Although Skryabin spent much time abroad giving concerts, he paid considerable attention to the decor of his apartment. The lofty rooms house his pianos, autographed manuscripts and Style-Moderne furniture. The museum also houses his original colour keyboard, which he used to combine musical notes with colours. Concerts are held in the rooms on the ground floor.

## ㉙ Spasopeskovskiy Pereulok

Спасопесковский переулок

*Spasopeskovskiy pereulok*

**Map** 3 A1. Ⓜ Smolenskaya.

The charms of the Old Arbat have been preserved in this secluded lane and the adjoining square,

Spasopeskovskaya ploshchad. In 1878, Vasily Polenov painted *A Moscow Courtyard*, depicting the square as a bucolic haven in the midst of the city.

At the centre of Polenov's picture, now in the State Tretyakov Gallery (*see pp98–9*), is the white bell tower of the Church of the Saviour on the Sands (Tserkov Spas na Peskakh), from which the lane gets its name. This 18th-century church still dominates the square, which is otherwise known as the site of Spaso House. This Classical-style mansion has been the home of US ambassadors since 1933.

## ㉚ Melnikov House

Дом Мельникова

*Dom Melnikova*

Krivoarbatskiy pereulok 10. **Map** 3 A2. Ⓜ Smolenskaya. **Closed** to public.

This unique Modernist house was designed by Konstantin Melnikov, one of Russia's greatest Constructivist architects (*see p33*), in 1927. Made from brick overlaid with stucco, it consists of two interlocking cylinders studded with hexagonal windows, creating a honeycomb effect. A spiral staircase rises through the space where the cylinders overlap, linking the airy living spaces.

Though it was built for Melnikov's family, it was meant as a prototype for future housing developments, until Stalin encouraged architects to adopt a new monumental style. Although he had won the Gold Medal at the 1925 Paris World

Fair, Melnikov's work was later ignored. However, he lived in this house for the rest of his life, one of the few residents of central Moscow allowed to live in a privately built dwelling.

## ③ Pushkin House-Museum

Музей-квартира АС Пушкина
*Muzey-kvartira AS Pushkina*

Ulitsa Arbat 53. **Map** 3 A2. **Tel** (499) 241 92 95. Ⓜ Smolenskaya. **Open** 10am–6pm Wed & Fri–Sun, noon–9pm Thu. **Closed** last Fri of the month. 🅿️ 📷 English (book in advance).

Alexander Pushkin rented this elegant Empire-style flat for the first three months of his marriage to Natalya Goncharova. Soon, however, Pushkin tired of life in Moscow and the couple moved to St Petersburg *(see p169)*, where gossip began to circulate that Pushkin's brother-in-law George d'Anthès, a French officer, was making advances to Natalya. Pushkin challenged him to a duel, was mortally wounded, and died two days later.

The exhibition on the museum's ground floor gives an idea of what Moscow would have been like before the Great Fire. On display are wax figures of a serf orchestra that belonged to the Goncharova family. Pushkin and Natalya lived upstairs. There are few personal possessions other than Pushkin's writing bureau and some family portraits, but the atmosphere is reverential.

Detail of a plaque outside Pushkin House-Museum

## ③ Ministry of Foreign Affairs

Министерство Иностранных дел
*Ministertsvo Inostrannikh del*

Smolenskaya ploshchad X. **Map** 3 A2. Ⓜ Smolenskaya. **Closed** to public.

Old Arbat meets the Garden Ring at Smolenskaya ploshchad, a wide expanse dominated by a Stalin-Gothic "skyscraper". Built between 1948 and 1953 to house the Soviet Foreign Ministry (known to Russians as "MID"), the 27-storey central block is crowned by a spire, taking it to a height of 172 m (564 ft). The original design was without a spire; when Stalin remarked on this, a metal spire was hastily added, painted to match the rest of the building.

## ③ Shalyapin House-Museum

Дом-музей Ф.И. Шаляпина
*Dom-muzey FI Shalyapina*

Novinskiy bulvar 25. **Map** 1 A5. **Tel** (495) 605 62 36. Ⓜ Smolenskaya, Barrikadnaya. **Open** check website for timings. 🅿️ 📷 book in advance. 🌐 **shalyapin-museum.org**

The renowned Russian bass, Fyodor Shalyapin, occupied this mansion from 1910 until he emigrated from Soviet Russia in 1922. Born in Kazan in 1873, he worked as a stevedore on the *Volga* before his unique vocal talent was discovered. He went on to sing such great operatic bass roles as *Don Quixote*, *Ivan the Terrible* and *Boris Godunov*. He died in Paris

The Ministry of Foreign Affairs building, an example of Stalin-Gothic architecture

in 1938, but his remains were later returned to Russia for reburial in the Novodevichiy Cemetery *(see p105)*.

Shalyapin rehearsed with renowned musicians and composers in the concert room, where visitors can now listen to recordings of the master at work. There is also a Bachstein grand piano, which was presented to Shalyapin in 1913.

Items on display in the house include the singer's much treasured velvet armchair. A selection of his playing cards are laid out on a side table. The mementoes on the second floor include amusing portraits of the singer in his various operatic roles, as well as a collection of theatrical costumes.

### Alexander Pushkin

Born in 1799 into Russia's aristocracy, Alexander Pushkin had established a reputation as both a poet and a rebel by the time he was 20. In 1820, he was exiled by the state for his liberal verse, but eventually allowed back to Moscow. Following early narrative poems such as *The Robber Brothers* (1821), he created his famous novel in verse, *Eugene Onegin* (1823–30). Later he wrote mostly prose, developing a unique style in pieces such as *The Queen of Spades* (1834). He is revered for giving Russian literature its own identity.

# ZAMOSKVORECHE

First settled in the 13th century, Zamoskvoreche (literally "beyond the Moscow river") acted as an outpost against the Mongols. The district's main road, Bolshaya Ordynka, was the route to the *Orda*, or Golden Horde, the Mongol headquarters on the Volga river. Later, under Ivan the Terrible, the Streltsy (royal guard) was stationed here. Artisans serving the court also moved in, living in areas according to their trade, each of which sponsored a church. These historic churches, now in varying states

of repair, and the fact that the district was almost untouched by the replanning of the 1930s, give it a more old-fashioned atmosphere than the centre, which is dominated by massive Soviet architecture. In the 19th century, wealthy merchants settled here, many of whom, such as Aleksey Bakhrushin and Pavel Tretyakov, were patrons of the arts. Today, the State Tretyakov Gallery, home to its founder's collection, is the nation's most important collection of Russian art.

**Locator Map**
*See Street Finder, map 4*

## Sights at a Glance

### Museums and Galleries

❶ *The State Tretyakov Gallery pp98–9*

❻ Bakhrushin Theatre Museum

### Churches and Cathedrals

❷ Church of the Resurrection in Kadashi

❸ Church of the Consolation of All Sorrows

❹ Church of St Nicholas in Pyzhy

❺ Convent of SS Martha and Mary

0 metres 400
0 yards 400

◀ *The Appearance of Christ to the People by Alexander Ivanov in the State Tretyakov Gallery*   For keys to symbols *see back flap*

# Street-by-Street: Around Pyatnitskaya Ulitsa

An old-fashioned atmosphere still prevails in the area around Pyatnitskaya ulitsa. The well-established streets are lined with attractive 19th-century churches and imposing Neo-Classical mansions. The busiest part of the district is the area around Tretyakovskaya metro. The market stalls on the station forecourt spill over onto Klimentovskiy pereulok, and nearby Pyatnitskaya ulitsa is the main shopping street. A short walk to the west is the stunning State Tretyakov Gallery. To the north, the area is bordered by the Vodootvodnyy Canal, which was built in 1783–6 to prevent the regular spring flooding of the Moskva river.

Vodootvodnyy Canal

**❷ ★ Church of the Resurrection in Kadashi**
With its five onion domes and lavish limestone ornamentation, this magnificent church is a fine example of the style known as Moscow Baroque *(see p32)*.

**Key**

— Suggested route

0 metres    100
0 yards     100

**❶ ★ The State Tretyakov Gallery**
The world's largest collection of Russian art is housed here. Taken down in the Soviet era, the statue of Pavel Tretyakov has now been restored to its rightful place in front of the gallery.

**The Demidov House** was built in 1789–91 by a family of well-known industrialists.

**❸ Church of the Consolation of All Sorrows**
Two of Moscow's best-known architects contributed to this much-loved church. Vasily Bazhenov designed the bell tower and Osip Bove the rotunda.

*For hotels and restaurants in this area see p266 and p282*

**The Church of SS Michael and Fyodor**, dating from the late 17th century, is named after two martyrs killed by Mongols when they refused to renounce Christianity.

**Church of St John the Baptist** has a distinctive green bell tower and was built in the 18th century.

Kremlin

PYATNITSKAYA ULITSA

KLIMENTOVSKIY PEREULOK

Tretyakovskaya

Area illustrated

ZAMOSKVORECHE

**Novokuznetskaya Metro Station**
Designed by Ivan Taranov and Natalia Bykova, this metro station was opened in 1943 at the height of World War II. The design of the interior is based on military subjects.

**The Church of St Clement**
Built in stages between 1720 and 1774, this splendid church is an outstanding example of Moscow Baroque. It has four black, star-spangled onion domes and a central golden one.

**The Dolgov House**
This town house, with an elaborately decorated Neo-Classical exterior, was built in the 1770s for a wealthy merchant named Dolgov, possibly by his son-in-law, Vasily Bazhenov.

# ❶ The State Tretyakov Gallery

Третьяковская галерея
*Tretyakovskaya galereya*

The Tretyakov Gallery was founded in 1856 by the wealthy merchant Pavel Tretyakov who presented his private museum of Russian art to the city in 1892. His brother Sergei also donated a number of works and the gallery's collection has been expanding ever since. Today, the Tretyakov has the largest collection of Russian art in the world. The building has a striking façade, designed by artist Viktor Vasnetsov, with a bas-relief of St George and the dragon at its centre. Many of the early 20th-century works from the collection are now housed in the State Tretyakov Gallery on Krymsky Val *(see p107)*.

Stairs down to ground floor

Portraits by Ivan Kramskoy, head of the Wanderer's Movement

**The Appearance of Christ to the People** (1837–57) is by the 19th-century Romantic artist, Aleksandr Ivanov.

**The Rooks Have Come** (1871) This bleak winter scene by Aleksey Savrasov contains a message of hope: rooks are taken by Russians as a sign of the coming spring.

**Portrait of Arseny Tropinin, the Artist's Son** (around 1818) This portrait was painted by the renowned artist Vasily Tropinin. He was a serf for 47 years before gaining his freedom and finding commercial success.

First floor

Stairs from basement

Portraits by Ilya Repin

★ **Demon (Seated)** (1890) This is one of several paintings by Mikhail Vrubel, who adopted a new, strikingly modern style. They are inspired by Mikhail Lermontov's Symbolist poem, *The Demon*, with which Vrubel became obsessed.

## Gallery Guide

*The gallery has 62 rooms on two main floors. On entering the museum, visitors first descend to the basement ticket office, then head straight up to the first floor. Paintings are hung in chronological order in rooms 1–48, while rooms 49–54 display drawings and engravings. The Russian Treasury is housed on the ground floor in room 55, while rooms 56–62 contain icons.*

**Ivan the Terrible and his Son Ivan on 16 November, 1581**
Painted in 1885 by Ilya Repin, this intense painting depicts the mighty tsar's face fraught with guilt as he cradles the mortally wounded body of his son.

## VISITORS' CHECKLIST

**Practical information**
Lavrushinskiy pereulok 10.
**Map** 4 D2.
**Tel** (495) 951 13 62.
🆆 tretyakovgallery.ru
**Open** 10am–6pm Tue, Wed, & Sun, 10am–9pm Thu–Sat.

**Transport**
🚌 6, K, 25. Ⓜ Novokuznetskaya, Tretyakovskaya. 🚎 1, 4, 8, 33, 62.

**The Morning of the Execution of the Streltsy** (1881) is by Vasily Surikov, who specialized in using historical subjects to illustrate contemporary social issues

Ground floor

★ **The Trinity** (1420s) This beautiful icon was painted by Andrei Rublev for the Trinity Monastery of St Sergius *(see p114)*, where he had been a novice monk. He dedicated the painting to the monastery's founder, St Sergius of Radonezh.

Stairs from first floor

Stairs down to basement

Exit

Main entrance leading to basement for tickets, information, toilets and cloakrooms

Russian Treasury

### Key to Floorplan

🔲 18th and early 19th centuries
🔲 Second half of the 19th century
🔲 Late 19th and early 20th centuries
🔲 Drawings and engravings of the 18th–20th centuries
⬜ Icons and treasury
🔲 Non-exhibition space

**Main Façade**
The gallery's façade was designed in 1902–1904 by Viktor Vasnetsov. An example of the Russian-Revival style, it has a frieze inspired by medieval manuscripts.

## ❷ Church of the Resurrection in Kadashi

Храм Воскресения в Кадашах

*Khram Voskreseniya v Kadashakh*

2-oy Kadashevskiy pereulok 7.
**Map** 4 D2. Ⓜ Tretyakovskaya.
**Open** 8am–7pm daily. 🎧 English, call
(495) 953 22 91 to book in advance.

This five-domed church is a fine
example of Moscow Baroque
*(see p32)* and is thought to
have been designed by Sergei
Turchaninov. It was paid for
by a wealthy guild of weavers
who moved into the district of
Kadeshevo in the 17th century.
In 1493, an earlier wooden
church stood here, in what was
at that time the district of
Kadeshevo, hence the name
that survives today.

The church was built around
1687, and a slender, tapering
bell tower was added in 1695.
Apart from the five gilded
onion domes, the most notable
features are the tiers of lace-
like limestone balustrades just
below the drums supporting

the domes. The church has had
a turbulent history, having
previously been used as a
stables by Napoleonic troops
and as a KGB archive.

## ❸ Church of the Consolation of All Sorrows

Церковь Богоматери Всех
Скорбящих Радость

*Tserkov Bogomateri Vsekh
Skorbyashchikh Radost*

Ulitsa Bolshaya Ordynka 20.
**Map** 4 D3. Ⓜ Tretyakovskaya.
**Open** 7am–8pm daily.

Both the Church of the
Consolation of All Sorrows
and the Neo-Classical mansion
opposite belonged to the
Dolgovs, a wealthy merchant
family. After completion of their
house in the 1770s, they
commissioned the church from
architect Vasiliy Bazhenov, a
relation by marriage. He first
built a new belfry and refectory
and then replaced the existing
medieval church, but his
creation was destroyed in the

The Empire-style Church of the
Consolation of All Sorrows

1812 Great Fire of Moscow.
A new church was designed
by Osip Bove, the architect in
charge of Moscow's recon-
struction after the fire. His
Empire-style rotunda and
dome were finished in 1833.

The interior is unusual for
an Orthodox church due to its
lavish Empire-style colonnade,
theatrical iconostasis and
exuberant sculpted angels.
On display in the church's
left aisle is the *Icon of Our Lady
of Consolation of All Sorrows*,
which is said to have
miraculously cured the ailing
sister of Patriarch Joachim in
the 17th century.

## ❹ Church of St Nicholas in Pyzhy

Церковь Николая в Пыжах

*Tserkov Nikolaya v Pyzhakh*

Ulitsa Bolshaya Ordynka 27a/8.
**Map** 4 D3. **Tel** (495) 951 37 42.
Ⓜ Tretyakovskaya. **Open** 7:30am–
8pm daily. ✉

Small crowns as well as the
traditional crosses decorate
the silver domes of this church,
indicating that its construction
(1670–72) was financed by the
Streltsy, or royal guard. Some of
these men were later executed
by Peter the Great for their role
in the 1682 Streltsy Revolt.
The exterior decoration includes
fretted cornices and a tiered bell
tower. In 1934, the church was
closed by the Communists and
turned into a laboratory, only
being returned to the Orthodox
Church in 1990.

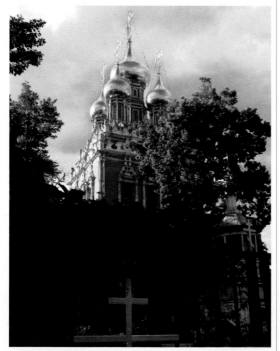

The Church of the Resurrection in Kadashi

## ❺ Convent of SS Martha and Mary

Марфо-Мариинская обитель
*Marfo-Mariinskaya obitel*

Ulitsa Bolshaya Ordynka 34. **Map** 4 D3.
**Tel** (495) 951 11 39. Ⓜ Tretyakovskaya,
Polyanka. **Open** 7:30am–8pm daily.

A low archway leads from the street to this compound, containing what appear at first glance to be medieval buildings. In fact they date from 1908–12 and were designed by Aleksey Shchusev, who later built Lenin's Mausoleum *(see p69)*.

The convent was conceived to house a dispensary, a clinic, a small women's hospital and a school. It was run by the Order of the Sisters of Charity, which was founded in 1908 by Grand Duchess Yelizaveta Fyodorovna, the sister-in-law of Tsar Nicholas II. She had turned to charitable work after her husband, Grand Prince Sergei (the tsar's uncle), was assassinated in a terrorist attack in the troubled year of 1905. Yelizaveta also met a violent death – the day after the shooting of Tsar Nicholas II and his family in 1918, the Bolsheviks pushed her down a mine shaft.

When designing the Church of the Intercession, the convent's main building, Shchusev carried out considerable research into Russian religious architecture, particularly that of the Pskov and Novgorod schools. His design juxtaposed a traditional style with Style-Moderne features

Set design by Mikhail Fokin, on show in the Bakhrushin Theatre Museum

such as boldly pointed gables, limestone carvings of mythical creatures and Slavonic script on the outer walls.

The artist Mikhail Nesterov, a protegé of industrialist and art patron Savva Mamontov *(see p114)*, was commissioned to design and paint the frescoes in the interior of the church. He also designed the pale grey and white habits of the nuns.

After the Revolution, the Order of the Sisters of Charity was suppressed and the church was used as a workshop for restoring icons. The nuns have returned to staff the clinic since 1991, when the convent was restored to the Orthodox Church.

## ❻ Bakhrushin Theatre Museum

Театральный музей имени
А.А. Бахрушина
*Teatralnyy muzey imeni
AA Bakhrushina*

Ulitsa Bakhrushina 31/12.
**Map** 4 E4. **Tel** (495) 953 44 70.
Ⓜ Paveletskaya. **Open** noon–7pm
Tue & Fri–Sun; 1–9pm Wed–Thu
(last ticket 30 mins before closing).
**Closed** last Fri of the month. 🎫 🚫
English, book in advance. ✉

Founded in 1894 by Aleksey Bakhrushin, a merchant and theatrical impresario, this museum contains probably the most important collection of theatre memorabilia in Russia. Spread over two floors, the exhibits range from sets and costumes to theatre tickets, programmes, advertisements and signed photographs.

The permanent exhibition begins in a study, where visitors can peruse a selection of Bakhrushin's belongings, as well as photographs and paintings depicting family life. From here, stairs lead down into the basement, which hosts temporary exhibitions on a variety of themes related to acting and the theatre.

Exhibits on 19th-century theatre include costumes and sets from the Ballets Russes. This company, formed by Sergei Diaghilev in 1909, revolutionized ballet. The sets include some designed by Mikhail Fokin, the company's inspired choreographer. A foot cast and pair of ballet shoes belonging to Marie Taglioni (1804–1884), the renowned Swedish dancer, are also displayed. She rose to fame when she featured in *La Sylphide* (1832), a ballet choreographed by her father. She is thought to be the first ballerina to dance *en pointe*, establishing her as a reformer in the history of ballet.

The room on 20th-century avant-garde theatre has changing temporary exhibitions.

Convent of SS Martha and Mary, designed by Aleksey Shchusev

# FURTHER AFIELD

Moscow's suburbs are generally rather bleak, but they conceal a surprising number of attractions, all accessible by metro. To the south of the centre lie a number of fortified monasteries, built to defend the city against the Mongols and the Poles. The most spectacular of them is the Novodevichiy Convent, a serene, fortified complex dating from the 16th century that boasts a glorious cathedral and a Baroque bell tower. Also worth a visit is the Donskoy Monastery with its ensemble of old and new cathedrals. The area is also known for the beauty and variety of its green spaces. Gorky and Izmaylovo parks are the perfect places to relax, while Sparrow Hills offers fantastic views. The city's best-kept secrets, however, are its grand estates situated away from the centre in what used to be countryside. Notable among these are the Neo-Classical summer residences of the Sheremetev family: Kuskovo and Ostankino. Both have beautifully preserved gardens and palaces full of fine paintings and period furnishings.

## Sights at a Glance

### Churches and Cathedrals
1 Novodevichiy Convent pp104–105
3 Church of St Nicholas of the Weavers
6 Donskoy Monastery

### Museums
2 Tolstoy House-Museum
4 State Tretyakov Gallery on Krymsky Val
8 Kolomenskoe
9 Tsaritsyno
12 Vasnetsov House-Museum
13 Gulag History Museum
16 Memorial Museum Of Space Exploration

### Parks
5 Gorky Park
7 Sparrow Hills
11 Izmaylovo
15 Exhibition of Achievements of National Economy (VDNKh)

### Palaces
10 Kuskovo
14 Ostankino Palace

### Key
■ Central Moscow
━━ Motorway
━━ Main road
═══ Minor road
── Railway

**Greater Moscow**

◀ Picturesque view of the Novodevichiy Convent from across a verdant lake

**For keys to symbols** see back flap

# ❶ Novodevichiy Convent

Новодевичий монастырь

*Novodevichiy monastyr*

Probably the most beautiful of the semi-circle of fortified religious institutions to the south of Moscow is Novodevichiy Convent, founded by Basil III in 1524 to commemorate the capture of Smolensk from the Lithuanians. The only building to be built at this time was the Cathedral of the Virgin of Smolensk. Most of the other buildings were added in the late 17th century by Peter the Great's half-sister, the Regent Sophia. After Peter deposed her and reclaimed his throne in 1689, he confined her here for the rest of her life. In 1812, Napoleon's troops tried to blow up the convent but, according to a popular story, it was saved by the nuns, who snuffed out the fuses.

**Gate Church of the Intercession**
It is not known who designed this church, but it is believed to have been built in the second half of the 17th century.

## KEY

① **Shoemaker's Tower**

② **Vorobeva Tower**

③ **Maria's Chambers** were used by Maria, the daughter of Tsar Alexis Mikhailovich.

④ **Church of St Ambrose**

⑤ **The Palace of Irina Gudunova** was home to the widow of Tsar Fyodor I.

⑥ **Setunskaya Tower**

⑦ **Faceted Tower**

⑧ **Refectory**

⑨ **The Church of the Assumption** and adjoining refectory were built in the 1680s on the orders of the Regent Sophia.

⑩ **Nuns' cells**

⑪ **Saviour's Tower**

⑫ **Naprudnaya Tower**

⑬ **The guard house** is where the Regent Sophia was imprisoned.

⑭ **Tsaritsa's Tower**

⑮ **St Nicholas's Tower**

⑯ **Tailor's Tower**

⑰ **Hospital**

Novodevichiy Cemetery

★ **Cathedral of the Virgin of Smolensk**
Built in 1524, this cathedral is the oldest building in the convent. The five-tier iconostasis, the rich frescoes and the onion domes all date from the 17th century.

0 metres    25
0 yards    25

## Novodevichiy Cemetery

Many famous Russians are buried in this cemetery. Among the leading cultural figures are playwright Anton Chekhov, writer Nikolai Gogol, composers Sergei Prokofiev, Aleksandr Skryabin *(see p92)* and Dmitri Shostakovich and opera singer Fyodor Shalyapin *(see p93)*. The cemetery is also the final resting place for numerous military and political dignitaries from the Soviet era, including the former Russian premier Nikita Khrushchev *(see p45)* and the first President of the Russian Federation, Boris Yeltsin.

Tomb of Boris Yeltsin, Novodevichiy Cemetery

Entrance

Sportivnaya metro

**★ Gate Church of the Transfiguration**
A cornice of scallop-shell gables, topped by five gilded domes and crosses, crowns this grand Baroque church. It stands over the main gate to the convent and was completed in 1688.

**★ Bell Tower**
Completed in 1690, this tower is one of the most exuberant examples of Baroque architecture in Moscow. The Church of St John the Divine occupies the second storey of the six-tiered, octagonal tower, which stands 72 m (236 ft) high.

**Lopukhin Palace**
This palace was built in 1687–9. After Peter the Great's death in 1725 his first wife, Yevdokiya Lopukhina, moved here from the Convent of the Intercession in Suzdal where she had been sent after Peter tired of her.

## ❷ Tolstoy House-Museum

Музей-усадьба ЛН Толстого
*Muzey-usadba LN Tolstovo*

Ulitsa Lva Tolstovo 21. **Tel** (499) 246
94 44. Ⓜ Park Kultury. **Open** 10am–
6pm Wed & Fri–Sun, noon–8pm Tue
& Thu. **Closed** last Fri of the month.
📷 ✓ English, book in advance. ✉
🅦 tolstoymuseum.ru

The presence of one of Russia's
greatest novelists can be felt in
every corner of this evocative
house. It was here that Leo
Tolstoy (1828–1910) spent the
winters between 1882 and
1901 with his long-suffering
wife, Sofya Andreevna, and their
nine surviving children. The
summers were spent on the
Tolstoy ancestral estate at
Yasnaya Polyana *(see p116)*.

Their house in Moscow was
turned into a museum in 1921
on Lenin's orders and has been
preserved much as it would
have been when Tolstoy and
his family lived here.

On the ground floor, the large
table in the dining room is still
laid with crockery. The evening
meal in the Tolstoy household
always began at 6pm at the
summons of the cuckoo clock
on the wall. Adjacent to the
dining room is the "corner room"
where, at one time, the elder
sons, Sergei, Ilya and Lev, would
retire to play Chinese billiards.

The house exudes a sense of
ordered, comfortable family life,
but Tolstoy and his wife often
quarrelled violently, largely on
account of his wish to renounce
society and live as simply as

### Leo Tolstoy

By the time Tolstoy was in his 50s, he was
an author of international renown and
had written his two masterpieces *War
and Peace* (1863–9) and *Anna Karenina*
(1873–7). He continued to write fiction,
but later renounced his earlier books
and the world they depicted. Instead,
Tolstoy concentrated on his highly
individual brand of Christian Humanism,
a doctrine that included non-violence,
vegetarianism and sexual abstinence. It was in
this period that he wrote the stories *The Death of Ivan Ilych* and
the *Kreutzer Sonata* and his last great novel, *Resurrection*, which
strayed so far from Orthodoxy that the Holy Synod excommu-
nicated him in 1901. Tolstoy left Moscow the same year for Yasnaya
Polyana, where he devoted himself to helping the poor and
peasants on the estate.

The dining room with a painting of Tolstoy's favourite daughter Mariya

The simple desk at which Tolstoy wrote his
final novel, *Resurrection*

possible. The couple were
reconciled for a short time when
Vanya, their youngest child,
died from scarlet fever before
reaching his seventh birthday.
His memory is preserved in his
bedroom near the scullery,
where his high chair, rocking
horse and books can be seen.

The room of Tolstoy's second
daughter, Tatyana, is crammed
with ornaments and keepsakes.
It features a tablecloth that has
70 autographs including those
of her family members and
distinguished visitors, such as the
artist Ilya Repin. Her paintings and
sketches are hung on the walls.

The stairs to the first floor open
into the salon, a large hall where
frequent guests were treated to
supper. They included the young
Sergei Rachmaninov who
accompanied the opera singer,
Fyodor Shalyapin, on the piano
here; Ilya Repin, whose bas-relief
of Tatyana now hangs in the
"corner room"; and the writer

Maxim Gorky with whom
Tolstoy would play chess. The
drawing room was decorated
by Sofya Andreevna herself.
The bedroom of Tolstoy's
favourite child, Mariya, is
rather spartan, testifying to
her sympathy for her father's
ideals and way of life.

At the far end of the upstairs
passage is Tolstoy's study.
Reflecting his passion for
austerity, the room is simply
furnished in black oilskin. The
plain, solid desk where he wrote
his novel *Resurrection* is lit by
candles. Rather than admit to
being short-sighted, Tolstoy
sawed off the ends of his chair
legs to bring himself closer to his
papers. In the adjoining
workroom are dumbbells and a
bicycle – evidence of his
interest in keeping fit. Also on
show are the tools he used for
his hobby of shoe-making, with
some of the pairs he made. The
back stairs lead to the garden.

## ❸ Church of St Nicholas of the Weavers

Храм Святителя Николая в Хамовниках

*Khram Svyatitelya Nikolaya v Khamovnikakh*

Ulitsa Lva Tolstovo 2. **Tel** (499) 246 72 08. Ⓜ Park Kultury. **Open** 7:30am–8pm daily. ✉

Dedicated to the patron saint of weavers, sailors and farmers, this church was founded in 1679 by *khamovniki* (local weavers). Their aim was to surpass the Church of the Resurrection in Kadashi, which was built a few years before by rival weavers across the river.

While staying at their winter home nearby, Tolstoy and his family used to attend services here until his rift with the church authorities.

The church continued to function throughout the Soviet era. Built in the Moscow Baroque style, the exterior is decorated with vivid orange and green gables and topped with five golden domes, while the walls are decorated with beautiful patterned tiles.

Inside, the iconostasis features a 17th-century icon of St Nicholas. A separate icon of the Virgin, Helper of Sinners, is reputed to perform miracles.

Luxurious interior of the Church of St Nicholas of the Weavers

Church of St Nicholas of the Weavers, topped by golden domes

## ❹ State Tretyakov Gallery on Krymsky Val

Третьяковская галерея на Крымском Валу

*Tretyakovskaya galereya na Krymskom Valu*

Krymskiy val 10. **Tel** (499) 230 77 88. Ⓜ Park Kultury, Oktyabrskaya. **Open** 10am– 6pm Tue, Wed, Sun, 10am–9pm Thu–Sat. 🎧 🇬🇧 English. ♿ 🌐 tretyakovgallery.ru

This huge white box of a building is an annexe of the superb State Tretyakov Gallery *(see pp98–9)* in Zamoskvoreche. It is devoted to Russian art from the early 1900s to the present. Most of the canvases here belong to the official move-ment known as socialist realism and reflect the cultural strait-jacket imposed by Stalin. It had its roots in the Wanderers Movement of the 1860s, which was based on the principle that art has, first and foremost, a social role to play; Stalin interpreted this to mean that art must serve the state's interests and reflect socialist goals and achievements. A few examples of the titles given to the paintings say it all: *Life is Getting Better, Building New Factories* and *Unforgettable Meeting* (between Stalin and a spellbound young woman). Technological achievements were also immortalized in pictures such as *The First Russian Airship.*

Many people will find the Modernist paintings at the start of the exhibition more aesthetically pleasing. These include Futurist works such as Kazimir Malevich's *Black Square* and also photomontages by Aleksandr Rodchenko.

Behind the gallery is the Muzeon Sculpture Park, a mixture of discarded monuments from the Soviet era and contemporary sculptures. Pride of place belongs to the statue of the secret police chief, Feliks Dzerzhinskiy, which once stood outside the FSB head-quarters on Lubyanka Square *(see p74)*. A striking addition to the view is the vast Monument to Peter the Great, which towers 95 m (312 ft) above the Moskva river. It was built in 1997 by the sculptor Zurab Tsereteli at a reputed cost of US $11 million.

Boating on the lake in the green, luxuriant surrounds of Gorky Park

## ❺ Gorky Park

Парк культуры и отдыха
имени М. Горького
*Park Kultury i otdykha imeni M.
Gorkovo*

Krymskiy val 9. **Tel** (495) 995 00 20.
Ⓜ Park Kultury, Oktyabrskaya.
**Open** 24 hrs daily.
Ⓦ park-gorkogo.com

Named in honour of the writer
Maxim Gorky, but known locally
as Park Kultury, this green space
extends for more than 1 sq km
(half a sq mile) along the banks
of the Moskva river. Opened in
1928 as the Park of Culture and
Rest, it incorporates the Golitsyn
Gardens, laid out in the late
18th century, and a 19th-century
pleasure park. During the Soviet
era, loudspeakers delivered
speeches by Communist leaders
across the park. Today, visitors will
find a modern park with wood-
land walks, a skatepark, boating
lakes, a 10,000-seat outdoor
theatre, an observatory and, in
the winter months, an ice rink,
which is the largest in Europe.

## ❻ Donskoy Monastery

Донской монастырь
*Donskoy monastyr*

Donskaya ploshchad 1–3. **Tel** (495) 952
14 81. Ⓜ Shabolovskaya. **Open** 7am–
7pm daily. 📷 ♿ grounds only. ✉

The Donskoy Monastery was
founded in 1593 by Boris
Godunov to honour *The Icon
of the Our Lady of the Don*,
credited with having saved

Russia from the Mongols twice.
The first time was in 1380 when
Prince Dmitri Donskoy carried
the icon into battle at Kulikovo.
Boris Godunov also used it to
rally his troops in 1591 against
the army of Khan Kazy Girei,
which retreated after minor
skirmishes. The crescent moons
below the golden crosses on top
of the monastery symbolize the
church as a ship of salvation.

The modest scale of the
original monastery is reflected
in the beautifully understated
Old, or Small Cathedral. The
Orthodox prelate Archbishop
Amvrosiy, killed by a mob during
a riot in 1771, is buried within.
The remains of Patriarch Tikhon,
who was imprisoned by the
Bolsheviks after the Revolution,
were secretly buried here until
1992 when they were moved to
the New, or Grand Cathedral.
The fortified outer walls and

Donskoy Monastery's imposing
17th-century Grand Cathedral

Grand Cathedral were added
in the late 17th century when
the monastery acquired greater
prestige under the patronage
of the Regent Sophia.

Built in 1684–98 in the Moscow
Baroque style, the brick Grand
Cathedral has five domes. Inside
is a stunning seven-tiered iconostasis and frescoes, painted in
1782–5 by Italian artist Antonio
Claudio. *The Icon of Our Lady of
the Don* is in the State Tretyakov
Gallery *(see pp98–9)*, but a copy is
on show in the Small Cathedral.

## ❼ Sparrow Hills

Воробьёвы горы
*Vorobevy gory*

Ⓜ Universitet.

The summit of this wooded
ridge offers unsurpassed views
across the city. There is an
observation point on ulitsa
Kosygina and newly wed
couples traditionally come
here to have their photograph
taken against the panorama.
It is also a favourite pitch for
souvenir sellers.

The hills are dominated by
the Moscow State University
(MGU) building commissioned
by Stalin, designed by Lev
Rudnev and completed in 1953.
With 36 floors, it is the tallest
of the seven skyscrapers built in
the Stalin-Gothic style in Moscow
in the 1940s and 1950s.

On prospekt Vernadskovo, on
the southeastern edge of the
hills, is the silver-roofed New
Moscow Circus and the Nataliya
Sats Children's Musical Theatre.

# ❽ Kolomenskoe

Коломенское

*Kolomenskoe*

Prospekt Andropova 39. **Tel** (499) 615 27 68. **M** Kolomenskaya. Front Gate Museum: **Open** May–Sep: 10am–6pm Tue–Fri & Sun, 11am–7pm Sat; Oct–Apr: 10am–6pm Tue–Sun. Church and Grounds: **Open** 7am–10pm daily. 🎫 🎧 English, book in advance. 📷 ♿ Grounds. 🚻 📸 **w** mgomz.com

Set on the steep west bank of the Moskva river, Kolomenskoe was a favourite country estate of the tsars. The oldest surviving building is the soaring tent-roofed Church of the Ascension in 1532, erected by Vasily III to celebrate the birth of his son Ivan (later, the Terrible). Between 1667 and 1672, Peter the Great's father, Tsar Alexis Mikhailovich, built an astonishing wooden palace with barrel-shaped roofs, onion domes and carvings, described by visiting diplomats as the eighth wonder of the world. This was demolished by Catherine the Great, but a model was made, now on display in the Front Gate Museum.

In 1925, the park was designated a museum of wooden architecture, and historic buildings, such as Peter the Great's cabin from Archangel, were moved here from all over Russia. Folkloric festivals and historical pageants are staged here throughout the year.

# ❾ Tsaritsyno

Царицыно

*Tsaritsyno*

Ulitsa Dolskaya 1.
**Tel** (495) 322 68 43. **M** Tsaritsyno, Orekhovo. **Open** 11am–6pm Tue–Fri (till 8pm Sat & 7pm Sun). Grounds: **Open** 6am–midnight daily. 🎫 🎧 English, book in advance. ♿

Catherine the Great bought this tract of land in 1775 and changed its name from Chyornaya Gryaz (Black Mud) to Tsaritsyno (Empress's Village). She commissioned architect Vasily Bazhenov to build a lavish imperial palace here. Bazhenov designed an innovative complex, combining Gothic,

Model of the wooden palace, displayed in the Front Gate Museum at Kolomenskoe

Baroque and even Moorish styles, but when Catherine visited the site in 1785 she proclaimed herself dissatisfied. Bazhenov's young colleague Matvei Kazakov was told to rebuild the palace but, after a further decade of construction, lack of funds left it incomplete.

After centuries as a roofless shell, Kazakov's Great Palace has finally been completed and now serves as a museum of antique tapestries, Central Asian folk art, ceramics and contemporary glassware. Some of Bazhenov's smaller structures in Tsaritsyno are equally impressive, such as the Figured Gate, with its Gothic-style towers and lancet windows, the Figured Bridge and the ornate two-storey Opera House, one of the few buildings Catherine approved. The extraordinary Bread Gate, with its arch of sharply pointed stone "teeth", leads to the kitchens, while the Octahedron was built as the servants' quarters.

# ❿ Kuskovo

Кусково

*Kuskovo*

Ulitsa Yunosti 2. **Tel** (495) 375 31 31. 🚌 133, 208, 620. **M** Ryazanskiy prospekt, Vykhino. **Open** mid-Apr–mid-Oct: 10am–6pm Wed–Sun; mid-Oct–mid-Apr: 10am–4pm Wed–Sun. **Closed** last Wed of the month. 🎫 tickets sold at main entrance for individual sights. 🎧 English, book in advance. ♿ Palace and grotto only. 📸 **w** kuskovo.ru

For over 200 years before the Revolution, Kuskovo was the country seat of one of Russia's wealthiest aristocratic families, the Sheremetevs. The present buildings were commissioned by Count Pyotr Sheremetev after his marriage to the heiress Varvara Cherkasskaya in 1743. Among their 200,000 serfs were the architects Fyodor Argunov and Aleksey Mironov, who played a major role in Kuskovo's construction under the supervision of architect Karl Blank.

The Neo-Classical palace, made entirely of wood, has a magnificent ballroom. The gardens boast a shell-encrusted grotto, luxurious "cottages" and an orangery exhibiting paintings, ceramics and other treasures. The Ceramics Museum has an impressive collection of ceramics and glass from antiquity to the present age.

Beautiful orangery in Kuskovo, now converted into a ceramics museum

The stately 17th-century Cathedral of the Intercession, Izmaylovo

## ⓫ Izmaylovo

Измайлово

*Izmaylovo*

Gorodok Baumana 2. **Tel** (499) 165 13 36. Ⓜ Partizanskaya. **Open** 10am–6pm Tue–Sun. ♿ 🖥 🌐 mgomz.ru

One of Moscow's largest wooded areas, Izmaylovo park covers nearly 12 sq km (5 sq miles). Acquired by the Romanov family in the 16th century, it became one of their favourite hunting estates where, in 1663, Tsar Alexis built an enormous wooden palace and dedicated the land to experiments in animal and vegetable husbandry. His son, the future Tsar Peter the Great, spent an idyllic childhood here, secluded from palace intrigues as he learned to sail an old boat on a lake – the genesis of his lifelong fascination with the sea. The boat was later nicknamed the "grandfather of the Russian Navy".

The former royal estate is on an island, approached via the white, triple-arched Ceremonial Gate, to the northeast of Izmaylovskiy Park metro station.

While the wooden palace has long since disappeared (demolished by Catherine the Great in 1767), visitors can still see the royal estate's walls and the imposing 17th-century Cathedral of the Intercession, whose five black domes are tiled with metallic scales. The *zakomary* (arched) gables beneath them are beautifully decorated with "peacock's eye" tiles by Stepan Polubes, a Belorussian ceramicist working in Moscow.

To the cathedral's right is the Bridge Tower. Built in 1671, this tiered red-brick arch is all that remains of a 14-span bridge that once crossed the estate's waterways. The top tier of the bridge offers fine views of the estate.

The road northwards leads to the Izmaylovo flea market *(see p118)*. Known to Muscovites as the Vernissazh, it is a boisterous melange of stalls selling folk crafts and Soviet memorabilia. It is at its busiest at weekends, when buskers strum away on the stage-set medieval wooden palace just inside the market's entrance.

## ⓬ Vasnetsov House-Museum

Дом-музей ВМ Васнецова

*Dom-muzey VM Vasnetsova*

Pereulok Vasnetsova 13. **Tel** (495) 681 13 29. Ⓜ Sukharevskaya, Prospekt Mira. **Open** 10am–5pm Wed–Sun. **Closed** last Thu of the month. ♿ 🖼 🌐 tretyakovgallery.ru

A sculptor, painter, theatre designer and architect, Viktor Vasnetsov (1848–1926) was a member of the artists' colony at Abramtsevo *(see p114)*. He designed the façade of the State Tretyakov Gallery *(see pp98–9)* and also his own family home, where he lived until his death. An enthusiastic advocate of traditional Russian folk art and architecture, he employed peasant carpenters from Vladimir to build his log-cabin-like timber house with green roofs.

The ground-floor rooms display highly individual pieces of furniture, many designed by Vasnetsov and his similarly talented younger brother, Arkady (1856–1933). A spiral staircase hung with 17th-century chain mail and weaponry leads up to the artist's studio, which resembles a vaulted medieval hall. This is the perfect backdrop for Vasnetsov's arresting canvases, which depict Russian legends such as the forest witch Baba Yaga stealing children. *The Sleeping Princess,* showing a scene from the classic fairy tale *Sleeping Beauty,* was painted in the last year of Vasnetsov's life, at a time when Stalin was tightening his grip on Russia.

Ornate roof of the wooden house designed by Viktor Vasnetsov

### ⓭ Gulag History Museum

Музей истории ГУЛАГа

*Muzey Istorii GULAGa*

1 Samotechny pereulok, 9–1.
**Tel** (495) 621 73 10. Ⓜ Dostoyevskaya,
Novoslobodskaya. **Open** 11am–
7pm Tue–Wed & Fri–Sun, noon–
8pm Thu. **Closed** last Fri of the month.
▨ ◪ Russian only. ▧ ⓦ gmig.ru

Housed in a large early 20th-century building, this museum recounts the grim history of Soviet prisons and labour camps (collectively known by their Russian acronym, GULAG). Prisoners' clothing, eating utensils, handmade chess sets, paintings, drawings and photographs show how millions suffered in the "white hell" of Kolyma in Siberia and other infamous sites across the Soviet Union. There were hundreds of prisons and camps, constituting what the writer Aleksandr Solzhenitsyn called the "Gulag Archipelago". The museum is equipped with multimedia interactive displays. The interior, with its iron doors, open pipes and exposed brick walls, matches the sinister mood of the exhibits.

### ⓮ Ostankino Palace

Московский музей-усадьба Останкино

*Moskovskiy muzey-usadba Ostankino*

1-ya Ostankinskaya ulitsa 5. **Tel** (495)
683 46 45. Ⓜ VDNKh. **Closed** for
renovation until further notice.

Like the Sheremetev estate at Kuskovo (*see p109*), Ostankino was built by the serf architects Pavel Argunov and Aleksey Mironov. It was commissioned by Count Nikolai Sheremetev, a patron of the arts, who had the palace built around a theatre, where a company of 200 serf actors and actresses performed plays of his choosing.

Built of wood skilfully plastered over to resemble brick and stone, the palace was completed in 1792–8. Its halls are a wonder of *trompe l'oeil* decor, with carved wooden mouldings painted to resemble bronze, gold and marble. The *pièce de résistance* is the ballroom.

The splendid Fountain of the Republics at the Exhibition of Achievements of National Economy

### ⓯ Exhibition of Achievements of National Economy (VDNKh)

Выставка достижений народного хозяйства (ВДНХ)

*Vystavka Dostizheniy Narodnogo Khozyaistva (VDNKh)*

Prospekt Mira 119. **Tel** (495) 544 34 00.
Ⓜ VDNKh. Grounds: **Open** 24 hours.
Pavilions: **Open** 9am–7pm (or till 8pm
or 9pm depending on the exhibition).
Botanical Gardens: **Open** May–Oct:
10am–8pm daily. Moskvarium: **Open**
10am–10pm daily ⓦ vdnh.ru

One of Moscow's main tourist attractions in Soviet times, the Exhibition of Achievements of National Economy (VDNKh) is a vast exhibition and recreation site. The entrance is via a huge triumphal arch topped by the figures of a tractor driver and collective farmer, holding up a sheaf of corn. VDNKh remains a fascinating place, especially for lovers of Soviet architecture.

The centrepiece is the Fountain of the Republics, consisting of 16 gilded statues of maidens in national dress representing the former Soviet republics. They surround a basin from which jets of water are sprayed 24 m (79 ft) into the air, illuminated at night by 525 spotlights. Nearby is a 75-m (246-ft) high ferris wheel, which offers a superb view of northern Moscow. VDNKh is also home to Russia's largest centre of oceanography and marine biology, Moskvarium, with

80 aquariums and 8,000 species of marine creatures. At the northern gate to VDNKh stands a major sculpture of monumental art, *Worker and Kolkhoz Woman* by Vera Mukhina. Adjoining VDNKh are Botanical Gardens, which include a Japanese Garden where tea is served.

### ⓰ Memorial Museum of Space Exploration

Музей космонавтики

*Muzei kosmonavtiki*

Prospekt Mira 111. **Tel** (499) 750 23 00.
Ⓜ VDNKh. **Open** 10am–7pm Tue–
Sun (till 9pm Thu). ▨ ◪ English. ♿
▧ ⓦ kosmo-museum.ru

It is hard to miss the titanium Space Obelisk near the VDNKh metro station. Over 100 m (328 ft) high, it represents a rocket blasting off, and was erected three years after Yuri Gagarin's historic flight in 1961. Underneath it is the Memorial Museum of Space Exploration, containing models of Belka and Strelka, the two dogs who were the first creatures to come back alive from space, and Vostok 1, the tiny capsule in which Gagarin famously orbited the Earth. The exhibits also include space suits and equipment used by astronauts. It is recommended to tour the museum with a guide, as they can narrate interesting details about the life of astronauts aboard spacecraft.

# BEYOND MOSCOW

As well as the numerous attractions of Moscow, there are some magnificent monasteries and historic sites in the surrounding region, which make for rewarding day trips. To the north is the spectacular Trinity Monastery of St Sergius. Once a place of pilgrimage for the tsars, this huge complex has several superb cathedrals. To the west lies Borodino, site of the great battle between Napoleon's army and Russian forces in 1812. Located to the northeast are the towns of the Golden Ring, including Vladimir, Suzdal and Yaroslavl. Founded by Russians seeking shelter from invading tribes, these attractive settlements still have many historic buildings. Also situated outside Moscow are several country estates. Significant among them are Abramtsevo Estate-Museum, a former artists' colony; the house in Klin rented by Pyotr Tchaikovsky; and Yasnaya Polyana, where Leo Tolstoy lived for many years. Although parts of the landscape are unappealingly industrial, there are large tracts of wooded countryside dotted with villages of small wooden cottages or *dachas*, each with a small plot of land that is used for growing fruit and vegetables. One of the best ways to visit sights outside Moscow is on an organized tour since public transport can be erratic, but bus and train travel are perfectly feasible for those who prefer a taste of everyday local life.

## Sights at a Glance

**Museums**
1. Abramtsevo Estate-Museum
3. Tchaikovsky House-Museum
5. Yasnaya Polyana

**Churches and Cathedrals**
2. Trinity Monastery of St Sergius

**Historic Sites**
4. Borodino
6. Vladimir
7. Suzdal
8. Yaroslavl

**Key**
=== Motorway
=== Main road
=== Minor road
— Railway

**Beyond Moscow**

0 km    50
0 miles    50

◄ Impressive church building in the Museum of Wooden Architecture, Suzdal

**For keys to symbols** *see back flap*

# ❶ Abramtsevo Estate-Museum

Музей-усадьба Абрамцево
*Muzey-usadba Abramtsevo*

60 km (37 miles) N of Moscow,
Ulitsa Muzeinaya 1, Abramtsevo.
**Tel** (495) 993 00 33. 🚃 from
Yaroslavskiy station to Abramtsevo.
**Open** 10am–6pm Wed–Sun.
Park: 10am–8pm daily. **Closed** last
Thu of the month. 🎟 📷
**W** abramtsevo.net

In the second half of the
19th century, this rural retreat
became a hive of cultural activity
after arts patron Savva Mamontov
established an artists' colony here.
Viktor Vasnetsov, Mikhail Nesterov
and others were inspired by the
work of local peasant craftsmen,
and used folk motifs and
traditional techniques in their art.

Dotted around the estate are
a number of remarkable buildings. The Church of the Saviour
Not Made by Human Hand
is modelled on the medieval
churches of Novgorod, its
whitewashed brickwork
enlivened by bands of painted

The fortified Trinity Monastery of St Sergius
as seen from the southeast

majolica tiles. The *teremok* is a free
improvisation on the *izba* (typical
peasant hut), with wooden
furnishings and ornaments,
and a tiled stove. Even more
eye-catching is the House on
Chicken Legs, which stands
on stilts. In Russian folklore, the
witch Baba Yaga lived in a house
built on giant chicken's legs.

# ❷ Trinity Monastery of St Sergius

Троице-Сергиева Лавра
*Troitse-Sergieva Lavra*

75 km (47 miles) N of Moscow.
**Tel** (496) 541 56 58, (496) 540 57 21
(excursions). 🚃 from Yaroslavskiy
station to Sergiev Posad.
Monastery and Church of St Sergius:
**Open** 5am–8pm daily. Cathedral of the
Assumption: 5am–9pm daily. Trinity
Cathedral: **Open** 5am–9pm daily.
Grounds: **Open** 5am–9pm daily. 📷
🎫 book in advance. ♿ grounds
only. 📷 💻 🏠 **W** stsl.ru

Founded around 1335 by
Sergius of Radonezh, the Trinity
Monastery of St Sergius in
Sergiev-Posad is one of
Russia's most important
religious centres and places of
pilgrimage. Sergius persuaded
Russia's princes to unite against
the Mongol invaders, and the
monastery later withstood a
Polish siege during the Time of
Troubles *(see p40)*. In the 1680s,
the young Peter the Great
found refuge here during the
Streltsy Revolt *(see p41)*.

The huge complex is
enclosed by white walls around
2 km (1 mile) in length, and its
stunning churches are among
the most beautiful in Russia.

The monks' refectory in the
complex was built in 1686–92
using money donated by
Peter the Great and his half-
brother, Ivan V, in gratitude for
the refuge given them by the
monastery during the Streltsy
Revolt. The exterior walls are
divided into a series of panels,
each painted so that it looks as
though it has three-dimensional
facets similar to those of the
Faceted Chamber *(see p61)* in
the Kremlin. The refectory's
main façade features a covered
terrace with a wealth of ornamentation. At the eastern end
of the refectory is the **Church
of St Sergius**.

The magnificent **Cathedral
of the Assumption**, with
its central golden cupola
surrounded by four blue,
star-spangled domes, lies at the
heart of the monastery. It was
commissioned by Ivan the Terrible
in 1559 to celebrate his defeat of
the Mongols at Kazan *(see p225)*,

The superb 17th-century iconostasis in the Cathedral of the Assumption

The reception area in the Tchaikovsky House-Museum, containing the composer's piano

and completed 26 years later to a design inspired by the Cathedral of the Assumption *(see pp58–9)* in the Kremlin.

The oldest stone building in the monastery, the exquisite white **Trinity Cathedral** is decorated with *kokoshniki* (tiered gables) above a triple-banded frieze. It was built over the tomb of St Sergius in 1422, the year of his canonization. His remains, encased in a silver shrine inside, are a focus for visiting pilgrims. The iconostasis contains two icons by the renowned painter Simon Ushakov, *The Holy Face* and *Christ Enthroned*, plus a copy of Andrei Rublev's masterpiece *The Trinity*, the original of which is housed in the State Tretyakov Gallery *(see pp98–9)*.

*Christ in Majesty* (1425–7) by Rublev, part of the Trinity Cathedral's iconostasis

## ❸ Tchaikovsky House-Museum

Дом-музей ПИ Чайковского

*Dom-muzey PI Chaykovskuvo*

90 km (56 miles) NW of Moscow. Ulitsa Tchaikovskaya 48, Klin. **Tel** (496) 245 81 96. ⬚ from Leningradskiy station to Klin. **Open** 10am–6pm Fri–Tue. **Closed** last Mon of the month. ⬚ ⬚ English. ⬚ **tchaikovsky-house-museum.ru**

In May 1892, Pyotr Tchaikovsky rented a house in Klin. Previous stays near Klin had inspired some of his best music, including the ballets *The Sleeping Beauty* and *The Nutcracker*. Tchaikovsky died in 1893, and his brother, Modest, opened the estate to visitors.

The walls of the reception area are covered with photographs of family and fellow musicians. In the centre is a grand piano and on a shelf behind the piano is a Statue of Liberty inkpot, which Tchaikovsky brought back from his triumphant tour of the United States in 1891. The winner of the Tchaikovsky International Competition gives a recital here every four years. On 7 May, the composer's birthday, famous musicians stage a concert and some even play the grand piano. The bedroom, separated from the reception by a curtain, is where Tchaikovsky finished his *Symphony No. 6*, the *Pathétique*.

Also open to visitors are the library and the study where Tchaikovsky worked as the Klin archivist until his death in 1893.

## ❹ Borodino

Бородино

*Borodino*

120 km (75 miles) W of Moscow. **Tel** (496) 385 15 46. ⬚ from Belorusskiy station. **Open** May–Oct: 10am–6pm Tue–Sun; Nov–Apr: 9am–4:30pm Tue–Sun. **Closed** last Fri of the month. ⬚ ⬚ ⬚ **borodino.ru**

One of the fiercest battles of the 19th century took place at Borodino on 7 September 1812. For over 15 hours Napoleon Bonaparte's Grande Armée and the Russian army, led by Field Marshal Mikhail Kutuzov, fought each other to a bloody impasse. The Russians were forced to abandon Moscow. However, their agents started a fire *(see p42)* that levelled the city. Faced with a Russian winter in the open, Napoleon's army was forced to retreat, vindicating Kutuzov's "scorched earth" strategy.

The battlefield covers over 100 sq km (38 sq miles), but the main places of interest are reasonably accessible. A museum, 1 km (half a mile) south of the village, recounts the story of the battle and a re-enactment takes place every 7 September. The inn, where Tolstoy stayed to conduct research for the novel *War and Peace*, is now a museum.

Monument to the fallen of Borodino

## ➎ Yasnaya Polyana
Ясная Поляна
*Yasnaya Polyana*

200 km (124 miles) S of Moscow. **Tel** (487) 517 61 18. 🚃 to Tula, then bus. **Open** Nov–Mar: 9am–5pm Tue–Sun (memorial buildings 10am–3:30pm); Apr–Oct: 9am–2pm Tue–Sun (memorial buildings 10am–4:30pm). **Closed** last Tue of the month. 📷 📹 English, book in advance. ✉ 📱 🏠 **w** ypmuseum.ru

The beloved country estate of Leo Tolstoy *(see p106)*, Yasnaya Polyana, is located in a peaceful valley surrounded by forests. Tolstoy was born on the estate in 1828. From the mid-1880s he spent summers here with his family, and moved here permanently in 1901. The house and its contents are much as they were in Tolstoy's day. The rooms on show include the study, where Tolstoy wrote *War and Peace* and *Anna Karenina*. The estate also includes the Volkonsky House, where the serfs lived, and a pavilion for guests. A literary museum is housed in the former peasants' school that Tolstoy established.

Tolstoy's study where he wrote *War and Peace* and *Anna Karenina*, Yasnaya Polyana

## ➏ Vladimir
Владимир
*Vladimir*

170 km (106 miles) NE of Moscow. 🏙 360,000. 🚃 🚌 🚐 daily.

Vladimir was founded on the Klyazma river by Prince Vladimir Svyatoslavich, the Baptizer of Russia, in the late 10th century. The city began to flourish under Prince Yuri Dolgorukiy's son Andrey Bogolyubskiy, who made it the capital of the new principality of Vladimir-Suzdal. Had it not been for the Mongols, who dev-

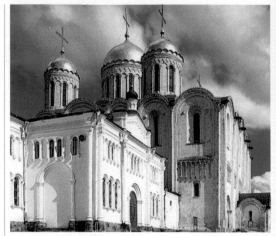

The 12th-century Cathedral of the Assumption in Vladimir

astated Vladimir in 1238, the city might today be Russia's capital. Today, Vladimir looks like any industrial city of the Soviet era, but fortunately its chemical plants and tractor and automobile appliance factories are away from the picturesque old part of the town.

Visitors arriving by train will see the town's landmarks arrayed along a ridge beside bolshaya Moskovskaya ulitsa, the road to Moscow. The most prominent among them is the **Cathedral of the Assumption**. It was built in 1158–60 and originally decorated with prodigious quantities of gold and silver, gems and majolica tiles. Craftsmen came from all over Russia, Poland and the Holy Roman Empire to contribute to what was then the tallest building in Russia, where the coronation of many princes, including Dmitri Donskoy *(see p40)* and Aleksandr Nevsky, subsequently took place. Some superb frescoes by artists such as Andrei Rublev and Daniil Cherny are still visible under the choir's gallery on the west wall.

Nearby stands the **Cathedral of St Demetrius**, built in 1194–7 by Prince Vsevolod III. A single-domed church of white limestone, its exterior is covered by bas-reliefs featuring griffons, centaurs, birds and lions as well as a portrait of Prince Vsevolod and his family.

A short stroll down bolshaya Moskovskaya ulitsa takes visitors past the 18th-century trading arcades and shops to the **Golden**

**Gate**. Constructed in 1164, it combines the functions of a triumphal arch and defensive bastion. Over the centuries the gate has sunk 2 m (6 ft) into the ground due to its weight. Vladimir might have withstood the Mongol siege had not the young prince Vsevolod lost his nerve and ventured forth bearing gifts, whereupon Genghis Khan's grandson Batu Khan slew him on the spot and laid waste to the city. This is depicted by a diorama within the Golden Gate.

🏛 **Cathedral of the Assumption**
Bolshaya Moskovskaya 56. **Tel** (4922) 32 52 01. **Open** 1pm–4:30pm Tue–Sun. 📷 📹 ✉ ♿ 📱

🏛 **Cathedral of St Demetrius**
Bolshaya Moskovskaya 60. **Tel** (4922) 32 42 63. **Open** May–Oct: 11am–6pm Wed–Fri; Nov–Apr: 10am–5pm Wed–Fri. **Closed** last Wed of the month. 📷 📹 ♿

## ➐ Suzdal
Суздаль
*Suzdal*

200 km (124 miles) NE of Moscow. 🏙 12,100. 🚃 to Vladimir, then bus or taxi. 🚌 🚐 Sun.

Nestling on the banks of the Kamenka river, Suzdal is the best preserved of the Golden Ring towns. Its clusters of 17th- and 18th-century churches, built by local merchants, and its low, wooden houses with traditional carved eaves and windows, make this the most attractive town in the Vladimir region.

The first records of Suzdal date from 1024, a century after which, Moscow's founder Prince Yuri Dolgorukiy built Suzdal's Kremlin on a grassy rampart above the river. Today, it is one of the several historic buildings that constitute the **Vladimir & Suzdal Museum of History, Art & Architecture**. The Kremlin's dominant building is the **Cathedral of the Nativity** with its blue, star-spangled domes. Although it was built in the 13th century, most of the current building dates from the 16th century. The south and west doors are of gilded copper, etched with biblical scenes.

The former Archbishop's Palace next door houses exhibitions on the history of Suzdal. The main room of the palace, the magnificent Cross Chamber, is one of the largest unsupported vaults in Russia. Within the Annunciation Church in the western part of the palace is the Old Russian Painting Exhibition, featuring icons and art from the 15th to 17th centuries.

Suzdal also contains five important religious foundations, including the **Monastery of the Saviour and St Euphemius**. Once the richest monastery in the area, with more than 10,000 serfs at its disposal, it has a commanding position overlooking the town, behind fortified walls almost 6 m (20 ft) thick. The monks' cells and all the other buildings of the monastery contain impressive collections of exhibits, including religious paintings and jewellery.

To the south of the monastery is the **Aleksandrovskiy Convent**, founded in 1240 and rebuilt in the 17th century. Its Cathedral of the Ascension was built by Nataliya Naryshkina, mother of Peter the Great.

Across the river is the **Convent of the Intercession**, where Peter the Great incarcerated his first wife, Yevdokiya Lopukhina, following the example set by tsars Basil III, Ivan the Terrible and Boris Godunov.

On the southwest edge of town is the **Museum of Wooden Architecture** – an open-air exhibition of wooden

Fifteenth-century icon of St Nicholas on display at the Old Russian Painting Exhibition

buildings brought from across the Vladimir region. Particularly impressive is the 1756 Church of the Transfiguration. With domes made with overlapping shingles, it was built without using metal nails.

🏛 **Vladimir & Suzdal Museum of History, Art & Architecture**
Ulitsa Bolshaya Moskovskaya 43.
**Tel** (4922) 32 42 63. **Open** call ahead of visit. 🔲 🗐 🚻 🏠
🌐 vladmuseum.ru

⛪ **Monastery of the Saviour and St Euphemius**
Ulitsa Lenina. **Tel** (49231) 2 07 46.
**Open** 10am–6pm Tue–Sun.
**Closed** last Thu of the month.
🔲 🗐 🖵 🏠

🏛 **Museum of Wooden Architecture**
Ulitsa Pushkarskaya. **Tel** (49231) 2 35 10.
**Open** May–Oct: 9am–7pm Thu–Tue (closed last Wed of the month); Nov–Apr: 9am–6pm Thu–Tue (closed last Tue of the month). 🔲 🗐 🏠

## ❽ Yaroslavl

Ярослваль

*Yaroslavl*

250 km (155 miles) NE of Moscow.
🚗 592,000. 🚉 from Yaroslavlsky station. ▭

Founded in 1010 on the banks of the Volga river by Prince Yaroslav the Wise after he reputedly gained the trust of local villagers by slaying a bear with an axe, Yaroslavl later became a wealthy commercial and industrial town that rivalled Moscow until the 17th century. Yaroslavl's merchants endowed it with splendid churches, many of them within the complex of the **Monastery of Our Saviour and Transfiguration**. An annual festival of classical music is held here in May.

A walk along the scenic Volga embankment leads to the **Museum of Music and Time**, a collection of antique clocks and musical instruments belonging to the eccentric magician and actor Ivan Mostoslavsky, who conducts tours in English if booked in advance.

⛪ **Monastery of Our Saviour and Transfiguration**
Bogoyavlenskaya ploshchad 25.
**Tel** (4852) 30 38 69. Churches:
**Open** May–Sep: 10am–5:30pm Tue–Sun (except rainy days).
**Closed** last Wed of the month.
🌐 yarmp.yar.ru

🏛 **Museum of Music and Time**
Volzhskaya naberezhnaya 33a.
**Tel** (4852) 232 86 37.
**Open** 10am–7pm daily.
🌐 music-and-time.narod.ru

View of the Monastery of Our Saviour and Transfiguration, Yaroslavl

# SHOPPING IN MOSCOW

In contrast to the long queues and shortages during the Soviet era, Moscow now boasts not just supermarkets and department stores stocking imported goods, but also exclusive boutiques selling international brands. Ulitsa Arbat and Tverskaya ulitsa are the main shopping hubs and are popular among shoppers looking for chic boutiques and other meccas of consumerism. However, high import duties, transportation costs and the relative lack of competition can make certain consumer goods more expensive than in the West. The colourful Russian arts and crafts available at many locations throughout the city are popular with visitors, as are exotic goods from the ex-Soviet Republics of Central Asia.

## Opening Hours

Moscow's shops and businesses rarely open before 10am and often not until 11am. Most stay open until around 7pm. A few state-run stores close for an hour at lunchtime, either from 1pm to 2pm, or from 2pm to 3pm. Shops are usually open all day on Saturdays, and most are also open on Sundays, although often for shorter hours. However, a large number of shops and services, from bookshops to beauty salons, are now open around the clock to cater for increasing consumer demands.

Outdoor markets are usually open from 10am to 4pm, but it is advisable to go in the morning to get the best choice of goods.

## Food and Drink

Many Muscovites buy meat, cheese and fresh fruit and vegetables at one of the number of big food markets across the city. One of the largest and most picturesque food markets is the **Danilovskiy Market**, which takes its name from the nearby Danilovskiy Monastery. The **Cheremushkinskiy Market** offers a wide variety of fresh produce; there is also sometimes a market across the road, at which vendors from distant Russian regions sell produce and souvenirs. The **Dorogomilovsky Market**, located near Kievsky train station, displays a colourful selection of fresh produce from Russia and the former Soviet republics. The upmarket **Farmers' Market** on the fifth floor of Tsvetnoy Central Market is also worth a visit. Visitors can buy ingredients here and have them cooked at one of the restaurants nearby.

A variety of traditional *matryoshka* dolls on sale at a souvenir stall

## Crafts and Souvenirs

The best place to buy crafts and souvenirs such as Soviet memorabilia and *matryoshka* dolls (see p294), icons, samovars, fur hats and Central Asian rugs is the Izmaylovo Crafts Market, which is held on the edge of Izmaylovo Park (see p110). Note that the crafts market is open on weekends only.

In the city centre, Arbat Square (see p89) is the place to shop for crafts. Handmade lace and embroidery are sold at **Russkaya Vyshivka**; Russian jewellery and amber at **Samotsvety**; and lacquer trays and painted china at **Arbatskaya Lavitsa**. Elsewhere in the city, **Dom Farfora** sells hand-painted porcelain tea sets and crystal bowls. Art lovers can browse through whimsical sculptures at the **Salon of the Moscow Cultural Fund**, which also has old lamps and samovars. **Roza Azora**, a small art gallery, stocks Soviet bric-a-brac, including lamps, old biscuit tins and hats. Soviet posters and badges, amber and lacquer boxes can be bought at the superb souvenir shop in the Museum of Contemporary History (see p85).

## Antiques

Any item made before 1945 officially counts as an antique and can only be legally exported after being cleared. The duty is paid at the **Ministry of Culture**. The area around ulitsa Arbat has many of the best antiques shops. **Eurasia Gallery**, one of the largest galleries of eastern antiques in Europe, specializes in Chinese and Japanese art, while **Ivan Tsarevich** has superb Soviet porcelain. For larger pieces and furniture, check out **Rokoko**.

## Fashion and Accessories

**GUM** (ГУМ) is Moscow's premier department store (see p69). A beautiful edifice beside Red Square (see p68), GUM contains three arcades of shops under a glass roof. It stocks a wide variety of international designer brands of clothing, perfumes and cosmetics, besides many smaller, more exclusive labels from Italy, France and Scandinavia.

A wide variety of merchandise on display at the Izmaylovo Crafts Market

Another popular downtown arcade is **Petrovskiy Passage,** which sells high-quality Russian fur hats and coats. The modern, three-storey **Gallery Aktyor** contains designer stores selling French perfumes, clothes and jewellery from Tiffany and Cartier.

Besides global brands, visitors will find works by Russian designers such as **Masha Tsigal**, who makes clothes, handbags and sunglasses. Both international and Russian designers are featured in the **Atrium** mall, which has boutiques, cafés, bars and a cinema.

Shoppers enjoying a meal at the café in the fashionable Atrium mall

## Books and Music

For English-language books, **Dom Inostrannoy Knigi** is probably the best shop to visit. The enormous **Moscow House of Books** sells a good range of English-language books and also old icons and Soviet propaganda posters. **Biblio Globus** is another good bookshop that you can browse. Both the Pushkin State Museum of Fine Arts *(see pp90–91)* and the State Tretyakov Gallery *(see pp98–9)* have shops selling art books in English.

The **Gorbushkin dvor** is a factory-size mart for CDs, DVDs and second-hand LPs, as well as video cameras and audio equipment. For vintage and specialist music, visit **Transylvania**.

## Toys

The best children's shop is **Malenkiy Genii** (Little Genius), selling imported and Russian educational toys, CDs, cartoon books, puzzles and board games.

# DIRECTORY

## Food and Drink

**Cheremushkinskiy Market**
Prospekt Lomonosovskiy 1/64.

**Danilovskiy Market**
Mytnaya ulitsa 74.
**Tel** (495) 958 17 25.

**Dorogomilovsky Market**
Mozhaysky val 10.
**Tel** (499) 249 55 53.

**Farmers' Market**
Tsvetnoy bulvar 15, building 1.
**Map** 2 D3.
**Tel** (495) 737 77 73.

## Crafts and Souvenirs

**Arbatskaya Lavitsa**
Ulitsa Arbat 27.
**Map** 3 B1.
**Tel** (495) 690 56 89.

**Dom Farfora**
Leninskiy prospekt 36.
**Tel** (495) 995 60 23.

**Roza Azora**
Nikitskiy bulvar 14.
**Map** 1 B5.
**Tel** (495) 695 81 19.

**Russkaya Vyshivka**
Ulitsa Arbat 31.
**Map** 3 B1.
**Tel** (499) 241 28 41.

**Salon of the Moscow Cultural Fund**
Pyanitskaya ulitsa 16.
**Map** 4 E2.
**Tel** (495) 680 24 06.

**Samotsvety**
Ulitsa Arbat 35.
**Map** 3 A1.
**Tel** (495) 241 07 65.

## Antiques

**Eurasia Gallery**
Nikitskiy bulvar 12A.
**Map** 1 B5.
**Tel** (495) 690 05 49.

**Ivan Tsarevich**
Ulitsa Arbat 4.
**Map** 3 B1.
**Tel** (495) 691 74 44.

**Ministry of Culture**
Malyy Gnezdnikovskiy pereulok 7/6.
**Map** 1 C4.
**Tel** (495) 629 20 08.

**Rokoko**
Frunzenskaya naberezhnaya 54.
**Map** 3 A5.
**Tel** (499) 242 36 64.

## Fashion and Accessories

**Atrium**
Zemlyanoy Val 33.
**Tel** (495) 970 15 55.
**W** atrium.su

**Gallery Aktyor**
Tverskaya ulitsa 16/1.
**Map** 1 C4.
**Tel** (495) 935 82 99.

**GUM**
Krasnaya ploshchad 3.
**Map** 4 D1.
**Tel** (495) 788 43 43.

**Masha Tsigal**
Ulitsa Yauzskaya 1/15.
**Map** 4 F1.
**Tel** (495) 660 56 44.

**Petrovskiy Passage**
Ulitsa Petrovka 10.
**Map** 2 D4.
**Tel** (495) 625 31 32.

## Books and Music

**Biblio Globus**
Myasnitskaya ulitsa 6/3.
**Map** 2 E5.
**Tel** (495) 781 19 00.

**Dom Inostrannoy Knigi**
Kuznetskiy Most 18/7.
**Map** 2 D5.
**Tel** (495) 628 20 21.

**Gorbushkin dvor**
Bagrationovskiy proyezd 7/1.
**Tel** (495) 737 74 74.
**W** gorbushkin.ru

**Moscow House of Books**
Ulitsa Novyy Arbat 8.
**Map** 3 B1.
**Tel** (495)789 35 91.

**Transylvania**
Tverskaya ulitsa 6/1.
**Map** 1 C5.
**Tel** (495) 629 87 86.

## Toys

**Malenkiy Genii**
Bolshoy Kozikhinskiy pereulok 6.
**Map** 1 B4.
**Tel** (495) 691 21 47.

# ENTERTAINMENT IN MOSCOW

From great theatres hosting the gamut of acclaimed operas and ballets to umpteen bars and clubs offering thriving nightlife, Moscow boasts a myriad of entertainment options. Attending a performance at the Bolshoi Theatre is considered by many to be the high point of a visit to the imperial city. Other theatres also put on an enormous range of productions, including musicals and shows for children. Many international artists include the city on their tours, so there are also performances by visiting reggae bands and DJs, orchestras and dance troupes, as well as local talent. In addition, there is plenty of lively entertainment from street performers.

A spectacular production of *The Sleeping Beauty* at the Bolshoi Theatre

## Information and Tickets

Moscow does not have any conventional tourist information offices. The English-language newspaper *The Moscow Times* has listings for clubs, concerts, plays and exhibitions in its Friday edition. Full listings of clubs, concerts and children's events also appear on Russian-language websites. Matinees start at noon, and most evening performances at 7pm.

Tickets are available at any large hotel. However, this is often more expensive than buying directly from the venue. Visitors who speak Russian will be able to buy cheap tickets from theatre kiosks, found all over the city. Ticket-booking website **Parter.ru** charges 10 per cent commission on the face-value of tickets. Prices are lowest at the venue's box office. Opening hours are generally from 11am to 3pm and 4pm to 7pm, but may vary.

## Ballet and Opera

The **Bolshoi Theatre** *(see pp82–3)* is the best venue to see ballet and opera. Best known abroad for performing Tchaikovsky's *Swan Lake* and *The Nutcracker*, its repertoire includes works such as *Boris Godunov* by Mussorgsky and European classics such as *Giselle*. Tickets can be booked by phone, online or at the box office.

Originally built as a convention hall for the Communist Party, the State Kremlin Palace *(see p56)* now hosts the Kremlin Ballet Company, while the **Helikon Opera** specializes in risqué re-workings of obscure operas.

## Music and Nightlife

Moscow's rich tradition of classical music is embodied in the **Tchaikovsky Concert Hall** and the Moscow Conservatory *(see p87)*. The annual December Nights held in the Pushkin State Museum of Fine Arts *(see pp90–91)* attract an array of talent, while the **Tchaikovsky International Competition** is a mecca for classical pianists. In summer both indoor and outdoor concerts are held at Kuskovo Palace *(see p109)* on Tuesday and Thursday evenings.

Moscow also has a vibrant jazz scene, and is well used to hosting international rock and pop stars, who perform at stadiums or on Red Square. The best in local talent play at clubs such as **B2**, which has established itself as one of the capital's best live music venues, hosting a variety of acts from rock to ska. **Sixteen Tons** favours bands playing alternative and indie music. **Liberty**, a lively South American bar and restaurant, is a good venue to see Latin American bands and hosts lively merengue and salsa nights.

Russians like to party hard and long into the night. Entrance is usually cheaper or free before 11pm, although the queues can be long. Most clubs do not close until 4am; some are open until 6am at weekends. **Propaganda** plays everything from the latest electronic sounds to classic disco. **Fabrique** is a huge split-level basement club, mostly playing house. **Krysha Mira**, a funky rooftop bar offers electronic music and beautiful views of

Indie band Race 7 performing at the Sixteen Tons club

the city. **Night Flight**, with the atmosphere of a London night club, is also popular. "Art cafés" such as **Tochka Sborki** host live music one night and an alternative fashion show or film screening the next.

The gay scene includes venues such as **Central Station**, a flamboyant club with nightly shows and karaoke. **Sharm** is set on two floors and offers a karaoke room and live shows.

## Theatre and Film

Repertory theatres stage a different play every night. The **Moscow Arts Theatre** is best known for its productions of Anton Chekhov's plays. An excellent dramatization of *The Master and Margarita*, by Mikhail Bulgakov, is staged by the **Taganka Theatre**, while the **Mossovlet Theatre** presents alternative interpretations of

Shakespearean dramas. For English-language cinema, there are a few options within the city centre. **Pioneer** shows dubbed films as well as English-language screenings. **35mm** specializes in independent foreign films.

## Children's Entertainment

The **Obraztsov Puppet Theatre** puts on matinee shows for children and evening performances for over 18s. The **Nataliya Sats Children's Musical Theatre** also stages fabulous shows.

Moscow's world-famous circus features clowns, acrobats, trapeze artists and performing animals. Visitors can attend shows at the **Old Circus** in the city centre, or the **New Circus** near Sparrow Hills.

The **Durov Animal Theatre** has performing cats and dogs as well as farm animals. Yuri

Kuklachev's **Moscow Cats Theatre**, established in 1990, has a troupe of over a hundred feline actors performing all manner of tricks. Performances include *Cats of the Universe* and are a must-see for cat lovers.

Performing artist and clown rehearsing for a show at Moscow's Old Circus

# DIRECTORY

## Information and Tickets

**Parter.ru**
w parter.ru

## Ballet and Opera

**Bolshoi Theatre**
Teatralnaya ploshcad 1.
**Map** 2 D5
**Tel** (495) 455 55 55.

**Helikon Opera**
Bolshaya Nikitskaya ulitsa 19/16.
**Map** 1 B5.
**Tel** (495) 250 22 22.

## Music and Nightlife

**B2**
Bolshaya Sadovaya ulitsa 8/1.
**Map** 1 A4.
**Tel** (495) 650 99 10.

**Central Station**
Ulitsa Yuzhny proezd 4.
**Tel** (916) 478 27 82.

**Fabrique**
Kosmodamianskaya naberezhnaya 2.
**Map** 4 F2.
**Tel** (495) 953 65 76.

**Krysha Mira**
Kutuzovsky prospekt 12/3.
**Tel** (901) 519 56 92.

**Liberty**
Slavyanskaya ploschad 2/5/4, building 3.
**Map** 2 D5.
**Tel** (495) 784 68 68.

**Night Flight**
Ulitsa Tverskaya 17.
**Map** 1 B4.
**Tel** (495) 629 41 65.

**Propaganda**
Bolshoi Zlatoustinskiy pereulok 7. **Map** 2 E5.
**Tel** (495) 624 57 32.

**Sharm**
Ulitsa Dubininskaya 69, Korpus 74.
**Tel** (495) 645 07 66.

**Sixteen Tons**
Ulitsa Presnenskiy Val 6.
**Tel** (499) 253 53 00.

**Tchaikovsky Concert Hall**
Triumfalnaya ploshchad 4.
**Map** 1 B3.
**Tel** (495) 232 53 53.

**Tochka Sborki**
Starosadskiy pereulok 5/8, building 6. **Map** 2 F5.
**Tel** (962) 267 76 14.

## Theatre and Film

**35mm**
Ulitsa Pokrovka 47/24.
**Map** 2 F5.
**Tel** (965) 423 60 33.

**Moscow Arts Theatre**
Kamergerskiy pereulok 3.
**Map** 1 C5.
**Tel** (495) 629 87 60.

**Mossoviet Theatre**
Ulitsa Bolshaya Sadovaya 16.
**Map** 1 B4.
**Tel** (495) 150 01 20.

**Pioneer**
Kutuzovsky prospekt 21.
**Tel** (499) 240 52 40.

**Taganka Theatre**
Ulitsa Zemlyanoy Val 76/21.
**Tel** (495) 915 12 17.

## Children's Entertainment

**Durov Animal Theatre**
Ulitsa Durova 4. **Map** 2 D2.
**Tel** (495) 631 30 47.

**Moscow Cats Theatre**
Kutuzovsky prospekt 25.
**Tel** (499) 243 40 05.

**Nataliya Sats Children's Musical Theatre**
Prospekt Vernadskovo 5.
**Tel** (495) 930 70 21.

**New Circus**
Prospekt Vernadskovo 7.
**Tel** (495) 930 03 00.

**Obraztsov Puppet Theatre**
Sadovaya-Samotechnaya ulitsa 3.
**Map** 1 A5.
**Tel** (495) 699 53 73.

**Old Circus**
Tsvetnoy bulvar 13.
**Map** 2 D3.
**Tel** (495) 625 89 70.

# MOSCOW STREET FINDER

The map below shows the areas of Moscow covered by the Street Finder maps. The map references in the Moscow section for sights of interest, restaurants, hotels, shops and entertainment venues refer to the maps in this section. The symbols used to represent sights and useful information on the Street Finder maps are shown in the key. The first figure in the map reference indicates which Street Finder map to turn to, and the letter and number that follow refer to the map's grid. An index of key street names can be found on the following pages. The index lists street names in transliteration, followed by the Cyrillic script (on the maps, the Cyrillic is only given for major roads).

Visitors strolling along the busy Arbat Street, in central Moscow

## Key to Street Finder

- Major sight
- Place of interest
- Other building
- 🚇 Train station
- Ⓜ Metro station
- 🚋 Main tram stop
- 🚎 Main trolleybus stop
- 🚌 Main bus stop
- ⛴ River boat pier
- ➕ Hospital
- 🏛 Police station
- ✠ Orthodox church
- ✝ Non-Orthodox church
- ✡ Synagogue
- ☪ Mosque
- ⚌ Railway line
- Pedestrian area

**Scale of Maps 1–4**

| 0 metres | 400 |
| 0 yards | 400 |

| 0 km | 2 |
| 0 miles | 2 |

# Street Finder Index

1-ya Brestskaya ulitsa
   1-Я БРЕСТСКАЯ УЛИЦА     1A3
1-ya Frunzenskaya ulitsa
   1-Я ФРУНЗЕНСКАЯ УЛИЦА     3A5
1-ya Miusskaya ulitsa
   1-Я МИУССКАЯ УЛИЦА     1B2
1-ya Tverskaya-Yamskaya ulitsa
   1-Я ТВЕРСКАЯ-ЯМСКАЯ УЛИЦА     1A2
1-ya Yamskovo Polya, ulitsa
   1-Я ЯМСКОГО ПОЛЯ, УЛИЦА     1A2
1-yy Kadashevskiy pereulok
   1-ЫЙ КАДАШЕВСКИЙ ПЕРЕУЛОК     4D2
1-yy Novokuznetskiy pereulok
   1-ЫЙ НОВОКУЗНЕЦКИЙ ПЕРЕУЛОК     4E4
1-yy Zachatevskiy pereulok
   1-ЫЙ ЗАЧАТЬЕВСКИЙ ПЕРЕУЛОК     3B3
2-oy Lesnoy pereulok
   2-ОЙ ЛЕСНОЙ ПЕРЕУЛОК     1A2
2-ya Tverskaya-Yamskaya ulitsa
   2-Я ТВЕРСКАЯ-ЯМСКАЯ УЛИЦА     1A2
3-iy Monetchikovskiy pereulok
   3-ИЙ МОНЕТЧИКОВСКИЙ ПЕРЕУЛОК     4E4
3-iy Samotechnyy pereulok
   3-ИЙ САМОТЕЧНЫЙ ПЕРЕУЛОК     1C2
3-ya Tverskaya-Yamskaya ulitsa
   3-Я ТВЕРСКАЯ-ЯМСКАЯ УЛИЦА     1B3
4-yy Dobryninskiy pereulok
   4-ЫЙ ДОБРЫНИНСКИЙ ПЕРЕУЛОК     4D5

## A

Akademika Sakharova, prospekt
   АКАДЕМИКА САХАРОВА, ПРОСПЕКТ     2E4
Aleksandra Nevskovo, ulitsa
   АЛЕКСАНДРА НЕВСКОГО, УЛИЦА     1A2
Arbat, ulitsa
   АРБАТ, УЛИЦА     3A1

## B

Bakhrushina, ulitsa
   БАХРУШИНА, УЛИЦА     4E4
Bersenevskaya naberezhnaya
   БЕРСЕНЕВСКАЯ НАБЕРЕЖНАЯ     3C3
Bolotnaya naberezhnaya
   БОЛОТНАЯ НАБЕРЕЖНАЯ     3C2
Bolotnaya ulitsa
   БОЛОТНАЯ УЛИЦА     4D2
Bolshaya Bronnaya ulitsa
   БОЛЬШАЯ БРОННАЯ УЛИЦА     1B5
Bolshaya Dmitrovka, ulitsa
   БОЛЬШАЯ ДМИТРОВКА, УЛИЦА     1C4
Bolshaya Lubyanka, ulitsa
   БОЛЬШАЯ ЛУБЯНКА, УЛИЦА     2D5
Bolshaya Nikitskaya ulitsa
   БОЛЬШАЯ НИКИТСКАЯ УЛИЦА     1A5
Bolshaya Ordynka, ulitsa
   БОЛЬШАЯ ОРДЫНКА, УЛИЦА     4D2
Bolshaya Pereyaslavskaya ulitsa
   БОЛЬШАЯ ПЕРЕЯСЛАВСКАЯ УЛИЦА     2F1
Bolshaya Pionerskaya ulitsa
   БОЛЬШАЯ ПИОНЕРСКАЯ УЛИЦА     4E5
Bolshaya Polyanka, ulitsa
   БОЛЬШАЯ ПОЛЯНКА, УЛИЦА     4D3
Bolshaya Sadovaya ulitsa
   БОЛЬШАЯ САДОВАЯ УЛИЦА     1A4
Bolshaya Serpukhovskaya ulitsa
   БОЛЬШАЯ СЕРПУХОВСКАЯ УЛИЦА     4D5
Bolshaya Tatarskaya ulitsa
   БОЛЬШАЯ ТАТАРСКАЯ УЛИЦА     4E3
Bolshaya Yakimanka, ulitsa
   БОЛЬШАЯ ЯКИМАНКА, УЛИЦА     3C4

## Useful Words and Abbreviations

| | | |
|---|---|---|
| | most | bridge |
| | podezd | entrance |
| | proezd | small street/passage/lane |
| | sad | garden |
| | shosse | road |
| | stroenie | building |
| | tupik | cul-de-sac |
| ul | ulitsa | street |
| pl | ploshchad | square |
| pr | prospekt | avenue |
| per | pereulok | small street/passage/lane |

Bolshoi Kamennyy most
   БОЛЬШОЙ КАМЕННЫЙ МОСТ     3C2
Bolshoi Krasnokholmskiy most
   БОЛЬШОЙ КРАСНОХОЛМСКИЙ МОСТ     4F4
Bolshoi Levshinskiy pereulok
   БОЛЬШОЙ ЛЕВШИНСКИЙ ПЕРЕУЛОК     3A3
Bolshoi Moskvoretskiy most
   БОЛЬШОЙ МОСКВОРЕЦКИЙ МОСТ     4D1
Bolshoi Sergievskiy pereulok
   БОЛЬШОЙ СЕРГИЕВСКИЙ ПЕРЕУЛОК     2E4
Bolshoi Sukharevskiy pereulok
   БОЛЬШОЙ СУХАРЕВСКИЙ ПЕРЕУЛОК     2E3
Bolshoi Tolmachevskiy pereulok
   БОЛЬШОЙ ТОЛМАЧЕВСКИЙ ПЕРЕУЛОК     4D3
Bolshoi Ustinskiy most
   БОЛЬШОЙ УСТЬИНСКИЙ МОСТ     4E2
Bolshoi Vlasevskiy pereulok
   БОЛЬШОЙ ВЛАСЬЕВСКИЙ ПЕРЕУЛОК     3A2
Bolshoi Znamenskiy pereulok
   БОЛЬШОЙ ЗНАМЕНСКИЙ ПЕРЕУЛОК     3B2
Butyrskiy val, ulitsa
   БУТЫРСКИЙ ВАЛ, УЛИЦА     1A2

## C

Chayanova, ulitsa
   ЧАЯНОВА, УЛИЦА     1B2

## D

Delegatskaya ulitsa
   ДЕЛЕГАТСКАЯ УЛИЦА     1C2
Denezhnyy pereulok
   ДЕНЕЖНЫЙ ПЕРЕУЛОК     3A2
Dobryninskiy pereulok
   ДОБРЫНИНСКИЙ ПЕРЕУЛОК     4D5
Dolgorukovskaya ulitsa
   ДОЛГОРУКОВСКАЯ УЛИЦА     1B2
Donskaya ulitsa
   ДОНСКАЯ УЛИЦА     3C5
Dostoevskovo, ulitsa
   ДОСТОЕВСКОГО, УЛИЦА     1C1
Dubininskaya ulitsa
   ДУБИНИНСКАЯ УЛИЦА     4E5
Durova, ulitsa
   ДУРОВА, УЛИЦА     2E2

## F

Fadeeva, ulitsa
   ФАДЕЕВА, УЛИЦА     1B3
Frunzenskaya naberezhnaya
   ФРУНЗЕНСКАЯ НАБЕРЕЖНАЯ     3A5

## G

Gagarinskiy pereulok
   ГАГАРИНСКИЙ ПЕРЕУЛОК     3A2

Gasheka, ulitsa
ГАШЕКА, УЛИЦА 1A3
Gazetnyy pereulok
ГАЗЕТНЫЙ ПЕРЕУЛОК 1C5
Georgievskiy pereulok
ГЕОРГИЕВСКИЙ ПЕРЕУЛОК 1C5
Glinishchevskiy pereulok
ГЛИНИЩЕВСКИЙ ПЕРЕУЛОК 1C4
Gogolevskiy bulvar
ГОГОЛЕВСКИЙ БУЛЬВАР 3B2
Goncharnaya ulitsa
ГОНЧАРНАЯ УЛИЦА 4F2
Granatnyy pereulok
ГРАНАТНЫЙ ПЕРЕУЛОК 1A5

## I

Ilinka, ulitsa
ИЛЬИНКА, УЛИЦА 4D1

## K

Kadashevskaya naberezhnaya
КАДАШЕВСКАЯ НАБЕРЕЖНАЯ 4D2
Kalanchevskaya ulitsa
КАЛАНЧЕВСКАЯ УЛИЦА 2F2
Kamergerskiy pereulok
КАМЕРГЕРСКИЙ ПЕРЕУЛОК 1C5
Karetnyy ryad, ulitsa
КАРЕТНЫЙ РЯД, УЛИЦА 1C3
Khlebnyy pereulok
ХЛЕБНЫЙ ПЕРЕУЛОК 1A5
Kitaygorodskiy proezd
КИТАЙГОРОДСКИЙ ПРОЕЗД 4E1
Koroviy val, ulitsa
КОРОВИЙ ВАЛ, УЛИЦА 4D4
Kosmodamianskaya naberezhnaya
КОСМОДАМИАНСКАЯ НАБЕРЕЖНАЯ 4F2
Kotelnicheskaya naberezhnaya
КОТЕЛЬНИЧЕСКАЯ НАБЕРЕЖНАЯ 4F2
Kozhevnicheskaya ulitsa
КОЖЕВНИЧЕСКАЯ УЛИЦА 4F4
Krasina, ulitsa
КРАСИНА, УЛИЦА 1A3
Krasnoproletarskaya ulitsa
КРАСНОПРОЛЕТАРСКАЯ УЛИЦА 1C2
Kremlevskaya naberezhnaya
КРЕМЛЁВСКАЯ НАБЕРЕЖНАЯ 4D1
Krymskaya naberezhnaya
КРЫМСКАЯ НАБЕРЕЖНАЯ 3B4
Krymskiy most
КРЫМСКИЙ МОСТ 3B4
Krymskiy val, ulitsa
КРЫМСКИЙ ВАЛ, УЛИЦА 3C4

## L

Lavrushinskiy pereulok
ЛАВРУШИНСКИЙ ПЕРЕУЛОК 4D2
Leninskiy prospect
ЛЕНИНСКИЙ ПРОСПЕКТ 3B5
Leontevskiy pereulok
ЛЕОНТЬЕВСКИЙ ПЕРЕУЛОК 1B5
Lesnaya ulitsa
ЛЕСНАЯ УЛИЦА 1A2
Letnikovskaya ulitsa
ЛЕТНИКОВСКАЯ УЛИЦА 4F5
Lva Tolstovo, ulitsa
ЛЬВА ТОЛСТОГО, УЛИЦА 3A3
Lyusinovskaya ulitsa
ЛЮСИНОВСКАЯ УЛИЦА 4D5

## M

Malaya Bronnaya ulitsa
МАЛАЯ БРОННАЯ УЛИЦА 1A4

Malaya Dmitrovka, ulitsa
МАЛАЯ ДМИТРОВКА, УЛИЦА 1C3
Malaya Nikitskaya ulitsa
МАЛАЯ НИКИТСКАЯ УЛИЦА 1A5
Malaya Ordynka, ulitsa
МАЛАЯ ОРДЫНКА, УЛИЦА 4D4
Malaya Pionerskaya ulitsa
МАЛАЯ ПИОНЕРСКАЯ УЛИЦА 4E4
Malyy Gnezdnikovskiy pereulok
МАЛЫЙ ГНЕЗДНИКОВСКИЙ ПЕРЕУЛОК 1B5
Malyy Tolmachevskiy pereulok
МАЛЫЙ ТОЛМАЧЕВСКИЙ ПЕРЕУЛОК 4E4
Malyy Znamenskiy pereulok
МАЛЫЙ ЗНАМЕНСКИЙ ПЕРЕУЛОК 3B2
Manezhnaya ulitsa
МАНЕЖНАЯ УЛИЦА 3C1
Maroseyka, ulitsa
МАРОСЕЙКА, УЛИЦА 2E5
Mira, prospekt
МИРА, ПРОСПЕКТ 2E2
Mokhovaya ulitsa
МОХОВАЯ УЛИЦА 3C1
Moskvoretskaya naberezhnaya
МОСКВОРЕЦКАЯ НАБЕРЕЖНАЯ 4E1
Myasnitskaya ulitsa
МЯСНИЦКАЯ УЛИЦА 2E5
Mytnaya, ulitsa
МЫТНАЯ, УЛИЦА 3C5

## N

Nikitskiy bulvar
НИКИТСКИЙ БУЛЬВАР 3B1
Nikitskiy pereulok
НИКИТСКИЙ ПЕРЕУЛОК 1C5
Novaya ploshchad
НОВАЯ ПЛОЩАДЬ 2D5
Novokhokhlovskaya ulitsa
НОВОХОХЛОВСКАЯ УЛИЦА 1B1
Novokuznetskaya ulitsa
НОВОКУЗНЕЦКАЯ УЛИЦА 4E3
Novoslobodskaya ulitsa
НОВОСЛОБОДСКАЯ УЛИЦА 1B1
Novyy Arbat, ulitsa
НОВЫЙ АРБАТ, УЛИЦА 3A1

## O

Olimpiyskiy prospekt
ОЛИМПИЙСКИЙ ПРОСПЕКТ 2D3
Orlikov pereulok
ОРЛИКОВ ПЕРЕУЛОК 2F3
Oruzheynyy pereulok
ОРУЖЕЙНЫЙ ПЕРЕУЛОК 1B3
Ostozhenka, ulitsa
ОСТОЖЕНКА, УЛИЦА 3B3
Ovchinnikovskaya naberezhnaya
ОВЧИННИКОВСКАЯ НАБЕРЕЖНАЯ 4E2
Ozerkovskaya naberezhnaya
ОЗЕРКОВСКАЯ НАБЕРЕЖНАЯ 4E2

## P

Pechatnikov pereulok
ПЕЧАТНИКОВ ПЕРЕУЛОК 2D4
Petrovka, ulitsa
ПЕТРОВКА, УЛИЦА 2D4
Petrovskiy bulvar
ПЕТРОВСКИЙ БУЛЬВАР 2D4
Petrovskiy pereulok
ПЕТРОВСКИЙ ПЕРЕУЛОК 1C4
Plotnikov pereulok
ПЛОТНИКОВ ПЕРЕУЛОК 3A2
Podgorskaya naberezhnaya
ПОДГОРСКАЯ НАБЕРЕЖНАЯ 4F2
Pokrovka, ulitsa
ПОКРОВКА, УЛИЦА 2F5

Povarskaya ulitsa
ПОВАРСКАЯ УЛИЦА   1A5
Prechistenka, ulitsa
ПРЕЧИСТЕНКА, УЛИЦА   3A3
Prechistenskaya naberezhnaya
ПРЕЧИСТЕНСКАЯ НАБЕРЕЖНАЯ   3C2
Priyutskiy pereulok
ПРИЮТСКИЙ ПЕРЕУЛОК   1A1
Protopopovskiy pereulok
ПРОТОПОПОВСКИЙ ПЕРЕУЛОК   2E2
Pushkinskaya naberezhnaya
ПУШКИНСКАЯ НАБЕРЕЖНАЯ   3B5
Pyatnitskaya ulitsa
ПЯТНИЦКАЯ УЛИЦА   4D4

## R

Raushskaya naberezhnaya
РАУШСКАЯ НАБЕРЕЖНАЯ   4E1
Rozhdestvenskiy bulvar
РОЖДЕСТВЕНСКИЙ БУЛЬВАР   2D4

## S

Sadovaya-Karetnaya ulitsa
САДОВАЯ-КАРЕТНАЯ УЛИЦА   1C3
Sadovaya-Kudrinskaya ulitsa
САДОВАЯ-КУДРИНСКАЯ УЛИЦА   1A5
Sadovaya-Samotechnaya ulitsa
САДОВАЯ-САМОТЕЧНАЯ УЛИЦА   2D3
Sadovaya-Spasskaya ulitsa
САДОВАЯ-СПАССКАЯ УЛИЦА   2E3
Sadovaya-Sukharevskaya ulitsa
САДОВАЯ-СУХАРЕВСКАЯ УЛИЦА   2D3
Sadovaya-Triumfalnaya ulitsa
САДОВАЯ-ТРИУМФАЛЬНАЯ УЛИЦА   1B3
Sadovnicheskaya naberezhnaya
САДОВНИЧЕСКАЯ НАБЕРЕЖНАЯ   4E2
Sadovnicheskaya ulitsa
САДОВНИЧЕСКАЯ УЛИЦА   4F3
Sadovnicheskiy proezd
САДОВНИЧЕСКИЙ ПРОЕЗД   4E2
Samotechnaya ulitsa
САМОТЕЧНАЯ УЛИЦА   2D2
Sandunovskiy pereulok
САНДУНОВСКИЙ ПЕРЕУЛОК   2D4
Seleznevskaya ulitsa
СЕЛЕЗНЕВСКАЯ УЛИЦА   1B2
Shabolovka, ulitsa
ШАБОЛОВКА, УЛИЦА   3C5
Sivtsev Vrazhek, pereulok
СИВЦЕВ ВРАЖЕК, ПЕРЕУЛОК   3B2
Skatertnyy pereulok
СКАТЕРНЫЙ ПЕРЕУЛОК   1A5
Smolenskaya ploshchad
СМОЛЕНСКАЯ ПЛОЩАДЬ   3A2
Smolenskiy bulvar
СМОЛЕНСКИЙ БУЛЬВАР   3A2
Sofiyskaya naberezhnaya
СОФИЙСКАЯ НАБЕРЕЖНАЯ   3C2
Solyanka, ulitsa
СОЛЯНКА, УЛИЦА   4F1
Sovetskoy Armii, ulitsa
СОВЕТСКОЙ АРМИИ, УЛИЦА   2D2
Soymonovskiy prospekt
СОЙМОНОВСКИЙ ПРОСПЕКТ   3B2
Spiridonovka, ulitsa
СПИРИДОНОВКА, УЛИЦА   1A5
Sretenka, ulitsa
СРЕТЕНКА, УЛИЦА   2E5
Sretenskiy bulvar
СРЕТЕНСКИЙ БУЛЬВАР   2E4
Starokonyushennyy pereulok
СТАРОКОНЮШЕННЫЙ ПЕРЕУЛОК   3B2
Staromonetnyy pereulok
СТАРОМОНЕТНЫЙ ПЕРЕУЛОК   4D2

Stoleshnikov pereulok
СТОЛЕШНИКОВ ПЕРЕУЛОК   1C5
Strastnoy bulvar
СТРАСТНОЙ БУЛЬВАР   1C4
Stremyannyy pereulok
СТРЕМЯННЫЙ ПЕРЕУЛОК   4E5
Sushchevskaya ulitsa
СУЩЕВСКАЯ УЛИЦА   1B1

## T

Tatarskaya ulitsa
ТАТАРСКАЯ УЛИЦА   4E3
Teatralnyy proezd
ТЕАТРАЛЬНЫЙ ПРОЕЗД   2D5
Timura Frunze, ulitsa
ТИМУРА ФРУНЗЕ, УЛИЦА   3A3
Troitskaya ulitsa
ТРОИЦКАЯ УЛИЦА   2D3
Tverskaya ulitsa
ТВЕРСКАЯ УЛИЦА   1B4
Tverskoy bulvar
ТВЕРСКОЙ БУЛЬВАР   1B5

## U

Uspenskiy pereulok
УСПЕНСКИЙ ПЕРЕУЛОК   1C3
Ustinskaya naberezhnaya
УСТЬИНСКАЯ НАБЕРЕЖНАЯ   4F2

## V

Valovaya, ulitsa
ВАЛОВАЯ, УЛИЦА   4E4
Varsonofevskiy pereulok
ВАРСОНОФЬЕВСКИЙ ПЕРЕУЛОК   2D4
Varvarka, ulitsa
ВАРВАРКА, УЛИЦА   4E1
Vasilevskaya ulitsa
ВАСИЛЬЕВСКАЯ УЛИЦА   1A3
Vishnyakovskiy pereulok
ВИШНЯКОВСКИЙ ПЕРЕУЛОК   4E3
Volkhonka, ulitsa
ВОЛХОНКА, УЛИЦА   3B2
Vozdvizhenka, ulitsa
ВОЗДВИЖЕНКА, УЛИЦА   3B1
Voznesenskiy pereulok
ВОЗНЕСЕНСКИЯ ПЕРЕУЛОК   1B5

## Y

Yakimanskaya naberezhnaya
ЯКИМАНСКАЯ НАБЕРЕЖНАЯ   3C3
Yauzskaya ulitsa
ЯУЗСКАЯ УЛИЦА   4F2
Yauzskiy bulvar
ЯУЗСКИЙ БУЛЬВАР   4F1

## Z

Zatsepa, ulitsa
ЗАЦЕПА, УЛИЦА   4E4
Zatsepskiy val, ulitsa
ЗАЦЕПСКИЙ, УЛИЦА   4E4
Zhitnaya, ulitsa
ЖИТНАЯ, УЛИЦА   3C4
Znamenka, ulitsa
ЗНАМЕНКА, УЛИЦА   3B1
Zoologicheskaya ulitsa
ЗООЛОГИЧЕСКАЯ УЛИЦА   1A4
Zubovskiy bulvar
ЗУБОВСКИЙ БУЛЬВАР   3A3
Zvonarskiy pereulok
ЗВОНАРСКИЙ ПЕРЕУЛОК   2D4

# ST PETERSBURG AREA BY AREA

The Islands      134–143

Palace Embankment      144–157

Gostinyy Dvor      158–169

Sennaya Ploshchad      170–177

Further Afield      178–183

Beyond St Petersburg      184–191

# St Petersburg at a Glance

Located at the head of the Gulf of Finland, St Petersburg covers an area of 605 sq km (234 sq miles). Founded by Tsar Peter the Great in 1703, this 300-year-old settlement has gradually evolved into a modern European city. Straddling a series of islands in the Neva delta, St Petersburg is justly known as the Venice of the North, thanks to its magnificent waterfront panorama of Baroque and Neo-Classical palaces, which are reflected in the waters of its canals. A network of bridges affords splendid views of the city, which can often seem like a gigantic stage set for real-life historical dramas.

**Locator Map**

**Kunstkammer** *(see p142)* was Russia's first museum, established by Peter the Great. Originally built to exhibit the intriguing collection of curios that the tsar purchased from anatomist Frederik Ruysch in 1717, the building now houses a Museum of Anthropology and Ethnography. Nearby are the red-coloured Rostral Columns.

**The Islands**
*(see pp134–143)*

**Sennaya Ploshchad**
*(see pp170–177)*

**St Nicholas's Cathedral** *(see p174)*, with its ice-blue façade and gilded domes, is a superb example of Russian Baroque, and a St Petersburg landmark. Founded as a sailors' church, it contains memorials to the victims of Russian naval battles and submarine disasters.

| 0 metres | | 600 |
| 0 yards | | 600 |

◄ A frozen canal overlooked by the giant bell tower of St Nicholas's Cathedral

**The Islands**
*(see pp134–143)*

**Peter and Paul Fortress** *(see pp136–7)* was originally built to secure Russia's hold on the Neva delta but later became a prison for generations of revolutionaries. It contains the Cathedral of SS Peter and Paul, where members of the Tsarist royalty were buried, and a prison museum.

**Palace Embankment**
*(see pp144–157)*

**Gostinyy Dvor**
*(see pp158–169)*

**The Hermitage** *(see pp154–5)* houses a world famous collection of art and antiquities, including prehistoric Scythian gold and Siberian mummies as well as Post-Impressionist works by Gauguin, Matisse and Picasso.

**Church on Spilled Blood**
*(see p162)* marks the spot where Tsar Alexander II was fatally wounded by "Nihilist" revolutionaries. This dramatically named church is recognized by its psychedelically painted onion domes and gilded mosaics.

# THE ISLANDS

St Petersburg was founded in 1703 as a wooden fortress on an island in the Neva delta. Tsar Peter the Great envisaged a city on the northern shores of the Neva – later known as the Petrograd side – with an administrative centre on Vasilevskiy Island. However, lack of access and the hazards of floods and stormy crossings led to the abandonment of Peter's project, and the centre developed around the Admiralty instead. The Petrograd side

remained a backwater until the Troitskiy Most (Trinity Bridge) made it accessible from the city centre. A penchant for Style-Moderne archi-tecture in the 1900s endowed the area with many fine buildings such as the Kshesinskaya Mansion. The most notable structure, however, is the Peter and Paul Fortress with its golden-spired cathedral and grim history. The eastern end of Vasilevskiy Island, known as the Strelka, or "spit", is home to various museums.

## Sights at a Glance

### Historic Buildings and Monuments
❶ St Peter's Gate
❺ Neva Gate
⓮ Rostral Columns
⓳ Twelve Colleges

### Museums
❷ Engineer's House
❹ Commandant's House
❻ Trubetskoy Bastion
❼ Artillery Museum
❿ Kirov Museum
⓫ Kshesinskaya Mansion
⓬ Cabin of Peter the Great
⓭ Cruiser Aurora
⓯ The Institute of Russian Literature (Pushkin House)
⓰ Zoological Museum
⓱ Kunstkammer
⓳ Menshikov Palace

### Churches and Cathedrals
❸ Cathedral of SS Peter and Paul

### Streets, Squares and Parks
❽ Aleksandrovskiy Park
❾ Kamennoostrovskiy Prospekt

**Locator Map**
*See Street Finder, maps 1, 2 & 3*

0 metres 500
0 yards 500

◀ Aerial view of the formidable Peter and Paul Fortress

For keys to symbols *see back flap*

# Street-by-Street: Peter and Paul Fortress

The establishment of the Peter and Paul Fortress on 27 May 1703, on the orders of Peter the Great, is considered to mark the founding of St Petersburg. It was first built in wood and was later replaced, section by section, in stone by Domenico Trezzini. Its history is gruesome, since hundreds of forced labourers died while building the fortress and its bastions were later used to guard and torture many political prisoners, including Peter's own son Aleksey. The cells where prisoners were once kept are open to the public, along with a couple of museums and the magnificent cathedral, which houses the tombs of the Romanovs.

Zotov Bastion

Kronverkskiy Most

**The Archives of the War Ministry** occupy the site of the "Secret House", a prison for political criminals in the 18th and 19th centuries.

**6 Trubetskoy Bastion**
From 1872 to 1921, the dark, damp solitary-confinement cells in this bastion served as a grim prison for enemies of the state. Today, the bastion is open to visitors.

**The Mint,** founded in 1724, still produces ceremonial coins, medals and badges.

**The Beach**
During summer, the beach is full of sunbathers. In winter, members of "The Walruses" swimming club break through the ice to dip into the waters beneath.

**The Naryshkin Bastion**, dating from 1725, is where the noon cannon is fired. The tradition began in 1873, stopped after the Revolution and was resumed in 1957.

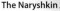

**5 Neva Gate** is also known as Death Gateway. It leads to the Commandant's pier from which prisoners embarked on their journey to execution or exile. The Neva river's flood levels are recorded under the arch.

**4 Commandant's House**
For 150 years, this attractive Baroque house was the scene of interrogations and trials of political prisoners. It now houses a museum of local history.

**❸ ★ Cathedral of SS Peter and Paul**
Marbled columns, glittering chandeliers and painted decor combine with Ivan Zarudnyy's carved and gilded iconostasis to create a magnificent setting for the tombs of the Romanov monarchs.

**The Boat House** is now a ticket office and souvenir shop.

Golovkin Bastion

**The Grand Ducal Mausoleum** is the last resting place of several Grand Dukes shot by the Bolsheviks in 1919 and of Grand Duke Vladimir who died in exile in 1992.

THE ISLANDS

THE ISLANDS

PALACE EMBANKMENT

☐ Area illustrated

**❶ St Peter's Gate**
The entrance to the fortress was completed in 1718 and features the Romanov double eagle with an emblem of St George and the dragon.

**Key**

— Suggested route

| 0 metres | 100 |
| 0 yards | 100 |

Cosmonautics Museum

**Ivan Gate**, in the outer wall, was constructed in 1731–40. It now serves as a ticket office and information centre.

Ioannovskiy Most

Kamennoostrovskiy prospekt, Gorkovskaya Metro and Troitskiy Most

**This statue of Peter the Great** (1991) is by Mikhail Shemiakin.

**Sovereigns' Bastion** was where Tsarevich Aleksey was tortured to death.

**❷ Engineer's House**
This building, dating from 1748–9, houses temporary exhibitions of artifacts used in everyday life in St Petersburg before the Revolution.

## ❶ St Peter's Gate

Петровские ворота

*Petrovskie vorota*

Petropavlovskaya krepost.
**Map** 2 D3. 🚋 46, 49, 76, 183, 223.
Ⓜ Gorkovskaya. 🚎 6, 40.
Cosmonautics Museum: **Tel** (812)
230 64 31. **Open** 11am–5pm Tue,
11am–6pm Thu–Mon.

The main entrance to the Peter
and Paul Fortress is through two
contrasting arches. The sombre
Ivan Gate, dating from the 1730s,
leads to the more imposing
St Peter's Gate. Built in 1708–18,
it structure with scrolled wings
and a rounded-gable pediment.
Domenico Trezzini's redesign
retained Karl Osner's carved bas-
relief that depicts St Peter casting
down the winged sorcerer
Simon Magus. It allegorizes
Peter the Great's victory over
Charles XII of Sweden.

The rampart behind the Ivan
Gate houses the **Cosmonautics
Museum**, which traces the
history of the Soviet space programme from Sputnik to the Mir
orbital station, paying homage
to the rocket-scientist Konstantin
Tsiolkovskiy (1857–1935).

The impressive Baroque façade of
St Peter's Gate

## ❷ Engineer's House

Инженерный дом

*Inzhenernyy dom*

Petropavlovskaya krepost. **Map** 2 D3.
**Tel** (812) 230 64 31 Ⓜ Gorkovskaya.
**Open** 11am–5pm Tue, 11am–6pm
Thu–Mon. 🗺 🏛 English.
Ⓦ **spbmuseum.ru**

The Engineer's House, built
in 1748–9, has a changing
exhibition that gives a
fascinating glimpse of daily life

Style-Moderne furnishings in the Engineer's House

in St Petersburg before the
Revolution. Architectural back-
drops and historical paintings
give way to an engaging
miscellany of artifacts, ranging
from model boats to duelling
pistols and court costumes.

A section on vintage
technology features Singer
sewing machines, typewriters,
Bakelite telephones and box
cameras. In the child-friendly
exhibition called the Street of
Time, visitors can try writing
with ink pens, and smell
perfumes that were popular
with Soviet women in the 1950s.

## ❸ Cathedral of SS Peter and Paul

Петропавловский собор

*Petropavlovskiy sobor*

Petropavlovskaya krepost. **Map** 2 D3.
**Tel** (812) 230 64 31. Ⓜ Gorkovskaya.
**Open** 10am–6pm Mon & Thu–Sat,
10am–5pm Tue, 11am–7pm Sun. 🗺
🏛 English. Ⓦ **spbmuseum.ru**

Domenico Trezzini designed
this magnificent church within
the fortress in 1712. A Baroque
masterpiece, it reflects Peter the
Great's rejection of traditional
Russian church architecture.
The bell tower was completed
first to test the foundations
and this served as an excellent
viewpoint from which Peter
could oversee the construction
of his new city. The cathedral
was completed in 1733, but was
badly damaged by fire in 1756,
when the soaring 122-m (400-ft)
spire was struck by lightning.
The gilded needle spire,
crowned by a weather-vane
angel, remained the tallest
structure in St Petersburg until

the building of a
TV transmitter in
the 1960s.

The interior,
with its dazzling
chandeliers, pink
and green
Corinthian
columns and
overarching vaults,
is a far cry from the
traditional Russian
Orthodox church.
Even the icono-
stasis is a Baroque
flight of fancy. This masterpiece
of gilded woodcarving was
designed by Ivan Zarudnyy and
executed in the 1720s by
craftsmen from Moscow.

After Peter's death in 1725,
the cathedral became the last
resting place of the tsars. The
sarcophagi are all of a uniform
white Carrara marble, except
the tombs of Alexander II and
his wife Maria Alexandrovna,
which are carved from Altai
jasper and Ural rhodonite.
Peter the Great's tomb lies
to the right of the iconostasis.
In 1998, the remains of the

Cathedral of SS Peter and Paul, with the
Dvortsovyy Bridge in the foreground

last tsar, Nicholas II, his wife and children, and the servants who died with them in Yekaterinburg *(see p235)* were buried in a side chapel.

The Grand Ducal Mausoleum, where relatives of the tsars are buried, was added to the cathedral at the end of the 19th century.

## ❹ Commandant's House
Комендантский дом
*Komendantskiy dom*

Petropavlovskaya krepost. **Map** 2 D4. **Tel** (812) 230 64 31. Ⓜ Gorkovskaya. **Open** 11am–5pm Tue, 11am–6pm Thu–Mon. 🎦 📷 English.

Dating from the 1740s, the plain brick, two-storey Commandant's House served both as the residence of the fortress commander and as a courthouse. Over the years, political prisoners, including the Decembrist rebels, were brought here for interrogation and sentencing.

The house is now a museum, with a ground-floor exhibition on medieval settlements in the St Petersburg region. Upstairs, visitors can see a doll's-house-style model of a 1900s apartment block, and watch an animated video of the erection of the Alexander Column on Palace Square.

## ❺ Neva Gate
Невские ворота
*Nevskie vorota*

Petropavlovskaya krepost. **Map** 2 D4. Ⓜ Gorkovskaya.

This austere river entrance to the fortress was once known as the Death Gate. Prisoners to be transported to Schlüsselburg Fortress on Lake Ladoga *(see p209)* for capital punishment, or to a "living death" in penal servitude, were led down the granite steps and taken away by boat. The appropriately dour grey gateway (reconstructed in 1784–7) is unornamented apart from an anchor in the pediment. In the archway, brass plaques record flood levels.

Neva Gate leading from the river into the Peter and Paul Fortress

The catastrophic inundation of November 1824 is the one commemorated in Pushkin's poem, *The Bronze Horseman*.

## ❻ Trubetskoy Bastion
Трубецкой бастион
*Trubetskoy bastion*

Petropavlovskaya krepost. **Map** 1 C4. **Tel** (812) 230 64 31. Ⓜ Gorkovskaya. **Open** 10am–5pm Tue, 10am–6pm Thu–Mon. 🎦 📷 English.

Peter the Great's son, Tsarevich Aleksey (1690–1718), was the first political prisoner to be detained in the grim fortress prison. Unjustly accused of treason in 1718 by his father, Aleksey escaped abroad only to be lured back to Russia with the promise of a pardon. Instead, he was tortured to death, aged 28,

almost certainly with Peter's consent and participation.

For the next 100 years prisoners were incarcerated in the much feared Secret House, since demolished. In 1872 a new prison block opened in the Trubetskoy Bastion, which has existed as a museum since 1924. On the ground floor there is a small exhibition of period photographs, prison uniforms and a model of the guardroom. Upstairs are 69 isolation cells, while downstairs there are two unheated, unlit punishment cells where recalcitrants were locked up for 48 hours at a time. Once every two weeks, all detainees were taken to the Bath House in the exercise yard for de-lousing. Here, prisoners were chained before they were made to trek all the way to penal servitude in Siberia.

### Political Prisoners

The fortress' sinister role as a prison for political activists continued until after the Revolution. Generations of rebels and anarchists

Russian revolutionary Leon Trotsky (1879–1940)

were interrogated and imprisoned here, including Leon Trotsky in the wake of the 1905 Revolution. Other prominent detainees were the leading Decembrists in 1825, writer Fyodor Dostoëvsky in 1849 and, from 1874 to 1876, the anarchist Prince Pyotr Kropotkin. In 1917 it was the turn first of the tsar's ministers, then of members of the Provisional Government. Then, in the Civil War, the Bolsheviks held hostage four Romanov Grand Dukes, who were executed in 1919.

Rocket launcher in the courtyard of the Artillery Museum

## ❼ Artillery Museum
### Музей Артиллерии
*Muzey Artillerii*

Alexandrovskiy Park 7, Kronverkskaya Embankment. **Map** 1 C3. **Tel** (812) 232 02 96. Ⓜ Gorkovskaya. **Open** 11am–5pm Wed–Sun. **Closed** last Thu of the month. ♿ Ⓦ **artillery-museum.ru**

This vast, horseshoe-shaped building in red brick stands on the site of the Kronverk, the outer fortifications of the Peter and Paul Fortress. Designed by Pyotr Tamanskiy and constructed from 1849 to 1860, the building was originally used as an arsenal.

There are more than 600 pieces of artillery and military vehicles, including tanks and the armoured car in which Lenin rode in triumph from Finland Station *(see p180)* to Kshesinskaya Mansion on 3 April 1917. There are uniforms, regimental flags, muskets and small arms dating to medieval times, as well as many rooms devoted to World War II.

## ❽ Aleksandrovskiy Park
### Александровский парк
*Aleksandrovskiy park*

Kronverkskiy prospekt. **Map** 1 C3. Ⓜ Gorkovskaya. ♿

The park's character as a centre of popular entertainment was established in the year 1900 with the inauguration of the Nicholas II People's House. This was where pantomime artists, magicians and circus acts entertained the crowds, while

the more serious-minded were drawn to the lecture halls, reading galleries and tearooms. The *pièce de résistance* was the magnificent domed Opera House, built in 1911, where the legendary bass singer, Fyodor Shalyapin, sometimes gave performances.

Today, the Opera House offers less highbrow entertainment, as its change of name to Music Hall suggests. The adjoining 1930s buildings include the innovative Baltic House Theatre and a planetarium. The biggest draw, however, is the park's funfair.

Further west is the city zoo, which dates back to 1865. In winter visitors can see polar bears, sables, elk and deer, when their fur is at its thickest.

Turreted House, built between 1913–15, Kamennoostrovskiy prospekt

## ❾ Kamennoostrovskiy Prospekt
### Каменноостровский проспект
*Kamennoostrovskiy prospekt*

**Map** 1 C1. 🚌 46, K-30, K-76, K-223. Ⓜ Gorkovskaya or Petrogradskaya.

Laid out during the late 1890s, this elegant avenue is notable for its Style-Moderne architecture. The first house (No. 1–3), designed by Fyodor Lidval, epitomizes this Russian version of Art Nouveau, with its multi-textured façade, windows of contrasting shapes and sizes, ornate iron balconies and fanciful carvings. The neighbouring house (No. 5) was once occupied by Count Sergei Witte, a leading industrialist who negotiated the peace treaty with Japan in 1905.

Just off the start of the avenue stands the city's only mosque, constructed from 1910 to 1914.

Griffon, No. 1–3 Kamennoostrovskiy

Its minarets, majolica tiling and rusticated granite walls are fully in keeping with the surrounding architecture, but were in fact modelled on the Mausoleum of Tamerlane in the city of Samarkand.

At the intersection with ulitsa Mira, each house has individually designed turrets, spires, reliefs and iron balconies, forming a striking Style-Moderne ensemble. Other buildings of interest include No. 24, with its handsome red-brick, majolica and terracotta façade; No. 26–28, where Sergei Kirov lived; and the Turreted House with portal, on the corner of Bolshoi prospekt.

## ❿ Kirov Museum
### Музей С. М. Кирова
*Muzey S M Kirova*

Kamennoostrovskiy prospekt 26–28, 4th floor. **Map** 1 C1. **Tel** (812) 346 02 17, (812) 346 02 89. Ⓜ Petrogradskaya. **Open** 11am–6pm Thu–Mon (till 5pm Tue). ♿ 🎧 English. Ⓦ **spbmuseum.ru**

From 1926 this apartment was home to Sergei Kirov, the charismatic first Secretary of the

Leningrad Communist Party. His popularity led Stalin to see in him a potential rival, and on 1 December 1934 Kirov was gunned down at the Smolnyy Institute (see p182) by a party malcontent. His assassination gave Stalin a pretext to launch the Great Terror (see p45).

Although most historians believe that Stalin instigated his murder, Kirov was cynically elevated to the status of a Soviet martyr, with countless buildings named in his honour. His apartment, preserved as it was in his lifetime, is an example of the near cult status awarded to party leaders, with documents and photographs chronicling his political career, and an array of memorabilia.

Portrait of Sergei Kirov (1930s), in the Kirov Museum

## ⑪ Kshesinskaya Mansion
Особняк М. Кшесинской
*Osobnyak M Kshesinskoy*

Ulitsa Kuybysheva 4. **Map** 2 D3. **Tel** (812) 233 70 52. Ⓜ Gorkovskaya. **Open** 10am–6pm Fri–Tue (till 8pm Wed). **Closed** last Mon of the month. 🎫 📷 English. 🌐 **polithistory.ru**

This Style-Moderne residence was built in 1904 for the prima ballerina Matilda Kshesinskaya, who was the mistress of the future Tsar Nicholas II at that time. Designed by court architect Von Gogen, the mansion is almost playfully asymmetric, with an octagonal tower and façades in contrasting bands of pink and grey granite and cream-coloured bricks ornamented with iron railings and majolica tiles.

An elegant recital hall in the Kshesinskaya Mansion

In March 1917 the mansion was commandeered by the Bolsheviks, and upon returning to Russia, Lenin addressed the crowds from its balcony. Formerly home to a museum glorifying the October Revolution, the mansion now houses the Museum of Russian Political History. The Bolshevik Party secretariat and Lenin's office on the first floor have been faithfully restored. Upstairs is a collection of revolutionary memorabilia, such as Communist posters, Nicholas II coronation mugs and a police file on Rasputin's murder (see p176).

## ⑫ Cabin of Peter the Great
Музей-домик Петра I
*Muzey-domik Petra I*

Petrovskaya naberezhnaya 6. **Map** 2 E3. **Tel** (812) 232 45 76, (812) 314 03 74. Ⓜ Gorkovskaya. **Open** 10am–5:30pm Mon, Wed & Fri–Sun, 1–9pm Thu. **Closed** last Mon of the month. 🎫 ♿

This humble pine-log cabin was built for Peter the Great by his soldier-carpenters in just three days in 1703. Peter lived here for

six years while overseeing the construction of his new city. Catherine the Great later had a protective brick shell built around the cabin.

There are only two rooms, both with period furnishings, and a hallway, which doubled as a bedroom. Among Peter's possessions are a compass, a frock coat and his rowing boat. Outside are two statues of the Shih Tze lions, brought from Manchuria during the Russo-Japanese War (1904–5).

## ⑬ Cruiser Aurora
Крейсер Аврора
*Kreyser Avrora*

Petrogradskaya naberezhnaya 3. **Map** 2 F3. **Tel** 230 84 40. 🚌 49, K-30, K-183. 🚃 6, 40. **Open** Call to check times.

The ship entered service in 1903, and took an active part in the Russo-Japanese War of 1904–5. According to the annals of the Revolution, at 9:40pm on 25 October 1917, the cruiser *Aurora* signalled the storming of the Winter Palace (see pp156–7), by firing a single blank round from its bow gun. It was later converted into a training ship and at the start of the Siege of Leningrad in 1941 it was sunk to protect it from German forces. The ship was raised in 1944 and has been a museum since 1956. The gun, bell and the crew's quarters can be viewed, along with an exhibition on the history of the *Aurora*. It underwent major restoration in 2014–16.

The cruiser *Aurora*, moored in front of the Neo-Baroque Nakhimov Naval Academy

One of the two russet-coloured Rostral Columns on the Strelka

## ⑭ Rostral Columns
Ростральные колонны
*Rostralnye kolonny*

Birzhevaya ploshchad. **Map** 1 C5.
🚎 7, 10, 24, 47, 191, K-187, K-209, K-252. 🚊 1, 7, 10, 11.

Situated on the eastern end of Vasilevskiy Island, known as the Strelka, the twin russet-coloured Rostral Columns were designed as lighthouses by Thomas de Thomon in 1810. During the 19th century the oil lamps were replaced by gas torches, which are still lit on ceremonial occasions. The columns are decorated with protruding ships' prows in celebration of naval victories and the figures around the base represent four of Russia's rivers – the Neva, Volga, Dnieper and Volkhov.

## ⑮ The Institute of Russian Literature (Pushkin House)
Институт русской литературы (Пушкинский Дом)
*Institut Russkoy Literatury (Pushkinskiy Dom)*

Naberezhnaya Makarova 4. **Map** 1 B5.
**Tel** (812) 328 05 02. 🚎 7, 10, 47, 187, K-209, K-252. 🚊 1, 7, 10, 11.
**Open** 11am–4pm Mon–Fri. 🎨
🇬🇧 English, book in advance.
🌐 **pushkinskijdom.ru**

Founded at the beginning of the 20th century, this museum focuses on preserving the

legacy of Russian literary culture from the distant past to the present. It houses numerous manuscripts and exhibits connected to Russia's greatest poet, Alexander Pushkin, as well as rare and unusual artifacts connected with some of Russia's eminent writers, including Gogol, Turgenev, Tolstoy and Dostoevsky.

Today, Pushkin House contains more than 3 million autographed manuscripts, including 12,000 pages from Pushkin alone. In addition to more than 700,000 books and print editions reflecting the history of Russian literature, the museum also preserves thousands of images, paintings, drawings and objects.

## ⑯ Zoological Museum
Зоологический музей
*Zoologicheskiy muzey*

Universitetskaya naberezhnaya 1/3.
**Map** 1 C5. **Tel** (812) 328 01 12. 🚎 7, 10, 24, 47, 191, K-187, K-209, K-252. 🚊 1, 7, 10, 11. **Open** 11am–6pm Wed–Mon.
🎨 free every third Thu of the month.
🇬🇧 English. 💻 🏛 🌐 **zin.ru**

One of the largest of its kind in the world, this museum contains more than 1.5 million specimens, and is renowned for its collection of prehistoric mammoths. One prized carcass exhumed from the frozen wastes of Siberia in 1902 is almost 44,000 years old.

Some of the stuffed animals on display belonged to Tsar Peter the Great's Kunstkammer collection, including the horse he

rode at the Battle of Poltava. Dioramas re-create natural habitats for giant crabs, weasels, polar bears and blue whales.

## ⑰ Kunstkammer
Кунсткамера
*Kunstkamera*

Universitetskaya naberezhnaya 3.
**Map** 1 B5. **Tel** (812) 328 08 12. 🚎 7, 10, 24, 47, 191, K-187, K-191, K-209, K-252. 🚊 1, 7, 10, 11. **Open** 11am–6pm Tue–Sun. **Closed** last Tue of the month. 🎨 🇬🇧 English.
🌐 **kunstkamera.ru**

Russia's first museum, the Baroque Kunstkammer (art chamber) was built between 1718 and 1734 to exhibit Peter the Great's infamous collection of curios. While touring Holland in 1697, he attended the lectures of anatomist Frederik Ruysch (1638–1731) and was so impressed with Ruysch's collection of rarities that on a return visit in 1717, he purchased the entire collection of over 2,000 anatomical preparations.

It was transported to St Petersburg and was exhibited to a wide-eyed public. At the time, Peter's collection also included live exhibits of deformed or unusual people, including a hermaphrodite.

Today the Kunstkammer houses the Museum of Anthropology and Ethnography, with the remnants of Peter's bizarre collection on the first floor. Beside a cabinet of teeth extracted by the tsar (an amateur dentist) are pickled oddities such

Mammoth skeleton on display at the Zoological Museum

*For restaurants in this area see pp283–4*

The grandiose Baroque Menshikov Palace, built for nobleman Alexander Menshikov

as a two-headed sheep. The surrounding halls contain exhibits on the peoples of the world. Often neglected by visitors, these marvellously old-fashioned displays present a wide range of artifacts, from an Inuit kayak to Javanese shadow puppets.

## ⑱ Twelve Colleges

Двенадцать коллегий

*Dvenadtsat kollegiy*

Universitetskaya naberezhnaya 7. **Map** 1 B5. 🚌 7, 24, 47, 129, K-187, K-209. 🚊 1, 10, 11. **Closed** to public.

This red-and-white Baroque building, almost 400 m (1,300 ft) in length, was intended for Peter the Great's newly streamlined administration of 12 colleges or ministries. The uninterrupted façade was designed to symbolize the government's unity of purpose. Its curious alignment, at right angles to the embankment, is supposedly due to Prince Menshikov changing the plan in Peter's absence so that the building would not encroach on his grounds.

The building's function gradually changed, and in 1819 part of it was acquired by St Petersburg University. A string of revolutionaries, including Lenin, were educated here. Famous lecturers who taught here include the chemist Dmitri Mendeleev (1834–1907) and the physiologist Ivan Pavlov (1849–1936).

Outside the Twelve Colleges, overlooking the Neva, is an engaging bronze statue of the 18th-century polymath Mikhail Lomonosov. A fisherman's son, dubbed the "Russian Leonardo", Lomonosov wrote poetry, systematized Russian grammar, and explored mathematics and the physical sciences. His discoveries led to the intro-duction of porcelain, glass and mosaic production in Russia.

## ⑲ Menshikov Palace

Меншиковский дворец

*Menshikovskiy dvorets*

Universitetskaya naberezhnaya 15. **Map** 1 B5. **Tel** (812) 323 11 12 🚌 7, 24, 47, 191, K-209. 🚊 1, 10, 11. **Open** 10:30am–6pm Tue, Thu & Sat–Sun, 10:30am–9pm Wed & Fri. 🅿️ 📷 compulsory, available in English, French and German.

Completed in 1720, the Menshikov Palace was one of the city's earliest stone buildings. It was built for Peter the Great's close friend, Alexander Menshikov, who rose from

A section of the detailed west façade of the Twelve Colleges

humble origins to the nobility, by helping Peter to crush the Streltsy Revolt of 1862 and defeat the Swedes at Poltava. Prince Menshikov entertained here on a lavish scale, often on the tsar's behalf. His palace is now a branch of the Hermitage with exhibitions on early 18th-century Russian culture, reveal-ing the extent to which Peter's court was influenced by Western tastes.

The compulsory tour begins on the ground floor. Besides the kitchen there are displays of Peter's cabinet-making tools, period costumes, oak chests and ships' compasses. The hallway is adorned with marble statues from Italy; Menshikov and Peter's monograms are entwined on its grand stairway.

Upstairs, a secretariat decorated with engravings of Dutch cities is followed by a series of rooms lined with 18th-century hand-painted blue-and-white Dutch tiles. The bedroom of Menshikov's sister-in-law features a German-made four-poster bed and Flemish tapestry. Guests were often received in the Walnut Study, with its commanding views of the Neva. Paintings hang from coloured ribbons, as was the fashion then, while the mirrors were a novelty at that time, condemned by the Orthodox Church as vanity.

Balls and banquets were held in the Great Hall, decorated in gold and stucco, which once hosted a dwarfs' wedding that Menshikov arranged for Peter's amusement.

# PALACE EMBANKMENT

In terms of sheer scale and grandeur, St Petersburg's magnificent southern waterfront has few equals. Its formidable granite quays, stretching over 2 km (1 mile) from the Senate building in the west to Peter the Great's Summer Palace in the east, and the surrounding area of stately aristocratic palaces and ornamental canal bridges, are justly famous worldwide. Every aspect of the city's history is palpable in this atmospheric area. Etienne Falconet's statue of Peter the Great, The Bronze Horseman, is a testimony to imperial ambition, while the square in which it stands was formerly named in honour of the Decembrist rebels who rose up against the Tsarist regime in 1825. Bartolomeo Rastrelli's Winter Palace evokes the opulence of imperial Russia, whereas the Eternal Flame, flickering in the Field of Mars, is a sombre reminder of revolutionary sacrifice. Dominating St Petersburg's skyline are the splendid dome of St Isaac's Cathedral and the gilded spire of the Admiralty. Some of the best views can be appreciated by making a boat trip along the waterways, or by strolling through the delightful Summer Garden.

## Sights at a Glance

**Historical Buildings and Monuments**
1. The Admiralty
3. The Bronze Horseman
4. Horseguards' Manège
7. Angleterre Hotel

**Streets and Squares**
2. Senate Square
6. St Isaac's Square
8. Palace Square
10. Millionaires' Street
12. Field of Mars

**Churches and Cathedrals**
5. St Isaac's Cathedral pp150–51

**Museums**
9. The Hermitage pp154–7

**Palaces and Gardens**
11. Marble Palace
13. Summer Garden
14. Summer Palace

**Locator Map**
*See Street Finder, maps 1–4*

◀ The pretty central passageway of the Summer Garden, flanked by statues

**For keys to symbols** *see back flap*

# Street-by-Street: St Isaac's Square

The highlight of St Isaac's Square is the imposing cathedral at its centre, which opened in 1858 and is the fourth church to stand on this site. The cathedral, and subsequently the square, were named after St Isaac of Dalmatia, because Peter the Great's birthday fell on the saint's day. The busy square, used as a market place in the first half of the 19th century, is now at the heart of an area teeming with buildings and statues of historical and architectural interest. Among them are the Admiralty, the Mariinskiy Palace and The Bronze Horseman.

❹ **Horseguards' Manège** was built in 1804–7 by Giacomo Quarenghi. It housed the Life Guards' Mounted Regiment.

ADMIRALTEYSKAYA NABEREZHNAYA

PROEZD DEKABRISTOV

❸ **The Bronze Horseman**
Etienne Falconet's impressive statue of Peter the Great, his horse trampling the serpent of treason, captures the spirit of the city's uncompromising and wilful founder.

ULITSA YAKUBOVICHA

**The Glory Columns**, topped by bronze angels, were erected in 1845–6.

ISAAKIEV
PLOS

❷ **Senate Square**
Dominating the western side of the square are Carlo Rossi's monumental Senate and Synod buildings, linked by a triumphal arch.

Myatlev House

BOLSHA

❺ ★ **St Isaac's Cathedral**
The magnificent golden dome of the cathedral is visible all across the city. Its surface is covered with 100 kg (220 lb) of gold leaf.

**The former German Embassy** was designed by the German architect Peter Behrens in 1911–12.

The Hermitage
and Winter Palace

Area illustrated

**❶ The Admiralty**
Sculptures and reliefs
celebrating the power
of Russia's Navy decorate
the Admiralty's façade.
The archway of the main
entrance is framed by
nymphs carrying globes
on their shoulders.

ADMIRALTEYSKIY PROSPEKT

GOROKHOVAYA UL

**The former Prince
Lobanov-Rostovskiy
Mansion** is now
a luxury hotel.
The lions in front
of the arcade are
by Italian sculptor
Paolo Triscorni.

**❼ Angleterre Hotel**
Originally built in the 1850s, the Angleterre
Hotel was the site of the first major public
protest in the history of the Soviet Union.
The hotel has been restored to its
19th-century splendour.

VOZNESENSKIY PROSPEKT

MALAYA MORSKAYA UL

Nevskiy
prospekt

**The former Ministry of
State Property**, designed
by Nikolai Yefimov in 1844,
is a fine example of Neo-
Renaissance architecture.

MORSKAYA UL

Siniy Most

REKI MOYKI

**The Mariinskiy Palace**, named
in honour of Maria, daughter
of Nicholas I, now houses the
St Petersburg city hall.

**Key**

— Suggested route

0 metres          100
0 yards           100

**❻ St Isaac's Square**
Overlooking the square is Pyotr Klodt's
statue of Tsar Nicholas I. The reliefs on
the pedestal depict episodes from his
reign. Significantly, two of them show
the suppression of rebellions.

The gilded spire and detailed façade of the Admiralty

# ❶ The Admiralty

Адмиралтейство

*Admiralteystvo*

Admiralteyskaya naberezhnaya 2. **Map** 3 C1. 7, 10, 24, 100, 191, K-169, K-209, K-252. 1, 5, 7, 10, 11, 17, 22. **Closed** to public.

Having founded a city and built a fortress, Peter the Great's next priority was to create a Russian Navy. The Admiralty was built as a fortified shipyard from 1704 to 1711, which soon employed some 10,000 men constructing the first battleships.

In 1806, Andrei Zakharov, one of Russia's most inspired architects, began to rebuild the Admiralty, creating a remarkable façade 407 m (1,335 ft) in length, adorned with an abundance of sculptures and reliefs symbolizing Russian naval glory. Zakharov retained some of the original features, including the central gate tower and spire, which he recast in Neo-Classical style with columned porticos and pavilions. The heightened spire was gilded and topped with a model frigate. This has become a symbol of the city, just like the trumpet-blowing pair of angels on the portals of the façade overlooking the Neva.

In the 1840s, shipbuilding was moved downstream and the Admiralty was handed over to the Russian Navy. It has been occupied by the Naval Engineering School since 1925.

# ❷ Senate Square

Сенатская площадь

*Senatskaya ploshchad*

**Map** 3 B1. 3, 10, 22, 27, 71, 100, K-169, K-187, K-306. 5, 22.

The momentous Decembrist uprising took place in this square on 14 December 1825. During the inauguration of Tsar Nicholas I, army officers intent on imposing a constitutional monarchy attempted to stage a coup d'état. After a confused stand-off lasting several hours, the rebels were routed with grapeshot. Five of the ring-leaders were later executed and 121 others exiled to Siberia, thus effectively ending Russia's first revolution.

The imposing Neo-Classical buildings commanding the western side of the Senate Square were intended to harmonize with the Admiralty. Designed by Carlo Rossi between 1829 and 1834, they housed the headquarters of two important institutions originally created by Peter the Great: the Supreme Court, or Senate, and the Holy Synod, responsible for the administration of the Orthodox Church. The two buildings, which now house historical archives, are linked to each other by a triumphal arch supported by Corinthian columns and decorated with a Neo-Classical frieze and a plethora of statuary.

# ❸ The Bronze Horseman

Медный Всадник

*Mednyy Vsadnik*

Senatskaya ploshchad. **Map** 3 B1. 3, 10, 22, 27, 71, 100, K-169, K-187, K-306. 5, 22.

Immortalized in Alexander Pushkin's famous poem, this equestrian statue of Peter the Great was unveiled in Senate Square in 1782 as a tribute from Catherine the Great. The eminent French sculptor, Etienne Falconet, spent more than 12 years over-seeing this ambitious project.

The pedestal alone weighs 1,625 tonnes (1,790 US tons) and was hewn from a single block of granite hauled from the Gulf of Finland. It bears the inscription, "To Peter I from Catherine II". A serpent, under-neath the horse's hooves, symbolizes treason.

# ❹ Horseguards' Manège

Конногвардейский манеж

*Konnogvardeyskiy manezh*

Isaakievskaya ploshchad 1. **Map** 3 B2. **Tel** (812) 312 22 43, (812) 571 41 57 (ticket office). 3, 22, 27, 71, 100, K-169, K-187, K-306. 5, 22. **Open** variable.

The enormous indoor riding school of the Life Guards' Cavalry was built by Giacomo Quarenghi in 1804–7 to resemble a Roman basilica.

Romanesque façade of Horseguards' Manège

St Issac's Cathedral, statue of St Nicholas I and the Angleterre Hotel in St Issac's Square

Two clues to its original function are the frieze of a horse race beneath the pediment and the naked statues on either side of the portico, copied from the statues of the twin sons of Zeus reining in wild horses outside the Quirinale Palace in Rome. The statues were removed after the Holy Synod objected to this display of nudity so near to St Isaac's Cathedral, but they were re-erected in 1954.

Like its namesake in Moscow, the Manège is now used as an exhibition hall.

## ❺ St Isaac's Cathedral

*See pp150–51.*

## ❻ St Isaac's Square

Исаакиевская площадь
*Issakievskaya ploshchad*

**Map** 3 C2. 🚃 3, 10, 22, 27, 71, 100, K-169, K-187, K-306. 🚎 5, 22.

Dominated by the majestic St Isaac's Cathedral, this square was created during the reign of Nicholas I, although a few buildings date from the 18th century. The tsar was post-humously honoured in 1859 by an equestrian monument sculpted by Pyotr Klodt, whose pedestal is embellished with allegorical sculptures of the tsar's wife and daughters, representing Faith, Wisdom, Justice and Might. The Holy Synod insisted that the horse's rump face away from the cathedral.

On the western side of the square, the Neo-Classical Myatlev House at No. 9 hosted the French encyclopedist Denis Diderot in 1773–4, following an invitation from Catherine the Great. In the 1920s, it became the premises of the State Institute of Artistic Culture, where some of Russia's most influential avant-garde artists, including Kazimir Malevich and Vladimir Tatlin, worked.

The impressive granite-faced building alongside is the former German embassy, which was looted by a frenzied crowd at the outbreak of war between Russia and Germany in 1914.

Across the 100-m (330-ft) wide Blue Bridge (Siniy Most), which was the site of a serf market until 1861, the Mariinskiy Palace dominates the southern end of the square.

## ❼ Angleterre Hotel

Гостиница Англетер
*Gostinitsa Angleter*

Malaya Morskaya ulitsa 24. **Map** 3 C2. **Tel** (812) 494 56 66. 🚃 3, 10, 22, 27, K-169, K-190, K-306. 🚎 5, 22.

The seven-storey Angleterre was designed between 1910 and 1912 by Fyodor Lidval in the Style Moderne form.

The American journalist, John Reed, author of the eyewitness account of the Revolution, *Ten Days that Shook the World*, was staying here when the Bolsheviks seized power in 1917.

In 1925, the poet Sergei Yesenin, husband of Isadora Duncan, hanged himself in the hotel's annexe, after daubing the walls of his room with a farewell verse in his blood, "To die is not new – but neither is it new to be alive."

The banqueting hall was to be the venue for Hitler's prematurely planned victory celebration, so sure was he that he would conquer Leningrad in 1941.

Style-Moderne foyer in the Angleterre Hotel

### *The Bronze Horseman* by Alexander Pushkin

The famous statue of Peter the Great is brought to life in Alexander Pushkin's epic poem *The Bronze Horseman* (1833). In this haunting vision of the Great Flood of 1824, the hero is pursued through the mist-shrouded streets by the terrifying bronze statue. Pushkin's words evoke the domineering and implacable will for which the tsar was renowned, "How terrible he was in the surrounding gloom! … what strength was in him! And in that steed, what fire!"

# ❺ St Isaac's Cathedral

Исаакиевский собор

*Isaakievskiy sobor*

One of the world's largest cathedrals, St Isaac's was designed in 1818 by the then unknown architect Auguste de Montferrand. The construction of the colossal building was a major engineering feat. Thousands of wooden piles were sunk into the marshy ground to support its weight of 300,000 tonnes (330,700 US tons) and 48 huge columns were hauled into place. The cathedral opened in 1858 but it was deconsecrated and became a museum of atheism during the Soviet era. Officially still a museum, the church is filled with hundreds of 19th-century works of art.

**Angels with Torch**
Ivan Vitali created many of the cathedral's sculptures, including the pairs of angels supporting gas torches that crown the four attic corners.

## KEY

① **The north pediment** is ornamented with a bronze relief of the Resurrection, designed by François Lemaire in 1842–4.

② **This chapel** honours Alexander Nevsky who defeated the Swedes in 1240.

③ **The mosaic icons** on the iconostasis are by Russian masters Bryullov, Neff and Zhivago.

④ **Malachite** and lapis lazuli columns frame the iconostasis. About 16,000 kg (35,280 lb) of malachite decorate the cathedral.

⑤ **St Catherine's Chapel** has a white marble iconostasis, crowned by a sculpted Resurrection, built by Nikolai Pimenov in 1850–54.

⑥ **The silver dove** (1850) hanging in the cupola is a symbol of the Holy Spirit.

⑦ **Portraits of the apostles and evangelists**

⑧ **Statue of St Matthew**

⑨ **The walls** are adorned with 14 coloured marbles and 43 other types of semi-precious stones and minerals.

⑩ **The relief of St Isaac** blessing the Roman Emperor Theodosius and his wife Flaccilla is by Ivan Vitali. On the extreme left, de Montferrand is depicted clutching a model of his cathedral.

⑪ **Red granite columns**, each weighing 114 tonnes (125 US tons), were transported from Finland in specially constructed ships.

⑫ **The vast interior** covers 4,000 sq m (43,000 sq ft).

**★ Iconostasis**
Three rows of icons surround the royal doors through which a stained-glass window is visible. Above the doors is Pyotr Klodt's gilded sculpture, *Christ in Majesty*, dating from 1859.

Exit

**The Dome**
From the dome there are panoramic views over the city, including the Admiralty (*see p148*) and the Hermitage (*see pp154–7*). Adorning the gilded dome are angels sculpted by Josef Hermann.

**VISITORS' CHECKLIST**

**Practical information**
Isaakievskaya ploshchad 4.
**Map** 3 C1.**Tel** (812) 315 97 32.
**Open** May–Sep: 10:30am–10:30pm Thu–Tue; Oct–Apr: 10:30am–6pm Thu–Tue.
🗓 🏛 ♿ ✝ religious festivals.

**Transport**
🚌 3, 10, 22, 27, 71, 100, K-169, K-190, K-289. Ⓜ Admiralteskaya, Sadovaya. 🚌 5, 22.

★ **Ceiling Painting**
The celestial *Virgin in Majesty* by Karl Bryullov, dating to 1847, covers an area of 816 sq m (8,780 sq ft). It is ringed by exuberant gilded stucco mouldings and white marble.

The entrance is through the side doors on St Isaac's Square

**South Doors**
Three great doors of oak and bronze, built from 1841 to 1846, are decorated with carved reliefs by Ivan Vitali. The exteriors of the doors show scenes from the life of Christ and saints, including Alexander Nevsky.

## ❽ Palace Square
Дворцовая площадь
*Dvortsovaya ploshchad*

**Map** 2 D5. 🚌 7, 10, 24, 191, K-209.
🚎 1, 7, 10, 11.

Palace Square has played a unique role in Russian history. In January 1905, it was the site of the Bloody Sunday massacre, when troops fired on thousands of unarmed demonstrators. Then, on 7 November 1917, Lenin's Bolsheviks seized power by attacking the Winter Palace *(see pp156–7)* from the square. It remains a favourite venue for political meetings and cultural events such as rock concerts.

Designed by architect Carlo Rossi *(see p167)*, the resplendent square is dominated by the giant arc of the General Staff Building that was built between 1819 and 1829. Its two curving wings are connected by a double arch leading through to Nevskiy prospekt. The arch is crowned by a sculpture of Victory in her chariot.

The impressive Alexander Column in the centre of the square is dedicated to Tsar Alexander I. Designed by Auguste de Montferrand, the red-granite pillar is balanced by its own 600-tonne (661-US-ton) weight. It took 2,400 workmen two years to hew and transport the granite, but less than 2 hours to erect the column in 1834. Topped by a bronze angel, it is 47 m (154 ft) high.

## ❾ The Hermitage
*See pp154–7.*

## ❿ Millionaires' Street
Миллионная улица
*Millionnaya ulitsa*

**Map** 2 D5.

This street takes its name from the aristocrats and members of the imperial family who once inhabited its opulent residences.

No. 26, on the embankment, was the home of Grand Duke Vladimir Aleksandrovich, who ordered the shooting of peaceful demonstrators on Bloody Sunday. Putyatin's house, at No. 12, witnessed the end of the Romanov dynasty. It was here that Grand Duke Mikhail Aleksandrovich, Nicholas II's designated successor, signed the decree of abdication in March 1917.

The street crosses the tapering Winter Canal, providing a superb view of the Neva river through an archway between the Large Hermitage and the Hermitage Theatre.

## ⓫ Marble Palace
Мраморный дворец
*Mramornyy dvorets*

Millionnaya ulitsa 5 (entrance from the Field of Mars). **Map** 2 E4.
**Tel** (812) 595 42 48. 🚌 46, 49, K-76.
**Open** 10am–6pm Mon, Wed, Fri–Sun, 1pm–9pm Thu. ♿ 📷 English.
Ⓦ **rusmuseum.ru**

The Marble Palace was a gift from Catherine the Great to her lover Grigori Orlov, who had helped her seize power in 1762. An early example of

The magnificent Gala staircase of the Marble Palace

Neo-Classical architecture, dating from 1768–85, it is considered to be Antonio Rinaldi's masterpiece.

The palace takes its name from the marbles used in its construction. Most of the interiors were reconstructed in the 1840s, although the gala staircase and the Marble Hall, with marbled walls in pastel hues and lapis lazuli, are Rinaldi's work.

Having housed a Lenin museum for 55 years, it is now a branch of the Russian Museum *(see pp164–5)*. It exhibits modern art bequeathed by two German collectors, including a Picasso and works by Andy Warhol and Roy Lichtenstein.

In the courtyard is an equestrian statue of Alexander III, which originally stood half-way down Nevskiy prospekt. Its sculptor said, "I simply depicted one animal on another."

The formidable red-granite Alexander Column in Palace Square

## ⑫ Field of Mars
Марсово Поле
*Marsovo Pole*

**Map** 2 E5. 🚌 46, 49, K-76.

Once a vast marshland, this area was drained during the 19th century and utilized for military manoeuvres and parades, fairs and other festivities. Named after Mars, the Roman god of war, the sandy expanse was nicknamed the "Petersburg Sahara". Following the Revolution, it was landscaped and transformed into a memorial to revolutionary martyrs (some of whom were buried here), and the Eternal Flame was added in 1957.

The western side is dominated by an imposing Neo-Classical edifice by Vasily Stasov, built in 1817–19 as the barracks of the Pavlovskiy Guards. The regiment's founder, Tsar Paul, is said to have only recruited guardsmen with snub noses like his own. Its soldiers were among the first to turn against the Tsarist government in the 1917 Revolution.

Today, the huge square is a popular spot for locals on summer evenings, when the flowers are in full bloom.

The Eternal Flame, a memorial to martyrs at the Field of Mars

## ⑬ Summer Garden
Летний сад
*Letniy sad*

**Map** 2 E4. 🚌 46, 49, K-76, K-212. **Open** May–Oct: 10am–10pm Wed–Mon; Nov–Apr: 10am–8pm Wed–Mon. ♿ 🖥

In 1704, Peter the Great commissioned this beautiful formal garden, which was among the first in the city. Designed in the style of Versailles, it was

Ivan Krylov's statue amidst pretty autumn foliage, Summer Garden

planted with imported elms and oaks and adorned with fountains, pavilions and statues. A flood in 1777 destroyed most of the garden. The English-style garden that exists today is the result of Catherine the Great's tastes. A lofty filigree iron grille along the Neva embankment gives the garden an air of seclusion.

For a century the Summer Garden was reserved for the nobility, until Nicholas I opened it to "respectably dressed members of the public". Two Neo-Classical pavilions, the Tea House and the Coffee House were erected, and these are now used for art exhibitions by local artists.

Nearby, the bronze statue of Ivan Krylov, Russia's most famous writer of fables is a favourite with children. It has bas-reliefs on the pedestal depicting animals from his fables.

## ⑭ Summer Palace
Летний дворец
*Letniy dvorets*

Naberezhnaya Kutuzova. **Map** 2 F4. **Tel** (812) 595 42 48. 🚌 46, 49, K-76, K-212. **Closed** for renovation.

Peter the Great's two-storey Summer Palace is the oldest stone building in the city. Built in the Dutch style by Domenico Trezzini in 1714, it is grander than Peter's cabin but hardly comparable to the magnificent palaces of his successors. The tsar's bedroom has a four-poster bed and a ceiling painting showing the triumph of Morpheus, the god of sleep. Next door, the turnery contains Peter's lathes and a meteorological instrument connected to a weathervane on the roof.

The palace boasted the city's first plumbing system with water piped into the kitchen, which opened directly on to the dining room, so that dishes arrived hot at the table. This was only used for family gatherings; major banquets were held at the Menshikov Palace *(see p143)*.

On the first floor is the suite of Peter's wife, Catherine I, whose throne is ornamented with sea deities. The glass cupboards in the Green Room once displayed Peter's collection of curios, before it was transferred to the Kunstkammer *(see p142)*.

Peter the Great's original four-poster bed in the Summer Palace

# ❾ The Hermitage

Эрмитаж

*Ermitazh*

One of the world's great museums, the Hermitage comprises a grand ensemble of buildings. The most impressive is the Winter Palace *(see pp156–7)*, to which Catherine the Great added the Small and Large Hermitages to house her collection of over 2,500 paintings, 10,000 drawings, gems, silver and porcelain. Her successors added to the collection, which was opened to the public in 1852. After the Revolution, the nationalization of private collections brought many more artworks, including Post-Impressionist masterpieces, into the Hermitage. In 1993 it became the first museum in Russia to admit possession of "trophy art" seized from Nazi Germany, kept hidden for decades.

**The Knights' Hall** is used for displays of armour and weapons from the former imperial arsenal.

Stairs to ground floor

**The Gallery of Ancient Painting**, constructed between 1842 and 1851, is decorated with scenes from ancient literature. It houses a superb display of 19th-century European sculpture.

Copies of Raphael's original frescoes in the Vatican

Skylight Rooms

★ **Litta Madonna** (around 1491) One of two works by Leonardo da Vinci in the museum, this masterpiece was admired by his contemporaries and was frequently copied.

★ **Abraham's Sacrifice** (1635) In the 1630s Rembrandt was painting religious scenes in a High Baroque style, using dramatic and striking gestures rather than detail to convey his message.

European Gold Collection

**The Hall of Twenty Columns**, built in 1842–51, is painted in Etruscan style.

**The Kolyvan Vase**, carved from Altai jaspar, weighs 19 tonnes (21 US tons). The Large Hermitage was built around it.

Main Entrance

Ground floor

Siberian Antiquities

## Key to Floorplan

- Large Hermitage
- Small Hermitage
- The Winter Palace

Stairs to
first floor

Stairs to
second floor

Second Floor

First Floor

Entrance from
Palace Square

Greek and Oriental
Gold Collection

### VISITORS' CHECKLIST

**Practical information**
Dvortsovaya ploshchad 2.
**Map** 1 C5.
**Tel** (812) 710 90 79.
**W** hermitagemuseum.org
**Open** 10:30am–6pm Tue, Thu,
Sat & Sun, 10:30am–9pm Wed &
Fri (last adm: 1 hr before closing).
English, call (812) 571 84
46 to book.

**Transport**
7, 10, K-141, K-187, K-209,
K-228. 1, 7, 10, 11.

★ **Ea Haere Ia Oe** (1893)
Entitled "Woman Holding a
Fruit; Where Are you
Going?", this is one of the
first paintings by Paul
Gauguin after he had left
France for Tahiti. His desire
to escape convention and
artificiality found expression
in his innovative use of
primitive art as inspiration.

**The State Rooms**
(see pp156–7)
contain magnificent
Russian and
European
*objets d'art*.

★ **La Danse** (1909–10)
Henri Matisse used strong tones of three colours –
blue, green and red – to heighten the drama and
concentration of the figures, totally lost in their dance.

## Gallery Guide

*Enter via Palace Square, then cross the main courtyard:
group tours use other entrances. Start with the interiors of
the State Rooms on the first floor of the Winter Palace to get
an overview of the museum. For 19th- and 20th-century
European Art use either of the staircases on the Palace Square
side of the Winter Palace. Note that collections may move.*

## Key to Floorplan

- Prehistoric: Rooms 11–24, 26, 33
- Classical: 102, 107–117, 121, 127–131
- Far East and Central Asia: 34–47, 55–66, 69, 100, 351–371, 381–397
- Russian: 147–153, 155–189, 190–198, 204, 260, 269–271, 282, 304–307
- Italian and Spanish: 207–223, 226–242
- Flemish, Dutch and German: 243, 245–254, 258–259, 261–268
- French and European: 272–281, 283–287, 290–302
- Caucasus: 314–325, 328–350
- Temporary exhibition space
- Non-exhibition space
- No access

# The Winter Palace

Built for Tsarina Elizabeth in 1754–62, this opulent winter residence was considered to be the finest achievement of Bartolomeo Rastrelli. A superb example of Russian Baroque, the existing palace was preceded by three structures, all of them built within half a century of each other. Although the exterior has changed little, the interiors were altered by a number of architects and then largely restored after a fire gutted the palace in 1837. After the assassination of Alexander II in 1881, the imperial family rarely lived here. During World War I, a field hospital was set up in the Nicholas Hall and other state rooms. Then, in July 1917, the Provisional Government took the palace as its headquarters, which led to its storming by the Bolsheviks.

**Small Throne Room**
Dedicated to the memory of Peter the Great in 1833, this room houses a silver-gilt English throne, made in 1731.

## KEY

① **North façade** overlooking the Neva.

② **The Nicholas Hall**, the largest room in the palace, was always used for the first ball of the season.

③ **The Field Marshals' Hall** (1833) was the reception room where the devastating fire of 1837 broke out.

④ **The Hall of St George** (1795) has monolithic columns and wall facings of Italian Carrara marble.

⑤ **The 1812 Gallery** (1826) has portraits of Russian military heroes of the Napoleonic War, most of them painted by English artist George Dawe (1781–1829).

⑥ **The Armorial Hall** (1839), with its vast gilded columns, covers over 800 sq m (8,600 sq ft). Hospital beds were set up here during World War I.

⑦ **The French Rooms**, designed by Bryullov in 1839, house a collection of 18th-century French art.

⑧ **South façade** on Palace Square

⑨ **The White Hall** retains decorations from the wedding of Alexander II in 1841.

⑩ **West wing**

⑪ **The Gothic Library** and other rooms in the northwestern part of the palace were adapted to suit Nicholas II's bourgeois lifestyle. This wood-panelled library was created by Meltzer in 1894.

⑫ **The rotunda** (1830) connected the private apartments on the west with the state apartments on the palace's north side.

**★ Main Staircase**
This sweeping staircase built in 1762 was Rastrelli's masterpiece. It was from here that the imperial family watched the Epiphany ceremony of baptism in the Neva, which celebrated Christ's baptism in the Jordan.

**Alexander Hall**
Architect Aleksandr Bryullov employed Gothic vaulting in this reception room dating from 1837. He combined it with Neo-Classical stucco bas-reliefs on military themes.

## Bartolomeo Rastrelli

The Italian architect Rastrelli (1700–71) came to Russia with his father in 1716 to work for Peter the Great. His rich Baroque style became highly fashionable, and he was appointed Chief Court Architect in 1738. During Elizabeth's reign, Rastrelli designed several buildings, including the Winter Palace, Tsarkoe Selo *(see pp188–9)* and Smolnyy Convent *(see p182)*. Unlike Elizabeth, Catherine the Great preferred classical simplicity and Rastrelli retired in 1763, after she came to power.

**Dark Corridor**
The French and Flemish tapestries here include *The Marriage of Emperor Constantine*, made in Paris in the 17th century to designs by Rubens.

**★ Gold Drawing Room**
Created in the 1850s, this room was given an extravagant all-over gilding covering the walls and ceiling in the 1870s. It houses a display of carved gems from Western Europe.

**★ Malachite Room**
Over 2 tonnes (2.2 US tons) of ornamental stone were used in this sumptuous room (1839), which is decorated with malachite columns and vases, gilded doors and a gilded ceiling, and rich parquet flooring.

# GOSTINYY DVOR

Dating from the earliest days of St Petersburg, Gostinyy Dvor, or the Great Bazaar, forms the commercial heart of the city. With modern shopping centres standing next to Tsarist-era churches, this vast square is also a major social and cultural hub of St Petersburg. Until the mid-19th century, shops in this area catered almost exclusively for the luxury end of the market, fulfilling the immense demand created by the royal and aristocratic households for gold and silverware, jewellery and haute couture. Increasing commercial and financial activity created a new middle class of business

entrepreneurs. By the time of the Revolution, banks proliferated around Nevskiy prospekt, their imposing new offices introducing diverse architectural styles to a largely Neo-Classical setting. Today, the wheels of capitalism are turning again, and Nevskiy prospekt continues to attract a wealthy clientele. In contrast to the bustling commercial atmosphere of much of the area is the peace and quiet of secluded Arts Square, with the Russian Museum and other institutions acting as a reminder of St Petersburg's rich cultural heritage.

## Sights at a Glance

### Churches and Cathedrals
**1** Church on Spilled Blood p162
**13** Cathedral of Our Lady of Kazan

### Museums
**2** Mikhaylovskiy Castle
**3** Russian Museum pp164–5
**16** Pushkin House-Museum

### Streets, Square and Bridges
**4** Arts Square
**6** Malaya Sadovaya Ulitsa
**7** Anichkov Bridge
**9** Nevskiy Prospekt
**11** Ostrovskiy Square
**12** Ulitsa Zodchevo Rossi

### Historic Buildings
**5** Grand Hotel Europe
**10** Gostinyy Dvor
**15** Academic Capella
**17** Imperial Stables

### Palaces
**8** Anichkov Palace
**14** Stroganov Palace

**Locator Map**
*See Street Finder, maps 2 & 4*

For keys to symbols *see back flap*

# Street-by-Street: Around Arts Square

The aptly named Arts Square, one of Carlo Rossi's finest creations, is surrounded by buildings showcasing the city's impressive cultural heritage. The grand palace housing the Russian Museum is flanked by theatres and the Great Hall of the Philharmonia. Behind it is the leafy Mikhaylovskiy Garden, a haunt of St Petersburg's intellectuals. The gardens stretch down to the beautiful Moyka river, which together with two other waterways, the Griboedov and Fontanka, create a shimmering frame for this picturesque area.

**❶ ★ Church on Spilled Blood**
Colourful mosaics and elaborate stone carvings are the main features of the church's exterior, which emulates traditional 17th-century Russian style.

Mikhaylovskiy Garden

NABEREZHNAYA REKI MOYKI

MOYKA

**❸ ★ Russian Museum**
Located in Rossi's Mikhaylovskiy Palace, this famous gallery boasts a fabulous collection of Russian painting, sculpture and applied art. The grand staircase and White Hall are original features.

KANAL GRIBOEDOVA

NAB KANALA GRIBOEDOVA

INZHENERNAYA ULITS

ITALYANSKAYA UL

Statue of Pushkin (1957)

To Nevskiy prospekt

**The Great Hall of the Philharmonia** is one of the major concert venues in St Petersburg.

**❹ Arts Square**
The square's present name derives from the number of cultural institutions situated here. Located on the western side, the Mikhailovskiy Theatre opened in 1833 for opera performances.

**❺ Grand Hotel Europe**
This famous St Petersburg hotel was constructed by Ludwig Fontana in 1873–5. Mighty atlantes adorn its eclectic façade, which stretches all the way down to Nevskiy prospekt.

*For hotels and restaurants in this area see p268 and pp285–6*

Area illustrated

**The Panteleymon Bridge**
Rebuilt in 1907–8 to support a new tramway, this bridge
retains its original Empire-style decor by Lev Ilyin.

**The bird statue**, cast in
1995 by Rezo Gabriadze,
alludes to a popular rhyme
about vodka drinking.

Statue of Peter
the Great (1747)

❷ **Mikhaylovskiy Castle**
Originally built for Paul I
between 1797 and 1801, this
castle was acquired by the
Corps of Engineers in 1823.
Today, it forms part of the
Russian Museum and displays
historical portraits.

**Key**

— Suggested route

0 metres 100
0 yards 100

To Nevskiy prospekt

**The Museum of Hygiene**,
with macabre displays of
preserved human organs, was
set up in 1919 to teach the public
about health and hygiene.

**The Circus**
The *tsirk* began performing in the 19th
century when it was known as the Ciniselli
Circus. It still offers traditional performances
in this historic site by the Fontanka. The
building was completely restored in 2015.

# ● Church on Spilled Blood

Храм Спаса-на-Крови

*Khram Spasa-na-Krovi*

Also known as the Resurrection Church of Our Saviour, this church was built on the spot where Tsar Alexander II was assassinated on 1 March 1881. In 1883, his successor, Alexander III launched a competition for a permanent memorial. The winning design, in the Russian-Revival style favoured by the tsar himself, was by Alfred Parland and Ignatiy Malyshev. The foundation stone was laid in 1883. The overall effect of the church is a riot of colour, created by the imaginative juxtaposition of materials. Inside, more than 20 types of minerals, including jasper, rhodonite, porphyry and Italian marble are used unsparingly on the mosaics of the iconostasis, icon cases, canopy and floor. The interior reopened in 1998 after more than 20 years of restoration.

**VISITORS' CHECKLIST**

**Practical information**
Kanala Griboedova 2b.
**Map** 2 E5.
**Tel** (812) 315 16 36.
**Open** May–Sep: 10:30am–10:30pm Thu–Tue; Oct–Apr: 10:30am–7pm Thu–Tue. ▨ ▣ ▨

**Transport**
Ⓜ Gostinyy Dvor, Nevskiy Prospekt.

**Mosaic Tympanum**
Mosaic panels showing scenes from the New Testament adorn the exterior. They were based on designs by artists such as Viktor Vasnetsov and Mikhail Nesterov.

**Jewellers' enamel** was used to cover the 1,000 sq m (10,760 sq ft) surface of the five domes.

**The tent-roofed steeple** is 81 m (266 ft) high.

**Coat of Arms**
The 144 mosaic coats of arms on the bell tower represent the regions, towns and provinces of the Russian Empire. They were intended to reflect the grief shared by all Russians in the wake of Alexander's assassination.

**Intricate Detailing**
The flamboyant Russian-Revival style of the exterior provides a dramatic contrast to the Neo-Classical and Baroque architecture that dominates the centre of St Petersburg.

**Glazed ceramic** tiles enliven the façade.

**Mosaic portraits** of the saints are set in *kokoshniki* arches. Almost 7,000 sq m (75,350 sq ft) of mosaics embellish the church's extravagant exterior.

**Twenty dark red plaques** of Norwegian granite are engraved in gilt letters with the most outstanding events of Alexander II's reign (1855–81). Among the historic events recorded are the emancipation of the serfs in 1861 and the conquest of Central Asia in 1860–81.

**Window Frames**
The windows are flanked by carved columns of ornate Estonian marble. The casings are in the form of double and triple *kokoshniki* (tiered gables).

South façade of Mikhaylovskiy Castle, which hosts a branch of the Russian Museum

## ❷ Mikhaylovskiy Castle

Михайловский замок

*Mikhaylovskiy zamok*

Sadovaya ulitsa 2. **Map** 2 F5. **Tel** (812) 595 42 48. 🚌 46, K-76, K-212. **Open** 10am–6pm Mon, Wed & Fri–Sun, 1–9pm Thu. 📷 🎫 call to book. ♿

This imposing fortified castle overlooking the Moyka and Fontanka rivers was commissioned by Tsar Paul shortly after his coronation in 1796. To clear the site, Paul had the wooden palace in which he had been born razed to the ground: a revealing act by a man plagued by rumours of illegitimacy and who blamed his mother, Catherine the Great, for murdering his father. Terrified of being assassinated himself, Paul ordered architects Vasily Bazhenov and Vincenzo Brenna to surround his new residence with moats and drawbridges, and construct a secret escape tunnel leading to the Field of Mars (*see p153*). Unfortunately, these precautions proved futile; after living here for just 40 days Paul was strangled in his bedroom by conspirators.

The castle was shunned by his successors and was acquired in 1823 by the Corps of Engineers as a training school known as the Engineers' Castle. Its most famous graduate was the writer Fyodor Dostoevsky. Today, the castle serves as a branch of the Russian Museum and is used to house 18th–19th-century sculptures and portraits, as well

as temporary exhibitions. The inner courtyard contains a statue of Paul, who also commissioned the bronze statue of Peter the Great on horseback on the castle's driveway. Its inscription "To great grandfather from great grandson" was intended to quell rumours of his illegitimacy.

## ❸ Russian Museum

*See pp164–5.*

## ❹ Arts Square

Площадь Искусств

*Ploshchad Iskusstv*

**Map** 4 E1. Ⓜ Nevskiy Prospekt, Gostinyy Dvor.

Several of the city's leading cultural institutions are located on this leafy Neo-Classical square – hence its name. The square was designed by Carlo Rossi in the early 19th century to harmonize with the splendid Mikhaylovskiy Palace (now the Russian Museum), which stands on its northern side.

On the opposite side of the square is the Great Hall of the Philharmonia, also known as the Shostakovich Hall. This is where the Philharmonic Orchestra has been based since the 1920s. Constructed by Paul Jacot over 1834–9, it started as a Nobles' Club where concerts were held. Works premiered here include Beethoven's *Missa Solemnis* in 1824 and Tchaikovsky's *Pathétique* in 1893.

On the square's western side is the Mikhailovskiy Theatre, rebuilt by Albert Kavos in the mid-19th century. In the centre of the square is a sculpture of one of Russia's greatest literary figures, Alexander Pushkin. The statue was executed by leading post-war Soviet sculptor, Mikhail Anikushin.

## ❺ Grand Hotel Europe

Гранд Отель Европа

*Grand Otel Evropa*

Mikhaylovskaya ulitsa 1/7. **Map** 4 E1. **Tel** (812) 329 60 00. Ⓜ Nevskiy Prospekt, Gostinyy Dvor. ♿

One of Russia's most famous hotels (known locally as the Yevropeyskaya), the Grand Hotel Europe was built in the 1870s. However, it owes much of its character to alterations made in the 1910s by Style-Moderne architect Fyodor Lidval. Before the Revolution, the hotel's magnificent restaurant was a favourite rendezvous for diplomats and spies; later, the hotel became an orphanage.

Opulent Style-Moderne interiors of the Grand Hotel Europe

# ❸ Russian Museum

## Русский музей
*Russkiy Muzey*

Built in 1819–25 for Grand Duke Mikhail Pavlovich, the Mikhaylovskiy Palace – a fine Neo-Classical creation by Carlo Rossi – is home to one of Russia's most illustrious museums. Alexander III's plans to create a public museum were realized by his son, Nicholas II, when the Russian Museum opened here in 1898. Today, it holds what is arguably the greatest collection of Russian art in the world.

**The Benois Wing**, named after its main architect Leontiy Benois, was added in 1913–19.

Stairs to ground floor

★ **Princess Olga Konstantinovna Orlova** (1911)
This painting is by Valentin Serov, one of the most successful portrait painters in Russia.

Benois Wing

Entrance

Ground floor

## Gallery Guide

*The main entrance on Arts Square leads to the ticket office on the lower ground floor. The exhibition starts on the first floor. It is arranged chronologically, starting with icons in Room 1. It continues on the ground floor of the main building and the Rossi Wing, then the first floor of the Benois Wing. Exhibitions change regularly.*

**Temporary exhibitions** featuring 20th-century art are often held here.

Stairs to first floor of Benois Wing

**Folk Art Toy** (1930s)
This clay toy from Dykomovo is part of the colourful selection of folk art which also includes lacquer boxes, painted ceramics and textiles.

### Key to Floorplan

- Old Russian art
- 18th-century art
- Early 19th-century art
- Late 19th-century art
- Late 19th–early 20th-century art
- 20th-century art
- 18th–20th-century sculpture
- Folk art
- Temporary exhibitions
- Non-exhibition space

**The Last Day of Pompeii** (1833) Karl Bryullov's Classical subject embodies the aesthetic principles of the Academy of Arts. This vivid depiction of the eruption of Mount Vesuvius won him the Grand Prix at the Paris Salon.

First floor

Stairs to ground floor

14

15

12

16

13

17

11

10

9

8

**The White Hall** contains original Empire-style furniture by Carlo Rossi.

1 2 3

7

6

Rossi Wing

Start of exhibition

5

4

★ **Barge Haulers on the Volga** (1870–73) Ilya Repin was the most famous member of the Wanderers *(see p29)*, a group of artists dedicated to socialist realism and Russian themes. His powerful indictment of wage slavery imbues the oppressed victims with sullen dignity.

43 42 41 40 39

33

32

52 53 54 55 56

34

35

36

37

38

31

30

29 28 27 26

25

24

Stairs to first floor

**Phryne at the Festival of Poseidon in Eleusin** (1889) Henryk Siemiradzki's paintings are fine examples of late European Neo-Classicism. He is renowned for his academic scenes of life in ancient Greece and Rome.

18 19 20 21 22 23

Entrance points from ticket office on lower ground floor

**The portico** of eight Corinthian columns is the central feature of Carlo Rossi's façade.

**The main entrance** is via a door leading to the lower ground floor with a ticket office, toilets and a café.

**A Meal in the Monastery** (1865–76) Vasiliy Perov's canvas exposes the hypocrisy of the Orthodox clergy, with the juxtaposition of good and evil, rich and poor, false piety and true faith.

# ❻ Malaya Sadovaya Ulitsa

Малая Садовая Улица
*Malaya Sadovaya ulitsa*

**Map** 4 F1. Ⓜ Gostinyy Dvor.

This pedestrianized side street is known for its many sculptures. Notable among these is a statue of the great photographer Karl Bulla (1853–1929) with his tripod camera, with which he captured life in St Petersburg before the Revolution. Beyond this, two sculpted cats watch each other from the second-floor ledges of buildings on opposite sides of the street. At the intersection of Malaya Sadovaya ulitsa and Nevskiy prospekt, a model of a loudspeaker recalls the public-address systems that broadcast air-raid warnings during the Siege of Leningrad.

# ❼ Anichkov Bridge

Аничков мост
*Anichkov most*

**Map** 4 F2.

This bridge spanning the Fontanka river is named after Colonel Mikhail Anichkov, who set up camp on this site at the time of the founding of the city, and built a wooden drawbridge here. Today's bridge, built in the mid-19th century, is famous for the statues at its four corners, each portraying a near-naked youth taming a stallion. It is said that their sculptor Pyotr Klodt got so annoyed with repeated meddling by Tsar Nicholas I that he depicted the tsar's face in the groin of the horse nearest to the Anichkov Palace.

Bronze sculpture of a boy taming a stallion, Anichkov Bridge

Colonnaded wing overlooking the Fontanka river, Anichkov Palace

# ❽ Anichkov Palace

Аничков дворец
*Anichkov dvorets*

Nevskiy prospekt 39. **Map** 4 F2. 🚌 3, 7, 22, 24, 27, 191. Ⓜ Gostinyy Dvor. 🚎 1, 5, 7, 10, 11, 22. **Closed** to public except for special events.

Built in 1741–50, the Anichkov Palace beside the Fontanka river was a gift from Tsarina Elizabeth to her lover Aleksey Razumovskiy. After his death, Catherine the Great in turn gave it to her own lover, Prince Potemkin. The palace became the traditional winter residence of the heir to the throne after 1817, although when Alexander III became tsar in 1881, he continued to live here rather than move to the Winter Palace, as was customary. His widow Maria Fyodorovna stayed on until the Revolution.

The palace originally had large gardens to the west but these were truncated in 1816, when Ostrovskiy Square was created and two Neo-Classical pavilions were added. The elegant colonnaded wing overlooking the Fontanka river was built for storing goods from the imperial factories before they were distributed to various palaces. Later, the building was converted into government offices. It now houses the Palace of Youth Creativity.

# ❾ Nevskiy Prospekt

Невский проспект
*Nevskiy prospekt*

**Map** 4 D1. Ⓜ Nevskiy Prospekt, Gostinyy Dvor.

Russia's most famous street, Nevskiy prospekt is also St Petersburg's main thoroughfare. In the 1830s, novelist Nikolai Gogol declared with pride,

"There is nothing finer than Nevskiy Avenue…in St Petersburg it is everything… is there anything more gay, more brilliant, more resplendent than this beautiful street of our capital?"

Laid out in the early days of the city, the street was originally named the Great Perspective Road, and ran 5 km (3 miles) from the Admiralty *(see p148)* to the Alexander Nevsky Monastery *(see p183)*. Despite roaming wolves and periodic flooding, mansions such as the Stroganov Palace *(see p168)* were built, followed by shops and bazaars catering to the nobility, and inns for travelling merchants. A magnet attracting rich and poor alike, the avenue became the place to meet for gossip, business and pleasure.

Today, the theatres, shops, cinemas and eateries along the stretch between the Admiralty and Anichkov Bridge, and the many cultural landmarks in the vicinity, are a big draw for visitors.

# ❿ Gostinyy Dvor

Гостиный двор
*Gostinyy dvor*

Nevskiy prospekt 35. **Map** 4 E2. **Tel** (812) 630 54 08. Ⓜ Gostinyy Dvor. **Open** 10am–1pm daily. 🌐 bgd.ru

The term *gostinyy dvor* originally meant a coaching inn, but as trade developed around the inns, with travelling merchants setting up their stalls, it later came to mean trading rows. The original wooden structure of this *gostinyy dvor* was destroyed by fire in 1736. It was replaced between 1761 and 1785 by a huge brick structure designed by Vallin de la Mothe. The columned arcades of the building form an irregular quadrangle, and the combined length of its façades is nearly 1,006 m (3,300 ft).

Serious damage during the Siege of Leningrad in 1941 led to major reconstruction, but even now, the original layout of "stalls" of individual trading units has been retained. The arcade offers a wide range of products and is the city's central supplier of basic goods and souvenirs.

Columned arcades at Gostinyy Dvor, St Petersburg's biggest department store

## ⓫ Ostrovskiy Square

Площадь Островского
*Ploshchad Ostrovskovo*

**Map** 4 F2. 🚌 3, 7, 22, 24, 27. 🚎 1, 5, 7, 10, 11, 22. Ⓜ Gostinyy Dvor. Russian National Library: **Tel** (812) 310 71 37. **Open** 9am–9pm Mon–Fri, 11am–9pm Sat & Sun. **Closed** last Tue of the month. Theatre Museum: **Tel** (812) 571 21 95. **Open** 11am–6pm Thu–Mon, 1–7pm Wed. **Closed** last Fri of the month and public hols. 🏛 📷
🌐 theatremuseum.ru

One of Russia's most brilliant architects, Carlo Rossi, created this early 19th-century square, now named in honour of the dramatist Aleksandr Ostrovskiy (1823–86). Its focal point is the elegant Alexandrinskiy Theatre, designed by Rossi in the Neo-Classical style, with a six-columned portico crowned by a chariot of Apollo. The theatre puts on an engaging repertoire, with productions of plays by dramatists from Checkhov and Gogol to Shakespeare.

### Carlo Rossi

Architect Carlo Rossi (1775–1849) was one of the last great exponents of Neo-Classicism in St Petersburg. He found an ideal client in Alexander I, who shared his belief in the use of architecture to express the power of the ruling autocracy. Rossi created no fewer than 12 of St Petersburg's streets and 13 of its squares. His status as Alexander I's favourite architect encouraged rumours that Rossi was the tsar's illegitimate son.

The palatial Russian Museum, designed by Carlo Rossi

In the garden is a monument to Catherine the Great. Unveiled in 1873, it depicts her surrounded by generals and statesmen. On the west side of the square is a colonnade decorated with Classical sculptures, which Rossi designed as an extension of the **Russian National Library**. Founded in 1795, the library currently holds more than 28 million items, including the personal library of the French philosopher Voltaire, which Catherine the Great purchased to show her appreciation of her mentor and correspondent.

In the southeast corner of the square, at No. 6, the **Theatre Museum** traces the evolution of the Russian stage from its origins in mid 18th century serf and imperial theatres. Amidst the eclectic array of playbills, photo-graphs, costumes, set designs and other artifacts, there are also some set designs by one of the great innovators of modern theatre, the director Vsevolod Meyerhold (1874–1940).

## ⓬ Ulitsa Zodchevo Rossi

Улица Зодчего Росси
*Ulitsa Zodchevo Rossi*

**Map** 4 E2. Ⓜ Gostinyy Dvor.

There could be no better memorial to Carlo Rossi than the architectural ensemble of arcades and colonnades forming Architect Rossi Street. The 22-m (72-ft) high buildings stand precisely 22 m (72 ft) apart and stretch for 220 m (720 ft). Seen from ploshchad Lomonosova, the perspective coaxes the eye towards the Alexandriinskiy Theatre.

At No. 2 is the home of the former Imperial Ballet School, now named after the teacher Agrippina Vaganova. The school began in 1738, when Jean-Baptiste Landé began training the children of palace servants to take part in court entertain-ment. It has produced many famous dancers, including Anna Pavlova and Rudolf Nureyev.

Porticoed façade of Alexandrinskiy Theatre, Ostrovskiy Square

# ⓭ Cathedral of Our Lady of Kazan

Собор Казанской Богоматери

*Sobor Kazanskoy Bogomateri*

Kazanskaya ploshchad 2. **Map** 4 D1. **Tel** (812) 314 46 63. ▣ 3, 7, 22, 24, 27, 191. Ⓜ Nevskiy Prospekt. ▣ 1, 5, 7, 10, 11, 22. **Open** 8:30am–8pm daily. ▣

This majestic cathedral was commissioned by Tsar Paul and took over a decade to build. Completed in 1811, it is linked with the wars against Napoleon fought during the same period. In fact, Field Marshal Mikhail Kutuzov (1745–1813), who masterminded the strategic retreat from Moscow following the invasion of Napoleon's Grande Armée in 1812, is buried here. His statue and that of his comrade-in-arms, Mikhail Barclay de Tolly (1761–1818), have stood outside the cathedral since 1837.

The cathedral is named after the miracle-working *Icon of Our Lady of Kazan*, kept within. Its design by serf architect Andrei Voronikhin was inspired by St Peter's Basilica in Rome. The 111-m (364-ft) long colonnade disguises the orientation of the building, which runs parallel to Nevskiy prospekt, conforming to a religious stipulation that the main altar face east. The 80-m (262-ft) high dome and the pink Finnish granite columns with bronze capitals and bases are its most impressive features.

Occupied in the Soviet era by a Museum of Atheism, the cathedral was returned to religious use in 1999.

Pink granite columns and mosaic floor in the main nave, Cathedral of Our Lady of Kazan

# ⓮ Stroganov Palace

Строгановский дворец

*Stroganovskiy dvorets*

Nevskiy prospekt 17. **Map** 4 D1. **Tel** (812) 571 82 38. ▣ 3, 7, 22, 24, 27, 191. Ⓜ Nevskiy Prospekt. ▣ 1, 5, 7, 10, 11, 17. **Open** 10am–6pm Mon, Wed & Fri–Sun, 1–9pm Thu. ▣

This Baroque masterpiece was designed in 1752–4 by Bartolomeo Rastrelli (*see p157*), for the enormously wealthy Count Sergei Stroganov, whose descendants occupied the palace until the Revolution. The Stroganov fortune was amassed mainly through the monopoly the family held on salt, mined from their territories in Siberia.

The pink-and-white palace, overlooking both Nevskiy prospekt and the Moyka river, was one of the city's most impressive private residences. Its splendid façade overlooking the Moyka is decorated with Doric columns, cornices and pediments. The windows proffer stunning views across the river.

The Stroganovs were noted collectors of everything from Egyptian antiquities and Roman coins to icons and Old Masters. After the Revolution, the family's collection was expropriated by the state, and the palace was turned into a museum on the life of the decadent aristocracy. The building now belongs to the Russian Museum (*see pp164–5*) and features temporary exhibitions.

The Stroganov family chef is believed to have invented the dish beef stroganoff.

The west façade of the Stroganov Palace overlooking the Moyka river

## ⓯ Academic Capella

Академическая капелла
*Akademicheskaya kapella*

Naberezhnaya Reki Moyki 20.
**Map** 2 D5. **Tel** (812) 314 10 58.
Ⓜ Nevskiy Prospekt. **Open** for concerts only. 🎷 📷

Enclosed within a courtyard off the Moyka river is this ochre-coloured concert hall with a façade in the French Classical style of Louis XV. The Academic Capella was designed by Leontiy Benois in 1887–9 as the residence of the Imperial Court choir. Founded during the reign of Peter the Great, the choir is hence almost as old as the city itself. Its former directors have included the distinguished Russian composers Mikhail Glinka (1804–57) and Nikolai Rimsky-Korsakov (1844–1908).

With its superb acoustics, the Academic Capella claims to be one of the best concert halls in the world. Outside is the Singers' Bridge (Pevcheskiy Most), which was designed by Yegor Adam between 1837 and 1840.

Academic Capella concert hall, known for its excellent acoustics

## ⓰ Pushkin House-Museum

Музей-квартира А. С. Пушкина
*Muzey-kvartira AS Pushkina*

Naberezhnaya Reki Moyki 12. **Map** 2 D5.
**Tel** (812) 571 35 31. **Open** 10:30am–6pm Wed–Mon. **Closed** last Fri of the month and public hols. 🎷 📷

Every year on the anniversary of Alexander Pushkin's death on 10 February 1837, loyal devotees of Russia's greatest poet come to lay floral tributes outside his apartment. Pushkin was born in Moscow in 1799 but spent many years in St Petersburg.

Pushkin's study, with his desk and library carefully preserved, Pushkin House-Museum

He settled in this fairly opulent apartment overlooking the Moyka, with his wife Natalya, their four children and Natalya's two sisters, from the autumn of 1836 until his death. It was here on the couchette in the study that he bled to death after his duel with d'Anthès *(see p93)*.

Some half a dozen rooms on the first floor have been refurbished in the Empire style of the period. The most evocative of them is Pushkin's study, which is arranged exactly as it was when he died. On the writing table is an ivory paper knife given to the poet by his sister, a bronze handbell and a treasured inkstand. Embellished with the figure of an Ethiopian boy, the inkstand is a reminder of Pushkin's Ethiopian great-grandfather, Abram Hannibal. Bought by the Russian ambassador in Constantinople as a slave in 1706, Hannibal served as a general under Peter the Great and was the inspiration for the unfinished novel on which Pushkin was working at the time of his death.

On the wall in front of his desk is a Turkish sabre presented to Pushkin in the Caucasus, where he had been exiled in 1820 for his radical views, and where he spent some of his happiest years. It was there that he began his most famous work, *Eugene Onegin*, a novel in verse written from 1823 to 1830. Pushkin's library contains more than 4,500 volumes

in 14 European and Oriental languages, including works by Shakespeare, Byron, Heine, Dante and Voltaire.

## ⓱ Imperial Stables

Конюшенное Ведомство
*Konyushennoe Vedomstvo*

Konyushennaya ploshchad 1.
**Map** 2 E5. Church: **Open** 10am–7pm daily. 📷

The long, salmon-coloured building running parallel to the Moyka embankment is the former Imperial Stables. Originally built in the first part of the 18th century, the stables were reconstructed by Vasily Stasov between 1817 and 1823.

The only part of the building open to the public lies behind the central section of the long south façade, crowned by a silver dome and cross. This is the church where Alexander Pushkin's funeral took place on 10 February 1837. Its Neo-Classical interior is in the form of a basilica and is decorated with yellow marble pillars. It is now a functioning Orthodox church.

North façade of the Imperial Stables

# SENNAYA PLOSHCHAD

The western part of St Petersburg is an area of contrasts. While it boasts some of the city's wealthiest residences, the area is also home to poverty-stricken dwellings. The palatial 18th-century architecture along the Neva embankment is a world away from the decrepit living quarters around bustling Sennaya Ploshchad, which have changed little since Fyodor Dostoevsky described them in *Crime and Punishment*. In between these two areas lies the old maritime quarter. Once extending from the timber warehouses in New Holland to St Nicholas's Cathedral,

it was inhabited by Peter the Great's shipwrights. This serene area, however, has much to offer. Its focal point is the marvellous Theatre Square, which has been a major entertainment hub since the mid-18th century. Dominated by the Mariinskiy Theatre and the Rimsky-Korsakov Conservatory, this is where many of Russia's greatest artists began their careers. Before the 1917 Revolution, many theatre directors, actors, ballerinas and musicians lived in the surrounding area. Today, artists are returning here, attracted by the tranquility of its tree-lined canal embankments.

## Sights at a Glance

**Theatres**
1 Mariinskiy Theatre

**Churches and Cathedrals**
2 St Nicholas's Cathedral

**Historic Buildings and Areas**
3 Rimsky-Korsakov Conservatory
4 New Holland
6 Main Post Office

**Palaces**
5 Yusupov Palace

**Museums**
7 Railway Museum

**Streets and Squares**
8 Sennaya Ploshchad

*See Street Finder, maps 3 & 4*

◀ Sumptuous interior of Yusupov Palace

**For keys to symbols** *see back flap*

# Street-by-Street: Theatre Square

Known as Carousel Square till the 1780s, Theatre Square was frequently used as the site for fairs and festivals. During the 19th century, when St Petersburg became the cultural capital of Russia, the Mariinskiy Theatre and Rimsky-Korsakov Conservatory were established and the neighbourhood became home to many artists. Today, the tradition of entertainment is still thriving and Theatre Square remains a focal point for theatrical and musical life. Nearby, the tree-lined canal embankments and the gardens surrounding the beautiful St Nicholas's Cathedral are enchanting places to explore.

NAB REKI MOYKI

ULITSA DEKABRISTOV

Mariinskiy II

TEATRA

NAB KRYUKOVA KANALA

PRO

**5 Yusupov Palace**
Historic site of the gruesome murder of Rasputin, this grand palace belonged to the wealthy Yusupov family. Its opulent interiors include an Italian marble staircase and a tiny Rococo theatre.

**The monument to Rimsky-Korsakov**, who taught at the Conservatory for 37 years, was designed by Veniamin Bogolyubov and Vladimir Ingal and erected here in 1952.

**3 Rimsky-Korsakov Conservatory**
Tchaikovsky, Prokofiev and Shostakovich were among the talents nurtured by Russia's first conservatory, founded in 1862 by pianist and composer Anton Rubinstein.

Monument to Mikhail Glinka

**1 ★ Mariinskiy Theatre**
This theatre has been home to the world-famous Mariinskiy (Kirov) Opera and Ballet Company since 1860. Hidden behind its imposing façade is the sumptuous auditorium where many of Russia's greatest dancers have performed.

*For hotels and restaurants in this area see p268 and p286*

**The Lion Bridge**
This bridge is one of a number of quaint suspension bridges on the tree-lined Griboedov Canal. They are well-known meeting places, notably for romantic trysts.

Area illustrated

**The House of Mikhail Fokin** at No. 109 is where the renowned ballet master and choreographer lived before the Revolution.

**The Benois House** belonged to an artistic dynasty that included the co-founder of the World of Art movement, Alexandre Benois.

**The Belfry**, an elegant four-tiered structure with a gilded spire, was built to mark the main entrance to St Nicholas's Cathedral.

NAB KANALA GRIBOEDOVA

KOVO-KORSAKOVA

NIKOLSKIY PEREULOK

KANAL GRIBOEDOVA

SADOVAYA ULITSA

**2 St Nicholas's Cathedral**
A fine example of 18th-century Russian Baroque, the lofty upper church is richly decorated with icons, gilding and a carved iconostasis. The lower church, beautifully lit with candles, is also open for worship.

**The Former Nicholas Market**
Characterized by its long arcade and steep roof, this building was constructed in 1788–9. In the 19th century, it became an unofficial labour exchange and many unemployed workers gathered here.

**Key**

— Suggested route

| 0 metres | 100 |
| 0 yards | 100 |

The ornately decorated royal box in the Mariinskiy Theatre

# ❶ Mariinskiy Theatre

Мариинский театр

*Mariinskiy teatr*

Teatralnaya ploshchad 1 and ulitsa Dekabristov 34 & 37. **Map** 3 B3. **Tel** (812) 346 41 41. 🚎 2, 3, 6, 22, 27, 71, K-1, K-2, K-62, K-124, K-154, K-169, K-186, K-350. 🚋 5, 22. **Open** for performances. 🎭🎫🎬🏛 **W** mariinsky.ru

Named in honour of Tsarina Maria Alexandrovna, wife of Alexander II, the Mariinskiy Theatre is still better known abroad by its Soviet title, the Kirov, despite having reverted to its original name. The original building was erected in 1860 by the architect Albert Kavos, who designed the Bolshoi Theatre *(see pp82–3)* in Moscow. It stands on the site of an earlier theatre that was destroyed by fire. The Neo-Renaissance façade was remodelled between 1883 and

Imperial eagle on the royal box

1896 by Viktor Schröter, who added a lot of ornamental detail.

The pale blue-and-gold auditorium, where so many illustrious dancers have made their debut, creates a dazzling impression. Its architectural design comprising columns, atlantes, cherubs and cameo medallions has remained unchanged since the theatre's completion, and the imperial eagles have been restored to the royal box. The painting of dancing girls and cupids on the ceiling by Enrico Franchioli dates from around 1856, while the superb stage curtain was added during Russian ballet's golden age in 1914. Equally remarkable is the festive foyer, decorated with fluted pilasters, bas-reliefs of Russian composers and mirrored doors.

Although the Mariinskiy Theatre is better known abroad for its ballet company, it is also

one of Russia's leading opera houses. Most of the great 19th-century Russian operas premiered here, including Mussorgsky's *Boris Godunov* (1874), Tchaikovsky's *Queen of Spades* (1890) and Shostakovich's controversial opera *Lady Macbeth of Mtsensk* (1934).

A concert hall, built in 2007, and a second opera and ballet stage, created in 2013, complete the original theatre complex.

# ❷ St Nicholas's Cathedral

Никольский собор

*Nikolskiy sobor*

Nikolskaya ploshchad 1/3. **Map** 3 B4. **Tel** (812) 714 08 62. 🚎 2, 3, 22, 27, 49, 71, 181, K-2, K-19, K-154, K-212. **Open** 6:30am–7:30pm daily.

This stunning Baroque cathedral was built between 1753 and 1762 by Savva Chevakinsky, one of Russia's great 18th-century architects. Founded for sailors and Admiralty employees housed in the neighbourhood, and named after St Nicholas, the patron saint of sailors, the cathedral came to be known as the "Sailors' Church".

The magnificent exterior is decorated with white Corinthian pilasters and surmounted by five gilded cupolas. Nearby, within the cathedral's leafy grounds and overlooking the intersection of the Kryukov and Griboedov canals, is a slender, four-tiered bell tower crowned by a spire.

Pale blue-and-white Baroque façade of St Nicholas's Cathedral

Following the Russian tradition, there are two churches within the cathedral. The lower church, intended for daily use, is lit by icon lamps, candles and chandeliers, creating a magical effect. Painted in 1755–7, the icons are the work of the brothers Fedot and Menas Kolokolnikov.

In total contrast, the upper church, used mainly on Sundays and for weddings, has a brighter, more airy feel and a typically Baroque exuberance, with gilt and stucco ornamentation and Italianate paintings. Its most impressive feature is the magnificent gilded iconostasis dating from 1755–60.

## ❸ Rimsky-Korsakov Conservatory

Консерватория
Римского-Корсакова
*Konservatoriya imeni
Rimskovo-Korsakova*

Teatralnaya ploshchad 3. **Map** 3 B3.
**Tel** (812) 571 85 74. 🚌 2, 3, 6, 22, 27, 71, K-1, K-2, K-62, K-124, K-154, K-169, K-186, K-350. 🚋 5, 22. **Open** for performances only. 📷 📷 by appointment, call (812) 312 25 07.

Russia's oldest music school, the Rimsky-Korsakov Conservatory was founded in 1862 by Anton Rubinstein. The present building was designed in 1896 by Vladimir Nicolas.

Among those to graduate from the school before the Revolution were Pyotr Tchaikovsky *(see p115)* and Sergei Prokofiev. In the Soviet years, the school continued to flourish, and the greatest musical figure to emerge from this era was composer Dmitri Shostakovich (1906–75).

In the forecourt outside the school are two statues. On the left, a 1952 memorial honours the school's influential teacher, Nikolai Rimsky-Korsakov, after whom the conservatory is now named. On the right, the statue of Mikhail Glinka by Robert Bach is a reminder that the conservatory stands on the site where Russia's first opera, Glinka's *A Life for the Tsar*, was premiered in 1836 in the old Kamennyy (Stone) Theatre.

Vallin de la Mothe's impressive arch on the Moyka, leading into New Holland

## ❹ New Holland

Новая Голландия
*Novaya Gollandiya*

Admiral Teyskovo kanala 2. **Map** 3 A2.
🚌 3, 6, 22, 27, 70, 100, K-169, K-350.
🚋 5, 22. **Open** 11am–10pm Mon–Thu (till 11pm Fri–Sun).

Created when the Kryukov canal was constructed between the Moyka and Neva rivers in 1719, this island was originally used for storing flammable ship timber. It is named after Dutch shipbuilders, who inspired Peter the Great's naval ambitions. In 1765, the original wooden warehouses were rebuilt in red-brick by Savva Chevakinsky, while Vallin de la Mothe designed an austere but impressive arch facing the Moyka. Barges would pass through the arch and into a turning basin beyond, then return loaded with timber along the canals towards the Admiralty shipyards. A cultural complex is now open to visitors after years of reconstruction.

### Russian Ballet

Admired throughout the world, Russian ballet traces its origins back to 1738 when a French dancing master, Jean-Baptiste Landé, established a school in St Petersburg to train the children of palace employees. The Imperial Ballet School, as it soon became known, flourished under a string of distinguished foreign teachers, culminating in Marius Petipa. French-born Petipa first joined the school in 1847 as a principal dancer, and later choreographed over 60 ballets.

Following the 1905 Revolution, a reaction against Classicism led to numerous defections from the imperial theatres to Sergei Diaghilev's Ballets Russes, which took Europe by storm in 1909. Diaghilev's vision of a spectacle that would fuse music, ballet and decor in a seamless whole was shared by the choreographer Mikhail Fokin, and such talented costume and set designers as Léon Bakst and Alexandre Benois.

After the Bolsheviks seized power in 1917 many artists went into exile abroad. Fortunately for Soviet Russia, the prima ballerina Agrippina Vaganova remained to train the next generation of dancers. St Petersburg's Russian Ballet Academy now bears her name.

Vera Fokina and Mikhail Fokin in a production of *Scheherazade*

## ❺ Yusupov Palace
Юсуповский дворец
*Yusupovskiy dvorets*

Naberezhnaya Reki Moyki 94.
**Map** 3 B2. **Tel** (812) 314 98 83.
🚌 3, 22, 27. **Open** 11am–5pm daily.
🎧 guided tours only. 🔊 English.
**W** yusupov-palace.ru

Overlooking the Moyka river, this yellow, colonnaded building dating from the 1760s was designed by Vallin de la Mothe. The palace was acquired in 1830 by the Yusupov family to house their collection of paintings. Four generations of Yusupovs have lived here and, with the help of architects such as Andrei Mikhailov, Ippolito Monighetti and Andrei Vaitens, added their personal styles to the interiors.

The palace and its ceremonial rooms can be viewed by guided or audio tour. Notable rooms include the Moorish Room, with its fountain, mosaics and arches and the Turkish Study, built at the same time for Prince Nikolai Yusupov. His father, Prince Boris, commissioned the ballroom, and a Rococo-style family theatre that seats just 180. Today, it is a

wonderful venue for concerts. Separate tickets are needed for the tour of the cellars, which house an exhibition on Grigori Rasputin, the infamous "holy man" who was murdered here by Prince Felix Yusupov.

## ❻ Main Post Office
Главпочтамт
*Glavpochtamt*

Pochtamtskaya ulitsa 9. **Map** 3 B2.
**Tel** (812) 314 23 71. 🚌 3, 22, 27, 70, 100, K-169, K-187, K-306. 🚎 5, 22.
**Open** 24 hrs daily.

The main exterior feature of this building is the arched gallery spanning Pochtamtskaya ulitsa. Built as an extension to architect Nikolai Lvov's main building, the gallery was added by Albert Kavos in 1859. Under the "Pochtamt" (Post Office) sign on the arch is a clock showing the time in major cities around the world.

Inside the post office, behind Lvov's porticoed Neo-Classical façade built between 1782 and 1789, is a splendid Style-Moderne hall. It is characterized

Porticoed façade and arched gallery, Main Post Office

by decorative ironwork and a glass ceiling over the vast, tiled floor space. The hall was created in the early 20th century when a roof was constructed over what had originally been the courtyard stables.

### The Grim Death of Rasputin

The Siberian peasant and mystic Grigori Rasputin (1869–1916) exercised an extraordinarily powerful influence over the court and government of Russia. The mysterious circumstances of his dramatic death on 30 December 1916 are legendary. Lured to Yusupov's palace on the pretext of a party, Rasputin was poisoned, then shot by Prince Felix Yusupov and left for dead. On returning to the scene, the prince found Rasputin still alive, and a struggle ensued before Rasputin fled into the courtyard. He was pursued by the conspirators, shot another three times and brutally battered before being dumped in the Neva river. His corpse was found three days later, clinging to the supports of a bridge. Water in his lungs indicated death by drowning.

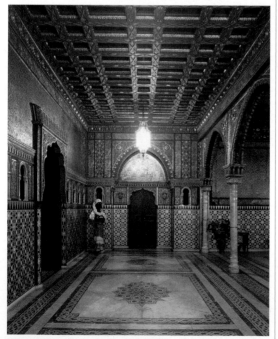

Islamic arches and coffered ceiling in the Moorish Room, Yusupov Palace

## ❼ Railway Museum

Музей железнодорожного
транспорта
*Muzey zheleznodorozhnovo
transporta*

Sadovaya ulitsa 50. **Map** 3 C3. **Tel** (812)
315 14 76. **M** Sennaya ploshchad,
Sadovaya, Spasskaya. **Open** 10:30am–
5pm Sun–Thu. **Closed** last Thu of the
month. 🗆 English.

This museum houses more than
6,000 exhibits that illustrate the
history of the Russian railway
system since 1813. The most
interesting sections of the
museum deal with the earliest
railways, including Russia's first
railway line from Tsarskoe Selo
*(see pp188–9)* to St Petersburg,
which began running in 1837,
and the 650-km (404-mile) line
from Moscow to St Petersburg,
which began operating in 1851.

Exhibits include models of
the first Russian steam engine,
built by the Cherepanovs in
1834, and an armoured train
used in the defence of the city
during the Civil War. The walk-
through section of a first-class
sleeping compartment offers an
insight into luxury travel in the
late Tsarist period. The compartment is furnished with Style-
Moderne decoration.

## ❽ Sennaya Ploshchad

Сенная площадь
*Sennaya ploshchad*

**Map** 4 D3. **M** Sennaya Ploshchad,
Sadovaya, Spasskaya.

One of the oldest squares in
St Petersburg, Sennaya Ploshchad,
meaning Haymarket, derives
from the original market that
opened here in the 1730s,
where livestock, fodder and
firewood were sold. A 10-minute
stroll from Nevskiy prospekt,
the area around the square was
inhabited by the poor and the
market was the cheapest and
liveliest in the city. The oldest
building at the centre of the
square is the former guard-
house. A Neo-Classical structure
with a columned portico, it dates
from 1818. By that time the
neighbourhood had become
synonymous with dirt, squalor,

Model of a 1830s engine for the Tsarskoe Selo railway, Railway Museum

crime and vice. The guards'
duties ranged from supervising
traders to flogging serfs for mis-
demeanours. At No. 3 is the site
of Vyazemskiy's Monastery,
the nickname for a notorious
tenement overrun with pubs,
gambling dens and brothels
in the 1850s and 1860s.

This was the squalid world
so vividly evoked in Fyodor
Dostoevsky's masterpiece *Crime
and Punishment*. As the con-
temptuous hero of the novel,
Raskolnikov, wanders around
the market, he absorbs the
"heat in the street… the
airlessness, the bustle and
the plaster, scaffolding, bricks
and dust… that special St
Petersburg stench… and the
numerous drunken men" which
"completed the revolting misery

of the picture". The novel
was completed in 1866 while
Dostoevsky was living at Alonkin's
House at No. 7 Przhevalskovo
ulitsa to the west of the square.

During the Soviet era, the
square was given a new image –
stallholders were banished, trees
were planted and it was
optimistically renamed Peace
Square (ploshchad Mira). The
five-storey, yellow-and-white
apartment blocks that surround
the square today were also
built then, in Stalin's version of
Neo-Classicism. Sadly, in 1961,
the square's most attractive
monument, the Church of the
Assumption, was pulled down
to make way for one of the city's
earliest metro stations. Today,
there are numerous fast-food
stalls and all-night shops here.

### Fyodor Dostoevsky

One of Russia's greatest writers,
Fyodor Dostoevsky was born in
1821 in Moscow but spent most
of his adult life in St Petersburg,
where many of his novels and
short stories are set. A defining
moment in his life occurred in
1849 when he was arrested
and charged with revolutionary
conspiracy. After eight months'
solitary confinement in the Peter
and Paul Fortress *(see pp136–7)*,
Dostoevsky and 21 other
"conspirators" from the socialist
Petrashevsky Circle were subjected
to a macabre mock execution
before being exiled to hard
labour in Siberia until 1859.
The experience turned him from a socialist into an ardent
supporter of autocracy and Orthodoxy. Unfortunately for him,
the police continued to regard him as a subversive. He died of
tuberculosis in 1881.

# FURTHER AFIELD

While the majority of St Petersburg's sights are centrally located, the outlying areas of the city have a number of places of architectural, cultural and historical importance. To the east is the Smolnyy district, taking its name from the tar yard that supplied the city's ship-building industry in the 18th century. The highlight of this area is the dazzling Baroque Smolnyy Convent. Designed by Bartolomeo Rastrelli, the convent is a brilliant amalgamation of Western and Russian Baroque styles. Part of the same architectural complex, the Smolnyy Institute is famed for its historic role as the headquarters of the Bolshevik movement during the October Revolution. Southeast of the centre lies the Alexander Nevsky Monastery, where many of Russia's celebrated artists, architects and composers are buried. The southern suburbs offer a different perspective of the city, with rows of imperious-looking houses dating from the 1930s – a legacy of Stalin's urban planning. Other intriguing sights in the south are the stunning Chesma Church and the Victory Monument, a memorial to the victims of the Siege of Leningrad.

## Sights at a Glance

### Historic Buildings and Monuments

❶ Yelagin Palace
❸ Piskarevskoe Memorial Cemetery
❹ Finland Station
❼ Tauride Palace
❾ Smolnyy Institute
❿ Sheremetev Palace
⑭ Victory Monument

### Museums

❷ Erarta
❺ Stieglitz Museum
⑪ Dostoevsky House-Museum

### Churches and Cathedrals

❻ Cathedral of the Transfiguration
❽ Smolnyy Convent
⑫ Alexander Nevsky Monastery
⑬ Chesma Church

### Key

▬ Central St Petersburg
▬ Main road
═ Minor road
— Railway

◀ Snow-covered monastic buildings, Alexander Nevsky Monastery

**For keys to symbols** *see back flap*

The Neo-Classical Yelagin Palace and its spacious grounds, designed by Carlo Rossi

# ❶ Yelagin Palace

Елагин дворец

*Yelagin dvorets*

Yelagin ostrov 1. **Tel** (812) 430 11 31.
Ⓜ Krestovskiy ostrov. **Open** 10am–
6:30pm Tue–Sun. **Closed** last Tue of
month. 🏛 🖼 🚹 ground floor.

One of the northernmost islands
of St Petersburg, Yelagin Island is
named after a court official who
built a palace here at the end of
the 18th century. Alexander I
then bought the island in 1817
for his mother, Maria Fyodorovna,
and commissioned Carlo Rossi
to rebuild the palace. The Neo-
Classical edifice, built from 1818
to 1822, includes an orangery, a
horseshoe-shaped stable block
and porticoed kitchens.

The palace interior was
destroyed by fire during World
War II but has now been restored
to its former glory. The Oval Hall
is resplendent with statuary and
*trompe l'oeils* while the rooms
leading from it are exquisitely
decorated with stucco, *faux
marble* (false marble) and
painted friezes, executed by
gifted artists and craftsmen.

Statue of Mother Russia at the Piskarevskoe
Memorial Cemetery

In the Soviet era, the island
became the Central Park of
Culture and Rest. Today, it is a
venue for festivals and entertainment, and the palace's former
stables display decorative art.

# ❷ Erarta

Эрарта

*Erarta*

29-ya Liniya 2, Vasilievskoy Ostrov.
**Tel** (812) 324 08 09. Ⓜ Primorskaya.
**Open** 10am–10pm Wed–Mon. 🖼 🖳
🆆 **erarta.com**.

Housed within a former Soviet-
era research institute, Erarta
is Russia's largest contemporary
art museum. Its permanent
collection consists of over 2,000
paintings, drawings, sculptures,
installations and other forms of
art by more than 170 artists from
across Russia, dating from 1945
to the present day. It also hosts
temporary exhibitions, concerts,
film screenings and lectures.

# ❸ Piskarevskoe Memorial Cemetery

Пискаревское мемориальное
кладбище

*Piskarevskoe memorialnoe
kladbishche*

Prospekt Nepokorennykh 72–74.
**Tel** (812) 297 57 16. 🚌 61, 80, 123,
138, 178. Ⓜ Akademicheskaya,
Ploschad Muzhestva. **Open** 24 hrs
daily. Memorial Halls: **Open** 9am–
6pm daily. 🖼

This vast, bleak cemetery is a
memorial to the two million
people who died during the
Siege of Leningrad *(see p45)*. With
little food and no electricity,

water or heating, the citizens of
Leningrad perished from
starvation, cold and disease.
Corpses were taken for burial to
mass cemeteries on the outskirts of town. Piskarevskoe was
the largest, with 490,000 burials.

Today, the cemetery is a place
of pilgrimage. The memorial
opened in 1960, on the 15th
anniversary of the end of the
war. Two halls, one of which
contains an exhibition on the
siege, flank the stairs down to
an avenue, which culminates in
a towering, heroic bronze statue
of Mother Russia.

# ❹ Finland Station

Финляндский вокзал

*Finlyandskiy vokzal*

Ploschad Lenina 6.
Ⓜ Ploschad Lenina.

On the night of 3 April 1917,
the exiled Vladimir Lenin and his
Bolshevik companions arrived
at Finland Station after travelling
from Switzerland on a sealed
train. A triumphant reception
awaited them, and, Lenin spoke
to cheering crowds from the
turret of an armoured car. A 1926
statue outside the station depicts
Lenin delivering his speech.

The modern terminal at
Finland Station was opened in
the 1960s. On platform 5 there is
a huge glass case containing
Locomotive 293 in which Lenin
fled the capital for a second time
in July 1917, disguised as an
engine stoker. After spending
the summer as a fugitive in
Russian Finland, Lenin returned
on the same train and spurred
on the October Revolution.

## ❺ Stieglitz Museum

Музей Штиглица
*Muzey Shtiglitsa*

Solyanoy pereulok 13–15. **Tel** (812)
273 32 58. 🚌 46, K-76, K-100, K-217.
**Open** Sep–Jul: 11am–5pm Tue–Sat.
**Closed** last Fri of month. 🅿️ ✅

The millionaire industrialist
Baron Aleksandr Stieglitz
founded the Central School of
Industrial Design in 1876. His
aim was to provide a top-quality
collection of original works for
the use of Russian students of
applied arts and design.

With a large budget and the
good taste of Stieglitz's son-in-
law, the collection soon outgrew the school, and in 1896 a
Museum of Applied Arts opened
next door. This building, designed
by Maximilian Messmacher, was
inspired by Italian Renaissance
palaces. Inside, the halls and
galleries were decorated in
national and period styles,
echoing French and German
Baroque and Italian Renaissance
monuments, such as St Mark's
Library in Venice and the
Raphael Loggias of the Vatican.

Situated on the ground floor,
the exhibition features opulent
displays of glassware, ceramics
and majolica, as well as porcelain
from all the great European
manufacturers. One room,
decorated in the style of the
medieval Terem Palace *(see p60)*
in the Kremlin, provides a
superb backdrop for a collection

of embroidered dresses and
headgear made by Russian
peasant women. The workman-
ship seen on the wooden
furniture is breathtaking. A Neo-
Gothic cabinet with finely inlaid
doors, depicting church naves
in perspective, opens to reveal
sculpted biblical scenes.

A last look at the Grand
Exhibition Hall with its curving
staircase of Italian marble and
magnificent glass roof is a fine
way to end the visit.

## ❻ Cathedral of the Transfiguration

Спасо-Преображенский собор
*Spaso-Preobrazhenskiy sobor*

Preobrazhenskaya ploshchad 1.
**Tel** (812) 272 36 62. 🚌 46, K-76,
K-90, K-177, K-258. 🚎 3, 8, 15.
Ⓜ Chernyshevskaya.
**Open** 8am–8pm daily.

Despite its monumental
Neo-Classicism and the
surrounding fence made of
guns captured during the
Russo-Turkish wars, Vasily
Stasov's church has an intimate
air, nestled in its leafy square.
The original church on this site
was built by Tsarina Elizabeth
to honour the Preobrazhenskiy
Guards, but it was rebuilt after
a fire in 1825. Today, the church
is famous for its excellent
choir – second only to that
in the Alexander Nevsky
Monastery *(see p183)*.

Tauride Palace, nestled among abundant
gardens on the banks of a quiet lake

## ❼ Tauride Palace

Таврический дворец
*Tavricheskiy dvorets*

Shpalernaya ulitsa 47.
Ⓜ Chernyshevskaya. 🚌 46, 136.
**Closed** to public.

This finely proportioned palace
by Ivan Starov was built
between 1783 and 1789 as
a present from Catherine the
Great to her influential lover
Prince Grigori Potemkin. Having
successfully annexed the
Crimea (Tauris) to Russia in
1783, Potemkin was given the
title of Prince of Tauris, hence
the palace's name. The building,
with its austere yellow façade
and distinctive six-columned
portico, was one of Russia's
first Neo-Classical structures.

Despite its magnificent
interiors having been ruined
by Catherine's son, Paul, who
turned the palace into barracks
after 1799, it went on to play
a vital role in 20th-century
political life. After the 1905
Revolution forced Tsar Nicholas II
to permit a Russian parliament,
or State Duma, the palace
became the seat of parliament.
Following the overthrow of the
monarchy after the February
Revolution of 1917, it became
the headquarters of the
Provisional Government, and
then the Petrograd Soviet of
Workers' and Soldiers' Deputies,
in 1918. Today, it is still a
government building.

The palace's gardens, with
winding streams, bridges and
an artificial lake, are among
the city's most popular parks.

Dolls in 17th- to 19th-century Russian folk costumes, Stieglitz Museum

Façade of the cathedral with adjacent buildings, Smolnyy Convent complex

## ❽ Smolnyy Convent

Смольный монастырь
*Smolnyy monastyr*

Ploshchad Rastrelli 3/1.
**Tel** (812) 710 31 59. 🚌 46, 136.
**Open** 10:30am–6pm Thu–Tue. 🎧
🎫 English. ♿

In 1748, Tsarina Elizabeth commissioned Bartolomeo Rastrelli to design a convent for the education of young noblewomen. He conceived a brilliant fusion of Russian and Western Baroque styles and incorporated it into the design of this architectural ensemble, whose centrepiece is the stunning cathedral. Work advanced very slowly; 50,000 wooden piles had to be sunk into the marshy soil before construction could begin.

When Catherine the Great came to power in 1762, funding stopped, and it was only in 1835 that Nicholas I commissioned Vasiliy Stasov to complete the cathedral. His austere white interior contrasts dramatically with the florid exterior.

Exhibitions and weekly concerts are now held here.

## ❾ Smolnyy Institute

Смольный Институт
*Smolnyy Institut*

Smolnyy proezd 1. **Tel** (812) 576 74 61, (812) 576 77 46. 🚌 46, 54, 74, 136, K-15, K-76, K-136. 🚃 5, 7, 11, 15, 16.
Smolnyy Museum: **Open** 11am–4pm Mon–Fri, by appointment only.
🎧 🎫 English. ♿

As the school for noblewomen outgrew its premises at the Smolnyy Convent, Giacomo

Quarenghi built an adjacent Neo-Classical structure between 1806 and 1808, which came to be known as the Smolnyy Institute.

It was from here, in October 1917, that Lenin directed the Bolshevik coup d'état against the Provisional Government. The Smolnyy Institute remained Lenin's seat of government until March 1918, after which it became the headquarters of the Leningrad Communist Party. On 1 December 1934, the First Secretary of the party, Sergei Kirov *(see p141)* was murdered here, providing the pretext for Stalin's great purges *(see p45)*.

The rooms where Lenin lived and worked can be viewed by appointment. The rest of the institute is now the Mayor's Office. The imperial eagle has replaced the hammer and sickle, but the statue of Lenin has survived.

Painting of Vladimir Lenin, Smolnyy Institute Assembly Hall

## ❿ Sheremetev Palace

Шереметевский дворец
*Sheremetevskiy dvorets*

Naberezhnaya Reki Fontanki 34.
🚌 15, 22, 27, K-15, K-90, K-187, K-258.
Ⓜ Mayakovskaya, Gostinyy Dvor.
🚃 1, 5, 7, 10, 22. Museum of Musical Life: **Tel** (812) 272 44 41. **Open** 1–9pm Wed, 11am–7pm Thu–Mon.
**Closed** last Wed of the month. 🎧
🎫 Anna Akhmatova Museum:
**Tel** (812) 579 72 39. **Open** 10:30am–6pm Tue & Thu–Sun, noon–8pm Wed.
🎧 🎫 English.

Also known as the "Fountain House" after the fountains that once adorned its grounds, this palace was the home of the Sheremetev family from 1712 until the Revolution. The family were great artistic patrons, and the palace is now home to the **Museum of Musical Life**. Exhibits include period instruments and several scores, some composed by the Sheremetevs themselves.

The great poetess Anna Akhmatova (1889–1966) lived in one of the service blocks from 1933 to 1941 and then between 1944 and 1954. Her flat is now the **Anna Akhmatova Museum** and is reached through the courtyard of No. 53 Liteynyy prospekt. Visitors can see some of her personal possessions, and listen to recordings of the poetess reading her poems. Her most famous poem, *Requiem*, relating her experiences during the purges when both her son and her lover were arrested, was written in fragments in 1935–40.

## ⓫ Dostoevsky House-Museum

Музей Достоевского
*Muzey Dostoevskovo*

Kuznechnyy pereulok 5/2. **Tel** (812) 571 40 31. Ⓜ Vladimirskaya. 🚃 49.
**Open** 11am–6pm Tue–Sun. 🎧
🎫 English.

This evocative museum was the final home of Russian author Fyodor Dostoevsky, who lived here from 1878 until his death in 1881. It was here that he completed his last great novel, *The Brothers Karamazov,* in 1880.

Although his public image was dour and humourless, he was a devoted and affectionate husband and father. The delightful nursery contains a rocking horse, silhouettes of his children and the book of fairy tales that he read aloud to them. In Dostoevsky's study are his writing desk and a reproduction of his favourite painting, Raphael's *Sistine Madonna*.

## ⑫ Alexander Nevsky Monastery

Александро-Невская лавра
*Aleksandro-Nevskaya lavra*

Ploshchad Aleksandra Nevskovo. **Tel** (812) 274 17 02. 8, 27, 46, 55, 58, 191, K-156, K-187, K-209. Ploshchad Aleksandra Nevskovo. 1, 14, 16, 22. 7, 65. Church of the Annunciation: **Tel** (812) 274 17 02. **Open** 11am–5pm Tue, Wed & Fri–Sun (till 6pm in summer). Holy Trinity Cathedral: **Open** 6am–8pm daily. Cemeteries & Church of the Annunciation:

Founded by Peter the Great in 1710, this monastery is named after Prince Alexander Nevsky of Novgorod, who defeated the Swedes in 1240. From the entrance, a path runs between two walled cemeteries into the monastic complex. Many leading cultural figures are buried in these cemeteries. The Lazarus Cemetery, to the east, contains the graves of the polymath Mikhail Lomonosov and Carlo Rossi *(see p167)*. Clustered together along the northern wall of the Tikhvin Cemetery, to the west, are the tombs of some of Russia's most famous composers; many of the tombs

Reliquary with Alexander Nevsky's remains, Holy Trinity Cathedral

are inscribed with musical motifs. Fyodor Dostoevsky is buried here, to the right of the entrance.

The oldest building in the monastery complex is the **Church of the Annunciation**, built in 1717–25. Non-ruling members of the royal family are buried here. However, the Neo-Classical **Holy Trinity Cathedral**, constructed from 1776 to 1790 by Ivan Starov, dominates the complex. To the right of the iconostasis is a silver reliquary with the remains of Alexander Nevsky, who has been venerated as a saint in Russia since the mid-16th century.

## ⑬ Chesma Church

Чесменская церковь
*Chesmenskaya tserkov*

Ulitsa Lensoveta 12. **Tel** (812) 373 61 14. 16, 39. Moskovskaya. 29, 45. **Open** 9am–7pm.

There is hardly anything Russian about the Chesma Church built by Yuri Velten between 1777 and 1780. Its "pastry Gothic" façade is decorated with

vertical stripes which direct the eye upwards to its zig-zagged crown and cupolas. The name commemorates the Russian naval victory over the Turks at Chesma in the Aegean in 1770.

Across the street is the Chesma Palace that served as a staging post for Catherine the Great en route to Tsarskoe Selo *(see pp188–9)*. Rasputin's body lay in state here after his murder. The palace now serves as a home for the elderly.

## ⑭ Victory Monument

Монумент Защитникам Ленинграда
*Monument Zashchitnikam Leningrada*

Ploshchad Pobedy. **Tel** (812) 371 29 51, (812) 373 65 63. 3, 11, 13, 39, 59, 90, 150, 187, K-13, K-100, K-350. Moskovskaya. 27, 29, 45. Memorial Hall: **Open** 11am–6pm Thu & Sat–Mon (till 5pm Tue). **Closed** last Tue of the month. book by phone.

Erected in 1975 to coincide with the 30th anniversary of the end of World War II, this monument commemorates the victims of the Siege of Leningrad. A red granite obelisk rises beside a circular enclosure, which symbolizes the grip of the siege, fronted by statues of soldiers, nurses and grieving mothers.

An underpass leads to the subterranean **Memorial Hall**, where solemn music gives way to the beat of a metronome, the wartime radio signal that represented the city's heartbeat. Among the artifacts on display is a morsel of bread, which was many people's daily ration.

The vertically striped façade of the Chesma Church, designed by Yuri Velten

# BEYOND ST PETERSBURG

Before St Petersburg was founded in 1703, the surrounding landscape was a marshy, inhospitable wilderness. When Russia was victorious in the Great Northern War, Peter the Great celebrated by building a summer residence on the shore of the Gulf of Finland. Known as the "Russian Versailles", Peterhof is dominated by water; the Gulf and the fountains mirror Peter's maritime interest. Yet, the Great Palace remains the centrepiece of the estate and owes much of its opulence to Peter's daughter, Tsarina Elizabeth, who commissioned Bartolomeo Rastrelli to expand it and redecorate its interiors. Wilfully extravagant, she also created her own stunning residence at Tsarskoe Selo, with a Baroque palace for hosting legendary costume balls. Her successor Catherine the Great added private apartments and secluded pavilions to the palace. Catherine's son Paul had his own estate at Pavlovsk, not far away, but, due to his untimely death, its Neo-Classical decor largely reflected the tastes of his wife, Maria Fyodorovna, who outlived him by 28 years. These magnificent palaces suffered extensive damage during World War II, and it took 50 years of painstaking restoration to return them to their former glory. All three sights are easily accessible from the city, on organized excursions or by public transport.

## Sights at a Glance

**Palaces**

1 Peterhof
2 Tsarskoe Selo
3 Pavlovsk

**Key**

━ Main road
═ Minor road
─ Railway

◀ The famous Visconti bridge over the Slavyanka river, Pavlovsk

For keys to symbols *see back flap*

# ➊ Peterhof

Петергоф

*Petergof*

With its commanding views of the Baltic, Peterhof is a perfect expression of triumphalism. Originally designed by Jean Baptiste Le Blond in 1714–21, the Great Palace was transformed during the reign of Tsarina Elizabeth when Bartolomeo Rastrelli added a third storey and wings with pavilions at either end. He tried to preserve Le Blond's early Baroque exterior, but redesigned the interiors, which demonstrate his love for gilded Baroque decoration. Peterhof stands at the centre of a magnificent landscaped park, with both French and English gardens.

View from the palace of the Grand Cascade leading down to the Gulf of Finland

**The Imperial Suite**

Situated in the palace's eastern wing, the Imperial Suite comprises several rooms. Peter's Oak Study is one of the few rooms to have survived unaltered from Le Blond's design. Some of the oak panel motifs are originals by Nicholas Pineau, designed between 1718 and 1721.

## KEY

➀ **The Upper Gardens** are framed by borders and hedges and punctuated with ornamental ponds.

➁ **Mezheumnyy Fountain**

➂ **Neptune Fountain**

➃ **Oak Fountain**

➄ **Samson Fountain**

➅ **The Marine Canal** enabled the tsars to sail from the Gulf of Finland up to the Great Palace.

➆ **Eve Fountain**

➇ **Adam Fountain**

## Peter the Great's Palace

After his victory over the Swedes at Poltava in 1709, Peter the Great decided to build a palace "befitting to the very highest of monarchs". A visit to Versailles in 1717 furthered Peter's ambitions and he employed more than 5,000 labourers, serfs and soldiers, supported by architects, water-engineers, landscape gardeners and sculptors. Work proceeded at a frenetic pace from 1714 until Peterhof was officially opened in 1723. Le Blond's Great Palace was completed in 1721 and has changed considerably over the decades. Catherine the Great commissioned Yuri Velten to redecorate some of Rastrelli's interiors in the 1770s, including the Throne Room and the Chesma Room.

Jean Baptiste Le Blond's original two-storey Great Palace

★ **Main Staircase**
Caryatids and gilded carvings adorn Rastrelli's glittering staircase. The fresco on the ceiling depicts Aurora and Genius chasing away the night.

## VISITORS' CHECKLIST

**Practical information**
Petrodvorets, 30 km (19 miles) W of St Petersburg.
**Tel** (812) 450 52 87. Great Palace: **Open** 10:30am–6pm Tue–Sun (till 9pm Sat). **Closed** last Tue of the month. Other Pavilions: **Open** 10:30am–6pm daily. Fountains: **Open** May–early Oct: 10:30am–5pm. 🚶 🛍 🎨 🏛

**Transport**
🚌 344, 348, 350, 351, 352, 355, 356. 🚆 from Baltiysky station to Novyy Petergof. 🚢 Hermitage (May–Oct).

★ **State Rooms**
The highlight of the State Rooms is the opulent Throne Room, redesigned by Yuri Velten in 1770. The relatively restrained stucco ornamentation, red velvet hangings and parquet floor provide an exquisite setting for portraits of Russia's imperial family.

0 metres 25
0 yards 25

Gulf of Finland

★ **The Grand Cascade**
The dazzling cascade, built between 1715 and 1724, is a sequence of 37 gilded bronze sculptures, 64 fountains and 142 water jets, descending from the terraces of the Great Palace to the Marine Canal and the sea.

# ❷ Tsarskoe Selo

Царское Село

*Tsarskoe Selo*

The imperial palace at Tsarskoe Selo was designed by Bartolomeo Rastrelli in 1752 for Tsarina Elizabeth. She named it the Catherine Palace in honour of her mother, Catherine I, who originally owned the estate. The next ruler to leave a mark on the palace was Catherine the Great, and during her reign she commissioned the Scotsman Charles Cameron to redesign the Baroque interiors according to her Neo-Classical taste. Cameron also designed a two-storey ensemble – as a summer pavilion – comprising the Agate Rooms, the Imperial Baths and the Cameron Gallery. The Amber Room, looted by the Nazis, has been reconstructed.

**★ The Great Hall**
Light streams into Rastrelli's glittering hall illuminating the mirrors, gilded carvings and the vast ceiling painting, *The Triumph of Russia* (around 1755), by Giuseppe Valeriani.

**★ Atlantes**
The stunning 300-m (980-ft) long Baroque façade is adorned with a profusion of atlantes, columns, pilasters and ornamented window framings.

Entrance

## KEY

① **The Cameron Gallery** is part of Catherine's private apartments.

② **The Agate Rooms** are part of the Imperial Baths and faced with semi-precious stones from the Urals.

③ **The Great Staircase**, designed by Ippolito Monighetti in 1860, leads to the state rooms on the first floor.

④ **The small Enfilade** comprises several unrestored rooms that exhibit a varied selection of furniture and *objets d'art*. These include Chinese lacquer furniture and Oriental rugs used to furnish the palace in the 19th century.

⑤ **The Picture Gallery** displays canvases by Italian, French, Dutch and Flemish masters of the 17th and 18th centuries.

⑥ **The Royal Chapel** is decorated in dark blue and gold. Built by Chevakinskiy in the 1740s, it contains an elaborate six-tiered iconostasis.

⑦ **The French-style formal gardens** were laid out in the 1740s. Their formality and symmetry contrasts with the naturalistic English-style landscaping of the park, created in 1768.

**The Cavaliers' Dining Room**
The table is laid for Tsarina Elizabeth's gentlemen-in-waiting, in the refined gold-and-white room created by Rastrelli.

★ **Amber Room**
The original amber panels by Andreas Schlüter, dating from 1709, were a gift from Friedrich Wilhelm I of Prussia to Peter the Great. The room has been recreated from photographs, with carved reliefs and panels of Florentine mosaics.

## VISITORS' CHECKLIST

**Practical information**
Tsarskoe Selo, 25 km (16 miles) S of St Petersburg.
Palace: **Tel** (812) 465 20 24
**Open** noon–8pm Mon, noon–5pm Wed–Sun. Agate Rooms: **Open** Jun–Oct: 11am–6pm Fri–Wed. **Closed** last Mon of the month. 🎫 🖼 💻 📷
Grounds: **Open** 7am–9pm daily.
🎫 May–Oct: 9am–6pm.

**Transport**
🚉 from Vitebskiy station to Detskoe Selo, then bus 371 or 382.

**Blue Drawing Room**
This room is characterized by blue floral motifs painted on silk. Among the royal portraits hanging here is a painting of Peter the Great, dating from around 1720, by Ivan Nikitin.

★ **Green Dining Room**
Cameron's restrained Neo-Classical style contrasts with the Baroque flamboyance of Rastrelli's work. The exquisite stucco bas-reliefs, sculpted by Ivan Martos, were based on motifs from frescoes discovered in Pompeii.

# ❾ Pavlovsk

Павловск
*Pavlovsk*

To celebrate the birth of his heir, Grand Duke Paul was presented this land by Catherine the Great in 1777. She also "gave" him their favourite architect, Charles Cameron, to design both the palace and park. Work at Pavlovsk (from Pavel or Paul) began in 1780 and was continued by Paul's grieving widow, Maria Fyodorovna, long after his death. "English gardens" were at the height of fashion and inspired Cameron's design of a seemingly natural landscape dotted with pavilions (used for informal parties), romantic ruins and attractive vistas around the Slavyanka river.

**The Apollo Colonnade**
Cameron's colonnade, built between 1782 and 1783, encircles a copy of the Apollo Belvedere above a romantically dilapidated cascade.

**★ Pavlovsk Palace**
Cameron's elegant Palladian mansion, built from 1782 to 1786, forms the central block of today's palace, with wings added in 1789 by Paul's favoured architect, Vincenzo Brenna.

## KEY

① **Cameron's Dairy** (1782) housed both a milking shed and a salon.

② **Aviary**

③ **Three Graces Pavilion**

④ **The Centaur Bridge** by Voronikhin (1805) nestles in a bend of the Slavyanka river.

⑤ **The Cold Baths** were built by Charles Cameron in 1799. This austere pavilion was used as a summer swimming pool, complete with an elegant vestibule, paintings, furniture and rich wall upholstery.

⑥ **Green Woman Alley**

⑦ **The Beautiful Valley** was the favourite spot of Elizabeth, wife of Alexander I.

⑧ **Paul's Mausoleum** bears the inscription "To my beneficient consort".

⑨ **The Rose Pavilion** was the favourite haunt of Maria Fyodorovna from 1812. She held many concerts and literary evenings in this cottage.

**★ Temple of Friendship** (1780)
This Doric temple was the first building to use the Greek form of architecture in Russia.

**Visconti Bridge**
One of the most famous bridges that cross the winding Slavyanka, it was designed by Andrei Voronikhin in 1807.

Pavlovsk
Railway Station

## VISITORS' CHECKLIST

**Practical information**
Pavlovsk, 26 km (16 miles) SE of St Petersburg.
**Tel** (812) 452 15 36.
Palace: **Open** 10am–6pm Sat–Thu. **Closed** Oct–Apr: first Mon of the month.
English.
Grounds: **Open** May–Nov: 6am–midnight.

**Transport**
from Vitebskiy, Kupchino or Moscovskay stations to Pavlovsk, then bus 370, 383, 383a, 493, K-286, K-299.

**The Etoile**
The earliest landscaped area in the park, L'Etoile, was laid out by Cameron in 1780. The circle of statues represents the nine Muses, protectors of the arts and sciences.

0 metres 200
0 yards 200

**Pil Tower and Bridge**
Brenna's tower, constructed between 1795 and 1797, contained a spiral staircase, lounge and library. The bridge was a later addition and dates from 1808.

# ST PETERSBURG STREET FINDER

The map below shows the areas of St Petersburg covered by the Street Finder maps. The map references given in the St Petersburg section for sights of interest, restaurants, hotels, shops and entertainment venues refer to the maps in this section. The symbols used to represent sights and useful information on these maps are listed below in the key. The first figure in the map reference indicates which Street Finder map to turn to, and the letter and number that follow refer to the map's grid. An index of street names can be found on the following pages. The index lists street names in transliteration, followed by Cyrillics (on maps, Cyrillics are only given for major roads).

Backpackers referring to a map in order to get around St Petersburg

## Key

- ▢ Major sight
- ▢ Place of interest
- ▢ Other building
- 🚉 Train station
- Ⓜ Metro station
- 🚊 Main tram stop
- 🚎 Main trolleybus stop
- 🚌 Main bus stop
- 🚤 River boat pier
- ✚ Hospital
- 🏛 Police station
- ✝ Orthodox church
- ✝ Non-Orthodox church
- ✡ Synagogue
- ☪ Mosque
- ═ Railway line
- ▬ Pedestrian area

**Scale of Maps 1–4**

0 metres        300
0 yards         300

0 kilometres              2
0 miles                 1

# Street Finder Index

10-ya Krasnoarmeyskaya ulitsa
  10-Я КРАСНОАРМЕЙСКАЯ УЛИЦА — 3A5
13-ya Krasnoarmeyskaya ulitsa
  13-Я КРАСНОАРМЕЙСКАЯ УЛИЦА — 3B5
1-ya Krasnoarmeyskaya ulitsa
  1-Я КРАСНОАРМЕЙСКАЯ УЛИЦА — 3C5
2-ya I 3-ya linii
  2-Я и 3-Я ЛИНИИ — 1A5
2-ya Krasnoarmeyskaya ulitsa
  2-Я КРАСНОАРМЕЙСКАЯ УЛИЦА — 3C5
3-ya Krasnoarmeyskaya ulitsa
  3-Я КРАСНОАРМЕЙСКАЯ УЛИЦА — 3C5
4-ya Krasnoarmeyskaya ulitsa
  4-Я КРАСНОАРМЕЙСКАЯ УЛИЦА — 3C5
8-ya Krasnoarmeyskaya ulitsa
  8-Я КРАСНОАРМЕЙСКАЯ УЛИЦА — 3B5
9-ya Krasnoarmeyskaya ulitsa
  9-Я КРАСНОАРМЕЙСКАЯ УЛИЦА — 3B5

| Useful words and abbreviations | | |
|---|---|---|
| | most | bridge |
| | podezd | entrance |
| | proezd | small street/passage/lane |
| | sad | garden |
| | shosse | road |
| | stroenie | building |
| | tupik | cul-de-sac |
| ul | ulitsa | street |
| pl | ploshchad | square |
| pr | prospekt | avenue |
| per | pereulok | small street/passage/lane |

## A

Admiralteyskaya naberezhnaya
  АДМИРАЛТЕЙСКАЯ НАБЕРЕЖНАЯ — 3B1
Admiralteyskiy proezd
  АДМИРАЛТЕЙСКИЙ ПРОЕЗД — 3C1
Admiralteyskiy prospekt
  АДМИРАЛТЕЙСКИЙ ПРОСПЕКТ — 3C1
Admiralteyskovo Kanala, naberezhnaya
  АДМИРАЛТЕЙСКОВО КАНАЛА, НАБЕРЕЖНАЯ — 3A2
Angliyskaya naberezhnaya
  АНГЛИЙСКАЯ НАБЕРЕЖНАЯ — 3A2
Angliyskiy prospekt
  АНГЛИЙСКИЙ ПРОСПЕКТ — 3A4
Antonenko, pereulok
  АНТОНЕНКО, ПЕРЕУЛОК — 3C2
Apraksin pereulok
  АПРАКСИН ПЕРЕУЛОК — 4D2
Aptekarskiy pereulok
  АПТЕКАРСКИЙ ПЕРЕУЛОК — 2E5

## B

Bankovskiy pereulok
  БАНКОВСКИЙ ПЕРЕУЛОК — 4D2
Batayskiy pereulok
  БАТАЙСКИЙ ПЕРЕУЛОК — 4D5
Birzhevaya liniya
  БИРЖЕВАЯ ЛИННЯ — 1B4
Birzhevoy pereulok
  БИРЖЕВОЙ ПЕРЕУЛОК — 1A4
Birzhevoy proezd
  БИРЖЕВОЙ ПРОЕЗД — 1B5
Blagoeva, ulitsa
  БЛАГОЕВА, УЛИЦА — 1B3
Blokhina, ulitsa
  БЛОХИНА, УЛИЦА — 1B3
Bolshaya Konyushennaya ulitsa
  БОЛЬШАЯ КОНЮШЕННАЯ УЛИЦА — 4D1
Bolshaya Monetnaya ulitsa
  БОЛЬШАЯ МОНЕТНАЯ УЛИЦА — 1C2
Bolshaya Morskaya ulitsa
  БОЛЬШАЯ МОРСКАЯ УЛИЦА — 3B2
Bolshaya Podyacheskaya ulitsa
  БОЛЬШАЯ ПОДЬЯЧЕСКАЯ УЛИЦА — 3C4
Bolshaya Posadskaya ulitsa
  БОЛЬШАЯ ПОСАДСКАЯ УЛИЦА — 2D2
Bolshaya Pushkarskaya ulitsa
  БОЛЬШАЯ ПУШКАРСКАЯ УЛИЦА — 1B2
Bolshaya Zelenina ulitsa
  БОЛЬШАЯ ЗЕЛЕНИНА УЛИЦА — 1A1
Bolshoi prospekt
  БОЛЬШОЙ ПРОСПЕКТ — 1B2
Bolshoy Sampsonievskiy prospekt
  БОЛЬШОЙ САМПСОНИЕВСКИЙ — 2F1
Borodinskaya ulitsa
  БОРОДИНСКАЯ УЛИЦА — 4E3
Borovaya ulitsa
  БОРОВАЯ УЛИЦА — 4F5
Boytsova, pereulok
  БОЙЦОВА, ПЕРЕУЛОК — 3C4
Bronnitskaya ulitsa
  БРОННИЦКАЯ УЛИЦА — 4D5

## C

Chapaeva, ulitsa
  ЧАПАЕВА, УЛИЦА — 2E1
Chaykovskovo, ulitsa
  ЧАЙКОВСКОГО, УЛИЦА — 2F4
Chernomorskiy pereulok
  ЧЕРНОМОРСКИЙ ПЕРЕУЛОК — 3C1
Chkalovskiy prospekt
  ЧКАЛОВСКИЙ ПРОСПЕКТ — 1A2

## D

Dekabristov, proezd
  ДЕКАБРИСТОВ, ПРОЕЗД — 3B1
Dekabristov, ulitsa
  ДЕКАБРИСТОВ, УЛИЦА — 3A3
Derptskiy pereulok
  ДЕРПТСКИЙ ПЕРЕУЛОК — 3A5
Divenskaya ulitsa
  ДИВЕНСКАЯ УЛИЦА — 2D2
Dobrolyubova, prospekt
  ДОБРОЛЮБОВА, ПРОСПЕКТ — 1A3
Drovyanaya ulitsa
  ДРОВЯНАЯ УЛИЦА — 3A5
Dumskaya ulitsa
  ДУМСКАЯ УЛИЦА — 4E2
Dvortsovaya naberezhnaya
  ДВОРЦОВАЯ НАБЕРЕЖНАЯ — 1C5

## E

Egorova, ulitsa
  ЕГОРОВА, УЛИЦА — 3C5

## F

Fonarnyy pereulok
  ФОНАРНЫЙ ПЕРЕУЛОК — 3B2

## G

Gagarinskaya, ulitsa
  ГАГАРИНСКАЯ УЛИЦА — 2F4
Galernaya ulitsa
  ГАЛЕРНАЯ УЛИЦА — 3A2
Glinki, ulitsa
  ГЛИНКИ, УЛИЦА — 3B3
Gorokhovaya ulitsa
  ГОРОХОВАЯ УЛИЦА — 3C1
Grazhdanskaya ulitsa
  ГРАЖДАНСКАЯ УЛИЦА — 3C3
Griboedova, naberezhnaya kanala
  ГРИБОЕДОВА, НАБЕРЕЖНАЯ КАНАЛА — 3A4

## I

Inzhenernaya ulitsa
ИНЖЕНЕНАЯ УЛИЦА    4E1
Italyanskaya ulitsa
ИТАЛЬЯНСКАЯ УЛИЦА    4E1
Izmaylovskiy prospekt
ИЗМАЙЛОВСКИЙ ПРОСПЕКТ    3C5

## K

Kadetskaya 1-ya liniya
КАДЕТСКАЯ И 1-Я ЛИНИЯ    1A4
Kamennoostrovskiy prospekt
КАМЕННООСТРОВСКИЙ ПРОСПЕКТ    1C1
Kanonerskaya ulitsa
КАНОНЕРСКАЯ УЛИЦА    3A4
Karavannaya ulitsa
КАРАВАННАЯ УЛИЦА    4F1
Kazachiy pereulok
КАЗАЧИЙ ПЕРЕУЛОК    4E4
Kazanskaya ulitsa
КАЗАНСКАЯ УЛИЦА    3C3
Kirpichnyy pereulok
КИРПИЧНЫЙ ПЕРЕУЛОК    4D1
Klimov pereulok
КЛИМОВ ПЕРЕУЛОК    3B4
Klinskiy prospekt
КЛИНСКИЙ ПРОСПЕКТ    4D5
Konnogvardeyskiy bulvar
КОННОГВАРДЕЙСКИЙ БУЛЬВАР    3A2
Konnogvardeyskiy per
Конногвардейский переулок    3B2
Konnyy pereulok
КОННЫЙ ПЕРЕУЛОК    2D2
Korpusnaya ulitsa
КОРПУСНАЯ УЛИЦА    1A1
Kotovskovo, ulitsa
КОТОВСКОГО, УЛИЦА    2E1
Krasnovo Kursanta, ulitsa
КРАСНОГО КУРСАНТА, УЛИЦА    1A2
Kronverkskaya naberezhnaya
КРОНВЕРКСКАЯ НАБЕРЕЖНАЯ    1C3
Kronverkskaya, ulitsa
КРОНВЕРКСКАЯ, УЛИЦА    1C1
Kronverkskiy prospekt
КРОНВЕРКСКИЙ ПРОСПЕКТ    1C2
Kropotkina, ulitsa
КРОПОТКИНА, УЛИЦА    1C2
Kryukova Kanala, naberezhnaya
КРЮКОВА КАНАЛА, НАБЕРЕЖНАЯ    3B4
Kutuzova, naberezhnaya
КУТУЗОВА, НАБЕРЕЖНАЯ    2E4
Kuybysheva, ulitsa
КУЙБЫШЕВА, УЛИЦА    2D3

## L

Labutina, ulitsa
ЛАБУТИНА, УЛИЦА    3A5
Lazaretnyy pereulok
ЛАЗАРЕТНЫЙ ПЕРЕУЛОК    4E4
Lebyazhevo Kanala, naberezhnaya
ЛЕБЯЖЬЕГО КАНАЛА, НАБЕРЕЖНАЯ    2E4
Lenina, ulitsa
ЛЕНИНА, УЛИЦА    1C2
Lermontovskiy prospekt
ЛЕРМОНТОВСКИЙ ПРОСПЕКТ    3A3
Levashovskiy prospekt
ЛЕВАШОВСКИЙ ПРОСПЕКТ    1A1
Lizy Chaykinoy, ulitsa
ЛИЗЫ ЧАЙКИНОЙ, УЛИЦА    1B2
Lomonosova, ulitsa
ЛОМОНОСОВА, УЛИЦА ·    4E2
Lva Tolstovo, ulitsa
ЛЬВА ТОЛСТОГО, УЛИЦА    1C1

## M

Makarenko, pereulok
МАКАРЕНКО, ПЕРЕУЛОК    3B4
Makarova, naberezhnaya
МАКАРОВА, НАБЕРЕЖНАЯ    1A4
Malaya Konyushennaya ulitsa
МАЛАЯ КОНЮШЕННАЯ УЛИЦА    4D1
Malaya Monetnaya ulitsa
МАЛАЯ МОНЕТНАЯ УЛИЦА    2D1
Malaya Morskaya ulitsa
МАЛАЯ МОРСКАЯ УЛИЦА    3C1
Malaya Posadskaya ulitsa
МАЛАЯ ПОСАДСКАЯ УЛИЦА    2E3
Malaya Pushkarskaya ulitsa
МАЛАЯ ПУШКАРСКАЯ УЛИЦА    1C2
Malaya sadovaya ulitsa
МАЛАЯ САДОВАЯ УЛИЦА    4F1
Malodetskoselskiy prospekt
МАЛОДЕТСКОСЕЛЬСКИЙ ПРОСПЕКТ    4D5
Malyy prospekt
МАЛЫЙ ПРОСПЕКТ    1B1
Malyy prospekt
МАЛЫЙ ПРОСПЕКТ    1A3
Marata, ulitsa
МАРАТА, УЛИЦА    4E4
Markina, ulitsa
МАРКИНА УЛИЦА    1C2
Masterskaya ulitsa
МАСТЕРСКАЯ УЛИЦА    3A3
Matveeva, pereulok
МАТВЕЕВА ПЕРЕУЛОК    3A3
Mendeleevskaya liniya
МЕНДЕЛЕЕВСКАЯ УЛИЦА    1B5
Michurinskaya ulitsa
МИЧУРИНСКАЯ УЛИЦА    2E2
Millionaires street
МИЛЛИОННАЯ УЛИЦА    2D5
Minskiy pereulok
МИНСКИЙ ПЕРЕУЛОК    3A3
Mira, ulitsa
МИРА, УЛИЦА    1C2
Moskatelnyy pereulok
МОСКАТЕЛЬНЫЙ ПЕРЕУЛОК    4D2
Moskovskiy prospekt
МОСКОВСКИЙ ПРОСПЕКТ    4D3
Mozhayskaya ulitsa
МОЖАЙСКАЯ УЛИЦА    4E4
Muchnoy pereulok
МУЧНОЙ ПЕРЕУЛОК    4D2
Mytninskaya naberezhnaya
МЫТНИНСКАЯ НАБЕРЕЖНАЯ    1B4
Mytninskiy pereulok
МЫТНИНСКИЙ ПЕРЕУЛОК    1B3

## N

Nesterova, pereulok
НЕСТЕРОВА, ПЕРЕУЛОК    1B3
Nevskiy prospekt
НЕВСКИЙ ПРОСПЕКТ    4D1
Nikolskiy pereulok
НИКОЛЬСКИЙ ПЕРЕУЛОК    3B3

## O

Obvodnovo Kanala, naberezhnaya
ОБВОДНОГО КАНАЛА, НАБЕРЕЖНАЯ    4E5
Ofitserskiy pereulok
ОФИЦЕРСКИЙ ПЕРЕУЛОК    1A3
Orenburgskaya ulitsa
ОРЕНБУРГСКАЯ УЛИЦА    2F2

## P

Penkovaya ulitsa
ПЕНЬКОВАЯ УЛИЦА    2E3
Pestelya, ulitsa
ПЕСТЕЛЯ, УЛИЦА    2F5

Petrogradskaya naberezhnaya
ПЕТРОГРАДСКАЯ НАБЕРЕЖНАЯ 2E1

Petrovskaya naberezhnaya
ПЕТРОВСКАЯ НАБЕРЕЖНАЯ 2E3

Pevcheskiy pereulok
ПЕВЧЕСКИЙ ПЕРЕУЛОК 2D2

Pinskiy pereulok
ПИНСКИЙ ПЕРЕУЛОК 2E3

Pionerskaya ulitsa
ПИОНЕРСКАЯ УЛИЦА 1A2

Pirogova, pereulok
ПИРОГОВА, ПЕРЕУЛОК 3B2

Pirogovskaya naberezhnaya
ПИРОГОВСКАЯ НАБЕРЕЖНАЯ 2F1

Pisareva, ulitsa
ПИСАРЕВА, УЛИЦА 3A3

Pochtamtskaya ulitsa
ПОЧТАМТСКАЯ УЛИЦА 3B2

Pochtamtskiy pereulok
ПОЧТАМТСКИЙ ПЕРЕУЛОК 3B2

Podezdnoy pereulok
ПОДЪЕЗДНОЙ ПЕРЕУЛОК 4E4

Podolskaya ulitsa
ПОДОЛЬСКАЯ УЛИЦА 4D5

Prachechnyy pereulok
ПРАЧЕЧНЫЙ ПЕРЕУЛОК 3B2

Pravdy, ulitsa
ПРАВДЫ, УЛИЦА 4F4

Pryadilnyy pereulok
ПРЯДИЛЬНЫЙ ПЕРЕУЛОК 3A5

Pushkarskiy pereulok
ПУШКАРСКИЙ ПЕРЕУЛОК 1C2

## R

Reki Fontanki, naberezhnaya
РЕКИ ФОНТАНКИ, НАБЕРЕЖНАЯ 4F1

Reki Moyki, naberezhnaya
РЕКИ МОЙКИ, НАБЕРЕЖНАЯ 3A3

Rentgena, ulitsa
РЕНТГЕНА, УЛИЦА 2D1

Repina, ulitsa
РЕПИНА, УЛИЦА 1A5

Revelskiy per
РЕВЕЛЬСКИЙ ПЕРЕУЛОК 3A5

Rimskovo-Korsakova, prospekt
РИМСКОГО-КОРСАКОВА, ПРОСПЕКТ 3B3

Rizhskiy prospekt
РИЖСКИЙ ПРОСПЕКТ 3A5

Rubinshteyna, ulitsa
РУБИНШТЕЙНА, УЛИЦА 4F3

Ruzovskaya ulitsa
РУЗОВСКАЯ УЛИЦА 4E4

Rybatskaya ulitsa
РЫБАЦКАЯ УЛИЦА 1B2

## S

Sablinskaya ulitsa
САБЛИНСКАЯ УЛИЦА 1C2

Sadovaya ulitsa
САДОВАЯ УЛИЦА 2F5

Saratovskaya ulitsa
САРАТОВСКАЯ УЛИЦА 2F3

Serpukhovskaya ulitsa
СЕРПУХОВСКАЯ УЛИЦА 4D5

Sezzhinskaya ulitsa
СЪЕЗЖИНСКАЯ УЛИЦА 1B3

Shchepyanoy pereulok
ЩЕПЯНОЙ ПЕРЕУЛОК 3B4

Shvedskiy pereulok
ШВЕДСКИЙ ПЕРЕУЛОК 4D1

Sovetskiy pereulok
СОВЕТСКИЙ ПЕРЕУЛОК 3C5

Soyuza Pechatnikov, ulitsa
СОЮЗА ПЕЧАТНИКОВ, УЛИЦА 3A4

Spasskiy pereulok
СПАССКИЙ ПЕРЕУЛОК 4D2

Sredniy prospekt
СРЕДНИЙ ПРОСПЕКТ 1A4

Srednyaya Podyacheskaya ulitsa
СРЕДНЯЯ ПОДЬЯЧЕСКАЯ УЛИЦА 3B3

Stolyarnyy pereulok
СТОЛЯРНЫЙ ПЕРЕУЛОК 3C3

Sytninskaya ulitsa
СЫТНИНСКАЯ УЛИЦА 1C2

## T

Tatarskiy pereulok
ТАТАРСКИЙ ПЕРЕУЛОК 1B3

Telezhnaya ulitsa
ТЕЛЕЖНАЯ УЛИЦА 1B5

Torgovyy pereulok
ТОРГОВЫЙ ПЕРЕУЛОК 4E3

Troitskiy prospekt
ТРОИЦКИЙ ПРОСПЕКТ 3B5

Truda, ulitsa
ТРУДА, УЛИЦА 3A2

Tuchkov pereulok
ТУЧКОВ ПЕРЕУЛОК 1A4

## U

Universitetskaya naberezhnaya
УНИВЕРСИТЕТСКАЯ НАБЕРЕЖНАЯ 1B5

## V

Vereyskaya ulitsa
ВЕРЕЙСКАЯ УЛИЦА 4D4

Volkhovskiy pereulok
ВОЛХОВСКИЙ ПЕРЕУЛОК 1A5

Volynskiy pereulok
ВОЛЫНСКИЙ ПЕРЕУЛОК 4D1

Voskova, ulitsa
ВОСКОВА, УЛИЦА 1C2

Voznesenskiy prospekt
ВОЗНЕСЕНСКИЙ ПРОСПЕКТ 3C2

Vvedenskaya ulitsa
ВВЕДЕНСКАЯ УЛИЦА 1B2

Vvedenskovo Kanala, naberezhnaya
ВВЕДЕНСКОГО КАНАЛА, НАБЕРЕЖНАЯ 4D4

## Y

Yablochkova, ulitsa
ЯБЛОЧКОВА, УЛИЦА 1B3

Yakobshtadtskiy pereulok
ЯКОБШТАДТСКИЙ ПЕРЕУЛОК 3C5

Yakubovicha, ulitsa
ЯКУБОВИЧА, УЛИЦА 3B2

Yefimova, ulitsa
ЕФИМОВА, УЛИЦА 4D3

## Z

Zagorodnyy prospekt
ЗАГОРОДНЫЙ ПРОСПЕКТ 4D5

Zamkovaya ulitsa
ЗАМКОВАЯ УЛИЦА 2F5

Zhdanovskaya ulitsa
ЖДАНОВСКАЯ УЛИЦА 1A3

Zodchevo Rossi, ulitsa
ЗОДЧЕГО РОССИ, УЛИЦА 4E2

Zvenigorodskaya ulitsa
ЗВЕНИГОРОДСКАЯ УЛИЦА 4F4

Zverinskaya ulitsa
ЗВЕРИНСКАЯ УЛИЦА 1A3

# RUSSIA REGION BY REGION

Russia at a Glance            202–203

Northern Russia              204–211

Kaliningrad                  212–219

Central and Southern Russia  220–235

The Caucasus                 236–245

Siberia and the Far East     246–259

# Russia at a Glance

Dominating the eastern end of Europe and all of northern Asia, Russia's longitudinal extent is phenomenal, and its topography incredibly varied. The country's fascinating cultural heritage is manifested in its many ancient towns and cities, of which Moscow and St Petersburg are foremost with their wealth of historical and architectural attractions. Beyond the Urals to the east, the Trans-Siberian Railway traverses the epic tracts of dense forest and featureless steppe that lie between Siberia's reassuringly civilized cities. Intrepid visitors can venture north to the desolate city of Magadan and beyond to the mesmerizing volcanic peninsula of Kamchatka, so remote that helicopters are often the only means of transport.

**Kizhi** *(see pp208–209)*, with its magnificent pair of 18th-century wooden churches topped with a profusion of tiny onion domes, has long attracted both pilgrims and tourists.

**Curonian Spit** *(see p218)* is a spectacular landform created by sand deposition millions of years ago. This strip of sandy wilderness stretches for almost 100 km (60 miles) between Kaliningrad and Lithuania and has some of the best beaches in the region. Known as Kurshkaya Kosa locally, it is also a UNESCO World Heritage Site.

*Baltic Sea*

**St Petersburg**
*(see pp130–199)*

**Kaliningrad**
*(see pp212–219)*

**Veliky Novgorod**

**Northern Russia**
*(see pp204–211)*

*Bare Sea*

**Moscow**
*(see pp48–129)*

**Kazan**

**Central and Southern Russia**
*(see pp220–235)*

**Yekaterinbu**

**Rostov-na-Donu**

**Krasnodar**

*Black Sea*

**The Caucasus**
*(see pp236–245)*

*Caspian Sea*

**Volga Delta**

**Sochi National Park**
*(see p242)* runs parallel to the Black Sea coast. The densely forested park encompasses mountains, canyons, rivers and caves, and is home to diverse wildlife.

◀ Magnificent view of the front of the Church on the Blood, Yekaterinburg

**Volga Delta** *(see p233)*, a picturesque labyrinth of waterways and islands sheltering an abundance of wildlife, lies at the end of the great Volga river where it meets the Caspian Sea.

**Kamchatka** *(see p259)* is a remote volcanic peninsula that offers unforgettable vistas of brown bears roaming the pristine natural landscapes dotted with mighty geysers and rumbling volcanoes.

*Arctic Ocean*

*Laptev Sea*

*Bering Sea*

**Siberia and the Far East** *(see pp246–259)*

Magadan

*Sea of Okhotsk*

Krasnoyarsk

Irkutsk

| 0 km | 800 |
|------|-----|
| 0 miles | 800 |

Vladivostok

**Lake Baikal** *(see p253)* is the oldest and deepest lake on earth, containing an astonishing 20 per cent of the planet's unfrozen freshwater supplies. Its largely unspoilt shoreline offers numerous opportunities for hiking and camping.

# NORTHERN RUSSIA

Sharing a 1,000-km (621-mile) border with Finland and a tiny sliver of Norway in the Arctic far north, much of Northern Russia's lake-covered wilderness resembles the terrain of its Scandinavian neighbours and lies within the Russian Republic of Karelia. With its potent blend of rugged nature, complex medieval history and rich cultural heritage, the region is a treasure-trove of attractions and is only just beginning to be appreciated by locals and foreigners alike.

To the north of St Petersburg lie vast stretches of rocky wilderness strewn with dense coniferous forests and myriad rivers once used as trade routes into Russia by the Vikings. Dotted with 100,000 glacial lakes, the northern region includes two of Europe's largest lakes: Ladoga and Onega. The island of Valaam on Lake Ladoga has been home to a monastic community for hundreds of years, while Kizhi island on Lake Onega features the iconic wooden churches that were built by god-fearing farmers who settled here in the 16th century.

With temperatures dropping as low as -40°C (-40°F) in some parts during winters, Northern Russia is popular among visitors in search of dazzling frozen landscapes. The northwestern area has the most hospitable climate in the region. This, combined with

the region's proximity to Western Europe, made it the obvious location for some of Russia's earliest settlements.

Founded around the 10th century, the towns of Pskov and Veliky Novgorod prospered from the lucrative trade in furs and developed into powerful city-states that rivalled Moscow. Both built mighty kremlins to withstand frequent aggression from their hostile neighbours.

Today, crumbling kremlin walls have been rebuilt and the once splendid churches and monasteries that were woefully neglected during the Soviet era are being painstakingly restored. Infrastructure has improved over the years and despite the numbing temperatures there is access to plenty of adventure activities, from snowmobiling to ice-hole swimming.

Detail of one of the panels in an iconostasis on display in the Pskov Museum of History, Architecture and Art

◀ The striking Transfiguration Church and the hexagonal bell tower at Kizhi

# Exploring Northern Russia

Dominated by lush wilderness and lakes, Northern Russia is a sparsely populated area. Although the landscape is punctuated by sleepy villages of faded wooden cottages and log cabins hemmed in by vegetable gardens, a vast majority of the population is concentrated around St Petersburg. Located up north, Petrozavodsk serves as the gateway to Kizhi, which is famous for its striking wooden churches. The grand cathedrals on the island of Valaam are another architectural attraction. South of St Petersburg, the impressive kremlins and medieval churches of Veliky Novgorod and Pskov are well worth an overnight trip. Alexander Pushkin's picturesque ancestral estate at Mikhaylovskoye makes for a superb day trip by bus from Pskov. Hiking and cycling trails in the region are poorly marked; it is advisable to register with one of the several travel agencies in Petrozavodsk to arrange organized trips.

NORTHERN RUSSIA

☐ Area illustrated

## Sights at a Glance

1. Petrozavodsk
2. Kizhi
3. Valaam
4. Veliky Novgorod
5. Pskov
6. Mikhaylovskoye

## Key

━━━ Major road
═══ Minor road
╍╍╍ Major railway
─── Minor railway
━━━ International border
━━━ Federal border

0 km        100
0 miles        100

FINLA

Lakhdenpok
Svetogor
Prioze
Vyborg
Sos
Primorsk
M
St Peter
Petrodvorets
Narva    Gatchi
Kingisepp
Slantsy    Luga
Lake Peipus    Gdov    Luga
Plyussa
Strugi-Krasnyye
Lake Pskov
A212   5 PSKOV   A11
M20   Cherekha   Porkho
A116
PSKOV OBLA
Ostrov
A116
Pushkinskiye Gory   6   Novor
P58
MIKHAYLOVSKOY
Opochka
Sebezh   Pusto
M9
M20
Neve

Cruising Lake Ladoga aboard a high-speed river boat

*For hotels and restaurants in this region see p270 and pp288–9*

Austere façade of the bell tower of Trinity
Cathedral within the Kremlin, Pskov

## Getting Around

Russia's extensive rail network connects
St Petersburg with most of the major cities
in Northern Russia such as Petrozavodsk,
Sortavala, Pskov and Veliky Novgorod as
well as with settlements further north. Buses
run throughout the region, although poor
road surfaces often make for a rough ride.
During winter, road conditions can be
extremely hazardous due to snow and ice.
Kizhi and Valaam are well connected to the
mainland by hydrofoil services between
June and September. These islands can also
be reached on a cruise from St Petersburg.

Picturesque view of the red-brick Kremlin watchtowers, Veliky Novgorod

**For keys to symbols** see back flap

# ❶ Petrozavodsk

Петрозаводск
*Petrozavodsk*

410 km (255 miles) NE of St Petersburg.
🗻 260,000. ✈ 🚃 🚌 🚇 🚢
ℹ Ulitsa Kuybushev 5, (8142) 76
48 35. 🔲 ticrk.ru

Surprisingly attractive for an industrial city, Petrozavodsk, meaning Peter's Factory, is the capital of the Republic of Karelia, a vast area of largely untouched wilderness bordering Finland. Petrozavodsk's boulevards and Neo-Classical city centre lie on the gently sloping shore of Lake Onega, Europe's second largest lake. In summer the city is a popular stop for visitors on their way to Kizhi island; in winter, when the temperature drops to as low as -40°C (-40°F) it is mostly visited by locals.

Petrozavodsk was established by Peter the Great in 1703 to process local iron ore deposits into munitions for the Great Northern War with Sweden *(see p41)*. The foundry was later used during the Russo-Turkish Wars in the 18th and 19th centuries. The munitions factory has since been replaced by a tractor plant, but an 1873 statue of Peter the Great still marks the spot near the hydrofoil station where the city was founded. A short walk southwest through the park from here leads up to ploshchad Kirova, dominated by the colonnaded **Musical Theatre of the Republic of Karelia**. Facing the theatre on

Statue of Peter the Great on the embankment of Lake Onega, Petrozavodsk

one side is the **Kizhi Museum** with rotating exhibitions about Kizhi island, while opposite is the **Karelia Fine Arts Museum**, with modern works by regional artists. From ploshchad Kirova, Karl Marx prospekt passes the tractor factory, reaching ploshchad Lenina, with a statue of Lenin.

🎭 **Musical Theatre of the Republic of Karelia**
Ploshchad Kirova 4. **Tel** (8142) 78 44 42.
**Open** 11am–8pm Mon–Fri, 10am–6pm Sat & Sun (ticket office).
🔲 mrteatr.ru

🏛 **Kizhi Museum**
Ploshchad Kirova 10A. **Tel** (8142) 79 98 66. **Open** 10am–6pm daily. 🎫 📷 📱
🔲 kizhi.karelia.ru

🏛 **Karelia Fine Arts Museum**
Prospekt Marksa 8. **Tel** (8142) 78 37 13.
**Open** 10am–6pm Tue, Wed & Fri–Sun, noon–8pm Thu. 🎫 📷
🔲 artmuseum.karelia.ru

# ❷ Kizhi

Кижи
*Kizhi*

68 km (42 miles) NE of Petrozavodsk.
🚢 from Petrozavodsk. ℹ Ploshchad Kirova 10a, Petrozavodsk, (8142) 79 98 77. 🔲 kizhi.karelia.ru Note: The island is icebound between Oct and May; the only access is by helicopter, snowmobile or hovercraft. In summer, a hydrofoil from Petrozavodsk provides daily connections.

With its profusion of medieval wooden churches and home-steads set amidst lakeside scenery, Kizhi island is the highlight of a visit to Northern Russia.

One of over a thousand islands on Lake Onega, this island's main attraction is the Kizhi *pogost* (enclosure), which is part of the **Kizhi State Open-Air Museum**. A UNESCO World Heritage Site, the *pogost* comprises an iconic pair of multi-domed wooden churches that date from the 18th century. The stunning Transfiguration Church with its 22 cascading onion domes was built in 1714 and was used as a summer church, while the heated nine-domed Intercession Church was used in winter. The Transfiguration Church has been closed to the public since restoration work began in 1980, but the smaller Intercession Church is open to visitors. A hexagonal bell tower from 1862 stands between the two churches. A short walk south is the tiny **Resurrection of Lazarus**

The spectacular Transfiguration Church (left), the Intercession Church (centre) and the bell tower (right), Kizhi

**Church**, built in the 14th century and considered one of Russia's oldest wooden buildings.

Populated by peasant farmers in the 16th century, Kizhi island once supported 14 small settlements, of which only two, Yamka and Vasilyevo, remain. These two restored villages now form part of the "living museum" where visitors can see traditional craft making and observe a few members of the Old Believer community going about their daily life.

🏠 **Kizhi State Open-Air Museum**
**Tel** (8142) 53 57 22. **Open** year-round, see website for timings.
🖼️ 💻 🅿️ ♿ 🌐 kizhi.karelia.ru

🏠 **Resurrection of Lazarus Church**
**Tel** (8142) 53 57 22. **Open** year-round; call ahead for timings.

Façade of the Valaam Monastery with the bell tower rising in the background

## ❸ Valaam

Валаам

*Valaam*

239 km (149 miles) SW of Kizhi. 🚢 🚢
🛈 (812) 902 86 11. 🌐 **valaam.ru**
Note: Daily motor ships from St Petersburg and hydrofoils from Sortavala May–Oct. Icebound late Jan–Apr, when the only access is by helicopter, or, Jan–Mar, by hovercraft.

A trip across Lake Ladoga, Europe's largest lake, to Valaam Monastery is another highlight of a tour to Northern Russia.

Churches and chapels belonging to the monastery are scattered throughout the Valaam archipelago, which has been inhabited by monks since the 10th century. Its heyday was in the late 19th century under the perspicacious abbotship of

A hydrofoil ferrying visitors across Lake Ladoga to Valaam

Father Damaskin (1795–1881). Valaam was then part of Russian Finland and home to a thriving monastic community replete with its own brickworks, tannery and farm. The **Transfiguration Cathedral**, Valaam's spiritual centre, dates from 1887 to 1896. Following over half a century of neglect after the Soviets took over the territory in 1940, the cathedral was fully restored in 2005. Its splendid pale blue domes and a gold-tipped bell tower can be seen from afar.

The islands of the Valaam archipelago are home to a number of *sketes* (settlements of monks). One of the most famous is the red-brick Resurrection

Skete, consecrated in 1906. Nearby are the Gethsemane Skete and the Konevsky Skete, close to which is the refuge where Father Damaskin spent seven years in solitude before he was made abbot. All Saints Skete is closer and makes for an idyllic one-hour walk through the woods. Built in the late 18th century, it stands within a walled compound and is renowned for its strict monastic rules, which allow women to enter for only one day a year.

🏠 **Transfiguration Cathedral**
**Tel** (812) 902 85 72. **Open** 10am–5pm Mon–Fri, 10am–7pm Sat, 1–5pm Sun.
💻 ♿ 🌐 **valaam.ru**

### White Sea Canal

The White Sea Canal was built between 1931 and 1933 to connect the Baltic Sea with the White Sea through Lake Onega. It was an early pet project of Stalin's for which there was little need at the time. The construction was assigned to the thousands of political prisoners who were pouring into Gulag prison camps in the region. The project also provided the Soviet regime with the opportunity to portray the gruelling prison labour as necessary for "reforging" these "class enemies".

Prisoners at the construction site of the White Sea Canal

Stalin wanted the canal completed within 20 months and infamously demanded that it be built cheaply and quickly. As many as 170,000 convict labourers were put to work, but without mechanized equipment. Instead, shovels and picks were used to hack out the canal in appalling conditions, which led to an estimated 100,000 deaths. Terrified of failing to meet Stalin's impossible deadline, the construction chiefs had the canal dug shallower than necessary, which allowed them to complete the project four months early to great Soviet acclaim. However, as it wasn't deep enough to transport most seagoing ships, larger vessels had to have their cargo unloaded and transported by barge.

## ❹ Veliky Novgorod

Великий Новгород

*Velikiy Novgorod*

508 km (316 miles) SW of Petrozavodsk. 🚗 220,000. 🚉 🚌 Ⓜ 🚢 ℹ Ploshchad Sennaya 5, (8162) 77 30 74. 🌐 **visitnovgorod.com**

Thought to be Russia's oldest city, Veliky Novgorod celebrated its 1,150th anniversary in 2009 despite the exact date of its foundation being a matter of academic dispute. However, less contentious is the assertion that Novgorod was the birthplace of Russian democracy. It was here, between the 12th and 15th centuries, that a citizens' assembly had the power to make laws and to select or dismiss their leaders. Novgorod's historic centre, dominated by the walled Kremlin, dates back to the period when the city was a partner of the Hanseatic League and profited handsomely from exporting Russian furs to the West. As the capital of an independent state, Novgorod was powerful enough to rival Moscow, but Ivan the Terrible brought its supremacy to an end when his troops slaughtered 60,000 Novgorodians in 1570.

The restored **Kremlin**, on the left bank of Volkhov river, remains Veliky Novgorod's central feature, but the city's power has long since ebbed. It is a peaceful place with numerous churches, well-kept parks and a leisurely air. In summer, locals gather by the river to swim or sunbathe and to promenade across the footbridge.

Built within the Kremlin in 1045, the **Cathedral of St Sophia** is one of Russia's oldest surviving church buildings. As is typical of church construction from that period, the lavish iconostasis, giant chandeliers and bright frescoes were intended to inspire awe, while the almost window-less exterior and thick walls were designed to resist attack. Next to the cathedral is a 15th-century belfry that can be climbed for views over the river. The multiple arches that house bells are known as *zvonitsa* and are characteristic of the region's church architecture. The 17th-century **Kokuy Tower**, rising 41 m (135 ft) above the Kremlin's red-brick walls, offers sweeping views of the city.

Kokuy Tower, one of the major attractions within the Kremlin in Veliky Novgorod

Nearby is the **Museum of History, Architecture and Art** whose collection includes a chronological display of hundreds of icons dating from the 12th century and over a thousand medieval letters written on birch bark that were excavated in the 1950s.

Opposite the museum is the grand **Millennium Monument**, built in 1862 to commemorate the city's 1,000th anniversary. Cast from 65 tonnes (72 US tons) of bronze, it resembles a bell adorned with sculptures of famous Russian figures from bygone years. An ensemble of pretty medieval churches known as **Yaroslav's Court**, once the city's main square, lies across the footbridge east of the Kremlin.

🏛 **Cathedral of St Sophia**
**Tel** (8162) 77 35 56. **Open** 8am–8pm daily.

🏛 **Museum of History, Architecture and Art**
**Tel** (8162) 90 93 92. **Open** 10am–6pm Wed–Mon. **Closed** last Thu of the month. 🌐 **novgorodmuseum.ru**

## ❺ Pskov

Псков

*Pskov*

211 km (131 miles) SW of Veliky Novgorod. 🚗 200,000. ✈ 🚉 🚌 Ⓜ ℹ Ploshchad Lenina 3, (953) 242 57 00. 🌐 **tourism.pskov.ru**

Pskov benefited hugely from trade between the East and West in medieval times, becoming

The Millennium Monument, celebrating Novgorod's 1,000 years of history

*For hotels and restaurants in this region see p270 and pp288–9*

Splendid interior of the Trinity Cathedral in Pskov's Kremlin

Pokrovskaya Tower, a part of Pskov's outer ring of fortifications

a member of the powerful Hanseatic League and gaining independence from Veliky Novgorod, its overbearing neighbour, in the 14th century. This led to frequent attacks and sieges, but the heavily fortified city famously withstood all barring a few.

Following the region's belated acceptance of Christianity in the 12th century, churches were erected throughout Pskov. Many of these were destroyed during the course of World War II and those that survived were neglected during the Soviet era. Efforts have been made in recent years to restore them.

The **Kremlin** lies at the heart of Pskov, opposite ploshchad Lenina. Ensconced within its mighty walls is **Trinity Cathedral**, founded in the 10th century and rebuilt several times since; the current building was consecrated in 1699. Its austere, defensive exterior belies the stunning iconostasis within, which rises some 20 m (66 ft) to the base

of the central dome, and gleams with multiple rows of bright gilt-framed icons. South of the Kremlin, on the opposite bank of the Velikaya river, **Mirozhky Monastery** shelters the pretty turquoise-domed Transfiguration Cathedral whose interior walls are covered with well-preserved 12th-century frescoes that have earned it a place on the UNESCO World Heritage List. Facing the monastery across the river is the massive **Pokrovskaya Tower**, the southernmost point of Pskov's fortifications. It bore the brunt of 31 Polish and Lithuanian attacks during their unsuccessful siege of the city from 1581 to 1582.

Nearby is the **Pskov Museum of History, Architecture and Art**, which consists of several buildings. Foremost is the imposing 17th-century **Pogankin's Chambers**, built for a wealthy merchant and now home to a comprehensive display of 14th- to 17th-century Pskov icon painting and an impressive collection of antique silverware.

The adjoining museum has an exhibition devoted to Pskov's involvement in World War II.

🏠 **Mirozhky Monastery**
Mirozhskaya Naberezhnaya 2.
**Tel** (8112) 57 64 03. **Open** 11am–6pm Tue–Sun. 📷 🏠 🌐 mirozhsky-monastery.ru

🏛 **Pskov Museum of History, Architecture and Art**
Ulitsa Nekrasova 7. **Tel** (8112) 66 33 11.
**Open** 11am–6pm Tue–Sun. 📷 🏠
🌐 museums.pskov.ru

## ❻ Mikhaylovskoye
Михайловское
*Mikhaylovskoye*

130 km (81 miles) S of Pskov. **Tel** (81146) 2 23 21. 🚌 **Open** 10am–5pm Tue–Sun. **Closed** last Tue of the month.

This idyllic lakeside country estate in the settlement of Pushkinskie Gory belonged to Alexander Pushkin's mother. It was here, amidst lush meadows, lakes and dense forest, that the author and poet spent several happy summers during his childhood. After the authorities intercepted a letter in which Pushkin had expressed support for atheism, he was exiled to Mikhaylovskoye from Odessa. From 1824 to 1826, he lived in the family's small wooden house on the estate as a virtual prisoner but found the inspiration to complete several of his literary masterpieces. The house has been rebuilt several times since and was wholly restored in time for the 200th anniversary of his birth in 1999.

Pushkin was killed in a duel at the age of 37 (*see p93*) and was buried beside his mother in the nearby Svyatagorsky Monastery.

The family house at Mikhaylovskoye where Pushkin spent two years in exile

# KALININGRAD

Dotted with tumbledown castles where Teutonic knights once engaged in bloody battles, this isolated piece of Russia with its half-forgotten history, vast deposits of amber and expanses of desolate sea-bound dunes exudes a strong sense of romance. The regional capital Kaliningrad, formerly Königsberg, has awakened from its Soviet slumber and is a vibrant city replete with great museums, historic monuments and a thriving social scene.

Known as Eastern Prussia and ruled by the Teutonic knights during the Middle Ages, this region had been coveted by many for centuries before it fell to the Soviet Union. To resist the Poles in the south and Lithuanians in the north and east during the 15th-century Teutonic wars, castles and fortresses were built throughout the region. The province was reorganized within the Kingdom of Prussia in 1773, and Königsberg became the seat of government. Prussian kings had successive defensive rings of massive fortresses constructed around the city in the 18th and 19th centuries. However, these were no match for the relentless Allied bombardments in 1944–5 that razed most of Königsberg's historic buildings; a huge Soviet offensive in 1945 brought the territory to its knees.

As the Soviet Union's westernmost point, the Kaliningrad region gathered immense strategic value. It became a militarized zone that was completely off limits to foreigners, and was only opened to visitors in 1991, when the Union collapsed.

Although the symbols of Kaliningrad's Prussian heritage have long been neglected, the ruined architecture still evinces the region's glorious past. The Insterburg and Georgenburg castles are gradually being restored by enthusiastic local volunteers. The region's other attractions include the charming Baltic Sea resorts of Svetlogorsk, Yantarny and Zelenogradsk as well as the Curonian Spit, a UNESCO-listed strip of shifting dunes that stretches for 98 km (61 miles) between Kaliningrad and Lithuania.

A stretch of sandy beach against the calm waters of the Baltic Sea, Zelenogradsk

◄ The ancient water tower in the town of Svetlogorsk, an example of the region's impressive architecture

# Exploring Kaliningrad

Separated from the Russian mainland by Lithuania and Poland, and fringed by the Baltic coast, Kaliningrad *oblast* (region) is Russia's smallest territory. Most of the region comprises low-lying land dotted with patches of forest, and enjoys a temperate climate. Kaliningrad, the region's capital, sits to the west and boasts architecture redolent of its Prussian past. The city is punctuated by captivating museums and leafy avenues, and has the best choice of shops, restaurants, bars and clubs in the region. Easily accessible from Kaliningrad are the northwestern seaside towns of Zelenogradsk, Yantarny and Svetlogorsk. Yantarny is particularly delightful with its golden sand beach and incredible amber reserves. Further northeast lies the enigmatic Curonian Spit – a 5,000-year-old landform that has been recognized as a UNESCO World Heritage Site. Chernyakhovsk, the region's second-largest city, lies to the east and makes a good base for exploring the haunting castle ruins of nearby Insterburg and Georgenburg.

## Sights at a Glance

1. Kaliningrad pp216–17
2. Zelenogradsk
3. Curonian Spit
4. Svetlogorsk
5. Yantarny
6. Chernyakhovsk

## Key

— Major road
===== Minor road
—•— Major railway
— Minor railway
▬ International border

The Gothic Königsberg Cathedral with its towering steeple, on the waterfront in Kaliningrad

*For hotels and restaurants in this region see p270 and p289*

The golden domes of the Cathedral of Christ the Saviour towering above Kaliningrad's skyline

**KALININGRAD OBLAST**

## Getting Around

Regular bus and train services connect the city of Kaliningrad with coastal and inland towns, but roads are often single-lane highways, so traffic can be slow. Tours of the Curonian Spit can be arranged in either Kaliningrad or Zelenogradsk. It is advisable to check the final departure times of return buses and trains when planning day trips. Taxis are plentiful but drivers will often overcharge tourists. Car hire is best arranged in Kaliningrad.

A ship's steering mechanism at the Museum of the World Ocean, Kaliningrad

**For keys to symbols** *see back flap*

# ❶ Kaliningrad
## Калининград
### *Kaliningrad*

Capital of Eastern Prussia in the 13th century, Kaliningrad – then known as Königsberg – took great pride in its architecture, which was as exquisite as Prague's. However, the Allied bombardments and Soviet occupation in 1945 devastated its rich heritage. Renamed in 1946, Kaliningrad was closed to foreigners under the Soviet regime. After the collapse of the Soviet Union in 1991, the city struggled through a decade of economic uncertainty before its transformation into today's buzzing regional capital. Kaliningrad's 750th anniversary in 2005 saw the restoration of many historic buildings – a sign that the city is coming to terms with its traumatic past.

### 🏛 Königsberg Cathedral
Кафедральный собор
Кенигсберга
*Kafedralniy sobor Kjonigsberga*
Kneiphof Island, Ulitsa Kanta 1.
**Tel** (4012) 63 17 05. **Open** 9am–5pm daily. 🌐 sobor-kaliningrad.ru
The striking redbrick Gothic cathedral with its 60-m (197-ft) steeple has dominated the city's skyline for centuries. Built in the early 1300s shortly after Prussia's conquest by the Teutonic knights, it was virtually destroyed during the Soviet bombardments of Königsberg in 1944. The ruined cathedral barely escaped total annihilation in the Soviet era by those intent on eradicating symbols of the city's German past. Its Gothic grandeur was restored in the 1990s with the aid of German and Russian funding.

Today, the cathedral has an Orthodox and a Lutheran chapel and two museums dedicated to its history and to the philosopher Immanuel Kant (1724–1804), who is buried under the edifice's northeastern wall. The cathedral also houses Russia's largest organ.

### 🏛 Museum of the World Ocean
Музей Мирового Океана
*Muzey Mirovogo Okeana*
Petra Velikogo Embankment 1.
**Tel** (4012) 53 17 44. **Open** 10am–6pm Wed–Sun (check website for detailed opening hours). 🐟 🎥 🖥
🌐 world-ocean.ru

Aquariums packed with all manner of oceanic creatures, the remains of an 18th-century shipwreck and a 16-m- (52-ft-) long sperm whale skeleton are among the exhibits to be found within this quayside museum.

Its main draw is the chance to board the exhibition vessels moored nearby, including the B143 diesel-electric submarine, built in 1968 and operational throughout the Cold War. Its cramped crew quarters jammed with instruments, a working periscope and torpedo tubes emblazoned with Soviet stars provide a fascinating glimpse into life on board. Alongside is the *Vityaz*, a research ship famed for using a cable to measure the ocean's maximum depth for the

first time. It is now home to dozens of exhibit-filled rooms. Representing Kaliningrad's booming fishing industry during the Soviet era is the German-built SRT-129 trawler, capable of carrying up to 110 tonnes (121 US tons) of herring in its hold. It has since been converted into an exhibition space.

### 🏛 Art Gallery
Художественная Галерея
*Khudozhestvennaya Galereya*
Moskovskiy prospekt 60. **Tel** (4012) 46 71 43. **Open** 10am–6pm Tue, Wed & Fri–Sun, 10am–9pm Thu). 🚶
🌐 kaliningradartmuseum.ru

The gallery has a collection of contemporary works by both Russian and international artists. There are a number of Socialist Realism pieces as well as a small display of early 20th-century paintings by artists from pre-Soviet Königsberg. Temporary exhibitions are held regularly.

### 🏛 Museum of History and Art
Историко-Художественный Музей
*Istonko-Khudozhestvenniy Muzey*
Ulitsa Klinicheskaya 21. **Tel** (911) 868 31 76. **Open** 10am–5pm daily. 🚶
Housed in a beautifully restored building that served as the city hall from 1912 until World War II, this museum has exhibits from the pre-war, wartime and post-war periods with an emphasis on the Soviet era. Archaeological findings from local Viking settlements and early Prussian villages are also on display.

### 🏛 Bunker Museum
Музей Блиндаж
*Muzey Blindazh*
Ulitsa Universitetskaya 2a. **Tel** (4012) 53 65 93. **Open** 10am–5pm daily. 🚶
Tucked away in a park off the main street is the nondescript entrance to the bunker built in February 1945 for the German commander Otto Lasch. It was from here that he directed the defence of the city before surrendering Königsberg to the Soviet Army in April 1945 after days of relentless bombardments. One of the rooms re-creates the scene of Lasch signing the surrender document.

Giant sperm whale skeleton on display in the Museum of the World Ocean

*For hotels and restaurants in this region see p270 and p289*

The steep towers of the Cathedral of Christ the Saviour, ploshchad Pobedi

## ⛪ Cathedral of Christ the Saviour

Собор Христа Спасителя

*Sobor Khrista Spasitelyu*

Ploshchad Pobedi 2a. **Tel** (4212) 61 69 49. **Open** 9am–7pm daily.

Facing the main square and with its brilliant white marble façade and golden domes, this cathedral is testament to the bold resurgence of the Orthodox faith in Russia. Built in 2006, it is one of the largest cathedrals in Russia.

## 🏛 Amber Museum

Музей Янтаря

*Muzey Yantarya*

Ploshchad Marshala Vasilevskogo 1. **Tel** (4012) 46 68 88. **Open** May–Sep: 10am–7pm Tue–Sun; Oct–Apr: 10am–6pm Tue–Sun. 🌐 📷 📱
**W** ambermuseum.ru

Ninety per cent of the world's amber reserves are buried underneath the Kaliningrad region from where the "sun stone" has been mined for thousands of years. Housed in the Dona Tower, the Amber Museum has displays on the history of amber extraction and processing and a splendid array of amber artworks. Besides intriguing Soviet-era pieces such as "Epoch", a clock stand depicting technological achievements, there are many copies of 17th- and 18th-century amber artworks. The museum also exhibits replicas of the 4,000-year-old carved amber figures found near Juodkrante on the Curonian Spit and boasts a superb array of rare "inclusions": nuggets of amber with pre-historic insects trapped inside.

## 🏰 King's Gate

Королевские Ворота

*Korolevskie Vorota*

Ulitsa Frunze 112. **Tel** (4012) 58 12 72. **Open** May–Sep: 11am–7pm Tue, Wed & Fri–Sun, 1–8pm Thu; Oct–Apr: 11am–7pm Wed & Fri–Sun, 1–8pm Thu. 🌐 📷

Built in the 1840s as part of the city's second defensive ring, this mighty red-brick gate with thick walls features statues of Frederick I, Prussia's first king; Ottokar II, the king of Bohemia and Duke Albert, the last Grand Master of the Teutonic Order. It weathered the Soviet bombardment of 1944, and the damage was not repaired until 2005. Since then it has been used as a cultural centre and has a small museum dedicated to Peter the Great's visit to Königsberg in 1697.

## 🏰 Friedland Gate

Музей Фридландские Ворота

*Muzey Fridlandskie Vorota*

Ulitsa Dzerzhinskogo 30. **Tel** (4012) 64 40 20. **Open** 10am–6pm daily. 🌐

One of the last gates of the defensive ring to be constructed, Friedland Gate has the same red-brick Gothic structure as King's Gate. A statue of Siegfried von Feuchtwangen, a Grand Master of the Teutonic Order, that originally adorned its outer wall was restored in 2005, and the gate is now home to a museum exhibition dedicated to the history of Königsberg from 1862 to 1945.

Imposing red-brick façade of King's Gate

## Sights at a Glance

1. Königsberg Cathedral
2. Museum of the World Ocean
3. Art Gallery
4. Museum of History and Art
5. Bunker Museum
6. Cathedral of Christ the Saviour
7. Amber Museum
8. King's Gate
9. Friedland Gate

0 metres    800
0 yards     800

Holidaymakers enjoying the beach at Zelenogradsk

# ❷ Zelenogradsk

Зеленоградск

*Zelenogradsk*

30 km (19 miles) N of Kaliningrad. 🚇 13,000. 🚉 🚌 Ⓜ

Just half an hour by train from Kaliningrad, Zelenogradsk is the closest seaside resort to the region's capital. Originally an unassuming fishing village called Cranz, it first attracted tourists in the 19th century owing to its dune-backed beach that stretches for kilometres along the Curonian Spit. The village was soon overrun by wealthy Prussians who built wooden villas and guesthouses here. Renamed by the Russians, Zelenogradsk was neglected during the Cold War *(see p45)* and its status as a prime destination was usurped by Svetlogorsk.

Today, a new generation of middle-class Russians are replacing Zelenogradsk's German-era buildings with characterless modern villas, yet the resort's palpable sense of faded glory remains.

# ❸ Curonian Spit

Куршская Коса

*Kurshskaya Kosa*

1 km (half a mile) NE of Zelenogradsk. 🚌 from Zelenogradsk. ℹ No. 402, Ulitsa Sergeeva 2, Kaliningrad, (4012) 53 29 07. 🚗 W **park-kosa.ru**

Split equally between Lithuania and Russia, this intriguing land formation, known locally as Kurshskaya Kosa, was created around 5,000 years ago when retreating glaciers deposited a strip of glacial rubble off the shore of the Baltic Sea. Sand gradually accumulated along the 98-km- (61-mile-) long spit

to form a natural barrier between the Baltic Sea and the freshwater Curonian Lagoon.

A single road runs the entire length of the spit, which is just 400 m (1,312 ft) wide at its narrowest point and 4 km (2 miles) at its widest. Its landscape consists largely of pine forests and sandy beaches, from which Europe's largest drifting sand dunes rise to a height of up to 60 m (197 ft).

Although the region is home to just three small villages today, it was relatively densely inhabited in the past. However, deforestation in the 18th century damaged the ecosystem, as a result of which the sand dunes began to shift dramatically, burying entire villages. The spit was saved by the Prussian government's reforestation initiative in the 19th century, when a vast number of trees were planted in the area. It now enjoys national park status in Russia and UNESCO recognized it as a World Heritage Site in 2000.

# ❹ Svetlogorsk

Светлогорск

*Svetlogorsk*

33 km (21 miles) W of Zelenogradsk. 🚇 11,000. 🚉 🚌 🚕 ℹ Ulitsa Karla Marksa 7a, (40153) 2 20 98. W **svetlogorsk-tourism.ru**

Up until the early 19th century, Svetlogorsk was a humble Prussian fishing village called Rauschen. Once a path had been cut through its steep wooded hills to access the narrow strip of sandy beach below, it soon, however, evolved into a pleasant summer resort. A promenade and short pier were built to make the beach accessible to public, and several quirky sculptures and mosaics were added by resident sculptor Hermann Brachert (1890–1972). Installed on Svetlogorsk's promenade is one of his most famous works, *Nymph* (1938), a mosaic clam shell sheltering a life-size bronze statue of Venus.

The town's characterful 19th-century architecture includes the Water Tower, which offers mud baths and sea-water therapies. In recent years, an open cable car has been installed to save holidaymakers the walk between the town centre and the beach below.

### Environs

About 2 km (1 mile) west of Svetlogorsk is the village of Otradnoe – home to the cosy

The busy promenade and beach on a summer's day, Svetlogorsk

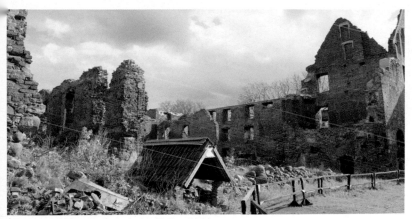

Impressive ruins of the Insterburg Castle – bastion of the Teutonic knights

**Hermann Brachert House-Museum**. The charming garden here features works by the sculptor, along with other pieces by contemporary artists.

**Hermann Brachert House-Museum**
Ulitsa Tokareva 7. **Tel** (40153) 2 11 66. **Open** 10am–5pm daily.

## ❺ Yantarny

Янтарный
*Yantarnyy*

21 km (13 miles) SW of Svetlogorsk.
6,400.

Meaning "amber" in Russian, Yantarny is an appropriate name for a town that sits upon 90 per

A shop in Yantarny selling luminous amber souvenirs

cent of the world's amber reserves. The town also boasts a breathtaking beach that is considered by many to be the best in the Kaliningrad region. Holidaymakers can make a day out of gathering small chunks of amber that are washed up onto the beach or found floating in the sea.

Amber, or "sun stone", has been fashioned into jewellery for millennia. In fact, an open-cast mine just outside Yantarny has been industrially extracting the precious fossilized tree resin since 1861. It currently produces around 200 tonnes (223 US tons) of raw amber every year. Visitors can watch the extraction process from a viewing platform.

## ❻ Chernyakhovsk

Черняховск
*Chernyakhovsk*

116 km (72 miles) SE of Zelenogradsk.
40,500.

Renamed after General Ivan Chernyakhovsky who led the Soviet forces against East Prussia in 1945, Chernyakhovsk started life as Insterburg, an isolated settlement that developed around the 14th-century Teutonic castle of the same name. The town was heavily bombed by the Allies during World War II, but a number of historic buildings have since been restored. Among them are the bright yellow house on ulitsa Pionerskaya where Napoleon stayed in 1812, a

crenellated 14th-century mill and a three-tiered church built in 1883 for the Lutherans, which now functions as St Michael's Orthodox Church.

Built by Teutonic knights in the 14th century, the red-brick **Insterburg Castle**, just outside town, now stands in ruins. The castle houses a gallery of local artworks and a small museum with a collection of donated antique exhibits from the old town. Visitors can also see the 14th-century castle vault. Several informative displays outline the exploits of the Teutonic knights who defended their order against Lithuanian attacks from here. A team of local volunteers runs the castle and organizes popular medieval-themed events in the summer.

Another formidable 14th-century Teutonic relic is the nearby **Georgenburg Castle**. Standing on a steep hillside above the Insterburg river, its façade still dominates the land-scape, but the interior is in need of restoration, for which locals are attempting to raise funds. Next door is the Georgenburg Stud Farm originating from the 18th century, when Trakehner horses were first bred here.

**Insterburg Castle**
Ulitsa Zamkovaya. **Tel** 8 906 233 78 63. **Open** 11am–6pm daily.

**Georgenburg Castle**
Ulitsa Centralnaya 10. **Tel** 8 911 473 26 58. **Open** by prior arrangement only.

# CENTRAL AND SOUTHERN RUSSIA

Colossal kremlins, gleaming golden-domed cathedrals, majestic mosques and monolithic Soviet-era buildings welcome visitors to this historic heartland of Russia. Winding its course through the region, the Volga river has played a crucial role in Russia's history. A vital trade and transport route, its banks are home to some of the country's finest cities.

Locally known as "Mother Volga", Europe's largest river meanders for 3,219 km (2,000 miles) through Central Russia's fertile grasslands before reaching the lush wet-lands of the Volga Delta where it drains into the Caspian Sea. For centuries, the river nurtured medieval citadels and trading posts, which came to be established along its course during Ivan the Terrible's forceful expansion of the Russian Empire in the 16th century. Fortified by kremlins and enriched by trade along the river, the settlements developed into glorious cities adorned with grand mansions, churches and state buildings.

Religion in all its forms was repressed during the Soviet era, but most religious buildings have since been returned to their communities. The cultural revival that began after the collapse of the Soviet Union in 1991 is in full swing. Since Russia's selection as host of the 2018 FIFA World Cup™, massive investment is being made in infrastructure projects to modernize the region.

A melting pot of cultures, the central and southern regions are inhabited by numerous ethnic groups, notably the Tatars, whose roots can be traced back to the 10th century when Islam was first adopted in Bolgar. The mosques and churches of Astrakhan and Kazan are a testament to the harmonious relations between the various cultures here.

Although tourism is still in its infancy in this region, its cities are a joy to explore. Today, the Volga is a source of summer leisure for locals who stroll along well-kept embankments or sunbathe on the riverside beaches. In winter, when the river freezes over, ice-hole fishing is a popular pastime.

Locals watching jugglers perform at Samara Embankment

◄ Multicoloured domes of the Church of the Blessed Virgin, Nizhny Novgorod

# Exploring Central and Southern Russia

Packed with sites of both historical and natural interest, the central and southern regions form the heart of Russia, although it covers only a fraction of the country's territory. Located along the Volga river, the cities of Kazan, Astrakhan and Nizhny Novgorod boast immaculate kremlins. Kazan also makes an excellent base from which to visit the ruins of Sviyazhsk and Bolgar that are currently being restored. The region is home to several cities famous for their historic quarters of wooden houses. Some of the best examples can be seen in Ulyanovsk and Yekaterinburg, where many have been converted into house-museums. Northwest of Yekaterinberg, Perm is a draw among art enthusiasts for its contemporary art scene. A must for history lovers, Volgograd counts striking war monuments and museums among its attractions. Astrakhan is the obvious base for trips into the Volga Delta, which delights with labyrinthine waterways that are home to lotus flowers, flamingoes and some of Russia's largest sturgeon.

CENTRAL AND SOUTHERN RUSSIA

■ Area illustrated

## Sights at a Glance

1. Nizhny Novgorod
2. Kazan
3. Staroye Arakchino
4. Sviyazhsk
5. Bolgar
6. Ulyanovsk
7. Saransk
8. *Samara pp228–9*
9. Volgograd
10. Astrakhan
11. Volga Delta
12. Perm
13. Perm-36 Memorial Centre of Political Repression
14. Kungur Ice Cave
15. Yekaterinburg

## Key

— Major road

::::: Minor road

-·-·- Major railway

-·-·- Trans-Siberian Railway

—— Minor railway

▬ International border

▬ Federal border

△ Peak

Buildings in the Old Tatar Quarter in Kazan

**For keys to symbols** *see back flap*

Wooden house with brightly painted shutters, Sviyazhsk

## Getting Around

Regular bus services connect most of the region's settlements. Road conditions, however, range from good to poor and tend to get worse in winter. Trains are a safe and efficient means of getting around; the Trans-Siberian route passes through Perm, Yekaterinburg and Nizhny Novgorod. Visitors seeking a quicker means of transportation can fly between the major cities in the region. A long-distance cruise on the Volga river is worth considering, although it is relatively slow and expensive.

The well-kept promenade overlooking the Volga river, Nizhny Novgorod

*For hotels and restaurants in this region see pp270–71 and pp289–90*

The splendid Annunciation Monastery overlooking the picturesque riverside, Nizhny Novgorod

# ❶ Nizhny Novgorod

Нижний Новгород

*Nizhniy Novgorod*

430 km (267 miles) NE of Moscow.
🌆 1,250,000. ✈ 🚆 🚌 🚊 🚕 🚇
🚢 🚢 **w** admgor.nnov.ru

This refreshingly upbeat city with its robust **Kremlin**, elegant 19th-century architecture and a sprinkling of golden-domed churches sits on a hilltop above the confluence of two great rivers: the Volga and the Oka.

Nizhny Novgorod was founded in 1221 by Grand Prince Yuri II to defend the northeastern frontier of the Vladimir-Suzdal Principality that later merged with Muscovy. The city's first Kremlin was razed by the Crimean Tatars in 1408. A century later, a red-brick Kremlin, the region's strongest, was built to protect Muscovy's eastern border from the Tatars of Kazan. By the 19th century, the city had developed into a wealthy centre of commerce due to its port on the Volga river. Many of its elegant buildings, especially those lining the pedestrianized ulitsa Pokrovskaya, date from that period. During the Soviet era, it was renamed Gorky after Stalin's favourite Soviet writer, who grew up here.

Today, the Kremlin's reconstructed towers and walls give a definite sense of past glory. But the grounds within lack the atmosphere of other walled cities, as many of the original churches were demolished to make way for 19th-century and Soviet-era administration buildings. The view of the Volga river

from within the Kremlin never fails to disappoint. The early 16th-century Dmitri Tower, the Kremlin's main gate, was rebuilt between 1949 and 1969.

A museum within the tower tells the story of its reconstruction. The tent-roofed **Archangel Mikhail Cathedral**, dating from 1628, houses the tomb of Nizhny Novgorod's celebrated son, Kuzma Minin, a butcher who famously raised an army of local volunteers with Prince Dmitri Pozharskiy to rescue Moscow from Polish invaders in the early 17th century *(see p41)*. An obelisk near the cathedral commemorates their heroism. The arsenal building running along the wall to the right of Dmitri Tower houses the National Centre of Contemporary Art, which regularly hosts exhibitions by Russian and international artists. A short walk northwest is the **State Art Museum**, with a collection of Russian and Western European works.

Below the Kremlin, on the banks of the Oka river, is the 18th-century **Church of the Blessed Virgin** with its wedding-cake structure and multicoloured domes. Equally impressive is the nearby **Annunciation Monastery**, founded in 1229. On the other side of the city is the AM Gorky Museum-Apartment, one of the three museums dedicated to the life of

Maxim Gorky. The open-air **Museum of Volga People's Architecture**, which lies south of the city centre, contains 18th- and 19th-century wooden houses and churches that have been moved here from around the Volga region.

🏛 **Kremlin**
pl. Minina i Pozharskogo. **Tel** (831) 422 10 80. **Open** 10am–5pm Tue–Sun.
**w** ngiamz.ru

🏛 **State Art Museum**
Kreml, Korpus 3. **Tel** (831) 439 13 73. **Open** 11am–6pm Wed & Fri–Mon, noon–8pm Thu. 🎨 📷
**w** artmuseumnn.ru

⛪ **Annunciation Monastery**
Melnichny pereulok. **Tel** (831) 430 07 97. 📷 call ahead to book.

🏛 **Museum of Volga People's Architecture**
Shchelokovsky Kutor Park. **Tel** (831) 422 10 88. **Open** 10am–5pm Tue–Sun.
🎨 📷 **w** ngiamz.ru

The imposing Dmitri Tower, Nizhny Novgorod

*For hotels and restaurants in this region see pp270–71 and pp289–90*

# ❷ Kazan

Казань
*Kazan'*

387 km (240 miles) SE of Nizhny Novgorod. 🚂 1,160,000. ✈ ✈
🚉 🚌 🚊 🚇 Ⓜ 🚋 🚢 ℹ Ulitsa Kremlovskaya 15, (843) 292 30 10.
Ⓦ gokazan.com

A thriving, progressive city, Kazan has invested massively in modernization programmes yet has deep historic roots. Originally part of the ancient Volga Bulgaria kingdom, it was not until the 15th century that the Kazan khanate was formed, with Kazan as its powerful Islamic capital. Trade along the Volga river brought immense wealth to the khanate. Soon this attracted the attention of Russia's Ivan the Terrible, who captured the city in 1552. Under Russian rule, the white-stone **Kremlin** was constructed and onion-domed churches were built alongside Kazan's ancient mosques. But Soviet rule after 1917 stifled the city's multiculturalism by razing many oreligious buildings. Since the collapse of the Soviet Union, Kazan has emerged as a city proud of its mixed-faith heritage. Officially recognized as Russia's third city, Kazan is also known as the country's sporting capital.

Kazan's focal point is its hilltop Kremlin, overlooking the confluence of the Kazanka and Volga rivers. The 16th-century Spasskaya Tower is the main entrance to the Kremlin. The Cadet School now houses the Hermitage Centre, a branch of the St Petersburg Hermitage. The minarets of the grand **Kul Sharif Mosque** rise behind the Cadet School. Built in 2005 for Kazan's millennium celebrations, this huge mosque has an observation balcony on the third floor. The six-tiered Suyumbike Tower, which leans at a rather alarming angle, was named after the last queen of Kazan and stands at the heart of the Kremlin alongside the presidential palace and the **Annunciation Cathedral**, commissioned by Ivan the Terrible in 1552.

Across from the Kremlin's main entrance is the **National**

Empress Catherine I's carriage in the National Museum of the Republic of Tatarstan, Kazan

**Museum of the Republic of Tatarstan.** Housed in a palatial 19th-century building, the museum's exhaustive collection covers the region's history in great detail. Among the notable exhibits is Empress Catherine I's carriage, used during her visit to Kazan in 1767. Nearby, the **St Peter and Paul's Cathedral** is one of the city's finest buildings, built to commemorate Peter the Great's visit to Kazan in 1722.

The far end of pedestrianized ulitsa Bauman, Kazan's central street, is dominated by the red-brick Epiphany Bell Tower, erected in 1897 to accompany

the modest 18th-century Epiphany Church to its rear.

South of the city centre lies the Old Tatar Quarter. Sadly, most of its characterful wooden buildings have been replaced with modern blocks. Of the quarter's surviving mosques, Nurallah Mosque, built in 1849, is Kazan's oldest working one. The late 19th-century **Azimov Mosque**, with its elaborate decorative brickwork, is considered the city's most beautiful.

🕌 **Kremlin**
Kazan. **Tel** (843) 567 80 74.
**Open** 8am–10pm daily.
Ⓦ kazan-kremlin.ru

🕌 **Annunciation Cathedral**
**Open** 9am–6pm daily.

🏛 **National Museum of the Republic of Tatarstan**
Ulitsa Kremlenskaya 2. **Tel** (843) 292 89 84. **Open** 10am–6pm Tue, Wed, Sat & Sun, 1–9pm Thu, 10am–5pm Fri. 📷 📷 Ⓦ tatmuseum.ru

🕌 **St Peter and Paul's Cathedral**
Ulitsa Musy Dzhalilya 21.
**Open** 9am–6pm daily.

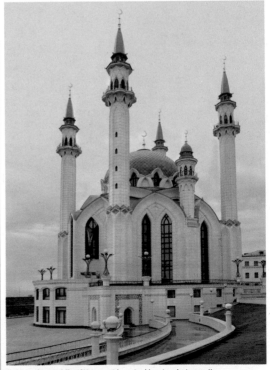
The magnificent Kul Sharif Mosque with soaring blue-tipped minarets, Kazan

## ❸ Staroye Arakchino

Старое Аракчино

*Staroe Arakchino*

10 km (6 miles) W of Kazan. 🚉 🚌
ℹ️ Ulitsa Kremlovskaya 15/25, (843)
292 30 10. 🆆 **gokazan.com**

A small suburb of Kazan until 1994, Staroye Arakchino has since been put on the map by sculptor and healer Ildar Khanov's inspiration to build the **Temple of All Religions** beside the local railway station. Relying on donations and volunteer labour has meant slow progress, but the unusual structure is finally nearing completion. A gloriously eclectic blend of colours, styles and shapes, the temple has a tower, dome, minaret or spire for each of the world's 12 major religions.

The striking Temple of All Religions, Staroye Arakchino

## ❹ Sviyazhsk

Свияжск

*Sviyazhsk*

60 km (37 miles) SW of Kazan. 🔼 300.
🚌 ⛴ 🚉 from Kazan. ℹ️ Ulitsa
Kremlovskaya 15, Kazan, (843) 292 30 10.

The settlement of Sviyazhsk has been considered an island since the Kuybyshev Reservoir, a hydro-electric dam, raised water levels in 1957, but it is still accessible by a strip of road. Ivan the Terrible chose the spot in 1551 to build a base after his attempt to conquer Kazan ended with a humiliating retreat. His troops turned the barren hilltop into a fortress larger than Moscow's before laying siege to Kazan and finally taking the city in 1552. In a curious historical parallel, the Bolshevik Red Army used Sviyazhsk as a base from which to defeat their White Army foes at Kazan in 1918.

Following huge local government investment, Sviyazhsk's decaying collection of ancient

ruins has recently been transformed into a major tourist attraction. The restored 16th-century church and cathedral within the walled **Assumption Monastery** are the island's oldest buildings and contain fragments of frescoes painted during the reign of Ivan the Terrible. Typically for the period, both are simple structures that were built with defence in mind. Across from these are the Monastery Stables, where local craftsmen demonstrate their traditional skills and children can ride horses in the yard.

Further inland is the **John the Baptist Monastery** with its red-brick Church of Our Lady from 1898 and a replica 16th-century wooden church. At the opposite end of the island, the town square overlooks the river port.

🏛 **Assumption Monastery**
Ulitsa Uspenskaya. **Tel** (917). 919
03 95. **Open** 8am–6pm daily.
♿ 🆆 **ostrovgrad.org**

🏛 **John the Baptist Monastery**
Ulitsa Troitskaya. **Tel** (917) 279
60 92. **Open** 10am–5pm daily.
🆆 **ostrovgrad.org**

## ❺ Bolgar

Болгар

*Bolgar*

198 km (123 miles) S of Kazan. 🔼 8,300.
🚌 from Kazan. ⛴ from Kazan. 🚉
from Kazan. ℹ️ Ulitsa Kremlovskaya 15,
Kazan, (843) 292 30 10.

The ancient riverside capital of Volga Bulgaria is of great significance to Russia's Muslims as it was here in AD 922 that Islam was first accepted on what is now Russian soil. Bolgar's historic ruins are part of the open-air **Great Bulgar Museum**, just outside modern Bolgar. Although they were neglected during the Soviet era, the region's influential Muslim community has since attracted local government investment to enhance the site.

Of the ruins spread over a vast expanse of grassland, the 13th-century Main Mosque forms the centrepiece. Its restored minaret is the focus of annual celebrations to mark Bolgar's acceptance of Islam. Nearby are the restored 14th-century Eastern and Northern Mausoleums and the 18th-century Assumption Church, which is seen as a symbol of the region's harmonious inter-faith relations. To the north is the small minaret that offers great views from its balcony, and the Black Chamber that served as a courtroom in the 14th century.

Opposite the museum stands the Monument to the Adoption of Islam that houses Kazan's Great Koran, the largest printed one in the world. Near the southern

Stunning view of the island town of Sviyazhsk on the frozen Volga river

gate to the museum is the splendid **White Mosque**, next to which is the **Museum of Bread**, which focuses on agricultural cycles and bread-making techniques.

**🏛 Great Bulgar Museum**
Ulitsa Nazarovyk 67. **Tel** (843) 473 94 14. **Open** 8am–5pm daily. 🖼 💻 🏛

## ❻ Ulyanovsk
Ульяновск
*Ulyanovsk*

231 km (143 miles) SW of Kazan.
🏛 610,000. ✈ 🚍 🚌 🚆 🚇 ⛴
🌐 welcometoulyanovsk.com

Named after one of the 20th century's most influential figures, Ulyanovsk is the birthplace of Vladimir Ilyich Ulyanov (1870–1924), better known as Lenin. Known as Simbirsk when the city was founded, it was here that Lenin, the mastermind of the October Revolution, spent his first 17 years. The various houses that his wealthy middle-class family rented or owned have been preserved; two of them form the core of the **Lenin Memorial Centre**. Built in 1970 to commemorate his 100th anniversary, the museum is packed with Lenin-related memorabilia.

Ulyanovsk's position above the Volga river affords superb views and many of its 19th-century wooden houses in the leafy suburbs are in remarkably good condition. Lined with pretty wooden houses is ulitsa Lenina, one of Simbirsk's oldest

One of the many wooden houses on ulitsa Lenina, Ulyanovsk

The Military Museum, Saransk

streets. **Melochnaya Lavka** at No. 78 is a small museum that has re-created the interior of a 19th-century general store. On the next street, the **Simbirsk Museum of Architecture** is housed in a wooden building, with elaborately decorated eaves and window frames.

**🏛 Lenin Memorial Centre**
Ploshchad 100-Letiya Lenina 1. **Tel** (8422) 44 24 43. **Open** 10am–5pm Tue–Sun. 🖼 🏛

**🏛 Melochnaya Lavka**
Ulitsa Lenina 76. **Tel** (8422) 32 18 79. **Open** 9am–5pm Tue–Fri & Sun, 11am–7pm Sat. 🖼 🏛

**🏛 Simbirsk Museum of Architecture**
Ulitsa L Tolstogo 24. **Tel** (8422) 42 04 63. **Open** 10am–5pm Tue–Sun. 🖼

## ❼ Saransk
Саранск
*Saransk*

229 km (142 miles) SW of Ulyanovsk.
🏛 295,500. 🚍 🚌 🚆

The capital of the Russian Republic of Mordovia, Saransk is home to a significant minority of ethnic Mordovians who speak either Moksha or Erzya. Both languages have Finno-Ugric roots and are listed as endangered by UNESCO. Mordovian culture can be traced back to the 6th century, but Saransk was founded only in 1641 as a fortress to protect Russia's eastern frontier. Although fires in the 19th century and decades of Soviet city planning left Saransk with little architectural heritage, in recent years the city has invested heavily in a reconstruction programme due

for completion before it hosts the FIFA World Cup™ in 2018. The city's new centrepiece is the golden-domed **Theodore Ushakov Cathedral**, consecrated in 2006 and fronted by immaculate flowerbeds. Just behind is the War Memorial dedicated to Mordovian soldiers who died in World War II, and the circular **Military Museum**, which tells the stories of Russia's 20th-century wars. The **Mordovian Museum of Visual Arts** houses works by acclaimed Mordovian sculptor Stepan Erzia (1876–1959).

**🏛 Theodore Ushakov Cathedral**
Ulitsa Bolshevistskaya. **Open** 7am–9pm daily. 🏛

**🏛 Military Museum**
Ulitsa Sovetskaya 34. **Tel** (8342) 47 50 00. **Open** 10am–6pm Tue–Sun. **Closed** last Tue of the month. 🏛

**🏛 Mordovian Museum of Visual Arts**
Ulitsa Kommunisticheskaya 61. **Tel** (8342) 47 80 04. **Open** 9am–6pm Tue, Wed & Fri–Sun, 11am–8pm Thu. 🖼 🏛 🌐 erzia-museum.ru

The splendid 21st-century Theodore Ushakov Cathedral, Saransk

# ❽ Samara
Самара
*Samara*

Founded as a fortress in the 16th century to protect Russia's eastern border, Samara soon developed into a bustling city because of its location along the Volga trading route. Known as Kuybyshev in 1935 after Stalin's key economic advisor, Valerian Vladimirovich Kuybyshev, the city was chosen as the Soviet Union's alternative capital should Moscow fall to the Germans during World War II. The city regained its original name in 1991 when it was also fully opened to foreigners. Today, the charming historic centre and the lovely embankment, with sweeping views of the Volga river, make Samara a pleasant city to visit.

### 🏛 Regional Art Museum
Самарский Областой
Художественный Музей
*Samarskiy Oblastoy
Khudozhestvenniy Muzey*
Ulitsa Kuybysheva 92. **Tel** (846) 333 46 50. **Open** 10am–6pm Wed, Fri–Mon & 1–9pm Thu. **Closed** second Mon of the month. 🅿 🏛 ♿ 🆆 artmus.ru

A short walk north of the Lenin Statue that dominates ploshchad Revolyutsii, this museum is worth visiting for a glimpse of the splendid interior alone. Its large collection includes a significant number of pieces from the Soviet era such as the evocative *Lenin on Red Square* (1934) by Boris Yohansen, a leading Soviet painter in the 1930s. In addition, the museum contains Russian 18th- to 19th-century and avant-garde paintings, along with an impressive collection of exhibits from the Middle East and Asia.

### 🏛 Children's Art Gallery
Детская картинная галерея
*Detskaya Kartinnaya galereya*
Ulitsa Kuybysheva 139. **Tel** (846) 332 43 98. **Open** 9am–5:30pm daily. 🅿

Dedicated to exhibiting and encouraging children's art

since 1991, this unique gallery has a delightful collection. The museum occupies a fantastic 19th-century mansion that was built for a wealthy merchant who made his fortune by importing Edison's electric light bulbs. The mansion's combination of Russian and German architectural styles, replete with a fairytale turret, make it one of the city's most iconic buildings.

### 🏛 Alabin Museum
Музей Им П.В. Алабина
*Muzey IM PV Alabina*
Ulitsa Leninskaya 142. **Tel** (846) 333 64 23. **Open** 10am–6pm Tue–Sun, 1–9pm Thu. **Closed** second Wed of the month. 🅿 🖥 🏛
🆆 alabin.ru

One of the region's oldest, the Alabin Museum was founded by city mayor Petr Alabin in 1886. Although the museum has a somewhat uninviting, concrete exterior, its collection of over 180,000 exhibits is worth visiting. The wide range of displays includes 14th-century weapons, ancient coins and clothes as well as dinosaur fossils.

### 🏛 Stalin's Bunker
Бункер Сталина
*Bunker Stalin*
Ulitsa Frunze 167. **Tel** (846) 333 35 71. **Open** 11am–3pm Mon–Fri. 🅿 🏛 🏛
🆆 bunkerstalina.com

A well-guarded secret until 1990, this 37-m (121-ft) deep bunker was constructed between February and December 1942. It was intended to accommodate Stalin and his State Defence Committee in the event of their evacuation from Moscow as German troops advanced towards the capital. But Stalin stayed in Moscow and never made use of the bunker. Now open as a museum, visitors descend five floors to the lowest level to see a 70-sq m (753-sq ft) copy of the Kremlin's meeting hall as well as the private office intended for Stalin's use.

### Zhiguli Brewery
Жигулёвский
Пивоваренный Завод
*Zhigulevskiy Pivovarenniy Zavod*
Volzhsky prospekt 4. **Tel** (846) 332 41 75. 🆆 samarabeer.ru

This imposing red-brick brewery was built on the bank of the Volga river in 1881 by an Austrian entrepreneur. Within a few years, his award-winning Vienna Beer was being distributed throughout Russia and was regarded as one of the country's best. During the Soviet era, the beer's bourgeois name was changed to Zhiguli, after the Zhiguli Hills nearby. It became the country's most popular beer following its production in vast quantities at hundreds of breweries across Russia. Zhiguli beer remains hugely popular, and Samara is considered the best place to sample it. Locals can be seen queuing outside the brewery through the year to buy fresh draught beer from its shop.

A bottle of
Zhiguli Beer

### 🏛 Monument of Glory
Монумент Славы
*Monument Slavy*
Ploshchad Slavy.

This striking monument features a tapering 40-m (131-ft) high pedestal upon which a gleaming

The austere façade of the Alabin Museum

*For hotels and restaurants in this region see pp270–71 and pp289–90*

The magnificent Monument of Glory, dedicated to aviation workers

statue of a worker holds aloft a pair of silver wings. It was erected in 1971 to celebrate the heroic achievements of Samara's aviation workers, who produced the IL-4 bomber and over 36,000 IL-2 ground attack planes during World War II. The neighbouring War Memorial and eternal flame were also built in 1971. In the northeastern corner of the square stands the golden domed St George's Cathedral, which was added in 1997 to commemorate the 55th anniversary of the Soviet Union's victory in World War II.

### Samara Embankment
Самарская набережная
*Samarskaya naberezhnaya*
With a sandy beach stretching for several kilometres along the shore of the Volga river, the Samara embankment is the city's most attractive feature during summer. The embankment has a raised promenade, which is thronged with locals walking, roller-skating, cycling

and jogging past a seemingly endless succession of cafés and bars. The beach below is a major draw for sunbathers.

### 🏛 Samara Space Museum
Самара Космическая
*Samara Kosmicheskaya*
Prospekt Lenina 21. **Tel** (846) 263 39 35.
**Open** 10am–6pm Tue–Fri, 10am–5pm Sat, 11am–3pm Sun. **Closed** first Tue of the month. 🅿 ♿ w
samaracosmos.ru

The highlight of this museum's exterior is the awe-inspiring 50-m- (164-ft-) high Soyuz rocket that seems to puncture the skyline like a modern-day church spire. Opened in 2007, the museum's well-presented exhibits cover the Russian space industry's recent history. Samara has a long history of involvement in the space industry. In 1961, Yuri Gagarin was brought to rest in the city after successfully orbiting the Earth in his Vostok 1 spacecraft, which, along with the later Soyuz rockets, was designed and built here.

Summer crowds at the beach along the Samara Embankment

## Sights at a Glance

① Regional Art Museum
② Children's Art Gallery
③ Alabin Museum
④ Stalin's Bunker
⑤ Zhiguli Brewery
⑥ Monument of Glory
⑦ Samara Embankment
⑧ Samara Space Museum

The splendid Kul Sharif Mosque, iconic of Kazan's multicultural heritage ▶

A tank on display in the Battle of Stalingrad Panorama Museum

# ❾ Volgograd
Волгоград
*Volgograd*

810 km (503 miles) SW of Samara.
🏙 1,020,200. ✈ 🚉 🚌 🚇 🚢

Built to defend Russia's southern border, Volgograd was founded in the 16th century as a fortress called Tsaritsyn. It did not bear witness to major warfare until 1918, when the Russian Red and White armies clashed here repeatedly *(see p44)*. But it was in August 1942 that the city, renamed Stalingrad, saw the Soviet Union fight the invading Axis armies in the landmark Battle of Stalingrad. By February 1943, the battle had claimed around two million lives, and the city was in ruins. Renamed Volgograd in 1961, the city has since been rebuilt, but the horrors of war are unlikely to be forgotten.

### 🏛 Mamayev Kurgan
Мамаев Курган
*Mamaev Kurgan*
Mamayev Kurgan hill. **Open** 24 hrs daily.

A strategic location that witnessed intense fighting during the Battle of Stalingrad, Mamayev Kurgan hill is now the site of a remarkable memorial complex to all who perished in the battle. Broad flights of steps, flanked by relief sculptures of battle scenes, lead visitors to the centrepiece – a mighty statue of Mother Russia wielding a 27-m (89-ft) sword. Built in 1967, it is one of the largest freestanding statues in the world. Just below is the cylindrical Hall of Glory, with a huge statue of a hand holding an eternal flame in the centre. A guard of honour keeps constant vigil.

### 🏛 Battle of Stalingrad Panorama Museum
Музей-панорама Сталинградская Битва
*Muzey-panorama Stalingradskaya bitva*
Ulitsa Chuykova 47. **Tel** (8442) 23 72 72.
**Open** Apr–Oct: 10am–6pm Tue–Sun (till 9pm Thu & 8pm Sat); Nov–Mar: 10am–6pm Tue, Wed & Fri–Sun (till 8pm Sat), 1–9pm Thu. 🅿 📷
**W** stalingrad-battle.ru

A visit to this enthralling museum is a must. The ground floor shows the stages of the Battle of Stalingrad chronologically, from the German advance during Operation Barbarossa to the eventual Soviet victory. Exhibits include mangled weapons found on the battlefield, a General's greatcoat riddled with bullet holes, military vehicles and battle plans. The central spiral staircase ends in a model of Mamayev Kurgan hill surrounded by a panoramic painting of the battle. The war-damaged flour-mill building outside the museum has been left untouched as a monument to the horrors of war.

The grand arch on the Volga-Don Canal opposite the Volga-Don Canal Museum

### 🏛 Regional Museum
Краеведческий Музей
*Kraevedcheskiy Muzey*
Prospekt Lenina 7. **Tel** (8442) 38 84 46.
**Open** 10am–6pm Wed–Mon. 📷

This museum offers a glimpse of life in pre-Soviet Volgograd (Tsaritsyn). Scale models and maps of the old town are on display alongside big-barrelled flintlock muskets and pistols from the 18th century. Peter the Great's felt cap and cane, which he donated to the museum during a visit to the town, hold pride of place. A copy of his death mask can also be seen.

### 🏛 Old Sarepta Ethnographic Museum
Музей этнографический "Старая Сарепта"
*Muzey-Zapovednik "Staraya Sarepta"*
Ulitsa Izobilnaya 10. **Tel** (8442) 67 33 02. **Open** 9am–5pm Tue–Sun. 📷 📷
📷 **W** altsarepta.ru

Located far enough from the battle scene to have survived World War II relatively unscathed, this small cluster of 18th- and 19th-century buildings was built by Germans invited to the region by Catherine the Great. The Ethnographic Museum has a fine display of agricultural tools, traditional outfits, early medical instruments and household objects used by the Volga German community.

### 🏛 Volga-Don Canal Museum
Музей Истории Волго-Донского канала
*Muzey Istorii Volgo-Donskogo Kanala*
Ulitsa Fadeeva 35A. **Tel** (8442) 69 57 44.
**Open** 10am–noon & 1–4:30pm Tue, Wed & Fri. **W** volgodon-museum.ru

Located opposite the Volga-Don Canal, this museum features impressive exhibits on the history of the canal's construction. After two failed attempts under Peter the Great in the early 18th century, the 101-km (63-mile) canal was completed by Soviet political prisoners between 1948 and 1952. This connection between the two great rivers, the Volga and the Don, was the final link in the European waterway ring that served to shorten shipping routes.

# ⑩ Astrakhan
Астрхань
*Astrakhan'*

424 km (263 miles) SE of Volgograd.
520,000. 🚉 🚌 🚍 🚏 🚤

The immaculate 16th-century **Kremlin** in Astrakhan is one of Russia's best, but most visitors flock to this "capital of the Caspian Sea" to see the region's diverse flora and fauna. The city also has a pleasant riverside embankment and an atmospheric old quarter of mosques and weathered wooden houses.

Although Astrakhan today is mainly populated by ethnic Russians, it also has a significant minority of Tatars, whose roots date back to the once powerful Astrakhan khanate that fell to Ivan the Terrible in 1552. Construction of the Kremlin began soon after, with walls up to 5 m (16 ft) wide in places designed to withstand heavy bombardments. The Russian defenders knew that, in the event of an attack, there would be no reinforcements from Moscow. Of its seven towers, only three – the Zhitnaya, Crimean and Artillery towers – were part of the original complex. East of the Kremlin, the Prechistensky Gate serves as the

Exterior of the three-storey Dogadin Art Gallery, Astrakhan

main entrance. It is topped with a bell tower, built in 1912 to complement the adjacent 18th-century **Assumption Cathedral**. Its lower church is heated for winter use, while the upper cathedral, with its marble-clad walls, is used in summer. Opposite lies the 17th-century **Trinity Monastery**. Currently under renovation, it is one of the Kremlin's oldest buildings.

A short walk east of the Kremlin along ulitsa Sovetskaya is the **Regional Museum**. A collection of exquisite Sarmatian gold jewellery from the 4th and 5th centuries is among the museum's highlights. Further

east is the **Dogadin Art Gallery** with mostly Russian works that include paintings by Kazimir Maleevich (1879–1935), Vasily Kandinsky (1866–1944) and by Astrakhan-born painter Boris Kustodiev (1878–1927). The best of Kustodiev's works can be seen at the **Kustodiev House Museum** northeast of the city centre.

South of the May 1st Canal lies the old Kirushi Quarter. Part of former Tatar and Persian suburbs, it is dotted with dilapidated wooden residences. Several of the quarter's mosques have been renovated in recent years, but it is still in dire need of restoration.

🏛 **Assumption Cathedral**
Ulitsa Trediakovskogo 2, Kreml.
**Open** 8am–7pm daily. 📷
🌐 **astrsobor.ru**

🏛 **Regional Museum**
Ulitsa Sovetskaya 15. **Tel** (8512) 51 18 22. **Open** 9am–5pm Mon, Wed, Sat & Sun, 10am–9pm Thu. 📷 📷

🏛 **Dogadin Art Gallery**
Ulitsa Sverlova 81. **Tel** (8512) 51 11 21. **Open** 10am–6pm Tue, Wed & Fri–Sun, 1–9pm Thu. **Closed** last day of the month. 📷 📷 🌐 **agkg.ru**

# ⑪ Volga Delta
Астрахань
*Astrakhan*

70 km (43 miles) S of Astrakhan.
🚉 from Astrakhan. Note: A permit is required to enter the delta. Several tour agencies in Astrakhan organize trips to the delta.

Europe's largest river delta is a labyrinth of lakes and water channels formed from sediment dumped by the Volga river as it drains into the Caspian Sea. Although hunting and fishing are big business here, the wetlands also attract bird-watchers and nature-lovers in search of pristine beauty.

The star attraction of the Volga Delta is the **Astrakhan Biosphere Reserve**. Established in 1919, the huge reserve is home to a variety of exotic species of birds, fish and plants. The Museum of Nature within the reserve details its history and provides an insight into scientific studies.

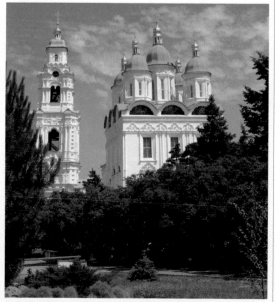
The Prechistensky Gate and the adjacent Assumption Cathedral, Astrakhan

## ⓬ Perm

Пермь

*Perm'*

663 km (412 miles) NE of Kazan. 🗺 990,000. ✈️ 🚆 🚐 🚌 🚕 🚢 🚢 *i* Ulitsa Sovetskaya 56, (342) 291 91 21. 📷 Jun: Perm Kaleidoscope. 🌐 **visitperm.ru**

Perm is blighted by its typically unappealing Soviet architecture, but progressive local policies have given a new lease of life to the city. Dotted with modern artworks and some lovely 19th-century buildings, the city centre has a Green Line, a walking and cycling route that links all the city's sights. The Perm Kaleidoscope summer festival is a regular feature of the city's cultural calendar, with dance shows, theatre and exhibitions.

An industrial centre since its foundation by Vasily Tatishchev in 1723, Perm was a centre of weapons production during World War II. Many west Russian factories were relocated to the city when Nazi armies threatened the Soviet capital. The city was subsequently rendered off-limits to foreigners until 1991.

Recent excavations suggest that the area has been inhabited since the Paleolithic Era. Related artifacts are on display at the **Perm Regional Museum**, housed in a palatial 19th-century mansion overlooking the Kama river. Among the museum's other intriguing exhibits are the "Perm

Exhibits on display at the Perm Museum of Contemporary Art

animal-style" bone ornaments carved with animal motifs that date back to the 5th century BC; copies are sold as souvenirs throughout the city. Opposite the museum is the former building of the River Boat Station, which is now occupied by **Perm Museum of Contemporary Art (PERMM)**. A capacious contemporary art gallery, it regularly hosts rotating exhibitions and is the hub of the city's thriving modern art scene. West of PERMM along the river bank is the **Perm State Art Gallery**, located in the grand Transfiguration Cathedral since 1922. Among its huge collection of Russian and West European artworks are numerous crude wooden figures, which were made for local churches but were often venerated as pagan idols in the 17th and 18th centuries. The gallery is due to be relocated to a building next to the Transfiguration Cathedral.

🏛 **Perm Regional Museum**
Ulitsa Monastyrskaya 11. **Tel** (342) 257 18 09. **Open** 10am–7pm Tue, Wed & Fri–Sun, noon–9pm Thu. 📷

🏛 **Perm Museum of Contemporary Art (PERMM)**
Bulvar Gagarina 24. **Tel** (342) 254 35 73. **Open** noon–9pm Tue–Sun. 🔲 📷 🌐 **permm.ru**

🏛 **Perm State Art Gallery**
Komsomolsky prospekt 4. **Tel** (342) 212 95 24. **Open** 10am–7pm Tue, Wed, Fri & Sat, noon–9pm Thu, 11am–7pm Sun. 🔲 📷 🌐 **gallery.permonline.ru**

## ⓭ Perm-36 Memorial Centre of Political Repression

Пермь-36 музей истории политических репрессий

*Muzey Istorii politicheskikh repressiy*

120 km (74 miles) NE of Perm; Kutchino, (342) 212 61 29. 🚐 **Open** 10am–6pm (last tour starts at 3pm) Tue–Sun. 🔲 📷 call ahead to book a tour. 🌐 **itk36.ru**

Of the many brutal Gulag prison camps set up during Stalin's repressive regime, Perm-36 is the only one to have survived. Now a memorial and museum, it was built in a remote forest in 1946. Unlike other camps that were relocated once they had served their purpose, Perm-36 remained in operation until 1987, when most political prisoners were pardoned. The preserved buildings include an original timber hut, the punishment block, bathhouse and infirmary. The museum details the life of prisoners who were woken at 6am for a meagre breakfast before a 90-minute march to work in temperatures as low as -40°C (-40°F).

Permian wooden sculptures at the Perm State Art Gallery

*For hotels and restaurants in this region see pp270–71 and pp289–90*

# ⓮ Kungur Ice Cave

Кунгурская ледяная пещера

*Kungurskaya Ledyanaya Peshchera*

98 km (61 miles) SE of Perm, Kungur District, Philippovka. **Tel** (342) 716 26 10. **Open** 10am–5pm daily (check website for tour times). 🚷 📷
Ⓦ **kungurcave.ru**

Located near the town of Kungur and accessible by taxi, the Kungur Ice Cave is one of Russia's most famous caves. Legend has it that the Cossack leader Yermak (1532–84) hid his looted treasure here. The cave, with its 6-km- (4-mile-) long subterranean passages, is best visited in February and March when the underground temperature averages -12°C (10°F) and the stalactite icicles and frozen stalagmites reach up to 2 m (7 ft) in length. There is an 80-minute tour that passes through a series of caverns and a 90-minute tour that ends with a laser show loosely based on the cave's mythological past.

Frozen stalagmites and stalactites in the fascinating Kungur Ice Cave

# ⓯ Yekaterinburg

Екатеринбург

*Ekaterinburg*

357 km (222 miles) SE of Perm. 🚉
1,400,000. ✈ �æ 🚌 🚐 🚇 Ⓜ
ℹ (343) 222 24 45. Ⓦ **ekburg.ru**

Situated on the eastern slopes of the Ural Mountains, Yekaterinburg straddles the border between Europe and Asia. The city was named after Peter the Great's wife and, like Perm, was founded in the early 18th century during the tsar's drive to industrialize the Ural region. As many as 50 factories were moved here from the west of the country during World War II. Despite being a major industrial zone, the city has retained much of its Neo-Classical architecture and exudes an air of cultural sophistication.

Among the city's notable attractions is the **Fine Arts Museum**. Founded in 1936, this museum houses the excellent Kasli Iron Pavilion, which showcases the Urals' traditional Kasli iron sculptures. It also contains a great collection of 16th to 19th- century Russian paintings. Northeast of the museum lies the **Literary Quarter**. The city had a lively literary scene in the 19th century, and several local authors' wooden houses have since been turned into house-museums. Nearby is the golden-domed **Church on the Blood**, built on the spot where Tsar Nicholas II and his family were

The splendid Church on the Blood, Yekaterinburg

executed under orders from the Bolshevik Party after the tsar's abdication in 1918 *(see p44)*. The cellar in which they were shot is now a shrine along with memorial stones to the tsar, his wife and their five children who have all recently been canonized by the Orthodox Church.

🏛 **Fine Arts Museum**
Ulitsa Voevodina 5. **Tel** (343) 371 06 26.
**Open** 11am–7pm Tue & Fri–Sun, 11am–8pm Wed & Thu. 🚷 📷

⛪ **Church on the Blood**
Ulitsa Tolmachev 34. **Open** 9am–9pm daily. 📷

## The Demise of the Romanovs

The Romanov family's 300-year rule of Russia came to an abrupt end following the February Revolution of 1917 when Tsar Nicholas II abdicated. Kept under house arrest until July 1917, the tsar and his family were then exiled to Tobolsk in Siberia. Their comfortable living conditions deteriorated after the October Revolution of 1917, but Nicholas II maintained his spirit by teaching Russian history to his children. In April 1918, the Bolsheviks moved them to Yekaterinburg, where they were accommodated in a house owned by Nikolai Ipatiev, a local engineer. Fearful of the Romanovs being rescued by White Russian forces that were approaching the region, the Bolsheviks hastily ordered their execution, gunning them down in the basement of Ipatiev House on the night of 17 July 1918.

Tsar Nicholas II (1868–1918) with his wife Alexandra and their five children

# THE CAUCASUS

With the enchanting open steppe to its north, the indomitable Caucasus Mountains at its heart and the sea and lush forests to the south, the Caucasus is a geographically diverse region that has long attracted settlers in search of fertile lands. Although it has been inhabited by a succession of native groups since ancient times, the northern Caucasus region is associated most strongly with its relatively recent and culturally rich Cossack past.

First colonized by the Greeks in the 6th century BC, the Black Sea coast was the scene of the Russo-Turkish wars from the 17th to the 19th centuries, when Russia and the Ottoman Empire fought for political control over the region. The native Slavic people, or Cossacks, helped realize the Russian tsars' dream and Russia eventually gained the territory through the 1829 Treaty of Adrianople. Over the next few decades, the coast's fishing villages were developed into resorts with sanatoriums providing specialist treatments. Concerned for their own health after Lenin's early death in 1924, Stalin and other high-ranking party members chose Sochi as the place for ministerial summer recuperation. This boosted the resort's popularity, earning it the title of Russia's summer capital.

However, after destructive occupation of the region by Axis forces during World War II, it was many years before the region returned to a state of normality.

Since the fall of the Soviet Union, the coast has drawn an ever-increasing number of wealthy Russian and foreign tourists. The selection of Sochi to host the 2014 Winter Olympics attracted huge investments to update the coast's ageing infrastructure, while simultaneously developing its winter sports facilities. Sochi also makes a good base for exploring the region. Day trips to the picturesque Sochi National Park or the ski resort of Krasnaya Polyana are a must on any itinerary. The quintessentially Cossack settlements of Krasnodar and Rostov-na-Donu are other favoured destinations.

The tranquil seaside promenade of Gelendzhik, with the hazy promontory jutting out into the Black Sea

◀ Hikers soaking up views of the pristine Caucasus Mountains

# Exploring The Caucasus

Sandwiched between the Black Sea and the Caspian Sea, this region derives its name from the mighty Caucasus mountain range that is considered to be a natural border between Europe and Asia. The southern Caucasian republics are politically unstable and hence unsuitable for tourism, but the north remains rather tourist friendly. Set against the tropical backdrop of the Black Sea coast, Sochi is a bustling resort city. Famed for its restorative santoriums, it was one of the host cities for the 2014 Winter Olympics. It also serves as a gateway to the expansive Sochi National Park, the ski-resort of Krasnaya Polyana and other provincial towns along the palm tree-lined coast. Watered by the Don and Kuban rivers, after which the local Cossack groups were named, Krasnodar and Rostov-na-Donu are steeped in Cossack history that is best explored by a visit to their regional museums.

THE CAUCASUS

■ Area illustrated

## Sights at a Glance

1. *Sochi pp240–41*
2. Sochi National Park
3. Adler
4. Krasnaya Polyana
5. Gelendzhik
6. Anapa
7. Krasnodar
8. Rostov-na-Donu
9. Starocherkassk

## Key

— Major road
⋯⋯ Minor road
⁓ Major railway
— Minor railway
▬ International border
— Federal border

Sochi's elegant tree-fringed promenade, against the backdrop of the Caucasus mountain range

*For hotels and restaurants in this region see pp271–2 and p290*

Kamensk-
Shakhtinskiy
Belaya Kalitva
Sinegorskiy
Novoshakhtinsk
Shakhty
Kamenolomni
Konstantinovsk
Tsimlyansk
ROSTOV-
NA-DONU
Novocherkassk
Volgodonsk
STAROCHERKASSK
Bolshaya Martynovka
zov
Bataysk
Don
ROSTOV
OBLAST
Zimovniki
Zernograd
Veselovskoye
Vodokhranilishche
Mechetinskaya
Proletarsk
Egorlykskaya
Tselina
Kushchevskaya
Gigant
Salsk
ningradskaya
REPUBLIC OF
KALMYKIA
Pavlovskaya
Gorodovikovsk
RASNODARSKY
KRAY
Novopokrovskaya
Tikhoretsk
Krasnogvardeyskoye
Kropotkin
Novoalexandrovsk
Izobilny
Ust-Labinsk
STAVROPOL
KRAI
Kurganinsk
Armavir
Stavropol
Kuban
REPUBLIC OF
lorechensk
ADYGEA
Maykop
Labinsk
Tulskiy
Apsheronsk
eftegorsk
Otradnaya
Kamennomostkiy
Shedok
Psebay
KRASNAYA
POLYANA
OCHI
SOCHI
NATIONAL PARK
ADLER

Monument to Kuban Cossacks, Krasnodar

## Getting Around

Sochi, Rostov-na-Donu and Krasnodar are served by airports with regular flights to destinations within Russia and Europe. Trains link all the major towns and cities and also run along the Black Sea coast connecting Gelendzhik and Adler. An efficient bus network covers the entire region and road conditions are generally good. Car hire is the quickest way to get around and can be arranged by hotels or travel agencies.

**For keys to symbols** *see back flap*

# ❶ Sochi

Сочи

*Sochi*

Nestling beneath the forested foothills of the Caucasus Mountains, Russia's summer capital is as popular as ever, especially following extensive regeneration for the 2014 Winter Olympic Games. Controlled by a succession of mountain peoples until it was ceded to Russia in 1829, Sochi was transformed into a sprawling health resort during the Soviet era after Stalin and his top ministers built their summer *dachas* here. Since then, the balmy seaside city has prospered and the massive Olympic investment in infrastructure and facilities has further enhanced its reputation.

Neo-Classical Maritime Terminal building topped by a steeple

## 🚆 Train Station

Железнодорожная станция

*Vokzal*

Ulitsa Gorkogo.

Conceived by renowned Soviet architect Alexei Dushkin (1904–77), the Sochi Train Station is a grandiose example of Stalinist-era architecture and design. Built between 1950 and 1952 from local sandstone and polished granite, the station is a complex architectural composition. Its huge arches, stately columns and high-ceilinged halls are based around a 55-m (180-ft) high clock tower that is adorned with zodiac symbols and topped with a gleaming red star.

## 🏛 History Museum

Музей истории

*Muzey Istorii*

Ulitsa Vorovskogo 54/11. **Tel** (862) 264 23 26. **Open** Jun–Aug: 9am–7:30pm daily. Sep–May: 9am–5:30pm Tue–Sun. 🎫 🏛

The museum's chronologically arranged exhibition space boasts an engaging series of mock-ups

Elegant façade of Sochi's History Museum

that include a prehistoric cave dwelling, a typical peasant cottage and the interior of a 19th-century ship. Early agricultural tools are also on display, along with Greek and Roman finds from the region. Black-and-white photographs tell the story of Sochi's architectural heritage being replaced by concrete blocks during the development of the city in the Soviet era. There is also a section devoted to the cosmonauts who have recuperated at Sochi's sanatoriums between space missions.

## 🚢 Maritime Terminal

Морской Вокзал

*Morskoy Vokzal*

Kurortny prospekt 74.

Built in 1955, the Maritime Terminal's elegant design was influenced by Sochi's earlier Neo-Classical buildings. Centred upon a tapering tower topped with the Soviet Union's ubiquitous red star, the terminal's vaulted upper floor is decorated with murals. A highly exclusive restaurant catering to luxury yacht owners has lovely views of the harbour.

## 🏖 Sochi's beaches

Пляжи

*Plyazhi*

Sochi's narrow pebble beaches and murky sea are not its most alluring features, but tourists flock to them nonetheless, and sun umbrellas and plastic deckchairs clog the limited beach space in summer. Centrally located restaurants and hotels often have private sections of beach reserved for clientele. However, for a more relaxing seaside experience, it is well worth travelling north of Sochi to access several cleaner and less crowded beaches.

## 🎭 Winter Theatre

Зимний Театр

*Zimniy Teatr*

Teatralnaya ulitsa. **Open** 10am–2pm daily (ticket office). 🎬 June: Kinotavr Film Festival. 🔲 **kinotavr.ru**

Another of Sochi's Neo-Classical Soviet-era buildings, the Winter Theatre's imposing colonnaded façade supports a portico topped with sculptures of Terpsichore, Melpomene and Thalia – the Greek muses of dancing, tragedy and comedy. Opened in 1938, it still hosts regular theatre performances as well as Kinotavr, one of Russia's major film festivals.

## 🌳 Arboretum

Дендрарий

*Dendrariy*

Kurortny prospekt 74. **Tel** (862) 262 18 42. **Open** 8am–8pm daily (till 6pm ticket office). 🎫 🏛
🔲 **dendrarium.ru**

The delightful arboretum (Dendrarium) dotted with fountains and monuments is among the city's highlights. Its 48 ha (119 acres) of lush grounds are home to over 2,000 plants and trees collected from around the world since its foundation in

*For hotels and restaurants in this region see pp271–2 and p290*

1892. A cable car runs to the top of the arboretum, affording superb views.

### 🏛 Art Museum

Художественный музей
*Khudozhestvenniy muzey*
Kurortny prospekt 51. **Tel** (862) 262 29 47. **Open** 10am–5:30pm Tue–Sun (till 8:30pm Sat).

The Art Museum is housed in a grand building with elaborate Neo-Classical motifs typical of Sochi's Stalinist-era architecture. Its interior is equally impressive with three floors of high-ceilinged halls that are packed with works by Russian and foreign artists from the 19th and 20th centuries. Notable among the numerous seascapes on display is *Heroic Landscape*, a gigantic work in pastel hues painted by Konstantin Bogaevski in 1930. Other artworks include a dramatic depiction of a sea battle by Viktor Samorezov and an image of a tumbledown seaside cottage painted in 1890 by Vyacheslav Korenev.

### 🞉 Riviera Park

Парк Ривьера
*Park Riv'era*
Kurortny prospekt. **Open** 10am–1am.
Hugely popular with children and promenading locals since it was opened in 1898, Riviera Park's expanse of woods and gardens that runs along the seafront is packed with play areas, eateries and fairground rides that stay open till dusk. Among the attractions is Cosmonaut Alley, where 45 Magnolia trees have been planted by American and Russian astronauts who have recuperated in Sochi since Yuri Gagarin started the tradition in 1961.

### Environs

Camouflaged by green paint that renders it virtually invisible from the surrounding countryside, Stalin's unpretentious summer *dacha*, **Zelenaya Roscha** *(see p272)*, is tucked away on a steep forested hill just outside the city. Built in 1937 for the infamous dictator, and featuring oak panelled interiors throughout, the quadrangular villa is in remarkably

good condition despite having been neglected for decades. The vaulted conference hall with its floor-to-ceiling windows and broad terrace with sweeping coastal view is open to the public, as is the hall where Stalin personally vetted every new Soviet film before its release.

### 🞉 Zelenaya Roscha

Green Grove, Kurortny prospekt 120.
**Tel** (862) 269 53 30. **Open** 8am–5pm by prior arrangement only.

Welcoming entrance to the lush Riviera Park

---

## Sights at a Glance

① Train Station
② History Museum
③ Maritime Terminal
④ Sochi's beaches
⑤ Winter Theatre
⑥ Arboretum
⑦ Art Museum
⑧ Riviera Park

| 0 metres | 800 |
| 0 yards | 800 |

Riviera Park ⑧   Train ① Station
② History Museum
③ Maritime Terminal
*Black Sea*
⑦ Art Museum
Sochi's beaches ④
⑤ Winter Theatre
*Sochi International Airport* 24 km (15 miles) ✈
Arboretum ⑥

**For keys to symbols** *see back flap*

Spectacular karst topography in the Vorontsovskaya cave, Sochi National Park

## ❷ Sochi National Park

Сочинский Национальный Парк

*Sochinskiy Natsionalnyy Park*

4 km (2 miles) NE of Sochi. **Tel** (8622) 62 18 42. from Sochi. Ulitsa Moskovskaya 21, 9am–5pm Mon–Fri.
**W** sochinp.ru

Established in 1983, this vast 1,940-sq km (749-sq mile) expanse of protected area is one of Russia's first national parks. All industrial activity in the region was halted when it was first created and strict planning laws were implemented to preserve the area's lumber.

Stretching from the sub-alpine meadows of the Caucasus Mountains through beech- and fir-covered foothills to the oak and chestnut forests that extend along the Black Sea coast, Sochi National Park has a diverse ecosystem. It is home to an enormous number of rare and endemic plants and animals that include several species of eagle, vulture and falcon besides wolves, bears, Persian squirrels and the endangered Caucasian

otter. Numerous trails link its wealth of canyons, rivers, waterfalls and karst caves, including Vorontsovskaya, the largest in the Caucasus region. The park attracts thousands of wildlife enthusiasts every year.

## ❸ Adler

Адлер

*Adler*

7 km (4 miles) SE of Sochi.
76,000.

Far more relaxed than its upmarket neighbour Sochi, this Black Sea resort boasts cleaner and more easily accessible beaches – a combination that appeals to young families and elderly tourists in particular. Restaurants and shops liven up its seaside promenade, which is the town's main attraction.

Although Adler was one of the host towns for the 2014 Winter Olympics, the acres of purpose-built accommodation were built just beyond its suburbs. The impact of the games on the town was limited to initiatives to spruce up the seafront.

## ❹ Krasnaya Polyana

Красная Поляна

*Krasnaya Polyana*

43 km (27 miles) NE of Adler.
4,600.

From the day Sochi was chosen as the venue for the 2014 Winter Olympics, Krasnaya Polyana was rapidly transformed from an unassuming mid-range ski centre into a high-end ski resort called Roza Khutor with slopes of varying levels of difficulty, from long and easy runs to off-piste options and state-of-the-art ski-lifts.

During the Olympics, the resort hosted all the ski and toboggan competitions. Many new accommodation options, commercial complexes, various shops and Gallaktika, an excellent entertainment centre, emerged around this time.

The best time for skiing at the resort is mid-January to mid-March.

A modern commercial complex in Krasnaya Polyana

Sparsely populated beach with a pier extending into the Black Sea, Adler

*For hotels and restaurants in this region see pp271–2 and p290*

Crowds strolling down the pleasant promenade, Gelendzhik

## ❺ Gelendzhik

Геленджик

*Gelendzhik*

310 km (193 miles) NW of Krasnaya Polyana. 🚶 55,000. 🚌 🚇 🚢

A charming seaside resort, Gelendzhik is overlooked by densely forested hills sporting a huge sign that once spelt "Lenin is with us" and has since been replaced by "Gelendzhik". It combines pleasant nightlife with child-friendly water parks and play areas, and is a laid-back alternative to busy Anapa.

Bronze-Age tribes left dolmen scattered throughout the forests surrounding Gelendzhik. However, records of the first settlement date from the 6th century BC, when the Greeks established a trading port here. During the Middle Ages, Genoese traders followed suit and maintained an outpost in the bay area. The town was occupied by the Ottomans from the 15th century until its annexation to Russia under the Treaty of Adrianople in 1829.

Gelendzhik welcomed its first tourists in the early 20th century and gradually evolved into today's bustling resort town with its fetching tree-shaded promenade. The **Regional Museum** has displays related to its role as a Soviet base during World War II as well as re-created interiors of local homes in the 1950s.

**🏛 Regional Museum**
Ulitsa Ostrovska 1. **Tel** (86141) 213 61. **Open** 9am–6pm daily (till 9pm Thu).
🚫 📷

Dolmen dating from the Bronze Age in the forests surrounding Gelendzhik

## ❻ Anapa

Анапа

*Anapa*

93 km (58 miles) NW of Gelendzhik. 🚶 59,000. 🚗 🚌 🚇 🚢

Popular with Russian tourists since the first sanatoriums were built here in the late 19th century, Anapa is an attractive family resort. Its wooded parks and neat flowerbeds provide the perfect backdrop for a central beach that is gridlocked with sun umbrellas throughout the busy summer season.

First settled by the Greeks and named Gorgipia in the 6th century BC, the area was later colonized by the Genoese before it fell to the Ottoman Empire in 1475. After the Russo-Turkish War of 1828–9, it was formally annexed to Russia and gradually developed into a thriving resort, but was totally destroyed during its occupation by German and Romanian troops during World War II.

Today, modern hotels, bars, discos and restaurants line the seafront and the town throngs with Russian holidaymakers. The reconstructed ruins of Gorgipia are on display at the central **Archaeological Museum** along with various ancient Greek artifacts from the region.

**🏛 Archaeological Museum**
Ulitsa Naberezhnaya 4. **Tel** (86133) 431 54. **Open** 9am–6pm Tue–Sun (till 5pm Fri). 🚫 📷

### Sanatoriums

An extensive network of sanatoriums, or wellness centres, was established in Russia in the 1930s. The Caucasus region especially abounds in them, owing to its curative mineral water springs. These relics of the Soviet era prove to be good alternatives to hotels. Seaside resorts such as Sochi have sanatoriums offering traditional and modern spa therapies for just about any ailment imaginable. Visitors traditionally stay for a three-week cure, but shorter treatments are also available.

The sanatorium at Zelenaya Roscha, Sochi

## ❼ Krasnodar

Краснодар

*Krasnodar*

170 km (106 miles) E of Anapa.
🚹 832,000. ✈ 🚆 🚌 🚎 🚇

A welcoming city, Krasnodar enjoys an almost Mediterranean climate that fuels an appealing outdoor culture. Locals promenade through its parks and along its boulevards until late into the night during the long hot summers.

Granted to the Kuban Cossacks by Catherine the Great in 1792 for defending Russia's southern border against the Circassians, the settlement was originally named Yekaterinodar – meaning Catherine's Gift. Initially a fort town, it developed into a major transport and trading hub with the arrival of the railway in the late 19th century. Many Cossacks remained loyal to the tsar during the Civil War and held the town against the Red Army until 1920 when it was annexed by the Bolsheviks and renamed Krasnodar or Gift of the Reds.

The German occupation between 1942 and 1943 saw the extermination of an estimated 13,000 locals in gas chambers by the Nazis. A memorial in Chistyakovskaya Roscha park denotes the mass grave where the victims are buried. A short walk from the park is the Aurora Cinema, a superb example of Soviet architecture from the 1960s. It marks one end of ulitsa Krasnaya,

Alexander's Triumphal Arch and St Martyr Catherine Memorial, Krasnodar

a boulevard that stretches for 7 km (4 miles) through the city centre. The street is adorned with statues, fountains and monuments to the Cossacks and Catherine the Great.

The city's **Regional Museum** has a collection of artifacts that recount the area's Cossack past as well as its natural history, archaeology and ancient roots. The nearby **Art Museum** exhibits 19th-century paintings by Russian artists.

### 🏛 Regional Museum

Ulitsa Gimnazicheskaya 67. **Tel** (861) 262 40 86. **Open** 10am–6pm Tue–Sun (till 9pm Thu & 5pm Fri). 🎟 📷

### 🏛 Art Museum

Ulitsa Krasnaya 13. **Tel** (861) 268 09 00. **Open** 10am–6pm Tue, Wed & Fri–Sun, 1–9pm Thu. 🎟 📷

## ❽ Rostov-na-Donu

Ростов-на-Дону

*Rostov-na-Donu*

280 km (174 km) NE of Krasnodar.
🚹 1,100,000. ✈ 🚆 🚌 🚎 🚇 🚢

Spread out along the northern banks of the great Don river lies the modern city of Rostov-na-Donu with its appealing blend of 19th- and-20th-century architecture interspersed by parks and broad squares.

Empress Elizabeth established a customs post here in the late 18th century to control trade with Turkey and the settlement soon evolved into a thriving commercial centre. Owing to its unique riverside location between European Russia and the Caucasus region, it came to be known as the "gateway to the Caucasus".

The area's fascinating history is documented by the **Regional Museum**, where Scythian and Sarmatian golden ornaments dating back to the 3rd century BC are on display. Additionally, Don Cossack outfits replete with fur hats and jewel embroidery from the 18th and 19th centuries can be found upstairs alongside Cossack uniforms and weaponry from World War II. The museum is flanked by parks on both sides. To the east is the Revolutsii Park, which is dotted with monuments and fountains, while Gorky Park, to the west, is popular for its fairground rides and bustling eateries. The two parks lie between the city's parallel thoroughfares – ulitsa Sadovaya, a traffic-clogged street, and ulitsa Pushkinskaya, a much calmer tree-lined boulevard.

The splendid **Nativity of the Blessed Virgin Cathedral**, built in 1860, stands on the northern slopes of the steep riverbank. Its striking golden domes and neighbouring bell tower are surrounded by the city bazaar, a maze of open market stalls selling pungent spices, fresh fish from the Don and local produce. Downhill is the great river itself. Lined with floating bars and restaurants, the city side of the river is a popular hangout, but locals

Golden domes of the Nativity of the Blessed Virgin Cathedral, Rostov-na-Donu

frequent the opposite side, known as the Left Bank, where a number of good restaurants and bars abut the sandy beaches.

Rostov-na-Donu is also slated to act as one of Russia's host cities for the 2018 FIFA World Cup™. A brand new football stadium is under construction, with a seating capacity of 43,700.

### 🏛 Regional Museum

Ulitsa Bolshaya Sadovaya 79. **Tel** (863) 240 93 04. **Open** 10am–6pm Tue–Sun. 🅿 📷 🌐 **rostovmuseum.ru**

### 🏛 Nativity of the Blessed Virgin Cathedral

Ulitsa Stanislavskogo 58. **Open** 8am–7pm daily.

Tree-lined ulitsa Pushkinskaya running the length of Rostov-na-Donu

## ❾ Starocherkassk

Старочеркасск

*Starocherkassk*

35 km (22 miles) NE of Rostov-na-Donu. 🔼 5,000. 🚌 🏛 🚐

It is hard to believe that this tranquil museum village, formerly known as Cherkassk, used to be the fortified island capital of the Don Cossacks between the 17th and 19th centuries. Peter the Great visited the area several times during his attempts to conquer the fortress at nearby Azov. Held by the Turks, the fortress prevented Russian access to the Black Sea. When it was eventually captured by Russian troops in 1696, it was in Cherkassk that

Ataman Palace and its lovely gardens, Starocherkassk

Peter the Great celebrated his victory with Russia's first ever fireworks display.

Starocherkassk's **Historical and Architectural Museum Reserve** was established in 1970 on the initiative of Mikhail Sholokhov – author of the classic Cossack novel *And Quiet Flows the Don* – and has since developed into one of the region's principal tourist attractions. It is a unique complex with over 30 architectural monuments that reflect the life and customs of the Don Cossacks. Just down the road from the museum is the **Resurrection Cathedral**, which dates back to 1706 and boasts an incredible iconostasis flanked by balconies decorated with

vivid depictions of biblical scenes. Displayed nearby are the hefty iron gates known as the Azov Trophies that were captured by local Cossacks during their first occupation of Azov between 1637 and 1641. Another draw is the impressive Ataman Palace – an 18th-century mansion – that houses exhibits relating to the Cossack culture. From May to September, the village hosts lively Cossack fairs.

### 🏛 Historical and Architectural Museum Reserve

Pochtovyi pereulok 6. **Tel** (863) 502 97 49. **Open** 9am–5pm daily. 🌐 **siamz-ro.ru**

### 🏛 Resurrection Cathedral

**Open** 9am–5pm daily.

## The Turbulent South

The South Caucasian republics have struggled bitterly for independence since the break up of the Soviet Union in 1991. Chechnya finally submitted to Russia's authority in 2009 after the Second Chechen War; Azerbaijan fought over territory with neighbouring Armenia until 1994; Dagestan has remained a Russian republic but suffers from internal Islamic tensions; and Abkhazia is recognized by Russia as an independent state yet is considered part of neighbouring Georgia by much

Ramzan Kadyrov, Head of the Chechen Republic

of the international community. Most recently, Russia's brief war with Georgia in 2008 confirmed Russian control of South Ossetia. Although the region has been comparatively calm for the past few years, mutual mistrust and simmering tensions between the neighbouring states have created a volatile climate that has resulted in occasional attacks and kidnappings of Russian and foreign citizens by minority groups. Travel in the region is currently considered dangerous and potential visitors are advised to consult their embassies for the latest security information.

# SIBERIA AND THE FAR EAST

A land of enormous proportions, this region offers stunning landscapes, fascinating museums and exciting adventures. The architecture and culture of its cities are similar, yet each has its own unique gems to be discovered. Beyond these urban centres lies a vast wilderness where indigenous peoples, some of whom still practise shamanism, can sometimes be found.

Stretching from the Ural Mountains in the West to the Pacific Ocean in the east, the Siberia and Far East region shares its border with China, Mongolia and Central Kazakhstan. Russia began exploring the region in the 16th century when pioneering Cossacks forced local tribes to pay regular tributes in furs to the tsar or face annihilation. By the 18th century, Siberia had become a prime location for imprisonment and exile, a convenient way to populate the unappealing region.

The construction of the Trans-Siberian Railway in the late 19th century had a massive social and economic impact on the region. It not only boosted trade and shortened travel time between cities across the country, but also led to the settlement of remote areas in Siberia. The 20th century saw the Soviet government establish thousands of Gulag prison camps across the region to run factories, mines and logging operations; these became an integral part of the Soviet economy.

Rich in natural resources, the region has attracted heavy investment from energy companies all over the world since the collapse of the Soviet Union in 1991. The region is also emerging as a major tourist destination. Cities such as Tomsk and Irkutsk have made efforts to restore and preserve their pre-Soviet architectural heritage. Much of the eastern part offers glorious mountain scenery and a host of thrilling adventure sports. Reached via Irkutsk, Lake Baikal is not just famous for scenic views, but also for amazing hiking and trekking trails.

A shepherd with reindeer in a typical Siberian snow-covered landscape

◄ Conifers lining the banks of a meandering mountain river in the Altai Republic

# Exploring Siberia and the Far East

Extending across seven time zones from the Ural Mountains in the west to Kamchatka in the east, this region has plenty in store for the relatively few foreign visitors it receives. It is still largely unpopulated, and the vast majority of its inhabitants live in the cities lining the route of the Trans-Siberian Railway, so wilderness is seldom far away. While the stunning Altai Mountains are accessible from Krasnoyarsk, the utterly remote landscapes of Sakhalin Island in the Far East can be explored from Yuzhno-Sakhalinsk. Most Siberian cities were greatly changed during the Soviet era, but several cities such as Tobolsk, Tomsk and Irkutsk have preserved the remnants of their architectural heritage. Irkutsk is the best base for excursions to Lake Baikal, a natural gem. East of Lake Baikal lies the Buryat (an ethnic minority group in Siberia) capital of Ulan-Ude, from where there are bus links to Ivolginsky Datsan, the most important Buddhist monastery in Russia.

Areas illustrated

## Sights at a Glance

1. Omsk
2. Tobolsk
3. Novosibirsk
4. Tomsk
5. Krasnoyarsk
6. Barnaul
7. Irkutsk
8. Taltsy Architectural and Ethnographic Museum
9. Lake Baikal
10. Ulan-Ude
11. Ivolginsky Datsan
12. Vladivostok
13. Khabarovsk
14. Komsomolsk-na-Amur
15. Sakhalin Island
16. Magadan
17. Kamchatka

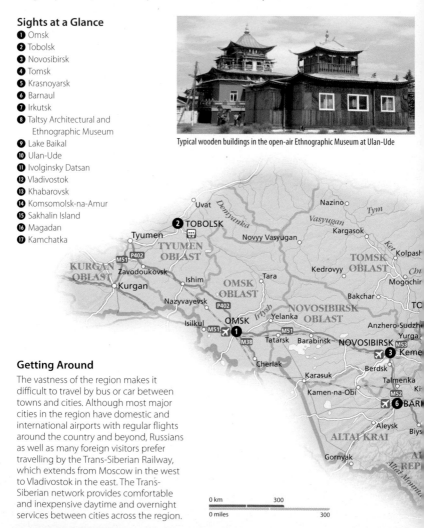

Typical wooden buildings in the open-air Ethnographic Museum at Ulan-Ude

## Getting Around

The vastness of the region makes it difficult to travel by bus or car between towns and cities. Although most major cities in the region have domestic and international airports with regular flights around the country and beyond, Russians as well as many foreign visitors prefer travelling by the Trans-Siberian Railway, which extends from Moscow in the west to Vladivostok in the east. The Trans-Siberian network provides comfortable and inexpensive daytime and overnight services between cities across the region.

*For hotels and restaurants in this region see pp272–3 and pp290–91*

A herd of reindeer crossing a river in northern Kamchatka

**Key**

— Major road

═══ Minor road

⌒ Major railway

⌒ Trans-Siberian Railway

⌒ Minor railway

▬ International border

▬ Federal border

**The Far East**

MAGADAN OBLAST

Yakutsk
Omsukchan
Manily
Pakhachi

M56

M56

Okhotsk
KAMCHATKA

KHABAROVSK KRAI
🛪 **16** MAGADAN
Nelkan Nelkan
KAMCHATKA KRAI
Bering Sea

M56

**17** 🛪

Klyuchi

Chumikan
Sea of Okhotsk

Svobodnyy
Ekimchan
Okha 🛪

Chegdomyn
🛪 **15** SAKHALIN ISLAND
Petropavlovsk-Kamchatsky 🛪

🛪 **14** KOMSOMOLSK-NA-AMUR
SAKHALIN OBLAST

JEWISH OBLAST
🛪 **13**
Yuzhno-Sakhalinsk

KHABAROVSK

Spassk-Dalniy
M60
PRIMORSKY KRAI

A181

🌿🏛 **12** 🛪 Olga
VLADIVOSTOK

0 km          800

0 miles          800

vonazimovo

Lesosibirsk

eguldet
Strelka
Zvezdnyy

Achinsk
Aban
IRKUTSK OBLAST
Severobaykalsk

M53

MEROVO
BLAST
Balakhta
🏛🛪🏛 **5** KRASNOYARSK
Tayshet
Vikhorevka
Surovo
Karam
Kurumkan

Uzhur
Zhigalovo
Ust-Barguzin

Krasnoyarskoye Vodokhranilishche
Tulun
Balagansk
LAKE BAIKAL

Artemovsk

Abakan
Minusinsk
M53
🏛🛪 **9** 🏛
Ust-Barguzin

REPUBLIC OF KHAKASSIA
Abaza
IRKUTSK **7**
🏛🏛 **10** ULAN-UDE

Abaza
TUVA REPUBLIC
TAITSY ARCHITECTURAL AND
ETHNOGRAPHIC MUSEUM **8** 🏛
🛪 **11**
IVOLGINSKY DATSAN

Turan
M55

Shagonar
Kyzyl
Gusinoozersk
A165

Ak-Dovurak
Balgazyn

Tashanta
Erzin

**For keys to symbols** *see back flap*

The Assumption Cathedral crowned by a massive onion dome, Omsk

# ❶ Omsk

Омск

*Omsk*

2,724 km (1,700 miles) E of Moscow.
🚉 1,150,000. ✈ ⛴ 🚌 🚋 🏢 🚆 ℹ **Tel** (3812) 27 06 20.
🌐 admomsk.ru

Stretching along the banks of the Irtysh river at its confluence with the Om river, Omsk is a lively city packed with restaurants, bars and clubs. It was founded in 1716 during the reign of Peter the Great to protect Russia's southern border from hostile Kazakh tribes. With the construction of the Trans-Siberian Railway in the 1890s, the city evolved into a prosperous trading outpost.

The **Assumption Cathedral**, the city's most central landmark, dominates ploshchad Sobornaya. Distinctive for its bulbous onion dome, it was built in 2007 to replace the original cathedral pulled down by the Soviets in 1935. A short distance south is the **Regional Museum** with artifacts related to the history and culture of the region. Nearby, the **MA Vrubel Regional Museum of Fine Arts** houses a superb collection of decorative and applied art.

🏛 **Regional Museum**
Ulitsa Lenina 23A. **Tel** (3812) 31 22 86.
**Open** 10am–6pm Tue–Sun. 🈲 📷
🌐 sibmuseum.ru

🏛 **MA Vrubel Regional Museum of Fine Arts**
Ulitsa Lenina 3. **Tel** (3812) 20 00 47.
**Open** 10am–7pm Tue–Sun. 🈲 📷

# ❷ Tobolsk

Тоболск

*Tobolsk*

862 km (536 miles) NW of Omsk.
🚉 100,000. 🚌 🚋 🚆 🏢 🚆
🌐 admtobolsk.ru

Founded in 1587 by Cossacks intent on expanding the Russian Empire eastwards, Tobolsk became Siberia's first capital. It was inhabited by wealthy merchants who built churches and wooden mansions all over the city. The merchants refused to allow the Trans-Siberian Railway to be routed through the city, fearing it would ruin their trade monopolies. However, Tobolsk's fortunes declined anyway when the railway was built.

Situated atop the high bank of the Irtysh river, Tobolsk's magnificent stone Kremlin overlooks the old town's wooden buildings. Restored during the Soviet era, it contains the elegant 17th-century **Cathedral of St Sofia**. To the right of the Kremlin is the Governor's Palace, which houses the **Regional Museum**.

🏛 **Cathedral of St Sofia**
Tobolsk Kremlin. **Open** 8am–8pm daily. 📷

🏛 **Regional Museum**
Dvorets Namestnika, ploshchad Krasnaya 1. **Tel** (345) 622 37 13.
**Open** 10am–6pm Tue–Sun. 🈲 📷

# ❸ Novosibirsk

Новосибирск

*Novosibirsk*

652 km (405 miles) E of Omsk.
🚉 1,500,000. ✈ ⛴ 🚌 🚋 🏢 🚆
Ⓜ 🚆 🌐 novo-sibirsk.ru

Russia's third-largest city was founded in 1893 as a small settlement of workers engaged in building a bridge across the Ob river for the Trans-Siberian Railway. Named Novonikolaevsk in honour of Tsar Nicholas, the town attracted local traders who capitalized on its river and rail connections to amass small fortunes. In due course the town expanded into a bustling city.

Despite the reluctance of the wealthier citizens to embrace Communism, Novonikolaevsk fell to the Bolsheviks in 1919 and was renamed Novosibirsk in 1926. The Soviet era saw an influx of huge industrial enterprises accompanied by the construction of monolithic state buildings and four-lane roads throughout the city. In spite of the fall of Communism, a great statue of Lenin dominates ploshchad Lenina, the city's central square. Just behind is the grand **Opera and Ballet Theatre**, which was completed in 1944 and is larger than the Bolshoi Theatre in Moscow. Opposite the Lenin Statue is the excellent **Regional Museum**, with an

Statue of Lenin in Novosibirsk

Crowds outside the impressive white stone Kremlin, Tobolsk

absorbing collection that includes a section on shamanism, which is still practised in some parts of the Altai Republic.

### 🎭 Opera and Ballet Theatre
Krasny prospekt 36. **Tel** (383) 222 60 40 (ticket office). **Open** check website for schedule. 🚪 🖥 W **novat.nsk.ru**

### 🏛 Regional Museum
Krasny prospekt 25. **Tel** (383) 227 15 43. **Open** 10am–6pm Mon–Fri. 🚪 📷 W **museum.nsk.ru**

One of the few well-preserved wooden mansions in Tomsk

## ❹ Tomsk
Томск
*Tomsk*

270 km (168 miles) NE of Novosibirsk. 🚂 525,000. ✈ 🚍 🚌 🚢

Founded in 1604 atop the Voskresenskaya Gora (Resurrection Hill), Tomsk is a lively university city famous for its intricately decorated wooden buildings that date back to the early 19th century. Though many of Tomsk's wooden houses are in a state of decay, some of the best examples of wooden architecture can be seen along Krasnoarmeiskaya ulitsa. The **Tomsk City History Museum** houses exhibits on the history of the city. Within the museum grounds is a wooden lookout tower. Once used for spotting fires, the tower offers sweeping views of the city. The nearby **Voskresenskaya Church** was first constructed from wood in 1622 and replaced by the current stone building in 1789.

### 🏛 Tomsk City History Museum
Ulitsa Bakunina 3. **Tel** (382) 265 72 55. **Open** 10am–7pm Tue–Sun. 🚪 📷 W **museum.tomsk.ru**

## ❺ Krasnoyarsk
Красноярск
*Krasnoyarsk*

582 km (362 miles) E of Tomsk. 🚂 1,000,000. ✈ 🚆 🚍 🚌 🚉 🚌 🚢

Described by Anton Chekhov in 1890 as a picturesque and cultured town, Krasnoyarsk is located along both banks of the broad Yenisei river beneath the craggy rock formations of the Stolby Nature Reserve. The city's central thoroughfares are lined with an eclectic mix of architectural styles, and the thousands of students at its numerous universities lend a youthful vibrancy, which finds expression in quirky contemporary artworks on display around the city.

Krasnoyarsk was founded in 1627 by pioneering Cossacks and the **Regional Museum** contains displays devoted both to the city's recent history and to the lifestyles of the indigenous peoples who have inhabited the region for millennia. Overlooking the Yenisei river is the Modernist **Museum of Culture and History**, which combines dated exhibitions of city history with impressive contemporary art installations.

### Environs
About 10 km (6 miles) west of the Yenisei river's south bank is the **Stolby Nature Reserve**, known for striking rock formations and outdoor activities such as hiking and rock climbing. The **Bobrovy Log Ski Resort**, some 30 minutes by car from Krasnoyarsk, on the northeastern edge of the nature reserve, is popular for winter sports.

### 🏛 Regional Museum
Ulitsa Dubrovinskogo 84. **Tel** (391) 227 05 80. **Open** 10am–6pm Tue–Sun. 🚪 📷 W **kkkm.ru**

### 🏛 Museum of Culture and History
Ploshchad Mira. **Tel** (391) 212 46 63. **Open** 11am–7pm Tue–Sun. 🎫 🚪 🖥 📷 W **mira1.ru**

### ⛷ Bobrovy Log Ski Resort
**Tel** (391) 256 86 86. **Open** 10am–10pm daily. 🚪 📷 W **bobrovylog.ru**

Yellow autumn foliage in the taiga forests of Stolby Nature Reserve near Krasnoyarsk

### Trans-Siberian Railway

A marvellous feat of late 19th-century engineering, the world's longest railway connects Moscow with the Sea of Japan at Vladivostok over a distance of 9,288 km (5,771 miles). During the week-long journey the train passes through vast forests, crosses immense rivers and trundles across seemingly endless vistas of steppes. A Trans-Siberian train journey is easy to arrange, conditions on board are comfortable and the trains well organized. The Trans-Siberian line runs from Moscow to Vladivostok, the Trans-Mongolian line connects Moscow with Ulan Bator, and the Trans-Manchurian line terminates in Beijing.

A section of the Trans-Siberian Railway near Lake Baikal

## ❻ Barnaul
Барнаул
*Barnaul*

241 km (150 miles) S of Novosibirsk.
🚇 621,700. ✈ ➔ 🚌 Ⓜ 🚰

The industrial city of Barnaul was founded in the mid-18th century and was once home to Russia's largest silver-smelting factory. The city serves as an excellent base for touring the mountainous Altai Republic. Although the region's wild landscape has attracted visitors since the early 20th century and popular sights are easily accessible, travelling deeper into the mountains is best arranged through a local tour operator. The **Altai Museum of Regional Studies and History** in Barnaul provides an absorbing overview of the region's past.

🏛 **Altai Museum of Regional Studies and History**
Ulitsa Polzunova 46. **Tel** (385) 263 47 58. **Open** 9:30am–5:30pm Wed & Fri–Sun, 11am–7pm Thu. **Closed** last Fri of the month. 🖼 📷

## ❼ Irkutsk
Иркутск
*Irkutsk*

2,090 km (1,300 miles) SE of Barnaul.
🚇 600,000. ✈ ➔ 🚉 🚌 🚰
ℹ Ulitsa Dekabrskikh Sobytii 77B, (395) 220 50 18. 🖥 itsirkutsk.com

Dubbed "the Paris of Siberia" by Anton Chekhov in the late 19th century, Irkutsk is a delightful city dotted with well-preserved wood and stone buildings. Largely unspoiled by concrete Soviet architecture, the city centre

The brightly painted Epiphany Cathedral, Irkutsk

features tree-lined avenues, punctuated with well-kept parks, and an elegant embankment promenade that follows the curve of the Angara river.

Established around 1661 on the right bank, Irkutsk profited from its proximity to Mongolia by importing tea, silk and porcelain into Russia. The discovery of gold and diamonds in the region attracted a surge of fortune-seekers, who were accompanied in almost equal numbers by exiled criminals. Among the exiles were the Decembrists *(see p43)*, whose arrival enhanced the city's cultural life, which soon revolved around the mansions of Prince Volkonsky (1788–1865) and Prince Trubetskoy (1790–1860); both mansions have been preserved as house-museums. Between the two mansions stands the late 18th-century Transfiguration Church where the aristocrats worshipped.

A short distance away is a restored complex of lovely mansions that house the **Museum of City Life**, which showcases how a typical 19th-century merchant-class family lived. Overlooking the Angara river, the city's oldest churches in ploshchad Kirova have been meticulously restored in recent years. The brightly painted Epiphany Cathedral was built in 1718, while the more sombre **Church of Our Saviour** dates back to 1706.

From ploshchad Kirov, ulitsa Lenina runs south past the **Sukachev Regional Art Museum**, whose superb collection includes Mongolian religious paintings and Russian Impressionist artworks. Further south, ulitsa Lenina connects with Irkutsk's main street, ulitsa Karla Marksa. This street leads to a pretty riverside square where a statue of Tsar Alexander III commemorates the construction of the Trans-Siberian Railway. Nearby, the **Regional Museum** contains a great collection of ethnographic exhibits and displays from the 20th century.

🏛 **Museum of City Life**
Ulitsa Dekabrskikh Sobytii 77. **Tel** (3952) 20 48 84. **Open** 10am–6pm Wed–Mon. 🖼 📷

⛪ **Church of Our Saviour**
Ploshchad Kirov. **Open** 7:30am–8:30pm daily. 📷

🏛 **Sukachev Regional Art Museum**
Ulitsa Dekabrskikh Sobytii 112. **Tel** (3952) 53 12 24. **Open** 10am–6pm Wed–Mon. 🖼 📷 🖥 sukachoff.ru

Spectacular mountains surrounding a lake, Altai Republic

*For hotels and restaurants in this region see pp272–3 and pp290–91*

## ❽ Taltsy Architectural and Ethnographic Museum

Музей Тальцы

*Muzey Taltsy*

47 km (29 miles) SE of Irkutsk. **Tel** (3952) 76 83 23. 🚌 from Irkutsk. **Open** 10am–5pm daily. 🚲 **W** talci.ru

Established in 1966, this fascinating outdoor museum is tucked away in the woods on the right bank of the Angara river. its exhibits were collected from flooded local villages in an attempt to preserve Siberia's traditional folk architecture.

The exhibition trail begins with a *chum*, a traditional house covered in pine-tree bark that was used by the north Siberian Evenk tribe. The hollowed out logs perched on trees nearby are examples of the Evenk's aerial graves. A 19th-century water mill consisting of three huts stands on a nearby hillside; stream water was channelled down through the huts to power the mills within. A series of Cossack homes lie beyond alongside a part of a stockade with the main watch-tower; there is also a pretty wooden church that dates from the end of the 17th century. Both the tower and church were rescued from the village of Ust-Ilimsk before it was flooded by a hydroelectric dam project in 1974. Traditional crafts are sold from stalls in a meadow setting surrounded by forested hills.

Tour boats moored along the beach at Listvyanka

## ❾ Lake Baikal

Озеро Байкал

*Ozero Baikal*

69 km (43 miles) E of Irkutsk. 🚌 from Irkutsk. 🛈 Ulitsa Narodnaya 10 Olkhon, Khuzhir, (3952) 65 06 52.
**W** discoverbaikal.ru

Sandwiched between the Baikal and Barguzin mountains to the north, Lake Baikal is the deepest and oldest lake in the world. A natural wonder, the lake was considered a living entity by local tribes who revered it for thousands of years. It contains around 20 per cent of the planet's unfrozen fresh water and is home to around 2,000 animal and plant species of which more than half are endemic. Its 3,219-km (2,000-mile) shoreline is scarcely populated and the majority of its few settlements are located along the southern shores.

Running right beside the lake between the villages of Sludyanka and Port Baikal, the Circum-Baikal Railway is a great way to experience the lake. Built between 1911 and 1915 to connect the eastern and western Trans-Siberian lines, the route was an incredible feat of engineering as it involved hacking a rail bed into the sheer cliffs rising from the lake. The Circum-Baikal Railway has since been bypassed by the faster Irkutsk–Sludyanka line, although there is still a twice-daily service used by locals and tourists.

Train on the Circum-Baikal Railway at Port Baikal station

Located at the mouth of the Angara river opposite Port Baikal, Listvyanka is the most popular of Baikal's villages. Fronted by shingle beaches, it stretches along the shore beneath steep forested hills. The village is the best spot to sample smoked omul, a delicious fish endemic to Baikal, and to learn more about the lake at the **Baikal Museum**.

Northeast of Listvyanka, Olkhon Island is Baikal's largest island and a place of pilgrim-age for the local Buryat shamans. Wooden guesthouses scattered around the island provide bases to explore Olkhon's hills, rocky bays and shamanic monuments.

🏛 **Baikal Museum**
Ulitsa Akademicheskaya 1. **Tel** (3952) 45 31 46. **Open** 9am–7pm daily. 🚲

Visitors aboard a horse-drawn carriage, Taltsy Architectural and Ethnographic Museum

A magnificent rock projection rising above the tranquil waters of Lake Baikal ▶

The magnificent Odigitria Cathedral with gold-tipped spires, Ulan-Ude

**Ethnographic Museum**
Verchnyaya Berezovka. **Tel** (3012) 33 25 10. **Open** 9:30am–6:30pm Tue–Fri, 9:30am–7:30pm Sat & Sun.

**Buryat History Museum**
Ulitsa Profsoyuznaya 29. **Tel** (3012) 21 06 53. **Open** 11am–7pm Tue–Sun.

# ⑪ Ivolginsky Datsan
Иволгинский Датцан
*Ivolginskiy Datsan*

23 km (14 miles) S of Ulan-Ude, Verkhnyaya Ivolga. **Tel** (9021) 69 81 08. from Ulan-Ude. **Open** 8am–7pm daily.

# ⑩ Ulan-Ude
Улан-Удэ
*Ulan-Ude*

450 km (280 miles) E of Irkutsk. 400,000.

Best known for the world's largest statue of Lenin's head that dominates the bleak Soviet-era upper end of the city, Ulan-Ude is steeped in history. Long before a group of Cossack soldiers erected a fort here in 1666, the indigenous Buryats considered the place to be sacred. Closely related to the Mongols, Buryats were originally nomadic herders. Today, they make up around 30 per cent of the city's population, and Ulan-Ude has been the capital of the autonomous Buryatia Republic since its creation in 1992. The simple Buryat tepees and yurts can be seen at the **Ethnographic Museum**, 5 km (3 miles) east of the city centre. A short walk southeast of ploshchad Sovetov, the **Buryat History Museum** has a great collection of relics rescued from the region's Buddhist monasteries before they were demolished by the Soviets.

Ulan-Ude's pleasant old town lies at the city's lower end on the banks of the Selenga and Uda rivers. A pedestrianized section of ulitsa Lenina, locally known as the Arbat, runs through the city centre where souvenir shops flank the small City Museum. A short distance southeast is the Fine Arts Museum, filled with fascinating paintings of Buryat culture. A little further south is the Odigitria Cathedral, which was consecrated in 1785 and is the city's oldest stone building.

Russia's spiritual centre of Buddhism occupies a remote piece of steppe beneath the Khamar Daban mountains. After having systematically destroyed the region's Buddhist temples in the 1930s, the Soviet government granted a plot of land to Buryatia's Buddhist community in 1945 as part of its postwar policy of easing the pressure on Russia's religious communities.

Ivolginsky Datsan has since developed into a thriving complex of temples, prayer wheels and souvenir stalls that attracts as many pilgrims as tourists, yet remains peaceful. Its most intriguing asset is the body of Ivolginsky's 12th Lama, Dashi-Dorzho Itegelov, who foresaw both his own death in 1927 and the fact that his corpse would never decay. His remains are exhibited to the public each year to mark Buddhist holidays.

Striking architecture of one of the temples within the monastery complex, Ivolginsky Datsan

Models of animals on display at the Regional Museum, Vladivostok

# ⑫ Vladivostok
Владивосток
*Vladivostok*

3,345 km (2,078 miles) SE of Ulan-Ude.
🚗 620,000. ✈ 🚆 🚌 🚋 ⛴

The final destination of the Trans-Siberian Railway, Vladivostok is Russia's largest Pacific port. The charming city sits on a hilly peninsula at the head of the Golden Horn Bay and offers superb sea views in every direction.

The Far East was loosely under Chinese control for centuries, but there was little resistance when Russia established Vladivostok, meaning "Owner of the East", in 1860. During the Russian Civil War *(see p44)*, thousands of foreign troops landed here to support the White Army, but the Bolsheviks' eventual triumph at Vladivostok in 1922 signalled the end of the war. Closed until 1991, the city has since flourished and massive investment was made to upgrade the city's infrastructure prior to the 2012 Asia-Pacific Economic Cooperation (APEC) summit.

The **Regional Museum** in the city centre provides a visual overview of Vladivostok's history. Its huge collection of artifacts includes sections on natural history, archaeology, trade with China and Japan, and a fascinating collection of Soviet statues and propaganda posters. A short distance north of the museum lies the pedestrianized ulitsa Fokina. Lined with small shops

Vintage car at the Antique Automobile Museum, Vladivostok

and cafés, this pretty street overlooks the Amur Gulf and is known as Vladivostok's Arbat *(see p89)*. A 10-minute walk northwest of the street leads to the cannons of the **Fortress Museum**. The fort was built in the early 20th century to protect Vladivostok against any military threat.

At the heart of Vladivostok next to the harbour lies ploshchad Bortsov Revolutsii and the grand Monument to the Fighters for Soviet Power in the Far East. The adjacent street runs along the seafront past a memorial to Vladivostok's founders before reaching the World War II S-56 Submarine on the grass verge. Inside the submarine is a fascinating museum replete with torpedo tubes, cramped sleeping quarters and the personal effects of its crew.

The funicular railway, about 15 minutes east of the city centre, takes passengers up to an observation point that offers brilliant views of the Golden Horn Bay on a clear day. A 30-minute bus ride from the city centre, the **Antique Automobile Museum** has a superb collection of Soviet limousines and motorcycles.

**🏛 Regional Museum**
Ulitsa Svetlanskaya 20. **Tel** (4232) 41 11 73. **Open** 9:30am–6pm daily. 📷 📸

**🏛 Antique Automobile Museum**
Ulitsa Sakhalinskaya 2. **Tel** (4232) 21 24 77. **Open** 10am–6pm daily. 📷 📸
**W** automotomuseum.vl.ru

# ⑬ Khabarovsk
Хабаровск
*Khabarovsk*

762 km (473 miles) NE of Vladivostok.
🚗 594,000. ✈ 🚆 🚌 🚋 🚉 ⛴

Named after the Cossack explorer Yerofey Khabarov (1603–71), whose heroic attempts to expand the Russian Empire into the Far East caused a series of conflicts with China, Khabarovsk sits on three hills beside the vast Amur river. The territory was not granted to Russia until the Treaty of Aguin in 1858, which established an official border with China and saw the construction of a Russian military fort here.

Khabarovsk is an upbeat city with boulevards connecting the several vast squares that were laid out during the Soviet era. In summer, locals flock to the City Park on the river bank where sandy beaches allow for sunbathing and swimming. Behind the park is the superb **Regional Museum**, which has exhibits devoted to the region's history. The **Far Eastern Arts Museum**'s absorbing collection of Russian artworks stands next door in an early 20th-century building opposite the Military Museum.

Just uphill is ploshchad Sobornaya, dominated by the **Dormition Cathedral**, whose onion domes are perched on an unusual high-rise structure.

**🏛 Regional Museum**
Ulitsa Shevchenko 11. **Tel** (4212) 31 63 44. **Open** 10am–6pm Tue–Sun. **Closed** last Fri of the month. 📷 📸

**🏛 Far Eastern Arts Museum**
Ulitsa Shevchenko 7. **Tel** (4212) 31 48 71. **Open** 10am–6pm Tue–Sun. 📷 📸 **W** dvhm.ru

Steps leading to the splendid Dormition Cathedral, Khabarovsk

Impressive stone sculptures of the World War II Memorial, Komsomolsk-na-Amur

## ⓮ Komsomolsk-na-Amur

Комсомольск-на-Амуре
*Komsomolsk-na-Amur*

399 km (248 miles) NE of Khabarovsk. ⛰ 268,000. ✈ 🚗 🚌 🚊 🚤 ⛴ 🚢 🚢

Built in remote, swampy taiga by a workforce of *Komsomol* (Communist Young League) volunteers and prison labour in 1932, Komsomolsk-na-Amur was a result of the Soviet regime's defensive policy to industrialize the Far East. The city was chosen as the location of a shipyard and an aircraft factory; the aviation industry continues to be the region's largest employer today.

Komsomolsk-na-Amur has progressed greatly since the days of canvas tents for shelter in winter, but living conditions here remain tough due to long, bitter winters and brief hot summers. The city is laid out according to typical Stalin-era town planning, with grandiose pastel-coloured buildings lining four- and six-lane streets. The dilapidated River Terminal lies at the heart of Komsomolsk-na-Amur's summer social scene, which sees open-air bars strung out along the river bank. North-west of the river terminal lies the stunning **World War II Memorial** featuring superb stone sculptures. Nearby, the small **Regional Museum** on prospekt Mira houses exhibits ranging from traditional clothing such as fish-skin jackets to a stuffed Amur tiger. Just north is the **Art Museum**, which showcases a selection of paintings by local artists. Although the city offers attractions worth a day's visit, it is also well known for rafting tours in the region that can be arranged by local travel agents.

**🏛 Regional Museum**
Prospekt Mira 8. **Tel** (4217) 54 14 40.
**Open** 10:30am–5pm Tue–Sun. 🎟 📷

**🏛 Art Museum**
Prospekt Mira 16. **Tel** (4217) 59 08 50.
**Open** 10am–6pm Tue–Fri (till 5pm Sat & Sun). 🎟 📷

## ⓯ Sakhalin Island

Сахалин
*Sakhalin*

354 km (220 miles) NE of Komsomolsk-na-Amur. 🚗 ⛴

Home to an abundance of diverse wildlife, this mountainous island draws nature enthusiasts from around the world. Rich in oil and gas reserves, the region is a magnet for international energy companies.

Inhabited since the Stone Age, Sakhalin Island is still occupied by three indigenous tribes who share the territory with ethnic Russians and a large number of international workers based in Yuzhno-Sakhalinsk, the island's main city. Following a series of bitter territorial disputes, Japan occupied the southern half of the island from 1905 until the end of World War II when the Soviets took control. A number of Japanese buildings have survived from that period, one of which in Yuzhno-Sakhalinsk now houses the excellent **Museum of Local Lore**. Exhibitions cover the island's indigenous tribes, the Japanese occupation and the Soviet era, when the island was used primarily as a penal colony. The Soviet era saw Gulag prisoners forced to dig a 10-km (6-mile) tunnel using hand tools from the mainland to the island. The project cost thousands of lives and was abandoned shortly after Stalin's death.

While it is possible to explore Sakhalin Island independently, it is more convenient to join an organized tour to access the island's natural beauty. Popular summer trips to the island include hiking up Mount Legushka and fishing in its vast lakes.

**🏛 Museum of Local Lore**
Kommunisticheskiy prospekt 29.
**Tel** (4242) 72 75 55. **Open** 11am–6pm Tue–Sun (till 8pm Sat). 🎟 📷
Ⓦ sakhalinmuseum.ru

Elegant whooper swans off the coast of Sakhalin Island

Dramatic rock formations on Sakhalin Island

Soviet-era concrete buildings on a street winding through Magadan

## ⓰ Magadan
Магадан

*Magadan*

2,225 km (1,382 miles) NE of Sakhalin Island. 🚇 95,000. ✈ ➤ 🚌 Ⓜ ⛴

Built in a region of permafrost by prison labour, the remote city of Magadan is rarely visited by tourists. The few who make the effort to visit the city do so not for its dreary Soviet-era architecture, but to experience what life was like at this former Gulag town. Winters in Magadan stretch over six months, with temperatures dropping below -35°C (-31°F), making living conditions harsh in the city.

The discovery of gold and platinum in the region inspired the Soviets to establish a port in the city in 1929. During the 1930s and 1940s, thousands of prisoners were sent by ship via Magadan to the Kolyma region beyond, where Gulag camps had been set up to mine gold and platinum in appalling conditions. The prisoners were also assigned the task of building the infamous Kolyma Highway by using hand tools to connect Magadan with Yakutsk, 2,025 km (1,258 miles) away. Later, the highway came to be known as the Road of Bones due to the countless lives that were lost while building it. An imposing concrete memorial to the Gulag victims, the **Mask of Sorrow** was erected on the hillside above Magadan in 1996. A decade later, the huge **Holy Trinity Cathedral** was built on the site of the unfinished House of the Soviets as an Orthodox memorial to the victims of Stalin's repression.

🏛 **Holy Trinity Cathedral**
Sobornaya ploshchad. **Open** 7:30am–8pm daily. 📷

## ⓱ Kamchatka
Камчатка

*Kamchatka*

400 km (249 miles) NE of Magadan. 🚇 320,000. ✈ ➤ 🚌 Ⓜ ⛴

The landscape of this mountainous peninsula is an intriguing mix of geographical features, ranging from rolling plains to geysers and glaciated volcanic brown bears roam freely across the peninsula, frolicking and lunging beneath a horizon of blunt-topped volcanoes, some of which belch sulphurous vapours. Thrilling helicopter flights over wide craters and jagged mountains are the only way to reach many parts of this remote territory, which was closed to non-Russians until 1991.

Among Kamchatka's many highlights is a visit to the **Valley of the Geysers**. A UNESCO World Heritage Site, the valley is a vast expanse of steam fields and spouting geysers. Lying in an ancient volcano crater, **Lake Kurilskoe** is a popular daytrip option; it is great for bear spotting and bird watching. **Mount Mutnovskaya**, a stunning 2,323-m (7,621-ft) active volcano that last erupted in 2000, is also a must see. Visitors can stand atop its two colossal craters and gaze at the volcanic activity below; in winter, it is possible to heli-ski down the volcano's side.

Kamchatka's largest city, Petropavlovsk-Kamchatsky is the starting point for most tours. Founded by Vitus Bering (1681–1741) on behalf of the Russians in 1740, the city boasts dramatic mountain scenery overlooked by drab Soviet buildings.

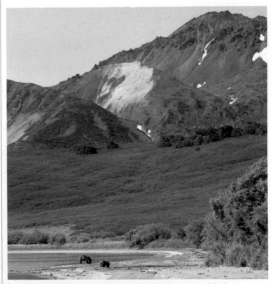

Brown bears foraging by a lake surrounded by majestic mountains, Kamchatka

# TRAVELLERS' NEEDS

| | |
|---|---|
| Where to Stay | **262–273** |
| Where to Eat and Drink | **274–291** |
| Shopping in Russia | **292–295** |
| Entertainment in Russia | **296–297** |
| Outdoor Activities | **298–299** |

# WHERE TO STAY

From luxury hotels in outstanding locations to wonderfully atmospheric bed and breakfast accommodation (B&Bs), Russia offers a range of places to stay to suit every budget. While Moscow abounds in high-end hotels, with cities such as St Petersburg not far behind, the provinces offer limited options. Out of the cities, hotels are mostly concrete blocks from the Soviet era where every floor is guarded by a *dezhurnaya* (concierge) who not only dispenses keys but also controls

room service. Travellers visiting on a package tour are usually housed in large, somewhat anonymous hotels outside the city centre. These hotels provide reasonable service and full amenities such as bars, restaurants and fitness facilities. Travelling off season cuts costs and offers the opportunity to book one of the many excellent deals available at the city-centre hotels. However, during peak season bookings for accommodation at all price levels should be made well in advance.

## Where to Look

Independent travellers should consider the location, price and facilities before making a reservation. Large, usually expensive hotels can be easily spotted in most city centres. But minihotels, as they are commonly known, and B&Bs may be tucked away in the courtyards of residential blocks, often with only a nameplate by the doorbell to identify them, whether they are located in the centre or in the suburbs. If they are in the suburbs, be sure to enquire about local transport links to the centre before making a booking.

Sign for a hotel on a quiet street off the city centre, Veliky Novgorod

debited if a cancellation is made less than 72 hours in advance. A number of hotels and agencies provide visa support. Be sure that the establishment where you are staying can register you with the authorities within 7 working days, otherwise you may face problems if asked to present this document by the police or authorities.

## Hotels

Hotels in Russia can be broadly divided into luxury options, mid-price places and the plainer

ex-Soviet hotels that were formerly run by the state. Rooms in most places have at least a shower, a TV and a telephone and possibly also air conditioning. Luxury hotels have comfortable rooms and offer modern facilities such as minibars. There is usually a luggage room for storing baggage after the midday check-out time. Bars are generally open until late at night, and fitness and sauna facilities are more or less standard in bigger establishments. A number of smaller, more modern hotels are emerging in the mid-price category. Rooms are generally clean and amenities include air conditioning and even sauna facilities. The cheaper ones in this category are mostly low-rises with small rooms, often without en-suite facilities. Ex-Soviet hotels are frequently lacklustre, with nondescript decor and poor-quality furniture. But the rooms are usually clean and of a good size.

The Russian word for hotel is *gostinitsa*, but some establishments may use the English

The Fifth Corner Business Hotel in St Petersburg's city centre *(see p269)*

## How to Book

Most hotels can be booked online or by fax. Some of the smaller hotels, which cannot be booked by email or phone, can be reserved through accommodation agencies such as **Ostrovok.ru**, **All Russian Hotels** and **Hotels.ru**. Guests are required to supply a credit card number, and money will be

The reception desk at the Park Inn, Astrakhan *(see p270)*

◀ Stylish interior of a shopping mall selling international brands in Moscow

The fine dining restaurant in Dvor Podznoeva, a luxury hotel in Pskov *(see p270)*

term, which is pronounced "khotyel". Taxi drivers should be able to understand either term.

## Price

The big city-centre hotels nearly all fall into the luxury category, offering everything from exclusive single rooms to imperial suites costing several thousand dollars a day. However, staying at a smaller but centrally located hotel or B&B costs less money.

Prices are often stated in euros or US dollars, but all cash transactions must be made in Russian roubles. Note that many small hotels and hostels do not accept credit cards. It is important to be prepared to pay in cash.

Accommodation costs rise considerably during events such as Stars of the White Nights (late May–early Jul) in St Petersburg, any major sports tournament, or even locally specific events such as during the summer season in Sochi. Christmas and New Year (by both the Western and Orthodox calendars) is another time when hotel rates tend to soar across the country. Prices return to normal during "mid-season" (usually from April to May and late July to late September), with good deals available from October to November and February to March.

## Hidden Extras

Upmarket hotels that provide visa support and obligatory passport registration for free may not include local taxes or breakfast in their quoted prices, and these can be a significant addition to the final bill. In smaller hotels, breakfast is usually included in the price, but expect to pay extra for the initial visa support. Phone calls made from hotels are usually far more expensive than those from public or cell phones.

## Tipping

A tip is expected if a hotel bellman or porter carries your bags to your room, but is not customary otherwise. However, in hotels that have a *dezhurnaya* on each floor, a small tip (as per your discretion) will ensure that room service is efficient and any requests or problems are attended to swiftly.

## Taxes

Local taxes vary from region to region. They usually range from 1.5 to 15 per cent. Tax is generally included in the cost of a room quoted on hotel websites or on tariff-boards at reception desks.

## Security

Many high-end hotels have metal detectors and bag searches at entrances, while smaller hotels have a doorman who may ask to see a visitor's card or identification. Most business-class hotels have a safe in the room or security deposit boxes at the front desk, where it is advisable to store any large sums of money or valuables.

## Disabled Travellers

Due to the thick snow in winter, most hotels have steps up to their entrances, making access difficult for disabled visitors. Only a few of the elite hotels are fully wheelchair accessible, with staff trained to be of assistance, although other hotels are increasingly adding ramps, widening doors and trying to adapt to meet the needs of disabled travellers. Anyone with special requirements should contact their preferred hotel before booking.

## Travelling with Children

Few hotels in Russia cater specifically for families. Large hotels, however, provide babysitting facilities. Most hotels will charge an additional fee for an extra bed in the room. It is worth checking this before making a reservation. Visitors are advised not to expect extensive facilities for children or favourable room rates for families.

The elegantly decorated lobby at the Radisson Hotel, Kaliningrad *(see p270)*

## Mini-Hotels

St Petersburg and Moscow have by far the widest range of mini-hotels, ranging from basic to boutique. Other cities may have only a handful, sometimes squeezed into unlikely premises such as office blocks.

Not always a budget option, considering some are extremely luxurious, mini-hotels can have anything from four to 15 or 20 rooms. In St Petersburg and Moscow, rooms may be elaborately furnished and decorated, but in the provinces the decor may be rather "Soviet", or garish in the "New Russian" style.

Many of St Petersburg's mini-hotels belong to the **Nevsky Hotels Group**, **Filippov Hotels** and **Rinaldi** networks. Mini-hotels elsewhere in the country can be booked through online agencies such as allrussiahotels.com, Lodging.ru and All Russian Hotels.

## Budget Accommodation

Truly cheap accommodation is hard to find in Russia. If hostels are not for you but your budget is tight, choose one of the more modest mini-hotels, which may describe themselves as a B&B. These establishments offer a small number of rooms in a converted flat in a residential building, with a housekeeper who makes breakfast. There may be a shared toilet rather than separate facilities.

Agencies such as **Apartment Reservation Network** and **Enjoy Moscow** offer short-term apartment rental. Note that the price drops considerably if more

A simply furnished room in the Filippov Hotel, St Petersburg

people share an apartment. Centrally located and refurbished, the apartments have one or more bedrooms, as well as satellite TV. In many cases, although the apartment has been refurbished, the communal staircase to the building may be on the grubby side, which can be off-putting at first.

**Couchsurfing** is another option, where you can find places to stay for free with Russian hosts. Travelling during off season is also a good idea.

## Hostels

For budget travellers seeking decent accommodation in a reasonably central location, there are hostels in most major cities. Guests can choose from private, double and dormitory-style rooms. Several hostels offer kitchen facilities and free Wi-Fi. Almost all hostels offer visa support and registration and are quite friendly. Few are "youth" hostels as such, although young people do tend to dominate in the summer months. Off season, it is not uncommon to see guests in the over-forty age range.

There are many hostels in Moscow, St Petersburg and Novgorod that are affiliated to the **Russian Youth Hostel Association**. In addition, **Hostelling International** and **HostelWorld** feature hostels in Russia on their websites.

Plush reception area of a Nevsky Moyka mini-hotel

However, no single booking site covers all hostels and some may not be on any network at all.

## Homestays

For an insight into Russian culture, staying with a family can be a worthwhile option, especially for visitors who plan to stay for a month or more. The system of homestays is similar to that of B&Bs in Europe, with prices including breakfast but no other meals. Extra meals can usually be provided at a small cost.

**International Homestay Agency** and **Worldwide Homestay** are good for booking homestays in Moscow and St Petersburg, while **OstWest** and **HOFA (Host Families Association)** are two reliable agencies covering a wide range of locations across Russia. OstWest focuses on St Petersburg and Lake Baikal, while HOFA also offers Moscow, Irkutsk, Kazan, Khabarovsk, Nizhny Novgorod, Veliky Novgorod, Novosibirsk, Omsk, Perm, Rostov-na-Donu, Samara, Saratov, Suzdal, Vladivostok, Volgograd, Yaroslavl and Yekaterinburg as homestay destinations. The host families are likely to be extremely hospitable. Many are well educated, speak several languages and are keen to talk to guests about life in Russia.

Many apartments are reached through scruffy entrance halls or courtyards, but do not let this act as a deterrent, as it gives little indication of the quality of the accommodation inside.

### Dachas and Camping

Russians love visiting the countryside for walks, swimming and mushroom gathering in warmer months. It is possible to do these on day trips, but finding accommodation out of town is difficult. Many Russians own *dachas* (country cottages), but these are seldom rented out except to people known to the owner. In fact, the demand for *dachas* located within 100 km (62 miles) from the city outstrips the supply. Be sure to book as early as February to ensure accommodation for the summer.

**Uncle Pasha** is an agency that can arrange *dacha* stays and horse-riding in a picturesque village beside the Volga river between Moscow and St Petersburg. The agency also recommends campsites.

Russia's climate means that camping is only feasible during summertime or until early autumn in temperate southern regions. Most campsites are geared towards travellers with cars, with motel-style rooms and guarded parking spots. Organized campsites are few and far between except around St Petersburg and Lake Baikal,

Cosy interior of a *dacha* listed on Uncle Pasha

but many people enjoy "wild" camping in the Altai Mountains, the Caucasus or even in the forests of Northern Russia.

### Extended Stays

Those intending to stay in any city for a month or more will find renting an apartment far cheaper than a hotel. This can be arranged by a number of agencies, such as HOFA (Host Families Association), OstWest, the Apartment Reservation Network or Enjoy Moscow. However, be sure to enquire about registration formalities.

### Recommended Hotels

The hotels listed in this guide have been carefully selected and are among the best in Russia in their categories: historic, hostel, guesthouse, business/chain and luxury. From guesthouses in picturesque settings to luxurious hotels in bustling city centres, accommodation in Russia can be found at all price levels. Befitting its rich history, the country boasts a host of splendid historic hotels. The hotels labelled "DK Choice" have been highlighted for their stunning location, spectacular interiors or inviting atmosphere.

## DIRECTORY

### Accommodation Agencies

**All Russian Hotels**
Pyatnitskaya ulitsa 3/4,
Moscow. **Map** 4 E2.
**Tel** (495) 225 50 12.
[w] allrussianhotels.com

**Hotels.ru**
**Tel** (312) 309 05 01.
[w] hotels.ru

**Ostrovok**
**Tel** (499) 215 65 25.
[w] ostrovok.ru

### Mini-Hotels

**Filippov Hotels**
St Petersburg.
**Tel** (812) 274 53 63.
[w] filippovhotel.ru

**Nevsky Hotels Group**
St Petersburg. **Tel** (812)
703 38 60. [w] hon.ru

**Rinaldi**
St Petersburg.
**Tel** (812) 325 41 88.
[w] rinaldi.ru

### Budget Accommodation

**Apartment Reservation Network**
**Tel** (495) 225 50 12.

**Couchsurfing**
[w] couchsurfing.org

**Enjoy Moscow**
**Tel** (495) 741 76 06.
[w] enjoymoscow.com

### Hostels

**Hostelling International**
[w] hihostels.com

**HostelWorld**
[w] hostelworld.com

**Russian Youth Hostel Association (RYHA)**
[w] hostelling-russia.ru

### Homestays

**HOFA (Host Families Association)**
Tavricheskaya ulitsa 5,
Apartment 25,
St Petersburg.
**Tel** (7911) 766 54 64.
[w] hofa.ru

**International Homestay Agency**
[w] homestayagency.com

**OstWest**
Ligovsky prospekt 10,
Office 2133,
St Petersburg.
**Tel** (812) 327 34 16.
[w] ostwest.com

**Worldwide Homestay**
[w] worldwidehomestay.com

### Dachas and Camping

**Uncle Pasha**
Ovchinnikovskaya naberezhnaya 8,
Flat 508, Moscow.
**Map** 4 E2.
**Tel** (985) 217 32 41.
[w] unclepasha.com

# Where to Stay

## Moscow
### Red Square and Kitay Gorod

### DK Choice

**Hotel Metropol**
Метрополь ⓇⓇⓇ
Luxury **Map** 2 D5
*Teatralnyy proezd 2*
**Tel** *(499) 501 78 00*
W metropol-moscow.ru
A wonderful example of Style-Moderne, the Metropol boasts spectacular interiors adorned with mosaics, golden chandeliers and stained glass. Many of the rooms are similarly lavish.

**Hotel Savoy** Савой ⓇⓇⓇ
Luxury **Map** 2 D5
*Ulitsa Rozhdestvenka 3/6*
**Tel** *(495) 620 85 00*
W savoy.ru
Stylish hotel with rich furnishings, artworks, soft lighting and all modern facilities.

### Garden Ring

**Marco Polo Presnya Hotel**
Марко Поло Пресня ⓇⓇ
Business/chain **Map** 1 B4
*Spiridonevskiy pereulok 9*
**Tel** *(495) 660 06 06*
W presnja.ru
Quiet and comfortable hotel in a lovely residential area, a short walk from Red Square.

**Peking Hotel** Пекин ⓇⓇ
Historic **Map** 1 A3
*Ulitsa Bolshaya Sadovaya 5*
**Tel** *(495) 650 09 00*
W hotelpeking.ru
Towering Empire-style building with rooms ranging from basic to luxurious. Free Wi-Fi.

### DK Choice

**Ararat Park Hyatt Moscow™**
Арарат Парк Хаятт ⓇⓇⓇ
Luxury **Map** 2 D5
*Neglinnaya ulitsa 4*
**Tel** *(495) 783 12 34*
W moscow.park.hyatt.com
Housed in a former Stalinist ministry, the eco-friendly Ararat offers superb views of the Bolshoi Theatre and the Kremlin from its terrace. The hotel has a health club with lounging areas, a sauna and a big Roman bath. Its restaurants serve Armenian, Japanese and European cuisines.

**Hotel Arbat** Арбат ⓇⓇⓇ
Business/chain **Map** 3 A2
*Plotnikov pereulok 12*
**Tel** *(499) 271 28 01*
W president-hotel.ru/arbat
Quiet hotel with large rooms and a nice veranda. Centrally located.

**Hotel Marriott Grand Moscow**
Марриотт Грандъ ⓇⓇⓇ
Business/chain **Map** 1 B4
*Tverskaya ulitsa 26/1*
**Tel** *(495) 937 00 00*
W marriott.com
Ultra-luxury establishment with all modern amenities. Great service.

**Hotel National** Националь ⓇⓇⓇ
Historic **Map** 1 C5
*Mokhovaya ulitsa 15/1*
**Tel** *(495) 258 70 00*
W national.ru
Lenin stayed here before moving into the Kremlin. Rooms are well-appointed. Free Wi-Fi.

**The Ritz-Carlton**
Ритц Карлтон ⓇⓇⓇ
Business/chain **Map** 1 C5
*Tverskaya ulitsa 3*
**Tel** *(495) 225 88 88*
W ritzcarltonmoscow.ru
Indulge in the spa and pool at this grand hotel opposite Red Square.

## Zamoskvoreche

### DK Choice

**Hotel Baltschug Kempinski**
Балчуг Кемпински ⓇⓇⓇ
Business/chain **Map** 4 D2
*Ulitsa Balchug 1*
**Tel** *(495) 287 20 00*
W kempinski-moscow.com
Located by the Moskva river, this elegant yet modern hotel offers magnificent views of the Kremlin and St Basil's Cathedral from its rooms on the riverside. Facilities include a business centre, spa and beauty centre. Taxi and transfer services are available from the hotel's fleet of luxury cars.

## Further Afield

**Godzillas Hostel**
Годзиллас Хостел Ⓡ
Hostel **Map** 2 D3
*Bolshoy Karetnyy pereulok 6*
**Tel** *(495) 699 42 23*
W godzillashostel.com
This amusingly named hostel has comfortable rooms and dorms. Kitchens are available for guest use. Friendly staff.

**Danilovskaya**
Даниловская ⓇⓇ
Business/chain
*Bolshoy Starodanilovskiy pereulok 5*
**Tel** *(495) 954 05 03*
W danilovsky.ru
Run by the Orthodox Church, Danilovskaya offers clean, quiet rooms. Portraits of patriarchs and icons adorn the hotel's walls.

**Domodedovo AirHotel**
Аэротель ⓇⓇ
Business/chain
*Domodedovo Airport*
**Tel** *(495) 795 38 68*
W airhotel.ru
Although lacking character, this place is well equipped with modern facilities, such as free Wi-Fi and business conference rooms.

**Holiday Inn Vinogradovo**
Холидей Инн Виноградово ⓇⓇ
Business/chain
*Dmitrovskoe shosse 171*
**Tel** *(495) 937 06 70*
W himv.ru
This lakeside hotel a 5-minute drive from Sheremetevo airport offers comfortable rooms and good sports and fishing facilities.

**Hotel Belgrade** Белград ⓇⓇ
Business/chain **Map** 3 A2
*Smolenskaya ulitsa 8*
**Tel** *(499) 248 16 43*
W hotel-belgrad.ru
Ex-Soviet budget hotel near the city centre. The restaurant serves good Eastern European food.

Gothic-Revival exterior of the stately Peking Hotel in Moscow

### Hotel Sherston Шерстон ⓇⓇ
Business/chain
*Gostinichniy proezd 8/1*
**Tel** *(495) 580 90 90*
Ⓦ **sherston.ru**
Rooms are clean and simple at this hotel far from the city centre but easily accessible by metro.

### Hotel Yunost Юность ⓇⓇ
Business/chain
*Khamovnicheskiy val 34*
**Tel** *(499) 242 48 61*
Ⓦ **hotelyunost.ru**
Once connected to the Soviet youth organization, *Komsomol*, Yunost has bright, airy rooms.

### Izmailovo Gamma-Delta
Измайлово Гамма-Дельта ⓇⓇ
Business/chain
*Izmaylovskoe shosse 71*
**Tel** *(495) 737 70 70*
Ⓦ **izmailovo.ru**
Simple and well-appointed rooms. Very close to Izmaylovo Market.

### Maxima Irbis Hotel
Гостиница Максима Ирбис ⓇⓇ
Business/chain
*Gostinichnaya ulitsa 1*
**Tel** *(495) 788 72 72*
Ⓦ **maximahotels.ru**
A friendly hotel near VDNKh (Exhibition of Achievements of National Economy), Maxim Irbis is well equipped and has free Wi-Fi.

### Maxima Zarya
Максима Заря ⓇⓇ
Business/chain
*Gostinichnaya ulitsa 4/9*
**Tel** *(495) 788 72 72*
Ⓦ **maximahotels.ru**
Zarya offers a wide range of accommodation options, from budget to luxurious studios.

### Novotel Новотель ⓇⓇ
Business/chain
*Sheremetevo 2 Airport*
**Tel** *(495) 626 59 00*
Ⓦ **novotel.com**
This clean and bright airport hotel has a great on-site restaurant.

### Proton Hotel Протон ⓇⓇ
Business/chain
*Novozavodskaya ulitsa 22*
**Tel** *(495) 797 33 00*
Ⓦ **protonhotel.ru**
Well equipped business hotel with comfortable rooms and excellent service.

### Sovietskiy Советский ⓇⓇ
Historic
*Leningradskiy prospekt 32/2*
**Tel** *(495) 960 20 00*
Ⓦ **sovietsky.ru**
Grand Stalinist decor with period furniture and a mirrored restaurant. Night club and lounge on site.

Plush waiting area at the Katerina City Hotel, Moscow

### Tourist Турист ⓇⓇ
Hostel
*Ulitsa Selskokhozyaystvennayav 17*
**Tel** *(495) 980 60 50*
Ⓦ **www.turist-hotel-moscow.ru**
Clean and basic rooms offer an authentic Soviet experience.

### Art Hotel Арт Отель ⓇⓇⓇ
Business/chain
*3-ya Peschanaya ulitsa 2*
**Tel** *(495) 725 09 05*
Ⓦ **arthotel.ru**
Centrally located hotel with cosy rooms, sauna and a beer garden.

### Azimut Moscow Olympic Hotel
Азимут ⓇⓇⓇ
Business/chain **Map** 2 D1
*Olimpiyskiy prospekt 18/1*
**Tel** *(495) 931 90 00*
Ⓦ **azimuthotels.com**
Rooms here are comfortable, with modern amenities. There's a pool and a free shuttle bus service to the city centre and metro.

### Crowne Plaza Краун Плаза ⓇⓇⓇ
Business/chain
*Krasnopresnenskaya naberezhnaya 12*
**Tel** *(495) 258 22 22*
Ⓦ **cpmow.ru**
A huge complex of rooms, offices, shops and restaurants in the riverside World Trade Center.

### Golden Apple Boutique Hotel
Голден Еппл Бутик ⓇⓇⓇ
Luxury **Map** 1 C3
*Ulitsa Malaya Dmitrovka 11*
**Tel** *(495) 980 70 00*
Ⓦ **goldenapple.ru**
A homage to design in wood, marble and slate. Rooms are much cheaper at weekends.

### Golden Ring Hotel Отель Золотое
Кольцо ⓇⓇⓇ
Business/chain **Map** 3 A2
*Smolenskaya ulitsa 5*
**Tel** *(495) 725 0100*
Ⓦ **hotel-goldenring.ru**
Disabled-friendly hotel. Restaurants serve a wide variety of cuisines.

### DK Choice

### Hilton Leningradskaya
Хилтон Ленинградская ⓇⓇⓇ
Historic
*Ulitsa Kalanchevskaya 21/40*
**Tel** *(495) 627 55 50*
Ⓦ **leningradskaya.ru**
With marble columns and bronze chandeliers, this hotel is one of the most famous in the city. Its elegant interiors and opulent rooms belie the modern amenities on offer. It has a well-equipped fitness room and a pool for guests.

### Katerina City Hotel
Катерина Сити ⓇⓇⓇ
Business/chain **Map** 4 F4
*Shluzovaya naberezhnaya 6*
**Tel** *(495) 795 24 44*
Ⓦ **katerinahotels.com**
Contemporary Swedish styled hotel with two relaxing bars and restaurants. The hotel has rooms for people with disabilities.

### Kebur Palace
Кебур Палас ⓇⓇⓇ
Guesthouse **Map** 3 B3
*Ulitsa Ostozhenka 32*
**Tel** *(495) 733 90 70*
Ⓦ **keburpalace.ru**
Near the Cathedral of Christ the Saviour, with some rooms overlooking a pretty cobbled patio.

### Korston Hotel
Корстон ⓇⓇⓇ
Business/chain
*Ulitsa Kosygina 15*
**Tel** *(495) 939 88 88*
Ⓦ **korston.ru**
Comfortable retro rooms, multi-cuisine restaurants and karaoke are offered at this hotel in the Sparrow Hills.

### Moscow Country Club
Москоу Кантри Клаб ⓇⓇⓇ
Luxury
*Nakhabino, Krasnogorsky District*
**Tel** *(495) 626 59 11*
Ⓦ **moscowcountryclub.ru**
A favourite weekend retreat for the city's elite, this hotel boasts Russia's only 18-hole championship golf course.

### President
Президент ⓇⓇⓇ
Historic **Map** 3 C3
*Ulitsa Bolshaya
Yakimanka 24*
**Tel** *(499) 271 28 00*
Ⓦ **president-hotel.ru**
A Communist-era haven for party leaders, the President has stately rooms, kitsch decor and tight security.

**For more information on types of hotels** *see pp264–265*

**Radisson Slavyanskaya**
Радиссон Славянская   Ⓡ Ⓡ Ⓡ
Business/chain
*Ploshchad Europa 2*
**Tel** *(495) 941 80 20*
Ⓦ radisson.com
Panoramic views and well-
furnished contemporary rooms.

### DK Choice

**Swissôtel Krasnye Holmy**
Красные Холмы   Ⓡ Ⓡ Ⓡ
Luxury     **Map** 4 F4
*Kosmodamianskaya*
*naberezhnaya 52/6*
**Tel** *(495) 787 98 00*
Ⓦ swissotel.com
One of Moscow's best hotels,
with stunning river-facing views
and two excellent restaurants.
Plush interiors and floor-to-
ceiling windows make for a
luxurious experience. Relax
in the heated indoor pool or
unwind at the hotel spa.

# St Petersburg
## Palace Embankment

**Prestige Hotel Centre**
Престиж Центр   Ⓡ Ⓡ
Business/chain   **Map** 3 C1
*Gorokhovaya ulitsa 5*
**Tel** *(812) 312 83 26*
Ⓦ prestige-hotels.com
Simply furnished rooms, a bistro
and a café. Tucked away near the
gardens fronting the Admiralty.

**Angleterre Hotel**
Отель Англетер   Ⓡ Ⓡ Ⓡ
Historic   **Map** 3 C2
*Malaya Morskaya ulitsa 24*
**Tel** *(812) 494 56 66*
Ⓦ angleterrehotel.com
Stylishly refurbished hotel with
views of St Isaac's Cathedral from
some rooms. Relax at the indoor
pool, spa or the turbo-solarium.

### DK Choice

**Casa Leto**
Лето   Ⓡ Ⓡ Ⓡ
Historic   **Map** 3 C2
*Bolshaya Morskaya ulitsa 34*
**Tel** *(812) 600 10 96*
Ⓦ casaleto.com
This ultra-chic family-owned
boutique hotel – reached by a
grand stairwell – boasts light-
filled rooms and a superb
central location. Non-smoking,
with many complimentary
extras such as fresh fruit and
refreshments. Airport transfer
facilities available upon
request. Free Wi-Fi.

**Comfort Hotel** Комфорт   Ⓡ Ⓡ Ⓡ
Business/chain   **Map** 3 C1
*Bolshaya Morskaya ulitsa 25*
**Tel** *(812) 560 67 00*
Ⓦ comfort-hotel.org
Simple, airy rooms in the heart of
the historic centre. Basic facilities,
but helpful staff.

**Petro Palace Hotel**
Петро палас   Ⓡ Ⓡ Ⓡ
Business/chain   **Map** 3 C1
*Malaya Morskaya ulitsa 14*
**Tel** *(812) 571 30 06*
Ⓦ petropalacehotel.com
Grand interiors and extensive facil-
ities, including a gym, a sauna and
a Jacuzzi, at competitive prices.

## Gostinyy Dvor

**Polikoff** Поликофф   Ⓡ Ⓡ
Guesthouse   **Map** 4 F1
*Karavannya ulitsa 11/64, apt 24–26*
**Tel** *(812) 995 34 88*
Ⓦ polikoff.ru
Mini-hotel with bright, cosy rooms.
Centrally located. Buffet breakfast.

### DK Choice

**Grand Hotel Europe** Гранд
Отель Европа   Ⓡ Ⓡ Ⓡ
Historic   **Map** 4 E1
*Mikhaylovskaya ulitsa 1/7*
**Tel** *(812) 329 60 00*
Ⓦ grandhoteleurope.com
In a superb location, the Europe
is close to all the main sights. It
boasts wonderful decor, espe-
cially the splendid Art Nouveau
L'Europe restaurant. Suites are
furnished with antiques.

**Kempinski Hotel Moika 22**
Кемпински Мойка 22   Ⓡ Ⓡ Ⓡ
Luxury   **Map** 2 D5
*Naberezhnaya Reki Moyki 22*
**Tel** *(812) 335 91 11*
Ⓦ kempinski.com
Some rooms offer great views of
the Hermitage. The restaurant
offers international cuisine.
Indulge in the Turkish bath.

Atrium café at the Grand Hotel Europe,
St Petersburg

**Pushka Inn**
Отель Пушка ИНН   Ⓡ Ⓡ Ⓡ
Guesthouse   **Map** 2 D5
*Naberezhnaya Reki Moyki 14*
**Tel** *(812) 644 71 20*
Ⓦ pushkainn.ru
Chic modern rooms in a historic
building right on the Moyka river.

## Sennaya Ploshchad

### DK Choice

**B&B Randhouse**
рэнд дом   Ⓡ Ⓡ
Guesthouse   **Map** 4 D3
*Pereulok Grivtsova 11, apt 83*
**Tel** *(812) 310 70 05*
Ⓦ randhouse.ru
Named after Ayn Rand, this loft-
based mini-hotel has open
fireplaces, bare brick walls and
king-size duvets. Some rooms
have private bathrooms, others
share facilities. Great location.

**Hotel Columb**
Отель Колумб   Ⓡ Ⓡ
Guesthouse   **Map** 3 C2
*Kazanskaya ulitsa 41*
**Tel** *(812) 315 70 93*
Ⓦ columbhotel.com
Quiet, comfortable hotel near the
metro. Free parking and Wi-Fi.

**Ambassador** Амбассадор   Ⓡ Ⓡ Ⓡ
Luxury   **Map** 3 C3
*Prospekt Rimskogo-Korsakova 5–7*
**Tel** *(812) 331 88 44*
Ⓦ ambassador-hotel.ru
Plush rooms with city views. Gym
and beauty services available.

## Further Afield

**Andersen Hotel**
Андерсен Отель   Ⓡ Ⓡ
Business/chain
*Ulitsa Chapygina 4*
**Tel** *(812) 740 51 40*
Ⓦ andersenhotel.ru
A hotel with pleasant rooms that
arranges tours of the city centre.

**Kronverk** Кронверк   Ⓡ Ⓡ
Business/chain   **Map** 1 B3
*Ulitsa Blokhina 9*
**Tel** *(812) 703 36 63*
Ⓦ kronverk.com
Very close to Peter and Paul
Fortress, this hotel offers rooms
with kitchenettes. Free Wi-Fi.

**Moskva** Москва   Ⓡ Ⓡ
Business/chain
*Ploshchad Aleksandra*
*Nevskogo 2*
**Tel** *(812) 333 24 44*
Ⓦ hotel-moscow.ru
Centrally located package-tour
establishment with good facilities.

**Okhtinskaya** Охтинская ⓡⓡ
Business/chain
*Bolsheokhtinskiy prospekt 4*
**Tel** *(812) 318 00 40*
🆆 **okhtinskaya.com**
Contemporary hotel, with airy
rooms overlooking the Neva river
near the Smolnny Cathedral.

**Rossiya** Россия ⓡⓡ
Business/chain
*Ploshchad Chernyshevskogo 11*
**Tel** *(812) 329 39 01*
🆆 **rossiya-hotel.ru**
Refurbished Soviet-era hotel
amidst the Stalinist buildings
of Moskovskiy prospekt.

**Stony Island Hotel**
Стоуни Айлэнд ⓡⓡ
Business/chain
*Kamennoostrovskiy prospekt 45*
**Tel** *(812) 337 24 34.*
🆆 **stonyisland.ru**
Housed in a historic building, with a
relaxed American bar and restaurant.

**Vesta Hotel** Веста Отель ⓡⓡ
Guesthouse
*Nevskiy prospekt 90*
**Tel** *(812) 272 13 22*
🆆 **vesta-hotel.ru**
Set in a quiet courtyard, this hotel
is located close to main sights.
Great service and hearty breakfast.

**AZIMUT Hotel St Petersburg**
АЗИМУТ Отель Санкт-
Петербург ⓡⓡⓡ
Business/chain **Map** 3 B5
*Lermontovskiy prospekt 43/1*
**Tel** *(812) 740 26 40*
🆆 **azimuthotels.com**
Over 1,000 budget rooms with
stunning views of Fontanka river.

**Baltic Star Hotel** Отель
Балтийская Звезда ⓡⓡⓡ
Luxury
*Berezovaya alleya 3, Strelna*
**Tel** *(812) 438 57 00*
🆆 **balticstar-hotel.ru**
A superb retreat for those seeking
elegance and comfort. Cottages
are available for greater privacy.

**Brothers Karamazov** Братя
Карамазовы ⓡⓡⓡ
Guesthouse **Map** 4 F4
*Sotsialisticheskaya ulitsa 11a*
**Tel** *(812) 355 11 85*
🆆 **karamazovhotel.ru**
Hotel with airy rooms named after
heroines in Dostoyevsky's novels.

**Corinthia Nevskij Palace**
Коринтия Невский Палас ⓡⓡⓡ
Business/chain
*Nevskiy prospekt 57*
**Tel** *(812) 380 20 01*
🆆 **corinthia.com**
This hotel is popular with
celebrities and has a DJ in the

Brightly lit reception area at the Fifth Corner Business Hotel, St Petersburg

lobby at weekends. Excellent
on-site restaurant.

**Fifth Corner Business Hotel**
Пятый угол ⓡⓡⓡ
Business/chain **Map** 4 F3
*Zagorodnyy prospekt 13*
**Tel** *(812) 407 81 81*
🆆 **5ugol.ru**
A simple eco-friendly hotel. All
rooms have a mini-bar and safe.

**Grand Hotel Emerald**
Гранд Отель Эмеральд ⓡⓡⓡ
Business/chain
*Suvorovskiy prospekt 18*
**Tel** *(812) 740 50 00*
🆆 **grandhotelemerald.com**
Modern hotel with opulent
rooms. It also has a great fitness
centre, sauna and Turkish bath.

**Holiday Inn St Petersburg**
Холидэй Инн Санкт-
Петербург ⓡⓡⓡ
Business/chain
*Moskovskiy prospekt 97a*
**Tel** *(812) 448 71 71*
🆆 **holidayinn.com**
Comfortable, well-equipped and
minimalist rooms. Great location.

**Hotel Dostoevsky** Отель
Достоевский ⓡⓡⓡ
Business/chain
*Vladimirskiy prospekt 19*
**Tel** *(812) 331 32 03*
🆆 **dostoevsky-hotel.ru**
Vibrant, modern hotel wrapped
around a shopping mall. Airport
shuttle available.

## DK Choice

**Hotel Shelfort** Шелфорт ⓡⓡⓡ
Historic **Map** 1 A5
*3-ya linlya 26, Vasilevskiy Island*
**Tel** *(812) 328 05 55*
🆆 **shelfort.ru**
With lovely tiled stoves in
elegantly minimalist rooms,
Shelfort will charm guests with
its understated beauty. It also
offers two luxury suites with
log fireplaces, one of them
with a balcony. There is no lift.

**Park Inn Pribaltiyskaya** Парк Инн
Прибалтийская ⓡⓡⓡ
Business/chain
*Korablstroiteley ulitsa 14*
**Tel** *(812) 329 26 26*
🆆 **parkinn.com**
Vast hotel looking out on to the
Gulf of Finland. Free shuttle bus
service to the city centre.

**Park Inn Pulkovskaya**
Парк Инн Пулковская ⓡⓡⓡ
Business/chain
*Ploshchad Pobedy 1*
**Tel** *(812) 740 39 00*
🆆 **parkinn.com**
Good selection of bars and restau-
rants, with great views of Victory
Monument. Close to the airport.

**St Petersburg Hotel**
Санкт-Петербург ⓡⓡⓡ
Business/chain **Map** 2 F2
*Pirogovskaya naberezhnaya 5/2*
**Tel** *(812) 380 19 19*
🆆 **hotel-spb.ru**
Splendid views from rooms on
the south side. Healthy breakfast
spread. Free Wi-Fi.

## Beyond St Petersburg

**Hotel Natali** Натали ⓡⓡ
Guesthouse
*Malaya ulitsa 56a, Pushkin*
**Tel** *(812) 466 27 68*
🆆 **hotelnatali.ru**
Cosy rooms, an excellent spa and a
bowling alley for guests. Free Wi-Fi.

## DK Choice

**New Peterhof**
Новый Петергоф ⓡⓡ
Business/chain
*Sankt-Peterburgskiy prospekt 34,
Petrodvorets*
**Tel** *(812) 319 10 10*
🆆 **new-peterhof.com**
Rooms at this award-winning
hotel are stylish and spacious –
many offer great views of
Peterhof's Upper Park. The amen-
ities include a spa and excellent
on-site restaurants serving
Russian and European cuisines.

**For more information on types of hotels** *see pp264–5*

# Northern Russia

**PETROZAVODSK: Petrozavodsk**
Петрозаводск ®
Hostel
*Ulitsa Krasnaya 28, 2nd floor*
**Tel** *(8142) 77 98 77*
W **petrohostel.ru**
Smartly furnished dorms and doubles are offered at this centrally located budget option.

**PETROZAVODSK: Zarechnaya**
Заречная ®
Business
*Naberezhnaya Lososinskaya 7A*
**Tel** *(8142) 59 22 20*
W **zarekoy.ru**
This pleasant hotel with friendly staff has comfortable rooms and a café-restaurant.

## DK Choice

**PSKOV: Dvor Podznoeva**
Двор Подзноева ®®
Historic
*Ulitsa Nekrasova 1B*
**Tel** *(8112) 79 70 00*
W **dvorpodznoeva.ru**
Enjoy all modern facilities within an ensemble of renovated 17th-century buildings. Located in the old town, this extremely atmospheric hotel is a short walk from the Kremlin.

**PSKOV: Rizhskaya** Рижская ®®
Business
*Rizhskiy prospekt 25*
**Tel** *(8112) 56 22 23*
W **rijskaya.ru**
A vast Soviet-era hotel, the renovated Rizhskaya still exudes period charm. Great service.

**VALAAM: Zimnaya** Зимняя ®®
Historic
*Valaam Monastery*
**Tel** *(921) 629 33 11*
W **valaam-hotel.ru**
Comfortable rooms are offered at this functional island hotel.

**VELIKY NOVGOROD: Voyage**
Вояж ®
Guesthouse
*Ulitsa Dvortsovaya 1*
**Tel** *(8162) 66 41 66*
W **hotel-voyage.ru**
This central hotel has big rooms, some with four-poster beds.

**VELIKY NOVGOROD: Park Inn (Radisson)** Парк Инн ®®
Business
*Ulitsa Studencheskaya 2*
**Tel** *(8162) 94 09 10*
W **parkinn.ru**
A classy hotel with barbecue areas, tennis courts and jogging trails.

**For key to prices** *see p266*

# Kaliningrad

**KALININGRAD: Amigos Hostel**
Амигос Хостел ®
Hostel
*Ulitsa Yablonevaya 34*
**Tel** *911 485 2157 (mobile)*
W **amigoshostel.ru**
Cosy dorm-style rooms are offered in this modern house in the leafy suburbs of Kaliningrad.

**KALININGRAD: Hotel Kaliningrad**
Гостиница Калининград ®
Business/chain
*Leninsky prospekt 81*
**Tel** *(4012) 53 60 21*
W **hotel.kaliningrad.ru**
Housed in a Soviet-era building, this central hotel has modern interiors and a billiards room.

## DK Choice

**KALININGRAD: Hotel Kaiserhof** Кайзерхоф ®®
Business
*Ulitsa Oktyabrskaya 6A*
**Tel** *(4012) 59 22 22*
W **heliopark.ru**
This stylish business hotel overlooks the Pregolya river and has splendid views of Königsburg Cathedral. Highlights include a lovely spa centre to unwind in and a fitness studio with sweeping views of the river. Helpful and professional staff.

**KALININGRAD: Radisson Hotel**
Радисон Отель ®®
Business/chain
*Ploshchad Pobedy 10*
**Tel** *(4012) 59 33 44*
W **radisson.ru**
In a superb central spot overlooking the main square, this hotel has state-of-the-art facilities.

Entrance to the ultra-chic Hotel Kaiserhof, Kaliningrad

**SVETLOGORSK: Dom Skazochnika** Дом Сказочника ®
Guesthouse
*Pereulok Gofmana 2*
**Tel** *(4015) 32 23 96*
W **hoffmanhouse.ru**
Close to the beach, this hotel is set in well-kept wooded gardens.

# Central and Southern Russia

**ASTRAKHAN: Park Inn**
Парк Инн ®®
Business
*Ulitsa Anri Barbusa 29*
**Tel** *(8512) 29 01 20*
W **parkinn.ru**
This 14-storey hotel close to the railway station has chic rooms and excellent standards of service.

**ASTRAKHAN: Victoria Palas**
Виктория Палас ®®
Business
*Ulitsa K Naberezhnaya 3*
**Tel** *(8512) 39 48 01*
W **victoriapalas.ru**
Amenities at this plush hotel on the banks of the Volga river include a spa and a piano bar.

**KAZAN: Vhostele** Вхостеле ®
Hostel
*Ulitsa Volkova 54A*
**Tel** *(843) 238 06 93*
W **vhostele.com**
All dorms and rooms at this hostel are non-smoking and air-conditioned. It is located near a bus stop.

**KAZAN: Giuseppe** Джузеппе ®®
Historic/luxury
*Ulitsa Kremliovskaya 15/25*
**Tel** *(843) 292 69 34*
W **giuseppe.ru**
In a historic building that exudes character, this hotel has spacious rooms. The restaurant serves Italian and Mediterranean cuisine.

**KAZAN: Shalyapin Palace**
Шаляпин Палас ®®
Luxury
*Ulitsa Universitetskaya 7*
**Tel** *(843) 231 10 00*
W **shalyapin-hotel.ru**
This recently refurbished hotel in a central location has elegantly furnished rooms. Helpful staff.

**NIZHNY NOVGOROD: Naberzhny Hostel** Чабержный Хостел ®
Hostel
*Naberezhnaya Nizhne-Volzhskaya 7/2*
**Tel** *(831) 413 90 41*
W **hostelbereg.ru**
Naberzhny is in a great location, has low prices, spacious dorms and all the usual hostel facilities.

**NIZHNY NOVGOROD:**
**Sergievskaya** Сергиевская ⓇⓇ
Historic
*Ulitsa Sergievskaya 12*
**Tel** *(831) 433 00 10*
🅦 hotel-sergievskaya.ru
Discover a delightful blend of the
old and new in this atmospheric
19th-century mansion.

**PERM: Hilton Garden Inn**
Хилтон Гарден Инн ⓇⓇ
Business
*Ulitsa Mira 45B*
**Tel** *(342) 227 67 87*
🅦 hi-perm.ru
Rooms are smart. Suites have a
whirlpool bath. Many rooms have
specialized accessible facilities.

**PERM: Ural** Урал ⓇⓇ
Business
*Ulitsa Lenina 58*
**Tel** *(342) 218 62 61*
🅦 hotel-ural.com
A colossal Soviet-era hotel domi-
nating the city centre with modern
business and wellness centres.

**SAMARA: Hotel Kolos** Колос Ⓡ
Historic
*Ulitsa Samarskaya, 69–71*
**Tel** *(846) 333 79 00*
🅦 gkolos.ru
Rooms are clean and basic at
this hotel housed in a late 19th-
century building close to the
picturesque city centre.

---

**DK Choice**

**SAMARA: Bristol-Zhiguly**
Бристоль Жигули ⓇⓇ
Historic/luxury
*Ulitsa Kuybyscheva 111*
**Tel** *(846) 331 65 55*
🅦 bristol-zhiguly.ru
A lovely historic hotel that has
been in business since the late
18th century. Pleasant, spacious
and well-appointed rooms offer
all modern amenities. The 24-
hour restaurant serves European
cuisine. Warm and friendly staff.

---

**SAMARA: Rossiya** Россия ⓇⓇ
Business
*Ulitsa M Gorkogo 82*
**Tel** *(846) 339 03 11*
🅦 hotel-rossia.ru
An ex-Soviet hotel with reasonable
service standards. Most rooms
come with fabulous river views.

**SARANSK: Hotel Saransk**
Саранск ⓇⓇ
Business
*Ulitsa Kommunicheskaya 35*
**Tel** *(8342) 47 88 82*
🅦 hotelsaransk.ru
A fully renovated hotel with com-
fortable rooms and a Turkish bath.

The Park Inn Ekaterinburg, a modern hotel in the heart of Yekaterinburg

**SARANSK: Park Hotel** Парк
Отель ⓇⓇ
Guesthouse
*Ulitsa Krasnaya 4*
**Tel** *(8342) 23 29 19*
🅦 parkhotel-saransk.ru
Resembling a chateau from the
outside, this lovely hotel is tucked
away in a quiet residential area.

**ULYANOVSK: Venets** Венец ⓇⓇ
Business
*Ulitsa Spasskaya 19/9*
**Tel** *(8422) 44 18 70*
🅦 venets-hotel.ru
This towering Soviet-era block has
modern interiors, a rooftop restau-
rant and views of the Volga river.

**VOLGOGRAD: Flamingo Motel**
Фламинго Мотель Ⓡ
Guesthouse
*Ulitsa Rokossovskogo 63*
**Tel** *937 725 9960 (mobile)*
Located above a car wash, this
popular budget option comprises
several modern en suites.

**VOLGOGRAD: Hotel Volgograd**
Волгоград ⓇⓇ
Business/luxury/historic
*Ulitsa Mira 12*
**Tel** *(8442) 55 19 55*
🅦 hotelvolgograd.ru
Rooms are tastefully decorated in
this grand 19th-century hotel.
Spa treatments are available.

**YEKATERINBURG: Domino Hostel**
Домино Хостел Ⓡ
Hostel
*Ulitsa Chelyuskintsev 60*
**Tel** *(343) 361 54 60*
🅦 dominohotel.ru
These basic apartments have clean
dorms and doubles. Free Wi-Fi.

**YEKATERINBURG: Park Inn**
**Ekaterinburg** Парк Ин ⓇⓇ
Business/chain
*Ulitsa Mamina-Sibiryaka 98*
**Tel** *(343) 216 60 00*
🅦 parkinn.ru
In a central location and popular
with business travellers, this large
hotel has well-furnished rooms.

**YEKATERINBURG: Viz' Avi**
Виз' Ави ⓇⓇ
Business
*Ulitsa Tatischeva 86*
**Tel** *(343) 381 50 27*
🅦 vizavi-hotel.ru
This modern hotel has uninspiring
decor but the rooms are spacious.

---

## The Caucasus

**ADLER: Ekodom** Екодом ⓇⓇ
Guesthouse
*Ulitsa Prosveshcheniya 160B*
**Tel** *(8622) 47 37 13*
🅦 ekodom-hotels.ru
Recently built, Ekodom has all mod
cons and a great breakfast spread.

**ADLER: Flamingo** Фламинго ⓇⓇ
Guesthouse
*Ulitsa Prosveshcheniya 15B*
**Tel** *(8622) 40 87 70*
🅦 adler-flamingo.ru
A few minutes from the beach,
this is a comfortable, friendly
hotel with efficient service.

---

**DK Choice**

**ANAPA: Starinnaya**
Старинная ⓇⓇⓇ
Luxury
*Ulitsa Naberezhnaya 2*
**Tel** *(86133) 322 11*
🅦 starinnaya-anapa.ru
The Starinnaya is a grand
colonnaded hotel with plush
carpets, polite staff and a
wonderful array of spa
treatments. Most rooms have
superb sea views. There are
both indoor and outdoor pools.

---

**GELENDZHIK: Gelendzhik**
Геленджик ⓇⓇ
Guesthouse
*Ulitsa Khersonskaya 1*
**Tel** *(86141) 211 45*
🅦 gelhotel.ru
This charming all-inclusive place
is right in the centre of the city, a
short distance from the seafront.

**GELENDZHIK: White House**
Белый Дом  ⓇⓇ
Guesthouse
*Ulitsa Lunacharskogo 127*
**Tel** *(86141) 320 08*
Ⓦ **whitehouse.azur.ru**
A calm alternative to the bustling
city centre, with an outdoor pool
and lovely sea views.

**KRASNAYA POLYANA: Piramida**
Пирамида  ⓇⓇ
Guesthouse
*Ulitsa Berezovaya 157*
**Tel** *918 401 1478 (mobile)*
Pleasant family-run guesthouse
located near the ski slopes.

**KRASNAYA POLYANA: Tulip Inn
Rosa Farm** Тюлип Инн
Роза Хутор  ⓇⓇ
Luxury
*Rosa Khutor Alpine Ski Resort*
**Tel** *(8622) 43 00 00*
Ⓦ **tulipinnrosakhutor.com**
This modern hotel is in the heart
of the Olympic ski resort.

**KRASNODAR: Intourist**
Интурист  ⓇⓇ
Business
*Ulitsa Krasnaya 109*
**Tel** *(861) 255 88 97*
Ⓦ **int-krd.ru**
Centrally located ex-Soviet hotel
with rooms decorated in warm
colours. High standards of service.

**KRASNODAR: Lux-Platan**
Люкс-Платан  ⓇⓇ
Business/luxury
*Ulitsa Rashpilevskaya 4/1*
**Tel** *(861) 262 86 84*
Ⓦ **platanhotel.ru**
Popular with rock stars, this hotel
boasts big rooms, a sauna and a
well-equipped fitness centre.

**ROSTOV-NA-DONU: Don-Plaza**
Дон-Плаза  ⓇⓇ
Business
*Ulitsa Bolshaya Sadoyova 115*
**Tel** *(863) 263 90 52*
Ⓦ **don-plaza.ru**
A stylish hotel with an impressive
open-plan lobby and spa centre.

**ROSTOV-NA-DONU:
Pushkinskaya** Пушкинская  ⓇⓇ
Business/historic
*Ulitsa Pushkinskaya 121*
**Tel** *(863) 299 92 70*
Ⓦ **hotel-pushkinskaya.ru**
Characterful 19th-century mansion
with graceful interiors. Free Wi-Fi.

**SOCHI: Villa Svetlana** Вила
Светлана  Ⓡ
Guesthouse
*Ulitsa Chernomorskaya 12/2*
**Tel** *918 200 3794 (mobile)*
This small guesthouse in a quiet
suburb is close to the beach.

A contemporary-style room at Tulip Inn Rosa Farm, Krasnaya Polyana

**SOCHI: Sochi Breeze**
Сочи Бриз  ⓇⓇ
Guesthouse
*Kurortny prospekt 72*
**Tel** *(8622) 66 38 00*
Ⓦ **sochibreeze.ru**
Smart hotel with a great spa and
an outdoor pool overlooking
the arboretum.

**SOCHI: Marins Park**
Маринс Парк  ⓇⓇⓇ
Business/luxury
*Morskoy pereulok 2*
**Tel** *(8622) 71 30 00*
Ⓦ **parkhotel-sochi.ru**
Swanky, central hotel with
spacious rooms. Private beach for
guests. Excellent breakfast spread.

**SOCHI: Zelenaya Roscha**
Зеленая Роща  ⓇⓇⓇ
Historic
*Kurortny prospekt 120*
**Tel** *(8622) 269 53 33*
Ⓦ **rosha-sochi.ru**
Stalin's camouflaged *dacha*, set
in the forested hills just outside
Sochi, has cavernous oak-
panelled guest rooms.

# Siberia and the
# Far East

**IRKUTSK: Luchshii Hostel**
Лучший Хостел  Ⓡ
Hostel
*Ulitsa Karla Marksa 41*
**Tel** *(3952) 24 20 91*
Ⓦ **hostel-irkutsk.com**
This modern, cosy hostel is
set in an ancient merchant house
located in the historic city centre.

**IRKUTSK: Courtyard Marriott**
Кортъярд Марриотт  ⓇⓇ
Business
*Ulitsa Chkalova 15*
**Tel** *(3952) 48 10 00*
Ⓦ **courtyardirkutsk.ru**
One of the city's best hotels
offers wheelchair-friendly rooms.
It has an elegant ballroom.

**IRKUTSK: Irkutsk** Иркутск  ⓇⓇ
Business
*Bulvar Gagarina 44*
**Tel** *(3952) 25 05 00*
Ⓦ **irkutsk-hotel.ru**
Huge riverfront hotel with superb
views from most of its rooms.

**KHABAROVSK: Intour** Интур  ⓇⓇ
Business
*Amurskiy Bulvar 2*
**Tel** *(4212) 31 23 13*
Ⓦ **intour-khabarovsk.ru**
Towering ex-Soviet hotel with
renovated rooms decorated in
elegant European style.

**KOMSOMOLSK-NA-AMUR:
Amur** Амур  Ⓡ
Guesthouse
*Prospekt Mira 15*
**Tel** *(4217) 55 20 60*
Ⓦ **amur-hotel.ru**
Constructed in the 1930s, this
place offers all the basic amenities.
Friendly and helpful staff.

**KOMSOMOLSK-NA-AMUR:
Voskhod** Восход  ⓇⓇ
Business
*Prospekt Pervostroiteley 31*
**Tel** *(4217) 53 51 31*
Ⓦ **hotel-voskhod.ru**
Soviet-era hotel with elegantly
furnished suites. Home to one
of the city's top restaurants.

**KRASNOYARSK: SibTourGuide
Hostel** СибТурГид  Ⓡ
Hostel
*Prospekt Mira 85, apt 72*
**Tel** *(391) 251 26 54*
Ⓦ **sibtourguide.com**
Centrally located hostel run by a
tour guide who organizes excur-
sions for guests around the city.

**KRASNOYARSK: Metelitsa**
Метелица  ⓇⓇ
Business
*Prospekt Mira 14/1*
**Tel** *(391) 227 60 60*
Ⓦ **hotel-metelitsa.ru**
Opulent rooms have luxurious
furnishings at this upmarket
hotel. Excellent restaurant on site.

## DK Choice

**LISTVYANKA: Hotel Mayak**
Маяк ®®
Business
*Ulitsa Gorkogo 85A*
**Tel** *(3952) 49 69 10*
W mayakhotel.ru
Set on the coast of Lake Baikal
in the legendary port village,
this hotel offers rooms with fine
views and a great on-site restau-
rant. Try the *banya (see p298)* or
sunbathe at the nearby beach.

**MAGADAN: Golden House**
Голден Хаус ®®
Business
*Ulitsa Transportnaya 1*
**Tel** *(4132) 20 11 11*
W hotel-goldenhouse.ru
Rooms are refreshingly modern
and comfortable at this hotel.

**NOVOSIBIRSK: Zokol Hostel**
Цоколь Хостел ®
Hostel
*Ulitsa Schetinkina 34*
**Tel** *(383) 223 36 11*
W zokolhostel.ru
Stylish dorms and doubles at
this inviting hostel. Outstanding
facilities and great location.

**NOVOSIBIRSK: Double Tree
Hilton** Даблтри Хилтон ®®®
Business/luxury
*Ulitsa Kamenskaya 7/1*
**Tel** *(383) 223 01 00*
W hilton.ru/hotels/doubletree-by-
hilton-novosibirsk/
The chic rooms here are well
appointed. Relax in the spa or
unwind in big whirlpool baths.

**OMSK: Ibis Sibir Omsk**
Ибис Сибирь Омск ®®
Business
*Ulitsa Lenina 22*
**Tel** *(3812) 31 15 51*
W ibis-sibir-omsk.com
Set in a 19th-century building, this
classy hotel has modern interiors.

**OMSK: Shato** Шато ®®
Luxury
*Ulitsa 1ya Severnaya 95*
**Tel** *(3812) 38 32 82*
W hotel.shato55.ru
This palatial hotel has elaborate
decor and excellent service, as
well as a great on-site restaurant.

**PETROPAVLOVSKY-
KAMCHATSKY: Avacha** Авача ®®
Business
*Ulitsa Leningradskaya 61*
**Tel** *(4152) 42 72 01*
W avacha-hotel.ru
Soviet-era hotel with comfortable
rooms and mountain views.

**PETROPAVLOVSKY-KAMCHATSKY:
Idelvels** Эдельвейс ®®
Business
*Prospekt Pobedy 27*
**Tel** *(4152) 29 50 00*
W idelveis.com
Idelvels offers basic but clean and
comfortable rooms in the town
centre. Helpful multilingual staff.

**SAKHALIN: Pacific Plaza**
Пацифик Плаза ®®
Business
*Prospect Mira 172*
**Tel** *(4242) 45 50 00*
W sakhalinpacificplaza.ru
Popular upmarket hotel with res-
taurants and conference facilities.

**SAKHALIN: Sakhalin Sapporo**
Сахалин Саппоро ®®
Business
*Ulitsa Lenina 181*
**Tel** *(424) 272 15 60*
W sakhsapporo.ru
Rooms are spacious and well
appointed with contemporary
furnishings. Good service.

**TOBOLSK: Georgievska**
Георгиевская ®®
Business
*Ulitsa Lenskaya 35*
**Tel** *(3456) 22 09 09*
W hotel-georgievskaya.ru
A centrally located hotel with cosy
rooms and adequate facilities.
Warm and personable staff.

**TOBOLSK: Sibir** Сибирь ®®
Business
*Ploshchad S Remezova 1*
**Tel** *(3456) 25 13 53*
W hotel-siberia.com
Although in need of refurb-
ishment, the Sibir still offers decent
rooms. Close to the Kremlin.

**TOMSK: Yoko** Йоко ®
Business
*Ulitsa Altayskaya 149*
**Tel** *(3822) 20 02 20*
W yoko.tomsk.ru
This pleasant Japanese-themed
mini-hotel has stylish interiors
and a good sushi bar.

**TOMSK: Toyan** Тоян ®®
Luxury
*Ulitsa Obrub 2*
**Tel** *(3822) 51 01 51*
W toyan.ru
Stunning hotel with cutting-edge
design features that include stone-
and marble-clad room interiors.

**ULAN-UDE: Traveller's House**
Трэвелерс Хаус ®
Hostel
*Ulitsa Lenina 63, apt 18*
**Tel** *950 391 6325 (mobile)*
W uuhostel.com
Popular hostel in a converted cen-
tral apartment with views of the
city's famed statue of Lenin's head.

**ULAN UDE: Buryatiya** Бурятия ®®
Business
*Ulitsa Kommunisticheskaya 47A*
**Tel** *(3012) 21 48 88*
W buryatiahotel.ru
Soviet-era hotel with great views
of the city and beyond. Good
value for money.

**VLADIVOSTOK: Optimum Hostel**
Оптимум Хостел ®
Hostel
*Ulitsa Aleutskaya 17*
**Tel** *(423) 272 91 11*
This budget-friendly hostel with
bright, funky design offers
singles, doubles and dorms.

**VLADIVOSTOK: Sibirskoe
Podvorie** Сибирское подворье ®®
Guesthouse
*Okeansky prospekt 26*
**Tel** *(4232) 22 52 66*
W otelsp.com
Centrally located hotel with
wooden floors and imaginatively
designed rooms.

**VLADIVOSTOK: Hyundai**
Хёндэ ®®®
Business
*Ulitsa Semenovskaya 29*
**Tel** *(423) 240 22 33*
W hotelhyundai.ru
Sleek hotel with high standards of
services and facilities. It features a
restaurant serving Korean cuisine.

Neatly arranged beds in a dorm at the Zokol Hostel, Novosibirsk

**For more information on types of hotels** *see pp264–5*

# WHERE TO EAT AND DRINK

Eating out in Russia was a rare privilege during the Soviet era, and a luxury for most people in the years immediately after *perestroika*. However, the country has seen a phenomenal boom in restaurants, cafés and bars since the 1990s. From cheap student cafés to staggeringly expensive eateries, all budgets are covered. Restaurants in Moscow, St Petersburg and other major cities offer the world's leading cuisines, including French, Italian, Japanese, Indian, Chinese and Thai. Restaurants serving cuisines of former Soviet Republics such as Georgia, Armenia and Uzbekistan provide a wide selection of vegetarian dishes. In provincial towns, non-Russian cuisine may be limited, but the standards of cooking and level of service has vastly improved since Soviet times.

Cosy bar at DoDo, a stylish restaurant in Moscow *(see p280)*

## Places to Eat

Restaurants located in city centres tend to be more expensive than those situated in the outer streets. However, a variety of dining options can be found outside the centres to suit most pockets and tastes.

Upmarket restaurants serve a mix of European and Russian dishes, with some Asian elements too. Style and fashion can overshadow the cuisine in some restaurants, but other eateries manage to combine food, decor and service in fine Russian style. Trends include "imperial Russian" in a historic interior, themed (Retro-Soviet style or based on characters in novels or films) and hybrid (Italian, Thai and Japanese under one roof).

In addition to individual restaurants and cafés, there are plenty of international and home-grown fast-food chains to choose from. Sit-down cafés serve traditional Russian dishes, while street kiosks sell *blinis* (pancakes) to take away.

Department stores, theatres and major museums offer a stand-up buffet serving open sandwiches with salami, pickled herring, caviar or other nibbles.

## Reading the Menu

Restaurants specializing in international cuisine usually have menus in Russian and English; the menu might be separately available in English. But in local eateries, knowledge of the Cyrillic alphabet will help to decipher the menu, as many ingredients are phonetic versions of their English equivalents. Most restaurants geared towards non-Russians usually have an English-speaking staff.

## Types of Cuisine

Much of the best Russian food is either wholesome dishes and soups from recipes passed down over generations, or cured and salted fish as well as caviar, for which preparation is more important at its source, as opposed to in restaurants.

Georgian or Armenian cooking, both of which are delicious and relatively inexpensive, are a better option. Mediterranean and other Western European restaurants, especially Italian ones, are very popular in most cities, but Chinese and Indian food is generally a bit bland and of variable quality. However, there are a few excellent Asian restaurants, particularly Japanese, with sushi being the most fashionable dish since 2000.

## What to Drink

Vodka is the alcoholic drink most often associated with Russia, but beer is usually

The bar at the English-style Dickens Restaurant, St Petersburg *(see p288)*

preferred as an accompaniment to meals. Most restaurants now offer imported and local beer on tap, along with a variety of bottled beers; Russian beer is light and generally very good. The better European restaurants have commendable wine lists, although good imported wine tends to be quite expensive. Be sure to sample a bottle of Georgian wine *(see p279)*, which is the perfect accompaniment to Georgian food. However, it can at times overpower the subtler flavours of European cuisine.

## Payment and Tipping

Prices vary widely – while a meal in a cheap *stolovaya* (local cafeteria) might cost 120 roubles, it could cost well over 2,500 roubles in classy restaurants.

Many restaurants in Russia, especially those outside of the big cities, accept payment only in cash. This is gradually changing, but it is still a consideration when deciding where to eat. It is advisable to call ahead and check which cards (if any) are accepted and whether there is a surcharge.

Tipping is not as ingrained in Russia as elsewhere. Service is rarely included in the bill. It is appropriate to tip between 10 to 15 per cent if satisfied with the quality of service. However, it is unnecessary to leave more than a few hundred roubles regardless of the amount spent in a restaurant.

## Opening Times

In major cities, most restaurants are open from noon–11pm. Many eateries in big cities have adopted the concept of the business lunch. These often take the form of a fixed-price menu and can be excellent value. They are usually served from noon to 4pm. Most restaurants start serving dinner at around 6pm and stop taking orders at 10:30pm; some family-run Georgian establishments close their kitchens as early as 9pm. Increasingly though, restaurants are staying open until the early hours of the morning and some are even open around the clock.

## Making a Reservation

Most international and tourist-oriented restaurants accept reservations and some of the more popular ones require them. It is best to book ahead whenever possible. However, some of the well-known Georgian and Caucasian restaurants do not take reservations and these can be busy, particularly at weekends.

## Dress Code

Casual or semi-formal dress is acceptable in the majority of restaurants, but formal dress is *de rigueur* at fashionable, upmarket restaurants. Trainers and tracksuits are acceptable in the less expensive cafés.

**Sign for a Japanese restaurant**

## Children

On the whole, Russians love children and will rarely refuse them entry to restaurants. Family-friendly restaurants are growing in number and most Western or Russian fast-food chains provide children's menus.

## Vegetarians

Much Russian cuisine consists of meat dishes. Salads generally contain meat, so the best option for vegetarians is often a beetroot or tomato platter. Georgian cuisine, featuring a number of excellent bean and aubergine dishes, is usually a better choice.

Restaurants are increasingly taking into account the demands of vegetarian visitors. European, Chinese and Japanese restaurants usually have some dishes suitable for vegetarians. For those who eat fish, however, there is always plenty of choice.

## Disabled Access

Besides expensive eateries and bars, few restaurants in Russia have facilities for disabled visitors, although waiters and doormen can at times be very helpful. It is best to check beforehand if there is full disabled access.

## Recommended Restaurants

The restaurants in this guide have been selected across a wide price range for their value, good food, ambience and location. Diners can look forward to a variety of cuisines, ranging from international to that of the ex-Soviet republics. Fusion cuisine blends elements of European and Asian cooking, while Oriental restaurants usually offer Caucasian and Central Asian fare, rather than Indian, Chinese or Japanese cuisine. Note that the establishments labelled as DK Choice have been highlighted in recognition of an exceptional feature – a celebrity chef, exquisite food or a highly inviting atmosphere.

View of Cathedral of Christ the Saviour from Bar Strelka in Moscow *(see p282)*

# The Flavours of Russia

The Tsarist and Soviet empires stretched from Poland in the west to the Pacific Ocean in the east, leaving behind a legacy of multi-cultural cuisines. Aubergine and tomatoes, from the Caucasus in the south, bring in the flavours of the Mediterranean, while spices from Central Asia lend an exotic touch. The stalls in farmers' markets sell caviar and crayfish alongside honey from Siberia and melons and peaches from Georgia. Yet, Russia's culinary reputation centres on warming stews full of wintry vegetables such as cabbage, beetroot and potatoes.

Wild mushrooms

Black caviar, or sturgeon roe, on lightly toasted slices of bread

## Russian Countryside

Many Russians have *dachas* (country cottages) within easy reach of the city, where they spend weekends from spring to early winter tending their immaculate vegetable gardens, or combing the countryside for wild berries and mushrooms. Much of this bountiful harvest is made into preserves and pickles. Restaurant menus regularly feature pickled mushrooms in sour cream along with a variety of fresh berry juices. Pickled cucumbers impart a delicious salty taste to a refreshing soup known as *solyanka*.

Very little is wasted in a country where food shortages remain a fairly recent memory. *Kvas*, a popular, mildly alcoholic drink is frequently made in homes by fermenting stale black or rye bread with sugar and a scattering of fruit. Summer visitors should make a point of trying the delicious cold soup *okroshka*, which is based on *kvas*.

Russia is also a land with hundreds of rivers and lakes, and it has a long tradition of fish-based dishes. These range

A range of cold appetizers, commonly known as *zakuski*

Labels: Salted fish, Blinis, Pickled mushrooms, Spiced feta, Rye bread, Gherkins, Sour cream, Pickled herrings

## Russian Dishes and Specialities

Beetroot

*Borsch* (beetroot soup) and *blinis* (buttery pancakes) served with caviar are perhaps two of the most famous Russian dishes. The former is a peasant dish, which varies with the availability of ingredients, while the latter is a staple for the week leading up to Lent, when rich food is eaten to fatten up for the forty days of fasting prior to Easter. Much of Russia's cuisine is designed to make use of produce that is readily available or else warming and filling. A popular main course dish is *kulebiaka*, a hearty fish pie, generously filled with eggs, rice, dill and onion and encased in a buttery crust. Another is beef stroganoff with its creamy mushroom sauce, created in 18th-century St Petersburg by the chef of the wealthy Stroganoff family.

**Borsch** is a beetroot soup made with meat or vegetable stock and usually served with dill and sour cream.

A wealth of fresh vegetables and herbs at a market, Moscow

from simple soups, such as *ukha* (clear fish soup) to caviar and sturgeon and salmon cooked in a bewildering variety of ways.

## The Caucasus

The former Soviet states of the Caucasus – Georgia, Azerbaijan and Armenia – are renowned for their legendary banquets, where tables are laden with an enormous quantity and variety of food and drink. They still supply Russia's cities with a tempting array of fine subtropical produce. Limes, figs, lemons, oranges, walnuts, pomegranates, peaches, beans, salty cheeses and herbs are all shipped in season to city markets and Georgian restaurants. The cuisine of Georgia, with its focus on freshly grilled meats, pulses, vegetables, yogurt, herbs and nut sauces, including *satsivi* (the hallmark walnut sauce), is famously healthy, and Georgians are known for their longevity.

## Central Asia

The Central Asian republics of the former Soviet Union contributed a range of culinary traditions to Russian cuisine,

*Plov*, a typical Uzbek dish prepared with rice, vegetables and lamb

which were based on the nomadic lifestyles of Russia's one-time overlords – the Mongol or Tartar Hordes. The meat of fat-tailed sheep, which thrive in the dry desert air, is used to make communal piles of *plov* (pilaf) around which guests sit, eating in the traditional manner with their hands.

In addition to *plov*, the menus in Uzbek restaurants also offer delicious flat breads, spicy noodle soups, *manti* (tasty dumplings reminiscent of Chinese cuisine) and a variety of melons and grapes, which proliferate in the desert oases, as well as apricots and nuts, grown in the mountains.

### ZAKUSKI

A traditional Russian meal generally begins with *zakuski*, which is a selection of cold appetizers. These may include *griby* (pickled mushrooms), *ogurtsy* (gherkins), *seliodka* (salted or pickled herrings), an assortment of smoked fish, *blinis* topped with caviar, various vegetable pâtés (sometimes known as vegetable caviars), *yaitsa farshirovanniye* (stuffed eggs), *brinza* (spiced feta cheese), *salat iz svyokly* (beetroot salad) and *pirozhki* (small meat pies) accompanied by rye bread and washed down with shots of vodka. A bowl of steaming soup often follows, before the main course reaches the table.

**Kulebiaka**, a rich, buttery puff pastry, is wrapped around a mixture of fish, hard-boiled eggs, rice, onion and chopped dill.

**Pelmeni** are meat-stuffed dumplings that are served in a clear broth, or with tomato sauce or sour cream.

**Kissel**, a soft fruit-based jelly, is made from a mixture of red berries and presented with a swirl of fresh cream on top.

# What to Drink

Russian vodka – famous throughout the world – is distilled in many cities across the country. Vodka first appeared in Russia sometime in the 14th or 15th century. Peter the Great was particularly fond of anise- or pepper-flavoured vodkas and devised modifications to the distillation process that improved the quality of the finished product. Tea is Russia's other national drink. Traditionally made using a samovar and served black, tea has been popular in Russia since the end of the 18th century when it was first imported from China.

Merchants from Nizhny Novgorod drinking tea at a pub

## Clear Vodka

Gzhelka vodka

Vodka is produced from grain, usually wheat, although some rye is also used. The 80° proof (40° ABV) standard was set by Tsar Alexander III, based on a formula by the famous scientist Dmitri Mendeleev. Russia's principal distilleries are St Petersburg's Liviz, whose best brands are Diplomat, Five Star and Russian Standard; Moscow's Cristall with brands such as Cristall, Gzhelka and Stolichnaya; and Flagman, official purveyor of vodka to the Kremlin. The range of vodkas available these days is overwhelming, but illegal bootlegging is still a problem. There is one golden rule: if it is under US$10 for half a litre, do not drink it.

Vodka is always served with food, most often with *zakuski (see pp276–7)*. It is not always served ice cold, but it should be chilled.

Stolichnaya    Russian Standard    Stolichnaya Cristall

## Flavoured Vodka

The practice of adding various flavours to vodka has entirely practical origins. When vodka was first produced commercially in the Middle Ages, the techniques and equipment were so primitive that it was impossible to remove all the impurities. This left unpleasant aromas and flavours, which were disguised by adding honey together with aromatic oils and spices. Over time distillation techniques

Pertsovka

improved and flavoured vodkas became a speciality in their own right. *Limonnaya*, which derives its taste from lemon zest, is one of the most traditional vodkas, as is *Pertsovka*, flavoured with red chilli pepper pods. *Okhotnichya* (hunter's vodka) has a wider range of flavourings including juniper, ginger and cloves. *Starka* (old vodka) is distilled from rye with an infusion of apple and pear leaves, aged in oak barrels. Some of the best flavoured vodkas are made at home by soaking peach stones or whole berries in alcohol for months.

Limonnaya    Okhotnichya    Starka

Georgian wines    Shampanskoe

### Wine

The Soviet Union was one of the world's largest producers of *vino* (wine), but many of the major wine regions are now republics in their own right. Several indigenous types of grape are cultivated in the different regions, along with many of the more familiar international varieties.

Georgia and Crimea (in southeastern Ukraine) have traditionally produced the best wines, although Georgian wines may be difficult to find in Russia due to frosty relations between the two countries. Wines such as Gurdzhaani are made from the Rkatsiteli grape, which imparts a unique, slightly bitter taste, and the Mtsvane grape that adds a subtle, fruity flavour and a floral aroma. Among Georgia's best red wines is the smooth Mukuzani. Moldova produces white, sparkling wines and a sweet, champagne-like wine called "Soviet Sparkling", widely known as *shampanskoe*.

### Other Alcoholic Drinks

*Konyak* (brandy) was originally a by-product of winemaking, and commercial production only began in Russia in the 19th century. Armenian brandy is one of the finest, with a distinctive vanilla fragrance, a result of its ageing in 70- to 100-year-old oak barrels. Georgia and Dagestan also produce good brandies. Baltika, Vena and Stepan Razin make a full range of beers in bottles and on draught. In addition, Tver beers such as Afanasy are well worth trying. Various imported beers are also available.

Baltika beer    Armenian brandy

Mineral water    Kvas    Mors

### Other Drinks

Made from barley and rye, *kvas* is a sweet, mildly alcoholic drink consumed by adults and children alike. Less commonly found but also traditional are *myod* (honey mead) and *sbiten*, a version flavoured with herbs. Russia's vast range of *mineralnaya voda* (mineral water) includes many types with unusually high mineral contents; those from the Caucasus, Siberia and Georgia are especially prized. Also available are *sok* (fruit juices), and *kompot* (sweetened drinks made by boiling fruit with sugar and water); the cranberry version is called *mors*.

### Tea

Russian tea is served black with a slice of lemon and may be drunk from tall glasses or cups. Sweetened with *varenye* (jam) instead of sugar, *chay* (tea) is an ideal accompaniment to rich cakes and pastries. The boiling water for tea traditionally comes from a samovar. The water is used to brew a pot of tea, from which a little is poured into a cup then it is diluted with more hot water.

Tall glass of tea with jam

### The Samovar

Made from brass or copper and heated by coals in the central chimney, samovars traditionally provided boiling water for a wide variety of domestic purposes and were an essential wedding gift. Modern electric ones are made of stainless steel and are used mainly for boiling water to make tea. The word samovar comes from *samo* meaning "itself" and *varit* meaning "to boil".

# Where to Eat and Drink

## Moscow

### Red Square and Kitay Gorod

**Jagannath** Джаганнат
Vegetarian ®
**Map** 2 D4
*Ulitsa Kuznetskiy Most 11*
**Tel** *(495) 628 35 80*
Tasty Indian, Mexican, Thai,
Chinese and European vegetarian
dishes are served at this stylish
café. Great ginger beer. No alcohol.

**Mu-Mu My-My**
Russian ®
**Map** 1 C5
*Manezhnaya ploschad 1/2*
**Tel** *(985) 129 82 76*
This popular café serves traditional
dishes and Russian, Georgian and
Ukrainian soups, such as *schi*
(cabbage soup), *borsch* (beetroot
soup) and *kharcho* (spicy soup).

**Dissident** Диссидент ®®
Mediterranean **Map** 2 D5
*Nikolskaya ulitsa 25*
**Tel** *(495) 500 27 67*
The focus at this restaurant-wine
bar is on French specialities.
Good selection of Italian and
French pâtés. Excellent wine list.

### DK Choice

**LavkaLavka** ®®
Russian **Map** 2 D4
*Ulitsa Petrovka 21–2*
**Tel** *(495) 621 20 36*
Enjoy a home-style spread
made with organic, traditional
ingredients sourced from local
farms. More unusual fare
includes pike burgers, deer
heart and *samogon* (home-
made vodka containing bread,
berries and even oak bark).
The rustic decor includes
lamps made from milk cans.

Tastefully decorated interior of Khachapuri, Moscow

**Noev Kovcheg** Ноев Ковчег ®®
Armenian **Map** 4 F1
*Malyy Ivanovskiy pereulok 9*
**Tel** *(495) 917 07 17*
Savour Armenian delights at "Noah's
Ark". Their bean stew and grilled
cheese appetizers are excellent, as is
the acclaimed Armenian cognac.

**Nostalgie** Ностальжи ®®®
French/fusion **Map** 2 F5
*Chistoprudnyy bulvar 12a*
**Tel** *(495) 258 56 68*
French haute cuisine with a
Japanese touch and a wine cellar
boasting 5,000 bottles should be
reason enough to try this place.
Reservation recommended.

### Garden Ring

**Bublik** Бублик ®
International **Map** 1 B4
*Tverskoy bulvar 24*
**Tel** *(495) 629 13 42*
Located on one of the city's most
historic boulevards, this deli-style
restaurant features an extensive
sandwich and brunch menu
alongside traditional Russian and
international confectionary items.

**Granvillano Caffe** ®
Italian **Map** 3 C5
*Leninsky prospekt 37A*
**Tel** *(916) 624 25 28*
Sip away at aromatic brews at
this excellent coffee house with
a well-stocked library and a shop
selling blends of coffee, gift
hampers and coffee sets.

**Montalto** Монтальто ®
Pizzeria **Map** 1 A4
*Ulitsa Sadovaya-Kudrinskaya 20*
**Tel** *(495) 234 34 87*
Thick-crust pizzas cooked in
a wood-fired oven. Toppings
come with an original twist – try
the pear, goat's cheese, fennel
and pistachio or spicy sausage.

**5-Spice** Пять Специй ®®
Chinese **Map** 3 B2
*Pereulok Sivtsev Vrazhek 3/18*
**Tel** *(495) 697 12 83*
Chinese restaurant specializing in
Cantonese food and dishes from
the northern provinces. Pleasant
interiors and good service.

**Akademiya** Академия ®®
Italian **Map** 1 C5
*Kamergerskiy pereulok 2*
**Tel** *(495) 692 96 49*
Dark-panelled pizzeria that is a
great place for delectable Italian
food and people-watching.

**Baba Marta** Баба Марта ®®
Bulgarian **Map** 3 B2
*Gogolevskiy bulvar 8*
**Tel** *(495) 232 92 09*
A family-run restaurant serving
diverse meat and vegetable
dishes, including mouthwatering
*banitsa* (pies with spinach, meat,
cheese, pumpkin and walnuts).

**Champagne Café**
шампанское кафе ®®
European **Map** 1 C5
*Bolshaya Nikitskaya ulitsa 12*
**Tel** *(495) 629 53 25*
Set in Venetian-style halls,
this eatery serves dishes such
as *foie gras* with berry sauce
and beef stroganoff.

**Clumba Club** Клумба Клаб ®®
International **Map** 1 A5
*Novinskiy bulvar 31*
**Tel** *(495) 644 96 69*
Clumba Club is home to Europe's
largest oyster bar. The menu is
international with an emphasis
on seafood. Extensive wine list.

**DoDo** ДоДо ®®
International **Map** 1 C4
*Ulitsa Petrovka 21/2*
**Tel** *(903) 105 10 10*
Enjoy European dishes with a
dash of the exotic in this laid-back
restaurant with outdoor seating.

**Dolkabar** Долькабар ®®
International **Map** 1 A3
*Ulitsa Krasina 7*
**Tel** *(499) 254 79 08*
Serving an international menu,
Dolkabar has travel-themed decor,
including maps on the tables and
photos of global sights on walls.

### Khachapuri Хачапури ®®
#### Georgian
*Bolshoi Gnezdnikovskiy pereulok 10*
**Tel** *(985) 764 31 18*
This inexpensive restaurant serves eight types of *khachapuri* (bread stuffed with cheese), and wonderful *khinkali* (dumplings).

### Mayak Маяк ®®
#### Russian/European **Map** 1 B5
*Bolshaya Nikitskaya ulitsa 19*
**Tel** *(495) 691 74 49*
A popular meeting place for actors and artists, with a wonderfully bohemian atmosphere. Good selection of wines. Must try the roast beef salad.

### Noor Нур ®®
#### International **Map** 1 C5
*Tverskaya ulitsa 23*
**Tel** *(903) 136 76 86*
More of a cocktail bar than a restaurant, Noor serves classic cocktails accompanied by dishes such as shrimps in filo pastry.

### Ararat Арарат ®®®
#### Armenian **Map** 2 D5
*Neglinnaya ulitsa 4*
**Tel** *(495) 783 12 34 (ext 5208)*
Relish Armenian specialities based on authentic recipes, plus a wide selection of vintage Armenian brandies and wines at the Ararat.

### Balzi Rossi Балзи Росси ®®®
#### Italian/Mediterranean **Map** 1 A5
*Kudrinskaya ploshchad 1*
**Tel** *(495) 144 74 14*
Set in one of Moscow's seven famous Stalinist skyscrapers, this restaurant offers an excellent multi-cuisine spread including seafood.

### Barashka Барашка ®®®
#### Azerbaijani **Map** 3 B1
*Ulitsa Novyy Arbat 21*
**Tel** *(495) 228 37 31*
Founded by famous restaurateur, Arkady Novikov, this upscale restaurant sources ingredients from Azerbaijan. Typical dishes include lamb *dolma* (lamb and rice-stuffed grape leaves) and sturgeon *shashlik* (kebab).

### Café Mart Кафе Март ®®®
#### International **Map** 1 C4
*Ulitsa Petrovka 25*
**Tel** *(495) 231 3661*
Café Mart offers a selection of light, international dishes, as well as tempting Georgian specialities.

### Central House of Writers
#### Центральный Дом Литераторов ®®®
#### Russian **Map** 1 A5
*Ulitsa Povarskaya 50/53, Bldg 1*
**Tel** *(495) 663 30 03*
This eatery features carved-oak wood decor, fireplaces,

Neatly arranged tables in Noor, a popular restaurant in Moscow

live music and tasty traditional dishes. Uniquely atmospheric, especially for devotees of Russian literature and popular with Russian actors, businessmen and politicians.

### DK Choice

#### Godunov Годунов ®®®
#### Russian **Map** 1 C5
*Teatralnaya ploshchad 5*
**Tel** *(495) 698 44 80*
Named after Tsar Boris Godunov and housed in a former monastic outbuilding, this restaurant serves excellent *borsch* and other rich soups, delicious game, *pirozhki* and a good choice of vegetarian main dishes. There is traditional Russian entertainment in the evenings.

### Mari Vanna Мари Ванна ®®®
#### Russian **Map** 1 B4
*Spiridonevskiy pereulok 10*
**Tel** *(495) 650 65 00*
Designed to replicate a 1930s Soviet flat, this restaurant offers delicious home cooking. Limited vegetarian options.

### Piazza Rossa Пьяцца Росса ®®®
#### Italian **Map** 1 C5
*Mokhovaya ulitsa 15*
**Tel** *(495) 258 70 68*
This restaurant, set in the historic Hotel National, offers stunning views of the Kremlin and authentic Italian cuisine complemented by an exclusive wine list.

### Polo Club Поло Клуб ®®®
#### Steakhouse/seafood **Map** 2 D4
*Ulitsa Petrovka 11*
**Tel** *(495) 937 10 00*
This renowned steakhouse also offers a good seafood menu and a large selection of sinful desserts. Superb wine list.

### Pushkin Пушкин ®®®
#### Russian/French **Map** 1 B4
*Tverskoy bulvar 26a*
**Tel** *(495) 739 00 33*
An aristocratic café with elegant decor, Pushkin offers an extensive menu and a rooftop terrace for dining in the summer.

### Scandinavia Скандинавия ®®®
#### European **Map** 1 B4
*Malyy Palashevskiy pereulok 7*
**Tel** *(495) 937 56 30*
A Swedish-run restaurant with quality European cuisine. Excellent steaks and desserts. Dine under chestnut trees in a pretty courtyard in fine weather.

### Steak House Bison Стейк Хаус Бизон ®®®
#### Steakhouse **Map** 2 D5
*Lubyansky Proezd 15*
**Tel** *(495) 231 92 82*
Come for some of the best steaks in Moscow served with delicious sauces. Specialities include flavourful Machete steak, tender butlers' steak and the signature Bison steak. Try the oxtail soup.

Classy decor at Barashka, an Azerbaijani eatery in Moscow

**For more information on types of restaurants** *see pp274–5*

## Zamoskvoreche

**Rodeo** Родео ⓇⓇ
European/Japanese **Map** 4 D4
*Ulitsa Bolshaya Polyanka 54/1*
**Tel** *(499) 230 73 33*
Rodeo offers an interesting menu featuring dishes such as duck breast, pork knuckle and grilled ice cream. Great cocktails.

**Discovery**
Дискавери ⓇⓇⓇ
Mediterranean **Map** 4 E4
*Novokuznetskaya ulitsa 24/2*
**Tel** *(495) 953 38 63*
Set in an old merchant's townhouse, Discovery offers a relaxed atmosphere. The second floor was designed to resemble a luxury yacht.

**Dorian Gray**
Дориан Грей ⓇⓇⓇ
Italian **Map** 4 D2
*Kadashevskaya naberezhnaya 6/1*
**Tel** *(499) 238 64 01*
A riverside restaurant with splendid views of the Kremlin, chic Italian decor and a traditional menu.

---

### DK Choice

**Oblomov** Обломов ⓇⓇⓇ
French/Russian **Map** 4 E4
*1-y Monetchikovskiy pereulok 5*
**Tel** *(495) 953 68 28*
A stylish restaurant with beautifully presented food and fine interiors. While the café on the first floor serves home-roasted coffee, the Eastern Room on the third floor has hookah pipes and live belly dancing.

---

## Further Afield

**Addis Abeba**
Аддис Абеба Ⓡ
Ethiopian
*Ulitsa Zemlyanoy Val 6*
**Tel** *(495) 916 24 32*
Try vegetarian, spicy dishes, mostly eaten from "plates" of *injera* (sourdough bread), at one of Moscow's few Ethiopian eateries.

**Avocado** Авокадо ⓇⓇ
Vegetarian **Map** 2 F4
*Chistoprudny bulvar 12, Bldg 2*
**Tel** *(495) 621 77 19*
This eatery is famed for its vegetarian versions of world cuisine, from *pelmeni* (dumplings) to pasta to curries.

**Korchma Taras Bulba**
Корчма Тарас Бульба Ⓡ
Ukrainian **Map** 3 A3
*Smolenskiy bulvar12*
**Tel** *(495) 488 89 89*
This café serves a range of traditional dishes including an assortment of *vareniks* (dumplings) stuffed with cherries, potatoes, cheese, meat or mushrooms.

**U Giuseppe** У Джузеппе Ⓡ
Italian **Map** 2 D2
*Samotechnaya ulitsa 13*
**Tel** *(495) 681 13 26*
A welcoming *osteria* (Italian wine and food joint) serving good home-made pasta. Caters to kids with board games and toys.

**Bar Strelka** Бар Стрелка ⓇⓇ
International **Map** 3 C2
*Bersenevskaya naberezhnaya 14, Bldg 5*
**Tel** *(495) 771 74 16*
Enjoy a bistro-style international menu, featuring dishes from New Zealand, Asia, Europe and Russia.

**Black Market** Блэк Маркет ⓇⓇ
American/fusion
*Ulitsa Usacheva 2, Bldg 1*
**Tel** *(495) 989 04 45*
Savour modern American fusion cuisine at this restaurant where the decor evokes a black market warehouse. Innovative burgers and desserts.

**China Garden** Китайский Сад ⓇⓇ
Chinese
*Krasnopresnenskaya naberezhnaya 12*
**Tel** *(495) 967 05 86*
Relish the range of tasty Szechwan, Peking and Cantonese dishes at China Garden. Most staff can speak English.

**Corner Burger**
Корнер Бургер ⓇⓇ
American
*Bolshaya Gruzinskaya ulitsa 76*
**Tel** *(499) 250 83 98*
Dig in to burgers made from beef, turkey, chicken or pork, or try the vegetarian soups and salads.

**Delicatessen**
Деликатессен ⓇⓇ
International **Map** 1 C3
*Sadovaya-Karetnaya ulitsa 20, Bldg 2*
**Tel** *(495) 699 39 52* **Closed** *Sun, Mon*
This family-run restaurant offers delicious home cooking and a good selection of wines and cocktails.

**Domozhilov in ARTPLAY**
Доможилов ⓇⓇ
Russian/International
*Nizhnyaya Syromyatnicheskaya 5/7, Bldg 10*
**Tel** *(499) 678 02 25*
The traditional *ponchiki* (doughnuts), served with a range of sweet sauces, are delicious at this café in the art and design complex.

**Italianets** Итальянец ⓇⓇ
Italian **Map** 2 D2
*Samotechnaya ulitsa 13*
**Tel** *(495) 688 56 51*
Try a range of macrobiotic Italian dishes, prepared using fresh produce flown in from Italy.

**Kavkazskaya Plenitsa**
Кавказская пленница ⓇⓇ
Georgian **Map** 2 E2
*Prospekt Mira 36*
**Tel** *(495) 680 51 11*
This restaurant offers Georgian favourites and a summer terrace facing a lovely garden.

**Ragout** Рагу ⓇⓇ
European
*Bolshaya Gruzinskaya ulitsa 69*
**Tel** *(495) 728 64 58*
Ragout has spacious interiors and a menu that leans towards British and French dishes, including shepherd's pie and Sunday roast.

Elegant interiors and bar at Delicatessen, Moscow

**For key to prices** *see p280*

### Red Pepper Красный перец ⓇⓇ
Italian                  **Map** 2 D4
*Tsvetnoy bulvar 2*
**Tel** *(495) 507 73 74*
Reminiscent of a seaside eatery, the interiors of this place have hues of red inspired by the name. Seasonal menu and a varied wine list.

### Rulet Рулет ⓇⓇ
Italian/International    **Map** 2 D3
*Trubnaya ulitsa 28C/1*
**Tel** *(495) 215 14 96*
Savour flavourful dishes, from pumpkin soup, risotto and filet mignon to strawberry gazpacho, at this multi-cuisine restaurant.

### Skazka Vostoka Сказка
Востока                  ⓇⓇ
Middle Eastern           **Map** 3 A5
*Krasnopresnenskaya naberezhnaya 16/1*
**Tel** *(499) 242 85 10*
Excellent Georgian, Azeri and Uzbek cuisine is served at this eatery in Bagration trade centre.

### U Pirosmani У пиросмани ⓇⓇ
Georgian
*Novodevichiy proezd 4*
**Tel** *(499) 255 79 26*
Delicious vegetable starters and meat dishes such as lamb shish kebab in wine and cognac.

### Volkonsky Волконский ⓇⓇ
International            **Map** 1 C2
*Seleznevskaya ulitsa 4*
**Tel** *(495) 258 54 40*
The best of Russian, Ukrainian and European cuisines are combined at this popular bakery serving freshly baked breads, decadent cakes and handmade chocolates.

### DK Choice

#### Chestnaya Kuhnya
Честная Кухня           ⓇⓇⓇ
European/Russian
*Ulitsa Sadovaya-Chernogryazskaya 10*
**Tel** *(495) 607 50 90*
A cosy restaurant in the heart of the city, Chestnaya Kuhnya offers superb home cooking. The wide-ranging menu includes meats cooked on an open fire, fresh salads, home-made pasta and delicious desserts. Extensive wine list. Good service.

### Ermak Ермак ⓇⓇⓇ
Russian
*Ulitsa Nizhniye Mnevniki 41*
**Tel** *(499) 191 25 23*
Built in the style of a Cossack log cabin, Ermak offers delicacies such as Siberian river fish and a range of traditional Russian and European recipes.

Well-stocked bar at Chestnaya Kuhnya, Moscow

### Genatsvale VIP
Генацвале VIP           ⓇⓇⓇ
Georgian                **Map** 3 B2
*Ulitsa Ostozhenka 14/2*
**Tel** *(495) 695 03 93*
The *khachapuri* (cheese-filled bread), *lobio* (beans with walnuts and spices), and vintage Georgian wines are delicious.

### Isola Pinocchio
Изола Пиноккио          ⓇⓇⓇ
Mediterranean
*Naberezhnaya Tarasa Schevchenko 23a*
**Tel** *(495) 730 44 00*
Enjoy river views through stained-glass windows while savouring Mediterranean cuisine and Spanish wines at Isola Pinocchio.

### Market Маркет ⓇⓇⓇ
Asian/seafood           **Map** 2 D3
*Ulitsa Sadovaya-Samotechnaya 18*
**Tel** *(495) 650 37 70*
Diners are served customized dishes with their choice of fish and vegetables. Special oyster dishes are served on holidays.

### Shinok Шинок ⓇⓇⓇ
Ukrainian
*Ulitsa 1905 Goda 2a*
**Tel** *(495) 651 81 01*
A rustically themed restaurant, Shinok serves the best Ukrainian food in Moscow. Efficient service.

Traditional Chinese lion statue at the entrance to China Garden, Moscow

### Simple Pleasures
Симпл Плэжерс           ⓇⓇⓇ
International            **Map** 2 E3
*Ulitsa Sretenka 22/1*
**Tel** *(495) 607 15 21*
The eclectic menu ranges from Mediterranean to South American at this chic, minimalist eatery with a long wine list and live music.

### Sky Lounge Скай Лаунж ⓇⓇⓇ
Asian/European
*Leninskiy prospekt 32a*
**Tel** *(495) 781 57 75*
Situated on the top floor of a 22-storey building, Sky Lounge offers great views and a wide range of Asian and European cooking. Lounge music by DJs at weekends.

### Tinatin Тинатин ⓇⓇⓇ
Georgian
*Ulitsa Plyushchikha 58, Bldg 1A*
**Tel** *(985) 761 66 36*
This elegant restaurant offers fine Georgian cuisine and an extensive selection of Russian and European wines. There are secluded balconies for private dining.

### Vanil Ваниль ⓇⓇⓇ
Fusion                  **Map** 3 B2
*Ulitsa Ostozhenka 1*
**Tel** *(495) 637 10 82*
Inventive blending of French, Asian and Russian cuisine, fine wines and elegant interiors. The summer veranda has fine views.

## St Petersburg

### The Islands

### Demyanova Ukha
Демьянова Уха           ⓇⓇ
Russian/Seafood         **Map** 1 C3
*Kronverkskiy prospekt 53*
**Tel** *(812) 232 49 14*
"Demyanova's Fish Soup", the city's oldest specialist fish restaurant, serves traditional Russian dishes. Enjoy live music in the evenings.

**DoZari Bar** ®®
European/Russian **Map** 1 B4
*Prospekt Dobrolyubova 14a*
**Tel** *(812) 928 60 70*
Traditional European and Russian fare is complemented by views of the Neva river. Karaoke and live stage shows take place after 10pm.

**Grand Café Neva** Гранд-кафе Нева
Russian/Italian **Map** 1 B5
*Tamozhennyy pereulok 2*
**Tel** *(812) 323 30 31*
This riverside restaurant specializes in European (notably, Italian cuisine) and offers spectacular views of Palace Bridge.

**Koryushka** Корюшка ®®
Russian **Map** 2 E3
*Peter and Paul Fortress 3*
**Tel** *(812) 640 16 16*
Enjoy impressive views of Neva river along with a menu featuring favourites including *koryushka* (lightly battered and fried smelt).

**Maria Karlotta** Мария Karlotta
European/Russian **Map** 3 B1
*Universitetskaya naberezhnaya 21*
**Tel** *(812) 313 66 22*
With its refined and traditional cuisine, excellent wine list and attentive service, this restaurant set in a restored palace is reminiscent of the Tsarist Russian era.

## DK Choice

**Salkhino** Салхино ®®
Georgian **Map** 1 D2
*Kronverkskiy prospekt 25*
**Tel** *(812) 232 78 91*
Generous home cooking is offered at this eatery run by two Georgian women. The *khachapuri* is the best in town. Gorge on aubergines stuffed with walnuts, savour roast beef or try the delicious fish in white sauce. The restaurant features paintings by Georgian artists.

**Tbiliso** Тбилисо ®®
Georgian **Map** 1 C2
*Sytninskaya ulitsa 10*
**Tel** *(812) 232 93 91*
The authentic menu at Tbiliso includes dishes such as *mamalyga* (ground corn with salted cheese) and *khachapuri*.

**Yakitoriya** Якитория ®®
Japanese **Map** 2 E2
*Petrovskaya naberezhnaya 4*
**Tel** *(812) 970 48 58*
One of the best sushi restaurants in St Petersburg, Yakitoriya serves high-quality sushi and sashimi.

Provincial cottage-style decor at Gosti, St Petersburg

**Casa del Myaso** Мясо ®®®
Steakhouse **Map** 1 B5
*Birzhevoy proezd 6*
**Tel** *(812) 320 97 46*
A short walk west of the Rostral Columns and the Kunstkammer, this cellar restaurant is squarely aimed at carnivores, with a wide variety of meat dishes on the menu.

**Flying Dutchman** Летучий Голландец
International **Map** 1 C4
*Mytninskaya naberezhnaya, Birzhevoy most*
**Tel** *(812) 313 88 66*
Choose from four different dining areas in this complex and savour European, Russian, Asian or Brazilian cuisine, while enjoying stunning views of the river and the architecture lining it.

**Gornyl Oryol** Горный Орел ®®®
Caucasian **Map** 1 C3
*Aleksandrovskiy park 1a*
**Tel** *(812) 323 05 05*
This atmospheric restaurant with its soaring columns, tall windows and fountains is a popular choice for large groups, weddings and events.

**Old Customs House** Старая Таможня
International **Map** 1 B5
*Tamozhennyy pereulok 1*
**Tel** *(812) 327 89 80*
This eatery serves mainly French meat or seafood dishes, accompanied by French wines.

**Volna** Волна ®®®
Fusion **Map** 2 E3
*Petrovskaya naberezhnaya 4*
**Tel** *(812) 322 53 83*
One of the cheaper fusion restaurants in town, the Volna has Japanese minimalist interiors. Try the Italian lettuce with salmon tempura, or grilled white salmon with mint and prawn sauce.

# Palace Embankment

## DK Choice

**1913** ®®
Russian **Map** 3 C3
*Voznesenskiy prospekt 13*
**Tel** *(812) 315 51 48*
Named after the last year of Russian imperial greatness, 1913 serves delicious regional dishes such as *draniki* (potato pancakes) with bacon and sorrel soup. Artists perform Russian songs in the evenings. Warm atmosphere and excellent service.

**Da Albertone** ®®
Italian **Map** 2 D5
*Millionnaya ulitsa 23*
**Tel** *(812) 315 86 73*
Ideal for those with children, Da Albertone offers a kids' menu, a playroom and 40 types of pizza and various pasta dishes.

**Gastronom** Гастроном ®®
Italian/Japanese **Map** 2 E5
*Naberezhnaya Reki Moyki 1/7*
**Tel** *(812) 314 38 49*
Try the horseradish and mustard at Gastronom, which is equally popular with locals and tourists.

**Gosti** Гости ®®
Italian/Russian **Map** 3 C1
*Malaya Morskaya ulitsa 13*
**Tel** *(812) 312 58 20*
Casual and cosy, Gosti serves Italian classics alongside Russian specialities, including pies with sweet and savoury fillings.

**Holst Maslo** Холст Масло ®®
Russian/French **Map** 4 D1
*Bolshaya Morskaya ulitsa 4*
**Tel** *(812) 570 40 69*
Located under an archway opposite the Hermitage Museum, this restaurant serves traditional Russian and French cuisine. It hosts art shows by local creatives.

**For key to prices** *see p280*

### Krokodil Крокодил
**International** ®® **Map** 3 B1
*Galernaya ulitsa 18*
**Tel** *(812) 314 94 37*
A small and intimate restaurant featuring fresh salads, great vegetarian dishes, a non-smoking room and board games for diners.

### Park Giuseppe Парк Джузеппе
**Italian** ®® **Map** 4 E1
*Naberezhnaya kanala Griboedova 2b*
**Tel** *(812) 571 73 09*
Park Giuseppe is the place for eating Neapolitan pizzas baked in a wood-burning stove and sipping Italian wine as the sun sets.

### T-Lounge
**International** ®® **Map** 3 B2
*Pochtamtskaya ulitsa 4*
**Tel** *(812) 380 40 00*
The T-Lounge within Renaissance Hotel offers delicious sandwiches, salads and pastries. Live music in the evenings.

### Borsalino Борсалино
**Italian** ®®® **Map** 3 C2
*Malaya Morskaya ulitsa 24*
**Tel** *(812) 494 51 15*
Inside the Angleterre Hotel, Borsalino has fabulous decor and excellent Italian food that attracts locals as well as tourists. Live jazz in the bar on most evenings.

### Canvas Канвас
**European** ®®® **Map** 3 B2
*Pochtamtskaya ulitsa 4*
**Tel** *(812) 380 40 00*
This elaborate breakfast room in the Renaissance Hotel turns into a restaurant serving fine European cuisine later in the day.

## Gostinyy Dvor

### Aragvi Арагви
**Georgian** ®® **Map** 2 F5
*Naberezhnaya Reki Fontanki 9*
**Tel** *(812) 570 56 43*
Take in enchanting views of the Fontanka river while savouring yummy *satsivi* (walnut sauce), *khachapuri* and pork *shashlik*.

### Baku Баку
**Caucasian/European** ®® **Map** 4 F1
*Sadovaya ulitsa 12/23*
**Tel** *(812) 941 37 56*
A Central Asian delight, Baku features a menu that is a mix of Continental and Caucasian cuisine.

### Clean Plates Society Общество Чистых Тарелок
**Fusion** ®® **Map** 4 D2
*Gorokhovaya ulitsa 13*
**Tel** *(812) 934 97 64*
Popular for its burgers, freshly made juices and inventive cocktails, this stylish restaurant is a favourite with the locals.

### Erivan Эривань
**Armenian** ®® **Map** 4 F2
*Naberezhnaya Reki Fontanki 51*
**Tel** *(812) 703 38 20*
Furnished in Armenian style, with rugs and brightly coloured tablecloths. Traditional dishes with lots of mutton and veal.

### Kavkaz-Bar Кавказ-бар
**Caucasian** ®® **Map** 4 F1
*Karavannaya ulitsa 18*
**Tel** *(812) 312 16 65*
Sink your teeth into the best vegetarian kebabs in town. Excellent wines and brandies on offer.

### Ket Кэт
**Georgian** ®® **Map** 4 F1
*Karavannaya ulitsa 24*
**Tel** *(812) 315 38 00*
A comfortable no-frills basement restaurant serving authentic Georgian food. A great place to mingle with the locals.

### Mama Roma Мама Рома
**Italian** ®® **Map** 4 F1
*Karavannaya ulitsa 3/35*
**Tel** *(812) 314 03 47*
One of the city's first authentic Italian restaurants, Mama Roma has light, airy interiors. There is a children's menu and toys.

### Metropole Метрополис
**Russian/European** ®® **Map** 4 F1
*Sadovaya ulitsa 22*
**Tel** *(812) 571 88 88*
Opened in 1847 and known for its luxurious interiors, this restaurant serves Russian and European classics and Belgian beer.

### Suliko Сулико
**Georgian** ®® **Map** 4 D2
*Kazanskaya ulitsa 6*
**Tel** *(812) 314 73 73*
Tucked away behind the Kazan Cathedral, Suliko is popular with Georgians. Plenty of options for meat lovers.

### Bellevue Brasserie Бельвью Брассери
**European** ®® **Map** 2 D5
*Naberezhnaya Reki Moyki 22*
**Tel** *(812) 335 91 11*
The Bellevue in the Kempinski Hotel offers superlative city views and great salads. Do not miss the Kamchatka crab salad.

### Caviar Bar and Restaurant Икорный Бар
**Russian** ®®® **Map** 4 E1
*Mikhaylovskaya ulitsa 1/7*
**Tel** *(812) 329 60 00*
Dine on elegantly served caviar and fish at this bar-restaurant in Grand Hotel Europe. The interior is tiny, but has a fountain, like a grotto in an 18th-century park.

### L'Europe Европа
**European/Russian** ®®® **Map** 4 E1
*Mikhaylovskaya ulitsa 1/7*
**Tel** *(812) 329 60 00*
Classic dishes are served in an Art Nouveau restaurant with a stained-glass ceiling at the Grand Hotel Europe.

### Jamie's Italian Джеймис Италиан
**Italian** ®®® **Map** 2 E5
*Konyushennaya ploshchad 2*
**Tel** *(812) 600 25 70*
Savour classic Italian dishes crafted by celebrity chef Jamie Oliver at this fine-dining restaurant. Relaxed ambience and excellent service.

### Literary Café Литературное кафе
**Russian** ®®® **Map** 4 D1
*Nevskiy prospekt 18*
**Tel** *(812) 312 60 57*
The former Wolff and Beranger Café serves rather delicious meat dishes in rich sauces.

Fine views and rooftop seating at the Bellevue Brasserie, St Petersburg

**For more information on types of restaurants** *see pp274–5*

**St Petersburg** Санкт-
Петербург ⓡⓡⓡ
Russian **Map** 4 E1
*Naberezhnaya kanala Griboedova 5*
**Tel** *(812) 314 49 47*
Generous portions of standard
Russian fare are served at this
eatery. Live music begins at 8pm.

### DK Choice

**Tsar** Царь ⓡⓡⓡ
Russian **Map** 4 F1
*Sadovaya ulitsa 12*
**Tel** *(812) 640 16 16*
Housed within a former noble's
palace, Tsar offers diners a
sumptuous setting in which to
enjoy first-rate Russian classics.
Be it the stylish decor or cut-
crystal glassware, everything
exudes opulence. The menu is
elaborate and features excellent
meat and fish dishes.

## Sennaya Ploshchad

**Brooklyn Local** Бруклин
Местное ⓡ
International **Map** 4 D2
*Naberezhnaya kanala
Griboedova 27a*
**Tel** *(812) 571 89 55*
This is the only place to offer
New York style-bagels in the city.
It is popular with students.

**Tokyo City** Токио-City ⓡ
Japanese **Map** 4 D3
*Sennaya ploshchad 7*
**Tel** *(812) 677 41 44*
A wide selection of freshly
prepared sushi and hot meals are
served at this chain restaurant.

**Denisov and Nikolayev**
Денисов и Николаев ⓡⓡ
European/Russian **Map** 3 C3
*Naberezhnaya kanala Griboedova 77*
**Tel** *(812) 571 01 26*
Relish extravagant pastries and
desserts along with the other

Model market stall selling fresh fruits and
nuts at Baklazhan, St Petersburg

Elegantly laid out tables at Tsar, an upmarket restaurant in St Petersburg

classics on the menu at this
modern, chic restaurant. The
cheesecakes are a highlight.

**Entrée** Антрэ ⓡⓡ
French **Map** 3 B4
*Nikolskaya ploshchad 6*
**Tel** *(812) 572 52 01*
This French bistro serves well-
prepared food such as beef, duck
and salmon carpaccio. The pastries
here are noted as the best in town.

**Russkaya Ryumochnaya No.1**
Русскя Рюмочная No. 1 ⓡⓡ
Russian **Map** 3 B2
*Konnogvardeiskiy bulvar 4*
**Tel** *(812) 570 64 20*
An old world-style dining room
serving modern interpretations
of classic Russian dishes.
Offers over 100 vodkas, of which
many are flavoured.

### DK Choice

**Percorso** Закорсо ⓡⓡⓡ
Italian **Map** 3 C1
*Voznesenskiy prospekt 1*
**Tel** *(812) 339 80 00*
Housed in a former palace
converted into the famous
Four Seasons hotel, this deluxe
restaurant serves sumptuous
Italian cuisine complemented
by an exclusive wine list. The
fine decor includes a massive
fireplace. All this, together
with the excellent service,
makes it a perfect venue for all
occasions and celebrations.

## Further Afield

**Bufet** Буфет ⓡ
Russian
*Pushkinskaya ulitsa 7*
**Tel** *(812) 764 78 88*
A cosy eatery near Nevskiy
prospekt with framed photo-
graphs and mementos on the
walls. Serves simple Russian fare.

**Kvartirka** Квартирка ⓡ
Russian **Map** 4 F2
*Nevskiy prospekt 51*
**Tel** *(812) 315 55 61*
A Soviet-era themed café that
packs in locals hungry for rustic
cooking as well as tourists in the
know. Quick service.

**Obedbufet** Обедбуфет ⓡ
International **Map** 4 D1
*Nevskiy prospekt 114*
**Tel** *(812) 640 16 16*
An inviting and upscale cafeteria
set in the Nevsky Centre shopping
mall, Obedbufet offers a range of
European, Asian and Russian food.

**Troitskiy Most**
Троицкий мост ⓡ
Vegetarian
*Kamennoostrovskiy prospekt 9/2*
**Tel** *(812) 942 23 97*
The emphasis is on vegetables at
this no-smoking café-restaurant.
Try the cheese and spinach salad
or tagliatelle with mushroom sauce.

**Alt Sherbet** Alt Шербет ⓡⓡ
Caucasian
*Ulitsa Vosstaniya 26*
**Tel** *(812) 272 76 13*
The menu combines European
cooking with some Caucasian
dishes at this charming, laid-back
restaurant with candlelit tables.

**Baklazhan** Баклажан ⓡⓡ
Oriental
*Ligovskiy prospekt 30*
**Tel** *(812) 640 16 16*
The menu at Baklazhan offers tasty
renditions of Georgian and Asian
classics. The home-made noodles
and baked goods are glorious.

**Beer House** Бир Хаус ⓡⓡ
International
*Ulitsa Nekrasova 25*
**Tel** *(812) 273 71 01*
Beer lovers can revel at the
extensive selection here. The
meat dishes are great too.

**Demidov** Демидов    ®®
Russian      **Map** 2 F5
*Naberezhnyaya Reki Fontanki 14*
**Tel** *(812) 2/2 91 81*
This touristy restaurant has an interesting menu that features quail's eggs, delectable pancakes and caviar. Enjoy gypsy music from 8pm onwards.

**Dom Byta**
Дом быта    ®®
Asian/European
*Razezzhaya ulitsa 12*
**Tel** *(812) 975 55 99*
Located on the ground floor of a Soviet era building, the menu includes pan-Asian and European classics. Music by a resident DJ.

**Fartuk** Фартук    ®®
Mediterranean    **Map** 4 F2
*Ulitsa Rubinshteyna 15–17*
**Tel** *(812) 764 52 56*
Relaxed outdoor dining at a communal country kitchen-style table. Delicious home-made lemonades. Reserve in advance.

**Geografia** Геoграфия    ®®
International    **Map** 4 F2
*Ulitsa Rubinshteyna 5*
**Tel** *(812) 340 00 74*
Feast on cuisine from around the world at this sophisticated restaurant with dining rooms decorated in different styles.

**Gulchatay**
Гульчатай    ®®
Oriental    **Map** 4 D5
*Zagorosnyy prospekt 70*
**Tel** *(812) 575 07 90*
Enjoy fantastic belly dances, live music and a game of backgammon. Excellent food and service.

**Jean-Jacques Rousseau**
Жан-Жак Руссо    ®®
French
*Ulitsa Marata 10*
**Tel** *(812) 315 49 03*
A stylish bistro, Jean-Jacques serves breakfast, lunch and dinner. Extensive wine list. Friendly staff.

**Khochu Kharcho** Хочу Харчо ®®
Georgian    **Map** 3 C3
*Sadovaya ulitsa 39/41*
**Tel** *(812) 640 16 16*
Enjoy authentic *kharcho* (beef-walnut soup) and *khachapuri* at this homely eatery. One of the best places in town to meet up with friends.

**Lagidze** Лагидзе    ®®
Georgian
*Ulitsa Belinskovo 3*
**Tel** *(812) 579 11 04*
Lagidze serves Georgian food in a modest but modern setting. Try the *lodka* (hot cheese-filled bread with egg) and *satsivi*, and finish the meal with Georgian brandy.

**Marcelli's** Марчелли's    ®®
Italian
*Ulitsa Vosstaniya 15*
**Tel** *(812) 986 91 11*
Casual and spacious, Marcelli's is the place for Italian food lovers. Affordable lunch specials.

**Na Zdorovye!**
На здоровье!    ®®
Russian    **Map** 1 B3
*Bolshoi prospekt 13, Petrograd Side*
**Tel** *(812) 232 40 39*
With garish 19th-century decor, gypsy cabaret and boisterous clientele, this is the place to revel in Russian kitsch and drink vodka.

**Palermo** Палермо    ®®
Italian    **Map** 4 F2
*Naberezhnaya Reki Fontanki 50*
**Tel** *(812) 764 37 64*
This friendly restaurant offers a classic Sicilian menu, plus a few Russian favourites – mainly hearty meat dishes.

**Pirosmani** Пиросмани    ®®
Georgian    **Map** 1 A3
*Bolshoi prospekt 14, Petrograd Side*
**Tel** *(812) 389 37 82*
Set out like a Georgian hill village, Pirosmani serves Georgian classics such as *lobio* (beans in spicy sauce).

**Povari** Повари    ®®
Italian    **Map** 1 B2
*Bolshoi prospekt 38/40, Petrograd Side*
**Tel** *(812) 233 70 42*
Specializes in all kinds of freshly made pasta such as fettuccini with mushrooms and truffle sauce.

**Russian Fishing**
Русская рыбалка    ®®
Fish
*Yuzhnaya doroga 11, Krestovskiy Island*
**Tel** *(812) 323 98 13*
A stylized fisherman's hut with a pond where guests can catch their own fish and then watch it being cooked. Great for families.

**Russian Kitsch** Русский китч ®®
Russian    **Map** 3 A1
*Universitetskaya naberezhnaya 25*
**Tel** *(812) 325 11 22*
The menu here is a mix of fusion cuisine and sushi rather than *pelmeni* and cabbage. Enjoy the very Russian dance floor.

**Schengen** Шенгенская    ®®
European    **Map** 3 B5
*Kirochnaya ulitsa 5*
**Tel** *(812) 922 11 97*
There is something for everyone at this friendly bistro serving hearty north European fare.

**Shinok** Шинок    ®®
Ukrainian    **Map** 4 F3
*Zagorodnyy prospekt 13*
**Tel** *(812) 571 82 62*
Elegant minimalism has no place at Shinok, which offers hearty food with three kinds of *salo* (salted pork belly), and Ukrainian vodka that hits the spot.

**Shurpa** Шурпа    ®®
Oriental
*Engelsa prospekt 27, 2nd floor*
**Tel** *(812) 640 16 16*
Shurpa offers an elaborate range of Oriental dishes such as *plov*, flat cakes and aromatic soups. Superb wine list to accompany the food.

**Staraya Derevnya**
Старая Деревня    ®®
Russian
*Ulitsa Savushkina 72*
**Tel** *(812) 431 00 00*
The decor at Staraya Derevnya resembles an old-fashioned apartment. Do not miss the cabbage pie and aubergine rolls.

**Sunduk** Сундук    ®®
European/Russian
*Furshtatskaya ulitsa 42*
**Tel** *(812) 272 31 00*
A trendy art café with Russian and European dishes and an extensive wine list. Live jazz in the evenings.

Brightly painted wall panels at Na Zdorovye! in St Petersburg

For more information on types of restaurants *see pp274–5*

**Tres Amigos** ®®
Latin American   **Map** 4 F3
*Ulitsa Rubinshteyna 25*
**Tel** *(812) 572 26 85*
Tres Amigos is notable for its
bizarre decor inspired by Aztecs
and beer halls. It has a children's
room with slides and swings.

## DK Choice

**Ukrop** Укроп ®®
**Russian**
*Ulitsa Marata 23*
**Tel** *(812) 946 30 36*
This centrally located
attractive café offers a healthy
menu with a fine selection of
creatively prepared vegetarian,
vegan and raw-food options.
Friendly service and welcoming
interiors make it an ideal spot
for a refreshing break.

**Xren** Хрен ®®
European   **Map** 4 F3
*Zagorodnyy prospekt 13*
**Tel** *(812) 347 88 50*
Xren comprises three dining
rooms, each with a different style
of decor. Try leek and potato soup
with prawns, duck and couscous.
DJs perform at weekends.

**Dickens Restaurant**
Диккенс ®®®
British   **Map** 4 D4
*Naberezhnaya Reki Fontanki 108,
2nd floor*
**Tel** *(812) 702 62 63*   **Closed** Sun
This cosy restaurant specializes
in steaks and game dishes. A
selection of fine cigars are offered
in the lounge. Fabulous views
of the Fontanka river.

**Karl & Friedrich**
Карл и Фридрих ®®®
International
*Yuzhnaya doroga 15,
Krestovskiy Island*
**Tel** *(812) 320 79 78*
Aimed at families, this place has a
nanny on weekdays and children's

Well-manicured gardens fronting the landmark windmill at Karl & Friedrich, St Petersburg

Façade of La Parisienne, a modern café-restaurant in Petrozavodsk

entertainment at weekends. There
is a strong meat orientation to the
menu. Great selection of beer.

**Ryba** Рыба ®®®
Italian/Asian
*Ulitsa Akademika Pavlova 5*
**Tel** *(812) 918 69 69*
Diners can choose from a wide
selection of pizzas, or try the delec-
table Asian wok-based dishes.

**SunDay Ginza**
Сандей Гинза ®®®
European/Japanese
*Yuzhnaya doroga 4/2*
**Tel** *(812) 640 16 16*
One of the best restaurants in the
area, SunDay Ginza is the ideal
place to try sushi or grilled dishes.

**Troika** Тройка ®®®
Russian   **Map** 4 F3
*Zagorodnyy prospekt 27*
**Tel** *(812) 407 53 43*
Enjoy circus acrobatics, folk
songs, Russian dancing, glitz
and glamour. The menu may not
offer much variety, but the food
is good.

## Beyond St Petersburg

**Krapiva** Крапива ®®
Russian
*Sankt-Peterburgskoe shosse 111,
Shuvalovka*
**Tel** *(812) 450 53 93*
Set in a stylized Russian tower,
Krapiva is a good place to try
traditional rural dishes.

**Podvorie** Подворье ®®
Russian
*Filtrovskoe shosse 16, Pavlovsk*
**Tel** *(812) 466 85 44*
Situated within a re-creation
of a 17th-century wooden house,
Podvorie offers plenty of meaty
soups and vodkas. Sample tradi-
tional fare such as *pelmeni* and
pancakes with caviar or sink your
teeth into a juicy beef stroganoff.
Great desserts.

## DK Choice

**Sofia** София ®®
European
*Pavlovskoye shosse 7*
**Tel** *(812) 451 98 02*
Not far from the main attractions of Pushkin and Pavlovsk,
Sofia offers a charming
ambience and excellent
service. It has two exquisitely
decorated dining rooms
for large groups. Savour the
delicious cream of cauliflower
soup or try the scrumptious
salmon on the grill. There are
plenty of meat dishes as well.

**Vena** Вена ®®
European/Russian
*Sankt-Peterburgskiy prospekt 30,
Petrodvorets*
**Tel** *(812) 450 64 47*
A Viennese-themed restaurant
near the upper garden of Peterhof
Palace, Vena serves beef
stroganoff, filled dumplings,
strudel, pancakes and other
central European favourites.

## Northern Russia

**PETROZAVODSK: La Parisienne**
Парижанка ®
European/Russian
*Prospekt Lenina 2*
**Tel** *(8142) 79 56 71*
This chain has 12 branches
scattered throughout the centre.
All are smart French-style café-
restaurants offering reliable pizza,
sandwiches, soups and pancakes.
Try the banana tempura.

**PSKOV: Dvor Podznoyeva**
Двор Подзноева
Russian ⓇⓇ
*Ulitsa Nekrasova 1B*
**Tel** *(8112) 79 70 00*
Come for authentic Russian
cuisine at this restaurant, set in
two restored buildings of 17th-
century merchant chambers.

**VELIKY NOVGOROD: Horoshie
Ludi** Хорошие Люди Ⓡ
International
*Ulitsa Meretskova-Volosova 1/1*
**Tel** *(8162) 73 08 79*
Diners can make their own salads
and slice their own freshly baked
bread here. Go for the home-
made sausages in cowberry sauce.

**VELIKY NOVGOROD: Teplo**
Тепло Ⓡ
Italian/Japanese
*Ulitsa Meretskova-Volosova 7/1*
**Tel** *(8162) 90 98 62*
A smart yet casual place with
rustic styling and excellent service.
Delectable desserts.

---

### DK Choice

**VELIKY NOVGOROD:
Dom Berga** Дом Берга ⓇⓇ
Russian
*Ulitsa Bolshaya Moskovskaya 24*
**Tel** *(8162) 94 88 38*
Housed in a historic 19th-century
mansion, this restaurant serves
traditional Russian dishes such
as Boyarsky *borsch*, stewed
rabbit and home-made
gingerbread. Wash it all down
with locally produced mead.

---

# Kaliningrad

**Solnechni Kamen**
Солнечный Камень Ⓡ
Russian
*Ploshchad Vasilevskogo 3*
**Tel** *(4012) 53 91 06*
This atmospheric restaurant near
the Amber Museum offers dishes
such as Siberian fried pork.

**Fish Club**
Рыбный Клуб ⓇⓇ
Seafood
*Oktyabrskaya ulitsa 4a*
**Tel** *(4012) 30 71 50*
Popular restaurant serving a range
of tasty fish dishes. The summer
terrace has fine river views.

---

### DK Choice

**Khmel**
Хмель ⓇⓇ
Russian
*Ploshchad Pobedy 10a*
**Tel** *(4012) 59 33 77*
Bare brick walls and industrial
piping provide a stylish backdrop for this popular eatery. The
menu covers most Russian
specialties, from Kaliningrad
quail to Kamchatka crab. There
is even smoked Omul from
Lake Baikal. Excellent service.

---

# Central and
Southern Russia

**ASTRAKHAN: Shollie** Шоли Ⓡ
Uzbek
*Ulitsa Uritskogo 3*
**Tel** *(8512) 51 28 88*
Lovely Oriental-style restaurant
specializing in delicious Uzbek
cuisine and other appetizing
dishes. Splendid river views.

**KAZAN: Dom Tatarskoy Kulinarii**
Дом Татарской Кулинарии ⓇⓇ
Tatar/Russian
*Ulitsa Baumana 31*
**Tel** *(843) 292 70 70*
One of Kazan's best restaurants,
this is a great place for traditional
Tatar dishes. Don't be surprised if
horsemeat is on the menu.

**NIZHNY NOVGOROD:
Pyatkin** Пяткинь ⓇⓇ
Russian
*Ulitsa Rozhdestvenskaya 25*
**Tel** *(831) 430 91 83*
The grand furnishings in Pyatkin
re-create the setting of a 19th-

Elegant dining area at Horoshie Ludi in
Veliky Novgorod

century mansion. Great spot
to try Russian staples such as
beef stroganoff.

**PERM: Nairi** Наири ⓇⓇ
Armenian/Russian
*Ulitsa Sovetskaya 67*
**Tel** *(342) 257 05 51*
A charming Armenian restaurant
offering excellent food and a
superb wine list. Live music and
traditional Armenian dancing on
most evenings.

---

### DK Choice

**SAMARA: Staraya Kvartira**
Старая Квартира Ⓡ
Russian
*Ulitsa Samarskaya 51/53*
**Tel** *(846) 332 22 60*
Dine at this fabulous retro
restaurant that rustles up
period dishes from all over the
ex-Soviet Union. Ensconced in
a warren-like cellar, it features
dining tables in the re-created
rooms of a Soviet-era apartment replete with elegant
decor that adds to the charm.

---

**SAMARA: U Vakano** У Вакано Ⓡ
Russian
*Volzhskiy prospekt 4*
**Tel** *(846) 332 60 73*
A menu featuring lots of meat
options and plenty of local fish is
offered at this delightful Soviet-
era restaurant with dining booths.

**SVIYAZHSK: Traktir**
Трактиръ Ⓡ
Russian
*Konnyi Dvor Ulitsa Uspenskaya 1a*
**Tel** *(8422) 44 18 80*
A medieval-themed eatery with
vaulted ceilings. The first-rate
three-course menu changes daily.

The elegantly furnished Dom Berga, Veliky Novgorod

**For more information on types of restaurants** *see pp274–5*

Bier Haus, a classy Bavarian-style beer hall in Irkutsk

### ULYANOVSK: Korchma Gopak
Корчма Гопак ®
Ukrainian
*Ulitsa Federatsii 9*
**Tel** *(8422) 94 95 96*
This atmospheric restaurant serves home-style cuisine such as sausages, *borsch* (beetroot soup) with *pampushki* (garlic doughnuts) and *medovukha* (mead).

### ULYANOVSK: Veprevo Koleno
Вепрево Колено ®
European
*Ulitsa Federatsii 11*
**Tel** *(9510) 94 51 15*
Classic Czech beer and generous portions of food are complemented by attentive service at this pub-restaurant.

### VOLGOGRAD: Shafran
Шафран ®
Uzbek
*Ulitsa Gvardeyskaya*
**Tel** *(8442) 23 57 52*
Plush Oriental-themed restaurant serving plenty of grilled meat options. Excellent *baklava* (sweet pastry filled with chopped nuts) and Armenian wine.

### VOLGOGRAD: Moliere
Мольер ®®
Traditional Russian
*Hotel Volgograd, Ulitsa Mira 12*
**Tel** *(8442) 55 12 55*
A classy restaurant dishing out exquisite fare with a pianist playing in the background.

### YEKATERINBURG: Troyekurov
Троекуровъ ®
Russian
*Ulitsa Malysheva 137*
**Tel** *(343) 378 81 18*
Sample traditional Russian cuisine at this restaurant housed in an historic two-storey 19th-century mansion.

## The Caucasus

### ADLER: Café Mayak
Кафе Маяк ®
Russian
*Ulitsa Prosvyasheniya 35A*
**Tel** *(8622) 44 41 86*
Fresh fish and dishes such as pancakes with red caviar feature on Mayak's menu. Pleasant open seafront terrace with comfortable furniture shaded by palms and umbrellas.

### ANAPA: Evrasia
Евразия ®
Asian/Russian
*200 m (656 ft) east of the sea port of Anapa*
Located right on the beach, Evrasia serves a reasonable range of sushi and Russian cuisine. Friendly staff.

### GELENDZHIK: Sea House
Си Хаус ®
International
*Ulitsa Mira 21*
**Tel** *(909) 450 60 20*
Sample sushi, pizza, panini and other Russian dishes. Wonderful sea views from the shaded terrace.

### KRASNODAR: Ekaterinodar
Екатеринодар ®
Russian/European
*Ulitsa Starokubanskaya 114*
**Tel** *(861) 231 44 20*
The ambience, along with the local and classic European fare, recreate old times at this charming restaurant.

### ROSTOV-NA-DONU: Drago Steakhouse
Драго Стейкхаус ®®
European
*Ulitsa Suvorova 75*
**Tel** *(8632) 00 08 52*
Savour excellent steaks paired with an extensive wine list at this family-friendly restaurant.

### SOCHI: Promenad
Променад ®
Russian/French
*Ulitsa Vorovskogo 3*
**Tel** *(862) 264 38 67*
Located in the centre of the city, this restaurant with fine interiors offers Russian and French cuisine made with local produce and organic ingredients.

### SOCHI: Ris Рис
International ®
*Kurortny prospekt 16*
**Tel** *(8622) 64 38 73*
This restaurant serves a good range of international cuisine with an emphasis on rice-based dishes and sushi.

### DK Choice

### SOCHI: Vostochny Kvartal Восточный
квартал ®®
Uzbek/Russian
*Ulitsa Primorskaya 7*
**Tel** *(8622) 66 10 99*
At this wonderfully atmospheric restaurant with glorious sea views, diners relax on cushions beneath the wood-panelled canopy and enjoy delicious Uzbek food served in traditional ceramic dishes. Lamb is roasted on the spit at weekends. There is live music in the evenings.

### SOCHI: Chayka
Чайка ®®®
International
*Voykova ulitsa 1*
**Tel** *(8622) 41 81 64*
A swanky restaurant within the Maritime Terminal building. Diners can sample delicious home-made pasta and locally caught fish.

## Siberia and the Far East

### IRKUTSK: Bier Haus
European ®
*Ulitsa Karla Marksa*
**Tel** *(3952) 55 05 55*
A German tavern-style restaurant, "Beer House" offers a selection of draft Czech, German and Irish beers and delicious beer sausages and pork shank to go with it.

### IRKUTSK: Kochevnik
Кочевник ®®
Mongolian
*Ulitsa Gorkogo 19*
**Tel** *(3952) 20 04 59*
The best place to sample Mongolian cuisine in Irkutsk, Kochevnik offers *pozi* (Mongolian dumplings) and plenty of horsemeat dishes.

### KHABAROVSK: Telegraph
Телеграф ®
European/Russian
*Ulitsa Sheronova 10*
**Tel** *(4212) 31 66 83*
Smart English-style pub and restaurant with a cosy wood-panelled interior that is popular with locals and business diners. Serves a good range of Russian and Western dishes that includes steak and braised ribs.

Charming wooden building housing Ladeynyi, Tobolsk

### KOMSOMOLSK-NA-AMUR:
**Escher** Эшер ®®
International
*Prospekt Pervostroiteley 31*
**Tel** *(4217) 53 51 31*
This restaurant in Hotel Voskhod boasts modern design, excellent service and an international menu, with dishes such as duck-breast salad and Munich sausage platter.

### KRASNOYARSK: Kalinka Malinka
Калинка Малинка ®
Russian
*Propekt Mira 91a*
**Tel** *(391) 211 50 81*
Vaguely Soviet-themed establishment with Russian staples such as *blini* and *pelmeni* plus a good selection of salads.

### NOVOSIBIRSK: People's Bar and Grill
Гриль-бар Пиплс ®
International
*Krasnyy prospekt 22*
**Tel** *(383) 209 25 90*
TV screens line the walls and Thai noodles, sausages and steaks are among the international offerings at this lively basement spot in the heart of the city.

### NOVOSIBIRSK: Paris
Пэрис ®®
International/Russian
*Ulitsa Kamenskaya 7/1*
**Tel** *(383) 223 01 00*
An exclusive fine dining restaurant in Doubletree by Hilton Hotel, Paris serves exquisite international and locally inspired dishes, a wide range of innovative cocktails and a good wine list.

### OMSK: Pertsi
Перцы ®
Italian
*Ulitsa Partizanskaya 2*
**Tel** *(3812) 20 20 65*
Excellent range of pizza and pasta dishes feature on the menu of this ultra-modern restaurant. Do not miss the locally renowned lasagne. Efficient service.

## DK Choice

### OMSK: Kolchak Колчак ®®
International
*Ulitsa Broz Tito 2*
**Tel** *(3812) 45 99 99*
An extraordinary establishment within a stunning Art Deco building, Kolchak has an Irish pub on the ground floor, an Italian restaurant on the second floor and an Uzbek restaurant on the third. There is even a cosy cocktail lounge and an elaborate banquet hall. Personable and friendly staff.

### PETROPAVLOVSK-KAMCHATSKIY:
**Yamato** Ямото ®
Japanese/Russian
*Ulitsa Lukashevskogo 5*
**Tel** *(4152) 26 77 00*
A pleasant, central restaurant that serves a mixture of Japanese and Russian dishes prepared with fresh local ingredients.

### TOBOLSK: Ladeynyi
Ладейный ®®
Russian
*Ulitsa Revolutsionnaya 2*
**Tel** *(3456) 22 21 11*
Lovely eatery in a reconstructed wooden building facing the Kremlin. Dishes on offer include "Cucumbers for Vodka", several tongue options and *vareniki* (Ukrainian stuffed dumplings).

### TOMSK: Vechny Zov
Вечный зов ®®
Siberian/Russian
*Ulitsa Sovetskaya 47*
**Tel** *(3822) 52 81 67*
An award-winning restaurant where diners can choose from a broad range of enticing Siberian dishes or Russian classics.

### ULAN-UDE: Kailash
Кайлаш ®®
Buryat/International
*Ulitsa Strelets 1*
**Tel** *(3012) 20 00 28*
Frequented by well-heeled locals, this modern restaurant has a hill-top location. Offers both European and Mongolian cuisine.

### VLADIVOSTOK: Ukh Ty Blin!
Ух Ты, Блин! ®
Russian
*Ulitsa Fokina 9*
**Tel** *(4232) 51 56 71*
The perfect place to try Russia's most popular dish – *blini*. Here the pancakes are cooked to order with every conceivable filling from gooey sweet cream to seafood.

### VLADIVOSTOK: Michelle
Мишель ®®
International
*Ulitsa Uborevicha 5A, 8th floor*
**Tel** *(4232) 30 81 16*
Worth visiting just for the panoramic sea and city views. Choose from a wide selection of fresh local seafood dishes.

### YUZHNO-SAKHALINSK:
**Cippolini** Чипполини ®®
International
*Ulitsa Chekhova 78*
**Tel** *(4242) 46 84 01*
A popular expat hangout offering dishes such as Angus beef tenderloin and grilled lamb chops.

Art Deco façade of Kolchak, Omsk

**For more information on types of restaurants** *see pp274–5*

# SHOPPING IN RUSSIA

Shopping in Russia is easier and more rewarding today than it was in Soviet times, when queues and shortages were the norm. However, there is one thing reminiscent of the Communist era and that is the country's export restrictions that cover a broad range of categories. Today, department stores offer everything from souvenirs to furs and supermarkets overflow with a variety of fresh produce. Most malls and boutiques stock clothes and accessories by international brands as well as little-known Italian and Scandinavian designers. In recent years imported goods have pushed out many local products, but Russian linen, chocolates and crafts and toys are still much sought after by tourists. Shoppers can head to specialist shops and flea markets to buy these wonderful gifts.

A typical flea market selling a selection of samovars

## Opening Hours

Shops across Russia are usually open from 10am until at least 7pm, although upmarket outlets may open later. A few small stores, especially inexpensive food shops, close for lunch. Department stores and large shops remain open on Sundays. However, smaller places are generally open for shorter hours and closed on weekends during summer. Most cities and towns have 24-hour food shops.

## How to Pay

Credit cards are accepted at many big stores, but cash is the preferred mode of payment in cities and towns across the country. The only legal currency in Russia is the rouble, and paying in non-Russian currency amounts to a criminal offence. While most shops in Moscow now use the one-stop cashier system, the Soviet *kassa* system of visiting several separate cashiers' desks is still common outside Moscow.

Self-service shopping is generally confined to supermarkets and retail chains. Shop assistants are usually helpful; they will write down the prices for you to hand to the cashier. Defective goods can be returned provided they are accompanied by a receipt.

The price of all goods includes Value-Added Tax (VAT), which is mostly 18 per cent, with a reduced rate of 10 per cent on basic food items, medical products and children's clothing. Note that there is no tax-free shopping for foreign visitors.

## Export Restrictions

All outgoing luggage is X-rayed by customs officials to check for items subject to export restrictions. The **Federal Customs Service** has set limits on the amount of caviar and alcohol that can be taken out of Russia.

Under Russian law, all objects made before 1956, and all objects made from valuable materials such as gold, silver, precious stones and fur, are subject to export controls. Contemporary art and books published before 1946 also fall under this ruling. Permission to export these can be obtained from the **Ministry of Culture** in Moscow or St Petersburg. Applications take about two weeks to process and entail paying an export tax of 50 per cent of the item's value according to the ministry's assessment.

It is best to buy items less than 50 years old and be able to prove their age. Books, medals and porcelain are all inscribed with a manufacturing date. For undated objects, ask for receipts from the vendor. The gallery from which art is purchased should assist with the paperwork.

Export restrictions are not applicable to mass-produced paintings, icons, amber, porcelain, books and clothing.

## Bargaining

Avoid bargaining if a set price is displayed at markets. In all other cases, you can usually get some reduction if you haggle, especially since non-Russian visitors are likely to be quoted a higher price than locals. However, bargaining in Russia is a serious matter; do not negotiate unless you genuinely intend to buy.

A dazzling variety of merchandise on sale at the Souvenir Market, St Petersburg

## Department Stores and Shopping Malls

Known as *univermag* (universal shop), the Russian department store evolved from Tsarist "trading rows" of kiosks owned by different merchants. After GUM (*see p69*) in Moscow, the most atmospheric of these shopping emporia is Gostinyy Dvor (*see pp166–7*) in St Petersburg. Other high-end shopping arcades include **Passazh** in St Petersburg and the **Pokrovskiy Passage** in Yekaterinburg.

Modern shopping malls are present in all big cities, often in residential suburbs or on the outskirts. One of the largest shopping centres in the Ural region, **Dirzhabl** stocks a wide variety of apparel, footwear and perfumes.

## Markets and Bazaars

Large indoor food markets, or *rynoks*, selling flowers, fruit, vegetables, home-made cream cheese, sausages and other delicacies can be found in every city. Visitors can buy jars of organic honey and sticks of *sera*, a traditional Siberian "chewing gum" at markets in the Altai Region. All kinds of food shopping can be done at **Andreevskiy Market** in St Petersburg, stacked high with Russian specialities.

Crafts and souvenir markets can be found in some towns and cities. In St Petersburg, the **Souvenir Market** offers

GUM, one of the most popular shopping malls in Moscow

a wide variety of *matryoshka* dolls and Soviet memorabilia. Flea markets such as **Unona** and the Friday- and Saturday-morning market at Udelnaya metro are worth visiting in St Petersburg. Shoppers are advised to be aware of pickpockets.

## Museum Shops

Museum shops are an excellent place to find reproduction prints, Soviet memorabilia (including ceramics), silk scarves and books on the museum's collection of exhibits, its home city as well as Russia in general. Besides Moscow, St Petersburg has the best museum shops in the Hermitage (*see pp154–5*) and the

Russian Museum (*see pp164–5*). In Kaliningrad, amber jewellery can be bought at the city's Amber Museum (*see p217*) or from vendors outside.

## Specialist Shops

Devoted to a local craft or product, specialist shops are popular in larger cities. In St Petersburg, the **Imperial Porcelain Factory** has two downtown outlets that stock wonderful tea sets and dinner services. **Russky Lyon** specializes in fine linen products such as skirts, shirts and duvet covers. The **Chocolate Museum** sells chocolates moulded into unusual shapes, such as busts of Lenin or chess sets.

---

# DIRECTORY

## Export Restrictions

### Federal Customs Service
W russian-customs.org

### Ministry of Culture
Malaya Morskaya ulitsa 17, St Petersburg. **Map** 3 C1.
**Tel** (812) 571 03 02.

## Department Stores and Shopping Malls

### Dirzhabl
Ulitsa Akademika Shvartsa, Yekaterinburg.
**Tel** (343) 278 09 89.

## Passazh
Nevskiy prospekt 48, St Petersburg.
**Map** 4 E1.
**Tel** (812) 313 74 00.
W passage.spb.ru

## Pokrovskiy Passage
Ulitsa Rosy Lyuksemburg 4, Yekaterinburg.
**Tel** (343) 365 87 87.
W pokrovskiy
passage.ru

## Markets and Bazaars

### Andreevskiy Market
Bolshoi prospekt 18, St Petersburg. **Map** 1 A3.
**Tel** (812) 323 66 87.

## Souvenir Market
Naberezhnaya kanala Griboedova, by the Church on Spilled Blood, St Petersburg. **Map** 4 E1.

## Unona
Ulitsa Marshala Kazakova 35, St Petersburg.
**Tel** (812) 747 02 00.
W spb-unona.ru

## Specialist Shops

### Chocolate Museum
Nevskiy prospekt 17, St Petersburg.
**Map** 4 D1.
**Tel** (812) 315 13 48.
W muzeyshokolada.ru

## Imperial Porcelain Factory
Vladimirskiy prospekt 7, St Petersburg.
**Tel** (812) 713 15 13.
Nevskiy prospekt 160, St Petersburg.
**Tel** (812) 717 48 38.
W ipm.ru

## Russky Lyon
Pushkinskaya ulitsa 3, St Petersburg.
**Tel** (812) 325 85 99.

# What to Buy

It is easy to find interesting and beautiful souvenirs in Moscow and St Petersburg. They range in price from small, enamelled badges, which sell for very little, through to hand-painted Palekh boxes and samovars, which can be very expensive. Traditional crafts were encouraged by the state in the old Soviet Union and many items, such as lacquered boxes and bowls, *matryoshka* dolls, wooden toys and chess sets, are still made by craftsmen and women using age-old methods. Memorabilia from the Soviet era also make good souvenirs and Russia is definitely the best place to buy the national specialities, vodka and caviar.

**Samovar** Used to boil water to make tea *(see p279)*, samovars come in all shapes and sizes. A permit is needed to export a pre-1956 samovar.

**Vodka and Caviar** An enormous variety of both clear and flavoured vodkas (such as lemon and pepper) is available *(see p278)*. They make excellent accompaniments to *ikra* (black and red caviar), which are often served with *blini (see p276)*.

Red caviar

Flavoured vodka

Clear vodka

Black caviar

Malachite egg        Amber ring

**Semi-precious Stones** Malachite, amber, jasper and a variety of marbles from the Ural Mountains are used to make a wide range of items – everything from jewellery and chess sets to inlaid table tops.

**Wooden Toys** These crudely carved wooden toys usually have moving parts. They are known as Bogorodskiye toys and make charming gifts.

**Chess Sets** Attractive chess sets made from all kinds of beautiful materials, including malachite, are widely available. This wooden chess set is painted in the same style as the *matryoshka* dolls.

**Matryoshka Dolls** These dolls fit one inside the other and come in a wide range of styles. The traditional dolls are the prettiest, but those painted as Russian, Soviet and world leaders are also very popular.

## Lacquered Artifacts

Painted wooden or papier-mâché artifacts make popular souvenirs and are sold all over the city. The exquisite hand-painted, lacquered Palekh boxes can be very costly, but the eggs decorated with icons and the typical red, black and gold bowls are more affordable.

**Palekh Box** The art of miniature painting on papier-mâché items originated in the late 18th century. Artists in the four villages of Palekh, Fedoskino, Mstera and Kholui still produce these hand-painted marvels. The images are based on Russian fairy tales and legends.

Painted wooden egg

**Bowl with Spoon** The brightly painted bowls and spoons, generally known as *Khokhloma*, have a lacquer coating, forming a surface which is durable, but not resistant to boiling liquids.

Russian hand-painted tray

Tuners

Strings

**Musical Instruments** Russian folk music uses a wide range of musical instruments. This *gusli* is similar to the Western psaltery and is played by plucking the strings with both hands. Also available are brightly painted balalaika and *bayan* (accordion).

**Russian Scarf** These brilliantly coloured traditional woollen shawls are good for keeping out the cold. Mass-produced polyester versions are also available, mostly in big department stores, but these are not so warm.

**Gzhel Ceramics** With a distinctive blue and white pattern, this style of ceramics takes its name from Gzhel, a village near Moscow. Ranging from figurines and vases to household crockery, they are popular with Russians and visitors alike.

### Soviet Memorabilia

An eclectic array of memorabilia from the Soviet era is on sale. Old banknotes, coins, pocket watches and Red Army kits, including belt buckles, badges and other items from uniforms, can be found alongside watches with cartoons of KGB agents on their faces.

Pocket watch

Badge with Soviet symbols

Red Army leather belt

# ENTERTAINMENT IN RUSSIA

Russia is a vibrant country where both mainstream and eclectic forms of entertainment have flourished. The range of cultural events and recreation here is wide and richly varied. Both Moscow and St Petersburg have an impressive choice of entertainment and their ballet, opera, classical music and theatre are among the best in the world. Both cities have a crowded cultural calendar, since international artistes, bands, soloists and conductors frequently come to visit. Additionally, Russia's great musical culture is manifested by the many music festivals that take place across the country throughout the year. Circuses remain an extremely popular form of entertainment. The Russian versions are highly stylized and elaborate, with a variety of impressive acts.

Ballerina warming up for a performance at the Mariinskiy Theatre

## Information and Tickets

There is never a dearth of things to do in Russia. St Petersburg can be quite a difficult city to keep up with as both official and unofficial events are organized at short notice. To keep abreast of what is on in the city, check out the weekly *St Petersburg Times* and the monthly magazine *Pulse*. Visitors who can read Russian can refer to two bi-weekly magazines, *Afisha* and *Time Out*, for detailed listings.

St Petersburg's Mariinskiy Theatre has an English-language website on which tickets can be bought. Ticket booking website **Artis** offers similar services for other theatres. Elsewhere, visitors can buy tickets in person from local ticket kiosks or the venue's box office, or online.

## Ballet, Opera and Classical Music

Russia's musical tradition has been upheld in its major cities. St Petersburg rivals, and occasionally surpasses, Moscow in the quality of its ballet, opera and classical music. The Mariinskiy Theatre *(see p174)* boasts some of the world's finest dancers, such as the prima ballerinas Ulyana Lopatkina and Diana Vishneva. The company tours abroad over summer, returning for the opening of the autumn season. One of the highlights of the year is the Christmas production of *The Nutcracker*, performed by children from the Vaganova Ballet School *(see p167)*. The Mariinskiy Concert Hall, near the theatre, is one of the main venues for the Stars of the White Nights Festival *(see p34)*.

While the Mariinskiy and the **Mikhailovskiy Theatre** are St Petersburg's main operatic venues, the **Great and Small halls of the Philharmonia** and the Academic Capella *(see p169)* are the city's best-known concert halls for classical music. The former is the home of the St Petersburg Philharmonic Orchestra. All are used during the city's annual International Early Music Festival *(see p36)*.

In Yekaterinburg, the local **Philharmonic** is home to the acclaimed Urals Academic Orchestra and often hosts visiting directors and soloists. The city's **Opera and Ballet Theatre**, with its Baroque auditorium, is a lovely place to see the Russian classics. Novosibirsk's silver-domed **Opera and Ballet Theatre** is bigger than Moscow's Bolshoi, with a grand interior to match.

## Cinema, Theatre and Circus

Russia's cinematic culture is showcased during film festivals, such as St Petersburg's **Festival of Festivals** held during the White Nights and **Open Cinema** (August), an acclaimed forum for short films. **The Russian International Film Fair** held in March has two venues – St Petersburg's **Dom Kino** cinema and Sochi's **Winter Theatre**.

After Moscow, St Petersburg is the second home of Russian drama. The **Bolshoi Dramatic Theatre** has a repertory that includes Chekhov, Gogol and other Russian classics. Plays by Shakespeare and Molière are staged at the **Theatre on Liteynyy**, the city's only wheelchair-accessible theatre.

Japanese pianist and composer Nobuyuki Tsujii performing at the Stars of the White Nights

A host of talented companies attend the **Festival of Russian Theatres** (mid-April) and the **Baltic House Festival** (October).

Circuses are popular with people of all ages. The **Bolshoi St Petersburg State Circus** is the oldest in Russia, having been based at its present site since 1877. Its shows include performing animals.

## Rock, Jazz and Folk Music

Russia boasts a unique pop culture. Every April, St Petersburg rock clubs such as **Kosmonavt** play host to SKIF, a three-day festival of DJs, performance artists and bands from all over Russia and abroad. Other events include the **White Nights Swing** and Autumn Rhythms, jazz festivals held in early July and mid-November respectively.

In the Siberian city of Perm, a summer festival, **Perm Kaleidoscope** in June with rock and folk bands, street theatre, exhibitions, traditional and modern dance, is followed in late July or early August by Kamwa, an ethno-futuristic celebration of ancient

Ugric culture and contemporary art, which brings together DJs, fashion designers and bands.

Other festivals include Ferma, a techno picnic festival with designer tents for hire, held at Tarusa in the Kaluga region in the first week of July, and **Nashestvie** (8–10 July) in the Tver region.

Traditional folk festivals include the Sadko Folklore Festival, held in Veliky Novgorod, and the Kizhi Volost Festival *(see p35)*.

## Children's Entertainment

Most big cities have theatres specializing in plays for children based on Russian fairy tales. In St Petersburg, the best-known are **Zazerkalye** and the **Large Puppet Theatre**. Shows are in Russian, but often transcend the language barrier.

Attending a dolphin show at St Petersburg's **Dolphinarium** is a must. By bringing a bathing costume, children may play and be photographed with the dolphins after the show. For a "real" Russian winter experience, try a *troika* (horse-drawn sleigh) ride.

Awe-inspiring performance of trapeze artists, Bolshoi St Petersburg State Circus

These are offered at **Shuvalovka**, a reproduction Russian village located 30 km (19 miles) south-west of St Petersburg. Open throughout the year, it includes 17th-century-style wooden houses, a museum of peasant life, a working smithy, a skating rink and ice slides. Take a minibus from Avtovo metro towards Peterhof and ask to stop at Shuvalovka.

# DIRECTORY

## Information and Tickets

**Artis**
w artis.spb.ru

## Ballet, Opera and Classical Music

**Great Hall of the Philharmonia**
Mikhaylovskiy ulitsa 2,
St Petersburg. **Map** 4 E2.
**Tel** (812) 710 42 90

**Mikhailovskiy Theatre**
Ploshchad Iskusstv 1,
St Petersburg. **Map** 4 E2.
**Tel** (812) 595 43 05.

**Opera and Ballet Theatre**
Krasnyy prospekt 36,
Novosibirsk.
**Tel** (383) 227 15 37.

**Opera and Ballet Theatre**
Prospekt Lenina 46A,
Yekaterinburg.
**Tel** (343) 350 32 07.

**Small Hall of the Philharmonia**
Nevskiy prospekt 30,
St Petersburg.
**Map** 4 E2.
**Tel** (812) 710 42 90.

**Yekaterinburg Philharmonic**
Ulitsa Karla Libknekhta
38a, Yekaterinburg.
**Tel** (343) 371 46 82.

## Cinema, Theatre and Circus

**Baltic House Festival**
Aleksandrovsky Park 4,
St Petersburg.
**Map** 1 C3.
**Tel** (812) 232 35 39.

**Bolshoi Dramatic Theatre**
Naberezhnaya Reki
Fontanki 65, St Petersburg.
**Map** 4 E3.
**Tel** (812) 244 10 71.

**Bolshoi St Petersburg State Circus**
Naberezhnaya Reki
Fontanki 3, St Petersburg.

Map 4 F1.
**Tel** (812) 570 51 98.

**Dom Kino**
Ulitsa Karavannaya 12,
St Petersburg. **Map** 4 F1.
**Tel** (812) 314 56 14.

**Festival of Festivals**
w filmfest.ru

**Open Cinema**
w opencinemafest.com

**Theatre on Liteynyy**
Liteynyy prospekt 51,
St Petersburg.
**Tel** (812) 273 53 35.

**Winter Theatre**
Ulitsa Teatralnaya 2,
Sochi.
**Tel** (862) 262 96 16.

## Rock, Jazz and Folk Music

**Kosmonavt**
Ulitsa Bronnitskaya 24,
St Petersburg.
**Map** 4 D5.
**Tel** (812) 303 33 33.

**Nashestvie**
w nashestvie.ru

**Perm Kaleidoscope**
w permfest.com

**White Nights Swing Festival**
w jazz-hall.ru

## Children's Entertainment

**Dolphinarium**
Konstantinovskiy
prospekt 19,
St Petersburg.
**Tel** (812) 235 46 31.

**Large Puppet Theatre**
Ulitsa Nekrasova 10,
St Petersburg.
**Tel** (812) 273 66 72.

**Shuvalovka**
Sankt-Peterburgskoe
shosse 111.
**Tel** (812) 450 53 93.

**Zazerkalye**
Ulitsa Rubinshteyna 13,
St Petersburg. **Map** 4 F2
**Tel** (812) 712 43 93.

# OUTDOOR ACTIVITIES

Russia's varied terrain offers a wide range of outdoor activities. From trekking in the Caucasus and the Altai Mountains and rafting in the Siberian rivers to volcano-watching in Kamchatka and pony trekking in the Urals, the country is an adventure-sports enthusiast's dream destination. In addition, those seeking more unusual experiences will find living in a nomad's yurt, dog-sledding in the Urals or visiting a *banya* especially rewarding. Specialist tour operators offering a variety of tour packages can be easily found in most big cities. However, for activities such as trekking and climbing, tourists can also contact local guides who usually have detailed knowledge of the area. Visitors must always check the safety gear before setting out for particularly risky adventure sports such as climbing and rafting.

Exploring a grotto in the spectacular Kungur Ice Cave

## Banya

The Russian steam bath or *banya* (баня) has been an integral part of the country's culture for many centuries. Its origins are rooted in village life, when peasants cleansed themselves communally once a week before spending Saturday drinking and Sunday in church. Today, well-equipped *banya*, such as **Kruglye Bani** and Sandunovskiy Baths *(see p75)*, can be found in cities and towns across the country.

Some *banya* have separate floors for men and women, while others operate on different days for each sex. Regardless of the set up, men and women do not bathe in the same area.

Towels, flip-flops and felt halts to protect hair from the intense heat can be rented at any *banya*. Many bathers buy a *venik*, a bunch of leafy birch twigs, with which they fan and flail themselves in the *parilka* (steam room) to open up the pores of the skin and enhance blood circulation.

In the countryside, visitors can experience a Siberian *banya* – a riverside log-built sweat lodge – from which bathers emerge to plunge into the icy water of the river. Russians believe the difference between the temperature inside and the weather outside makes the body stronger.

## Caving

The Kungur Ice Cave *(see p235)* in the Perm region of the Urals is the most accessible of Russia's many caves. The numerous grottoes and lakes inside the cave can be explored on three different tour routes of varying duration and difficulty. Trips can be arranged by **Krasnov**.

## Climbing and Volcano-watching

The Caucasus in the south offers superb trekking and climbing opportunities. Here, one of the best places to climb is the 5,642-m (18,510-ft) Mount Elbrus, the highest peak in Europe. Although it is popular with Russian climbers, foreign governments advise their citizens against going there due to ongoing separatist terrorism. It is far safer to go climbing in the Altai Mountains of Siberia. The area's snow-capped peaks, alpine meadows and pristine lakes provide some of the most picturesque trekking trails.

In the Far East, Kamchatka offers thrilling climbing opportunities, including the chance to climb Klyuchevskaya Sopka, Eurasia's highest active volcano at 4,750 m (15,584 ft). Expeditions are only allowed when the local volcano-monitoring station judges it safe.

**LenAlpTours** offers a variety of volcano-watching and climbing tour packages.

## Ethnographic Tourism

Visitors can experience the culture and traditions of ethnic minority groups in the Buryatia, Tuva and Altai regions of Siberia. In addition to living in a yurt, herding on horseback and sampling *kumis*, a mildly alcoholic beverage made of fermented mare's milk, tourists can also learn about the Buddhist and shamanic rituals practiced around these parts. Sayan Ring

Breathtaking views reward hikers in the Caucasus

*(see p315)* is one of the several Siberian travel companies that offers such tour packages.

## Kayaking and Rafting

With its great rivers swollen by snowmelt in early summer, Russia offers plenty of kayaking and rafting opportunities. In southern Russia, thousands of locals raft the Samara Bend in an annual event called the *Zhigulyovskaya krugosvetka* (Zhiguli Circuit). Samara Intour *(see p315)* arranges 10-day rafting trips in this area.

In the Altai Mountains, the Katun river offers high-speed rafting, where enthusiasts can test their skills in catamaran kayaks, rubber dinghies and other craft. The US-based tour company **Bio Bio Expeditions** offers a tour package that includes rafting, camping, fishing and a Siberian *banya* experience. **Kayak USSR**, Krasnov and LenAlpTours also organize kayaking trips on the Katun and other Siberian rivers.

## Pony Trekking and Dog-Sledding

Pony trekking is a great way to explore the rugged terrain of the Altai Mountains and visit settlements where traditional Altai culture, a fusion of Turkic, Mongol and indigenous shamanism, is still practised. LenAlpTours can arrange multi-day pony treks during the summer months.

A visitor dog-sledding in the Urals

From mid-December to mid-March, **Ural Expeditions & Tours** and **Visit Ural** offer dog-sledding in the Urals. The one-day excursion includes instructions on how to manage a sledge and feed a team of dogs, as well as a barbecue with vodka.

## Military Experiences

Since the collapse of the Soviet Union, Russia's Defence Ministry and arms factories have capitalized on their military equipment and expertise by offering a variety of sanitized military experiences. **Go Russia** offers package holidays with high-altitude aerobatics and supersonic flights to the edge of space in MiG-29 and MiG-31 jet fighters from airbases outside Moscow and Nizhny Novgorod. Visitors are required to undergo a medical examination before the flight.

## Spectator Sports

Football is the most popular spectator sport in the country. The Russian Championship runs from spring to autumn. It is dominated by four Moscow clubs and Zenit St Petersburg. Zenit's current home ground is the 21,000-seat **Petrovskiy Stadium**. Visitors can find a schedule of the year's matches on the **Russian Football Union**'s website.

Ice hockey runs a close second in popularity. The season starts in September and culminates in the annual world championships that are held in summer. In St Petersburg, **Ice Palace** and **Yubileynyy Sports Palace** host ice hockey matches.

Russia hosted the 2014 Winter Olympics in Sochi and is set to host another major international sporting event, the 2018 FIFA World Cup™ in a number of cities across the country.

# DIRECTORY

## Banya

**Kruglye Bani**
Karbysheva ulitsa 29,
St Petersburg.
**Tel** (812) 550 09 85.

## Caving

**Krasnov**
Ulitsa Borchaninova 4, Perm.
**Tel** (342) 238 35 20.
Ⓦ uraltourism.com

## Climbing and Volcano-Watching

**LenAlpTours**
Ulitsa Vosstania 9, Rm4,
St Petersburg.
Ⓦ russia-climbing.com

## Kayaking and Rafting

**Bio Bio Expeditions**
**Tel** (1800) 246 72 38.
Ⓦ bbxrafting.com

**Kayak USSR**
Novosibirsk.
**Tel** (909) 50 89 23.
Ⓦ kayakussr.com

## Pony Trekking and Dog-Sledding

**Ural Expeditions & Tours**
Posadskaya ulitsa 23A,
Yekaterinburg.
**Tel** (343) 253 57 75.
Ⓦ welcome-ural.ru

## Visit Ural

Ulitsa Radishcheva 28,
Level 13, Yekaterinburg.
**Tel** (343) 377 77 25.
Ⓦ visitural.com

## Military Experiences

**Go Russia**
Boundary House,
Boston Rd,
London W7 2QE.
**Tel** (020) 3355 7717.
Ⓦ justgorussia.co.uk

## Spectator Sports

**Ice Palace**
Prospekt Pyatiletok 1,
St Petersburg.

**Tel** (812) 718 66 20.
Ⓦ newarena.spb.ru

**Russian Football Union**
Ⓦ rfs.ru

**Petrovskiy Stadium**
Petrovskiy ostrov 2,
St Petersburg.
**Map** 1 A3.
**Tel** (812) 232 16 22.
Ⓦ petrovsky.spb.ru

**Yubileynyy Sports Palace**
Prospekt Dobrolyubova 18, St Petersburg.
**Map** 1 A3.
**Tel** (812) 702 36 05.
Ⓦ yubi.ru

# SURVIVAL
# GUIDE

Practical Information     302–311

Travel Information     312–317

# PRACTICAL INFORMATION

Russia can be a bewildering country for visitors. Besides the downtown areas of Moscow and St Petersburg, most street names and signs are only in Cyrillic, although bilingual signage can be occasionally found in other cities or at major tourist sights in the country. Staff at hotels, restaurants and in all service sectors, as well as passers-by are usually helpful to foreigners. However, it is a good idea for visitors to familiarize themselves with the Cyrillic alphabet in order to decipher signs. Conventional tourist offices are hard to find in Russia, but a number of cities now have online information portals. Hotels, restaurants and theatre tickets can be expensive; check the price carefully before booking something. Public transport is generally cheap and efficient.

## When to Go

Visitors should not be daunted by Russia's long, harsh winters. Temperatures fall to around -8°C (17.6°F), or even -31°C (-23.8°F), between November and late March across the country. However, most big cities are well equipped with an army of snow ploughs and street cleaners to deal with the ice and snow. Note that sturdy footwear, warm layers of clothing and hats are a must.

The height of the tourist season is from May to September, especially during Stars of the White Nights (see p34) in June and July, when prices are at their highest. Although fewer tourists visit during the low season, from October to April, it is the best time for skiing and visiting museums and galleries.

## Visas and Passports

Citizens of almost all countries will need a visa to visit Russia. Be sure to verify entry requirements with the Russian embassy in your country several weeks ahead of departure; visitors arriving by train from Europe will also need a transit visa for Belarus. Note that visas can be obtained only from a Russian consulate in a country where you have right of residence. However, EU citizens can apply from any EU country.

For those on a package tour, visas will be organized by the tour companies. Independent travellers can pay a modest fee and get a specialist agent, such as **Real Russia** or **Visa Express**, based in the UK, or **Peace Travel Services** in the US, to arrange it for them. Moscow-based **Visa House** can also arrange visas for visitors of any nationality.

Alternatively, apply to the Russian embassy. All visa applications must be accompanied by a letter of invitation, which is often referred to as a "visa support letter". This can be provided by your hotel (if booked in advance) or a tourist or accommodation agency in Russia, the UK or the US.

Visas take around 10 days to process. However, all specialist agents offer an express service for an extra fee. Overstaying your visa can lead to a hefty fine or having to remain until an extension is obtained.

## Customs Information

Passports and visas are thoroughly checked at immigration desks. On arrival, visitors are given an immigration card by immigration officials; it must be retained while in the country and presented upon departure. If you lose the exit half of your immigration card, you will need to visit the Immigration Service offices in the airport terminal to request a replacement card.

There are no limitations on the amount of foreign currency that can be brought into Russia, but visitors carrying more than US$10,000 in cash need to fill in a customs declaration form. Departure customs are generally stricter than in other countries, particularly in regard to art and antiques (see p292).

## Travel Safety Advice

Visitors can get up-to-date travel safety information from the Foreign and Commonwealth Office in the UK (www.gov.uk/foreign-travel-advice), the State Department in the US (travel.state.gov) and the Department of Foreign Affairs and Trade in Australia (dfat.gov.au or smartraveller.gov.au).

## Registration

All foreign nationals must register with the Federal Migration Service (FMS) within seven days of arrival. Hotels and hostels can do this for their guests. If you are travelling independently on a business visa, the agency that provided the visa support should register you at a local police station or

A Russian Railways Service office functioning as a tourist information centre, Kaliningrad

◀ Striking view of people standing next to their cars on frozen Lake Baikal

FMS office. Non-registration can lead to on-the-spot fines by local police of up to US$160.

## Embassies and Consulates

Every country that has diplomatic relations with Russia has an embassy or consulate in Moscow; some also have consulates in St Petersburg, Vladivostok or Yekaterinburg. Travellers intending to reside in Russia for longer than three months are advised to register with their consulate or embassy. If a visitor is robbed, hospitalized, imprisoned or otherwise rendered helpless, the embassy or consular officials will help make arrangements, find an interpreter or at least offer advice. They can also re-issue passports and, in some cases, provide a loan to get visitors home.

## Visitor Information

Walk-in tourist information centres can rarely be found in cities across Russia; there are walk-in offices in Kazan, Veliky Novgorod and St Petersburg. However, many Russian cities such as Königsberg have online "information portals". The **Moscow Tourist Helpline** provides information about the city's sights and public transportation in English.

In other cities, local tourist agencies and hotels are the main source of information. In addition, monthly or weekly publications, which are distributed at hotels and restaurants, and via online media (often in Russian only) are useful too.

## Opening Hours

Most sights open from 10am or 10.30am to 6pm and close one day a week. A number of sights also close one day each month for cleaning. Last tickets are usually sold about an hour before closing. All museums remain open on Sundays. Some cathedrals and churches are always open, but others open only for services.

Visitors outside a tourist information centre in Listvyanka

## Admission Charges

Many museums and theatres charge foreigners considerably higher admission fees than Russians, although well within European and North American norms. Such places include the State Tretyakov Gallery *(see pp98–9)*, the Armoury Chamber *(see pp62–3)*, the Pushkin State Museum of Fine Arts *(see pp90–91)* and the Bolshoi Theatre *(see pp82–3)* in Moscow as well as the Hermitage *(see pp154–5)*, the Russian Museum *(see pp164–5)* and the Mariinskiy Theatre *(see p174)* in St Petersburg. However, schoolchildren and students *(see p304)* are entitled to discounts. Credit cards are only accepted at some sights. A good option is to buy a Tourist Card from tourist information offices. It offers free entry to many state museums as well as discounts in some restaurants.

The *kassa* (ticket office) is often located at some distance from the entrance to the sight. It

Women entering the Cathedral of St Sophia in Tobolsk wearing headscarves

can be recognized by the "КАССА" sign; staff at the entrance will point you in its direction.

## Visiting Churches and Mosques

The most important Orthodox church services take place on Saturday evenings and Sunday mornings as well as on religious holidays. In general, services run for several hours. It is normal for visitors to drop in on a service for a while, but certain dress codes must be observed: shorts are not acceptable; men must remove their hats; women should cover their chest and shoulders and preferably wear a headscarf or hat. Although acceptable in town churches, women wearing trousers might be refused entry to monasteries.

Visitors should always seek permission before entering mosques. Besides observing the dress code specified for Orthodox churches, be sure to remove your shoes before entering the mosque premises.

## Language

Cyrillic, the alphabet used in the Russian language, is named after the 9th-century monks Cyril and Methodius who invented it. Various systems for transliterating Cyrillic into Roman characters exist, but they do not differ enough to cause confusion.

Many Russians who regularly come into contact with visitors can speak some English. However, knowledge of a few Russian words will be much appreciated and taken as a sign of respect.

An outdoor café where debit and credit cards are accepted, Krasnodar

## Addresses

Russian addresses are given in reverse order: post code, city, street name, *dom* (house) number, *kvartira* (apartment) number and finally the person's name.

Buildings on the corner of two streets are denoted by two numbers separated by a slash, the first referring to the larger street and the second to the smaller one.

If a flat is part of a complex, a *korpus (k)* or *stroinie (str)* number will also be given to indicate which block it is in.

## Social Etiquette

On public transport, young men are expected to give up their seats to women with young children or the elderly.

Smoking is prohibited in museums, cinemas, theatres and public transport. Special areas are usually reserved for smoking in restaurants. When invited to a private home, be sure to toast *za khozyayku* (the hostess) or *za khozyaina* (the host).

Photographing metro stations, official-looking buildings and any type of military structure is prohibited, and may lead to detention by the police. In some museums, visitors must buy a ticket to photograph or video.

## Travelling with Children

Russians adore children, and those accompanying visitors to Russia are likely to attract plenty of compliments. Children under six travel free on public transport, but over this they pay the full price. While museums are free for toddlers and babies, school-children pay a reduced price.

## Gay and Lesbian Travellers

Russian society is not in general very tolerant of homosexuality and its "promotion" is a criminal offence. Any public displays of affection will almost always be frowned upon. Despite hostility, the gay and lesbian scene continues to thrive in major cities. The **Russian LGBT Network** provides general information on gay and lesbian life in the country.

## Disabled Travellers

There are few facilities for the disabled in Russia. Public transport is difficult to access, entrances have steps and narrow doors and public lifts are rare. However, the Russian Museum and the Hermitage in St Petersburg, as well as the State Tretyakov Gallery in Moscow, all have wheelchair access. **Liberty**, a tour company in St Petersburg, specializes in wheelchair-accessible tours in and around the city and can book hotels with suitable

A day out with children at one of Saransk's many museums

facilities. Travel advice can also be obtained abroad, from **RADAR** in the UK and **SATH** in the US.

## Student Travellers

An ISIC (International Student Identity Card) entitles its holder to discounts in museums and on rail and air tickets booked through **STAR Travel**.

## Paying and Tipping

The rouble is the only official valid currency in Russia (*see p308*). Some hotels and agencies may display prices in US dollars or euros, but all cash payments must be in roubles. Debit and credit cards are accepted in some restaurants and most hotels, as well as in large retail stores in major cities.

Tipping is a matter of choice, but baggage handlers at airports and train stations may ask exorbitant sums. Visitors should simply pay what they consider to be appropriate.

## Public Toilets

Most cafés and bars have toilet facilities, but public toilets on the street are not pleasant. It is often best to find the nearest large hotel or McDonald's, or a pay toilet in a department store, where fees may range from 10 to 30 roubles. Although the attendant who takes the money also hands out toilet paper rations, it is a good idea to carry your own.

## Electricity

The electrical current in Russia is 220 V. Two-pin plugs are required, but some of the old Soviet two-pin sockets do not take modern European plugs, which have thicker pins. US appliances need a 220:110 volt current adaptor. Adaptors are best bought before travelling.

## Time

Since Russia abolished daylight savings time in 2014, Moscow time has been three hours ahead of Greenwich Mean Time (GMT).

Moscow time is the standard for Russia's nine time zones. Note that Trans-Siberian Railway schedules express Moscow time, not local time zones.

## Conversion Table

### Imperial to Metric
1 inch = 2.54 centimetres
1 foot = 30 centimetres
1 mile = 1.6 kilometres
1 ounce = 28 grams
1 pound = 454 grams
1 pint = 0.6 litres

### Metric to Imperial
1 centimetre = 0.4 inches
1 metre = 3 feet, 3 inches
1 kilometre = 0.6 miles
1 gram = 0.04 ounces
1 kilogram = 2.2 pounds
1 litre = 1.8 pints

## Responsible Travel

Despite the efforts of Greenpeace and other NGOs, Russia has a regrettably poor record in environmental issues. State funding to develop 12 nature reserves for eco tourism has

been greeted with scepticism: activists fear it will open them to property developers, as at Krasnaya Polyana, which hosted the 2014 Winter Olympics.

Tourists can support local communities by opting for homestays or B&Bs (see p264) over chain hotels. While Moscow is not renowned as a green city, there are a few eco-friendly, but expensive, hotels such as Ararat Park Hyatt Moscow (see p266) and Swissôtel Krasnye Holmy (see p268), which employ energy-saving systems and recycle much of their waste. The centrally located Dorgomilovsky Market (see p118) is one of the city's largest farmers' markets

selling fresh produce from regional farms. At local markets across Russia, the older women on the fringes often sell organic produce grown at their own *dachas*. Visitors can also buy organic fruits, vegetables and honey from the numerous markets in the Altai Republic.

Adventure travel agencies in the Urals and Siberia offer itineraries involving a variety of eco-friendly activities, such as rafting, dog sledding and pony-trekking. Based in Moscow, **Astravel** supports conservation projects through tours that include activities such as volcano-watching and surveying snow leopards.

Rafting, a popular pastime in the Urals

# DIRECTORY

## Visas and Passports

### Peace Travel Services
848 North Rainbow
Blvd #1224,
Las Vegas, 89107.
W go-russia.com

### Real Russia
3 The Ivories,
Northampton St,
Islington, London, N1 2HY.
W realrussia.co.uk

### Visa Express
Parnell House,
25 Wilton Rd,
London, SW1V 1LW.
W visaexpress.co.uk

### Visa House
22/2 Bolshaya Nikitskaya,
Office 18, Moscow.
Map 1 B5.
Tel (495) 721 10 21.
W visahouse.com

## Embassies and Consulates

### Australia
10A/2 Podkolokolny
pereulok, Moscow.

Map 4 F1.
Tel (495) 956 60 70.
W russia.embassy.
gov.au

### Canada
Starokonyushenny
pereulok 23, Moscow.
Map 3 B2.
Tel (495) 925 60 00.
W russia.gc.ca

### United Kingdom
Smolenskaya
naberezhnaya 10, Moscow.
Tel (495) 956 72 00.
W ukinrussia.fco.gov.uk

### United States
Bolshoy Deviatinsky
pereulok 8, Moscow.
Tel (495) 728 50 00.
W moscow.us
embassy.gov

## Visitor Information

### City Tourist Information Centre
Sadovaya ulitsa 14/52,
St Petersburg. Map 4 D1.
Tel (812) 310 28 22.

### Kazan Tourist Information Centre
Chernyshevskogo 27A,
Kazan.
Tel (843) 292 97 77.
W gokazan.com

### Königsberg.ru
Kaliningrad.
W konigsberg.ru/eng

### Moscow Tourist Helpline
Tel (800) 220 00 02.

### Red Izba
Sennaya ploshchad 5,
Veliky Novgorod.
Tel (816) 277 30 74.
W visitnovgorod.com

## Gay and Lesbian Travellers

### Russian LGBT Network
Ligovsky prospekt 87,
office 509,
St Petersburg.
Tel (812) 454 64 52.
W lgbtnet.ru

## Disabled Travellers

### Liberty
Ulitsa Polozova 12,
Office 1,
St Petersburg.
Map 1 B1.
Tel (812) 232 81 63
W libertytour.ru

### RADAR
W disabilityrights.org

### SATH
347 Fifth Ave, Suite 605,
New York, 10016.
W sath.org

## Student Travellers

### STAR Travel
Novoslobodskaya ulitsa 3,
Moscow
Map 1 B2.
Tel (495) 797 95 55.

## Responsible Travel

### Astravel
Novoslobodskaya ulitsa 31,
Moscow. Map 1 B2.
W astravel.ru

# Personal Security and Health

Despite lurid worldwide reporting on the Russian mafia, most visitors to Russia encounter little if any serious crime. Hazards such as pickpocketing and car-thefts are common, but they can usually be avoided by taking sensible precautions. Due to language reasons, it is a good idea to have a card with your Russian address written on it for use in taxis or emergencies. Medical insurance is essential, as local health care compares poorly with Western standards and English-speaking services and medical evacuation are expensive. Many medicines are readily available, but it is best to bring specific medicines if needed.

Bright red fire engine with the distinctive white stripe

## What to Be Aware Of

Visitors to Russia are advised to take out travel insurance. Once in the country, tourists can prevent trouble by following some simple measures. Pickpockets can be avoided by not carrying money in open pockets or displaying large sums of money in public; bags should be kept closed and roubles kept apart from foreign currency and credit cards. It is advisable to carry a small sum of money for purchases, and to keep the rest in the hotel safe.

Downtown areas are often frequented by "gypsies", ostensibly begging but often engaged in pickpocketing. If approached, hold tight to valuables and walk on without aggression.

Traveller's cheques are insured against loss or theft. However, if they are stolen report it immediately to the issuing company as they can easily be "laundered" in Russia.

It is essential to report thefts to the police in order to obtain certificates for insurance claims. Since the police station is unlikely

to have an interpreter, contact your hotel security staff for assistance. Embassies generally deal with more serious situations.

## In an Emergency

The emergency services can be reached by dialling 01 for the fire department, 02 for police and 03 for an ambulance. There is also a combined number, 112. If at all possible, seek help first from your embassy or consulate.

## Personal Safety

The greatest danger faced by travellers is posed by thieves who might become violent if they encounter resistance. It is advisable to hand over belongings if they are demanded with menace.

Although widespread, the mafia has scant contact with foreigners, particularly tourists, who are generally less wealthy than Russian businessmen.

Women on their own may be approached by kerb crawlers or may be propositioned in bars and restaurants. It is best to ignore such advances.

At night, it is safer to use taxis booked in advance rather than hailed on the street. The metro is usually safe.

Racism is unfortunately rampant in Russia. It is advisable to be vigilant on the streets, especially around Hitler's birthday on 20 April and National Unity Day on 4 November, when bands of neo-Nazi thugs usually roam the streets.

## Police

Several kinds of police operate in Russia. They change uniforms according to the weather, with the necessary addition of fur hats and big coats in winter. The *politsiya* (street officers), who always carry guns, can be frequently spotted on the streets. The riot police or OMON, who dress in blue camouflage fatigues, are seldom seen on the streets, except during demonstrations and football matches.

Separate from both these are the traffic police, whose uniforms carry the logo ДПС (DPS) on the chest and shoulder. They have the authority to stop any vehicle to check documents.

Both the *politsiya* and traffic police supplement their income by fining people for minor infringements of the law, and have unfortunately been known to stop tourists for document checks. Carry a photocopy of your passport and visa, and try to avoid handing over your original passport to the police.

## Pharmacies

*Apteka* (pharmacies) in Russia can be recognized by the "Аптека" sign and a green cross hanging

A police car patrolling a city street

outside. Although pharmacies in cities are well stocked with imported and locally made products, small-town pharmacies usually have limited stocks. Prescriptions are not necessary for any purchase, and antibiotics and other strong medications can be purchased over the counter. All assistants are trained pharmacists and should be able to suggest a Russian alternative to visitors who name the drug they are seeking. However, visitors with specific requirements, particularly insulin, should bring enough supplies to last the length of their stay. Every city has several all-night pharmacies, the addresses of which can be obtained from hotel receptionists.

Brightly painted kiosk selling bottled water and other beverages

Façade of a 24-hour city pharmacy stocking both local and imported medicines

## Medical Treatment

Most large hotels have their own doctor and this should be the first port of call for anyone who falls ill. Public health care is based on local polyclinics and hospitals, where the standard of care is variable. Since few physicians and nurses speak English, visitors generally prefer private companies such as the **European Medical Centre**, the **American Medical Clinic** and **Euromed**. These companies provide a wide range of facilities, from basic treatment to dental care and X-rays, ultrasound scans and even medical evacuation. **US Dental Care** offers a full range of dental treatment. Although expensive, they are experienced in dealing with foreign insurance policies.

Most of these companies are in Moscow and St Petersburg, but some can be found in other major cities. If you are taken to a local hospital and require further treatment, contact either your consulate or an international private facility. Hospital bills tend to be rather stiff, so it is best to have a comprehensive health insurance policy. However, most travel insurance policies cover medical treatment as well.

## Health Precautions

Visitors should not drink tap water in Russia as it contains heavy metals and giardia, a parasite that causes stomach ailments. Stick to bottled water and avoid fruit and raw vegetables that may have been washed in tap water. Avoid eating *pirozhki* (a type of pie) sold on the streets.

With an increasing incidence of diphtheria, and a low risk of rabies, polio and hepatitis A and B, visitors intending to spend much time in remote areas are advised to be inoculated against these. Sexually transmitted diseases are on the rise, so all due caution must be exercised.

*Komari* (mosquitoes) are rife from June to late September. Plug-in chemical mosquito coils are available and are good at night. Alternatives are sprays, or citronella oil repellents used in vaporizers.

A more serious issue is warding off encephalitis-bearing ticks, found in the taiga forests. Visitors planning to trek in the taiga from May to June are recommended to have encephalitis vaccinations, and should always wear insect repellent as well as cover exposed skin. If you find a tick, remove it carefully with tweezers; should any part remain, it can still infect you.

## DIRECTORY

### In an Emergency

**All emergencies**
**Tel** 112.

**Ambulance** (skoraya pomoshch)
**Tel** 03.

**Fire** (pozhar)
**Tel** 01.

**Police** (politsiya)
**Tel** 02.

### Medical Treatment

**American Medical Clinic**
Naberezhnaya Reki Moyki 78, St Petersburg.
**Map** 3 C2.
**Tel** (812) 740 20 90.
**w** amclinic.com

**Euromed**
Suvorovskiy prospekt 60, St Petersburg.
**Tel** (812) 327 03 01.
**w** euromed.ru

**European Medical Centre**
Spiridonievskiy pereulok 5, Building 1, Moscow.
**Tel** (495) 933 66 55.
**w** emcmos.ru

**US Dental Care**
Ulitsa Bolshaya Dmitrovka 7/5, Building 2, Moscow.
**Map** 1 C4.
**Tel** (495) 933 86 86.

# Banking and Local Currency

The official currency of Russia is the rouble. Major European debit and credit cards can be used to pay at hotels, restaurants and large retail stores across Russia, but cash is still the norm in some cities as well as in provincial towns and villages. Exchange bureaux and banks, where visitors can change their currency to roubles, are widespread. Money should never be changed on the street, where apparently better offers from individuals will lead to visitors being cheated.

An automatic cash dispenser

## Banks and Exchange Bureaux

Roubles can be obtained outside Russia, but rates are usually better once in the country. In cities and towns, there are numerous exchange bureaux, some of which are open 24 hours. They can be identified by the "Обмен валюты" (obmen valyutiy) sign. US dollars and euros are widely accepted, but other currencies may be difficult or impossible to exchange.

A passport has to be shown when changing money. Any defect on foreign banknotes, especially vertical tears or ink or water stains, can make them difficult to exchange. Make sure that all banknotes brought into Russia are in good condition and that any US dollars were issued after 1990.

There are few foreign banks in Russia and they rarely offer over-the-counter services. However, most Russian banks will exchange US dollars, euros and sometimes other currencies. They also offer cash advances on credit cards. **Alfa-Bank** and **Sberbank** offer the best rates, although this can vary across Russia. Master Bank and Bank Moskvy also offer money transfer and accept American Express traveller's cheques.

## ATMs

Recognized by the "Банкомат" (bankomat) sign, ATMs, or cash dispensers, can be easily found in cities. If unsure of where to find one, head to a big hotel. Visa and MasterCard are accepted in all ATMs, while American Express is taken at Sberbank and Russkiy Standart. Maestro and Diners Club cards, however, are rarely accepted. Prepaid currency cards can be used to withdraw cash at many ATMs. As always, it is advisable to be alert when withdrawing cash and to cover the keypad when entering your PIN, to avoid becoming the victim of credit card fraud.

**Western Union** is widely used for international money transfers, which can be made through almost any bank. Note that commissions are exorbitant (about US$40 to transfer US$300).

A sign displaying conversion rates outside an exchange bureau

## Credit Cards and Traveller's Cheques

Credit cards can be used to obtain cash, both roubles and US dollars, through the larger banks and from ATMs in some banks or hotels. Although the local commission is only 1 per cent (or zero), the credit card company will charge a fee for the transaction.

The most commonly accepted cards are Visa and MasterCard. Diners Club and American Express, however, are less widely recognized. Less commission is charged for cash in roubles.

Lost or stolen cards should be reported immediately to the credit card company in Moscow or St Petersburg.

Banks charge 1–3 per cent commission to refund or cash traveller's cheques. Note that only large banks, such as Alfa-Bank and Sberbank, offer this service. American Express cheques are most widely accepted, followed by those from Thomas Cook. Traveller's cheques can only be used as payment for goods or services in a few large hotels and are acceptable only in US dollars and euros. Recent customs regulations make it necessary to declare traveller's cheques on arrival in Russia.

## DIRECTORY

### Banks and Exchange Bureaux

**Alfa-Bank**
w alfabank.com/russia

**Sberbank**
w sberbank.ru

### ATMs

**Western Union**
w westernunion.co.uk

### Credit Cards and Traveller's Cheques

**American Express**
Moscow.
**Tel** (495) 933 84 00.
St Petersburg.
**Tel** (812) 329 60 60.

**Visa, MasterCard and Diners Club**
**Tel** (866) 654 01 64.

## Local Currency

The Russian currency is the rouble (or ruble), written as "рубль" and abbreviated to "р" or "руб." While the higher denominations are currently available in banknotes, all of which bear images of well-known Russian cities, the lower denominations are in coins. The kopek is issued in coins as well. Traditionally, the rouble always consisted of 100 kopeks. Today, however, kopeks have virtually no purchasing power.

## Banknotes

*There are six denominations of banknotes, with face values of 10, 50, 100, 500, 1,000 and 5,000 roubles. When changing money check that the notes correspond to those pictured here.*

10 roubles

50 roubles

100 roubles

500 roubles

1,000 roubles

5,000 roubles

## Coins

*The revaluation of the Russian rouble in 1998 led to the revival of the long-redundant kopek. Any coins issued before 1997 are essentially valueless. Visitors should therefore always examine change they receive and refuse to accept any old coins.*

50 kopeks

10 kopeks

10 roubles

5 roubles

2 roubles

1 rouble

# Communications

Telecommunications is one of the most dynamic sectors of Russia's economy. Cafés and restaurants in big cities have a Wi-Fi connection, which is usually free. Mobile phone shops can be found across cities, where a local SIM can be purchased upon presentation of a passport. The abundance of newspapers, magazines and TV channels on offer includes some in English. Russia's postal system has improved, but remains slow and unreliable.

## International and Local Telephone Calls

Phone calls can be made from one of the public phone boxes on the streets and in metro stations. A prepaid *telefonnaya karta* (phonecard), which is available from kiosks, telecom shops or Sberbank branches, is required to make a call. Some of the popular phonecards include Zebra, which can also be used for dial-up Internet access, MTU-Net, Matrix and Access. Cards come in 25, 50, 100, 120, 200, 400 and 1,000 units. However, you will need at least 100 units to call internationally. Note that international and inter-city calls are cheaper from 10pm to 8am all through the week.

In cities and towns, it may be cheaper to call abroad through a *peregovorniy punkt* (public communications centre). Here, you give the clerk the number that you want to call, pay a deposit and then go to your assigned booth to make the call, paying the difference afterwards.

Visitor at MTS office, one of the biggest telecom operators in Russia

## Mobile Phones

**MTS**, **Megafon** and **Beeline** are the main mobile network operators in Russia. They cover most cities and also areas along the Trans-Siberian Railway, but remote areas may lack coverage due to the size of the country.

Most visitors from the EU can use their mobile phones in Russia if "roaming" is activated, but those from the US and Australia, who do not have a GSM phone, may not be able to. It is advisable to contact your local service provider to enable your "roaming" access before travelling to the country. Bear in mind that "roaming" in Russia is expensive.

A cheaper option is to buy a prepaid Russian SIM card if your phone is unlocked. A passport is required for registration when buying a SIM. Offered by service providers and usually priced at 300 roubles, these SIMs give you a local telephone number and a sum of credit that can be topped up by prepaid cards sold in phone shops, ATMs and top-up points in city underpasses. Two reliable phone shop chains are **Euroset** and **Svyaznoy**. Call charges are low within networks. Since roaming charges across Russia are high, it may be worth changing SIM cards when crossing regional telecom boundaries.

## Internet

Major cities have 4G (mobile broadband Internet access) coverage. Internet cafés can be found in every city and town, and sometimes even in villages. They provide access for around 100 roubles per hour.

Wi-Fi coverage is widely available in hotels as well as at the airport. It is generally free, but some hotels may charge, where Internet is available only in a specific area. Wi-Fi hotspots can also be found in stations, malls, cafés and bars. It has been introduced on the circle line of Moscow metro as well.

Fax services are available at post offices, communications centres and hotel business

## Useful Dialling Codes

- To call Russia from abroad, dial the international access code, followed by Russia's country code (7), the city code, and finally the individual number.
- To call Moscow, dial 495 followed by the individual number.
- To call St Petersburg, dial 812 followed by the individual number.
- To make an inter-city call, dial 8, followed by the city code and the individual number.
- To make a call from a landline to a mobile number, dial 8, then the city code, and finally the mobile number.
- To use an international calling card, dial the local access number followed by the card number and the PIN, then dial the number along with the country code.
- To make an international call from a domestic phone, dial 8, then dial the international access number (10), followed by the country code.
- For Moscow or St Petersburg directory enquiries, dial 09.

A Svyaznoy outlet, Russia's leading mobile phone retailer

centres. Some hotels and travel agencies still require reservations or documentation for visa support, to be transmitted by fax.

## Postal Services

The state-run postal service has offices everywhere, even in villages. However, the service is very slow, and is best avoided except for sending postcards. Ordinary post offices, and those in hotels, sell normal and commemorative Russian stamps, postcards and envelopes. Russian postoffices are marked "Почта" (pochta) and can be found across cities.

For important documents, use a courier service such as **DHL**, **FedEx** or **TNT**, which have offices in Moscow, St Petersburg and other cities. Anything other than paper, especially computer discs, is checked by customs, which can delay despatch by an extra day or so.

## TV and Radio

Almost every hotel room in Russia has a television equipped to receive a variety of local, national, cable or satellite channels, including CNN, the BBC World Service TV and Eurosport. Russian-language television is dominated by detective shows, soap operas and talk shows. Russia Today,

A kiosk selling a variety of newspapers and magazines

the state-run English-language channel widely viewed as a mouthpiece for the Kremlin, is available in most hotels.

Since the BBC World Service stopped transmitting in Russia, there has been no regular English language radio station, but online radio stations from around the world are easily accessible. Local pop stations include Europa Plus (106.2 FM), Radio Maximum (103.7) and Russkoe Radio (105.7 FM). Radio Orfey (72.14 FM) plays classical music.

## Newspapers and Magazines

Quality national papers include *Izvestiya*, *Nezavisimaya Gazeta* and *Kommersant*, as well as the twice-weekly *Novaya Gazeta*, known for its investigative journalism. *Pravda* and *Komsomolskaya Pravda* (the former Communist Party and Communist Youth papers) are mass-market tabloids.

*The Moscow Times* is one of the best English-language newspapers and is available free of charge at hotels, cafés and bars. It is published from Tuesday to Saturday and includes event listings in its Friday edition. *Moscow In Your Pocket* is a free listings guide published every two months. Similarly *St Petersburg In Your Pocket*, published every two months, covers the northern capital with detailed listings and reviews.

## DIRECTORY

### Mobile Phones

**Beeline**
1ya Tverskaya-Yamskaya ulitsa 2, Moscow.
**Map** 1 B3.
**Tel** (495) 974 88 88.
W beeline.ru

**Euroset**
Tverskaya ulitsa 4, Moscow.
**Map** 1 C5.
**Tel** (495) 771 73 12.
W euroset.ru

**Megafon**
Myasnitskaya ulitsa 48, Moscow.
**Map** 2 F4.
**Tel** (495) 50 77 77.

Artilleriyskaya ulitsa 1, St Petersburg.
**Tel** (800) 300 05 00.
W english.megafon.ru

**MTS**
Sadovaya-Karetnaya ulitsa 2, Moscow.
**Map** 1 C3.
**Tel** (495) 766 0166.
Kazanskaya ulitsa 45, St Petersburg.
**Map** 3 C3.
**Tel** (800) 380 00 00.
W vis.mtsgsm.com

**Svyaznoy**
Ulitsa Arbat 1, Moscow.
**Map** 3 A2.
**Tel** (495) 788 52 55.
W svyaznoy.ru

### Postal Services

**DHL**
1ya Tverskaya-Yamskaya ulitsa 11, Moscow.
**Map** 1 B3.
**Tel** (495) 956 10 00.
Nevskiy prospekt 10, St Petersburg.
**Map** 4 D1.
**Tel** (812) 326 64 00.
W dhl.ru

**FedEx**
Sokolnicheskiy val 1L, Moscow.
**Tel** (495) 737 52 23.
Nevskiy prospekt 30, St Petersburg.
**Map** 4 E1.
**Tel** (812) 325 88 25.
W fedex.com.ru

**TNT**
Ulitsa Svobody 31, Moscow. **Tel** (495) 797 27 77. Sofiyskaya ulitsa 14, St Petersburg.
**Tel** (812) 718 33 30.
W tnt.com

### Newspapers and Magazines

**Pravda**
W english.pravda.ru

**The Moscow Times**
W themoscowtimes. com

**St Petersburg In Your Pocket**
W inyourpocket.com/ st-petersburg

# TRAVEL INFORMATION

Flying remains the easiest way of travelling to Russia from Europe or the US, although many Australasians from China take the famous Trans-Siberian Railway. Travelling overland, especially by road, can be difficult and often involves crossing many borders and negotiating road networks and pot-holed roads. However, if cost is a priority, arriving by train or coach are cheaper alternatives, especially for visitors from neighbouring countries such as Ukraine or Belarus. Ferries are an increasingly popular form of transport to reach cities such as St Petersburg, Sochi and Vladivostok. Irrespective of the route chosen, it is worth shopping around to find the best deal as flight prices fluctuate greatly throughout the year. Many companies also offer package deals.

The three-level air terminal complex at Sochi International Airport

## Arriving by Air

Direct flights run from London to Moscow on **British Airways** and the Russian airlines **Aeroflot**, while British Airways as well as the Russian carrier **Rossiya** fly to St Petersburg. The two cities can also be reached by inexpensive indirect flights such as **Finnair** via Helsinki, **SAS** via Stockholm or **Austrian Airlines** via Vienna.

Direct flights from the US to Moscow are limited to Aeroflot and **Delta Air Lines**. There are very few direct flights to other Russian cities from the US, Ireland, Canada, South Africa or Australia. The usual route from these places is to fly via a European city (often Helsinki) or via Moscow.

**Scott's Tours** in London and **Visit Russia** in New York are good for budget fares. Some agencies only sell flights, while others also book hotels or offer package deals, which can be cheaper than booking flights and accommodation separately.

## Main Airports

Moscow has three international airports: **Domodedovo**, **Sheremetyevo** and **Vnukovo**. Each of the airports is linked by

**Aeroexpress** trains to railway stations in the city centre and metro stations on the circle line. A one-way ticket costs 320 roubles and trains depart every 30 minutes from 5am to 12:30am.

There are also buses to outlying metro stations between 6am and midnight. However, traffic congestion often causes delays. Official airport taxis can be pre-booked by your hotel or at the terminal. Meters are rarely used; be sure to negotiate a price beforehand.

St Petersburg's **Pulkovo** airport is located 23 km (14 miles) south of the city centre and serves both international and domestic flights. The airport has a regulated taxi system with stands near the exit of the arrivals terminals. Visitors should expect to pay about 1,000 roubles to reach the city centre. A cheaper alternative is to take bus 39 from outside the airport terminal to Moskovskaya metro station. Minibuses travel the same route but charge twice as much.

The **Sochi International Airport** in Adler is linked to the central train station by buses and minibuses. The ski resort of Krasnaya Polyana can also be reached by bus from the airport. Taxi fares are negotiable; they start around 500 roubles. The main airport for Yekaterinburg is **Koltsovo**. It is connected to the central train station by buses and minibuses.

## Arriving by Train

From Paris, Brussels, Berlin, Prague or Warsaw, it takes at least 24 hours to reach Moscow and 48 hours to reach St Petersburg. Note that a transit visa is required for Belarus. **Seat 61** contains full details of all rail routes to Russia.

Trains from Western Europe, Poland and Belarus arrive in Moscow at Belorusskaya station; from the Baltic States at Rizhskaya station and from Eastern Europe at Kievskaya station. Yaroslavskiy and Kazanskiy serve domestic routes only. Komsomolskaya is the terminus for trains arriving from Finland and St Petersburg. Paveletskaya and Kurskaya stations handle trains from southern Russia and Ukraine.

In St Petersburg, trains from Helsinki arrive at Finlyandskiy station; from Tallinn and Riga

A Trans-Siberian train travelling on a route along Lake Baikal

at Baltiskaya station; and from Germany, Poland and Belarus at Vitebskiy station. The most central terminus is Moscow station, where trains from the capital and most other parts of Russia arrive.

There are two rail routes to Russia from China and Mongolia. Starting from Beijing, the Trans-Mongolian route runs via the Mongolian capital, Ulan Bator, while the Trans-Manchurian route runs via the Chinese city of Harbin. The routes converge at Ulan-Ude and head west across Siberia following the Trans-Siberian Railway.

One of Lux Express's luxury Wi-Fi-enabled coaches

## Arriving by Sea

From May to September, UK operators such as **Fred Olsen Cruises**, **P&O Cruises** and **Virgin Holidays** offer luxury cruises to St Petersburg. Cruise boats dock in the Neva basin in the heart of the city or at the Marine Facade Terminal on Vasilievskiy Island, linked to the centre by trolleybus 10 and bus 7. From February to December, there are regular **St Peter Line** ferries from Helsinki, Stockholm and Tallinn. On all these cruises, passengers may travel visa-free for up to 72 hours in St Petersburg. In summer, Sochi can be reached by hydrofoil or ferry from the Black Sea port of Trabzon in

Turkey. Hydrofoils take 4–5 hours and tickets cost 4,000 roubles; ferries take 12 hours. Contact **Abdullah CAKIR** for details.

Visitors from Asia can reach Vladivostok by a **DBS Cruise** boat that sails once a week from the Japanese port of Sakamintao via Donghae in South Korea.

## Arriving by Coach

Coach travel is suitable for visitors travelling on a very tight budget. There are **Eurolines** routes to Moscow from Germany, the Czech Republic, Slovakia, Poland and Hungary, Latvia and Estonia. All these routes usually terminate at the **Moscow Central Bus Station**.

For visitors to St Petersburg, **Sovavto** runs a daytime and an overnight service from Helsinki, which drops off passengers at several locations. The journey takes around 8 hours. **Ecolines** and **Lux Express** run services from the Baltic States,

terminating at the Baltiskaya train station near Baltiyskaya metro. One-way fares cost as little as 560 roubles from Tallinn, 520 roubles from Riga and 1,280 roubles from Vilnius.

## Green Travel

Travelling to Russia by train reduces the high ecological impact of flying. As green initiatives are limited in the country, an easy way to reduce your carbon footprint is by choosing a centrally located hotel for ease of access to the main sights. Cycle hire is possible and is also one of the most eco-friendly ways to get around a city. The public transport system in most cities is good enough to make travelling by car unnecessary.

However, if you do not hike or cycle, exploring the remoter regions without your own vehicle will be difficult, as buses are slow and infrequent.

## DIRECTORY

### Arriving by Air

**Aeroflot**
[w] aeroflot.ru

**Austrian Airlines**
[w] austrian.com

**British Airways**
[w] britishairways.com

**Delta Air Lines**
[w] delta.com

**Finnair**
[w] finnair.com

**Rossiya**
[w] rossiya-airlines.com

**SAS**
[w] flysas.com

**Scott's Tours**
[w] scottstours.co.uk

**Visit Russia**
[w] visitrussia.com

### Main Airports

**Aeroexpress**
[w] aeroexpress.ru

**Domodedovo**
[w] domodedovo.ru

**Koltsovo**
[w] koltsovo.ru

**Pulkovo**
[w] pulkovoairport.ru

**Sheremetyevo**
[w] svo.aero

**Sochi International Airport**
[w] sochi-airport.com

**Vnukovo**
[w] vnukovo.ru

### Arriving by Train

**Seat 61**
[w] seat61.com

### Arriving by Sea

**Abdullah CAKIR**
[w] al-port.com

**DBS Cruise**
[w] dbsferry.com/eng/main/main.asp

**Fred Olsen Cruises**
[w] fredolsencruises.com

**P&O Cruises**
[w] pocruises.com

**St Peter Line**
[w] stpeterline.com

**Virgin Holidays**
[w] virginholidays.co.uk

### Arriving by Coach

**Ecolines**
[w] ecolines.ru

**Eurolines/
Lux Express**
[w] luxexpress.eu

**Moscow Central Bus Station**
[w] busmow.ru

**Sovavto**
[w] sovavto.ru

# Travelling around Russia

The railway network is the mainstay of long-distance travel in Russia. Although European discount passes provide little or no reduction in fares, trains are still cheaper than internal flights, and also much safer. Inter-city buses are suitable only for short trips, while travelling around by car can be difficult due to the unpredictable weather and the vagaries of the traffic police. For a leisurely tour through Russia's heartland, a river cruise on the Volga or the northern lakes is a good idea.

Aeroflot airplanes docked at the Sheremetyevo Airport

## Travelling by Air

Flying is not only the fastest form of transport between cities, but often the only way to get to some Siberian cities during the winter months or spring thaw. However, domestic aviation in Russia does not have a great safety record, especially among the smaller carriers known as "Babyflots".

All airports in Moscow handle domestic flights. Aeroflot uses Sheremetyevo's Terminal D; the low-cost airlines Transaero and **S7** use Teminal B at Domodedovo, and the Siberian **UTair Aviation** flies from Terminal A at Vnukovo. In St Petersburg, all domestic flights arrive at Pulkovo.

Aeroflot and Rossiya run regular 50- to 90-minute flights between Moscow and St Petersburg. Prices range from 2,700 roubles for an economy class one-way ticket to 4,200 roubles for business class. Tickets are sold online at airports, or through hotels and travel agencies.

Passengers need to show their passport on departure despite the fact that they will not be leaving the country.

## Travelling by Train

Russia's rail network is one of the longest in the world and provides reliable service.

**Russian Railways'** (RZD) Russian-language website covers the entire network and has a journey planner, unlike the English version. Full instructions on how to use this feature can be found on Seat 61 (see p313). Tickets can be booked online through either of these websites, or agencies specializing in rail travel such as **Russiantrains** and **RussianRail.com**. Be sure to buy tickets in advance; tickets are not sold on trains.

Owing to the long distances covered, the majority of trains are overnight sleepers, but some standard trains operate on shorter routes. Trains fall into four categories: *ekspressy* (express) trains, which travel between Moscow and St Petersburg only; *skorye* (fast) trains, which operate on long journeys and stop at only a few stations; *passazhirskie* (passenger) trains, which also operate on long routes, but stop at most or all stations; and suburban trains (see p317). Sleepers offer a choice of *spalny vagon* (two-bed cabins), *kupe* (four-person compartments), or *platzkart* (dormitory-style carriages), which is a good option for travellers on a tight budget.

Trains are the most popular form of transport between Moscow and St Petersburg; there are ten or more trains daily. The fastest is the Sapsan train, which covers the distance in less than 4 hours at speeds of up to 250 kmph (155mph).

Prices vary depending on class and services included. There is a choice between *sidyashchyy* (sitting) tickets and more expensive sleeper options. One-way prices for standard trains range from 2,500 roubles for *kupe* to 400 roubles for *sidyashchyy*, while Sapsan tickets start at 3,300 roubles. Prices do not always include bed linen, for which there is an additional small charge. On cheaper trains, the *provodnik* (carriage attendant) will issue and charge for bed linen.

## Travelling by Bus

Buses are much less comfortable than trains and are worth taking only occasionally. They are useful for travelling to sights such as Vladimir (see p116) or Veliky Novgorod (see p210) rather than big cities. Elsewhere, the

The high-speed Sapsan train running between Moscow and St Petersburg

rail network may not reach certain attractions, making buses the only option for travellers.

## Travelling by Boat

In summer, river cruises are an enjoyable way to see more of Russia. Volga cruises between Moscow and St Petersburg stop at several historic towns, on 5- to 7-day itineraries. From both cities, there are longer river cruises to Kazan *(see p225)*, Samara *(see pp228–9)* or Nizhny Novgorod *(see p224)*, and cruises on Lake Ladoga to Valaam *(see p209)* and Kizhi *(see p208–209)*.

All cruises can be booked through **Noble Caledonia** or **Voyages Jules Verne** in the UK, and through **Visit Russia** *(see p313)* in the US, often as part of a package deal including flights. Cruises can also be booked within Russia at a fairly short notice, through agencies such as **Infoflot**. Note that some boats are less modern than others, and the standard of meals can vary.

In St Petersburg, cruises depart from the *Rechnoy Vokzal* (River Terminal), which is a 10-minute walk from Proletarskaya metro. Boats in Moscow depart from *Severnoy Rechnoy Vokzal* (Northern River Terminal), a 10-minute walk from Rechnoy Vokzal metro station, or from the *Yuzhniy Rechnoy Vokzal*

(Southern River Terminal). The routes to both termini are well-signposted.

## Travelling by Car

Driving in Russia can be gruelling and is not advisable for the uninitiated. Major cities suffer from chronic traffic congestion, with cars travelling in disorderly lanes, veering dangerously to avoid pot holes. Road signs mostly follow international conventions but are rarely bilingual, so drivers should familiarize themselves with the names of places in advance.

Russia's traffic police *(see p306)*, have the right to stop drivers and ask for documents. They can issue fines on the spot for infringements such as not having a fire extinguisher or first-aid kit and not wearing seat belts. It is compulsory for both drivers and front-seat passengers to wear seat belts, although many people do not. Drivers are

Traffic congested roads during rush hour, St Petersburg

not allowed to drink any alcohol at all and fines for drunk driving can be very high.

Priority is given to traffic approaching from the right unless a yellow, diamond-shaped sign indicates otherwise. Buying driving licences, rather than obtaining them through legitimate means, is common, so not all road users are qualified and responsible.

Driving is dangerous during winter and not advisable unless drivers have had experience in other northern climes. Drivers must use studded tyres as roads are icy and covered with snow. Car rental is possible in all cities, with **Avis**, **Europcar** and **Hertz** offices at international airports.

## Guided Tours and Excursions

Local tourist agencies such as **Patriarshy Dom Tours**, **Baikaler**, **Peter's Walking Tours**, **Intourist Delta Volga**, **Sayan Ring** and **Samara Intour** offer a wide range of tours and day trips around Russia. Many of the agencies can arrange visa support and accommodation too. Tours should generally be booked at least 48 hours in advance.

---

## DIRECTORY

### Travelling by Air

**S7 Airlines**
Tel (495) 777 99 99 or (8800) 200 00 07.
W s7.ru

**UTair Aviation**
W utair.ru/en

### Travelling by Train

**General enquiries**
Tel 055.

**Russian Railways**
W rzd.ru
W eng.rzd.ru

**RussianRail.com**
W russianrail.com

**Russiantrains**
W russiantrains.com

### Travelling by Boat

**Infoflot**
W infoflot.com

**Noble Caledonia**
W noble-caledonia.co.uk

**Voyages Jules Verne**
W vjv.com

### Travelling by Car

**Avis**
W avis.com

**Europcar**
W europcar.com

**Hertz**
W hertz.com

### Guided Tours and Excursions

**Baikaler**
Ulitsa Lenina 9, Apartment 11, Irkutsk.
Tel (395) 292 96 86.
W baikaler.com

**Intourist Delta Volga**
Ulitsa Zhelyabova 33, Astrakhan.
Tel (8512) 73 22 20.
W deltavolgy.narod.ru

**Patriarshy Dom Tours**
Vspolniy pereulok 6, Moscow.

Tel (495) 795 09 27.
W toursinrussia.com

**Peter's Walking Tours**
St Petersburg.
Tel (812) 943 12 29.
W peterswalk.com

**Samara Intour**
Ulitsa Samarskaya 51/53, Samara.
Tel (846) 279 20 40.
W samaraintour.ru

**Sayan Ring**
Ulitsa Uritskogo 41, Krasnoyarsk.
Tel (391) 245 4646.
W sayanring.com

# Travelling in the Cities

Public transport in Russian cities is abundant, efficient and cheap. In major cities, the metro has stops close to many sights, but it can get extremely crowded during peak hours. Buses, trams and trolleybuses are useful for travelling to areas beyond the metro network. Knowledge of the Cyrillic alphabet will help with reading signs on these services, although signs in English can be found in some cities. Taxis are the most flexible, but also the most expensive, way of getting around.

Lavish decoration on the metro system in Moscow

## Metro

Efficient, relatively inexpensive and usually safe, metro systems are possibly the best way to get around cities in Russia.

Moscow's 305-km (190-mile) metro network has 200 stations on 11 lines plus a monorail, and is one of the busiest in the world. The circle line, which follows the Garden Ring road, intersects with other metro lines and main railway stations. Intended by Stalin to be "palaces for the people", many metro stations are adorned with statuary, murals and mosaics.

St Petersburg's metro system is one of the deepest in the world due to the city's swampy subsoil. The 114-km (71-mile) network has 68 stations on five lines.

The metro network of Novosibirsk has two lines with 13 stations and a metro bridge over the Ob river, while Nizhny Novgorod's metro is confined to the west bank, where two lines meet beside the main railway terminus.

Volgograd's **Metrotram** has 22 stations on a single line that runs along the Volga river for

17 km (11 miles) and is mostly overground beyond the city centre. Yekaterinburg's metro – the last built in the Soviet Union – has a single line with eight stations decorated with semi-precious stones from the Urals.

Kazan's metro is Russia's most advanced, with automated, driverless trains on a single line with seven stations. All signs are bilingual in Russian and Tatar.

## Using the Metro

Metro stations at street level are usually indicated by a large "M" sign and use Cyrillic signage for directions. Bilingual signs in Russian and English are at present limited to Moscow and St Petersburg.

Most metro systems operate from 6am to midnight, with trains every 2 to 5 minutes. All have flat fares, whether the journey is a couple of stops or the length of the network. Travellers with large items of luggage will be asked to pay a surcharge.

In some metro systems, the stations where it is possible to change between metro lines often have two or more separate names, according to the line

they serve. When changing lines, it is, therefore, vital to know the name of the station on the other line. It is then easy to reach the right platform by following the "interchange" or *perekhod* signs indicating this name. Exits are marked "выход" *(vykhod)*.

It is advisable to buy enough rides for your stay in any city at the outset, to avoid queuing at the *kassa*. In Moscow, visitors can buy a smart card for 1, 2, 5, 10, 20 or 60 rides, or a travel pass that allows unlimited travel for three months. Any number of people can travel on the same card. When the card is swiped at the barrier, the number of journeys left will be reduced by one. The number of remaining journeys will then flash up on the barrier display.

In St Petersburg, travellers pay for rides with a *zheton* (plastic token) or magnetic cards that can be topped up with as many trips as needed. Monthly magnetic cards are valid for 70 metro journeys during a calendar month. Cards valid for 35 journeys for a two-week period can be bought between the 5th and 16th of each month. Note that all cards are valid from the 1st to the 15th of each month.

## Buses and Minibuses

In major cities, buses are useful for travelling to outlying suburbs. Bus stops are often shared with trolleybus stops and marked by a white and yellow sign showing the Cyrillic letter "A".

Bus routes are often duplicated by *marshrutki* (minibuses) serving the city centre, outlying suburbs and malls. Minibuses can be

A tram passing through Irkutsk en route to suburban areas

Double-decker boat cruising down the Moskva river

hailed or requested to stop anywhere along the route. Fares are fixed, usually 30 to 100 roubles, and are paid to the driver.

## Trolleybuses and Trams

Trolleybuses are an environmentally friendly way of travelling around towns and cities. The stops are marked by a sign with a bus symbol on a white background and the Cyrillic letter "T".

Trams remain the country's most traditional means of transport. Although services have been cut back over the years, the remaining services run frequently, especially in the suburbs, providing links to metro stations and apartment blocks. Stops are marked by a sign labelled "Tp" in Cyrillic with a tram symbol on a white background.

## Tickets and Travel cards

Tickets valid for 1, 2, 5, 10, 15, 20 or 60 local journeys can be bought in cities across Russia. The same tickets can be used on all buses, trolleybuses and trams for a single ride without changes. Tickets are bought from kiosks next to bus stops or from the vehicle's driver. In St Petersburg, visitors can also buy a monthly or a half-monthly travel card for all forms of transport.

## Taxis

For safety reasons, it is best to travel by official taxis, which should at least have a taxi light on the roof and some kind of chequered markings. However, in provincial cities, travellers rely on rides from local moonlighters,

which can mean travelling in a private car for a negotiable sum. This is best avoided if you are travelling alone at night. Visitors speaking little or no Russian should stick to pre-ordered cabs from firms such as **Taxi956** in Moscow or **Six Million** in St Petersburg. Fares must be negotiated in advance. You can ask hotel or restaurant staff to book a taxi by phone.

## Boat Trips

From May to October, some cities offer a variety of superb boat trips, which should not be confused with cruises on Russia's great waterways. The commentary is usually in Russian only.

In Moscow, the boat trips cover a long stretch of the Moskva river, offering a fabulous view of the Kremlin, run by **Capital Shipping Company** from May to October. You can hop on or off at ten sights, such as the Novodevichiy Convent and the Uritskiy Bridge.

In St Petersburg, large covered boats depart from the Anichkov Bridge on Nevskiy prospekt (see p166). A 60-minute trip for about 500 roubles takes in the Moyka and Fontanka rivers, and sometimes the Griboedov Canal. For 100 roubles more, you can get a guided tour in English from **Anglotourismo**.

## Suburban Trains and Buses

*Prigorodnye poezda* (suburban trains) depart from an annexe to mainline stations. Popularly known as *elecktrichki*, they are busy at weekends when Russians head for their *dachas*.

# DIRECTORY

## Metro

**Metrotram Volgograd**
Ⓦ volgograd.metro.ru

**Moscow**
Ⓦ engl.mosmetro.ru

**St Petersburg**
Ⓦ metro.spb.ru

## Taxis

**Six Million**
Ⓦ 6-000-000.ru

**Taxi956**
Ⓦ taxi956.ru

## Boat Trips

**Anglotourismo**
Ⓦ anglotourismo.com

**Capital Shipping Company**
Ⓦ cck-ship.ru

## Cycling

**Kruti-Pedali**
Ⓦ kruti-pedali.ru

**Rentbike**
Ⓦ Rentbike.org

**Skatprokat**
Ⓦ skatprokat.ru

**Velotour**
Ⓦ velotour-spb.ru

All cities have a network of *prigorodnye marshruty* (suburban buses) and one or more terminals for *mezhdugorodnye avtobusy* (inter-city buses). These buses are useful where trains are too slow or do not allow access to sights you might want to visit.

## Cycling

Traffic-congested roads make most cities far from ideal for cycling. Cyclists are advised to wear brightly coloured clothing – drivers will generally take care to avoid cyclists if they notice them.

In Moscow, **Kruti-Pedali** offers bikes and equipment for hire costing around 500–600 roubles. In St Petersburg, daily rental costs 600–800 roubles from **Rentbike**, **Skatprokat** or **Velotour**, who also deliver on request. Elsewhere in Russia, adventure-travel companies offer cycling tours of the great outdoors.

# General Index

Page numbers in **bold** refer to
main entries.

17th-century Life and Applied Arts
Museum (Moscow) 56
35mm (Moscow) 121

## A

Abkhazia 245
*Abraham's Sacrifice* (Rembrandt) 154
Abramovich, Roman 47
Abramtsevo Estate-Museum 110,
113, **114**
Academic Capella
(St Petersburg) **169**
Accessories 118–19
Accommodation agencies 265
Adam, Yegor 169
Addresses 304
Adler **242**, 271, 290
Admission charges 303
Adrianople, Treaty of 237, 243
Adventure sports 23, 298–9
Afghanistan, invasion of 45
Aguin, Treaty of 257
*Ahasuerus, Haman and Esther*
(Rembrandt) 91
Air travel
arriving in Russia 312, 313
travelling around Russia 314, 315
Akhmatova, Anna 31, 182
Alabin, Petr 228
Alabin Museum (Samara) **228**
Aleksandrovskiy Convent (Suzdal)
26, 117
Aleksandrovskiy Park (St Petersburg)
135, **140**
Aleksey, Tsarevich 136, 137, 139
Aleksey II, Patriarch 68
Alexander I, Tsar 42, 61, 152
Alexander II, Tsar 43, 133, 138, 162
assassination 43, 133, 156, 162
emancipation of the serfs 80
wedding 156
Alexander III, Tsar 43, 152, 162, 164
Alexander Column (St Petersburg)
152
Alexander Gardens (Moscow) **61**
Alexander Nevsky Monastery
(St Petersburg) 166, 178, 179, **183**
Alexandrinskiy Theatre
(St Petersburg) 167
Alexis, Tsar 41, 63, 72, 104, 109, 110
Altai Mountains 39, 248, 298, 299
Altai Museum of Regional Studies
and History (Barnaul) 252
Altai Republic 246, 252
Amber 213, 217, 219, 294
Amber Beach (Kaliningrad) 35
Amber Museum
(Kaliningrad) **217**
Amber Room (Tsarskoe Selo) 188,
189
Amur Gulf 257
Amur river 24, 257
Amvrosiy, Archbishop 108
Anapa 238, **243**, 271, 290
Andropov, Yuri 45, 69
Angara river 252, 253

Angleterre Hotel (St Petersburg) 147,
**149**
Anichkov, Colonel Mikhail 166
Anichkov Bridge (St Petersburg) **166**
Anichkov Palace (St Petersburg) **166**
Anikushin, Mikhail 163
Anna Akhmatova Museum
(St Petersburg) 182
Anna Ioannovna, Empress 42, 63
*Annunciation* (Botticelli) 90
Annunciation Cathedral (Kazan) 225
Annunciation Cathedral (Moscow)
27, 52, 55, **57**
Annunciation Church (Alexander
Nevsky Monastery) 183
Annunciation Monastery (Nizhny
Novgorod) 224
Anti-Semitism 43
Antique Automobile Museum
(Vladivostok) 257
Antiques 118, 119
Apartments 264, 265
*Apollo in the Chariot of the Sun*
(Klodt) 82
*The Appearance of Christ to the People*
(Ivanov) 94, 98
Arbat Square (Moscow) 12, **89**
Arboretum (Sochi) **240–41**
Archaeological Museum (Anapa)
243
Archangel Cathedral (Moscow)
55, **57**
Archangel Mikhail Cathedral
(Nizhny Novgorod) 224
Architecture **32–3**
Arctic Ocean 24, 25
Argunov, Fyodor 109
Argunov, Pavel 111
Armenia 245
Armoury Chamber (Moscow) 12, 33,
54, **62–3**
Arms industry 21
Art galleries *See* Museums and
galleries
Artillery Museum (St Petersburg) **140**
Arts 22, **28–9**
Arts Square (St Petersburg) 159,
160, **163**
Askoldov, Aleksandr 29
Assumption Cathedral (Astrakhan)
233
Assumption Cathedral (Moscow) 12,
32, 51, 55, **58–9**
Assumption Cathedral (Omsk) 250
Assumption Cathedral (Trinity
Monastery of St Sergius) 114–15
Assumption Cathedral (Vladimir)
32, 116
Assumption Monastery (Sviyazhsk)
14, 226
Astrakhan 10, 14, 40, 221, 222, **233**
Where to Eat and Drink 289
Where to Stay 270
Astrakhan Biosphere Reserve **233**
Ataman Palace (Starocherkassk) 245
ATMs 308
Autumn 36–7
Autumn Rhythms (St Petersburg) 36
Azerbaijan 245
Azimov Mosque (Kazan) 225
Azov 245

## B

B&Bs 262, 264
Babel, Isaac 31
*Bacchanalia* (Rubens) 91
Bach, Robert 175
Baikal, Lake 24, 203, 247, 248, **253**,
254–5
A week in Baikal Region 11, 15
Baikal Museum (Listvyanka) 253
Bakhrushin, Aleksey 95, 101
Bakhrushin Theatre Museum
(Moscow) 95, **101**
Bakst, Léon 175
Balabanov, Alexei 29
Ballet 22, 28–9, **175**, 296, 297
*See also* Entertainment
Ballets Russes 101, 175
Baltic House (St Petersburg) 36
Baltic Republics 46
Baltic Sea, resorts 213, 214, 218–19
Banking and Currency **308–309**
Banya 75, 298, 299
Baranovskiy, Pyotr 68, 72
Barclay de Tolly, Mikhail 168
Bargaining 292
*Barge Haulers on the Volga* (Repin)
165
Barnaul **252**
Baroque architecture 32
Basil III, Tsar 104
Battle of Stalingrad Panorama
Museum (Volgograd) 10, **232**
Batu Khan 40
Bazhenov, Vasily 33, 97, 100, 109,
163
Bears, brown 25, 203, 259
Beer 228, 274–5, 279
Behrens, Peter 146
Bekmambetov, Timur 29
Belarus 46
Bell Tower (Novodevichiy Convent)
105
Benois, Alexandre 173, 175
Benois, Leontiy 164, 169
Berezovsky, Boris 47
Béthencourt, General Augustin
de 81
Bicycle hire 313, 317
Biron, Count 42
Birzhevaya ploshchad (Moscow)
66, 73
Black Sea 20, 237, 238, 242
resorts and beaches 240, 242, 243
Blank, Karl 109
Blessed Virgin Church (Nizhny
Novgorod) 14, 220, 224
Blok, Alexander 31
Bloody Sunday 43, 152
Boat travel
around Russia 315
in cities 317
Bobrovy Log Ski Resort 251
Bogaevski, Konstantin 241
Bogolyubov, Veniamin 172
Bolgar 221, 222, **226–7**
Bolshaya Nikitskaya Ulitsa **87**
Bolsheviks 44, 179, 182
political prisoners 139
seize power 149
storm Winter Palace 141, 152, 156
Bolshoi Ballet, Soviet era **83**

Bolshoi Dramatic Theatre
(St Petersburg) 296, 297
Bolshoi Theatre (Moscow) 22, 29, 50,
79, **82–3**, 120
Bolshoi Zal (Moscow Conservatory)
**87**
Bondarchuk, Sergei 29
Booking
hotels 262
restaurants 275
Bookshops 119
Boris Godunov, Tsar 40, 56, 108
Borodin, Alexander 22, 28
Borodino 113, **115**
re-enactment of the Battle
of Borodino 36
Botanical Gardens (Moscow) 111
Botticelli, Sandro, *Annunciation* 90
Bove, Osip 33, 80, 82, 96, 100
Boyars 39, 40, 41
Brachert, Hermann 219
Bread Museum (Bolgar) 227
Brenna, Vincenzo 163, 190, 191
Brezhnev, Leonid 29, 45
tomb 69
Brik, Lilya 75
Brik, Osip 75
Brodsky, Joseph 31
Bronze Horseman, The
(St Petersburg) 145, 146, **148**
Bryullov, Aleksandr 157
Bryullov, Karl 150, 151, 165
Bryusov Pereulok (Moscow) 77, 78,
**84**
*Bucentaur's Return to the Pier by the
Palazzo Ducale* (Canaletto) 91
Buddhism 248, 256
Buddhist New Year 37
Budget accommodation 264, 265
Bulgakov, Mikhail 31, 84, 86
Bulgakov House and Museum
(Moscow) 77, **86**
Bulla, Karl 166
Bunin, Ivan 31
Bunker Museum (Kaliningrad) **216**
Buryat History Museum (Ulan-Ude)
11, 15, 256
Buryatia Republic 256
Buryats 11, 15, 248, 253, 256, 298
Bus travel
in cities 316–17
long-distance 314–15
Byzantine Orthodox Christianity
39, 40
Byzantine style 32

**C**

Cabin of Peter the Great
(St Petersburg) **141**
Cameron, Charles 188, 189, 190, 191
Camping 265
Canaletto 91
Carlo Rossi 33, 146, 148, 152, 160,
163, 164, **167**, 180, 183
Car rental 315
Car travel 315
Caspian Sea 10, 20, 221, 233
Castles and fortifications
Friedland Gate (Kaliningrad) 217
Georgenburg Castle
(Chernyakhovsk) 214, 219

Castles and fortifications (cont.)
Insterburg Castle (Chernyakhovsk)
214, 219
King's Gate (Kaliningrad) 217
Kremlin (Astrakhan) 10, 14, 233
Kremlin (Kazan) 10, 14, 225
Kremlin (Moscow) 52–63
Kremlin (Nizhny Novgorod) 14, 224
Kremlin (Pskov) 211
Kremlin (Veliky Novgorod) 207, 210
Mikhaylovskiy Castle
(St Petersburg) 161, 163
Peter and Paul Fortress
(St Petersburg) 13, 133, 134, 136–8
Schlüsselburg Fortress (Lake
Ladoga) 139
Trubetskoy Bastion (St Petersburg)
136, 139
Cathedrals
Annunciation Cathedral (Kazan)
225
Annunciation Cathedral (Moscow)
27, 52, 55, **57**
Archangel Mikhail Cathedral
(Nizhny Novgorod) 224
Assumption Cathedral (Astrakhan)
233
Assumption Cathedral (Omsk) 250
Cathedral of Archangel (Moscow)
55, 57
Cathedral of the Assumption
(Moscow) 12, 32, 51, 55, **58–9**
Cathedral of the Assumption
(Trinity Monastery of St Sergius)
114–15
Cathedral of the Assumption
(Vladimir) 32, 116
Cathedral of Christ the Saviour
(Kaliningrad) 215, **217**
Cathedral of Christ the Saviour
(Moscow) 12, 33, 76, **89**
Cathedral of Our Lady of Kazan
(St Petersburg) 13, 168
Cathedral of St Demetrius
(Vladimir) 116
Cathedral of St Sofia (Tobolsk) 250
Cathedral of St Sophia (Veliky
Novgorod) 210
Cathedral of the Nativity (Suzdal)
117
Cathedral of the Transfiguration
(St Petersburg) 181
Cathedral of the Virgin of Smolensk
(Novodevichiy Convent) 104
Dormition Cathedral (Khabarovsk)
257
Epiphany Cathedral (Irkutsk) 15,
252
Grand Cathedral (Donskoy
Monastery) 108
Holy Trinity Cathedral (Alexander
Nevsky Monastery) 183
Holy Trinity Cathedral (Magadan)
259
Kazan Cathedral (Moscow) 64, **68**
Königsberg Cathedral (Kaliningrad)
214, **216**
Nativity of the Blessed Virgin
Cathedral (Rostov-na-Donu)
244, 245
Odigitria Cathedral (Ulan-Ude) 256

Cathedrals (cont.)
Resurrection Cathedral
(Starocherkassk) 245
St Basil's Cathedral (Moscow) 12,
32, 51, 68, **70–71**
St Isaac's Cathedral (St Petersburg)
13, 19, 145, 146, **150–51**
St Nicholas's Cathedral (St
Petersburg) 132, 171, 173, **174–5**
SS Peter and Paul Cathedral (St
Petersburg) 13, 133, 135, 137,
**138–9**
St Peter and Paul's Cathedral
(Kazan) 225
Theodore Ushakov Cathedral
(Saransk) 227
Transfiguration Cathedral (Valaam)
209
Trinity Cathedral (Pskov) 207, 211,
211
Trinity Cathedral (Trinity Monastery
of St Sergius) 115
*See also* Churches; Convents;
Monasteries
Catherine I, Empress 41, 42, 153,
188, 225
Catherine II, the Great 42, 62, 63, 109,
110, 153, 154, 157, 167, 183, 185,
186, 188, 190, 244
death of husband 163
lovers 152, 154, 166, 181
tributes to Peter the Great 141,
148
The Caucasus 25, **236–45**
food 277
getting around 239
map 238–9
Where to Eat and Drink 290
Where to Stay 271–2
Caucasus Mountains 236, 237, 238,
240, 242, 298
Caviar 23, 292, 294
Caving 298, 299
Central and Southern Russia **220–35**
getting around 223
map 222–3
Where to Eat and Drink 289–90
Where to Stay 270–71
Ceramics 295
Cézanne, Paul 88
Chancellor, Richard 72
Chechnya 47, 245
Cheka 74
Chekhov, Anton 22, 28, 31, 78, 84,
86, 105, 167
Chekhov House-Museum
(Moscow) **86**
Cheremushkinskiy Market
(Moscow) 118, 119
Cherepanov, Yefim and Miron 177
Cherkasskaya, Varvara 109
Chernenko, Konstantin 45
Chernobyl disaster 46
Cherny, Daniil 116
Chernyakhovsk 214, **219**
Chesma Church (St Petersburg)
179, **183**
Chess sets 294
Chevakinsky, Savva 174, 175, 188
Children
entertainment 121, 297

Children (cont.)
  in hotels 263
  in restaurants 275
  travelling with 304
Children's Art Gallery (Samara) **228**
*Christ in Majesty* (Klodt) 150
Christ the Saviour Cathedral
  (Kaliningrad) 215, **217**
Christ the Saviour Cathedral
  (Moscow) 12, 33, 77, **89**
Christianity 23, 26–7, 39
Christmas 37
Churches 26–7, 303
  Chesma Church (St Petersburg)
    179, 183
  Church of the Annunciation
    (Alexander Nevsky Monastery) 183
  Church of the Blessed Virgin
    (Nizhny Novgorod) 14, 220, 224
  Church of the Consolation of All
    Sorrows (Moscow) 96, **100**
  Church of Laying Our Lady's Holy
    Robe (Moscow) 55, **60**
  Church of the Nativity of the Virgin
    in Putinki (Moscow) 85
  Church of Our Saviour (Irkutsk) 252
  Church of the Resurrection in
    Kadashi (Moscow) 96, **100**
  Church of St Clement (Moscow) 97
  Church of St Maxim the Blessed
    (Moscow) 67, 72
  Church of St Nicholas in Pyzhy
    (Moscow) **100**
  Church of St Nicholas of the
    Weavers (Moscow) **107**
  Church of the Saviour Not Made
    by Human Hand (Abramtsevo)
    114
  Church of the Trinity in Nikitniki
    (Moscow) 67, **73**
  Church of the Twelve Apostles
    (Moscow) 56
  Church on Spilled Blood
    (St Petersburg) 13, 33, 133, 158,
    160, **162**
  Church on the Blood
    (Yekaterinburg) 235
  Gate Church of the Intercession
    (Novodevichiy Convent) 104
  Gate Church of the Transfiguration
    (Novodevichiy Convent) 105
  Intercession Church (Kizhi) 32, 208
  Resurrection of Lazarus Church
    (Kizhi) 208–9
    Transfiguration Church (Kizhi) 32,
    204, 208
    Voskresenskaya Church (Tomsk)
    251  *See also* Cathedrals;
    Convents; Monasteries
Cinema 22, 29, 121, 296, 297
Circum-Baikal Railway 11, 15, 253
Circus
  Moscow 121
  St Petersburg 161, 297
City Day (Moscow) 36
City Day (St Petersburg) 34
City History Museum (Tomsk) 251
City Life Museum (Irkutsk) 15, 252
Civil War 44, 139, 257
Classical music 22, 28, 120, 121, 296,
  297
Claudio, Antonio 108
Climate 20, 36–7, 302
Climbing 298, 299

Clubs, Moscow 120–21
Coach travel 313
Cold War 45
Collective agriculture 44
Commandant's House
  (St Petersburg) 135, 136, **139**
Communications **310–11**
Communism 19, 44–7
  Fall 21, 46
  Party conferences 56
Composers' Union 84
Concert halls *See* Theatres and
  concert halls
Conservation 20, 305
Consolation of All Sorrows Church
  (Moscow) 96, 100
Constantine Monomachus, Emperor
  59, 63
Constructivism 33
Contemporary Art Museum (Perm)
  234
Contemporary History Museum
  (Moscow) **85**
Convents
  Aleksandrovskiy Convent (Suzdal)
    26, 117
  Convent of the Intercession
    (Suzdal) 117
  Convent of SS Martha and Mary
    (Moscow) **101**
  Novodevichiy Convent (Moscow)
    32, 102, **104–5**
  Smolnyy Convent (St Petersburg)
    157, 179, **182**
  *See also* Monasteries
Cosmonautics Museum
  (St Petersburg) 137, 138
Cossack Fairs (Starocherkassk) 34
Cossacks 237, 238, 244, 245, 247,
  250, 251, 253, 257
Courier services 311
Crafts 23, 294–5
  *See also* shopping
Credit cards 308
  at tourist sights 303
  in hotels 262, 304
  in restaurants 275, 304
  in shops 292
Crime 21, 306
Crimean War 43
Crown of Monomakh (Moscow) 63
Cruiser Aurora (St Petersburg) **141**
Cruises 313, 315
Cuban Missile Crisis 45
Cuisine 274
  *See also* Restaurants, cafés and bars
Culture 22
Culture and History Museum
  (Krasnoyarsk) 251
Curonian Spit 202, 213, 214, **218**
Currency 304, 308–9
Customs regulations 302
Cycling 313, 317
Cyril, St 26
Cyrillic alphabet 302, 303
Czechoslovakia, Prague Spring 45

**D**

*Dachas* 34, 113, 265, 276
Dagestan 245
Danilovskiy Market (Moscow) 118, 119
*La Danse* (Matisse) 155
Dawe, George 156
Day of National Unity 37

Day of Russia 35
Day of Slav Culture 34
December Nights (Moscow) 120
Decembrist Rebellion 43, 139, 145,
  148, 252
Defender of the Fatherland Day 37
Democracy, managed 47
Dental treatment 307
Department stores 293
Deserts 24
Dmitri, False 40–41, 56
Dmitri, Tsarevich 55
Dog-sledding 299
Dogadin Art Gallery (Astrakhan)
  233
Dolgorukiy, Prince Yuri 53, 78
Dolgov House (Moscow) 97
Dolphinarium (St Petersburg) 297
Dom Kino (St Petersburg) 296, 297
Dome (Moscow) 121
Don river 20, 232, 238, 244–5
Donskoy, Prince Dmitri 26, 40, 108,
  116
Donskoy Monastery (Moscow) 103,
  **108**
Dormition Cathedral (Khabarovsk)
  257
Dorogomilovsky Market (Moscow)
  118, 119
Dostoevsky, Fyodor 22, 30, 139, 163,
  171, **177**, 182, 183
Dostoevsky House-Museum
  (St Petersburg) **182–3**
Drama 22, 28, 121, 296–7
Dress code, in restaurants 275
Drinks *See* Food and drink
Driving 315
Duma 43
Durov Animal Theatre (Moscow) 121
Dushkin, Alexei 240
Dzerzhinskiy, Feliks 74, 107

**E**

*Ea Haere la Oe* (Gauguin) 155
Easter Sunday 34
Economy 20–21
Ecosystems 24–5
Edict of Emancipation 43
Eisenstein, Sergei 22, 29
Elections 46, 47
Electricity 304
Elizabeth, Empress 32, 42, 156, 166,
  181, 182, 185, 186, 188
Embassies and consulates 303, 305
Emergencies 306, 307
Engels, Freidrich 61
Engineer's House (St Petersburg)
  135, 137, 138
Entertainment **296–7**
  in Moscow **120–21**
Environmental issues 20, 305
Epiphany Cathedral (Irkutsk) 15,
  252
Era of Stagnation 45
Erarta (St Petersburg) 179, **180**
Erzia, Stepan 227

Ethnic mix 19, 23
Ethnographic Museum (Ulan-Ude) 15, 248, 256, 256
Ethnographic tourism 298–9
Etiquette
churches and mosques 303
social 304
Evenk tribe 253
Exchange bureaux 308
Exhibition of Achievements of National Economy (VDNKh), The **111**
Export restrictions 292

**F**

Fabergé eggs 62
Faceted Chamber (Moscow) 53, 55, **61**
Falconet, Etienne 145, 146, 148
Famine 44
Far Eastern Arts Museum (Khabarovsk) 257
Farmers' Market (Moscow) 118, 119
Fashion 22, 118–19
Fast-food chains 274
Fax services 310–11
Fayoum Portrait 91
February Revolution (1917) 181
Federal Customs Service 292, 293
Festival of Festivals 296, 297
Festival of Russian Theatres 297
Festivals and events 22, **34–7**
Feuchtwangen, Siegfried von 217
Field of Mars (St Petersburg) 145, **153**, 163
FIFA World Cup™ 221, 227, 245, 299
Film 22, 29, 121, 296–7
Fine Arts Museum (Yekaterinburg) 235
Finland Station (St Petersburg) 140, **180**
Fioravanti, Aristotele 58
Five-Year Plans 44
Fokin, Mikhail 101, 173, 175
Fokina, Vera 175
Folk music 297
Folk tales 30
Fontana, Ludwig 161
Fontanka river (St Petersburg) 160, 161, 163, 166
Food and drink
The Flavours of Russia **276–7**
health precautions 307
shopping for 118, 119
What to Drink 274–5, **278–9**
See also Restaurants, cafés and bars
Football 299
Forests 20, 25
Former Nicholas Market (St Petersburg) 173
Fortress Museum (Vladivostok) 257
Four Nations Tournament 37
Franchioli, Enrico 174
Frederick I of Prussia 217
Frescoes 27
Friazin, Marco Bon 56
Friedland Gate (Kaliningrad) **217**
Friedrich Wilhelm I of Prussia 189
Front Gate Museum (Kolomenskoe) 109
Futurism 29
Fyodor I, Tsar 40
Fyodor III, Tsar 41
Fyodor Filaret, Patriarch 73

**G**

Gabriadze, Rezo 161
Gagarin, Yuri 45, 69, 229, 241
Galleries See Museums and galleries
Gallery of 19th- and 20th-Century European and American Art (Moscow) 12, **88**
Garden Ring (Moscow) 50, **76–93**
area map 77
Street-by-Street map: Around Theatre Square 78–9
Where to Eat and Drink 280–1
Where to Stay 266
Gardens See Parks and gardens
Gate Church of the Intercession (Novodevichiy Convent) 104
Gate Church of the Transfiguration (Novodevichiy Convent) 105
Gauguin, Paul 88
Ea Haere Ia Oe 155
Gay and lesbian travellers 304, 305
Gelendzhik 237, 238, **243**, 271–2, 290
General Staff Building (St Petersburg) 33, 152
Genghis Khan 40
Geography 20
Georgenburg Castle 214, 219
Georgia 245
Geysers 25, 203, 259
Gilardi, Domenico 81
Glasnost 46
Glazunov, Ilya 88
Glazunov Picture Gallery (Moscow) **88**
Glinka, Mikhail 28, 169, 175
Gogen, Alexander von 141
Gogol, Nikolai 22, 28, 30, 166, 167
Golden Gate (Vladimir) 116
Golden Horde 40, 95
Golden Horn Bay 257
Golden Ring 113
Goncharova, Natalya 29, 87, 93
Gorbachev, Mikhail 29, 46, 74
Gorky, Maxim 69, 84, 86–7, 88, 106, 224
Gorky House-Museum (Moscow) 33, **86–7**
Gorky Park (Moscow) 103, **108**
Gorodetskiy, Prokhor 57
Gostinyy Dvor (St Petersburg) **158–69**
area map 159
Street-by-Street map: Around Arts Square 160–61
Where to Eat and Drink 285–6
Where to Stay 268
Gostinyy Dvor department store (St Petersburg) 166–7
Goths 39
Government 21
Grand Cathedral (Donskoy Monastery) 108
Grand Ducal Mausoleum (St Petersburg) 137, 139
Grand Dukes 139
Grand Hotel Europe (St Petersburg) 159, 160, **163**
Grand Kremlin Palace (Moscow) 33, 53, 54, **60**
Great Bulgar Museum (Bolgar) 226, 227
Great Fire of Moscow 32, 33, 77, 81, 87, 100
Great Hall of the Philharmonia (St Petersburg) 160, 163, 296, 297
Great Northern War 41, 185, 208

Greeks 237, 240, 243
Green travel 305, 313
Griboedov, Alexander 28
Griboedov Canal (St Petersburg) 160, 174
Grozny 47
Grushinsky Festival (Samara) 35
Guided tours and excursions 315
Gulag 31, 44, 45, 84, 209, 234, 247, 258, 259
Gulag History Museum (Moscow) 79, **111**
Gulf of Finland 132, 185, 186
GUM (Moscow) 12, 65, **69**, 118, 293
Gusinsky, Vladimir 47

**H**

Halloween Night 36–7
Hannibal, Abram 169
Hanseatic League 210, 211
Health 306–307
Helikon Opera (Moscow) 120, 121
Hermann Brachert House-Museum (Otradnoe) 219
Hermann, Josef 151
Hermitage (St Petersburg) 13, 42, 133, 147, **154–7**
Hermogen, Patriarch 58
Herodotus 39
Historical and Architectural Museum Reserve (Starocherkassk) 245
Historical Museum (Moscow) 10, 33, 68
Historicism 33
History of Russia, The **38–47**
History, Architecture and Art Museum (Pskov) 205, 211
History, Architecture and Art Museum (Veliky Novgorod) 210
History and Art Museum (Kaliningrad) **216**
History Museum (Sochi) **240**
Hitler, Adolf 149
Ho Chi Minh 69
Holy Trinity Cathedral (Alexander Nevsky Monastery) 183
Holy Trinity Cathedral (Magadan) 259
Homestays 264, 265
Horseguards' Manège (St Petersburg) 145, 146, **148–9**
Hospitals and clinics 307
Hostels 264, 265
Hot-air balloons 35
Hotel Metropol (Moscow) 77, 79, **80**
Hotel National (Moscow) 77, 78, **81**
Hotels 262–73
The Caucasus 271–72
Central and Southern Russia 270–71
general information 262–5
Kaliningrad 270
Moscow 266–8
Northern Russia 270
St Petersburg 268–9
Siberia and the Far East 272–3
House of Unions (Moscow) 77, 79, **80**
Huns 39
Hygiene Museum (St Petersburg) 161

**I**

Ice hockey 37, 299
Icon of the Kazan Virgin 68
Iconostasis 26–7
Icons 26–7, 29

Ilyin, Lev 161
Imperial Ballet School 167, 175
Imperial Stables (St Petersburg)
    **169**
Ingal, Vladimir 172
Insterburg Castle 214, 219
Institute of Russian Literature
    (Pushkin House) (St Petersburg)
    **142**
Insurance, medical 306, 307
Intercession Church (Kizhi) 32, 208
Intercession Convent (Suzdal) 117
International Early Music Festival 36
International Women's Day 34
Internet access 310
Invitations, letters of 302
Ipatiev, Nikolai 235
Irina Gudunova, Tsarina 104
Irkutsk 15, 247, 248, **252**
    Where to Eat and Drink 290
    Where to Stay 272
Irtysh river 250
Islam 23, 221, 225, 226
The Islands (St Petersburg) **134–43**
    area map 135
    Street-by-Street map: Peter and
        Paul Fortress 136–7
    Where to Eat and Drink 283–4
Istomin, Nazariy 60
ITAR-TASS news agency 87
Itegelov, Dashi-Dorzho 256
Itineraries, suggested **10–15**
Ivan I of Muscovy 40
Ivan III the Great, Tsar 40
    Kremlin 53, 55, 56, 57, 58, 61
Ivan III the Great Bell Tower
    (Moscow) 55, **56–7**
Ivan IV the Terrible, Tsar 40, 51, 57, 59,
    67, 70, 72
    birth 109
    defeat of Mongols 114
    expansion of Empire 70, 221, 225,
        226, 233
    Streltsy guard 95
*Ivan the Terrible and his Son Ivan on
    16 November, 1581* (Repin) 99
Ivan V, Tsar 41, 42
Ivanov, Alexander 94, 98
Ivolginsky Datsan 11, 15, 248, **256**
Izmaylovo (Moscow) 37, 103, **110**
Izmaylovo Crafts Market (Moscow)
    110, 118, 119
Izvestiya 85

**J**

Jacot, Paul 163
Jazz 297
John the Baptist Monastery
    (Sviyazhsk) 226

**K**

Kadyrov, Ramzan 245
Kalashnikov, Mikhail 60
Kaliningrad (city) 213, 214, 215, **216–17**
    map 217
    Where to Eat and Drink 289
    Where to Stay 270
Kaliningrad (region) 35, **212–19**
    getting around 215
    map 214–15
    Where to Eat and Drink 289
    Where to Stay 270

Kalmyk Steppe 24
Kalmyks 23
Kamchatka 25, 203, 249, **259**, 298
Kamennoostrovskiy Prospekt
    (St Petersburg) 135, **140**
Kaminskiy, Aleksandr 66
Kamwa Festival (Perm) 35
Kandinsky, Vasily 22, 29, 88, 233
Kant, Immanuel 216
Karelia 205, 208
Karelia Fine Arts Museum
    (Petrozavodsk) 208
Katun river 299
Kavos, Albert 79, 82, 163, 174, 176
Kayaking 299
Kazakh tribes 250
Kazakov, Matvei 33, 79, 80, 81, 109
Kazan 14, 40, 221, 222, **225**, 226,
    230–31
    Where to Eat and Drink 289
    Where to Stay 270
Kazan, Battle of 114
Kazan Cathedral (Moscow) 64, **68**
Kazanka river 225
KGB 74
Khabarov, Yerofey 257
Khabarovsk 248, **257**
    climate 37
    Where to Eat and Drink 290
    Where to Stay 272
Khanova, Ildar 226
Khazars 39
Khodorkovsky, Mikhail 47
Khrushchev, Nikita 45, 81, 85, 105
Kievan Rus 26, 39
King's Gate (Kaliningrad) **217**
Kirov, Sergei 44, 140–41, 182
Kirov Museum (St Petersburg) **140–41**
Kitay Gorod (Moscow) 50, 65
    Street-by-Street map **66–7**
    *See also* Red Square and Kitay Gorod
Kizhi 202, 204, 205, 206, **208–209**
    Kizhi Volost Festival 35
Kizhi Museum (Petrozavodsk) 208
Kizhi State Open-Air Museum 208, 209
Klein, Roman 90
Klin 115
Klodt, Pyotr 147, 149, 166
    *Apollo in the Chariot of the Sun* 82
    *Christ in Majesty* 150
Klyuchevskaya Sopka 298
Knipper-Chekhova, Olga 86
Knowledge Day 36
Kolokolnikov, Fedot and Menas 175
Kolomenskoe (Moscow) 103, **109**
Kolyma region 259
Kolyvan Vase 154
Komsomolsk-na-Amur 248, **258**
    Where to Eat and Drink 291
    Where to Stay 272
Königsberg *See* Kaliningrad
Königsberg Cathedral (Kaliningrad)
    214, **216**
Korenev, Vyacheslav 241
Kosmonavt (St Petersburg) 297
Kramskoy, Ivan 98
Krasnaya Polyana 237, 238, **242**, 272
Krasnodar 237, 238, 239, **244**, 272, 290
Krasnoyarsk 248, **251**, 272, 291
Kremlin (Astrakhan) 10, 14, 233
Kremlin (Kazan) 10, 14, 225
Kremlin (Moscow) **52–63**
    area map 53
    Street-by-Street map 54–5

Kremlin (Nizhny Novgorod) 14, 224
Kremlin (Pskov) 211
Kremlin (Veliky Novgorod) 207,
    210
Kropotkin, Prince Pyotr 139
Krylov, Ivan 86, 153
Kryukov Canal (St Petersburg) 174
Kshesinskaya, Matilda 141
Kshesinskaya Mansion (St Petersburg)
    33, 135, **141**
Kul Sharif Mosque (Kazan) 14, 225,
    230–31
Kulikovo, Battle of 40, 108
Kungur Ice Cave 222, **235**, 298
Kunstkammer (St Petersburg) 132,
    135, **142–3**
Kurilskoe, Lake 259
Kuskovo (Moscow) 35, 103, **109**
Kustodiev, Boris 233
Kustodiev House Museum
    (Astrakhan) 233
Kutuzov, Marshal Mikhail 115, 168
Kuybyshev, Valerian Vladimirovich
    228
Kuybyshev Reservoir 226

**L**

Labour Day 34
Lacquered artifacts 295
Ladoga, Lake 205, 206, 209
Lakes 24
    *See also* by name
Landé, Jean-Baptiste 167, 175
Landscape and Wildlife 20, **24–5**
Language 23, 303
Large Puppet Theatre (St Petersburg)
    297
Lasch, Otto 216
*The Last Day of Pompeii* (Bryullov) 165
Laying Our Lady's Holy Robe Church
    (Moscow) 53, 55, **60**
Le Blond, Jean Baptiste 186
Lemaire, François 150
Lena river 24
Lenin, Vladimir Ilyich 12, 14, 69, 81,
    101, 140, 141, 180, 227
    Bolshevik Revolution 44, 152, 182
    death 44, 69, 237
    Embalming Lenin **69**
    lying in state 80
    painting of 228
    statues 228, 250, 256
Lenin Mausoleum (Moscow) 12,
    65, **69**
Lenin Memorial Centre (Ulyanovsk)
    14, 227
Leningrad 44
    Siege of Leningrad 36, 45, 141, 166,
        179, 180, 183
    *See also* St Petersburg
Leonardo da Vinci, *Litta Madonna*
    154
Lermontov, Mikhail 30, 92, 98
Lermontov House-Museum
    (Moscow) 77, **92**
Lichtenstein, Roy 152
Lidval, Fyodor 33, 140, 149, 163
Lion Bridge (St Petersburg) 173
Listings magazines 120, 311
Listvyanka 15, 253, 273
Literature 22, **30–1**
*Litta Madonna* (Leonardo da Vinci)
    154
Lobanov-Rostovskiy, Prince 147

Local Lore Museum (Yuzhno-Sakhalinsk) 258
Lomonosov, Mikhail 74, 81, 143, 183
Lopukhin Palace (Moscow) 105
Lopukhina, Yevdokiya 105
Lubyanka Square (Moscow) 64, **74**
Luzhkov, Yuri 61, 81, 89
Lvov, Nikolai 176

# M

MA Vrubel Regional Museum of Fine Arts (Omsk) 250
Mafia 46, 306
Magadan 202, 248, **259**, 273
Main Post Office (St Petersburg) 171, **176**
Makovsky, Vladimir 43
MAKS Air Show 35
Malaya Sadovaya Ulitsa (St Petersburg) 159, **166**
Malevich, Kazimir 29, 107, 149, 233
Malls 293
Malyshev, Ignatiy 162
Malyy Theatre (Moscow) 79, 80
Mamayev Kurgan (Volgograd) 10, 14, **232**
Mamontov, Savva 80, 101
Mandelstam, Osip 31
Manège Square (Moscow) 77, **81**
Maps
The Caucasus 238–9
Central and Southern Russia 222–3
Kaliningrad (city) 217
Kaliningrad (region) 214–15
Moscow: At a Glance 50–51
Moscow: Beyond Moscow 113
Moscow: Further Afield 103
Moscow: Garden Ring area map 77
Moscow: Kitay Gorod Street-by-Street 66–7
Moscow: Kremlin area map 53
Moscow: Kremlin Street-by-Street 54–5
Moscow: Around Pyatnitskaya Ulitsa street-by-street 96–7
Moscow: Red Square and Kitay Gorod area map 65
Moscow: Street Finder 122–9
Moscow: Around Theatre Square Street-by-Street 78–9
Moscow: Zamoskvoreche area map 95
Northern Russia 206–207
Russia 16–17
Russia at a Glance 202–203
St Petersburg: Around Arts Square Street-by-Street 160–61
St Petersburg: At a Glance 132–3
St Petersburg: Beyond St Petersburg 185
St Petersburg: Further Afield 179
St Petersburg: Gostinyy Dvor area map 159
St Petersburg: The Islands area map 135
St Petersburg: Palace Embankment area map 145
St Petersburg: Peter and Paul Fortress Street-by-Street 136–7
St Petersburg: St Isaac's Square Street-by-Street 146–7
St Petersburg: Sennaya Ploshchad area map 171
St Petersburg: Street Finder 192–9

Maps (cont.)
St Petersburg: Theatre Square Street-by-Street 172–3
Samara 229
Siberia and the Far East 248–9
Sochi 241
Marble Palace (St Petersburg) 147, **152**
Maria Alexandrovna, Tsarina 138, 174
Maria Alexeyevna, Tsarevna 104
Maria Fyodorovna, Tsarina 166, 180, 185, 190
Mariinskiy Palace (St Petersburg) 146, 147, 149
Mariinskiy Theatre (St Petersburg) 13, 22, 29, 171, 172, **174**
Maritime Terminal (Sochi) **240**
Markets and bazaars
Moscow 118
St Petersburg 293
Martos, Ivan 71, 189
Marx, Karl 61, 80
Marxism 44
Mary, the Virgin 27
Mask of Sorrow (Magadan) 259
Maslenitsa 34
Matisse, Henri 88, 155
Matryoshka dolls 294
Mayakovsky, Vladimir 31, 75, 87
Mayakovsky Museum (Moscow) 65, **75**
Mayakovsky Theatre (Moscow) 87
*A Meal in the Monastery* (Perov) 165
Medical treatment 307
Medieval period 39–40
Medvedev, Dmitri 47
Melnikov, Constantin 33, 92–3
Melnikov House (Moscow) 33, 77, **92–3**
Melochnaya Lavka (Ulyanovsk) 227
Meltzer, Roman 156
Mendeleev, Dmitri 143, 278
Mensheviks 44
Menshikov, Prince Alexander 143
Menshikov, Prince Sergei 87
Menshikov Palace (St Petersburg) 135, **143**
Menus, reading 274
Messmacher, Maximilian 181
Methodius, St 26
Metro 316, 317
Meyerhold, Vsevolod 78, 84, 87, 101, 167
Mighty Five 28
Mikhail Aleksandrovich, Grand Duke 152
Mikhail Pavlovich, Grand Duke 164
Mikhail Romanov, Tsar 41, 60
Mikhailov, Andrei 176
Mikhalkov, Nikita 39
Mikhaylov, Andrei 82
Mikhaylovskiy Castle (St Petersburg) 159, 161, **163**
Mikhaylovskiy Garden (St Petersburg) 160
Mikhaylovskiy Palace (St Petersburg) 160, 163
Mikhaylovskiy Theatre (St Petersburg) 22, 160, 163, 296, 297
Mikhaylovskoye 206, **211**
Military experiences 299
Military Museum (Saransk) 227
Millennium Monument (Veliky Novgorod) 210

Millionaires' Street (St Petersburg) 145, **152**
Miloslavskiy family 41
Mini-hotels 264, 265
Minibuses 316–17
Minin, Kuzma 41, 71
Ministry of Culture 118, 119, 292, 293
Ministry of Foreign Affairs (Moscow) 12, 33, 77, **93**
Mironov, Aleksey 109, 111
Mirozhky Monastery (Pskov) 211
Mobile phones 310, 311
Monasteries 26
Alexander Nevsky Monastery (St Petersburg) 166, 178, 179, **183**
Annunciation Monastery (Nizhny Novgorod) 224
Assumption Monastery (Sviyazhsk) 14, 226
Donskoy Monastery (Moscow) 103, **108**
Ivolginsky Datsan 11, 15, 248, **256**
John the Baptist Monastery (Sviyazhsk) 226
Mirozhky Monastery (Pskov) 211
Monastery of Our Saviour and Transfiguration (Yaroslavl) 117
Monastery of Saviour and St Euphemius (Suzdal) 117
Monastery of the Sign (Moscow) 72
Trinity Monastery (Astrakhan) 233
Trinity Monastery of St Sergius 12, 41, **114**
Upper Monastery of St Peter (Moscow) 32, **84–5**
Valaam 209
Zaikonospasskiy Monastery (Moscow) 74
*See also* Convents
Mongols 22, 40, 95, 114
Monighetti, Ippolito 176, 188
Monomakh Throne (Moscow) **59**
Montferrand, Auguste de 150, 152
Monument to Glory (Samara) **228–9**
Mordovia, Republic of 227
Mordovian Museum of Visual Arts (Saransk) 227
Morozov Mansion **84**
Moscow **48–129**
climate 36
day trips 112–17
Entertainment 120–1
festivals and events 34–7
Further Afield 102–11
Garden Ring 76–93
history 19, 40, 41, 42, 46–7
The Kremlin 52–63
map: Moscow at a Glance 50–1
map: Street Finder 122–9
public transport 316–17
Red Square and Kitay Gorod 64–75
Shopping 118–19
travelling to 312–13
Two days itinerary 12
Where to Eat and Drink 280–3
Where to Stay 266–8
Zamoskvoreche 94–101
Moscow Arts Theatre 22, 28, 77, 78, **84**, 87, 121
Moscow Cats Theatre 121
Moscow Conservatory 77, **87**, 120
Moscow Forum 37
Moscow International Film Festival 35, 85

Moscow Old University 33, 81
Moscow Stars 34
Moscow State University (MGU) 33, 108
Moskva river 53, 96, 109
Mosques
  Azimov Mosque (Kazan) 225
  Kul Sharif Mosque (Kazan) 14, 225, 230–31
  visiting 303
  White Mosque (Bogar) 227
Mosquitoes 307
Mossoviet Theatre (Moscow) 121
Mount Elbrus 25, 298
Mount Legushka 258
Mount Mutnovskaya 259
Mountains 25
  *See also* by name
Moyka river 160, 163, 168, 169, 175, 176
Museum shops 293
Museums and galleries
  Abramtsevo Estate-Museum 113, **114**
  Alabin Museum (Samara) **228**
  Altai Museum of Regional Studies and History (Barnaul) 252
  Amber Museum (Kaliningrad) **217**
  Anna Akhmatova Museum (St Petersburg) 182
  Antique Automobile Museum (Vladivostok) 257
  Archaeological Museum (Anapa) 243
  Armoury Chamber (Moscow) 12, 33, 54, **62–3**
  Art Gallery (Kaliningrad) **216**
  Art Museum (Komsomolsk-na-Amur) 258
  Art Museum (Krasnodar) 244
  Art Museum (Sochi) **241**
  Artillery Museum (St Petersburg) **140**
  Baikal Museum (Listvyanka) 253
  Bakhrushin Theatre Museum (Moscow) **101**
  Battle of Stalingrad Panorama Museum (Volgograd) 10, **232**
  Bulgakov House and Museum (Moscow) **86**
  Bunker Museum (Kaliningrad) **216**
  Buryat History Museum (Ulan-Ude) 11, 15, 256
  Cabin of Peter the Great (St Petersburg) **141**
  Chekhov House-Museum (Moscow) **86**
  Children's Art Gallery (Samara) **228**
  Commandant's House (St Petersburg) 136, **139**
  Cosmonautics Museum (St Petersburg) 138
  Cruiser Aurora (St Petersburg) 141
  Dogadin Art Gallery (Astrakhan) 233
  Dostoevsky House-Museum (St Petersburg) **182–3**
  Engineer's House (St Petersburg) 137, **138**
  Erarta (St Petersburg) **180**
  Ethnographic Museum (Ulan-Ude) 15, 248, 256, 256
  Far Eastern Arts Museum (Khabarovsk) 257

Museums and galleries (cont.)
  Fine Arts Museum (Yekaterinburg) 235
  Fortress Museum (Vladivostok) 257
  Front Gate Museum (Kolomenskoe) 109
  Gallery of 19th- and 20th-Century European and American Art (Moscow) 12, **88**
  Glazunov Picture Gallery (Moscow) **88**
  Gorky House-Museum (Moscow) 33, **86–7**
  Great Bulgar Museum (Bolgar) 226, 227
  Gulag History Museum (Moscow) **111**
  Hermann Brachert House-Museum (Otradnoe) 219
  Hermitage (St Petersburg) 13, 42, 133, **154–7**
  Historical and Architectural Museum Reserve (Starocherkassk) 245
  Historical Museum (Moscow) 10, 33, 68
  History Museum (Sochi) **240**
  Institute of Russian Literature (Pushkin House) (St Petersburg) 142
  Karelia Fine Arts Museum (Petrozavodsk) 208
  Kirov Museum (St Petersburg) **140–41**
  Kizhi Museum (Petrozavodsk) 208
  Kizhi State Open-Air Museum 208, 209
  Kshesinskaya Mansion (St Petersburg) 33, **135**
  Kunstkammer (St Petersburg) 132, **142–3**
  Kustodiev House Museum (Astrakhan) 233
  Lenin Memorial Centre (Ulyanovsk) 227
  Lermontov House-Museum (Moscow) **92**
  MA Vrubel Regional Museum of Fine Arts (Omsk) 250
  Mayakovsky Museum (Moscow) **75**
  Melochnaya Lavka (Ulyanovsk) 227
  Memorial Museum of Space Exploration (Moscow) 103, **111**
  Military Museum (Saransk) 227
  Mordovian Museum of Visual Arts (Saransk) 227
  Morozov Mansion (Moscow) **84**
  Museum of 17th-Century Life and Applied Arts (Moscow) 56
  Museum of Bread (Bolgar) 227
  Museum of City Life (Irkutsk) 15, 252
  Museum of Contemporary History (Moscow) **85**
  Museum of Culture and History (Krasnoyarsk) 251
  Museum of History, Architecture and Art (Veliky Novgorod) 210
  Museum of History and Art (Kaliningrad) **216**
  Museum of Hygiene (St Petersburg) 161
  Museum of Local Lore (Yuzhno-Sakhalinsk) 258
  Museum of Music and Time (Yaroslavl) 117

Museums and galleries (cont.)
  Museum of Musical Life (St Petersburg) 182
  Museum of the World Ocean (Kaliningrad) 215, **216**
  Museum of Volga People's Architecture (Nizhny Novgorod) 224
  Museum of Wooden Architecture (Suzdal) 112, **117**
  National Museum of the Republic of Tatarstan (Kazan) 14, 225
  Old English Court (Moscow) 67, **72**
  Old Sarepta Ethnographic Museum (Volgograd) **232**
  Perm Museum of Contemporary Art (PERMM) 234
  Perm Regional Museum 234
  Perm State Art Galery 234
  Perm-36 Memorial Centre of Political Repression **234**
  Polytechnical Museum (Moscow) **75**
  Pskov Museum of History, Architecture and Art 205, 211
  Pushkin House-Museum (Moscow) **93**
  Pushkin House-Museum (St Petersburg) **169**
  Pushkin State Museum of Fine Arts (Moscow) 12, 50, **90–91**
  Railway Museum (St Petersburg) **177**
  Regional Art Museum (Samara) **228**
  Regional Museum (Astrakhan) 233
  Regional Museum (Gelendzhik) 243
  Regional Museum (Irkutsk) 252
  Regional Museum (Khabarovsk) 257
  Regional Museum (Komsomolsk-na-Amur) 258
  Regional Museum (Krasnodar) 244
  Regional Museum (Krasnoyarsk) 251
  Regional Museum (Novosibirsk) 250–51
  Regional Museum (Omsk) 250
  Regional Museum (Rostov-na-Donu) 244, 245
  Regional Museum (Tobolsk) 250
  Regional Museum (Vladivostok) 257
  Regional Museum (Volgograd) **232**
  Russian Museum (St Petersburg) 159, 160, 163, **164–5**, 168
  Samara Space Museum 14, **229**
  Shalyapin House-Museum (Moscow) **93**
  Simbirsk Museum of Architecture (Ulyanovsk) 227
  Skryabin House-Museum (Moscow) **92**
  Space Museum (Moscow) **111**
  Stalin's Bunker (Samara) **228**
  Stanislavskiy House-Museum (Moscow) **87**
  State Art Museum (Nizhny Novgorod) 224
  State Tretyakov Gallery on Krymsky Val (Moscow) **107**
  State Tretyakov Gallery (Moscow) 12, 51, 95, 96, **98–9**
  Stieglitz Museum (St Petersburg) **181**
  Sukachev Regional Art Museum (Irkutsk) 252

Museums and galleries (cont.)
Taltsy Architectural and
Ethnographic Museum 10, 15, **253**
Tchaikovsky House Museum (Klin)
113, 115
Theatre Museum (St Petersburg) 167
Tolstoy House-Museum (Moscow)
**106**
Tomsk City History Museum 251
Trubetskoy Bastion (St Petersburg)
136, **139**
Vasnetsov House-Museum
(Moscow) **110**
Vladimir & Suzdal Museum of
History, Art & Architecture 117
Volga-Don Canal Museum
(Volgograd) **232**
Zoological Museum (St Petersburg)
**142**
Music 22, 28, 120–21, 296, 297
Music shops 119
Music and Time Museum (Yaroslavl)
117
Musical instruments 295
Musical Life Museum (St Petersburg)
182
Musical Spring in St Petersburg 34
Musical Theatre of the Republic of
Karelia, The (Petrozavodsk) 208
Mussorgsky, Modest 22, 28, 174

**N**

Nabokov, Vladimir 31
Napoleon 42, 50, 54, 56, 89, 168,
219
Borodino 113, 115
Napoleonic Wars 42, 61, 71, 104, 156
Naryshkin family 85
Nashestive 297
Nataliya Sats Children's Musical
Theatre (Moscow) 121
National Museum of the Republic
of Tatarstan (Kazan) 14, 225
National parks and nature
reserves 20
Astrakhan Biosphere Reserve **233**
Sochi National Park 202, 237,
238, **242**
Stolby Nature Reserve 251
Nativity of the Blessed Virgin
Cathedral (Rostov-na-Donu)
244, 245
Nativity Cathedral (Suzdal) 117
Nativity of the Virgin in Putinki
Church (Moscow) 85
Natural resources 20, 21
Navy Day 35
Nazi Germany 45
Neff, Timofei 150
Neglinnaya river 53
Neizvestniy, Ernst 81
Nemirov-Danchenko, Vladimir 28,
74, 84
Nenets 23
Nesterov, Mikhail 101, 114, 162
Neva delta 41, 132, 135
Neva Gate (St Petersburg) 136, **139**
Neva river 135, 148, 152, 171, 175
Nevskiy Prospekt (St Petersburg) 13,
152, 159, **166**
Nevsky, Prince Alexander 116, 183
New Economic Policy 44
New Holland (St Petersburg) 171, **175**
New Year's Eve 37

Newspapers and magazines 311
Nicholas I, Tsar 43, 62, 72, 166, 182
inauguration 148
statue 147, 149
Nicholas II, Tsar 43, 164, 156
1905 Revolution 181
abdication 43, 152, 235
coronation 61, 141
execution 101, 235
Nicolas, Vladimir 175
Night of Ivan Kupala (near Veliky
Novgorod) 35
Nightlife 22
Moscow 120–22
Nihilists 43
Nikitin, Ivan 189
Nikitnikov, Grigori 67, 73
Nikolskaya Ulitsa (Moscow) 74
Nikon, Patriarch 32, 55, 56
Nikoskaya Ulitsa (Moscow) 66
Nizhny Novgorod 10, 14, 220, 222,
223, **224**
Where to Eat and Drink 289
Where to Stay 270–71
Northern Russia **204–11**
getting around 207
map 206–207
Where to Eat and Drink 288–9
Where to Stay 270
Novgorod 39, 40
Novodevichiy Cemetery (Moscow)
**105**
Novodevichiy Convent (Moscow)
32, 102, **104–105**
Novoluznetskaya Metro Station
(Moscow) 97
Novorossiysk Bikers' Festival 35
Novosibirsk 248, **250–51**, 273, 291
Novyy, Aleviz 57, 85
Nuclear weapons 45
Nureyev, Rudolf 167

**O**

Ob river 24
Obraztsov Puppet Theatre (Moscow)
121
Ocean World Museum (Kaliningrad)
215, 216
October Revolution 19, 44, 141, 179,
180
Odigitria Cathedral (Ulan-Ude)
256
Oil 20, 21
Oka river 10, 14, 224
Okudhava, Bulat 89
Old Arbat (Moscow) 77, 89, 92–3
Old Believers 208
Old English Court (Moscow) 65, 67,
**72**
Old New Year 37
Old Sarepta Ethnographic Museum
(Volgograd) **232**
Oleg, Prince 39
Oligarchs 21, 47
Olkhon Island 15, 253
Om river 250
Omsk 247, **250**, 273, 291
Onega, Lake 35, 205, 208, 209
Opekushin, Alexander 85
Open Cinema 296, 297
Opening hours
restaurants 275
shops 118, 292
tourist sights 303

Opera 22, 28, 296, 297
Moscow 120, 121
Opera and Ballet Theatre
(Novosibirsk) 250, 251, 296, 297
Opera and Ballet Theatre
(Yekaterinburg) 296, 297
Operation Barbarossa 232
Operetta Theatre (Moscow) 80
Orlov, Count Grigori 62, 152
Osner, Karl 138
Ostankino Palace (Moscow) 103, **111**
Ostrovskiy, Aleksandr 79, 80, 167
Ostrovskiy Square (St Petersburg)
33, 159, **167**
Ostrovsky, Nikolai 28, 31
Otradnoe 218–19
Ottokar II of Bohemia 217
Ottoman Empire 40, 237, 243
Our Lady of Kazan Cathedral (St
Petersburg) 13, 168
Our Saviour Church (Irkutsk) 252
Our Saviour and Transfiguration
Monastery (Yaroslavl) 117
Outdoor activities 23, **298–9**

**P**

Pacific Ocean 20, 25, 247, 257
Painting 22, 29
Paisein, Ivan and Boris 58
Palace Embankment (St Petersburg)
**144–57**
area map 145
Street-by-Street map: St Isaac's
Square 146–7
Where to Eat and Drink 284–5
Where to Stay 268
Palace Square (St Petersburg) 13,
**152**
Palaces
Anichkov Palace (St Petersburg)
**166**
Ataman Palace (Starocherkassk)
245
Grand Kremlin Palace (Moscow)
33, 54, **60**
Kuskovo Palace (Moscow) 35, 103,
**109**
Lopukhin Palace (Moscow) 105
Marble Palace (St Petersburg)
145, **152**
Mariinskiy Palace (St Petersburg)
146, 147, 149
Menshikov Palace (St Petersburg)
**143**
Mikhaylovskiy Palace
(St Petersburg) 160, 163
Ostankino Palace (Moscow) 103,
**111**
Palace of Romanov Boyars
(Moscow) 32, 67, **72–3**
Patriarch's Palace (Moscow) 12,
55, **56**
Pavlovsk 13, 184, 185, **190–91**
Peterhof 13, 32, 34, 36, 185, **186–7**
Sheremetev Palace (St Petersburg)
**182**
State Kremlin Palace (Moscow)
54, **56**, 120
Stroganov Palace (St Petersburg)
166, **168**
Summer Palace (St Petersburg)
145, **153**
Tauride Palace
(St Petersburg) **181**

Palaces (cont.)
Terem Palace (Moscow) 54, **60–61**, 181
Tsarskoe Selo 35, 157, 177, 185, **188–9**
Winter Palace (St Petersburg) 13, 32, 145, 152, 154, **156–7**
Yelagin Palace (St Petersburg) 180
Yusupov Palace (St Petersburg) 172, **176**
Palekh boxes 295
Panteleymon Bridge (St Petersburg) 161
Parks and gardens
Aleksandrovskiy Park (St Petersburg) **140**
Alexander Gardens (Moscow) **61**
Botanical Gardens (Moscow) 111
Dendrarium (Sochi) **240–41**
Gorky Park (Moscow) 103, **108**
Izmaylovo (Moscow) 37, 103, **110**
Mikhaylovskiy Garden (St Petersburg) 160
Riviera Park (Sochi) **241**
Sparrow Hills (Moscow) 103, **108**
Summer Garden (St Petersburg) 144, **153**
Parland, Alfred 162
Pashkov House (Moscow) 33, 77, **88**
Passports 302, 305
Pasternak, Boris 31
Patriarch's Palace (Moscow) 12, 55, **56**
Patriarch's Pond (Moscow) **86**
Paul I, Tsar 161, 163, 185, 190
assassination 42, 163
mausoleum 190
Pavlovskiy Guards 153
Pavlov, Ivan 143
Pavlova, Anna 167
Pavlovsk 13, 184, 185, **190–91**, 288
People 23
Perestroika 46
Perm 35, 222, **234**
Where to Eat and Drink 289
Where to Stay 271
Perm-36 Memorial Centre of Political Repression 222, **234**
Perm Kaleidoscope **234**
Perov, Vasiliy, *A Meal in the Monastery* 165
Personal Security and Health **306–307**
Peter the Great 41, 132, 138, 142, 145, 153, 157, 185, **186**, 187, 189, 208, 232, 245
administration 143, 148
Bronze Horseman 145, 148, 149
Cabin 109, 141
childhood 110
founding of St Petersburg 132, 135, 136
imprisonment of son 136, 139
monument 107
reclaims throne 104
Russian Navy 110, 148, 171, 175
statues 137, 148, 161, 163
Streltsy Revolt 61, 85, 100, 114, 143
victory over Swedes 138
victory over Turks 245
Winter Palace 156
Peter II, Tsar 41
Peter III, Tsar 42
Peter and Paul Fortress (St Petersburg) 13, 133, 134, 135, 136–8
Street-by-Street map **136–7**

Peterhof 13, 32, 43, 36, 185, **186–7**
Petipa, Marius 175
Petrashevsky Circle 177
Petrograd 43, 44
*See also* Leningrad; St Petersburg
Petropavlovsk-Kamchatsky 259, 273, 291
Petrozavodsk 206, **208**, 270, 288
Pharmacies 306–307
Philharmonic (Yekaterinburg) 296, 297
Philotey of Pskov 26
*Phryne at the Festival of Poseidon in Eleusin* (Siemiradzki) 165
Picasso, Pablo 88, 152
Pickpockets 306
Pimenov, Nikolai 150
Pineau, Nicholas 186
Pioneer (Moscow) 121
Piskarevskoe Memorial Cemetery (St Petersburg) 179, **180–81**
Poland, wars 41
Polenov, Vasily 92
Police 306, 307
Political prisoners 45, **139**, 209, 234, 247, 258, 259
Politics 21, 45–7
Poltava, Battle of 41, 142, 186
Polubes, Stepan 110
Polytechnical Museum (Moscow) **75**
Pomerantsev, Aleksandr 69
Pony-trekking 299
Population 23
Port Baikal 15, 253
*Portrait of Arseny Tropinin, the Artist's Son* (Tropinin) 98
Pospeev, Sidor 58
Postal services 311
Potanin, Vladimir 47
Potemkin, Prince Grigori 166, 181
Poverty 21, 23
Pozharskiy, Prince Dmitri 41, 68, **71**
Prices
in hotels 263
in restaurants 275
Primitivism 29
*Princess Olga Konstantinovna Orlova* (Serov) 164
Prokofiev, Sergei 28, 84, 172, 175
Prussia 213, 216
Pskov 205, 206, 207, **210–11**
Where to Eat and Drink 289
Where to Stay 270
Pskov school 60, 72, 211
Public holidays 37
Public transport 316–17
Pugachev Rebellion 42
Puppet theatre 121, 297
Pushkin, Alexander 22, 30, 81, 87, **93**, 169, 206, **211**
statues 85, 163
*The Bronze Horseman* 43, 139, **149**
Pushkin House-Museum (Moscow) 77, **93**
Pushkin House-Museum (St Petersburg) 159, **169**
Pushkin Square (Moscow) 77, **85**
Pushkin State Museum of Fine Arts (Moscow) 12, 50, 77, **90–91**
Putin, Vladimir 21, 47
Putyatin, Admiral 152
Pyatnitskaya Ulitsa (Moscow), Street-by-Street map **96–7**

**Q**
Quarenghi, Giacomo 72, 146, 148, 182

**R**
Rachmaninov, Sergei 28, 80, 87, 106
Radio 311
Rafting 299
Rail travel *See* Trains
Railway Museum (St Petersburg) **177**
Rainfall 36–7
Rasputin, Grigori 43, 141, 172, **176**, 183
Rastrelli, Bartolomeo 32, 42, 145, 156, **157**, 168, 179, 182, 185, 186, 187, 188, 189
Red Army 44, 45
Red Square and Kitay Gorod (Moscow) **64–75**
area map 65
Street-by-Street map: Kitay Gorod 66–7
Where to Eat and Drink 280–83
Where to Stay 266
Red Square (Moscow) 12, 65, **68–71**
Reed, John 69, 149
Registration 302
Religion 23, 26–7
Rembrandt 91, 154
Renoir, Pierre Auguste 88
Repin, Ilya 29, 88, 99, 106, 165
Rerberg, Ilya 81
Responsible travel 305
Restaurants, cafés and bars **274–91**
The Caucasus 290
Central and Southern Russia 289–90
general information 274–5
Kaliningrad 289
Moscow 280–83
Northern Russia 288–9
St Petersburg 284–8
Siberia and the Far East 290–91
Resurrection Cathedral (Starocherkassk) 245
Resurrection Gate (Moscow) 65, **68**
Resurrection in Kadashi Church (Moscow) 95, 96, **100**
Resurrection of Lazarus Church (Kizhi) 208–209
Revolution 1905 43, 139
Revolution 1917 19, 44, 141, 179, 180
Rimsky-Korsakov, Nikolai 169, 172
Rimsky-Korsakov Conservatory (St Petersburg) 171, 172, **175**
Rinaldi, Antonio 152
River cruises 315
Rivers 24
*See also* by name
Riviera Park (Sochi) **241**
Rock music 297
Rodchenko, Aleksandr 107
Romanov Boyars Palace (Moscow) 32, 65, 67, **72–3**
Romanov dynasty 41, 43, 152, 235, 138–9
Romanov, Nikita 67, 72
*The Rooks Have Come* (Savrasov) 98
Roslin, Alexander 42
Rossiya Musical Theatre (Moscow) 85
Rostov-na-Donu 237, 238, **244–5**, 272, 290
Rostral Columns (St Petersburg) 135, **142**

Rubens, Peter Paul 91, 157
Rubinstein, Anton 87, 172, 175
Rubinstein, Nikolai 87
Rublev, Andrei 29, 57, 99, 116
Rudnev, Lev 108
Ruffo, Marco 55, 61
Rurik, Prince 39
Rurik dynasty 39–40
Russian Academic Youth Theatre
    (Moscow) 80
Russian International Film Fair 296
Russian Museum (St Petersburg)
    159, 160, 163, **164–5**, 168
Russian National Library
    (St Petersburg) 167
Russian Orthodox Christmas 37
Russian Orthodox Church 23, **26–7**
Russian White House 47
Russian Winter Festival (Moscow) 37
Russian-Revival style 33, 162
Russo-Japanese War 43, 141
Russo-Turkish wars 42, 181, 237, 243

**S**
Sadko Folklore Festival (Veliky
    Novgorod) 35
St Basil's Cathedral (Moscow) 12, 32,
    51, 65, 68, **70–71**
St Clement Church (Moscow) 97
St Demetrius Cathedral (Vladimir) 116
St Isaac's Cathedral (St Petersburg)
    13, 19, 145, 146, **150–51**
St Isaac's Square (St Petersburg)
    147, 149
    Street-by-Street map **146–7**
St Maxim the Blessed Church
    (Moscow) 67, 72
St Nicholas Church in Pyzhy
    (Moscow) 95, **100**
St Nicholas of the Weavers Church
    (Moscow) 103, **107**
St Nicholas's Cathedral (St Petersburg)
    132, 171, 173, **174–5**
St Peter and Paul's Cathedral (Kazan)
    225
St Peter's Gate (St Petersburg) 136,
    137, **138**
St Petersburg **130–99**
    climate 37
    day trips 184–91
    entertainment 296–7
    festivals and events 34–6
    Further Afield 178–83
    Gostinyy Dvor 158–69
    history 19, 41, 42, 43
    The Islands 134–43
    map: St Petersburg at a Glance 132–3
    map: Street Finder 192–9
    Palace Embankment 144–57
    public transport 316–17
    Sennaya Ploshchad 170–77
    shopping 293
    travelling to 312–13
    Two days itinerary 13
    Where to Eat and Drink 283–8
    Where to Stay 268–9
    See also Leningrad; Petrograd
St Petersburg Palaces 35
St Sofia Cathedral (Tobolsk) 250
St Sophia Cathedral (Veliky
    Novgorod) 210
Sakhalin Island 248, **258**
    Where to Eat and Drink 291
    Where to Stay 273

Samara 10, 14, 35, 221, **228–9**, 299
    map 229
    Where to Eat and Drink 289
    Where to Stay 271
Samara Embankment 221, 228, **229**
Samorezov, Viktor 241
Samovars 279, 294
Sanatoriums 238, **243**
Sandunov, Sila 75
Sandunovskiy Baths (Moscow) 65, **75**
Saransk **227**, 271
Sarmatians 39
Saviour Not Made by Human Hand
    Church (Abramtsevo) 114
Saviour and St Euphemius
    Monastery (Suzdal) 117
Savrasov, Aleksey 98
*Scenes from the Life of Metropolitan
    Peter* (workshop of Dionysius) 59
Schliemann, Heinrich 90
Schlüsselburg Fortress (Lake Ladoga)
    139
Schröter, Viktor 174
Schülter, Andreas 189
Scriabin, Alexander 28
Scythians 39
Sea of Japan 251
Sea of Okhotsk 258
Sea travel
    arriving in Russia 313
    travelling around Russia 315
Security *See* Personal Security and
    Health
Selenga river 256
Semi-precious stones 294
Senate Square (St Petersburg) 145,
    146, **148**
Sennaya Ploshchad
    (St Petersburg) **170–77**
    area map 171
    Street-by-Street map: Theatre
        Square 172–3
    Where to Eat and Drink 286
    Where to Stay 268
Sennaya Ploshchad (St Petersburg)
    171, **177**
Serfs 43
Sergius of Radonezh 40
Serov, Valentin 164
Shalyapin, Fyodor 93, 105, 106, 140
Shalyapin House-Museum (Moscow)
    77, **93**
Shchusev, Aleksey 69, 101
Shekhtel, Fyodor 33, 84
Shemiakin, Mikhail 137
Sheremetev, Count Nikolai 111
Sheremetev, Count Pyotr 109
Sheremetev family 103, 109, 182
Sheremetev Palace (St Petersburg)
    179, **182**
Sherwood, Vladimir 68
Sholokhov, Mikhail 31, 245
Shopping **118–19**, **292–3**, **294–5**
Shostakovich, Dmitri 28, 44, 84, 87,
    105, 172, 174, 175
Shuvalovka 297
Siberia, exile in 43, 177, 235, 247,
    252
Siberia and the Far East **246–59**
    getting around 248
    landscape and wildlife 24, 25
    map 247–8
    Where to Eat and Drink 290–91
    Where to Stay 272–3

Siege of Leningrad Day
    (St Petersburg) 36
Siemiradzki, Henryk 165
Sikhote-Alin Mountains 25
Silk Road 39
Simbirsk Museum of Architecture
    (Ulyanovsk) 227
Sketes 209
SKIF Festival (St Petersburg) 34, 297
skiing 242, 251
Skryabin, Aleksandr 92, 105
Skryabin House-Museum (Moscow)
    77, **92**
Sky Fair of the Urals (Kungur) 35
Slavophile movement 22
Slavs 39
Slavyanka river 184, 190, 191
Sludyanka 253
Smolnyy Convent (St Petersburg)
    157, 179, **182**
Smolnyy Institute (St Petersburg)
    141, 179, **182**
Sochi 237, 238, **240–41**
    climate 37
    map 241
    Where to Eat and Drink 290
    Where to stay 272
Sochi National Park 202, 237, 238, **242**
Social etiquette 304
Socialist realism 29, 84
Society 23
Sokurov, Alexander 29
Solario, Pietro 55, 61
Solzhenitsyn, Alexander 31, 45, 60, 84
Sophia, Regent 41, 104, 108
South Caucasian republics 245
South Ossetia 245
Souvenirs 23, 118, 119, 294–5
Soviet memorabilia 23, 295
Soviet Union 19, 44–6
Space Museum (Moscow) 111
Space Museum (Samara) 14, **229**
Space programme 45, 111, 138, 229
Sparrow Hills (Moscow) 103, **108**
Spasopeskovskiy Pereulok (Moscow)
    77, **92**
Specialist shops 293
Sports *See* Outdoor activities
Spring 34
Sputnik 45
SS Martha and Mary Convent
    (Moscow) **101**
SS Peter and Paul Cathedral
    (St Petersburg) 13, 133, 135, 137,
    **138–9**
Stalin, Joseph 44–5, 69, 237, 240,
    241, 272
    architecture 33, 53, 56, 61, 68, 77,
        78, 81, 89, 92, 93, 108, 177, 179,
        240, 241, 258
    bunker 10, 14, 228
    culture under 29, 75, 86, 107, 224
    Great Terror 44–5, 79, 80, 84, 141,
        182, 234, 258, 259
    Palace of Soviets Plan 89
    White Sea Canal 209
Stalingrad, Battle of 14, 232
Stalin's Bunker (Samara) 10, 14, **228**
Standard of living 21, 23
Stanislavskiy, Konstantin 22, 28, 31,
    74, 84, 87, 101
Stanislavskiy House-Museum
    (Moscow) 77, **87**
Starocherkassk 34, 238, **245**

Starov, Ivan 181
Staroye Arakchino 222, **226**
Stars of the White Nights
(St Petersburg) 34
Stasov, Vasily 153, 169, 181, 182
State Art Galery (Perm) 234
State Art Museum (Nizhny
Novgorod) 224
State Diamond Fund 54, 62
State Kremlin Palace (Moscow) 54,
**56**, 120
State Tretyakov Gallery (Moscow)
12, 51, 95, 96, **98–9**
State Tretyakov Gallery on Krymsky
Val (Moscow) 103, **107**
Steppes 20, 24
Stieglitz, Baron Aleksandr 181
Stieglitz Museum (St Petersburg)
179, **181**
Stolby Nature Reserve 251
Stravinsky, Igor 28
Strelka, The (St Petersburg) 135, 142
Streltsy Revolt 41, 61, 85
Stroganov, Count Sergei 168
Stroganov Palace (St Petersburg)
159, 166, **168**
Student travellers 304, 305
Style-Moderne 33
Moscow 78, 80, 81, 86, 92, 101
St Petersburg 135, 140, 141, 149,
163, 176, 177
Sukachev Regional Art Museum
(Irkutsk) 252
Summer 34–5
Summer Garden (St Petersburg)
144, 145, **153**
Summer Palace (St Petersburg) 145,
**153**
Sunshine 36–7
Surikov, Vasily 99
Suzdal 12, 113, **116–17**
Svetlogorsk 212, 213, 214, **218–19**, 270
Sviyazhsk 10, 14, 222, 223, **226**, 289
Svyatki Masquerades (Moscow) 37
Symbolism 29

**T**

Taglioni, Marie 101
Tales of the Boy Onfim (Veliky
Novgorod) 35
Taltsy Architectural and
Ethnographic Museum 10, 15, **253**
Tamanskiy, Pyotr 140
Taranov, Ivan 97
Tarkovsky, Andrey 29
Tatars 23, 38, 221, 224, 225, 233
Tatishchev, Vasily 234
Tatlin, Vladimir 29, 149
Tauride Palace (St Petersburg)
179, **181**
Taxes
export 292
in hotels 263
VAT 292
Taxis 317
Tchaikovsky, Pyotr 22, 28, 87, 113,
115, 163, 172, 175
Tchaikovsky Concert Hall (Moscow)
120, 121
Tchaikovsky House Museum (Klin)
113, **115**
Tchaikovsky International
Competition 87, 120
Tea 279

Telephone services 310, 311
Television 311
Temperatures 36–7
Temple of All Religions (Staroye
Arakchino) 226
Terem Palace (Moscow) 53, 54,
**60–61**, 181
Terrorism 47, 298
Teutonic knights 213, 216, 217,
219
The Thaw 45
Theatre 22, 28, 296–7
Moscow 121
Theatre on Liteynyy (St Petersburg)
296, 297
Theatre Museum (St Petersburg)
167
Theatre Square (Moscow) 33, 79, **80**
Street-by-Street map **78–9**
Theatre Square (St Petersburg) 171
Street-by-Street map **172–3**
Theatres and concert halls
Academic Capella (St Petersburg)
**169**
Alexandrinskiy Theatre
(St Petersburg) 167
Bolshoi Dramatic Theatre
(St Petersburg) 296, 297
Bolshoi Theatre (Moscow) 22, 29,
50, 79, **82–3**, 120
Bolshoi Zal (Moscow Conservatory)
**87**
Durov Animal Theatre (Moscow)
121
Great Hall of the Philharmonia
(St Petersburg) 160, 163, 296, 297
Large Puppet Theatre
(St Petersburg) 297
Malyy Theatre (Moscow) 79, 80
Mariinskiy Theatre (St Petersburg)
13, 22, 29, 171, 172, **174**
Mayakovsky Theatre (Moscow)
87
Mikhaylovskiy Theatre
(St Petersburg) 22, 160, 163,
296, 297
Moscow Arts Theatre 22, 28, 78,
**84**, 87, 121
Moscow Cats Theatre 121
Mossoviet Theatre (Moscow) 121
Musical Theatre of the Republic
of Karelia (Petrozavodsk) 208
Nataliya Sats Children's Musical
Theatre (Moscow) 121
New Beethoven Concert Hall
(Moscow) 82
Obraztsov Puppet Theatre
(Moscow) 121
Opera and Ballet Theatre
(Novosibirsk) 250, 251, 296, 297
Opera and Ballet Theatre
(Yekaterinburg) 296, 297
Operetta Theatre (Moscow) 80
Philharmonic (Yekaterinburg)
296, 297
Rimsky-Korsakov Conservatory
(St Petersburg) 171, 172, **175**
Rossiya Musical Theatre (Moscow)
85
Russian Academic Youth Theatre
(Moscow) 80
Taganka Theatre (Moscow) 121
Tchaikovsky Concert Hall (Moscow)
120, 121

Theatres and concert halls (cont.)
Theatre on Liteynyy (St Petersburg)
296, 297
Winter Theatre (Sochi) **240**, 296,
297
Zazerkalye (St Petersburg) 297
Theodore Ushakov Cathedral
(Saransk) 227
Theophanes the Greek 29, 57
Tickets
entertainment 120, 121, 296, 297
public transport 316, 317
tourist sights 303
Ticks 307
Tigers, Siberian **25**
Tikhon, Patriarch 108
Tilsit, Treaty of 42
Time of Troubles 41
Time zone 304–305
Tipping 304
in hotels 263
in restaurants 275
Titov, Pyotr 83
Tobolsk 248, **250**
Where to Eat and Drink 291
Where to Stay 273
Toilets 304
Tolstoy, Leo 30, **106**, 115, 116
Tolstoy family 106
Tolstoy House-Museum (Moscow)
· 103, **106**
Tomsk 247, 248, **251**
Where to Eat and Drink 291
Where to Stay 273
Ton, Konstantin 33, 54, 60, 61, 89
Tourist information 303, 305
Tours *See* Itineraries
Toyshops, Moscow 74, 119
Trade routes 39, 40
Train Station (Sochi) **240**
Trains
arriving in Russia 312–13
suburban 317
travelling around Russia 314, 315
Trams 317
Trans-Siberian Railway 202, 247, 248,
250, **251**, 257
Transfiguration Cathedral
(St Petersburg) 179, **181**
Transfiguration Cathedral (Valaam)
209
Transfiguration Church (Kizhi) 32,
204, 208
Travel
around Russia 314–15
in cities 316–17
to Russia 312–13
Travel cards 317
Traveller's cheques 308
Trekking 298
Tretyakov, Pavel 95, 96, 98
Trezzini, Domenico 138, 153
Trinity Cathedral (Pskov) 207, 211, 211
Trinity Cathedral (Trinity Monastery
of St Sergius) 115
Trinity Monastery (Astrakhan) 233
Trinity Monastery of St Sergius 12,
41, 113, **114**
Trinity in Nikitniki Church (Moscow)
65, 67, 73
*The Trinity* (Rublev) 99
Trinity Sunday 35
Trinity Tower (Moscow) 53, 54, **56**
Triscorni, Paolo 147

Troika rides 297
Trolleybuses 317
Tropinin, Vasily 98
Trotsky, Leon 139
Trubetskoy Bastion (St Petersburg) 135, 136, **139**
Trubetskoy, Prince 252
Tsar Bell (Moscow) 12, 57
Tsar Cannon (Moscow) 12, 49, 55, **56**
Tsaritsyno (Moscow) 103, **109**
Tsarskoe Selo 35, 157, 177, 185, **188–9**
Tsereteli, Zurab 107
Tsiolkovskiy, Konstantin 138
Tsvetaeva, Marina 31
Tundra 20, 25
Turchaninov, Sergei 100
Turganev, Ivan 30
Tverskaya Ulitsa (Moscow) 77, 78, **81**
Twelve Apostles Church (Moscow) 56
Twelve Colleges (St Petersburg) 135, **143**

**U**

Uda river 256
Ukraine 46
Ulan-Ude 10, 15, 248, **256**, 273, 291
Ulitsa Ilinka (Moscow) 65, 66, **73**
Ulitsa Varvarka (Moscow) 65, 67, **72**
Ulitsa Zodchevo Rossi (St Petersburg) 159, **167**
Ulyanovsk 14, 32, 222, **227**, 271, 290
Upper Monastery of St Peter (Moscow) 32, 77, **84–5**
Ural Mountains 19, 24, 235, 247, 248
US Independence Day 35
Ushakov, Simon 56, 57, 67, 115

**V**

Vaccinations 307
Vaganova, Agrippina 167, 175
Vaitens, Andrei 176
Valaam 206, **209**
Where to Stay 270
Valaam Monastery 209
Valeriani, Giuseppe 188
Valley of the Geysers (Kamchatka) 259
Vallin de la Mothe, Jean-Baptiste 167, 175, 176
Van Gogh, Vincent 88
Varangians 39
Vasilevskiy Island (St Petersburg) 135, 142
Vasily III, Tsar 109
Vasnetsov, Viktor 98, 99, 110, 114, 162
Vasnetsov House-Museum (Moscow) 103, **110**
Vegetarians 275
Vegetation 20, 24–5
Veliky Novgorod 35, 205, 206, 207, **210**, 270, 289
Velten, Yuri 183, 186, 187
Victory Day 34
Victory Monument (St Petersburg) 179, **183**
Vikings 39, 205
*Virgin in Majesty* (Bryullov) 151
Virgin of Smolensk Cathedral (Novodevichiy Convent) 104
Visas 302, 305

Visconti Bridge (Pavlovsk) 184
Vitali, Ivan 150, 151
Vladimir 113, **116**
Vladimir, Prince 26, 29, 39
Vladimir & Suzdal Museum of History, Art & Architecture 117
Vladimir Aleksandrovich, Grand Duke 152
Vladimir Kirillovich, Grand Duke 137
Vladimir Monomakh, Prince 59
Vladivostok 248, 251, **257**
Where to Eat and Drink 291
Where to Stay 273
Vodka 23, 274, 278, 294
Vodootvodnyy Canal (Moscow) 96
Volcanoes 25, 259, 298, 299
Volga Bulgaria 225, 226
Volga Delta 14, 203, 221, 222, **233**
Volga People's Architecture Museum (Nizhny Novgorod) 224
Volga river 20, 203, 221, 223, 224, 225, 228–9, 232, 233
Two weeks itinerary 10, 14
Volga-Don Canal 232
Volga-Don Canal Museum (Volgograd) **232**
Volgograd 10, 14, 222, **232**, 271, 290
Volkonskaya, Princess Zinaida 81
Volkonsky, Prince 252
Voltaire 167
Voronikhin, Andrei 168, 190, 191
Voskresenskaya Church (Tomsk) 251
Vrubel, Mikhail 29, 80, 98
Vsevolod III, Prince 116

**W**

Walcot, William 79, 80
Wanderers Movement 29, 98, 107
Warhol, Andy 152
Warrior saints 26
Weights and measures 305
Where to Eat and Drink **274–91**
Where to Stay **262–73**
White Mosque (Bolgar) 227
White Nights Festival 34, 297
White Sea Canal 44, **209**
Wildlife 20, **24–5**
Wine 275, 279
Winter 37
Winter Olympics 47, 237, 238, 240, 242, 299
Winter Palace (St Petersburg) 13, 32, 141, 145, 152, 154, **156–7**
Winter Theatre (Sochi) **240**, 296, 297
Witte, Count Sergei 140
Wolves 25
Women travellers 306
Wooden Architecture Museum (Suzdal) 112, 117
Wooden toys 294
World War I 43
World War II 45
50th anniversary 68
Artillery Museum 140
The Caucasus 237, 243, 244
Field of Mars 61, 153
Kaliningrad 213, 216
Komsomolsk-na-Amur Memorial 258
Perm 234
Samara 228, 229
Victory Monument 179, 183

World War II (cont.)
Vladivostok 257
Volgograd 232
Yekaterinburg 235
*See also* Leningrad, Siege of; Operation Barbarossa; Stalingrad, Battle of

**Y**

Yakovlev, Postnik 70
Yakutsk 259
Yantarny 213, 214, 219
Yaroslav, Prince 117
Yaroslav the Wise 39
Yaroslavl 113, **117**
Yasnaya Polyana 106, 113, **116**
Yefimov, Nikolai 147
Yekaterinburg 222, **235**, 271, 290
Yelagin Island (St Petersburg) 180
Yelagin Palace (St Petersburg) 179, **180**
Yeliseev, Grigori 81
Yelizaveta Fyodorovna, Grand Duchess 101
Yeltsin, Boris 21, 46–7, 89, 105
Yenisei river 24, 251
Yesenin, Sergei 31, 149
Yohansen, Boris 228
Yuri II, Grand Prince 224
Yusupov, Prince Boris 176
Yusupov, Prince Felix 176
Yusupov, Prince Nikolai 176
Yusupov Palace (St Petersburg) 171, 172, **176**
Yuzhno-Sakhalinsk 248, 258
Where to Eat and Drink 291

**Z**

Zaikonospasskiy Monastery (Moscow) 74
Zakharov, Andrei 148
Zakusi 277, 278
Zamoskvoreche (Moscow) **94–101**
area map 95
Street-by-Street map: Around Pyatnitskaya Ulitsa 96–7
Where to Eat and Drink 282
Where to Stay 266
Zamyatin, Yevgeny 31
Zarudnyy, Ivan 137, 138
Zazerkalye (St Petersburg) 297
Zelenaya Roscha (Sochi) 241, 243, 272
Zelenogradsk 213, 214, **218**
Zhemchugova-Kovaleva, Praskovia 111
Zhiguli Brewery (Samara) **228**
Zhivago, Semion 150
Zhukov, Georgi 68
Zoological Museum (St Petersburg) 135, **142**

# Acknowledgments

Dorling Kindersley would like to thank the following people whose help and assistance contributed to the preparation of this book.

## Main Contributors

Daniel Richardson was born in England. Before joining Rough Guides, he worked as a sailor on the Red Sea and lived in Peru. Since then he has authored or co-authored guidebooks to Moscow, St Petersburg, Hungary, Romania, Budapest, Bulgaria and Egypt. He has also lectured at the Foreign Office and been a volunteer aid worker in Albania. When not abroad, he lives in London.

Matt Willis is a widely published travel writer, whose fascination with Russia can be traced back to an early obsession with the country's literary greats. Tentative trips to Moscow soon evolved into a period of residence during which he produced the *DK Eyewitness Top 10 Moscow* guide. Based since the early 2000s in Russia and Eastern Europe, Matt has also written *DK Eyewitness Top 10 Turkey's Southwest Coast*, and co-authored DK Eyewitness guides to Bulgaria and Central and Eastern Europe.

## Additional Photography

Jonathan Buckley; Demetrio Carrasco; Andy Crawford; Steve Gorton; John Heseltine; Nigel Hicks; Dave King; William Reavell; Rough Guides/Jonathan Smith; Jon Spaull; Clive Streeter; James Young; Leandro Zoppe.

**Fact Checkers** Andrei Bogdanov, Kiki Deere
**Proofreader** Sandhya Iyer
**Indexer** Helen Peters
**Editorial Consultant** Scarlett O'Hara

## Design and Editorial

*Publishing Director* Claire Currie
*Publisher* Vivien Antwi
*List Manager* Kate Berens
*Senior Editors* Michelle Crane, Georgina Palffy
*Managing Art Editor* Mabel Chan
*Designer* Tracy Smith
*Senior Cartographic Editor* Casper Morris
*Senior DTP Designer* Jason Little
*Senior Picture Researcher* Ellen Root
*Production Controller* Rita Sinha

## Revisions Team

Dipika Dasgupta, Chris Gordon, Rahul Kumar, Rada Radojicic, Rituraj Sing, Irina Titova.

## Special Assistance

Dorling Kindersley would like to thank the following for their assistance:

Kiki Deere; Public Relationship Office at Russian Museum; Public Relationship Office at The State Academic Bolshoi Theatre of Russia; Nikita Anikin at the State Central Museum of Contemporary History of Russia; Elena Obuhovich & Olga Novoseltseva at The State Hermitage Museum; Lara Bobkova at The State Tretyakov Gallery; Alex Dmitriev at Tsarskoye Selo State Museum.

## Photography Permissions

Dorling Kindersley would like to thank all the museums, galleries, churches and other sights that allowed us to photograph at their establishments:

16 Tons Club; Battle of Stalingrad Panorama Museum; Museum of the World Ocean; National Museum of the Republic of Tatarstan; Perm State Art Gallery; Regional Museum, Vladivostok; Samara Cosmos Museum; Zoological Museum.

Works of art have been reproduced with the kind permission of the following copyright holders:
La Danse © Succession H Matisse/DACS 2013 155crb.

## Picture Credits

a = above; b = below/bottom; c = centre; f = far; l = left; r = right; t = top

The publisher would like to thank the following for their kind permission to reproduce their photographs:

Works of art have been reproduced with the permission of the following copyright holders:

**Akg-images**: 63tl; Russian Picture Service 63cr.
**Alamy Images**: The Art Archive 8–9, Sergey Bogomyako 76; The Bridgeman Art Library Ltd. 91tl; Caro 202cl; Danita Dalmonte 170, Joeri De Rocker 34bl; Eastland Photo 84bl, Ekaterinburg 200–201; Bernie Epstein 27tr; Pavel Filatov 246; imagebroker 259tl; ITAR-TASS Photo Agency 21br, 62bl, 116cl, 130–131, 184, 278cr, 312cl; Frans Lemmens 59tc; Yadid Levy 108t; Steve Morgan 23tr; Joanne Moyes 292br; Andrey Nekrasov 300–301; Sergey Nezhinkiy 212; North Wind Picture Archives 41tl; 42clb; Prisma Bildagentur AG 2–3; RIA Novosti 35bl, 55cr, 62cl, 83cr, 91crb, 117br, 167tr, 209crb, 218br, 297tr; Russ Images 178; Peter Russian 148br; Helen Sessions 1c; Alexey Solodov 144; Travel Pictures 18; Universal Images Group/DeAgostini 121cr; Ivan Vdovin 203tl, 205b; ZUMA Press, Inc. 296br.
**Archives H. Matisse**: 155crb.
**AWL Images**: Amar Grover 236.
**Baklazhan Restaurant**: 286bl.
**Bar Strelka, Moscow**: Strelka Bar Archive 275br.
**Barashka Restaurant**: 281br.
**Bellevue Brasserie**: 285br.
**Bier Haus Restaurant**: 290br.
**Café Delicatessen**: 282b.
**Capital Shipping Company**: 317tl.
**Corbis**: 93br; Adoc-photos 106tr; The Art Archive/Alfredo Dagli Orti 41cb; Morton Beebe 37cl; Bettmann 43bc, 45cb, 45bl, 46tc; Alan Carey 25tr; Dean Conger 61tl; Fridman Damm 149tl; Design Pics/Keith Levit 13tr; DPA/Agentur Voller Ernst/Evgeny Khaldei 45tl; The Gallery

Collection 42tc; Global Look/Serguei Fomine 226bl; Jon Hicks 133tr, 133br, 260–261; Hulton-Deutsch Collection 83br, 176cr; ITAR-TASS Photo/Mudrats Alexander 29tc/Korotayev Artyom 12bl,/Katayev Igor 298cl,/ Shemetov Maxim 35crb,/ Shamukov Ruslan 4br, 22bc, 28tr,/ Krasilnikov Stanislav 28tr,/ Rodionov Vladimir 46br,/ Belinsky Yuri 36tr; JAI/Walter Bibikow 94, 158/Jane Sweeney 112,/ Katie Garrod 173cr; Braham Nowitz 89t; Diego Lezama Orezzoli 54cl; Steve Raymer 296cl; Robert Harding World Imagery/ Graham Lawrence 68c; Sygma/ Antoine Gyori 34cra; Peter Turnley 46clb.
**DoDo:** 274cl.
**Dom Berga Restaurant:** 289bl.
**Dreamstime.com:** 2bears 51cr; Alex_us 230–231; Alexsol 26tr; Alexvu 57tc; Andytv 244bl; Atovot 24c; Catthesun 202br, 242tl; Count 180bl; Definedtalent 52; Demian1975 211tl; Doroo 88tl; Ir717 24cl; Jackf 36cl; Joymsk 161br; Larshinksten 254–255; Lenikovaleva 220; Limp 20br; Loonara 276cl; Lvenok1968 177br; Markovskiy 15tr, 32bl, 208b; Mgrushin 119tr; Mil 21tl; Nebesnaya 56cl; Nobilior 35tl; Ortodoxfoto 314br; Photoniles 151cr; Pingvin121674 51br; Pokec 25bc; Ppl5806 245cl; Psv 102; Rogkoff 250tl; Roumyantseva 315c; Rudolft 55tc; Sborisov 10cl; Shap1964 258br; Silentiger 27br; Sportfoto 24cra; Stevart 46bl; Symphoni 252bl; Uralla 24tr; Valerii 24cb, 25cla; Vas177 26bc; Vitalyfoto 20t; Natalia Volkova 111tr; Voltan1 146cl, 180t; Vovez 172cl; Wrangel 251br; Yuryz 314cl; Zanskar 277br.
**Dvor Podznoeva Restaurant:** 263tl.
**Fotolia:** Alz 25cra; M. Bolot 203br; Evgeniy_golovko 243c; Gl0ck 214b; Donkey IA 13bl; Iva 163tl; JackF 14br; Mikhail Markovskiy 202tr; Maxximmm 44bl; Nikolny 259br, OlegDoroshin 132cl; Pavel Parmenov 40bc; RedTC 258crb; Maksim Shebeko 277c; WithGod 24crb.
**Getty Images:** 26–27c, 45crb; AFP/Gerard Julien 31tc,/ Stringer 47tr, 69br, 245crb; Age fotostock/Gonzalo Azumendi 58c; AWL Images/Gavin Hellier 215tr,/ Ken Scicluna 302c; The Bridgeman Art Library/Boris Mihajlovic Kustodiev 44tl,/ Carl Faberge 62tr,/ Russian School 44cb,/ Vladimir Egorovic Makovsky 43tr; Danita Delimont 5tr, 249t; Epsilon 47bc; Hemis.fr/Perousse Bruno 48–49; Hulton Archive/ Apic 31br,/ Imagno 28cla,/ Stringer 30tr, 41bc, 42bl, 175crb, 278tr,/ Topical Press Agency 139bc; The Image Bank/Frans Lemmens 55br,/ Bruno Morandi 312br; Lonely Planet Images/Jane Sweeney 26clb,/ Jonathan Smith 80tr,/ Richard I'Anson 50bl, 64; Mordolff 12tr; Moviepix/Keith Hamshere 30bl; New York Public Library/Wu Swee Ong 251crb; Photo Researchers 235br; Popperfoto/Bob Thomas 40clb; Robert Harding World Imagery/Gavin Hellier 217tl; Kevin Schafer 25cb; Slow

Images 19b; Stone/Paul Harris 247b; Stringer/Oleg Nikishin 90cla; Time & Life Pictures 39bc,/ Mansell 38; Universal Images Group 63crb.
**Gosti Restaurant:** 284tr.
**Horoshie Ludi:** 289tr.
**Khachapuri:** 280bl.
**Lux Express Group:** 313tr.
**Masterfile:** Robert Harding Images 74tl.
**Nevsky Hotel:** 264bl.
**Noor Restaurant:** 281tr.
**Park Inn by Radisson Astrakhan:** 262br.
**Park Inn by Radisson Ekaterinburg:** 271tr.
**Photoshot:** DeAgostini/UIG 134, Shamukov Ruslan 11br.
**Radisson Hotel:** 263br.
**Roses & Filippov Hotels:** 264tr.
**The State Academic Bolshoi Theatre of Russia:** Damir Yusupov 22t, 50cl, 82br, 83tc, 83bc, 120cl.
**State Central Museum of Contemporary History of Russia:** 85b.
**The State Hermitage Museum, St Petersburg:** 5cl, 154cl, 154bl, 155cr, 156tr, 156bc, 157tl, 157tr, 157cra, 157bl, 157br.
© 2013, **State Russian Museum, St Petersburg:** 164cl, 164bc, 165tl, 165cra, 165cr, 165br.
**The State Tretyakov Gallery:** 98tl, 98clb, 98bc, 99tl, 99cr, 99br.
**SuperStock:** age fotostock 14cl, 204, imagebroker.net 24cla, NaturePL 203tr.
**Tourist Information Centre of Perm Region:** 235cl.
**Tsar Restaurant:** 286tr.
**Tsarskoye Selo State Museum:** 189tl, 189crb.
**Tulip Inn Rosa Khutor Hotel:** 272tr.
**Uncle Pasha:** 265tr.
**Ural Expeditions & Tours:** 298br, 299tr.
**Zokol Hostel:** 273br.

**Front Endpaper**
**Alamy Images:** Pavel Filatov fbr, Sergey Nezhinkiy cl; **AWL Images:** Amar Grover bl; **Dreamstime**.com: Lenikovaleva br; **Getty Images:** Lonely Planet Images/ Richard I'Anson bc; **Photoshot:** DeAgostini/UIG tc; **SuperStock:** age fotostock tr.

**Jacket Images**
Front: **AWL Images:** Jane Sweeney main; **Corbis:** Abraham Nowitz bl; Spine: **AWL Images:** Jane Sweeney t.

All other images © Dorling Kindersley.
For further information see: www.dkimages.com

# Phrase Book

In this guide the Russian language has been transliterated into Roman script following a consistent system used by the US Board on Geographic Names. All street and place names, and the names of most people, are transliterated according to this system. For some names, where a well-known English form exists, this has been used – hence, Leo (not Lev) Tolstoy.

In particular, the names of Russian rulers, such as Peter the Great, are given in their anglicized forms. Throughout the book, transliterated names can be taken as an accurate guide to pronunciation. The Phrase Book also gives a phonetic guide to the pronunciation of words and phrases used in everyday situations, such as when eating out or shopping.

## Guidelines for Pronunciation

The Cyrillic alphabet has 33 letters, of which only five (a, к, м, о, т) correspond exactly to their counterparts in English. Russian has two pronunciations (hard and soft) of each of its vowels, and several consonants without an equivalent.

The right-hand column of the alphabet, below, demonstrates how Cyrillic letters are pronounced by comparing them to sounds in English words. However, some letters vary in how they are pronounced according to their position in a word. Important exceptions are also noted below.

On the following pages, the English is given in the left-hand column, with the Russian and its transliteration in the middle column. The right-hand column provides a literal system of pronunciation and indicates the stressed syllable in bold. The exception is in the Menu Decoder section, where the Russian is given in the left-hand column and the English translation in the right-hand column, for ease of use. Because of the existence of genders in Russian, in a few cases both masculine and feminine forms of a phrase are given.

## The Cyrillic Alphabet

| | | |
|---|---|---|
| А а | a | **a**limony |
| Б б | b | **b**ed |
| В в | v | **v**et |
| Г г | g | **g**et (see note 1) |
| Д д | d | **d**ebt |
| Е е | e | **ye**t (see note 2) |
| Ё ё | e | **yo**nder |
| Ж ж | zh | lei**s**ure (but a little harder) |
| З з | z | **z**ither |
| И и | i | s**ee** |
| Й й | y | bo**y** (see note 3) |
| К к | k | **k**ing |
| Л л | l | **l**oot |
| М м | m | **m**atch |
| Н н | n | **n**ever |
| О о | o | r**o**b (see note 4) |
| П п | p | **p**ea |
| Р р | r | **r**at (rolling, as in Italian) |
| С с | s | **s**top |
| Т т | t | **t**offee |
| У у | u | b**oo**t |
| Ф ф | f | **f**ellow |
| Х х | kh | **kh** (like loch) |
| Ц ц | ts | le**ts** |
| Ч ч | ch | **ch**air |
| Ш ш | sh | **sh**ove |
| Щ щ | shch | fre**sh sh**eet (as above but with a slight roll) |
| ъ | | hard sign (no sound, but see note 5) |
| ы ы | y | f**i**d |
| ь | | soft sign (no sound, but see note 5) |
| Э э | e | **e**gg |
| Ю ю | yu | **you**th |
| Я я | ya | **ya**k |

## Notes

1) Г   Pronounced as v in endings -oro and -ero.
2) Е   Always pronounced ye at the beginning of a word, but in the middle of a word sometimes less distinctly (more like e).
3) Й   This letter has no distinct sound of its own. It usually lengthens the preceding vowel.
4) О   When not stressed it is pronounced like a in across.
5) ъ, ь The hard sign (ъ) is rare and indicates a very brief pause before the next letter. The soft sign (ь, marked in the pronunciation guide as ') softens the preceding consonant and adds a slight y sound: for instance, n' would sound like ny in 'ca**ny**on'.

## In an Emergency

| | | |
|---|---|---|
| Help! | Помогите! Pomogite! | pam**a**g**ee**tye! |
| Stop! | Стоп! Stop! | Stop! |
| Leave me alone! | Оставте меня в покое! Ostavte menya v pokoe! | ast**a**vt'e my**e**n**ya** v pak**o**ye! |
| Call a doctor! | Позовите врача! Pozovite vracha! | paz**a**v**ee**tye vr**a**cha! |
| Call an ambulance! | Вызовите скорую помощь! Vyzovite skoruyu pomoshch! | vizav**ee**tye sk**o**ru-yu p**o**mash'! |
| Fire! | Пожар! Pozhar! | pazh**a**r! |
| Call the fire brigade! | Вызовите пожарных! Vyzovite pozharnykh! | vizav**ee**tye pazh**a**rnikh! |
| Police! | Милиция! Militsiya! | meel**ee**tseeya! |
| Where is the nearest… | Где ближайший… Gde blizhayshiy… | gdye bleezh**a**ysheey… |
| …telephone? | …телефон? …telefon? | …tyelyef**o**n? |
| …hospital? | …больница? …bolnitsa? | …bal'n**ee**tsa? |
| …police station? | …отделение милиции? …otdelenie militsii? | …atdyel**ye**nye meel**ee**tsee-ee? |

## Communication Essentials

| | | |
|---|---|---|
| Yes | Да Da | da |
| No | Нет Net | nyet |
| Please | Пожалуйста Pozhaluysta | pazh**a**lsta |
| Thank you | Спасибо Spasibo | spas**ee**ba |
| You are welcome | Пожалуйста Pozhaluysta | pazh**a**lsta |
| Excuse me | Извините Izvinite | eezveen**ee**t-ye |
| Hello | Здравствуйте Zdravstvuyte | zdr**a**stvooyt-ye |
| Goodbye | До свидания Do svidaniya | da sveed**a**nya |
| Good morning | Доброе утро Dobroe utro | d**o**bra-ye **oo**tra |
| Good afternoon/ day | Добрый день Dobryy den | d**o**bree dyen' |
| Good evening | Добрый вечер Dobryy vecher | d**o**bree v**ye**chyer |
| Good night | Спокойной ночи Spokoynoy nochi | spak**o**ynay n**o**chee |
| Morning | утро utro | **oo**tra |
| Afternoon | день den | dyen' |
| Evening | вечер vecher | v**ye**chyer |
| Yesterday | вчера vchera | fchyer**a** |
| Today | сегодня sevodnya | syev**o**dnya |
| Tomorrow | завтра zavtra | z**a**ftra |
| Here | здесь zdes | zdyes' |
| There | там tam | tam |

| What? | Что?<br>*Chto?* | *shto?* |
|---|---|---|
| Where? | Где?<br>*Gde?* | *gdye?* |
| Why? | Почему?<br>*Pochemu?* | *pachyemoo?* |
| When? | Когда?<br>*Kogda?* | *kagda?* |
| Now | сейчас<br>*seychas* | *seychas* |
| Later | позже<br>*pozzhe* | *pozhe* |
| Can I...? | можно?<br>*mozhno?* | *mozhna...?* |
| It is<br>possible/allowed | можно<br>*mozhno* | *mozhna* |
| It is not<br>possible/allowed | нельзя<br>*nelzya* | *nyelzya* |

## Useful Phrases

| How are you? | Как дела?<br>*Kak dela?* | *kak dyela?* |
|---|---|---|
| Very well, thank<br>you | Хорошо, спасибо<br>*Khorosho, spasibo* | *kharasho, spaseeba* |
| Pleased to meet you | Очень приятно<br>*Ochen priyatno* | *ochen' pree-yatna* |
| How do I get to...? | Как добраться<br>до...?<br>*Kak dobratsya do...?* | *kak dabrat'sya da...?* |
| Would you tell me<br>when we get<br>to...? | Скажите,<br>пожалуйста,<br>когда мы<br>приедем в...?<br>*Skazhite,<br>pozhaluysta,<br>kogda my<br>priedem v...?* | *skazheet' ye,<br>pazhalsta, kagda<br>mi pree-yedyem<br>v...?* |
| Is it very far? | Это далеко?<br>*Eto daleko?* | *eta dalyeko?* |
| Do you speak<br>English? | Вы говорите<br>по-английски?<br>*Vy govorite<br>po-angliyski?* | *vi gavareet-ye<br>po-angleeskee?* |
| I don't understand | Я не понимаю<br>*Ya ne ponimayu* | *ya nye<br>paneema-yoo* |
| Could you speak<br>more slowly? | Говорите<br>медленнее<br>*Govorite medlennee* | *gavareet-ye<br>myedlyenye-ye* |
| Could you say it<br>again please? | Повторите,<br>пожалуйста<br>*Povtorite,<br>pozhaluysta* | *paftareet-ye,<br>pazhalsta* |
| I am lost | Я заблудился<br>(заблудилась)<br>*Ya zabludilsya<br>(zabludilas)* | *ya zabloodeelsya<br>(zabloodeelas')* |
| How do you say...<br>in Russian? | Как по-русски...?<br>*Kak pa-rooskee...?* | *kak pa-rooskee...?* |

## Useful Words

| big | большой<br>*bolshoy* | *bal'shoy* |
|---|---|---|
| small | маленький<br>*malenkiy* | *malyen'kee* |
| hot (water, food) | горячий<br>*goryachiy* | *garyachee* |
| hot (weather) | жарко<br>*zharko* | *zharka* |
| cold | холодный<br>*kholodnyy* | *khalodnee* |
| good | хорошо<br>*khorosho* | *kharasho* |
| bad | плохо<br>*plokho* | *plokha* |
| okay/fine | нормально<br>*normalno* | *narmal'na* |
| near | близко<br>*blizko* | *bleezka* |
| far | далеко<br>*daleko* | *dalyeko* |
| up | наверху<br>*naverkhu* | *navyerkhoo* |
| down | внизу<br>*vnizu* | *fneezoo* |

| early | рано<br>*rano* | *rana* |
|---|---|---|
| late | поздно<br>*pozdno* | *pozdna* |
| vacant (unoccupied) | свободно<br>*svobodno* | *svabodna* |
| free (no charge) | бесплатно<br>*besplatno* | *byesplatna* |
| cashier/ticket office | касса<br>*kassa* | *kasa* |
| avenue | проспект<br>*prospekt* | *praspyekt* |
| bridge | мост<br>*most* | *most* |
| embankment | набережная<br>*naberezhnaya* | *nabyeryezhnaya* |
| highway/motorway | шоссе<br>*shosse* | *shasse* |
| lane/passage | переулок<br>*pereulok* | *pyeryeoolak* |
| square | площадь<br>*ploshchad* | *ploshat'* |
| street | улица<br>*ulitsa* | *ooleetsa* |
| flat/apartment | квартира<br>*kvartira* | *kvarteera* |
| floor | этаж<br>*etazh* | *etash* |
| house/block | дом<br>*dom* | *dom* |
| entrance | вход<br>*vkhod* | *fkhot* |
| exit | выход<br>*vykhod* | *vikhot* |
| river | река<br>*reka* | *ryeka* |
| summer country<br>house | дача<br>*dacha* | *dacha* |
| swimming pool | бассейн<br>*basseyn* | *basyeyn* |
| town | город<br>*gorod* | *gorat* |
| toilet | туалет<br>*tualet* | *tooalyet* |

## Making a Telephone Call

| Can I call abroad<br>from here? | Можно отсюда<br>позвонить за<br>границу?<br>*Mozhno ostyuda<br>pozvonit za<br>granitsu?* | *mozhna atsyooda<br>pazvaneet' za<br>graneetsoo?* |
|---|---|---|
| I would like to<br>speak to... | Позовите,<br>пожалуйста...<br>*Pozovite,<br>pozhaluysta* | *pazaveet-ye,<br>pazhalsta...* |
| Could you leave<br>him/her a<br>message? | Вы можете<br>передать ему/ей?<br>*By mozhete peredat<br>emy/ey?* | *vi mozhet-ye<br>pyeryedat'<br>yemoo/yay?* |
| My number is... | Мой номер...<br>*Moy nomer...* | *moy nomyer...* |
| I'll ring back later | Я позвоню позже<br>*Ya pozvonyu pozzhe* | *ya pazvanyoo<br>pozzhe* |

## Sightseeing

| castle | замок<br>*zamok* | *zamak* |
|---|---|---|
| cathedral | собор<br>*sobor* | *sabor* |
| church | церковь<br>*tserkov* | *tserkaf'* |
| circus | цирк<br>*tsirk* | *tseerk* |
| closed for cleaning<br>"cleaning day" | санитарный день<br>*sanitarnyy den* | *saneetarnee dyen'* |
| undergoing<br>restoration | ремонт<br>*remont* | *remont* |
| exhibition | выставка<br>*vystavka* | *vistafka* |
| fortress | крепость<br>*krepost* | *kryepost'* |
| gallery | галерея<br>*galereya* | *galeryeya* |
| garden | сад<br>*sad* | *sad* |

| | | |
|---|---|---|
| island | остров<br>*ostrov* | **o**straf |
| kremlin/fortified<br>stronghold | Кремль<br>*kreml* | kryeml' |
| library | библиотека<br>*biblioteka* | beeblee-at**ye**ka |
| monument | памятник<br>*pamyatnik* | p**a**myatneek |
| mosque | мечеть<br>*mechet* | mych**ye**t' |
| museum | музей<br>*muzey* | mooz**yey** |
| palace | дворец<br>*dvorets* | dvar**ye**ts |
| park | парк<br>*park* | park |
| parliament | дума<br>*duma* | d**oo**ma |
| synagogue | синагога<br>*sinagoga* | seenag**o**ga |
| tourist information | пункт информации<br>для туристов<br>*punkt informatsii<br>dlya turistov* | p**oo**nkt<br>eenfarm**a**tsee-ee<br>dlya toor**ee**staf |
| zoo | зоопарк<br>*zoopark* | zap**a**rk |

## Shopping

| | | |
|---|---|---|
| open | открыто<br>*otkryto* | atkr**i**ta |
| closed | закрыто<br>*zakryto* | zakr**i**ta |
| How much does<br>this cost? | Сколько это стоит?<br>*Skolko eto stoit?* | sk**o**l'ka eta st**o**eet? |
| I would like to<br>buy… | Я хотел (хотела) бы<br>купить…<br>*Ya khotel (khotela)<br>by kupit…* | ya khat**ye**l (khat**ye**la)<br>bi koop**ee**t'… |
| Do you have…? | У вас есть…?<br>*U vas yest…?* | oo vas yest'…? |
| Do you take credit<br>cards? | Кредитные<br>карточки вы<br>принимаете?<br>*Kreditnye kartochki<br>vy prinimaete?* | kryed**ee**tnye<br>kart**a**chkee vy<br>preeneem**a**yetye? |
| What time do you<br>open/close? | Во сколько вы<br>открываетесь/<br>закрываетесь?<br>*Vo skolko vy<br>otkryvaetes/<br>zakryvaetes?* | Va sk**o**l'ka vy<br>atkriv**a**yetyes'/<br>zakriv**a**yetyes'? |
| This one | этот<br>*etot* | **e**tat |
| expensive | дорого<br>*dorogo* | d**o**raga |
| cheap | дёшево<br>*deshevo* | dy**o**shyeva |
| size | размер<br>*razmer* | razm**ye**r |
| white | белый<br>*belyy* | b**ye**lee |
| black | чёрный<br>*chernyy* | ch**yo**rnee |
| red | красный<br>*krasnyy* | kr**a**snee |
| yellow | жёлтый<br>*zheltyy* | zh**o**ltee. |
| green | зелёный<br>*zelenyy* | zyel**yo**nee |
| dark blue | синий<br>*siniy* | s**ee**nee |
| light blue | голубой<br>*goluboy* | galoob**oy** |
| brown | коричневый<br>*korichnevyy* | kar**ee**chnyevye |

## Types of Shop

| | | |
|---|---|---|
| bakery | булочная<br>*bulochnaya* | b**oo**lachna-ya |
| bookshop | книжный магазин<br>*knizhnyy magazin* | kn**ee**zhnee magaz**ee**n |
| butcher | мясной магазин<br>*myasnoy magazin* | myasn**oy** magaz**ee**n |
| camera shop | фото-товары<br>*foto-tovary* | f**o**to-tav**a**ri |
| chemist | аптека<br>*apteka* | apt**ye**ka |
| delicatessen | гастроном<br>*gastronom* | gastran**o**m |

| | | |
|---|---|---|
| department store | универмаг<br>*univermag* | ooneevyerm**a**g |
| florist | цветы<br>*tsvety* | tsv**ye**ti |
| grocer | бакалея<br>*bakaleya* | bakal**ye**-ya |
| hairdresser | парикмахерская<br>*parikmakherskaya* | pareekm**a**khyerskaya |
| market | рынок<br>*rynok* | r**i**nak |
| newspaper stand | газетный киоск<br>*gazetnyi kiosk* | gaz**ye**tnee kee-**o**sk |
| post office | почта<br>*pochta* | p**o**chta |
| record shop | грампластинки<br>*gramplastinki* | gramplast**ee**nkee |
| shoe shop | обувь<br>*obuv* | **o**boof' |
| travel agent | бюро путешествий<br>*byuro puteshestviy* | byoor**o**<br>pootyesh**e**stvee |
| bank | банк<br>*bank* | bank |

## Staying in a Hotel

| | | |
|---|---|---|
| Do you have a<br>vacant room? | У вас есть<br>свободный номер?<br>*U vas yest<br>svobodnyy nomer?* | oo vas yest'<br>svab**o**dnee<br>n**o**myer? |
| double room with<br>double bed | номер с<br>двуспальной<br>кроватью<br>*nomer s dvuspalnoy<br>krovatyu* | n**o**myer s<br>dvoosp**a**l'noy<br>krav**a**t'-yoo |
| twin room | двухместный<br>номер<br>*dvukhmestnyy<br>nomer* | dvookhm**ye**stnee<br>n**o**myer |
| single room | одноместный<br>номер<br>*odnomestnyy nomer* | adnam**ye**stnee<br>n**o**myer |
| bath | ванная<br>*vannaya* | v**a**na-ya |
| shower | душ<br>*dush* | doosh |
| porter | носильщнк<br>*nosilshchik* | nas**ee**l'sheek |
| key | ключ<br>*klyuch* | kly**oo**ch |

## Eating Out

| | | |
|---|---|---|
| A table for two,<br>please | Стол на двоих,<br>пожалуйста<br>*Stol na dvoikh,<br>pazhalsta* | stol na dva-**ee**kh,<br>pazh**a**lsta |
| I would like to<br>book a table | Я хочу заказать<br>стол<br>*Ya khochu zakazat stol* | ya khach**oo** zakaz**a**t'<br>stol |
| The bill, please | Счёт,<br>пожалуйста<br>*Schet,<br>pozhaluysta* | shyot, pazh**a**lsta |
| I am a vegetarian | Я вегетерианец<br>(вегетерианка)<br>*Ya vegeterianets<br>(vegeterianka)* | ya vyegyetaree**a**nyets<br>(vyegyetaree**a**nka) |
| breakfast | завтрак<br>*zavtrak* | z**a**ftrak |
| lunch | обед<br>*obed* | ab**ye**t |
| dinner | ужин<br>*uzhin* | **oo**zhen |
| waiter! | официант!<br>*ofitsiant!* | afeetsee-**a**nt! |
| waitress! | официантка!<br>*ofitsiantka!* | afeetsee-**a**nka! |
| dish of the day | фирменное блюдо<br>*firmennoe blyudo* | f**ee**rmenoye<br>bly**oo**da |
| appetizers/starters | закуски<br>*zakuski* | zak**oo**skee |
| main course | второе блюдо<br>*vtoroe blyudo* | ftar**o**ye bly**oo**da |
| meat and poutry<br>dishes | мясные блюда<br>*myasnye blyuda* | m**ya**sniye blyu**oo**da |
| fish and seafood<br>dishes | рыбные блюда<br>*rybnye blyuda* | r**i**bniye bly**oo**da |
| vegetable dishes | овощные блюда<br>*ovoshchnye blyuda* | avashn**i**ye bly**oo**da |
| dessert | десерт<br>*desert* | dy**e**syert |

| | | |
|---|---|---|
| drinks | напитки *napitki* | *napeetkee* |
| vegetables | овощи *ovoshchi* | *ovoshshee* |
| bread | хлеб *khleb* | *khlyeb* |
| wine list | карта вин *karta vin* | *karta veen* |
| rare (steak) | недожаренный *nedozharennyy* | *nyedazharenee* |
| well done (steak) | прожаренный *prozharennyy* | *prozharenee* |
| glass | стакан *stakan* | *stakan* |
| bottle | бутылка *butylka* | *bootilka* |
| knife | нож *nozh* | *nosh* |
| fork | вилка *vilka* | *veelka* |
| spoon | ложка *lozhka* | *loshka* |
| plate | тарелка *tapelka* | *taryelka* |
| napkin | салфетка *salletka* | *salfyetka* |
| salt | соль *sol* | *sol* |
| pepper | переЦ *perets* | *pyeryets* |
| butter/oil | масло *maslo* | *masla* |
| sugar | сахар *sahar* | *sakhar* |

## Menu Decoder

| | | |
|---|---|---|
| абрикос *abrikos* | *abreekos* | upricot |
| апельсин *apelsin* | *apyel'seen* | orange |
| апельсиновый сок *apelsinovyy sok* | *apyel'seenavee sok* | orange juice |
| арбуз *arbuz* | *arbooz* | water melon |
| белое вино *beloe vino* | *byelaye veeno* | white wine |
| бифштекс *bifshteks* | *beefshtyeks* | steak |
| блины *bliny* | *bleeni* | pancakes |
| борщ *borshch* | *borshsh* | borsch (beetroot soup) |
| варенье *varene* | *varyen'ye* | Russian syrup-jam |
| варёный *varenyy* | *varyonee* | boiled |
| ветчина *vetchina* | *vyetcheena* | ham |
| вода *voda* | *vada* | water |
| говядина *govyadina* | *gavyadeena* | beef |
| грибы *griby* | *greebi* | mushrooms |
| груша *grusha* | *groosha* | pear |
| гусь *gus* | *goos* | goose |
| джем *dzhem* | *dzhem* | jam |
| жареный *zharenyy* | *zharyenee* | roasted/grilled/fried |
| икра *ikra* | *eekra* | black caviar |
| икра красная/кета *ikra krasna-ya/keta* | *eekra krasna-ya/kyeta* | red caviar |
| капуста *kapusta* | *kapoosta* | cabbage |
| картофель *kartofel* | *kartofyel'* | potato |
| квас *kvas* | *kvas* | kvas (sweet, mildly alcoholic drink) |
| клубника *klubnika* | *kloobneeka* | strawberries |
| колбаса *kolbasa* | *kalbasa* | salami sausage |
| кофе *kofe* | *kofye* | coffee |

| | | |
|---|---|---|
| красное вино *krasnoe vino* | *krasnoye veeno* | red wine |
| креветки *krevetki* | *kryevyetkee* | prawns |
| курица *kuritsa* | *kooreetsa* | chicken |
| лук *luk* | *look* | onion |
| малина *malina* | *maleena* | raspberries |
| минеральная вода *mineralnaya voda* | *mineral'naya vada* | mineral water |
| мороженое *morozhenoe* | *marozhena-ye* | ice cream |
| мясо *myaso* | *myasa* | meat |
| огурец *ogurets* | *agooryets* | cucumber |
| осетрина *osetrina* | *asyetreena* | sturgeon |
| пельмени *pelmeni* | *pyel'myenee* | meat or fish dumplings |
| персик *persik* | *pyerseek* | peach |
| печенье *pechene* | *pyechyen'ye* | biscuit |
| печёнка *pechenka* | *pyechyonka* | liver |
| печёный *pechenyy* | *pyechyonee* | baked |
| пиво *pivo* | *peeva* | beer |
| пирог *pirog* | *peerok* | pie |
| пирожки *pirozhki* | *peerashkee* | small parcels with savoury fillings |
| помидор *pomidor* | *pameedor* | tomato |
| продукты моря *produkty morya* | *pradookti morya* | seafood |
| рыба *ryba* | *riba* | fish |
| салат *salat* | *salat* | salad |
| свинина *svinina* | *sveeneena* | pork |
| сельдь *seld* | *sye'ld'* | herring |
| сосиски *sosiski* | *saseeskee* | sausages |
| сыр *syr* | *sir* | cheese |
| сырой *syroy* | *siroy* | raw |
| утка *utka* | *ootka* | duck |
| фасоль *fasol* | *fasol'* | beans |
| форель *forel* | *faryel'* | trout |
| чай *chay* | *chai* | tea |
| чеснок *chesnok* | *chyesnok* | garlic |
| шашлык *shashlyk* | *shashlik* | kebab |
| яйцо *yaytso* | *yaytso* | egg |
| слива *sliva* | *sleeva* | plum |
| фрукты *frukty* | *frookti* | fruit |
| яблоко *yabloko* | *yablaka* | apple |

## Transport

| | | |
|---|---|---|
| north | север *sever* | *syever* |
| south | юг *yug* | *yook* |
| east | восток *vostok* | *vastok* |
| west | запад *zapad* | *zapat* |
| airport | аэропорт *aeroport* | *aeraport* |
| aeroplane | самолёт *samolet* | *samalyot* |

| | | |
|---|---|---|
| traffic police | ГАИ | Ga-ee |
| | GAI | |
| bus | автобус | aftoboos |
| | avtobus | |
| bus station | автобусная | aftoboosna-ya |
| | станция | stantsee-ya |
| | avtobusnaya | |
| | stantsiya | |
| bus stop | остановка автобса | astanofka aftoboosa |
| | ostanovka avtobusa | |
| car | машина | masheena |
| | mashina | |
| flight | рейс | ryeys |
| | reys | |
| metro (station) | (станция) метро | (stantsee-ya) myetro |
| | (stantsiya) metro | |
| no entry | нет входа | nyet fkhoda |
| | net vkhoda | |
| no exit | нет выхода | nyet vikhada |
| | net vykhoda | |
| parking | автостоянка | aftostoyanka |
| | avtostoyanka | |
| petrol | бензин | byenzeen |
| | benzin | |
| railway | железная дорога | zhelyezna-ya |
| | zheleznaya doroga | daroga |
| railway station | вокзал | vagzal |
| | vokzal | |
| return ticket | обратный билет | obratnee beelyet |
| | obratniy bilet | |
| seat | место | myesta |
| | mesto | |
| suburban train | пригородный поезд | preegaradnee |
| | prigorodniy poezd | po-yezd |
| straight on | прямо | pryama |
| | pryamo | |
| taxi | такси | taksee |
| | taksi | |
| ticket | билет | beelyet |
| | bilet | |
| token (for a single | жетон | zheton |
| metro journey) | zheton | |
| to the left | налево | nalyeva |
| | nalevo | |
| to the right | направо | naprava |
| | napravo | |
| train | поезд | po-yezd |
| | poezd | |
| tram | трамвай | tramvay |
| | tramvay | |
| trolleybus | троллейбус | tralyeyboos |
| | trolleybus | |

## Numbers

| | | |
|---|---|---|
| 1 | один/одна/одно | adeen/adna/adno |
| | odin/odna/odno | |
| 2 | два/две | dva/dvye |
| | dva/dve | |
| 3 | три | tree |
| | tri | |
| 4 | четыре | chyetir-ye |
| | chetyre | |
| 5 | пять | pyat' |
| | pyat | |
| 6 | шесть | shest' |
| | shest | |
| 7 | семь | syem' |
| | sem | |
| 8 | восемь | vosyem' |
| | vosem | |
| 9 | девять | dyevyat' |
| | devyat | |
| 10 | десять | dyesyat' |
| | desyat | |
| 11 | одиннадцать | adeenatsat' |
| | odinnadtsat | |
| 12 | двенадцать | dvyenatsat' |
| | dvenadtsat | |
| 13 | тринадцать | treenatsat' |
| | trinadtsat | |
| 14 | четырнадцать | chyetirnatsat' |
| | chetyrnadtsat | |
| 15 | пятнадцать | pyatnatsat' |
| | pyatnadtsat | |
| 16 | щестнадцать | shestnatsat' |
| | shestnadtsat | |
| 17 | семнадцать | syemnatsat' |
| | semnadtsat | |

| | | |
|---|---|---|
| 18 | восемнадцать | vasyemnatsat' |
| | vosemnadtsat | |
| 19 | девятнадцать | dyevyatnatsat' |
| | devyatnadtsat | |
| 20 | двадцать | dvatsat' |
| | dvadtsat | |
| 21 | двадцать один | dvatsat' adeen |
| | dvadtsat odin | |
| 22 | двадцать два | dvatsat' dva |
| | dvadtsat dva | |
| 23 | двадцать три | dvatsat' tree |
| | dvadtsat tri | |
| 24 | двадцать четыре | dvatsat' chyetir-ye |
| | dvadtsat chetyre | |
| 25 | двадцать пять | dvatsat' pyat' |
| | dvadtsat pyat | |
| 30 | тридцать | treetsat' |
| | tridtsat | |
| 40 | сорок | sorak |
| | sorok | |
| 50 | пятьдесять | pyadyesyat' |
| | pyatdesyat | |
| 60 | шестьдесят | shes'dyesyat |
| | shestdesyat | |
| 70 | семьдесят | syem'dyesyat |
| | semdesyat | |
| 80 | восемьдесять | vosyem'dyesyat |
| | vosemdesyat | |
| 90 | девяносто | dyevyanosta |
| | devyanosto | |
| 100 | сто | sto |
| | sto | |
| 200 | двести | dvyestee |
| | dvesti | |
| 300 | триста | treesta |
| | trista | |
| 400 | четыреста | chyetiryesta |
| | chetyresta | |
| 500 | пятьсот | pyat'sot |
| | pyatsot | |
| 1,000 | тысяча | tisyacha |
| | tysyacha | |
| 2,000 | две тысяч | dvye tisyach |
| | dve tysyach | |
| 5,000 | пять тысяч | pyat' tisyach |
| | pyat tysyach | |
| 1,000,000 | миллион | meelee-on |
| | million | |

## Time and Days

| | | |
|---|---|---|
| one minute | одна минута | adna meenoota |
| | odna minuta | |
| one hour | час | chas |
| | chas | |
| half an hour | полчаса | polchasa |
| | polchasa | |
| day | день | dyen' |
| | den | |
| week | неделя | nyedyel-ya |
| | nedelya | |
| Monday | понедельник | panyedyel'neek |
| | ponedelnik | |
| Tuesday | вторник | ftorneek |
| | vtornik | |
| Wednesday | среда | sryeda |
| | sreda | |
| Thursday | четверг | chyetvyerk |
| | chetverg | |
| Friday | пятница | pyatneetsa |
| | pyatnitsa | |
| Saturday | суббота | soobota |
| | subbota | |
| Sunday | воскресенье | vaskryesyen'ye |
| | voskresene | |

# Moscow Metro Map

**Key**

| | | |
|---|---|---|
| — Line 1 | — Line 6 | — Line 11 |
| — Line 2 | — Line 7 | — Line M1 (monorail) |
| — Line 3 | — Line 8 | ⚏ Under construction |
| — Line 4 | — Line 9 | |
| — Line 5 (circle) | — Line 10 | |